NOTABLE WOMEN IN AMERICAN HISTORY

A Guide to Recommended Biographies and Autobiographies

LYNDA G. ADAMSON

GREENWOOD PRESS

Westport, Connecticut • London

Library of Congress Cataloging-in-Publication Data

Adamson, Lynda G.
 Notable women in American history : a guide to recommended
biographies and autobiographies / Lynda G. Adamson.
  p. cm.
 Includes index.
 ISBN 0–313–29584–0 (alk. paper)
  1. Women—United States—Biography—Bibliography.
2. Autobiography—Women authors—Bibliography. 3. American diaries—
Women authors—Bibliography. 4. Women—United States—
Correspondence—Bibliography. 5. United States—Biography—
Bibliography. I. Title.
 Z7963.B6A27 1999
 [CT3260]
 016.92072′0973—dc21   98–55350

British Library Cataloguing in Publication Data is available.

Library of Congress Catalog Card Number: 98–55350
ISBN: 0–313–29584–0

First published in 1999

Greenwood Press, 88 Post Road West, Westport, CT 06881
An imprint of Greenwood Publishing Group, Inc.
www.greenwood.com

Printed in the United States of America

The paper used in this book complies with the
Permanent Paper Standard issued by the National
Information Standards Organization (Z39.48–1984).

10 9 8 7 6 5 4 3 2 1

In honor of one Irma and in memory of another Irma, both teachers who dedicated themselves to their families and their students, and in memory of Noèmie, an unsung American naval officer wife who, through protecting her family and her husband, served her country during World War II.

Contents

Acknowledgments

Several people have made this project possible. First, my colleague and friend, William A. Fry, has offered continual encouragement throughout the years. Barbara Rader at Greenwood Press has made valuable suggestions and helpful comments during my research, and Elizabeth Meagher has thoughtfully guided the book's production. The interlibrary loan facilitator at my college, Veronica Coleman, has graciously searched for biographies missing from Library of Congress shelves. Lastly, my husband, Frank, with his editing skills, clarifying questions, and understanding, has given me the needed support to finish this endeavor. I thank them all.

Introduction

The best biographies leave their readers with a sense of having all but entered into a second life and of having come to know another human being in some ways better than [she] knew [herself].
Mary Cable in the *New York Times*, 1969

Women have often worked privately for the betterment of their world because society has too often disdained their public advocacy of a cause. One of the main ways that women have gained recognition is by their writing, an activity pursued in private, where no man could control their creativity. Yet some women could only hope for publication by masquerading behind a masculine pseudonym. Only after attracting a wide readership could they reveal themselves as women. Attitudes toward women as public figures in America have slowly changed since the mid-nineteenth century when Abby Kelley Foster and the Grimké sisters confronted charges of prostitution for lecturing on abolition to mixed crowds of men and women. In twentieth-century America, unlike much of the rest of the world in any century, women have had opportunities for careers other than writing or homemaking. But even in America, as feminist scholars will attest, only in recent decades have some, but not all, professions treated males and females equally in assessing their achievements. Fortunately, some of these women have now also become subjects for biographies.

The 500 women included here must fulfill three criteria. They must have lived in the United States or one of its territories, and if born abroad after 1900, be a naturalized American citizen; have enriched life for other Americans in some way; and have a full-length biography or autobiography for either adults or mature young adults published since 1970 which is available by interlibrary loan. For twentieth-century actors, authors, and poets, an additional criterion is that they must have won major recognition from their colleagues. Each entry features a brief biography and an annotated list of no more than five biographies, autobiographies, letter collections, or journals concerning their lives. The appendices list the women according to year of birth; acquired title, occupation, or main areas of interest; and ethnicity, if from a minority population. The work, aimed at high school and college students, will also serve as a general reference for interested adults.

When Barbara Rader at Greenwood Press suggested this book of notable women in American history, I thought identifying 500 worthy American women about whom at least five biographies and autobiographies had been published in English since 1970 would be simple. I was wrong. What I collected from a variety of sources such as *The Larousse Biographical Dictionary*, *Webster's New Biographical Dictionary*, *Chronology of Women's History* (Olsen, 1994), *Notable Asian Americans* (Zian, 1995), *Notable Black American Women* (Smith, 1996), *Notable Hispanic American Women* (Kamp, 1993), *Notable Black American Women* (Smith, 1992), *Notable American Women* (James, 1971), *Notable American Women: The Modern Period* (Sicherman, 1980), *Notable Latino Americans* (Meier, 1997), *Notable Women in the Physical Sciences* (Shearer, 1997), *Notable Women in the Life Sciences* (Shearer, 1996), and *Notable Women in Mathematics* (Morrow, 1998) was a list of nearly 2,000 American women who might fulfill my criteria for inclusion. After searching the Library of Congress catalog, I found that the only women who had at least five biographies or autobiographies about them were actors or women with noncontroversial backgrounds about whom only biographies for juvenile readers had been written. Specialists such as physicists or chemists, like Gertrude Elion, might have recognition in one biography for juveniles but nothing for mature readers. After examining the attributes of all the women who fulfilled my criterion for being the subject of a biography, I focused on the criterion that the woman must have enriched someone's life whether by a medical discovery or a particularly engrossing performance. My conclusion after this exercise was that women chosen as subjects for biographies, in a publisher's view, must attract a readership. Some American readers are interested in the sensational or the sexual rather than the scholarly or the scientific. Therefore, women who may be the subject of several biographies—an actor, author, or entertainer—are excluded here because they have achieved little worthy of recognition by their peers.

In the short biographical sketch of each woman, I have listed her general achievement, date and place of birth, parental heritage, education, occupation or interest information, and recognition or specific awards won. I use the family name, married name, or pseudonym by which each woman was known and have included cross-references for women known by both family and married names. Since current psychological and physiological studies show that the first three years of life are the most important in forming the adult, I have included each woman's father's known employment since his economic or social status indicates the circumstance in which her mother, father, or another person, was able to raise her. If marriage aided a woman's achievements, I have mentioned it. And finally, I have tried to summarize some of her accomplishments and awards or recognition that she received. Cross-references in entries to other subjects in the guide appear in **bold** print. Names with asterisks (*) in the entries refer to women whose biographies can be found in *Notable Women in World History* (Adamson, 1998).

Pearl S. Buck, in *Advice to Unborn Novelists*, says:

How could an actual person fit into the covers of a book? The book is not a continent, not a definite geographical measure. It cannot contain so huge a thing as an actual full-size person. Any person has to be scaled by eliminations to fit the book world.

In the annotated bibliography, I have broadened the traditional concept of biography, for the reason that sometimes women do not "fit the book." I include not only authentic biography (researched and documented), fictional biography (invented dialogue), and autobiography as a crafted work with a beginning, middle, and end but also correspondence, journals, and interviews as autobiographical, primary sources which biographers use, because they offer the immediacy of an autobiography although rarely shaped into a cohesive whole. Notable female writers often have biographical information commingled with critical analyses of their work. For this reason, I have included critical analyses when they are one of the few sources of biographical background available. Notable female artists often are subjects of exhibition catalogs which focus on biography but contain photographs and analyses of their work rather than traditional biographies. I have included those works as well. When a subject had more than five acceptable biographical works available, I selected the most informative works. Usually they were the best documented and most recently published works.

Reprints published after 1970 but originally written before are included when more recent information is unavailable. I have also incorporated a very few works written earlier when a woman has made an unusually important contribution in a field such as medicine but has not been the subject of a recent biography. All works are appropriate for the general reader unless otherwise noted in the annotation. Scholarly or critical biographies are usually more abstract than popular biographies, and therefore require additional attention. If the biographies have won literary prizes, I have named the prize at the end of the annotation.

Be they anthropologists or actors, singers or spies, the women included here have often had to counter expectations of society and culture, with members of both sexes often maligning their choices. But what these women have achieved has changed the lives of Americans for the better, and they deserve much more recognition than they have so far received. Women appear in this book because someone has appreciated their worth and taken time to write about their accomplishments in biographies that adults, and in some cases, young adults, may enjoy. Many other noteworthy women deserve that attention as well. Many who have made enormous achievements in their fields for the betterment of society have remained unknown because their silent but steady work has kept them from becoming the subjects of lurid gossip and its resultant eager readership. People need to know about them. Orlando Romero in *Nambé—Year One* (1976) states it best:

Today will be the past, and, since the future seems uncertain, we derive our strength to face each new day from the lingering warmth of what has gone by. Each one of us lives in [her] own time. Each one of us lives in [her] own world. It is the health of our own past and the health of our own world that will determine our future.

ABBOTT, BERENICE (1898–1991)
Photographer   Springfield, Ohio

Berenice Abbott's photographs of New York City in the 1930s remain a document of its architecture. She was born July 17, 1898, the youngest of four children, and in her early childhood was separated from the others and rarely saw her father. At 19, when she entered Ohio State to study journalism, she considered herself independent of her family. On a trip to New York in 1918, after meeting Marcel Duchamp and Man Ray, she decided to leave college and study drawing and sculpture. In 1921, she unsuccessfully tried to establish her reputation as a sculptor in Paris and Berlin, becoming instead Man Ray's assistant. Photography quickly became her interest, and in 1926, **Peggy Guggenheim** financed a studio for her. Two years later, she exhibited at the first Independent Salon of Photography to critical acclaim. She met Eugène Atget, whose photographs she later rescued and preserved, and photographed expatriates in Paris including Guggenheim, James Joyce, **Sylvia Beach**, and Leo Stein. When she returned to New York in 1929, she established a portrait studio and began photographing the city during her spare time as Atget had done in Paris. After six years, she received funding, and for the next four years, she captured New York's architecture. She then began working with wave form photographs, inventing the Projection Supersight System. She photographed examples of scientific principles and taught at the New School for Social Research. She also traveled along Route 1 between Maine and Florida to photograph significant sights. Among her awards were recognition as one of the Top Ten Woman Photographers by the Professional Photographers of America, induction into the Order of Arts and Letters by the French government, and three honorary degrees.

BIBLIOGRAPHY

Haaften, Julia Van, ed. *Berenice Abbott, Photographer: A Modern Vision*. New York: New York Public Library, 1989. 0–89381–327–3, 95p. This brief biographical overview of Abbott's life and career includes selected copies of both her realistic and artistic photographs.

O'Neal, Hank. *Berenice Abbott, American Photographer*. New York: McGraw-Hill, 1982. 0–07–047551–2, 255p. O'Neal knew Abbott well, and his biased biography, with commentary by Abbott, examines her techniques and importance as an artist.

Yochelson, Bonnie. *Berenice Abbott at Work: The Making of Changing New York*. New York: New Press, 1997. 1–565–84377–0, 399p. Yochelson discusses Abbott's difficulty in obtaining federal funds to finance the New York project and her work.

ABBOTT, GRACE (1878–1939)
Social Worker, Public Administrator, and Educator   **Grand Island, Nebraska**

Grace Abbott, social worker, public administrator, educator, and reformer, made important contributions to immigration and child labor legislation. She was born on November 17, 1878, to parents who had opposed slavery and supported woman suffrage. After earning a degree from Grand Island College, she taught before moving to Chicago to obtain her master's degree and to live at **Jane Addams**'s Hull-House. In 1908, she became director of the Immigrants' Protective League, and during this time, wrote articles for the *Chicago Evening Post* attacking exploitation of immigrants and literacy test requirements. While she served as director of the Child Welfare Division of the United States Children's Bureau, the first federal statute limiting child labor was declared unconstitutional, and during World War I, she initiated a child labor clause in all contracts for war goods between the federal government and private industry. As director of the entire Children's Bureau, she helped establish over 3,000 child health and prenatal clinics. Later a professor of public welfare at the University of Chicago, she also served as a delegate to the League of Nations' Advisory Committee on Traffic in Women and Children and helped write the first Social Security Act during Franklin Roosevelt's New Deal. Throughout her life, she and her sister, Edith Abbott, worked for social reform and for woman suffrage.

BIBLIOGRAPHY

Abbott, Edith. *Grace Abbott: A Sister's Memories*. Chicago: Social Service Review, 1939. No ISBN, 351p. The author recalls her sister's life and her achievements in welfare reform.

Costin, Lela B. *Two Sisters for Social Justice*. Urbana: University of Illinois, 1983. 0–252–01013–2, 315p. Costin's scholarly and thoroughly researched biography covers the social activism of Abbott and her sister Edith.

ABZUG, BELLA (1920–1998)
Attorney, Congresswoman, and Activist   New York, New York

Bella Abzug, an attorney and advocate for women's rights, served in Congress for six years. She was born Bella Savitsky on July 24, 1920, to an unsuccessful Russian-Jewish emigré businessman and his wife, who supported the family. After attending Hunter College, Abzug was editor of the *Columbia Law Review* while attending law school. During her early law practice, she represented civil rights workers and individuals whom Senator Joseph McCarthy accused of communist connections, choices identifying her as a liberal activist. In 1961, she formed Women Strike for Peace, and in 1970, after election to the House of Representatives for New York City's 19th District, she founded and chaired the National Women's Political Caucus. She also supported the Equal Rights Amendment, a women's credit-rights bill, abortion rights, and child-care legislation, earning such names as "Battling Bella," "Hurricane Bella," and "Mother Courage." In 1976, she lost the Democratic nomination for senator, and in 1977 was defeated in a primary for mayor of New York but refused to stop speaking for and writing about women's rights. In 1994, she was inducted into The National Women's Hall of Fame.

BIBLIOGRAPHY

Abzug, Bella S. *Bella! Ms. Abzug Goes to Washington.* New York: Saturday Review Press, 1972. 0-8415-0154-8, 314p. Abzug discloses, in diary form, her activities ånd diverse roles during her first year as a congresswoman.

Faber, Doris. *Bella Abzug.* New York: Lothrop, Lee & Shepard, 1976. 0-688-41776-0, 162p. This biography of Abzug balances her outspokenness, which alienated both press and staff, with her organizational abilities.

ADAMS, ABIGAIL SMITH (1744–1818)
First Lady   Weymouth, Massachusetts

Abigail Adams, wife of one American president and the mother of another, supported women's rights during and after the American Revolution. She was born Abigail Smith on November 22, 1744, into a colonial farmer's family. Even though she had no formal education, she read widely, and when she married John Adams, a Boston lawyer, she was intellectually prepared to communicate the history of the country through her letters to him during his 10-year tenure in Philadelphia, beginning in 1774. She supported colonial independence, thought women should be educated, and hated slavery—topics about which she elaborated in her letters. After 1783, she lived in Paris, The Hague, and London with her diplomat husband, and wrote to friends at home about customs in Europe. When her husband became president, she briefly lived in the new White House on the Potomac River before returning to her home in Braintree, Massachusetts. The National Women's Hall of Fame now honors her as a member.

BIBLIOGRAPHY

Akers, Charles W. *Abigail Adams: An American Woman*. Boston: Little, Brown, 1980. 0–316–02040–0, 207p. In a biography suitable for young adults, Akers used more than 2,000 of Adams's letters to illuminate political, social, and intellectual life and her feminist ideas.

Gelles, Edith Belle. *Portia: The World of Abigail Adams*. Bloomington: Indiana University Press, 1992. 0–253–32553–6, 227p. Using Adams's family correspondence in conjunction with various theories of the eighteenth century, Gelles explores Adams's ties to the American Revolution, to her daughter, and to the society in which she lived.

Keller, Rosemary Skinner. *Patriotism and the Female Sex: Abigail Adams and the American Revolution*. Brooklyn, NY: Carlson, 1994. 0–926019–69–4, 239p. Through examination of Adams's maturity, the author traces her testing of parameters for females, both political and intellectual.

Levin, Phyllis Lee. *Abigail Adams*. New York: St. Martin's, 1987. 0–312–00007–3, 575p. Levin's readable biography includes manuscripts, newspapers, histories, and fiction contemporary to Adams to detail her life.

Withey, Lynne. *Dearest Friend: A Life of Abigail Adams*. New York: Macmillan, 1981. 0–02–934760–2, 369p. Using Adams's letters and journals as sources, Withey recounts her life and describes her 54-year marriage, adding useful background information about her daily activities and social conventions of her time.

ADAMS, HARRIETT CHALMERS (1875–1937)
Author, Lecturer, and Humanitarian   Stockton, California

Harriet Chalmers Adams was an author and lecturer. She was born on October 22, 1875, to a mining engineer who inspired in her a love of travel when he took her at age two on horseback through the California mountains. After private tutoring and further travel with her parents, she married and began journeys with her husband, starting with an extended honeymoon to Mexico, followed by a three-year trip to primitive areas of South America where she was the first white woman to visit. She earned money for future trips by writing and lecturing about her discoveries, becoming the first lecturer to use color slides to illustrate her talks. She visited the Caribbean and the Far East looking for evidence to support her theory that ancestors of Native American were Asian, and in World War I, she was the first woman correspondent allowed to travel to the front. She was the third woman to become a member of the Royal Geographic Society of London, but the American National Geographic Society never granted her full membership, although she wrote and lectured for *National Geographic* magazine for nearly 30 years. Instead, she and nine other women founded the Society of Woman Geographers in 1925. She traveled worldwide by boat, by train, by burro, and on foot before airplanes became widely used and was especially pleased with having visited all countries that Spain and Portugal ever colonized.

BIBLIOGRAPHY

Anema, Durlynn. *Harriet Chalmers Adams: Explorer and Adventurer*. Greensboro, NC: Morgan Reynolds, 1997. 1–88384–618–8, 112p. With excerpts from Adams's writing, Anema recreates her life as a world traveler, but the text for young adults emphasizes neither the places nor the perils in Adams's life, stating, without elaboration, that she fell off a Spanish cliff and spent two years in a body cast.

ADAMS, MAUDE (1872–1953)
Actor   Salt Lake City, Utah

Maude Adams was an actor. She was born Maude Kiskadden on November 11, 1872, the youngest and only surviving child of a businessman and his actor wife. Adams got a job as an actor at age five in a San Francisco melodrama production and was often billed as "Little Maude" while playing with stock companies until she became too tall at age ten. Her father's sudden death when she was 11 cemented her decision to become a great actor as soon as possible, and she left school to tour in a stock company with her mother. Five years later, she reached New York. Charles Frohman noted her talent and hired her to play light comedies for four seasons. Adams carefully studied her roles and approached her profession seriously. Frohman knew the Scottish playwright James Barrie, and when Barrie saw Adams, he immediately adapted his novel *The Little Minister* as a stage play. Adams successfully played the title role and began working with Barrie, acting in *Peter Pan* and four other plays. She enjoyed his use of fantasy to reach a spiritual truth in his drama and changed Peter Pan's London costume to a round collar and a peaked hat. She also performed other dramatists' plays; for one she received 22 curtain calls at the opening performance. In 1918, she fell ill with influenza, and after her recovery, she stopped acting until 1931. After performing in radio plays, she became a lighting designer, and working with General Electric, helped develop the incandescent bulb used in color film. Lastly, she taught drama at Stephens College in Columbia, Missouri. At her death, she donated her estate to the Cenacle Convent in New York City.

BIBLIOGRAPHY
Patterson, Ada. *Maude Adams: A Biography*. 1907. New York: B. Blom, 1971. No ISBN, 109p. This adulatory biography of Adams has no documentation.
Robbins, Phyllis. *The Young Maude Adams*. Francestown, NH: M. Jones, 1959. No ISBN, 163p. This readable but undocumented biography of Adams emphasizes her place in show business history.

ADDAMS, JANE (1860–1935)
Reformer   Cedarville, Illinois

Jane Addams founded Hull-House in Chicago, one of America's first social settlements. Born on September 6, 1860, she was the youngest child of a community builder and politician. Her mother died when Addams was two. When she attended Rockford Female Seminary, she met Ellen Gates Starr with whom she first traveled to Europe while recovering from an illness exacerbated by family responsibilities coupled with medical school attendance in Philadelphia. Abroad, influenced by her father's concerns with freedom and equality, Addams came to realize that she wanted to help the poor and needy families she saw on her travels. The two returned to Chicago and opened Hull-House in 1889, offering hot lunches, child care, English instruction, educational lectures, social opportunities, and rooms for union meetings. After her election to the Chicago Board of Education, she attracted others who shared her values, including Edith and **Grace Abbott,** John Dewey, **Julia Lathrop, Florence Kelley,** and **Alice Hamilton.** In 1910, she became the first female president of the National Conference of Social Work. When World War I began, Addams worked for peace and helped form the Woman's Peace Party. She traveled in Europe again to advocate a permanent international peacekeeping organization while serving as chairman of the International Congress of Women. She then organized the Women's International League for Peace and Freedom, and in 1931, received the Nobel Prize for Peace. She was also elected to The National Women's Hall of Fame.

BIBLIOGRAPHY

Addams, Jane. *Twenty Years at Hull-House.* 1910. New York: Penguin, 1998. 0–14–118099–4, 320p. Addams approaches her 20 years at Hull-House from a topical rather than a chronological standpoint.

Davis, Allen Freeman. *American Heroine: The Life and Legend of Jane Addams.* New York: Oxford University Press, 1973. 0–19–501897–4, 339p. Davis's scholarly and recommended biography explores Addams's complexities.

Hovde, Jane. *Jane Addams.* New York: Facts on File, 1989. 0–8160–1547–3, 131p. In her biography, based on Addams's papers and comments of persons who knew her, Hovde discusses her Hull-House experiment.

Kittredge, Mary. *Jane Addams.* New York: Chelsea House, 1988. 1–555–46636–2, 111p. This biography for young adults covers Addams's life.

Levine, Daniel. *Jane Addams and the Liberal Tradition.* 1971. Westport, CT: Greenwood Press, 1980. 0–313–22691–1, 277p. Levine examines Addams's role in reform thought.

AGASSIZ, ELIZABETH CABOT (1822–1907)
Naturalist and Educator   **Arlington Heights, Massachusetts**

Elizabeth Cabot Agassiz was a naturalist and educator who became the first president of Radcliffe College. She was born on December 5, 1822, the second of seven children in the cultured Cary family. Her father was treasurer of his father-in-law's Lowell, Massachusetts, mills. As a sickly child, Agassiz studied at home, where she read widely and learned languages. She married the Swiss naturalist Louis Agassiz in 1850, and although she was not formally trained, she worked with him on scientific expeditions, wrote scholarly treatises, and helped him found the Anderson School of Natural History, a marine laboratory on Penikese Island in Buzzard's Bay, Massachusetts. After her husband died in 1873, Agassiz began working to establish a women's college taught by Harvard faculty so that women could benefit from Harvard's academic resources. Six years later, she helped open Harvard Annex, and when it became the Society for the Collegiate Instruction of Women (later Radcliffe College) in 1882, she became its president. She also helped develop the Natural History Museum in Cambridge.

BIBLIOGRAPHY

Agassiz, Louis, and Elizabeth Agassiz. *A Journey in Brazil.* 1868. New York: Praeger, 1969. No ISBN, 540p. Agassiz gives a day-by-day account of her travels in the Amazon Basin, describing the region and the social customs.

Paton, Lucy Allen. *Elizabeth Cabot Agassiz.* 1919. New York: Arno, 1974. No ISBN, 423p. While recreating Agassiz's life and travels, Paton also places her within the Boston community in which she worked.

ALBRIGHT, MADELEINE (1937–)
Cabinet Member   **Prague, Czechoslovakia**

Madeleine Albright, political scientist and educator, served as the permanent U.S. representative to the United Nations before her appointment as the first female secretary of state. She was born Madeleine Korbel on May 15, 1937, one of three children of a Czech diplomat and his wife. Before coming to the United States at the age of 11 with her parents, Albright lived in Prague, Belgrade, London (where she became fluent in English), and Switzerland (where she learned French). After attending a small private high school, she received a scholarship to Wellesley College. She married soon after graduation, followed her journalist husband, and by 1976, earned a Ph.D. from Columbia. In 1975, she volunteered in Senator Edmund S. Muskie's Democratic presidential campaign, and when he hired her to work for him, she gained experience with foreign affairs while he was a member of the Senate Foreign Relations Committee. She continued her foreign policy work by serving on the National Security Council and advising the presidential campaigns of Walter F. Mondale, Michael S. Dukakis, and Bill Clinton. After she received a Woodrow Wilson Fellowship at the Smithsonian Institution, she served on the faculty of Georgetown University where she won four teacher of the year awards and directed the Women in Foreign Service Program. She was the vice chairperson of the National Democratic Institute for International Affairs and headed the Center for National Policy. She has also written books and articles on various aspects of foreign relations. She received a W. Averell Harriman Democracy Award from the National Democratic Institute for International Affairs and was elected to The National Women's Hall of Fame in 1998.

BIBLIOGRAPHY

Byman, Jeremy. *Madam Secretary: The Story of Madeleine Albright.* Greensboro, NC: Morgan Reynolds, 1998. 1–88384–623–4, 96p. Byman focuses on Albright's career, using magazine and newspaper articles along with television news programs and press conferences, in this young adult biography.

Freedman, Suzanne. *Madeleine Albright: She Speaks for America.* New York: Franklin Watts, 1998. 0–531–11454–6, 111p. Freedman's young adult biography of Albright, based on newspapers, magazine articles, government publications, and speeches, gives a general overview of her life.

ALCOTT, LOUISA MAY (1832–1888)
Author   Germantown, Pennsylvania

Louisa May Alcott was an author known mainly for her children's books. Born November 29, 1832, she was the eldest of four daughters of Bronson Alcott. Among the contemporary intellectuals joining her father as her educators were Ralph Waldo Emerson and Henry Thoreau. Her father's formal schools failed, however, and his continuing inability to earn money led Alcott to begin supporting the family at age 18 by working as a domestic, a seamstress, and a writer. When she volunteered as a nurse during the Civil War in Washington, D.C., she caught typhoid, from which she never fully recovered, but her experiences led to fame when her letters were published in book form as *Hospital Sketches* (1863). Her work began to appear in the *Atlantic Monthly*, and in 1869, she published the autobiographical *Little Women*. Proceeds from that book paid all of the family debts. She wrote other books for young people, and some for adults, using a pseudonym. Throughout her life, even though in ill health, she continued to help her mother and sisters. By the time of her death on the day of her father's funeral, she had published over 300 pieces. Her accomplishments were honored with election to The National Women's Hall of Fame.

BIBLIOGRAPHY
Anderson, William. *The World of Louisa May Alcott*. New York: HarperCollins, 1995. 0–06–095156–7, 120p. This beautifully illustrated look at Alcott's world contains color photographs with lengthy descriptions covering the major events and main people in her life.
Delamar, Gloria T. *Louisa May Alcott and Little Women*. Jefferson, NC: McFarland, 1990. 0–89950–421–3, 350p. Delamar records Alcott's abolitionist views and role as a suffragist, critically analyzes *Little Women*, and examines her legacy.
Elbert, Sarah. *A Hunger for Home: Louisa May Alcott's Place in American Culture*. New Brunswick, NJ: Rutgers University Press, 1987. 0–8135–1199–2, 346p. Elbert sees Alcott as examining the duality of women in her work.
Saxton, Martha. *Louisa May Alcott: A Modern Biography*. 1977. New York: Farrar, Straus and Giroux, 1995. 0–374–52460–2, 428p. In a carefully researched text, Saxton emphasizes Alcott's feminist approach to issues.
Stern, Madeleine B. *Louisa May Alcott*. New York: Random, 1996. 0–679–76949–8, 422p. In a readable, well-researched, and documented biography, Stern suggests that Alcott's motivation for her writing, always based on her own life, was invariably her devotion to her family.

ALLEN, FLORENCE ELLINWOOD (1884–1966)
Judge and Attorney Salt Lake City, Utah

Florence Ellinwood Allen was the first woman judge to become an assistant county prosecutor, to try a first-degree murder trial, to pronounce a death sentence, to be elected to a court of appeals, and to be appointed to the United States Court of Appeals. She was born on March 23, 1884, the third of seven children of a professor of classical languages who taught her Latin and Greek by age seven and prepared her for college by thirteen. When she attended one of **Susan B. Anthony**'s lectures before entering college, Allen began supporting women's rights. After graduating as Phi Beta Kappa from Case Western Reserve, Allen planned to become a concert pianist in Europe, but when a nerve injury shortened her performing career, she returned to Cleveland as a music critic and became interested in law. Western Reserve's law school refused to admit women, but she eventually graduated from New York University in 1913 after supporting herself while a student. She established a practice in Cleveland, focusing on women's legal problems, before becoming a volunteer counselor for the Legal Aid Society and working for the Woman's Suffrage Party. She became assistant county prosecutor and then the first female judge of a Common Pleas Court in 1921. Her friendship with **Eleanor Roosevelt** led President Franklin D. Roosevelt to appoint her as the first female judge on the U.S. Court of Appeals, although he would not appoint her to the Supreme Court. In 1958, she became the first woman to serve as chief judge of a federal appellate court.

BIBLIOGRAPHY

Allen, Florence Ellinwood. *To Do Justly.* Cleveland, OH: Press of Western Reserve University, 1965. No ISBN, 201p. In her readable autobiography, Allen describes the pleasure that she has enjoyed as a lawyer and judge.

Tuve, Jeanette E. *First Lady of the Law, Florence Ellinwood Allen.* Lanham, MD: University Press of America, 1984. 0-8191-4311-1, 220p. Tuve's biography, based on letters and records, tries to reveal Allen's personal side.

ALLEN, GRACIE (1895–1964)
Entertainer San Francisco, California

Grace Ethel Cecile Rosalie Allen worked for more than 30 years with her husband, George Burns, in vaudeville, radio, motion pictures, and television. She was born on July 26, 1895, the youngest of five children, to a father who taught dancing and physical education. She wanted to be a secretary, but she joined her sisters in a vaudeville act when she was 14. In the 1920s, she met Burns, and they formed a comedy team that continued after their marriage in 1926. Their success in New York and London caused their radio audience to grow to 45 million by 1940. In their act, a young man chatted with his "dizzy" girlfriend, who used malapropisms in her responses, about topics that everyone could enjoy. When the two went to television, their humor focused on the family, with Burns functioning as the stage manager and smoking a cigar while Allen pretended to be a silly wife. Among her benevolent acts was a donation of pastels to a New York gallery to make money for the China Aid Council in 1938.

BIBLIOGRAPHY

Blythe, Cheryl, and Susan Sackett. *Say Good Night, Gracie! The Story of Burns and Allen.* New York: Dutton, 1986. 0-525-24386-0, 304p. Based on interviews and archives from libraries for the performing arts, this biography of Allen and her husband asserts that their fame was based on their timeless humor.

Burns, George. *Gracie: A Love Story.* New York: Putnam, 1988. 0-399-13384-4, 319p. Burns portrays his wife, Allen, as a strong, generous woman who worked hard and won them success.

Clements, Cynthia, and Sandra Weber. *George Burns and Gracie Allen: A Bio-Bibliography.* Westport, CT: Greenwood Press, 1996. 0-313-26883-5, 412p. The text gives a thorough overview of Allen's life and career.

AMES, JESSIE DANIEL (1883–1972)
Reformer   **Palestine, Texas**

Jessie Daniel Ames was an antilynching activist and suffragist who became the director of the women's committee of the Commission on Interracial Cooperation. Born on November 2, 1883, she was the third of four children. Her father was a self-educated orphan who worked as a train dispatcher and telegraph operator, and her mother was a teacher. When Ames's older sister became her father's favorite, Ames felt unloved and had difficulty forming friendships in school. After graduation from Southwestern University in 1902, she married and had children, but she and her husband were often separated, and at 31, she was widowed. The suffrage movement interested her, and after she organized a county association, the Texas association elected her treasurer in 1918. She helped Texas become the first southern state to ratify the Nineteenth Amendment. She then formed the Texas League of Women Voters and attended the league's national conference before helping found the Texas Federation of Women's Clubs. When racism became her major concern, she founded the Association of Southern Women for the Prevention of Lynching and showed from statistical studies that only one-third of the victims supposedly lynched for raping white women were convicted for that crime. Although she did not want federal control of lynching legislation because it would undermine her personal position, she educated women about its implications and how it affected their own lives.

BIBLIOGRAPHY

Hall, Jacquelyn Dowd. *Revolt Against Chivalry: Jessie Daniel Ames and the Women's Campaign Against Lynching.* New York: Columbia University Press, 1993. 0-231-08282-7, 405p. Hall interviewed Ames's daughter and used unpublished family correspondence and autobiographical writings in this readable biography, which is carefully researched and documented.

ANDERSON, MARIAN (1897-1993)
Opera Singer   Philadelphia, Pennsylvania

Marian Anderson was a distinguished classical singer about whom Arturo Toscanini, the famed conductor, noted, "Yours is a voice such as one hears only once in a hundred years." Her loving parents raised her in Philadelphia, where she was born on February 27, 1897, but her father died from a head wound when she was 10, and her family moved to his parents' home. Her church supported her singing and love of music in a variety of ways, and in 1919, **Lucie E. Campbell** introduced her as the vocalist in Atlantic City at the National Baptist Convention. She won her first vocal contest in a Philadelphia Philharmonic Society appearance and followed it with a New York City win in 1925 which offered her an appearance with the New York Philharmonic. In 1929, she went to Europe, and after success in Scandinavia, Germans invited her to sing, unaware of her race. When they discovered she was not Aryan, however, they rescinded the offer. Racial incidents continued to mar her career, especially in Washington, DC, where the Daughters of the American Revolution (DAR) refused to allow her to sing in their Constitution Hall. **Eleanor Roosevelt** resigned from the organization and arranged for Anderson to perform at the Lincoln Memorial, where a crowd of 75,000 heard her on Easter Sunday, April 9, 1939. She married in 1943, and after World War II sang engagements around the world. She returned to America in January 1955 became the first African American to sing at the Metropolitan Opera, as Ulrica in Verdi's *Un Ballo in Maschera*, before touring for another 40,000 miles as a goodwill ambassador in Asia. Among her awards were the Spingarn Medal, the United States Arts Medal, and election to The National Women's Hall of Fame. She sang at the presidential inaugurations of Dwight D. Eisenhower and John F. Kennedy and gave over 50 farewell concerts before her retirement in 1965.

BIBLIOGRAPHY

Anderson, Marian. *My Lord, What a Morning: An Autobiography*. Madison: University of Wisconsin Press, 1992. 0-299-13390-7, 314p. In her readable, recommended autobiography, Anderson recalls her life as an opera star and concert performer, emphasizing the importance to her of membership in the Metropolitan Opera company and her pleasure at the number of African Americans who succeeded her there.

Newman, Shirlee Petkin. *Marian Anderson: Lady from Philadelphia*. Philadelphia: Westminster Press, 1965. No ISBN, 175p. This biography for young adults covers Anderson's life and career.

Patterson, Charles. *Marian Anderson*. New York: Watts, 1988. 0-531-10568-7, 159p. Patterson relies on Anderson's autobiography for most of this young adult biography.

Vehanen, Kosti. *Marian Anderson: A Portrait*. 1941. Westport, CT: Greenwood Press, 1970. 0-8371-4051-X, 270p. Vehanen was Anderson's accompanist for 10 years, and this memoir covers the time they traveled together, which culminated with Anderson's performance at the Lincoln Memorial.

ANGELOU, MAYA (1928-)
Poet and Author   St. Louis, Missouri

Maya Angelou is an African American poet and author. Born Marguerite Johnson on April 4, 1928, to a doorman and a registered nurse, she grew up with her paternal grandmother when her parents divorced. After her mother's boyfriend raped Angelou when she was seven, she remained mute for nearly five years. At 16, Angelou had a son, an event she had not planned but which she thinks saved her life. When she could not answer her son's varied questions, she went to the library to search for the appropriate responses. After this initial education, and jobs including a dancer and songwriter, she and her son went to Africa for several years, where she taught at the University of Ghana. When she returned to America, an agent urged her to write her autobiography. The result, *I Know Why the Caged Bird Sings*, was nominated for a National Book Award. Angelou has been the Reynolds Professor of American Studies at Wake Forest University since 1981. In her work, she explores themes of oppression—racial, social, and economic—and in 1993, she read one of her poems at the presidential inauguration. She was elected to The National Women's Hall of Fame in 1998.

BIBLIOGRAPHY
Angelou, Maya. *All God's Children Need Traveling Shoes*. New York: Vintage, 1987. 0-394-75077-2, 209p. In the fifth volume of her autobiography, Angelou discusses living in Ghana, where she found that being African American did not mean that she would feel comfortable.

———. *The Heart of a Woman*. New York: Random, 1981. 0-394-51273-1, 272p. In this volume of her autobiography, Angelou writes about the years 1957 to 1962, when she moved to Cairo with her African common-law husband, separated, and enrolled her son in a college in Ghana.

———. *I Know Why the Caged Bird Sings*. New York: Random, 1970. No ISBN, 281p. This recommended autobiography of Angelou describes her painful childhood while simultaneously revealing the supportive nature of her southern African American community.

Hagen, Lyman B. *Heart of a Woman, Mind of a Writer, and Soul of a Poet*. Lanham, MD: University Press of America, 1996. 0-7618-0620-2, 180p. This thoroughly researched and documented critical text examines Angelou's use of autobiography in relationship to her writing.

Shapiro, Miles. *Maya Angelou*. New York: Chelsea House, 1994. 0-7910-1862-8, 111p. Using interviews and Angelou's autobiographical works, Shapiro focuses on her youth and early adulthood, enumerating her careers as cook, dancer, madam, singer, actress, poet, administrator, journalist, and professor.

ANTHONY, SUSAN BROWNELL (1820–1906)
Activist   Adams, Massachusetts

Susan Brownell Anthony spent her adult life crusading for woman suffrage, serving as president of the National American Woman Suffrage Association. She was born on February 15, 1820, the daughter of a Quaker abolitionist and cotton manufacturer who dominated the family. Anthony learned to read and write by age three and attended a boarding school before beginning to teach at a female academy. When she returned home in 1849, however, she met Frederick Douglass, William Lloyd Garrison, and Wendell Phillips, and heard them discuss needed reforms in society. She then became an active reformer, her first public project being the founding of the Woman's State Temperance Society of New York. More concerned about suffrage than temperance, she, **Elizabeth Cady Stanton**, and **Amelia Bloomer** began their crusade for women's rights. In 1854, she added the antislavery movement to her concerns and served as an agent for the American Anti-Slavery Society. After the Civil War, she campaigned for equal pay for women. When she tried to vote in 1872, she was arrested, but instead of hiding, she lectured and began her quest for federal woman suffrage. In 1888, she organized the International Council of Women, and in 1904 founded the International Woman Suffrage Alliance, a longtime dream. Throughout her life, she supported coeducation both vocally and financially. Participants at meetings she attended in London and Berlin during her activism repeatedly acknowledged her contributions to women's rights worldwide. Recently, she was elected to The National Women's Hall of Fame.

BIBLIOGRAPHY
Anthony, Katharine Susan. *Susan B. Anthony: Her Personal History and Her Era*. 1954. New York: Russell & Russell, 1975. 0-8462-1742-2, 521p. This scholarly, well-researched, and documented biography of Anthony gives a thorough view of her life and accomplishments.
Barry, Kathleen. *Susan B. Anthony: A Biography of a Singular Feminist*. New York: New York University Press, 1988. 0-8147-1105-7, 426p. Using feminist and sociological approaches, Barry examines Anthony's choice of social justice instead of marriage and a family life.
Dorr, Rheta Louise. *Susan B. Anthony: The Woman Who Changed the Mind of a Nation*. 1928. New York: AMS Press, 1970. 0-404-00626-4, 367p. Dorr's thorough and cogent account clearly presents Anthony's character and achievements.
Harper, Ida Husted. *Life and Work of Susan B. Anthony*. 1908. Salen, NH: Ayer, 1983. 0-405-00102-9, 1633p. Harper knew Anthony, and she wrote this readable biography after examining 20,000 letters, diaries of 50 years, financial accounts, scrapbooks, and Anthony's personal responses.
Sherr, Lynn. *Failure Is Impossible*. New York: Times Books, 1995. 0-8129-2430-4, 382p. Sherr's accessible text, based on Anthony's speeches, letters, interviews, and writings, examines her views and her attitudes toward her friends.

ANTIN, MARY (1881–1949)
Author   Polatsk, Belarus

Mary Antin's work described the immigrant experience in the United States. She was born June 13, 1881, the second of six children of a trader who lived in the pale of settlement. She migrated to America with her family when she was 13, following her father, who had left three years prior. The family remained poor, but Antin learned English rapidly and advanced through five grades in six months. Teachers arranged for publication of her compositions in Boston newspapers and encouraged her progress toward college. Her translation of the Yiddish letters she wrote to her uncle in Russia were published as a book, *From Plotzk to Boston* (1899). She married instead of attending college full-time, but then enrolled in Columbia, where her husband was a professor. She believed that immigrants were the backbone of the country, giving America the strength it needed, and she focused on the immigrant experience in both *The Promised Land* (1912) and *They Who Knock at the Gates* (1914). Antin separated from her husband when he remained loyal to Germany during World War I, and she began pursuing interests which included natural history. As she published fewer articles in her later life, she began lecturing to support herself.

BIBLIOGRAPHY

Antin, Mary. *From Plotzk to Boston*. 1899. New York: M. Wiener, 1970. 0-910129-45-2, 80p. When only 11, Antin wrote about the difficulties her family endured on shipboard in 1891 traveling from Plotzk to Boston.

———. *The Promised Land*. Ed. Walter Sollors. New York: Penguin, 1997. 0-14-018985-8, 305p. Sollors's informative introduction discloses Antin's attitudes during various periods of her publishing life, and in the autobiography, Antin recalls her life, from Plotzk schoolgirl to American writer and lecturer.

ARZNER, DOROTHY (1900–1979)
Film Director   San Francisco, California

Dorothy Arzner was one of Hollywood's most valued film directors. She was born on January 3, 1900, to a cafe owner in whose establishment she eventually waited on tables. At first Arzner wanted to become a doctor, but after serving in World War I as an ambulance driver, she chose to become a typist in the script department of Paramount Studios. She soon became an editor, and her editing of a silent film bullfight scene starring Rudolph Valentino established her as one of silent film's best editors. In 1927, she began to direct, and her debut film, *Fashions for Women*, was a success. She was one of the first directors to use theme music and overhead microphones, hanging from fishing poles. While earning her reputation as a "star-maker," she worked with actors including **Katharine Hepburn**, Clara Bow, and **Lucille Ball**. By 1943, she had directed 16 credited films. During World War II, she also created training films for the Women's Army Corps. When she stopped directing films, she initiated film courses at the Pasadena Playhouse, taught film at the University of California, and made television commercials.

BIBLIOGRAPHY

Johnston, Claire, ed. *The Work of Dorothy Arzner: Towards a Feminist Cinema*. London: British Film Institute, 1975. 0–85170–044–6, 34p. The text contains three brief researched and documented essays; two examine Arzner's work as a feminist challenging the male view in her cinema, and the third is an interview with Arzner about her life and work.

Mayne, Judith. *Directed by Dorothy Arzner*. Bloomington: Indiana University Press, 1994. 0–253–33716–X, 209p. Mayne recounts Arzner's directing career and offers a feminist critique of her films.

ASTOR, NANCY WITCHER (1879–1964)
Government Official   Greenwood, Virginia

Viscountess Nancy Witcher Langhorne Astor was the first woman to hold a seat in the British Parliament. Although born into a poor Greenwood, Virginia, family on May 19, 1879, Astor spent her adult life in England, raising five children prior to her election to the House of Commons after her second husband, Waldorf Astor, succeeded to his father's title in the House of Lords in 1919. She remained a Member of Parliament until she retired in 1945. She also served as a hostess, attracting many interesting and intelligent people to her home at Cliveden in Buckinghamshire. Her social activism began after a conversion to Christian Science in 1914, and during World War I, she set up a military hospital at Cliveden, visited the Soviet Union with George Bernard Shaw, and spoke against communism on her return. People either loved or hated her; she was rude and tyrannical, but she was also honest and loyal. She worked for women's rights, temperance, children's welfare, and progressive education. She advocated raising the age at which children were allowed to leave school, improving conditions in distributive and catering trades, and world peace.

BIBLIOGRAPHY

Grigg, John. *Nancy Astor: A Lady Unashamed*. Boston: Little, Brown, 1981. 0–316–32870–7, 192p. Grigg sees Astor as having the spirit of a pioneer with a brilliant and unique personality who worked to accomplish her historic mission.

Halperin, John. *Eminent Georgians: The Lives of King George V, Elizabeth Bowen, St. John Philby, and Nancy Astor*. New York: St. Martin's, 1995. 0–312–12661–1, 242p. In this collective biography, Halperin creates an interesting, affectionate, and conversational life of Lady Astor.

Langhorne, Elizabeth Coles. *Nancy Astor and Her Friends*. New York: Praeger, 1974. No ISBN, 277p. In her researched and readable biography, Langhorne says that Astor, who knew that she was not an original thinker, did not want her biography written because she thought that only people with new ideas were worth reading about.

Masters, Anthony. *Nancy Astor: A Biography*. New York: McGraw-Hill, 1981. 0–07–040784–3, 237p. Masters thinks that Astor might have been more successful politically if she had not tried to bring Prohibition to England and had not used Christian Science to suit her own needs.

Sykes, Christopher. *Nancy: The Life of Lady Astor*. Chicago: Academy Chicago, 1984. 0–89733–098–6, 637p. Using letters and accounts from friends and family along with Astor's unpublished autobiography in this balanced and recommended biography, Sykes gives an objective overview of her life.

AUSTIN, MARY HUNTER (1868–1934)
Author   Carlinville, Illinois

Mary Hunter Austin wrote novels and essays about Native American culture. She was born on September 9, 1868, the fourth of six children of a lawyer who had emigrated from Britain and his Scotch-Irish wife. Ignored by her mother after her father's early death, Austin developed her inner resources, discovered at age five when she had a mystical experience; she called her deeper self the "Inknower" or "Genius" and relied on it when she worked. She graduated in science from Blackburn College in 1888 and married three years later after moving to California with her family and falling in love with desert life. Her daughter was born mentally disabled, and her husband could not function at his job, so to support the family, she began writing seriously. Her first book, *The Land of Little Rain*, published in 1903, remains a Western classic. She wrote a book a year, and after traveling abroad, discovered in London that authors such as George Bernard Shaw, W. B. Yeats, and H. G. Wells greatly admired the intelligence of her writing. After her move to New Mexico in 1924, she worked to conserve the arts of the Native Americans, and the University of New Mexico gave her an honorary degree. She published 32 volumes and nearly 200 articles in her lifetime in which she discussed socialism, feminism, and other timely problems, but her main concern remained Native American heritage.

BIBLIOGRAPHY

Austin, Mary Hunter. *Earth Horizon: Autobiography*. 1960. Albuquerque: University of New Mexico Press, 1991. 0–8263–1316–7, 403p. Austin's autobiography, written partially in the third person, reflects her strong beliefs.

Church, Peggy Pond. *Wind's Trail: The Early Life of Mary Austin*. Ed. Shelley Armitage. Santa Fe: Museum of New Mexico Press, 1990. 0–89013–200–3, 215p. In her readable and well-researched biography of Austin, Church emphasizes the connection between Austin's objective and subjective experiences.

Fink, Augusta. *I-Mary: A Biography of Mary Austin*. Tucson: University of Arizona Press, 1983. 0–8165–0789–9, 310p. In her researched, documented, and readable biography, Fink examines Austin's difficult private life and her public image.

Lanigan, Esther F. *Mary Austin: Song of a Maverick*. New Haven, CT: Yale University Press, 1989. 0–300–04255–8, 269p. In her carefully researched biography, Lanigan identifies moments in Austin's life that reveal the complexities of her personality and her work.

Pearce, Thomas Matthews. *Mary Hunter Austin*. New York: Twayne, 1965. No ISBN, 158p. This carefully researched and documented critical biography examines Austin's life and work.

$\mathscr{B}$

BACALL, LAUREN (1924–)
Actor   New York, New York

Lauren Bacall has won awards for her work as an actor in film and on stage. She was born Betty Joan Perske on September 16, 1924, and her mother raised her. She attended the American Academy of Dramatic Arts in New York, but when a director's wife saw her picture on the cover of *Harper's Bazaar* in 1944, Bacall was cast in *To Have and Have Not* with Humphrey Bogart, whom she married. Her subsequent performances also received reviewers' praises. After Bogart died, Bacall returned to Broadway, and in 1970, she received a Tony Award and a Drama Desk Award for *Applause*. On tour with *Applause*, she received the *Sarah Siddons Award. She received another Tony in 1981 for *Woman of the Year*. In 1996, Bacall earned her first Academy Award nomination, along with a Golden Globe Award and a Screen Actors Guild Award, for *The Mirror Has Two Faces*. Other awards include the George Eastman Award, the Kennedy Center Honors Lifetime Achievement Award, and induction into the Theatre Hall of Fame.

BIBLIOGRAPHY
Bacall, Lauren. *Lauren Bacall by Myself*. New York: Knopf, 1979. 0-394-41308-3, 377p. Bacall covers her life and remembers the illness and death of her first husband, Humphrey Bogart. National Book Award.
———. *Now*. New York: Knopf, 1994. 0-394-57412-5, 214p. Bacall reflects on her relationships with her children and her friends.
Greenberger, Howard. *Bogey's Baby*. New York: St. Martin's, 1978. 0-312-08740-3, 216p. This readable biography about Bacall's marriage to her first husband,

Humphrey Bogart, includes many anecdotes but little insight into her life or relationships.

Quirk, Lawrence J. *Lauren Bacall: Her Films and Career*. Secaucus, NJ: Citadel, 1986. 0-8065-0935-X, 192p. In a chatty popular biography, Quirk examines each of Bacall's movies and briefly highlights major events in her life.

Royce, Brenda Scott. *Lauren Bacall: A Bio-Bibliography*. Westport, CT: Greenwood Press, 1992. 0-313-27831-8, 283p. The text details Lauren Bacall's life and career.

BAEZ, JOAN   (1941-)
Singer   Staten Island, New York

Joan Baez has used her singing to express her beliefs in civil rights and world peace. She was born on January 9, 1941. Her father was a Mexican-born physicist who taught at several American universities as well as in Paris and Baghdad and her mother was Scottish. Baez left Boston University in her first semester, began singing in Harvard Square coffeehouses, and then performed at the Newport Folk Festival. In 1960, she made her first recording and toured small African American colleges in the South. In 1963, she participated in the civil rights march on Washington, DC, and marched with Martin Luther King, Jr., from Selma to Montgomery, Alabama, in 1965. She participated in anti-Vietnam War demonstrations, protested taxes that paid for armaments, and founded and financed, with Ira Sandperl, the Institute for the Study of Nonviolence. She married David Harris, an antiwar activist, but they divorced in 1973 after the birth of a child. In tours abroad, Baez supported peace and human rights before founding Humanitas International in 1979. Of her more than 30 albums, 8 reached the gold status, as did several of her singles.

BIBLIOGRAPHY

Baez, Joan. *And a Voice to Sing With: A Memoir*. New York: Summit, 1987. 0-671-40062-2, 378p. Baez chronicles her life beginning in the 1960s.

———. *Daybreak*. New York: Dial, 1968. No ISBN, 159p. Baez recounts her childhood, her relationship with her parents, and her youthful aspirations.

Fuss, Charles J. *Joan Baez: A Bio-Bibliography*. Westport, CT: Greenwood Press, 1996. 0-313-28463-6, 252p. A biography and a chronology of Baez's career comprise this informative text.

Garza, Hedda. *Joan Baez*. New York: Chelsea House, 1991. 0-7910-1233-6, 119p. Garza's researched biography for young adults discusses Baez's life and career.

BAILEY, FLORENCE MERRIAM   (1863-1948)
Ornithologist   Locust Grove, New York

Florence Merriam Bailey was an ornithologist and nature writer who became the first female associate member and first female fellow of the American Ornithologists' Union. She was born on August 8, 1863, the youngest of four children of a banker and an educated mother. She grew up on the family's country estate and became interested in natural history under the tutelage of her father and brother. Although she attended Smith College as a special student for four years, she was not granted a degree until 1921. She became interested in birds while attending Smith and began contributing articles on bird lore to *Audubon* magazine, some of them later collected in her first book. While traveling for her health, she watched birds in the West before returning to Washington, DC, and marrying a man with similar interests. Together they took strenuous journeys connected with her husband's job with the United States Biological Survey, and on these trips, she recorded her ornithological observations, becoming one of the first explorers to study live birds in the field. In 1897, she helped establish the Audubon Society of the District of Columbia. In 1928 she published *Birds of New Mexico*, for which she became the first woman to win the American Ornithologists' Union's Brewster Medal. She also wrote *Birds of Village and Field*, one of the first popular American bird guides. Always concerned about social welfare, she held memberships in several groups, including the National Child Labor Committee. Although she made no new discoveries, she contributed much and was honored when a chickadee discovered in southern California was named *Farus gambeli baileyae*.

BIBLIOGRAPHY

Kofalk, Harriet. *No Woman Tenderfoot: Florence Merriam Bailey, Pioneer Naturalist.* College Station: Texas A and M University Press, 1989. 0-89096-278-9, 225p. Kofalk chronicles Bailey's life using quotes from her writings as a basis.

BAILEY, PEARL (1918–1990)
Singer   Newport News, Virginia

Pearl Bailey, born on March 29, 1918, gained international acclaim as an entertainer. When she was four, her parents separated. She stayed with her father at first, but eventually she and three siblings joined their mother and her husband in Philadelphia. Bailey won an amateur contest at Philadelphia's Pearl Theater when she was 15 and followed that victory with another at an Apollo Theater amateur night in New York City. She performed throughout the 1930s in a variety of places and settled in Washington, DC, before touring the country to sing for the troops in a series of USO tours during World War II. In 1946, she appeared on Broadway and won the Donaldson Award for most promising newcomer. In 1952, after a disastrous second marriage, she married the white drummer Louis Bellson. Among her honors were a Tony Award, the March of Dimes Award, and the *Britannica* Life Achievement Award. She wrote several books, became the special advisor to the U.N. Mission of the United Nations General Assembly, and received a B.A. in theology from Georgetown University. In 1988, she received the Presidential Medal of Freedom.

BIBLIOGRAPHY

Bailey, Pearl. *Between You and Me: A Heartfelt Memoir on Learning, Loving and Living.* New York: Doubleday, 1989. 0–385–27972–8, 270p. Bailey's conversational autobiography discusses her student life and after.

———. *Hurry Up, America, and Spit.* New York: Harcourt Brace Jovanovich, 1976. 0–15–143000–4, 106p. This collection of poetry, prose, and letters reveals Bailey's thoughts on self-reliance.

———. *Talking to Myself.* New York: Harcourt Brace Jovanovich, 1971. 0–15–187990–7, 233p. Bailey reflects on several subjects including politics, show business, friends, and religion.

BAKER, ELLA (1903–1986)
Reformer   Norfolk, Virginia

Ella Josephine Baker was an important link in the civil rights movement from the 1930s until her death. Born on December 13, 1903, to educated parents who were children of former slaves, Baker grew up in Littleton, North Carolina. Her father was a steamship waiter. Her grandfather had purchased some of the land on which he was a slave, and his character influenced Baker's thinking. She attended boarding school at age 15 in Raleigh and graduated as valedictorian of her college class at Shaw in 1927. She moved to New York in the Great Depression, and in her first few years in Harlem, she joined the Young Negroes Cooperative League and was elected its first national director. She also worked with the Workers Education Project of the Works Progress Administration. Although she married, she refused to take her husband's name and never allowed her private life to interfere with her political concerns. In 1940, she joined the NAACP, became an officer, and created contacts throughout the African American community in the South that became the foundation of the civil rights movement of the 1950s. In 1958, she moved to Atlanta to coordinate the Crusade for Citizenship, a voter rights campaign. Two years later, she and other Shaw graduates formed the Student Nonviolent Coordinating Committee, and from this group evolved the Mississippi Freedom Democratic Party in 1964. Baker's organizational skills helped start the civil rights movement. She was honored with election to The National Women's Hall of Fame.

BIBLIOGRAPHY

Dallard, Shyrlee. *Ella Baker: A Leader Behind the Scenes.* Englewood Cliffs, NJ: Silver Burdett, 1990. 0–382–09931–1, 130p. Dallard's young adult biography, based on interviews, newspaper articles, and magazines, emphasizes Baker's contribution to the civil rights movement.

Grant, Joanne. *Ella Baker: Freedom Bound.* New York: Wiley, 1998. 0–471–02020–6, 270p. For this biography, Baker's niece researched library archives and interviewed Baker's friends to establish her importance to the civil rights movement.

BAKER, JOSEPHINE (1906–1975)
Entertainer   St. Louis, Missouri

Josephine Baker, "the Black Venus of France," was the first African American singer and dancer to be famous as an entertainer. She was born on June 3, 1906, and started dancing at an early age. She began touring at 16 and performed in the African American show *Shuffle Along*, the major musical event of the era in Harlem. In 1925, she went to Paris and performed as an exotic dancer at the Folies Bergère and the Casino de Paris, where she introduced the Charleston and the Black Bottom. Baker began making films while in Europe, and when she returned to New York, she appeared in the Ziegfeld Follies, with her ability to sing in six languages broadening her appeal. To avoid racism in America, she became a French citizen in 1937. She entertained Allied soldiers in North Africa during World War II and worked as a Red Cross volunteer. In 1940, she became involved in underground intelligence, an effort for which Charles De Gaulle awarded her the Legion of Honor and the Rosette of Resistance. She married four times, but none of the marriages lasted. In the 1950s, she began adopting orphans from different races, and to support her 12 children, she had to keep working. When she died, France honored her with a 21-gun salute.

BIBLIOGRAPHY
Baker, Jean-Claude. *Josephine: The Hungry Heart.* New York: Random, 1993. 0-679-40915-7, 532p. The author researched and interviewed for over 20 years to learn more about Baker, who adopted him when he was a 14-year-old waiter.

Baker, Josephine. *Josephine.* 1977. New York: Paragon House, 1988. 1-55778-108-7, 302p. Baker's third husband used her autobiography for this readable memoir.

Haney, Lynn. *Naked at the Feast: A Biography of Josephine Baker.* New York: Dodd, Mead, 1981. 0-396-07900-8, 338p. Haney's carefully researched and readable text shows both Baker's public face and her private concerns.

Papich, Stephen. *Remembering Josephine Baker.* Indianapolis: Bobbs-Merrill, 1976. 0-672-52257-8, 237p. Papich, a close friend and Baker's choreographer, used anecdotes and memorabilia to document this readable biography.

Rose, Phyllis. *Jazz Cleopatra: Josephine Baker in Her Time.* New York: Doubleday, 1989. 0-385-24891-1, 321p. Rose's carefully researched biography of Baker places her within a larger social and historical context.

BALL, LUCILLE (1911–1989)
Actor and Businesswoman   Jamestown, New York

Lucille Désirée Ball was an actor and television comedy star. She was born on August 6, 1911, to a telephone lineman, who died when she was four, and a pianist. The family lived with her grandmother and her vaudeville-loving socialist grandfather. She decided to enter the theater at 15 and dropped out of school to enroll in a Manhattan drama school. She began modeling, and after posing as the Chesterfield Cigarette Girl in 1933, she won national attention and minor film roles. In 1940, she married Desi Arnaz, and in 1951, they began their television series, *I Love Lucy*. In the show, Ball played a band leader's wife who became involved in chaotic schemes and situations. The series won more than 200 awards, including five Emmys. After their divorce, Ball continued to work; as head of Desilu Productions, she was the first woman since **Mary Pickford** to run a major Hollywood studio. She then married Gary Morton, and they also created a company. She always worked hard for her success both on stage and behind it.

BIBLIOGRAPHY

Ball, Lucille. *Love, Lucy*. New York: Putnam, 1996. 0–399–14205–3, 286p. Ball wrote her autobiography before 1964, but her children did not discover it until 1989.

Brady, Kathleen. *Lucille: The Life of Lucille Ball*. New York: Hyperion, 1994. 0–7868–6007–3, 397p. Brady's carefully researched biography details Ball's life and career as well as her appearance before the House Un–American Activities Committee, a result of her grandfather's registering the family as Socialists in the 1930s.

Brochu, Jim. *Lucy in the Afternoon*. New York: Morrow, 1990. 0–688–08646–2, 271p. Brochu first saw Ball in 1960 on Broadway, and he bases his memoir on later interviews with her.

Harris, Warren G. *Lucy & Desi: The Legendary Love Story of Television's Most Famous Couple*. New York: Simon and Schuster, 1991. 0–671–74709–6, 351p. With reminiscences from Ball's friends, family, and colleagues, Harris divulges Ball's struggle through an unhappy marriage.

Sanders, Coyne Steven. *Desilu: The Story of Lucille Ball and Desi Arnaz*. New York: Morrow, 1993. 0–688–11217–X, 384p. This carefully documented biography of Ball is based on archives and interviews with her family.

BARRYMORE, ETHEL (1879–1959)
Actor   Philadelphia, Pennsylvania

Ethel Barrymore was a film and stage actor often called the "first lady of the American theater." She was born Ethel Blythe on August 15, 1879, one of three children and the only daughter of two actors. She lived mainly with her grandparents, studying intermittently at several schools. In 1894, she made her professional debut in her grandmother's company, but she did not have a major success until she performed in London in 1897. Her first Broadway show was *Captain Jinks of the Horse Marines* (1901). Other well-known plays in which she acted include *Déclassée* (1919), *The Second Mrs. Tanqueray* (1924), *The Constant Wife* (1928), and *The Corn Is Green* (1942). In 1928, she opened the Ethel Barrymore Theater in New York with *The Kingdom of God*. She also appeared in vaudeville, on radio, on television, and in film. In 1944, she won an Academy Award for *None but the Lonely Heart*.

BIBLIOGRAPHY

Barrymore, Ethel. *Memories: An Autobiography*. New York: Harper, 1954. No ISBN, 310p. Barrymore's autobiography, with entertaining anecdotes, covers her 60-year career in the theater through her seventieth year.

Fox, Mary Virginia. *Ethel Barrymore: A Portrait*. Chicago: Reilly and Lee, 1970. No ISBN, 133p. This biography of Barrymore for young adults reveals her dignity and the respect she achieved.

Peters, Margot. *The House of Barrymore*. New York: Knopf, 1990. 0-394-55321-7, 641p. Peters unearthed many sources to recreate the Barrymore family in a balanced, definitive biography.

Thorleifson, Alex. *Ethel Barrymore*. New York: Chelsea House, 1991. 1-555-46640-0, 109p. In a biography for young adults, Thorleifson recounts Barrymore's life.

BARTON, CLARA HARLOWE (1821-1912)
Nurse   North Oxford, Massachusetts

Clara Barton, the "Angel of the Battlefield," founded the American Red Cross. Clarissa Harlowe Barton was born on December 25, 1821, the youngest of five of a veteran soldier farmer who believed in helping needy persons. She attended school sporadically and helped her brother recover from a two-year illness. Her teaching career began at 18, and after 18 years, she left when a male became her boss. She took a job as a clerk in the United States Patent Office, but when the Civil War began, she created an agency to gather supplies and distribute them to wounded soldiers via mule team. She often spent her own money during this operation, refusing to join **Dorothea Dix**'s organization. President Abraham Lincoln requested that she set up a bureau of records in 1865 which would help locate missing men. She did so, and then lectured over 300 times about her experiences. In 1869, she went to Europe for a rest but, once there, preferred to help distribute supplies to victims of the Franco-Prussian War. While in Europe, she first heard of Henry Dunant's International Committee of the Red Cross, and when she returned to the United States, she established the American National Red Cross, serving as its president until 1904. During this time, she convinced the government to sign the Geneva Agreement in 1882 for uniform treatment of the sick, wounded, dead, and imprisoned during war. She then added an amendment to the Red Cross constitution to offer relief during earthquakes, floods, famines, cyclones, and pestilence. She helped with disasters in the 1880s and 1890s and went to Cuba during the Spanish-American War. For her work, she received medals and awards from several countries including Germany, Russia, Serbia, and Turkey. She was also elected to The National Women's Hall of Fame.

BIBLIOGRAPHY
Barton, William Eleazar. *The Life of Clara Barton, Founder of the American Red Cross*. 1922. New York: AMS Press, 1969. No ISBN, 2 vols. The author based his thorough and balanced biography on Barton's journals, unpublished autobiographical writings, letters, clippings, and records.

Burton, David Henry. *Clara Barton: In the Service of Humanity*. Westport, CT: Greenwood Press, 1995. 0-313-28945-X, 176p. Burton reveals in a balanced account that Barton's dedication to others was not always selfless.

Oates, Stephen B. *A Woman of Valor: Clara Barton and the Civil War*. New York: Macmillan, 1994. 0–02–923405–0, 527p. Using Barton's letters, Oates reconstructs a recommended, informative, and balanced look at her life.

Pryor, Elizabeth Brown. *Clara Barton: Professional Angel*. Philadelphia: University of Pennsylvania Press, 1987. 0–8122–8060–1, 444p. In her carefully researched, recommended biography, Pryor uses recently discovered diaries, letters, and other primary sources to examine Barton's motives as well as her achievements.

BEACH, AMY MARCY (1867–1944)
Pianist and Composer   **Henniker, New Hampshire**

Amy Beach (Mrs. H.H.A. Beach) was a pianist and composer who was the first American woman to write a symphony. Born Amy Cheney on September 5, 1867, as the only child to educated parents, her father a mathematician and paper manufacturer and her mother a musician, Beach could sing tunes when she was one year old and was composing by age four. She received her only formal instruction in music theory in a harmony course at 15. At 16, she made her debut in Boston as a pianist and received positive reviews. She married a surgeon 24 years older than herself when she was 18. He encouraged her to compose and study composition by herself because he thought formal study might destroy her originality. She examined Bach's fugues and learned orchestration by notating themes she had heard at concerts from memory and comparing her rendition with the original score. In 1892, she became the first woman composer whose works the Boston Symphony Orchestra performed. The same year, she received a commission for a composition to dedicate the Woman's Building at the World's Columbian Exposition in Chicago. Four years later she completed her *Gaelic Symphony*, and major orchestras performed it throughout the country. She continued her own performances as a pianist, and after her husband died, she went to Europe and established her reputation there. She helped found the Association of American Women Composers and became its first president. She received many awards including honorary degrees.

BIBLIOGRAPHY

Block, Adrienne Fried. *Beach, Passionate Victorian*. New York: Oxford University Press, 1998. 0–19–507408–4, 448p. The researched and documented text examines Beach's life and work.

Brown, Jeanell Wise. *Amy Beach and Her Chamber Music*. Metuchen, NJ: Scarecrow, 1994. 0–8108–2884–7, 407p. Brown used critical reviews, original papers, and correspondence to informatively analyze Beach's life and chamber music.

BEACH, SYLVIA (1887–1962)
Businesswoman and Publisher   **Baltimore, Maryland**

Sylvia Beach was a bookshop owner and publisher. She was born on March 14, 1887, as the second of three daughters to a Presbyterian minister and his wife, daughter of a missionary. When Beach was 14, her father took an appointment at the American Church in Paris, and Beach felt at home in the city during the family's tenure. After serving as a Red Cross volunteer in Belgrade during World War I, she established a business with an accompanying lending library in Paris called Shakespeare and Company. Her shop attracted American expatriates including Ezra Pound, **Gertrude Stein**, Sherwood Anderson, Ernest Hemingway, **Katherine Anne Porter, Janet Flanner,** and **Hilda Doolittle.** In 1920, Beach met James Joyce, and when he despaired that his legally obscene book, *Ulysses*, would never be printed, she offered to help. Until February 2, 1922, she acted as Joyce's unpaid secretary and editor. She relinquished her rights to royalties after the eleventh printing, and when the book was published in the United States, she did not benefit. During the Depression in the 1930s, she had financial difficulties, and in 1936, the same year the French government gave her the Legion of Honor, her French friends rescued her. After the Germans arrived in Paris, she refused to sell *Finnegan's Wake* to a German, and to stop him from confiscating her inventory, she removed the entire contents of her bookstore within two hours. She never reopened her shop, but in 1959, she created a catalog of the persons she had known during the 1920s for a Paris exhibition, and in 1962, she spoke at the opening of the center for Joyce studies at the Martello Tower in Dublin, the site of the first chapter of *Ulysses*.

BIBLIOGRAPHY

Beach, Sylvia. *Shakespeare and Company*. 1959. Lincoln: University of Nebraska Press, 1980. 0–8032–6056–3, 199p. Beach's memoirs impart anecdotes about the many writers and artists she knew in Paris.

Fitch, Noel Riley. *Sylvia Beach and the Lost Generation*. New York: Norton, 1983. 0–393–01713–3, 447p. The Beach family papers and reminiscences from those who lived in Paris between the world wars help Fitch to report Beach's work and life in chronological detail.

BEARD, MARY RITTER (1876–1958)
Historian and Activist   **Indianapolis, Indiana**

Mary Ritter Beard was a historian and a feminist. She was born on August 5, 1876, the daughter of a reformist lawyer father and a schoolteacher mother. She graduated from DePauw University, and after teaching German for three years, married a college friend with whom she went to England while he studied history at Oxford. She returned to the United States in 1902 and enrolled at Columbia, but remained active in suffragism and trade unionism, helping organize the National Women's Trade Union League. She joined **Alice Paul**'s militant group in 1913 but resigned in 1920 because she thought protective labor legislation would be more helpful to women than the Equal Rights Amendment. She became a lecturer and writer and collaborated with her husband on a series of American history books. At 70, she wrote her major work, *Woman as a Force in History*, and although it received criticism from historical scholars at publication, it has become recognized as a seminal work in women's studies. Contemporary critics acknowledge her contributions and the importance of her views of history to feminist research.

BIBLIOGRAPHY

Beard, Mary Ritter. *Mary Ritter Beard: A Sourcebook*. 1977. Ed. Ann J. Lane. Boston: Northeastern University Press, 1988. 1-55553-029-X, 252p. Lane wanted to write a biography, but Beard's destruction of her personal papers led Lane to examine Beard's views of history in a scholarly, researched edition.

Cott, Nancy F., ed. *A Woman Making History: Mary Ritter Beard Through Her Letters*. 1977. New Haven, CT: Yale University Press, 1991. 0-300-04825-4, 378p. Cott introduces Beard's letters written from 1912 to 1955 with a biographical essay and critically interprets them.

Turoff, Barbara K. *Mary Beard as Force in History*. Dayton, OH: Wright State University Press, 1979. No ISBN, 85p. Turoff discovered in her thorough research on Beard that she was a social reformer, a pioneering scholar in women's history, and a feminist leader.

BEAUX, CECILIA (1855-1942)
Artist   Philadelphia, Pennsylvania

Cecilia Beaux was an American painter known for her introspective portraits. She was born May 1, 1855, the youngest of three daughters of an unsuccessful businessman. Since her mother died 12 days after her birth, Beaux lived with her maternal grandmother. Her aunts instructed her in art and took her to art galleries before she began serious study of painting at 16. The next year, she entered the Philadelphia School of Art and became enamored with the effects of light. Further study with William Sartain in Philadelphia led her to open a studio and paint her first full-length portrait, *Les Derniers Jours d'Enfance*, which won the Mary Smith Prize at the Pennsylvania Academy of Fine Arts, and which the Paris Salon exhibited in 1885. She won two more Mary Smith prizes for her portraiture, and in 1893 was elected to the Society of American Artists. In 1895, she became the first female instructor at the Pennsylvania Academy of Fine Arts. The next year, the Paris Salon exhibited six of her paintings, and she was honored with election as an associate in the Société Nationale des Beaux-Arts. She held 14 one-woman shows and won medals from the Carnegie Institute, the Pennsylvania Academy of Fine Arts, and the Paris exposition. In 1903, she became a full member of the National Academy of Design. In 1919, she received commissions to paint Allied leaders of World War I, including Georges Clemenceau, and in 1925, she became the first American woman to be invited to paint her self-portrait for the Medici Gallery of famous artists. She won the American Academy of Arts and Letters' gold medal and was finally elected to membership in 1933. She received honorary degrees and was twice named one of America's greatest living women.

BIBLIOGRAPHY

Beaux, Cecilia. *Cecilia Beaux: Portrait of an Artist*. Philadelphia: Pennsylvania Academy of the Fine Arts, 1974. No ISBN, 126p. This recommended retrospective catalog includes a chronology of Beaux's life and plates of her portraits.

Tappert, Tara Leigh. *Cecilia Beaux and the Art of Portraiture*. Washington, DC: Smithsonian Institution Press, 1995. 1-560-98658-1, 148p. This exhibition catalog displays Beaux's talents and explains why she was one of the most popular portrait painters.

BEECHER, CATHARINE ESTHER (1800–1878)
Educator and Author   East Hampton, New York

Catharine Beecher was an educator and an author. She was born on September 6, 1800, the eldest daughter of eight surviving children of a Presbyterian evangelical minister and temperance activist. Her siblings included **Harriet Beecher Stowe** and Henry Ward Beecher. Her mother died when Beecher was 16, and she took responsibility for the family until her father remarried. She briefly attended school before becoming a teacher, and after her fiancé died at sea, she devoted her life to others by first establishing a girls' school with her sister Mary, which later incorporated with Hartford Female Seminary. Beecher added exercise to her school curriculum, suggested that teachers focus on a limited number of subjects, and required women to be trained in the arts of teaching and domestic science. She had periods of poor health, but in the 1840s, concerned that many children received no education, she traveled widely, persuading teachers to go west and create schools. She then established the American Woman's Educational Association, advocating that teachers start local schools and train their students to become teachers. Royalties from her book, *A Treatise on Domestic Economy* (1841), advising women on housekeeping, health, and education, supported her. Throughout her life, however, she railed against exploitation of women, a condition she believed men could easily change.

BIBLIOGRAPHY

Harveson, Mae Elizabeth. *Catharine Esther Beecher*. 1932. New York: Arno Press, 1969. No ISBN, 295p. In a carefully researched and documented biography, Harveson declares that Beecher spent her life trying to obtain independence for women.

Sklar, Kathryn Kish. *Catharine Beecher: A Study in American Domesticity*. New Haven, CT: Yale University Press, 1973. 0-300-01580-1, 356p. Sklar's well-researched and documented biography of Beecher examines her life and work.

BELMONT, ALVA VANDERBILT (1853–1933)
Activist   Mobile, Alabama

Alva Belmont was a militant suffragist. Born Alva Smith on January 17, 1853, the third of five children of wealthy parents, she was educated in France and moved to New York City after the Civil War. Married first to a Vanderbilt, she joined the suffrage movement after the death of her second wealthy husband in 1908 and devoted the rest of her life to the cause. She believed that women had to clear the chaos that men had created, and she published articles expressing her views in several magazines, including *Harper's Bazaar* and *Good Housekeeping*. She rented offices on Fifth Avenue in New York for suffrage movement headquarters, helped found the Political Equality League in New York, and arranged a lecture tour around America for the British suffragist *Christabel Pankhurst. In the New York City shirtwaist makers' strike of 1909, Belmont paid bail for arrested strikers and walked the picket line. She served on the executive board of **Alice Paul**'s Congressional Union, and after it became the National Woman's Party, she was elected president in 1921. She also supported the international suffrage movement and used her own money to finance other claims of injustice.

BIBLIOGRAPHY

Rector, Margaret Hayden. *Alva, That Vanderbilt-Belmont Woman: Her Story as She Might Have Told It*. Wickford, RI: Dutch Island Press, 1992. 0–934881–13–8, 324p. Rector carefully researched Vanderbilt-Belmont's life for 10 years, and in a biography written from Vanderbilt-Belmont's point of view, includes only documented information.

Stasz, Clarice. *The Vanderbilt Women: Dynasty of Wealth, Glamour, and Tragedy*. New York: St. Martin's, 1991. 0–312–06486–1, 449p. In a well-researched, balanced, and readable collective biography, Stasz notes that Vanderbilt-Belmont refused to live according to social expectations.

BENEDICT, RUTH (1887–1948)
Anthropologist   New York, New York

Ruth Benedict was an anthropologist and poet. She was born Ruth Fulton on June 5, 1887, as the oldest of two girls, but her father died when she was 21 months old, and her mother, educated at Vassar, supported the family by teaching. Measles left Benedict almost deaf, and physical manifestations of her depression over this affliction occurred until she was 35. In 1909, she graduated Phi Beta Kappa from Vassar. After working for the Charity Organization Society in Buffalo and teaching in California, she married, but unfulfilled without children, she enrolled in the New School for Social Research in 1919. There she discovered her love of anthropology and worked with **Elsie Clews Parsons** and Franz Boas. Her first field trip to study the Serrano Indians of California in 1922 was the beginning of her research, and she received her Ph.D. the following year. During this period, she influenced **Margaret Mead**'s work and wrote poetry published under the pseudonym Anne Singleton. Before Benedict and her husband divorced in 1930, Benedict received a low salary while working with Boas since married women supposedly did not need money. She was finally appointed assistant professor at Columbia, and as she developed what she termed "patterns of culture," she began to realize that each culture fostered one dominant type of personality. After identifying these differences in Native American cultures and noting that societies sometimes revered persons considered outcasts in other cultures, she published her seminal work, *Patterns of Culture*, in 1934. Her research led her to combat racism in the early 1940s. She worked for the Office of War Information from 1943 to 1945, and managed a grant at Columbia from the Office of Naval Research on contemporary cultures in 1947 while serving as president of the American Anthropological Association. In 1948, Columbia finally offered her a full professorship, after ignoring her as Boas's successor in the late 1930s.

BIBLIOGRAPHY

Caffrey, Margaret M. *Ruth Benedict: Stranger in This Land*. Austin: University of Texas Press, 1989. 0-292-74655-5, 432p. Caffrey used recently opened papers of Margaret Mead for her biography of Benedict.

Mead, Margaret. *Ruth Benedict*. New York: Columbia University Press, 1974. 0-231-03519-5, 180p. The biographical text precedes selections from Benedict's main work, but adds little insight about Benedict's personality.

Modell, Judith Schachter. *Ruth Benedict: Patterns of a Life*. Philadelphia: University of Pennsylvania Press, 1983. 0-8122-7874-7, 355p. Modell's carefully researched biography paints Benedict as painfully introspective, concerned about women, and desiring passionate relationships.

BERNARD, JESSIE (1903–1996)
Sociologist   Minneapolis, Minnesota

Jessie Bernard, a sociologist, studied feminist topics. Born Jessie Shirley Ravitch on June 8, 1903, into a Romanian-Jewish family of immigrant shopkeepers, she enrolled at the University of Minnesota at 16, and when she fell in love with her sociology professor, graduated early with an M.A. in 1924, married him, and followed him on various assignments before obtaining her Ph.D. in 1935. She co-authored books with her husband on sociology while working as a social science analyst for the U.S. Bureau of Labor Statistics, and in the late 1930s, she began teaching. Among her own titles as a sociologist are *American Family Behavior*, *Academic Women*, and *Marriage and Family Among Negroes*. She ended her professional career at Pennsylvania State University in 1964 but began writing on feminist topics as a well-informed participant having been both a wife and a single mother. Those titles included *The Sex Game* (1968), *Women and the Public Interest* (1971), *The Future of Marriage* (1972), *The Future of Motherhood* (1974), and *The Female World* (1981).

BIBLIOGRAPHY

Bannister, Robert C. *Jessie Bernard: The Making of a Feminist*. New Brunswick, NJ: Rutgers University Press, 1991. 0-8135-1614-5, 276p. This well-written, scholarly biography traces Bernard's life and career.

Bernard, Jessie Shirley. *Self-Portrait of a Family*. Boston: Beacon Press, 1978. 0-8070-3798-2, 344p. Bernard used letters to remember raising three children while following a career after her husband's death.

BERNSTEIN, ALINE (1881–1955)
Stage and Costume Designer   New York, New York

Aline Frankau Bernstein was an award-winning stage and costume designer. Although given the name Hazel Frankau by her actor father after her birth on December 22, 1881, her mother renamed her Aline. Her parents died while she and her sister were young, after which she lived with her aunt, a drug addict. A family friend thought Bernstein had artistic talent and helped her enter the New York School of Applied Design on scholarship. She married a broker and painted portraits after studying with Robert Henri, but she also began volunteer work backstage at **Lillian Wald**'s Henry Street Settlement. For nine years, she served an unofficial apprenticeship designing and creating costumes for over 15 plays. In 1924, she began working part-time for the Theatre Guild and created her first important designs for the Neighborhood Playhouse. The next year, she met the author Thomas Wolfe, who was younger than she, and began a relationship with him during which she encouraged him to forget writing plays and focus on novels. The same year, 1925, she designed the first United States production of *The Dybbuk*. Three years later, she began working with *Eva Le Gallienne and the Civic Repertory Theatre, becoming the resident designer. She created a unit setting which could be moved and used in later seasons because of the flexibility of its parts. In 1935, she designed two movies and **Lillian Hellman**'s *The Children's Hour*. Four years later, she worked on Hellman's *The Little Foxes*. After teaching at the Experimental Theatre at Vassar from 1943 to 1949, she won a Tony Award for costume design in the opera *Regina*. After her last show in 1953, she helped her friend Irene Lewisohn establish the precursor of the Costume Institute of the Metropolitan Museum of Art.

BIBLIOGRAPHY

Bernstein, Aline. *An Actor's Daughter*. 1941. Athens: Ohio University Press, 1987. 0–8214–0870–4, 227p. Bernstein recounts her childhood and expresses great admiration for her father.

Klein, Carole. *Aline*. New York: Harper and Row, 1979. 0–06–012423–7, 352p. Klein's biography, based on research and personal interviews, details the relationships between Bernstein and Thomas Wolfe and between Bernstein and her family.

Stutman, Suzanne, ed. *My Other Loneliness: Letters of Thomas Wolfe and Aline Bernstein*. Chapel Hill: University of North Carolina Press, 1983. 0–8078–1543–8, 390p. These letters between Bernstein and Thomas Wolfe reveal Bernstein's unselfish encouragement of his work.

BETHUNE, MARY McLEOD (1875–1955)
Educator   Mayesville, South Carolina

African American Mary McLeod Bethune spent her life trying to ensure that as many African Americans as possible received an education so that they could earn a living and oppose racial inequality. She was born on July 19, 1875, as the fifteenth of seventeen children to former slaves. She attended school a few miles from the family farm and continued her education in preparation for becoming a missionary. When the Presbyterian Church refused to help Bethune reach Africa, she realized that she should serve people at home. Although she married, she devoted her efforts to education, and her one son later produced a grandchild whom Bethune legally adopted. In 1904, Bethune moved to Daytona, Florida, to start a school where she taught children regardless of their ability to pay, and benevolence from others helped her eventually open another school and a hospital. She led the Florida Federation of Colored Women, and in 1924, she became president of the National Association of Colored Women, at that time the highest national office for an African American woman. In 1935, she formed the National Council of Negro Women with the aim of gaining equality for them. She continued work with various organizations and advised Presidents Calvin Coolidge, Herbert Hoover, and Theodore Roosevelt about education, employment, child welfare, and housing. A statue of her stands in Lincoln Park in Washington, DC, and she was elected to The National Women's Hall of Fame.

BIBLIOGRAPHY

Halasa, Malu. *Mary McLeod Bethune*. New York: Chelsea House, 1989. 1–55546–574–9, 111p. This biography of Bethune for young adults recounts her life.

Holt, Rackham. *Mary McLeod Bethune*. Garden City, NY: Doubleday, 1964. No ISBN, 306p. Holt's undocumented biography of Bethune, based on her diaries, recounts her struggle to establish her schools.

Poole, Bernice Anderson. *Mary McLeod Bethune*. Los Angeles: Melrose Square, 1994. 0–87067–783–7, 186p. This popular biography, appropriate for young adults, has an index but no list of sources.

BICKERDYKE, MARY ANN (1817–1901)
Nurse   Knox, Ohio

Mary Ann Bickerdyke, known as Mother Bickerdyke, was organizer and chief of nursing, hospital, and welfare services for the western armies under the command of General Ulysses S. Grant during the Civil War. She was born Mary Ann Ball on July 19, 1817, but her mother died when Bickerdyke was 17 months old. She went to live with her maternal grandparents, and she also lived with several other family members, moving too often to receive much schooling. She married an older man who died suddenly, leaving her with children to support. She nursed using botanic medicine, something she may have learned before her marriage. Soldiers preparing to fight in the Civil War but suffering from typhoid and dysentery at their camp needed volunteers to nurse, clean, and feed them, and, her children raised, she volunteered. In 1862, she joined Grant's army on the front lines, and two months later the Northwestern Sanitary Commission in Chicago appointed her agent in the field to launder, prepare food, distribute supplies, and nurse the wounded. She began lecturing on the horrid conditions, expressing her anger at slow military procedures for obtaining supplies. Throughout the war, Bickerdyke served at different places in support of Union soldiers, including Vicksburg, and helped build nearly 300 field hospitals with the help of Sanitary Commission agents. After the war, she became a pension attorney to help veterans organize homestead plans, returning to Washington several times to press their claims. She also helped the California branch of the Woman's Relief Corps before the government finally gave her a small pension of $25 a month in 1886. A statue of her stands in Galesburg, Illinois.

BIBLIOGRAPHY

Baker, Nina Brown. *Cyclone in Calico: The Story of Mary Ann Bickerdyke*. Boston: Little, Brown, 1952. No ISBN, 278p. For her readable biography of Bickerdyke, Baker consulted books, letters, manuscripts, newspapers, and scrapbooks.

De Leeuw, Adele. *Civil War Nurse, Mary Ann Bickerdyke*. New York: Messner, 1973. 0-671-32617-1, 158p. De Leeuw's young adult biography of Bickerdyke discusses her work during and after the Civil War.

BISHOP, ELIZABETH (1911–1979)
Poet and Author   Worcester, Massachusetts

Elizabeth Bishop was a poet and an author. Soon after her birth on February 8, 1911, her father died, and when her mother was committed to a mental institution, Bishop lived with her maternal grandparents and an aunt. She graduated from Vassar in 1934 and had already started writing seriously with **Marianne Moore** as a mentor, but did not publish her first book of poems, *North and South*, until 1946. Nine years later, the book, with additions, was republished and won a Pulitzer Prize. She served as the Library of Congress consultant in poetry during 1949 and 1950 before traveling abroad and living much of the 1950s and 1960s in Brazil. She eventually returned to teach at several American universities. In much of her work, she reflected on the thematic differences between North and South and examined the need to explore the self and to take responsibility in life. Among her many honors were the **Harriet Monroe** Award for Poetry, a National Book Award, the Neustadt International Prize for Literature, and honorary degrees.

BIBLIOGRAPHY

Fountain, Gary. *Remembering Elizabeth Bishop*. Amherst: University of Massachusetts Press, 1994. 0-8702-3936-8, 408p. Fountain interviewed nearly 120 relatives, colleagues, and students to analyze Bishop's life and work.

Kalstone, David. *Becoming a Poet*. New York: Farrar, Straus and Giroux, 1989. 0-374-10960-5, 299p. Kalstone quotes Bishop's letters to show their autobiographical relationship to her poems.

BLACK, SHIRLEY TEMPLE. *See* TEMPLE (BLACK), SHIRLEY

BLACKWELL, ANTOINETTE BROWN (1825-1921)
Clergy   Henrietta, New York

Antoinette Louisa Brown Blackwell was the first woman to be ordained a minister of a recognized denomination in the United States. She was born on May 20, 1825, as the seventh of ten children to a farmer with strong orthodox standards. At nine, she made a public profession of faith, and the Congregational elders decided to accept her into membership. She studied with boys, and after she had taught, her father helped her pay to attend Oberlin College. She graduated from the literary course and announced her intention to study theology. Although initially discouraged from this pursuit, she finished her study in 1850. Professors refused to allow her to officially graduate or to give her a student license to preach, but in 1853, a Wayne County, New York, Congregational church ordained her minister. The next year, however, she resigned because of theological disagreement with her congregation and became a Unitarian minister in Elizabeth, New Jersey. Having made friends with **Lucy Stone** while at Oberlin, Brown met Stone's brother-in-law, and since he agreed with her views, she married him. He encouraged her to lecture and write in support of abolition, temperance, and women's rights. She also inspired other women interested in the ministry. In 1911, she rode in a suffrage parade, and four years later, at 90, she preached her last sermon. In 1920, she exercised her right to vote even though in declining health and going blind. She was later inducted into The National Women's Hall of Fame.

BIBLIOGRAPHY

Cazden, Elizabeth. *Antoinette Brown Blackwell: A Biography.* Old Westbury, NY: Feminist Press, 1983. 0-935312-00-5, 315p. Manuscripts, letters, and other primary documents help Cazden recount Brown Blackwell's contributions to theology and social reform.
Lasser, Carol, and Marlene Deahl Merrill, eds. *Friends and Sisters: Letters Between Lucy Stone and Antoinette Brown Blackwell.* Urbana: University of Illinois Press, 1987. 0-252-01396-4, 278p. Although these letters between Stone and Antoinette Brown Blackwell span the period between 1846 and 1893, none date from the 1860s.

BLAINE, ANITA McCORMICK (1866-1954)
Reformer and Philanthropist   Manchester, Vermont

Anita Eugénie McCormick Blaine was a philanthropist and social reformer. She was born on July 4, 1866, as the fourth of seven children to the inventor and manufacturer of the reaper and his educated wife. While studying with tutors before graduating from Chicago's Kirkland School, she developed her family's attitudes toward stewardship and social welfare, believing that personal wealth should be used for the good of all. After the early death of her husband, she worked to alleviate urban problems. Later, she helped **Jane Addams** form the City Homes Association to investigate tenement conditions and served on committees and boards and in charity societies. Concerned about her son's education, she investigated various methods of instruction and decided that the child-centered approach was most effective. In 1899, she founded and funded the Chicago Institute at which Francis W. Parker trained teachers with his progressive methods. The school soon merged with the University of Chicago School of Education, and she replaced it with the Francis W. Parker School. After World War I, she campaigned for the League of Nations and financially backed the World Citizens Association. During World War II, she supported Chinese war orphans, and afterward, the Foundation for World Government. She personally gave away $10 million and willed another $20 million to educational and social welfare causes.

BIBLIOGRAPHY

Harrison, Gilbert A. *A Timeless Affair: The Life of Anita McCormick Blaine*. Chicago: University of Chicago Press, 1979. 0–226–31804–4, 253p. Harrison's biography presents Blaine's private relationships based on family records and anecdotal evidence from her granddaughter.

BLATCH, HARRIOT STANTON (1856–1940)
Reformer   Seneca Falls, New York

Harriot Stanton Blatch was a woman suffrage leader. She was born on January 20, 1856, the sixth of seven children of suffragist **Elizabeth Cady Stanton** and her abolitionist lawyer husband. Blatch was educated privately before graduating from Vassar in 1878 with honors in mathematics. Before marrying, she went to Germany as a tutor and companion and helped her mother write *History of Woman Suffrage*. She lived in England with her husband for over 20 years and worked for educational and social reform while participating in the British suffrage movement. In 1902, she returned to the United States and founded the Equality League of Self–Supporting Women, which held suffrage parades and open-air meetings. She joined **Alice Paul**'s militant Congressional Union (later the National Woman's Party) and worked for the passage of a federal Equal Rights Amendment. She participated in the Food Administration's Speakers' Bureau before returning to England to settle her husband's affairs after his accidental death, and saw the roles of women changing in that economy. During World War I, she directed the Women's Land Army, an organization promoting farm labor, and in her later years, she wrote four books supporting women's rights.

BIBLIOGRAPHY

Blatch, Harriot Stanton. *Challenging Years: The Memoirs of Harriot Stanton Blatch*. 1940. Westport, CT: Hyperion, 1976. 0–8835–5256–6, 347p. Blatch's memoirs are a social history of her time.
DuBois, Ellen Carol. *Harriot Stanton Blatch and the Winning of Woman Suffrage*. New Haven, CT: Yale University Press, 1997. 0–300–06562–0, 353p. This scholarly biography examines Blatch's life and her expansion of the suffrage movement.

BLOOMER, AMELIA JENKS (1818–1894)
Reformer   Homer, New York

Amelia Jenks Bloomer was a social reformer who campaigned for temperance and women's rights. She was born on May 27, 1818, one of the youngest in a family of six to a clothier and his wife. She was educated at home, and at 17 became a teacher and governess before marrying a law student, deleting the word "obey" from their vows. Her husband became an antislavery reformer and editor, and she wrote articles for his newspaper. In 1848, she became an officer in the Ladies' Temperance Society, and the next year, she began publishing *Lily*, a journal for temperance which soon gave equal coverage to women's rights. In 1850, she introduced **Elizabeth Cady Stanton** to **Susan B. Anthony**, and they began their joint campaign. When Bloomer introduced pantaloons in *Lily*, readers wanted patterns and information, and these pants, worn under a short skirt, became known as "bloomers." Bloomer moved to the Midwest in 1855, and during the Civil War organized a soldiers' aid society and worked to establish churches and Good Templar lodges. She was elected to The National Women's Hall of Fame.

BIBLIOGRAPHY

Bloomer, Dexter C. *Life and Writings of Amelia Bloomer*. Ed. Susan Kleinberg. New York: Schocken, 1975. 0-8052-0483-0, 387p. Kleinberg's introduction presents additional primary source material from articles, letters, and speeches supplementing the biography Bloomer's husband wrote the year after her death.
Gattey, Charles Neilson. *The Bloomer Girls*. New York: Coward-McCann, 1968. No ISBN, 192p. This collective biography and feminist history examines Bloomer's life and influence.

BLY, NELLIE   (1864–1922)
Journalist   Cochran's Mills, Pennsylvania

Nellie Bly was the pseudonym used by Elizabeth Seaman, a journalist. She was born Elizabeth Cochrane on May 5, 1864, daughter of a mill owner and lawyer and his second wife. When her father died, the family of 10 children moved to Pittsburgh. Seaman was educated at home, and when she was 18, she vigorously disagreed with an editorial saying that women belonged in the home. The editor, impressed with her work, tested her on other assignments before hiring her at the *Pittsburgh Dispatch*. Stephen Foster's song title, "Nelly Bly," became her byline. She wrote articles about factory working conditions, slums, life in Mexico, and divorce. After Mexico expelled her for her damning articles on conditions there, she went to New York and got a job with Joseph Pulitzer on the *World* to investigate the conditions inside an insane asylum by pretending to be mentally ill. Her work led to a public investigation and several reforms. She then exposed tenement conditions, mashers, and lobbyists in Albany. In 1889, Pulitzer sent her around the world to see if she could complete the trip in 80 days as had Jules Verne's character, Phileas Fogg. She beat the record by taking 72 days, 6 hours, 11 minutes, and 14 seconds. During the journey, she wrote articles describing her transportation on train, steamer, rickshaw, and sampan. She met Robert Seaman on a train in 1895 and married him a few days later, but after his death, she lost money trying to settle his business affairs. She returned to newspaper work in 1920. She has been elected to The National Women's Hall of Fame.

BIBLIOGRAPHY

Davidson, Sue. *Getting the Real Story: Nellie Bly and Ida B. Wells.* Seattle: Seal Press, 1992. 1-878067-16-8, 152p. Davidson's dual biography for young adults examines Bly's life and includes a chronology of its major events.

Ehrlich, Elizabeth. *Nellie Bly.* New York: Chelsea House, 1989. 1-55546-643-5, 111p. In this biography for young adults, Ehrlich relates Bly's professional achievements and personal difficulties.

Kroeger, Brooke. *Nellie Bly: Daredevil, Reporter, Feminist.* New York: Times Books, 1994. 0-8129-1973-4, 631p. Since Bly kept no journals and wrote few letters, Kroeger has developed this researched and recommended biography from her newspaper articles and court documents.

Rittenhouse, Mignon. *The Amazing Nellie Bly.* 1956. Freeport, NY: Books for Libraries, 1971. 0-8369-8074-3, 254p. This fictional biography of Bly, suitable for young adults, recounts her exploits but lacks an analysis of her personality.

BOGAN, LOUISE (1897–1970)
Poet and Literary Critic   Livermore Falls, Maine

Louise Bogan was a poet and literary critic. She was born on August 11, 1897, to a businessman unhappily married to a wife who often inexplicably disappeared for long periods of time. Bogan learned to read at eight, focusing on adventure books belonging to her older brother. At school in Boston, lonely from discrimination against the Irish, she began writing poetry at 14. After attending Boston University for one year, she decided to escape home through marriage, but her husband died in 1920 after the birth of their daughter, whom Bogan's mother helped raise, Bogan went to New York and began publishing in the *New Republic*, and after spending a year in Vienna, published a book of poetry to critical acclaim. After she remarried, a fire destroyed a decade of papers, one of several events that caused her to have an emotional breakdown. After her recovery, she began publishing poetry reviews in *The New Yorker*, and a Guggenheim Fellowship made travel in Europe possible. Her marriage dissolved, and after another emotional collapse, she gained renewed strength from facing her past and writing from personal experience. In 1945, she served as the Library of Congress poetry consultant, and in subsequent years lectured at universities. Among other honors was the Bollingen Prize in Poetry.

BIBLIOGRAPHY

Bogan, Louise. *What the Woman Lived: Selected Letters of Louise Bogan, 1920–1970.* Ed. Ruth Limmer. New York: Harcourt, Brace, 1973. 0-15-195878-5, 401p. Limmer edited and carefully annotated 500 letters that Bogan wrote to friends and associates.

Frank, Elizabeth. *Louise Bogan: A Portrait*. New York: Knopf, 1985. 0–394–52484–5,
    460p. Frank's balanced biography shows Bogan as both a gifted artist and a shrew.
    Pulitzer Prize.
Limmer, Ruth. *Journey Around My Room: The Autobiography of Louise Bogan*. New
    York: Viking, 1980. 0–670–40942–1, 197p. Limmer uses letters, poems, stories,
    literary criticism, and conversation interfaced with Bogan's two journals to give
    insight into her thought processes.

BOMBECK, ERMA (1927–1996)
Author   Dayton, Ohio

Erma Bombeck was an author whose work allowed many women to see the
humor in their frantic lives. She was born on February 21, 1927, to a city laborer
and a housewife. Her father died when she was nine, and her mother, with only a
fourth grade education, had to support them. Bombeck knew in seventh grade that
she wanted to be a humorist after reading James Thurber and Robert Benchley. In
high school, she worked part-time on the city newspaper at jobs no one else
wanted and then full-time after high school for a year before entering college. She
worked while in school, graduated with a degree in English, got married, and
became a reporter. In her written interviews she always sounded like she was
talking because she took no notes. She stopped writing to have children, but when
the youngest entered kindergarten, she published a column in the local newspaper
that quickly gained readers. Her column was syndicated the next year, and by
1970, it appeared in 200 newspapers. In 1976, her third book, *The Grass Is Always
Greener over the Septic Tank*, stayed on the *New York Times* best-seller list for
almost a year. During her career, she wrote over 4,000 columns. Among her
awards were the Mark Twain Award for Humor and the American Cancer Society
Medal of Honor.

BIBLIOGRAPHY
Edwards, Susan. *Erma Bombeck: A Life in Humor*. New York: Avon, 1997. 0–380–97482–7,
    222p. This popular readable biography contains no documentation.
King, Norman. *Here's Erma! The Bombecking of America*. Aurora, IL: Caroline House,
    1982. 0–89803–050–1, 166p. This conversational biography of Bombeck gives an
    overview of her life as a humorist.

BOURKE-WHITE, MARGARET (1904–1971)
Photographer   New York, New York

Margaret Bourke-White was a photojournalist who innovated the photo-essay. She
was born on June 14, 1904, as the second of three children, to an engineer-designer
in the printing industry and a stenographer. She attended Columbia for one
semester before her father died, and the next year won a scholarship to the
University of Michigan at Ann Arbor. After a brief marriage, she graduated with a
degree in biology from Cornell where she supported herself by selling prints of her

artistic photographs of campus buildings. In 1927, she began her professional career as an industrial and architectural photographer, and in 1929, Henry Luce hired her to work for his new magazine, *Fortune*. Simultaneously, she established a studio and worked part of the year as a freelancer. Photographs of the Krupp Iron Works in Germany and of the Dust Bowl area during the drought of the 1930s solidified her style and led to her employment by *Life* magazine in 1936. She collaborated with Erskine Caldwell on *You Have Seen Their Faces* (1937), about southern sharecroppers; *North of the Danube* (1939), on life in Czechoslovakia before the Nazi takeover; and *Say, Is This the U.S.A.* (1941), on America. After a brief marriage to Caldwell, Bourke-White covered World War II for *Life* and was the first woman photographer to travel with United States forces in North Africa; she covered the Italian campaign, the siege of Moscow, and the final trip across the Rhine into Germany. She photographed the shocking images of emaciated inmates in concentration camps and of the corpses in gas chambers. After the war, she went to India to photograph Mahatma Gandhi and the division of the Indian subcontinent. In Korea, she photographed the communists fighting the South Korean troops. Soon after the Korean War, she developed Parkinson's disease and took fewer photographs but continued to write and was later elected to The National Women's Hall of Fame.

BIBLIOGRAPHY

Bourke-White, Margaret. *Portrait of Myself*. New York: Simon and Schuster, 1963. No ISBN, 383p. Bourke-White discusses the story of her life and career and includes photographs.

Goldberg, Vicki. *Margaret Bourke-White: A Biography*. New York: Harper and Row, 1986. 0-06-015513-2, 426p. Goldberg's carefully researched and balanced biography, using archives and interviews with Bourke-White's family, friends, and colleagues, is recommended.

Silverman, Jonathan. *For the World to See: The Life of Margaret Bourke-White*. New York: Viking, 1983. 0-670-32356-X, 224p. Silverman has made selections from Bourke-White's articles, manuscripts, and books and juxtaposed them with her photographs to illuminate her professional career.

BOYD, BELLE   (1844–1900)
Spy   Martinsburg, Virginia

Belle Boyd was a Confederate spy, an actor, and a lecturer. She was born on May 9, 1844, to a tobacco plantation manager and general store owner as the oldest of eight children. After attending boarding school in Baltimore, she entered Washington society at age 16 in 1860. When the war began, she returned to Virginia, where Union officers interested in gaining her favors gave her information which she sent to Confederate leaders via both white and African American messengers. When the Union discovered her activity, it merely reprimanded her. In the fall of 1861, Generals Beauregard and Jackson ordered her to become a courier, and her excellent horsewomanship and knowledge of the

Shenandoah Valley helped her smuggle and run blockades. When she gained renown for helping save bridges near Front Royal, the Union treated her with more care, making sure that she was under surveillance when she was near the forces. After she boarded a ship to carry Confederate dispatches to London, Union soldiers captured her, but before being banished to Canada, she fell in love with a British soldier fighting for the Union. She later married him in London, but his sudden death forced her to support her daughter by acting professionally and writing *Belle Boyd in Camp and Prison*. Upon her return to the United States after the war, she continued acting and lecturing about her wartime experiences.

BIBLIOGRAPHY

Boyd, Belle. *Belle Boyd in Camp and Prison*. 1865. Ed. Curtis Carroll Davis. Baton Rouge: Louisiana State University Press, 1998. 0-8071-2214-9, 200p. An introduction to Boyd's experiences as a Civil War spy fills in details of her life.
Scarborough, Ruth. *Belle Boyd, Siren of the South*. Macon, GA: Mercer University Press, 1983. 0-86554-065-9, 212p. Scarborough used Boyd's memoirs in this biography suitable for young adults to reveal her as an active but perhaps not particularly important Confederate spy.

BRADSTREET, ANNE (1612?–1672)
Poet   Northampton, England

Anne Bradstreet was one of the first women to write her own poems in English and was the first female poet to write English verse in the American colonies. Born Anne Dudley around 1612, she was the second of five children of the chief steward to the Puritan Earl of Lincoln and his wealthy wife. As a child, she had private tutors and read freely in the Earl's library. She married when 16, and two years later, she came to America with her husband and parents. Her first poems were published in 1650 in England without her knowledge by a brother-in-law who had a manuscript copy. They reveal her life in England, while her poems published eight years after her death show her as fully integrated into colonial Puritan life as a pious wife and mother with status in her community.

BIBLIOGRAPHY

Martin, Wendy. *An American Triptych: Anne Bradstreet, Emily Dickinson, Adrienne Rich*. Chapel Hill: University of North Carolina Press, 1984. 0-8078-1573-X, 272p. Martin traces female poetics by examining Bradstreet and others in terms of their historical time and place.
Rosenmeier, Rosamond. *Anne Bradstreet Revisited*. New York: Twayne, 1991. 0-8057-7625-7, 200p. Rosenmeier joins Bradstreet's life and poetry in a thoroughly researched thematic scholarly biography.
White, Elizabeth Wade. *Anne Bradstreet, the Tenth Muse*. New York: Oxford University Press, 1971. 0-19-501440-5, 410p. White reconstructs Bradstreet's life through her verse and prose to illuminate her family relationships.

BRADWELL, MYRA COLBY (1831–1894)
Attorney   Manchester, Vermont

Myra Colby Bradwell was a lawyer and editor. She was one of five children, born on February 12, 1831, into an abolitionist family of Baptists. She attended school in Illinois before marrying the law student son of poor English immigrants. In Chicago, where her husband practiced law, Bradwell became active in the Northwestern Sanitary Commission and other charities growing out of the Civil War effort, such as the Soldiers' Aid Society. Throughout their marriage, Bradwell studied law with her husband, and in 1868, she began publishing the *Chicago Legal News*. The paper's broad and fair coverage of American legal news made it the most important legal publication west of the Alleghenies. After the Chicago Fire of 1871, only the subscription book remained, saved by Bradwell's 13-year-old daughter. Bradwell went to Milwaukee and published the paper there, on time, in three days. In her paper, she urged railroad legislation and zoning ordinances, advocated bar associations, and encouraged specialization of lawyers. She also served as a member of the executive committee of the Illinois Woman Suffrage Association, for which she drafted legislation giving married women legal rights to their own earnings and for widows to have rights in their husbands' estates. Although she passed the bar, Bradwell was initially denied admission because of her sex. Not until 1890 was she admitted to practice law in Illinois, but only two years later, she was admitted to practice before the Supreme Court of the United States. She also served four terms as vice president of the Illinois State Bar Association. She is now a member of The National Women's Hall of Fame.

BIBLIOGRAPHY
Friedman, Jane M. *America's First Woman Lawyer: The Biography of Myra Bradwell.* Buffalo, NY: Prometheus, 1993. 0–87975–812–0, 217p. In a carefully researched and recommended biography, Friedman emphasizes Bradwell's contributions to reform.

BRANT, MOLLY (MARY) (1736–1796)
Activist   Mohawk Valley, New York

A United Empire Loyalist, Molly Brant became the most influential Mohawk woman in the New World. She was born in 1736 to Margaret and Peter, a chief, who were Canajoharie Mohawks registered as Protestant Christians. Brant supposedly received her name from her stepfather who was part Dutch and a strong influence on her and her brother, Joseph. In a Mohawk ceremony which the British government did not recognize, she married Sir William Johnson, a widower 22 years her senior; he was a British official responsible for Native American relationships during the American Revolution. She retained her Native American dress and her name, as was the tribal custom. During her life with Johnson, she entertained both white guests from Great Britain and the Colonies and sachems from the Iroquois tribes. At the same time, she was responsible for the schooling and well-being of nine children and was the guardian of four others. As a young woman, she became a clan mother in her matrilineal tribe and eventually the head of all clan mothers. Her influence with members of the Native American community helped her husband communicate with them, and she influenced five of the six Iroquois Nations to ally with the British. Molly Brant's son Peter captured Ethan Allen, her brother Joseph Brant became the war's most famous Native American warrior, and she spied on the Patriots, sent ammunition to Loyalist troops, and hid Loyalist soldiers. The British gave her a lifetime pension for her efforts after she moved to Kingston, Ontario.

BIBLIOGRAPHY

Archibald, Mary. *Molly Brant.* Toronto: Dundurn, 1977. No ISBN, 4p. This brief look at Brant gives an overview of her life.
Earle, Thomas. *The Three Faces of Molly Brant: A Biography.* Kingston, Ontario: Quarry, 1996. 1-55082-176-8, 160p. Earle used government documents, land papers, wills, church records, and other disparate sources to write a balanced, researched, documented, and readable biography of Brant.

BRICE, FANNY (1891–1951)
Entertainer   New York, New York

Fanny Brice was a comedian. She was born Fannie Borach on October 29, 1891, as the third of four children to a gambler and his Hungarian immigrant wife. Brice's mother ran the family businesses, while her father encouraged Brice to sing on bar tables. Brice quit school at 14, won her first amateur contest, and assumed the name of a family friend. Too tall for the chorus the next year, she began to rely on humor in performances. In 1910, while touring on the burlesque circuit, she sang Irving Berlin's song "Sadie Salomé," a parody of the Salomé dance in Yiddish dialect. She wore a starched sailor suit that made her itch and squirm, and when the audience loved her behavior, she added dialect and parody to her act. In the Ziegfeld Follies, she combined serious songs, "Second Hand Rose" and "My Man," with comedy to become Ziegfeld's greatest star. She appeared in nine Follies before 1936 and toured while also playing musicals and films. She always insisted on controlling her own material and refused to change it even when threatened with being fired. She played her most distinctive character, Baby Snooks, on radio for seven years beginning in 1944. She married and divorced twice and raised two children with the help of servants, balancing time between children and career. Her characters focused on the false and the foolish, showing that women could be comedians without belittling themselves or emphasizing their sexuality.

BIBLIOGRAPHY

Goldman, Herbert G. *Fanny Brice: The Original Funny Girl.* New York: Oxford University Press, 1992. 0-19-505725-2, 308p. Goldman noted the difficulty of finding primary sources about Brice, but his research for this readable biography led him to reflect on Brice as both the wise mother and the romantic child.

Grossman, Barbara Wallace. *Funny Woman: The Life and Times of Fanny Brice*. Bloomington: Indiana University Press, 1991. 0–253–32653–2, 287p. For this carefully researched biography, Grossman used Brice's unpublished memoirs, interviews, contemporary newspapers, photographs, scrapbooks, sheet music, recordings, films, and extant script material to analyze her performances and the major events in her life.

BROOKS, GWENDOLYN (1917–)
Poet   Topeka, Kansas

Gwendolyn Brooks was the first African American poet to win a Pulitzer Prize. Born on June 7, 1917, to caring parents, Brooks lived mainly in Chicago, where she began to record poetry in her notebooks at age seven. She attended mainly white high schools, and to combat her loneliness, she read other poets who made her feel that poetry was important. When she was 16, she met Langston Hughes, and he encouraged her writing. She attended junior college for two years before marrying, and in 1941, she took a class in modern poetry at the South Side Community Art Center, where she first discussed poetry with other writers. She won an award at the Midwestern Writers' Conference in 1943, and in 1946 and 1947, she received Guggenheim fellowships. She published *Annie Allen*, her second book of poetry, and it won the Pulitzer Prize. She continued publishing, and in 1968 became the poet laureate of Illinois, succeeding Carl Sandburg. In this position, she initiated poetry contests for young people, often providing the prize money herself, offered poetry workshops, and read her poetry throughout the state. As her poetry matured, it developed a simplicity and clarity focusing on the optimism of the African American experience. She has served as the Library of Congress consultant in poetry and received honors for her contributions including election to The National Women's Hall of Fame.

BIBLIOGRAPHY

Brooks, Gwendolyn. *Report from Part One*. Detroit: Broadside, 1972. 0–910296–82–0, 215p. Brooks uses memoirs, mental notations, interviews, letters, and photographs to describe her life in Chicago during the 1920s and her growth as a poet.

Kent, George E. *A Life of Gwendolyn Brooks*. Lexington: University Press of Kentucky, 1990. 0–8131–1659–7, 287p. Kent uses Brooks's early notebooks along with anecdotes from friends and family to explore both the aesthetic and political changes in her life.

Melhem, D. H. *Gwendolyn Brooks: Poetry and the Heroic Voice*. Lexington: University Press of Kentucky, 1987. 0–8131–1605–8, 270p. Melhem presents biographical background on Brooks and discusses her contributions to poetry.

Shaw, Harry B. *Gwendolyn Brooks*. New York: Twayne, 1980. 0–8057–7287–1, 200p. In his analysis of Brooks's poetry, Shaw claims that she uses her locale of Chicago's South Side not to rise above the ghetto but as a way through which to understand the universals of life.

BROWN, CHARLOTTE HAWKINS (1883-1961)
Educator   Henderson, North Carolina

African American Charlotte Hawkins Brown, an educator, refused to accept injustice in her fight for civil rights. She was born on June 11, 1883, to an educated mother and a father whose mother, descended from the English navigator John D. Hawkins, worked as a housemaid on the Hawkins plantation. When Brown was seven years old, the family of 19, including her mother's new husband, moved to Cambridge, Massachusetts. They ran a laundry and boarded Harvard students while Brown attended school with Henry Wadsworth Longfellow's children. For her high school graduation, she had to earn money for a dress. While pushing the carriage of children she was tending, she read her Latin book and impressed **Alice Freeman Palmer**, who observed her. Brown's mother wanted her to teach, and Brown wanted to attend Radcliffe; they compromised by having Brown attend the State Normal School with Palmer's financial support. While in college, Brown decided to return to the South to teach, and she became the administrator, teacher, and fund-raiser for a school she named the Alice Freeman Palmer Memorial Institute. She met her husband at Harvard in 1911, although they remained married for only four years. She helped found the National Council of Negro Women and was the first African American woman chosen to join the Twentieth Century Club in Boston. She advocated civil rights through her speeches and her leadership as president of Palmer.

BIBLIOGRAPHY
Brown, Charlotte Hawkins. *Mammy: An Appeal to the Heart of the South.* New York: Hall, 1995. 0–8161–1632–6, 192p. Brown discusses her life, education, travels, and missionary work in South Africa.
Silcox-Jarrett, Diane. *Charlotte Hawkins Brown.* Winston-Salem, NC: Bandit, 1995. 1–878177–0–7, 113p. Interviews with Brown's friends and graduates of Palmer Institute form the basis for this fictional biography, suitable for young adults.

BROWN, OLYMPIA (1835-1926)
Clergy and Reformer   Prairie Ronde, Michigan

Olympia Brown was the first female minister to formally study with men. She was born on January 5, 1835, as the eldest in a family of four to Universalist farmers. She studied at the school on the farm and then at Mount Holyoke before enrolling at Antioch, where she received her B.A. in 1860. While in college, she heard **Antoinette Brown Blackwell** preach and wanted to emulate her. In 1863, Brown graduated from St. Lawrence University theological school, and the Northern Universalist Association ordained her as the first woman with full denominational authority in the United States. Always interested in reform, Brown became a charter member of the American Equal Rights Association; she campaigned throughout Kansas for woman suffrage in 1867, and the next year campaigned in Boston. In 1873, she married, and with her husband's approval, kept her maiden name. After moving to Wisconsin, Brown became president of the state Woman Suffrage Association in 1884, serving until 1912. When a vague statute passed saying that women could vote on a ballot with school-related matters, Brown theorized that all ballots in some way dealt with school matters and encouraged women to vote. When her own ballot was refused in 1887, she sued. Although she argued her case cogently and logically, she was denied, and she left her pastorate to devote full time to suffrage campaigning. She became vice president of the National Woman Suffrage Association, and in 1892 called a convention which formed the Federal Suffrage Association, for which she served as president from 1903 to 1920. As a member of **Alice Paul**'s Congressional Union (National Woman's Party), she denounced President Wilson in front of the White House. She also supported the American Civil Liberties Union and the Women's International League for Peace and Freedom with her effective speaking.

BIBLIOGRAPHY

Brown, Olympia. *Acquaintances, Old and New, among Reformers*. Milwaukee: S. E. Tate, 1911. No ISBN, 115p. In her memoirs, Brown acknowledges her mother as the first woman she knew concerned about women's rights.

Cote, Charlotte. *Olympia Brown: The Battle for Equality*. Racine, WI: Mother Courage Press, 1988. 0–941300–09–9, 216p. In an accessible, well-researched biography, Cote shows the conflict Brown felt between her calling to the ministry and the campaign for woman suffrage.

BROWN BLACKWELL, ANTOINETTE. *See* **BLACKWELL, ANTOINETTE BROWN**

BUCK, PEARL SYDENSTRICKER (1892–1973)
Author and Humanitarian   Hillsboro, West Virginia

Pearl Buck was the first woman to receive the Nobel Prize for Literature. She was born Pearl Sydenstricker on June 26, 1892, as the fifth of seven children to Presbyterian missionaries serving in China. She learned to speak Chinese before English and had to flee with her family during the Boxer Rebellion. She attended boarding school in Shanghai before going to Randolph-Macon Woman's College in Virginia, from which she graduated. In 1914, she returned to China, married, and began university teaching in Nanking. In 1923, American magazines began publishing her stories, but she did not gain a wide readership until her novel *The Good Earth* appeared in 1931. She followed it with two more novels as part of a trilogy published as *The House of Earth* in 1935. She divorced in 1934, married a New York publisher, and returned to live in the United States. In 1941, she founded the East and West Association and the Wellcome House adoption agency for Asian Americans. After World War II, she aided the illegitimate children of American servicemen in Asian countries by establishing the Pearl S. Buck Foundation. She also continued writing, publishing five works with atypical content under the name John Sedges. Among the awards she received were the Pulitzer Prize, the William Dean Howells Medal, and election as one of two women life-members to the American Association of Arts and Letters. She also received many honorary degrees and over 300 humanitarian awards including election to The National Women's Hall of Fame.

BIBLIOGRAPHY

Buck, Pearl S. *The Child Who Never Grew*. Rockville, MD: Woodbine House, 1992. 0–933149–49–2, 107p. Buck discusses her adjustment to the birth of her mentally retarded daughter and her resolve that her daughter's life be useful to other human beings.

Conn, Peter J. *Pearl S. Buck: A Cultural Biography*. New York: Cambridge University Press, 1996. 0–521–56080–2, 468p. In this balanced and scholarly biography using Buck's own words, Conn shows how she advanced women's, children's, and minorities' rights.

Rizzon, Beverly. *Pearl S. Buck: The Final Chapter*. Palm Springs, CA: ETC Publications, 1989. 0–88280–120–1, 435p. Rizzon, Buck's personal secretary for some years, has written a readable memoir about her years knowing a generous woman.

Sherk, Warren. *Pearl S. Buck: Good Earth Mother*. Philomath, OR: Drift Creek Press, 1992. 0–9626441–3–7, 232p. For his selective, carefully researched, and recommended biography, Sherk interviewed Buck's friends and used archives from her foundation.

Stirling, Nora B. *Pearl Buck, A Woman in Conflict*. Piscataway, NJ: New Win, 1983. 0–8329–0261–6, 357p. Stirling uses Buck's letters and information from friends and family for a carefully researched fictional biography suitable for young adults.

BURNETT, CAROL (1936–)
Entertainer   **San Antonio, Texas**

Carol Burnett is an award-winning actor and singer. On August 26, 1936, she was born to two alcoholic parents whose marriage survived eight more years. Then she, her mother, and her grandmother moved to Los Angeles and lived on welfare; there Burnett's religious grandmother became a major influence in her life. Burnett earned a scholarship to the University of California, where she first studied journalism before changing her major to drama. She left for New York and organized a group performance for actors searching for work, an endeavor that won her an agent who secured jobs for her in summer stock and nightclubs. She began appearing on television in the 1950s, and after a rendition of teenage love songs made her famous, she became a regular performer on *The Garry Moore Show*. She also starred off-Broadway before hosting her own television show, in which she rarely sang, playing a number of appealing characters, which her audiences liked, without music. Burnett continues to work in theater whenever possible and has won five Emmy Awards for her television comedy.

BIBLIOGRAPHY

Burnett, Carol. *One More Time: A Memoir*. New York: Random, 1986. 0–394–55254–7, 359p. Burnett relates the confusion and difficulty of her childhood.

Carpozi, George. *The Carol Burnett Story*. New York: Warner, 1975. 0–446–78639–X, 206p. Carpozi recounts Burnett's difficult childhood and later life.

Taraborrelli, J. Randy. *Laughing Till It Hurts: The Complete Life and Career of Carol Burnett*. New York: Morrow, 1988. 0–688–08103–7, 432p. This popular biography, based on interviews with Burnett's friends, emphasizes her friendliness as well as her reluctance for anyone to know her deepest feelings.

BURROUGHS, NANNIE HELEN (1879–1961)
Educator   Orange, Virginia

African American Nannie Helen Burroughs led women in their quest for equal rights. She was born on May 2, 1879, to an itinerant preacher and a former slave. Her mother took Burroughs and her sister to Washington, DC, to find work and to get an education. Burroughs attended M Street High, where teachers **Mary Church Terrell** and **Anna J. Cooper** greatly influenced her. She worked in several cities after graduation, becoming connected with the local churches, and in 1900, when she was only 21, she went to Richmond to speak at the National Baptist Convention about the underutilization of women in the church. At that time, she began the call for women's rights, antilynching laws, desegregation, and industrial education. Quickly appointed corresponding secretary for the newly formed Women's Convention Auxiliary (WC), she worked every day for the next year, and in 1907, claimed that 1.5 million women had joined. She never married, devoting herself to her causes and irritating her ministers but keeping the love of the women she served. She became president of the WC and kept the title until her death. Her support was so solid that over 5,500 people attended her funeral.

BIBLIOGRAPHY

Easter, Opal V. *Nannie Helen Burroughs*. New York: Garland, 1995. 0–8153–1861–8, 146p. The text focuses on Burroughs's career as an officer and president of the Women's Convention.

$\mathcal{C}$

CADY STANTON, ELIZABETH. *See* **STANTON, ELIZABETH CADY**

CALAMITY JANE (1852–1903)
Pioneer   Princeton, Missouri

Calamity Jane, a frontierswoman, has become legendary for her exploits. She was born Martha Jane Cannary on May 1, 1852, probably as one of five children of a farmer. Her family moved to Virginia City, Montana, when she was 13, and her parents died soon after. She supposedly became a camp follower in the West, working as a dance-hall girl or cook to earn a living. She masqueraded as a man and may have served undetected in calvary units. Supposedly, she married and moved to Denver, where her husband failed to change her into a lady. Records show that in 1876 she went to Deadwood, South Dakota, where she worked as a bullwhacker hauling goods and machinery to camps. There she met Wild Bill Hickok, and although some stories say they met earlier, married, and had a daughter, Jean Hickok McCormick, no one has verified Hickok as McCormick's father. Around 1878, Calamity Jane may have gained her nickname nursing smallpox victims during an epidemic. However she earned the name, she kept it and expanded the legend of being someone who could "outshoot, outride, outdrink, outcuss, outfight, outchew, and outlie" any of her companions. After living with a hack driver, Clinton (Charley) Burke, for seven years, she married him, and beginning in 1895, she toured with Wild West shows throughout the Midwest. In 1901, when she appeared at the Pan-American Exposition in Buffalo, New York, she was fired for her alcoholism, and returned to obscurity.

BIBLIOGRAPHY

Aikman, Duncan. *Calamity Jane and the Lady Wildcats.* 1927. Lincoln: University of Nebraska Press, 1987. 0–8032–1020–5, 356p. Aikman presents Calamity Jane and other notorious women of her pioneer era.

Foote, Stella. *A History of Calamity Jane: Our Country's First Liberated Woman.* New York: Vantage, 1995. 0–533–11273–7, 242p. This critical biography, based on 30 years of research, uses Cannary's authenticated diary and family Bible to analyze her life.

Sollid, Roberta Beed. *Calamity Jane: A Study in Historical Criticism.* 1958. Helena: Montana Historical Society, 1995. 0–917298–33–0, 163p. This critical history of Calamity Jane's life includes available factual information.

CALLAS, MARIA (1923–1977)
Opera Singer   New York, New York

Maria Callas was one of the great dramatic sopranos of the twentieth century. She was born Maria Cecilia Sophia Anna Kalogeropoulos on December 2, 1923, to a mother who early recognized her talent and took her to study with soprano Elvira de Hidalgo at the Athens Conservatory at age 14. Callas made her debut in Greece in 1938, and in 1945, she returned to the United States, where the Metropolitan Opera offered her a contract. She instead went to Italy for her first important performance, in *La Gioconda*, in Verona during 1947. In Milan, she joined La Scala and won critical acclaim singing the roles of Elvira, Tosca, Norma, and Lucia di Lammermoor. She made her debut in the United States as Norma with the Chicago Opera in 1954 and in New York at the Metropolitan Opera in the same role. She performed in New York for 11 years, and in 1971, she starred in the film *Medea* and started teaching at the Juilliard School of Music. During her career, she sang difficult roles from French, German, and Italian opera and reintroduced the operas of Bellini, Rossini, Donizetti, and Cherubini while displaying her large vocal range and strong acting ability. She performed more than 40 roles and recorded more than 20 complete operas before her last European and American concert tour in 1973.

BIBLIOGRAPHY

Callas, Jackie. *Sisters.* New York: St. Martin's, 1989. 0–312–03934–4, 249p. Callas's sister recalls their life in a personal, readable memoir.

Kesting, Jürgen. *Maria Callas.* Trans. John Hunt. Boston: Northeastern University Press, 1993. 1–55553–179–2, 416p. Kesting emphasizes Callas's voice and her misuse of it in his thoroughly researched biography.

Meneghini, G. B. *My Wife Maria Callas.* Trans. Henry Wisneski. New York: Farrar, Straus and Giroux, 1982. 0–374–21752–1, 331p. Meneghini, Callas's husband, used letters and reminiscences to re-create her life and career.

Scott, Michael. *Maria Meneghini Callas*. Boston: Northeastern University Press, 1992. 1-55553-146-6, 312p. In a carefully researched biography, Scott examines Callas, her performances, and her recordings.

Stancioff, Nadia. *Maria: Callas Remembered*. New York: Dutton, 1987. 0-525-24565-0, 258p. Stancioff, supposedly one of Callas's confidantes, also interviewed others for her balanced biography.

CAMERON, DONALDINA (1869–1968)
Reformer and Missionary   Clydevale, New Zealand

Donaldina MacKenzie Cameron was a missionary and social reformer. She was born on July 26, 1869, on a sheep station, the youngest of seven children of ranchers who had emigrated from Scotland. Her father took the family to the San Joaquin Valley of California when Cameron was two, and her mother died two years later. The family stayed together while her father worked on a ranch, and her sisters raised the other children. Cameron began teacher training in Los Angeles, but when her father died and funds ceased, an Oakland schoolmate's mother suggested that Cameron do mission work in San Francisco. She taught sewing and helped the director of the Mission Home for Foreign Missions, and in 1900 became the superintendent of the home. From this position, she began to attack and destroy San Francisco's Chinese slave trade by fighting it in the courts, through brothel raids, and by sheltering women sold as slaves. During this time, she rescued more than 2,000 women smuggled into the United States from China. At the home, she developed educational programs and found staff positions, schools, lodging, and husbands for the women assigned as her foster daughters. In 1925, she established a second refuge home in Oakland which **Julia Morgan** designed. After the slave trade slackened, the Mission Home became a social service center of the Presbyterian Church. The California legislature honored Cameron as a "distinguished Californian" for her work.

BIBLIOGRAPHY
Martin, Mildred Crowl. *Chinatown's Angry Angel: The Story of Donaldina Cameron*. Palo Alto, CA: Pacific, 1977. 0-8701-5225-4, 308p. Martin based her carefully researched but undocumented biography on conversations with Cameron's relatives, friends, and fellow-workers; her personal papers and correspondence; reports of the Mission Home; board minutes; and journals.

Wilson, Carol Green. *Chinatown Quest: One Hundred Years of Donaldina Cameron House*. 1930. San Francisco: California Historical Society, 1974. No ISBN, 190p. In this recommended biography, Wilson recounts Cameron's story mainly through the eyes of the young Chinese women whom Cameron rescued from prostitution.

CAMPBELL, LUCIE E. (1885–1963)
Composer and Educator   Duck Hill, Mississippi

Lucie E. Campbell was a major influence on the growth and development of African American religious music. The youngest of 11 children, Campbell was born on April 30, 1885. Her father died before she was two. Always self-disciplined, she won a penmanship award in elementary school and the top prize in Latin class. After graduation from high school as valedictorian, she taught American history and English at Booker T. Washington High School until her retirement, but earned her B.A. and M.S. while teaching. A self-taught musician, she served as the music director of the Sunday School and Baptist Young People's Union Congress of the National Baptist Convention for 47 years, directing 1,000 voice choirs, composing songs (heard more often now in the Grand Ole Opry than at Baptist conventions), staging original pageants, and selecting hymn book contents. In 1919, she accompanied **Marian Anderson** to Atlantic City and introduced her to those attending the National Baptist Convention. Critics recognize her hymns of the 1920s to 1940s to be excellent examples of gospel hymn writing. She was a superb orator, irritating males who envied her, and she held several leadership positions throughout the state of Tennessee in religious and educational organizations.

BIBLIOGRAPHY
Walker, Charles. *Miss Lucie*. Nashville, TN: Townsend Press, 1993. 0–910683–20–4, 175p. Walker's undocumented biography of Campbell emphasizes her importance to gospel music and her influence on her American history students.

CANNARY, MARTHA JANE. *See* CALAMITY JANE

CARROLL, ANNA ELLA (1815–1894)
Activist   Pocomoke City, Maryland

Anna Ella Carroll was a political pamphleteer who claimed to have helped formulate the Union strategy during the Civil War. She was born on August 29, 1815, as the eldest child of seven to a future governor of Maryland. When her father was elected, the family moved to Annapolis, where Carroll attended school and the Presbyterian Church. When the family had financial difficulty, she left home. In the mid-1850s, as a supporter of the American or Know-Nothing Party, she delivered and printed a series of anti-Catholic tracts in support of Millard Fillmore. In 1857, she published pieces praising William Walker's trips to Central America and advocated a transcontinental railroad. With the approval of Assistant Secretary of War, Thomas A. Scott, Carroll printed several pamphlets supporting the Lincoln administration, arguing that secession was unconstitutional and that Confederate citizens were breaking the law. She opposed abolitionists and emancipation, urging Lincoln to consider Latin American colonization schemes. After Scott left the War Department before paying

Carroll, she claimed to have created the plan of an invasion up the Tennessee River. Lemuel Evans, the former House member and later chief justice of the Texas Supreme Court who befriended Carroll, probably encouraged Scott to write letters supporting her allegation, but the government denied Carroll a hearing.

BIBLIOGRAPHY

Carroll, Anna Ella. *Anna Ella Carroll (1815–1893), American Political Writer of Maryland.* Lewiston, ME: Mellen Press, 1992. 0-7734-9244-5, 205p. The text recounts Carroll's life and work as a woman in the Civil War.

Coryell, Janet L. *Neither Heroine nor Fool: Anna Ella Carroll of Maryland.* Kent, OH: Kent State University Press, 1990. 0-87338-405-9, 177p. In her carefully researched and documented biography, Coryell examines Carroll's methods for achieving her goals.

Greenbie, Marjorie Latta Barstow. *My Dear Lady: The Story of Anna Ella Carroll.* 1940. New York: Arno Press, 1974. 0-405-06101-3, 316p. After visiting Carroll's home, interviewing friends and family, and conducting extensive research, Greenbie concluded that Carroll did help Lincoln and other leaders.

CARSON, RACHEL (1907–1964)
Biologist, Environmentalist, and Author   **Springdale, Pennsylvania**

Rachel Louise Carson used her college majors in English and biology to write about the environment. She was born on May 27, 1907, into a family controlled by her mother. After gaining a love of wildlife as a child, she received a graduate degree from Johns Hopkins and worked at the Woods Hole Marine Biological Laboratory before joining the United States Bureau of Fisheries. Her first book, *The Sea Around Us*, which she wrote at night and during brief leaves of absence from her job, won the National Book Award and a Guggenheim Foundation fellowship, allowing her to write full-time. It remained on the best-seller list for one and one-half years and was translated into 32 languages. Her next book, *The Edge of the Sea*, won her more awards. During this period, her niece died, and she adopted her niece's five-year-old son. The effects of DDT prompted her to write another book, *Silent Spring* (1962). Her warnings of environmental pollution infuriated pesticide companies, but this work marked the beginning of the ecological movement. She was later elected to The National Women's Hall of Fame.

BIBLIOGRAPHY

Brooks, Paul. *The House of Life: Rachel Carson at Work.* Boston: Houghton Mifflin, 1989. 0-395-13517-6, 350p. Brooks used letters, personal papers, Carson's writings, and reminiscences of friends for a carefully documented biography.

Carson, Rachel. *Always, Rachel: The Letters of Rachel Carson & Dorothy Freeman.* Ed. Martha Freeman. Boston: Beacon, 1983. 0-8070-7010-6, 608p. Freeman has edited over 750 of Carson's letters to her grandmother, Dorothy.

Lear, Linda J. *Rachel Carson: Witness for Nature.* New York: Henry Holt, 1997. 0–8050–3427–7, 634p. This definitive biography, based on Carson's letters and interviews with her friends, reveals Carson's life and work.

McCay, Mary A. *Rachel Carson.* New York: Twayne, 1993. 0–8057–3988–2, 123p. McCay's short but detailed biography traces Carson's concern with the environment.

Presnall, Judith Janda. *Rachel Carson.* San Diego: Lucent, 1995. 1–56606–056–5, 112p. Presnall's authentic biography for young adults shows Carson's dedication to her work and her beliefs.

CARTER, ROSALYNN (1927–)
First Lady and Activist   Plains, Georgia

Rosalynn Carter, a First Lady of the United States, has worked for international service projects helping those in need. She was born August 18, 1927, the oldest of four children of a mechanic and school bus driver father who died of leukemia when she was 13. She helped her mother support the family by babysitting, sewing, and shampooing hair in the local beauty parlor. In 1946, she graduated from Georgia Southwestern College and immediately married the area's most eligible bachelor, Jimmy Carter. While Carter and her husband rebuilt his family's company, Carter studied accounting. When her husband entered politics, she administered the business while he first campaigned and then served as a Georgia state senator. During his second gubernatorial quest, she, although shy, began to speak on his behalf. While First Lady of Georgia, she led initiatives for 134 daycare centers, served as a Georgia Regional Hospital volunteer, and supported the mentally retarded. During her husband's presidency and after he left office, Carter continued to serve on charity boards. She has also written books and held a fellowship at the Institute of Women's Studies at Emory University. She has received many awards and honorary degrees.

BIBLIOGRAPHY

Carter, Rosalynn. *First Lady from Plains.* 1984. Fayetteville: University of Arkansas Press, 1994. 1–55728–355–9, 394p. Carter uses recollections, diaries, and interviews to recall her life as First Lady.

Langford, Edna, and Linda Maddox. *Rosalynn, Friend and First Lady.* Tappan, NJ: Revell, 1980. 0–8007–1132–7, 160p. Langford, Carter's friend, reports Carter's role in the 1980 campaign.

Norton, Howard Melvin. *Rosalynn.* Plainfield, NJ: Logos International, 1977. 0–88270–260–2, 220p. Norton's popular biography of Carter, based on personal interviews, reveals her importance as an advisor to her husband.

Simmons, Dawn Langley. *Rosalynn Carter: Her Life Story.* New York: F. Fell, 1979. 0–8119–0301–X, 194p. Simmons went to Plains, Georgia, during the presidential campaign to interview people who knew the Carters for a popular biography.

CARY, MARY ANN SHADD (1823–1893)
Educator, Journalist, and Attorney   Wilmington, Delaware

Mary Ann Shadd Cary founded a newspaper to help transform slave refugees into Canadian citizens and established herself as the first African American female editor, publisher, and investigative reporter. She was born on October 9, 1823, the oldest of 13 children of free black parents; her father was a leader in the Underground Railroad movement. After she attended a Quaker school, she opened a school for African American children in Wilmington in 1840. When the Fugitive Slave Law passed in 1850, she and her brother went to Windsor, Canada, and there she established an integrated school supported by the American Missionary Association. She also began publishing emigration propaganda pamphlets to entice people to Canada. In 1853, she rejected the views of leaders who advocated moral, social, physical, intellectual, and political elevation of ex-slaves in a separatist organization instead encouraging ex–slaves to integrate and become independent in her newspaper, *Provincial Freeman*. She married in 1856 and had two children, but her husband left her a widow in 1860. She returned to the United States in 1863, became a Union Army recruiting officer, and after the war, attended Howard Law School, becoming the first African American woman lawyer in the United States in 1870. She promoted women's rights and independence throughout her life, using her paper's motto, "Self-Reliance Is the Fine Road to Independence." Her accomplishments achieved her the honor of election to The National Women's Hall of Fame.

BIBLIOGRAPHY
Bearden, Jim, and Linda Jean Butler. *Shadd: The Life and Times of Mary Shadd Cary*. Toronto: NC Press, 1977. 0–919600–73–5, 233p. This carefully researched and thoroughly documented biography follows Cadd's career.

Rhodes, Jane. *Mary Ann Shadd Cary: The Black Press and Protest in the Nineteenth Century*. Bloomington: Indiana University Press, 1998. 0–253–33446–2, 320p. Cary battled her male contemporaries for a public voice while insisting on her right to participate in the African American politics of her time.

CASSATT, MARY (1844–1926)
Artist   Allegheny City, Pennsylvania

Mary Cassatt was an artist who painted in the Impressionist style. She was born on May 22, 1844, as the fifth of seven children to a wealthy banker who preferred travel to work. The family went to Europe when Cassatt was seven, and she lived in Paris, Heidelberg, and Darmstadt. Delighted by paintings in museums abroad, Cassatt decided to become an artist. She attended the Pennsylvania Academy of the Fine Arts during the Civil War and then returned to Paris, where she copied old masters rather than studying formally. The Paris Salon first exhibited her work in 1872, but she left after five years at the Salon when Edgar Degas invited her to join the Impressionists. She exhibited with them and in America with the newly formed Society of American Artists. She enjoyed using her relatives as models but refused to teach or to accept portrait commissions. She urged friends and family to buy Impressionist paintings and influenced H. O. Havemeyer's collection in New York's Metropolitan Museum of Art. She declined exhibition prizes, but becoming a Chevalier of the Legion of Honor in France in 1904 pleased her. When her eyesight failed around 1910, she had to stop painting. She was elected into The National Women's Hall of Fame.

BIBLIOGRAPHY

Dillon, Millicent. *After Egypt: Isadora Duncan and Mary Cassatt*. New York: Dutton, 1990. 0-525-24846-3, 403p. This documented and researched biography using Cassatt's letters examines her artistic skills and her life.

Hale, Nancy. *Mary Cassatt*. Reading, MA: Addison-Wesley, 1987. 0-201-13305-9, 333p. Hale used Cassatt's unpublished letters and papers to create a carefully researched and readable biography.

Mathews, Nancy Mowll. *Mary Cassatt: A Life*. New York: Villard, 1994. 0-394-58497-X, 383p. Mathews examines the censures and criticisms Cassatt received for refusing to marry in a thoughtful, balanced biography.

———. *Mary Cassatt: A Retrospective*. New York: Simon and Schuster, 1996. 0-88363-256-X, 376p. Letters, essays, articles, and memoirs from those who knew Cassatt personally create a vital picture of a woman who chose art over marriage.

Roudebush, Jay. *Mary Cassatt*. Trans. Alice Sachs. New York: Crown, 1979. 0-517-53740-0, 95p. This straightforward, well-researched account of Cassatt includes photographs of some of her paintings and explanations of her different techniques.

CATHER, WILLA (SIBERT) (1873–1947)
Author   Winchester, Virginia

Willa Cather was a novelist who wrote about settlers and frontier life on the American plains. She was born on December 7, 1873, the oldest of seven children in a family that moved west to Nebraska when Cather was nine. Cather met educated immigrants who encouraged her reading, music study, and interest in school plays. She then attended the University of Nebraska and started writing fiction and journalism pieces. After graduation, she became a copy editor, music critic, and drama reviewer for the *Pittsburgh Leader*. In 1901, as companion to a daughter in the wealthy McClure family, she went abroad for the first time. *McClure's* hired her as managing editor upon her return, and she soon met **Sarah Orne Jewett**, who suggested that she seek themes for her writing from her personal experience. In 1912, Cather began writing full-time. Her novels *O Pioneers!* (1913) and *My Ántonia* (1918) show her main themes—the spirit and courage of the immigrants who settled the frontier. *One of Ours* (1922) won the Pulitzer Prize; along with *A Lost Lady* (1923), it notes the end of America's pioneer spirit. Cather decided to write about pioneers in other times, and her novel *Death Comes for the Archbishop* (1927) deals with the French Catholic missionaries in the Southwest. She set *Sapphira and the Slave Girl* (1940) in early Virginia. She received many honorary degrees and awards, including election to the National Institute of Arts and Letters, the Academy of Arts and Letters, and The National Women's Hall of Fame. She also won the first annual Prix Femina Américaine.

BIBLIOGRAPHY

Bennett, Mildred R. *The World of Willa Cather.* 1961. Lincoln: University of Nebraska Press, 1995. 0-8032-1151-1, 285p. Bennett interviewed people who knew Cather to write an anecdotal, undocumented biography.

Lee, Hermione. *Willa Cather: Double Lives.* New York: Pantheon, 1989. 0-394-53703-3, 410p. Lee posits in this study that Cather deserves membership in the canon of world literature.

O'Brien, Sharon. *Willa Cather: The Emerging Voice.* 1987. Cambridge, MA: Harvard University Press, 1997. 0-674-95322-3, 464p. O'Brien's scholarly, thoroughly researched, and balanced biography looks at Cather anew from a feminist perspective.

Wagenknecht, Edward. *Willa Cather.* New York: Continuum, 1994. 0-8264-0607-6, 203p. Wagenknecht establishes Cather's quality as a writer and reveals her personality.

Woodress, James Leslie. *Willa Cather: A Literary Life.* Lincoln: University of Nebraska Press, 1987. 0-8032-4734-6, 583p. This detailed, scholarly, and balanced biography presents Cather's unconventional private life and her distinctive public life.

CATLETT, ELIZABETH (1919-)
Artist   **Washington, District of Columbia**

Elizabeth Catlett is an African American sculptor and printmaker influential in both the United States and Mexico. She was born posthumously to a professor on April 15, 1919, the youngest of three children; her mother supported the family as a truant officer. Her father had been a musician and an artist, and her mother provided her with the materials to work and a place to do it. When Catlett graduated from Dunbar High School with honors, she took entrance examinations for the Carnegie Institute of Technology in Pittsburgh, but after the school rejected her, she heard one of the teachers lament, "It's too bad she's a Negro." She studied at Howard University instead with teachers such as **Loïs Mailou Jones** and Alain Locke, who suggested that African American artists look to their ancestors for influence. After graduating cum laude, she taught in Durham, North Carolina, where she protested the low salaries, and then attended graduate school at the University of Iowa, studying with Grant Wood and becoming the first student to earn an M.F.A. Later, she received a Julius Rosenwald Fellowship, with which she visited Mexico and worked with local printmakers. She remained in Mexico, marrying, raising a family, and teaching there. During the McCarthy era, she became a Mexican citizen, a decision prohibiting her travel in the United States until 1974. Her prints and sculpture appear in museums around the world as well as in churches and social clubs of her choice. She has won many awards and honorary degrees.

BIBLIOGRAPHY

Gedeon, Lucinda H., Michael Brenson, and Lowery Stokes Sims. *Elizabeth Catlett: Sculpture, A Fifty-Year Retrospective.* Seattle: University of Washington Press, 1998. 0-295-97722-1, 119p. This 50-year retrospective includes an overview of Catlett's life and photographs of her work.

Lewis, Samella S. *The Art of Elizabeth Catlett.* Claremont, CA: Hancraft Studios, 1984. 0-941248-06-2, 193p. The text, half biography and half color and black and white plates of Catlett's sculptures and drawings, reveals both her life and her art.

CATT, CARRIE (CHAPMAN) (1859–1947)
Activist and Politician   **Ripon, Wisconsin**

Carrie Chapman Catt, a leader in the women's rights movement, supported other important reform movements after passage of the Nineteenth Amendment. She was born Carrie Lane on January 9, 1859, one of three children in a farming family. As a child, she became a superb equestrian and a voracious reader who finished high school in three years. She earned a teacher's certificate and then paid to attend Iowa State College by washing dishes and working in the library. She graduated in three years and first became a high school principal before being appointed the first woman school superintendent in the country. Her first husband died after two years of marriage, and she became involved with the Iowa Woman Suffrage Association. She remarried only after her fiancé agreed to a prenuptial legal contract allowing her to work for woman suffrage four months each year. When he died, he left her financially independent to pursue her reform activities full-time. Catt reorganized the National American Woman Suffrage Association along political district lines and served as the group's president from 1915 until her death, lecturing continuously on behalf of suffrage, while also serving as president of the International Woman Suffrage Alliance, which she had founded in 1902. After Congress adopted the Nineteenth Amendment, Catt reorganized her suffrage association of 2 million into the League of Women Voters. She also fostered the peace movement, encouraged disarmament and Prohibition, and, following World War II, supported the United Nations. She received honorary degrees and other awards including the American Hebrew Medal, the gold medal of the National Institute of Social Sciences, and election to The National Women's Hall of Fame.

BIBLIOGRAPHY

Fowler, Robert Booth. *Carrie Catt: Feminist Politician.* Boston: Northeastern University Press, 1986. 0-930350-86-3, 226p. Fowler examines Catt's leadership as a feminist and a politician in his balanced biography.

Peck, Mary Gray. *Carrie Chapman Catt: A Biography.* 1944. New York: Octagon, 1975. 0-374-96336-3, 495p. Peck knew Catt and focused on her achievements as a woman suffrage leader.

Van Voris, Jacqueline. *Carrie Chapman Catt: A Public Life.* New York: Feminist Press, 1987. 0-935312-63-3, 307p. Since Van Voris found little material about Catt's private life, she used Catt's correspondence to detail her international experiences.

CHER (1946–)
Actor   El Centro, California

Cher is an award-winning vocalist and actor. She was born Cherilyn Sarkisian on May 20, 1946, one of two daughters. Her mother, a fashion model and country blues singer was married eight times, including three times to Cher's biological father. In the mid-1960s, Cher met and married Sonny Bono, with whom she performed in nightclubs and on television. After the birth of a daughter and their subsequent divorce, Cher developed her own career as an entertainer in Las Vegas. Known for her exotic costumes and her refusal to conform, she worked diligently to gain acceptance as a serious actor, with her Academy Award nomination for *Silkwood* in 1983 affirming her ability. She then won an Academy Award for her performance in *Moonstruck* in 1988. Her role in *Mask*, a film she especially liked, exposed her to children who had craniofacial deformities, and she has spent time raising funds for further research to find ways to correct these problems. After a hiatus from performing on stage, she has resumed her singing career with several successful albums.

BIBLIOGRAPHY
Carpozi, George. *Cher*. New York: Berkley, 1976. 0-425-02973-5, 178p. Carpozi investigates Cher's childhood and marriages in a reasonably balanced biography.

Cher. *Cher in Her Own Words*. New York: Music Sales, 1992. 0-7119-3030-0, 96p. This text is a collection of Cher's candid thoughts, not in any noticeable order, on many different topics.

Quirk, Lawrence J. *Totally Uninhibited: The Life and Wild Times of Cher*. New York: Morrow, 1991. 0-688-09822-3, 303p. Quirk focuses on Cher's intelligence and compassion.

Taraborrelli, J. Randy. *Cher: A Biography*. New York: St. Martin's, 1986. 0-312-13170-4, 322p. In this popular, undocumented biography, Taraborrelli emphasizes Cher's struggle to gain approval for her acting.

CHESNUT, MARY BOYKIN MILLER (1823–1886)
Author   Pleasant Hill, South Carolina

Mary Boykin Miller Chesnut's records of her experiences during the Civil War remain a unique historical view of the period. She was born on March 31, 1823, as the eldest of four children to a prominent South Carolina political leader who served as governor and as a member of the United States Congress and his second wife. Chestnut absorbed her father's political statements as a young girl and attended private schools where she learned French and German. At 13, she met James Chesnut, but her father quelled the relationship by making her return to the family's new home in Mississippi. When she married James, a Princeton graduate, in 1840, her intellectual preparation facilitated their compatibility. She remained childless, however, and was often ill. She spent two happy years in Washington, DC, while her husband served as a senator, but South Carolina's secession terminated her stay. Her husband became a Confederate staff officer, and she accompanied him on military missions, keeping notes in a daily journal from February 15, 1861, to August 2, 1865, in which she transcribed conversations, thoughts, and her responses to leisure reading. Since she had no way to validate what she heard, she recorded both facts and rumors. Although the Confederate government's weakness became obvious to her, she retained her loyalty throughout the war. She anticipated the diary's publication, but it did not appear until 20 years after her death. It is now recognized as one of the important annals of Civil War life.

BIBLIOGRAPHY

Chesnut, Mary Boykin Miller. *Mary Chesnut: The Unpublished Civil War Diaries*. New York: Oxford University Press, 1984. 0-19-503513-5, 292p. Chesnut's diaries in this text are those she revised in the 1880s.

———. *Mary Chesnut's Civil War*. Ed. C. Vann Woodward. New Haven, CT: Yale University Press, 1981. 0-300-02459-2, 886p. Woodward spent five years analyzing Chesnut's diary, and in this scholarly and definitive recommended text, he has also included portions from earlier versions.

DeCredico, Mary A. *Mary Boykin Chesnut: A Confederate Woman's Life*. Madison, WI: Madison House, 1997. 0-945612-46-X, 176p. Although supposedly a biography of Chesnut, the text instead discusses the Civil War.

Muhlenfeld, Elisabeth. *Mary Boykin Chesnut: A Biography*. Baton Rouge: Louisiana State University Press, 1981. 0-8071-0852-9, 271p. In a balanced biography, Muhlenfeld focuses on the last 20 years of Chesnut's life.

CHILD, JULIA (1912-)
Author and Chef   Pasadena, California

Julia Child, a chef, made traditional French cuisine available to Americans. She was born Julia McWilliams on August 15, 1912, the daughter of a prosperous financier and consultant. She graduated from Smith College in 1934 and worked in advertising before joining the Office of Strategic Services (OSS) during World War II and serving in Ceylon (Sri Lanka) and China. In Ceylon, she met Paul Child; she married him in 1945, and went with him to Paris. There she attended the Cordon Bleu cooking school for six months and studied privately with a master chef, Max Bugnard. In 1951, she and two French friends, Simone Beck and Louisette Bertholle, established L'École des Trois Gourmandes. Ten years later they published the important *Mastering the Art of French Cooking* in two volumes. The same year, the Childs returned to the United States, and in Boston, Child started her television series, *The French Chef*. Her informality, humor, and creativity along with her ability to adapt American ingredients to French recipes made her shows immediately and immensely popular. Since that time, she has conceived other television series and written cookbooks related to them.

BIBLIOGRAPHY

Fitch, Noel Riley. *Appetite for Life: The Biography of Julia Child*. New York: Doubleday, 1997. 0-385-48335-X, 569p. In this well-researched view of Child's life, Fitch discusses her collaboration with Simone Beck.

Reardon, Joan. *M.F.K. Fisher, Julia Child, and Alice Waters: Celebrating the Pleasures of the Table*. New York: Harmony, 1994. 0-517-57748-8, 302p. This collective biography examines Child's life before she went to Paris and her transformation once she and her husband arrived.

CHILD, LYDIA MARIA (FRANCIS) (1802–1880)
Reformer and Author   Medford, Massachusetts

Lydia Maria Francis Child authored influential antislavery works. She was born on February 11, 1802, as the youngest of six to a baker and his wife. She early became interested in books, an alarming attribute to her father. Her mother died when Child was 12, and after going to live with her sister in Maine, she continued reading and preparing herself to teach instead of focusing on domestic arts. After two years of teaching, she became bored and went to live with her brother Convers, a Harvard graduate, and his family near Boston. She met intellectuals who gathered in his home, including Ralph Waldo Emerson; Bronson Alcott and his wife, Abba May Alcott; John Greenleaf Whittier; and **Margaret Fuller**. She began writing, dropped her first name, and used Maria when she published her first novel. She conducted a private school and started *Juvenile Miscellany*, the first American periodical for children. Her impractical husband became an abolitionist, and Child began writing about slavery. In her most famous book, *An Appeal in Favor of that Class of Americans Called Africans* (1833), she traced the history of slavery and its evils. Bostonians, infuriated with her text, ostracized her, and her children's periodical ceased publication. In 1840, she became the editor of the *National Anti-Slavery Standard* for the American Anti-Slavery Society but resigned after a conflict with William Lloyd Garrison. She and her husband struggled to survive as farmers, and her articles, published in several publications, became their main financial support. After John Brown's attack at Harper's Ferry, over 300,000 copies of Child's vitriolic attacks on slavery were published and distributed throughout the North. Her home was a station on the Underground Railroad, and after the Civil War, she transcribed the recollections of freed slaves.

BIBLIOGRAPHY

Clifford, Deborah Pickman. *Crusader for Freedom: A Life of Lydia Maria Child*. Boston: Beacon Press, 1992. 0-8070-7050-5, 367p. Clifford's scholarly biography reveals Child's position as a member of Boston's elite until she began supporting the antislavery movement.

Karcher, Carolyn L. *The First Woman in the Republic: A Cultural Biography of Lydia Maria Child*. Durham, NC: Duke University Press, 1994. 0-88314-85-1, 804p. In this thoroughly researched and scholarly biography based on Child's writings and secondary sources, Karcher focuses on Child's concerns.

CHILDRESS, ALICE (1920–1994)
Author   Charleston, South Carolina

African American Alice Childress was a playwright, novelist, and actor. She was born on October 12, 1920 (some sources say 1916), and moved to Harlem at age five to live with her grandmother after her parents divorced. Although poor, her grandmother took Childress to museums, art galleries, and Wednesday night testimonials at Salem Church. Childress left school when her mother and grandmother died in the late 1930s and began teaching herself as she worked as an assistant machinist, salesperson, photo retoucher, domestic, and insurance agent to support her daughter. She began writing in the 1940s, and in 1943 became associated with the American Negro Theater. During the 1950s, she helped off-Broadway union actors receive guaranteed pay in New York City. In her dozen plays, she spoke against racism and stereotypes of African Americans, and for *Trouble in the Mind* she won the first Obie ever received by an African American woman. When a director tried to make changes in the play on Broadway, however, she refused to let it be produced. In her novels, including *A Hero Ain't Nothin' But a Sandwich* (1973), she reveals the struggle of the poor to survive in a capitalist society. Among her awards were a Rockefeller Grant.

BIBLIOGRAPHY
Jennings, La Vinia Delois. *Alice Childress*. New York: Twayne, 1995. 0–8057–3963–7, 157p. In a careful, scholarly study, Jennings looks at Childress's exploration of psychological and social themes.

CHISHOLM, SHIRLEY (1924–)
Congresswoman and Educator   Brooklyn, New York

Shirley Chisholm was the first African American woman elected to the United States Congress. She was born Shirley Anita St. Hill on November 30, 1924, one of three daughters, to immigrants from British Guiana and Barbados. When the family had financial difficulties, she lived in Barbados with her grandmother. She attended the island's strict British schools, and when she visited Brooklyn, her father's avid reading impressed her. After graduating from high school, she received scholarship offers from Vassar and Oberlin but decided to attend Brooklyn College. She graduated in 1946, taught, and worked on her M.A. at Columbia University. While managing daycare centers in Brooklyn and Manhattan, she became active in community and political groups, including her district's Unity Democratic Club. She won election to the New York legislature and served from 1964 until she was elected to the U.S. House of Representatives in 1968, defeating the civil rights leader James Farmer. She was a strong liberal opponent of weapons development, the Vietnam War, the draft, the foundation of the Department of Education, and tax credits to defray tuition for private schools. She favored full employment, consumer protection, and extended daycare funding. When she ran for the Democratic presidential nomination in 1972, she won 152 delegates before she withdrew. Then she helped found the National Women's Political Caucus and supported both the Equal Rights Amendment and legalized abortions during her Congressional service. She refused to run for reelection in 1982, citing the conservative political atmosphere growing in the country, and became the Purington Professor at Mt. Holyoke College. She was elected into The National Women's Hall of Fame.

BIBLIOGRAPHY

Brownmiller, Susan. *Shirley Chisholm: A Biography.* Garden City, NY: Doubleday, 1970. No ISBN, 139p. This biography for young adults recounts Chisholm's life as a New York politician.

Chisholm, Shirley. *The Good Fight.* New York: Harper and Row, 1973. 0–06–010764–2, 206p. Chisholm reflects on her campaign for president in 1972 and her desire to reform American politics with practical solutions.

Haskins, James. *Fighting Shirley Chisholm.* New York: Dial, 1975. 0–8037–4835–3, 211p. In a thorough juvenile biography, Haskins examines all aspects of Chisholm's life.

Marshall-White, Eleanor. *Women: Catalysts for Change: Interpretive Biographies of Shirley St. Hill Chisholm, Sandra Day O'Connor.* New York: Vantage, 1991. 0–533–09130–6, 115p. In a collective biography for young adults, based on interviews and articles, Marshall-White emphasizes Chisholm's role as a model for other women.

Scheader, Catherine. *Shirley Chisholm, Teacher and Congresswoman.* Hillsdale, NJ: Enslow, 1990. 0–89490–285–7, 128p. Scheader's balanced biography for young adults shows Chisholm's intelligence as she worked within the political system to achieve her goals.

CHOPIN, KATE (1851–1904)
Author   **St. Louis, Missouri**

Kate Chopin wrote novels and short stories with feminist themes about culture in New Orleans during a period when women had few rights. She was born Katherine O'Flaherty on February 8, 1851, to an Irish immigrant father who had become a prominent merchant and his aristocratic Creole wife. During her education at a St. Louis convent school, Chopin learned to speak French and German fluently. She loved music and writing, and after graduation, she read constantly until her marriage two years later to a member of a French-Creole family from Louisiana. On her way to New York for a honeymoon trip to Europe, Chopin met **Victoria Claflin Woodhull,** who told her not to settle for the useless life of a wife. When she returned, Chopin devoted herself to her husband and six children but dressed unconventionally and refused to follow social norms. She also watched the people in the streets of New Orleans, absorbing their attitudes and habits. After her husband died of swamp fever in 1882, Chopin managed the family plantation for a year and then took her children to St. Louis. The family doctor suggested that she read Charles Darwin, Thomas Henry Huxley, and Herbert Spencer and, based on the quality of her correspondence with him while she was visiting Louisiana, encouraged her to write. Chopin began writing in 1888 and published her first two stories the next year. Before her death, she wrote two novels and over 100 more stories, most set in Louisiana. She acknowledged that Guy de Maupassant, **Sarah Orne Jewett**, and **Mary E. Wilkins Freeman** all influenced her work. Critics reacted strongly to her novel *The Awakening*, declaring that Chopin was immoral. But since the 1920s, critics have reassessed her achievement and realize that in her treatment of themes such as female sexuality she was a pioneer in American literature and feminist writing.

BIBLIOGRAPHY

Seyersted, Per. *Kate Chopin: A Critical Biography*. Baton Rouge: Louisiana State University Press, 1969. 0–8071–0915–0, 246p. For his accessible biography, Seyersted examined Chopin's letters and notebooks to uncover what influenced her.

Toth, Emily. *Kate Chopin*. New York: Morrow, 1990. 0–688–09707–3, 528p. Toth used Chopin's personal writing as a child, lists of books read, and other minute details in a thoroughly researched biography.

CHUNG, CONNIE (1946–)
Broadcast Journalist   Washington, District of Columbia

Connie Chung is an Asian American broadcast journalist. She was born on August 20, 1946, to a former Nationalist Chinese diplomat and his wife. While majoring in biology at the University of Maryland, she became interested in politics and switched to journalism. During college, she began to work part-time as a copygirl with a Washington, DC, television station and took a full-time job as a secretary after she graduated in 1969. She soon became a news writer and on-air reporter. In 1971, Columbia Broadcasting System (CBS) in Washington hired her, and her careful reporting on George McGovern's 1972 presidential campaign and the Watergate scandal earned respect from her colleagues. On August 9, 1974, she made her first live broadcast report when Richard Nixon resigned from the presidency. A Los Angeles station then recruited her as an anchor for local news broadcasts and as a reporter. Between 1978 and 1980, she won two Emmys and a Peabody Award. Three years later, Chung had reportedly become the highest-paid newswoman on television, earning an annual salary estimated at $600,000. National Broadcasting Company (NBC) hired her for national news in New York, and by 1989 her salary had risen to nearly $1 million. Then CBS News lured her from NBC for $6 million over three years. Although she continued to do high-quality work, she decided to reduce her schedule to have a child with her husband, Maury Povich, whom she had married in 1984. Among her other awards are the Metro Area Mass Media Award, the Women in Communications Award, and several honorary degrees.

BIBLIOGRAPHY

Malone, Mary. *Connie Chung: Broadcast Journalist*. San Diego: Enslow, 1992. 0–89490–332–2, 128p. Malone traces Chung's movements upward from station to station and into the television networks as a first-generation Chinese American.

CICCONE, MADONNA LOUISE. *See* MADONNA

CISNEROS, SANDRA (1954-)
Author   Chicago, Illinois

Sandra Cisernos is a Latina American writer. She was born as the only girl in a family of seven on December 20, 1954, to a Mexican father upholsterer and a Mexican American mother. Cisernos had difficulty making the transition between schools and became very shy in elementary school even though bilingual. Not until high school would she permit others to read her writing. Her father let her attend Loyola College in Chicago because he thought she could find a husband there, but recognition for her writing as a junior and senior got her into the poetry workshop at the University of Iowa, where she received her M.F.A. in 1978. She hated Iowa when she realized that she was different from every other student in her class, but this separateness allowed her to find her own voice and identity in her writing as a Latina American. She began writing *The House on Mango Street* while still at Iowa, and after she left, the Latino immigrants to whom she taught English became the characters in her book. She decided to live alone, against her family's wishes, and when she worked at night, she gained strength from knowing that women like **Mary Cassatt** had also isolated themselves. When Turtle Bay publishers gave her a large contract, she knew that her Latina voice had been heard. Cisneros dislikes the term "Hispanic" because whites have given that name to persons of Latino origin while her people prefer the name "Latino" or "Latina." She refuses requests for her work to be published in any anthology with the word "Hispanic" in its title. Other works include *Woman Hollering Creek* and *Loose Woman*. Among her awards are the Before Columbus American Book Award and the MacArthur Award.

BIBLIOGRAPHY
Miriam-Goldberg, Caryn. *Sandra Cisneros: Latina Writer and Activist*. Springfield, NJ: Enslow, 1998. 0-7660-1045-7, 128p. This well-researched and documented biography for young adults overviews Cisneros's life and her career as a writer.

CLARK, EUGENIE (1922-)
Ichthyologist   New York, New York

Eugenie Clark, an ichthyologist, was the first American to successfully use artificial insemination experiments on fish. She was born on May 4, 1922, to a father who died while she was a baby and a Japanese mother who later married another Japanese. While her mother worked at a cigar and newspaper stand on Saturdays, Clark watched fish in the New York Aquarium. Later, she graduated from Hunter College before attending New York University for her M.S. and Ph.D. in zoology, during which time she researched the reproduction of platys and swordtail fish. Her life as a researcher has taken her to the West Indies to study fish vision and a fish's ability to transfer images from one eye to the other. She has collected and identified poisonous fish in the South Seas and searched for poisonous blowfish in Egypt. After she began her research on sharks in the 1960s and wrote two books about her experiences, she went to Israel's Hebrew University as a visiting professor in 1972 and became a full professor at the University of Maryland in 1973. Among her awards are several honorary degrees, the Dugan Award, the Cousteau Award, the Gold Medal from the Society of Women Geographers, and the David B. Stone Medal.

BIBLIOGRAPHY

Balon, Eugene K., et al., eds. *Women in Ichthyology*. Boston: Kluwer Academic, 1994. 0-7923-3165-6, 456p. In this well-documented collective biography, Balon includes a biography of Clark, a list of her published articles, and informative photographs.

Clark, Eugenie. *The Lady and the Sharks*. New York: Harper and Row, 1969. No ISBN, 269p. This sequel to Clark's *Lady with a Spear* describes her work and her responsibilities as a mother.

———. *Lady with a Spear*. 1952. New York: Ballantine, 1974. 0-345-23733-1, 246p. In this volume of her autobiography, Clark discusses her experiences in the West Indies, Florida, California, Micronesia, and the Red Sea.

CLINE, PATSY (1932–1963)
Entertainer   **Winchester, Virginia**

Patsy Cline was one of the first nationally successful female country and western singers. She was born on March 5, 1932, and began entertaining when she won a tap dance contest at age four. When she was 15, she began singing in nightclubs and auditioning to appear on the Grand Ole Opry. In 1955, she started recording but had no success until her appearance on *Arthur Godfrey's Talent Scouts* television show in January 1957. She sang "Walkin' After Midnight," and her recording, which was immediately released, climbed near the top of both the country and the pop charts. Not for four more years did she have a second hit. "I Fall to Pieces" stayed at the top of the country charts for many weeks, and she followed it with six more top ten hits. Although she had been performing for 20 years, she had been recording for only 8 when the airplane in which she was flying crashed in Tennessee. Her song "Sweet Dreams" was released posthumously, and it also became a top ten hit. Many female country singers continue to thank Cline for her pioneering path which made their career pursuits less hazardous.

BIBLIOGRAPHY

Bego, Mark. *I Fall to Pieces: The Music and the Life of Patsy Cline*. Holbrook, MA: Adams, 1995. 1-55850-476-1, 258p. A readable, researched but undocumented text, Bego's recommended biography covers Cline's career.

Brown, Stuart E., and Lorraine F. Myers. *Patsy Cline: Singing Girl from the Shenandoah Valley*. Berryville, VA: Virginia Book, 1996. 0-911578-00-5, 110p. The authors, who state that they have not meant for their collection to be a biography, examine Cline's rise to fame and her life after 1959.

Jones, Margaret. *Patsy: The Life and Times of Patsy Cline*. New York: HarperCollins, 1994. 0-06-016696-7, 335p. Jones used interviews with Cline's colleagues to trace her rise in the country music world.

Nassour, Ellis. *Honky Tonk Angel: The Intimate Story of Patsy Cline*. New York: St. Martin's, 1993. 0-312-08870-1, 270p. In his balanced biography, Nassour reveals differing accounts from Cline's associates to show a complex woman.

CLINTON, HILLARY RODHAM (1947-)
Attorney and First Lady   Chicago, Illinois

Hillary Rodham Clinton, a lawyer, has been First Lady of the United States. She was born on October 26, 1947, as the only daughter in a middle-class family of three children. She began her activism in public high school by organizing babysitting services for migrant workers and participating in civil rights activities. After graduating as a National Merit Scholarship finalist, she attended the all-female Wellesley College, and while there, campaigned for a higher African American student enrollment, actively opposed the Vietnam War, and delivered the commencement address, the first graduate to do so. While enrolled in Yale Law School, she spent summers interviewing children of migrant workers, serving at the Yale Child Study Center, and doing legal research for the Carnegie Council on Children. After she met and married her husband, Bill Clinton, at Yale, he became the attorney general of Arkansas and then governor. Clinton joined the Rose Law Firm and founded the Arkansas Advocates for Children and Families to help low-income children, and after the birth of her daughter, led efforts to improve education in the state. She campaigned for her husband both times when he ran for president of the United States. As First Lady, she has continued to support education, families, and children. In 1988 and 1991, the *National Law Journal* named her one of the most influential lawyers in the United States, and she has won many honorary degrees and other awards.

BIBLIOGRAPHY
Flaherty, Peter, and Timothy Flaherty. *The First Lady: A Comprehensive View of Hillary Rodham Clinton*. Lafayette, LA: Vital Issues Press, 1996. 1-56384-119-3, 238p. Using references to newspaper and magazine articles, the Flahertys try to understand the relationship between Clinton and her husband in a popular biography.

King, Norman. *The Woman in the White House: The Remarkable Story of Hillary Rodham Clinton*. New York: Carol, 1996. 1-55972-349-1, 233p. This popular but undocumented biography of Clinton emphasizes her role as wife, mother, and unofficial presidential advisor.

Nelson, Rex. *The Hillary Factor: The Story of America's First Lady*. New York: Gallen, 1993. 0-9636477-1-7, 364p. Nelson focuses on Clinton as a revolutionary figure in his popular biography based on files from the *Arkansas Democrat-Gazette*.

Radcliffe, Donnie. *Hillary Rodham Clinton: A First Lady for Our Time*. New York: Warner, 1993. 0-446-51766-6, 270p. This readable and researched biography examines Clinton's life as a professional female trying to balance marriage and family.

Warner, Judith. *Hillary Clinton: The Inside Story.* New York: Signet, 1993. 0-451-17808-4, 246p. This readable popular biography, based on interviews and archives in Arkansas newspapers, examines Clinton's life through her initial year as the First Lady.

COCHRAN, JACQUELINE (1910–1980)
Aviator   Pensacola, Florida

Jacqueline Cochran Odlum was an aviator who held more speed, distance, and altitude records than any other flyer during her career. She was born on May 11, 1910, but was orphaned as a young child and raised by foster parents. She went to work when she was eight in a Georgia cotton mill and then became a beauty shop operator before founding her own cosmetics firm. In 1932, she learned to fly as a way to promote her cosmetics business, but after her marriage in 1936 to an industrialist and banker, she began to break speed records as well as business records. In 1938, she set one of two speed records and established a record time for women by crossing North America in 10 hours, 12 minutes, and 55 seconds. She was the first woman to enter and win the Bendix Transcontinental Air Race. In World War II, Cochran served as a captain in the British Air Force Auxiliary and organized a group of female pilots to fly military aircraft throughout Europe from their places of manufacture to their places of deployment. When the United States joined the Allies, Cochran served as director of the Women's Air Force Service Pilots and taught American women to fly transport planes. In 1953, she broke the world speed records for both men and women in a Sabre jet. The same year, she became the first woman to fly faster than the speed of sound (Mach 1). In 1961, she broke her own 100- and 500-kilometer world records and became the first woman to fly at Mach 2. In 1964, she flew faster than any woman in previous history by flying 1,429 mph. When she retired as a colonel from the Air Force Reserve in 1970, she became a special National Aeronautics and Space Administration (NASA) consultant. She was later elected into The National Women's Hall of Fame.

BIBLIOGRAPHY

Cochran, Jacqueline. *Jackie Cochran: An Autobiography.* New York: Bantam, 1987. 0-553-05211-X, 358p. This text of Cochran's autobiography includes comments by her friends.
———. *The Stars at Noon.* 1954. New York: Arno Press, 1980. 0-405-12156-3, 274p. Cochran reveals in her lively autobiography, suitable for young adults, that she was willing to try almost anything.
Smith, Elizabeth Simpson. *Coming Out Right: The Story of Jacqueline Cochran, the First Woman Aviator to Break the Sound Barrier.* New York: Walker, 1991. 0-8027-6988-8, 114p. In a balanced biography for young adults, Smith recounts Cochran's life and her accomplishments.

COFER, JUDITH ORTIZ   (1952–   )
Author and Poet   Hormigueros, Puerto Rico

Latina American Judith Ortiz Cofer is both a poet and novelist. She was born on February 24, 1952, one of two children of a Navy sailor and his wife. Although the family address was New Jersey, her mother took the children to Puerto Rico to visit with relatives while Cofer's father was at sea. Cofer spoke only Spanish as a child, but began to learn English before attending school in the United States. She earned a degree in English literature from Augusta College and then an M.A. from Florida Atlantic University. She has taught at various colleges and universities including the University of Georgia. She published her first three books, *Latin Women Pray*, *The Native Dancer*, and *Among the Ancestors*, in the early 1980s and subsequently published three more poetry collections and a novel. In her fiction and in her poetry, she deals with the differences in identity, sex roles, and family values between the cultures in which she grew up. She has received acclaim for prose as well as poetry, with her honors including the Pushcart Prize and an O. Henry Award.

BIBLIOGRAPHY
Cofer, Judith Ortiz. *Silent Dancing: A Partial Remembrance of a Puerto Rican Childhood.* Houston: Arte Publico Press, 1990. 1-55885-015-5, 158p. In this *ensayos* (essay) about her life, appropriate for young adults, Cofer wonders how her family and events have led to inspiration for her poems.

COLEMAN, BESSIE   (1896–1926)
Aviator   Atlanta, Texas

Bessie Coleman was an African American aviator who starred in air exhibitions and shows. She was born the twelfth of thirteen children to an African American mother and a mixed Choctaw and African father on January 20, 1896. After her family moved to Waxahatchie, Texas, and began working in the cotton fields, her father left. Her mother recognized Coleman's mathematical ability and kept her at home to manage the family's meager money supply. She also allowed Coleman to keep the money she earned from taking in laundry for college, and Coleman attended the Colored Agricultural and Normal University in Langston, Oklahoma, for one year. In 1915, she went to Chicago and became a manicurist in a barbershop, where she heard men returned from World War I discuss aviation. Two African American philanthropists supported her aviation interests by sending her to a French school when local schools used Jim Crow laws to refuse her admission. She learned parachuting and stunt flying before becoming the first American with an international license. In America, she flew as a barnstormer but refused to perform in shows when the organizers would not revoke the Jim Crow order. She also lectured to African American groups, encouraging them to become involved in aviation, and she raised money to begin a school. During a dress rehearsal flight, she accidentally fell 2,000 feet and died.

BIBLIOGRAPHY

Freydberg, Elizabeth Hadley. *Bessie Coleman, the Brownskin Lady Bird*. New York: Garland, 1994. 0–8153–1461–2, 156p. Freydberg's researched, scholarly biography examines Coleman's achievements.

Rich, Doris L. *Queen Bess: Daredevil Aviator*. Washington, DC: Smithsonian Institution Press, 1993. 1–56098–265–9, 153p. Interviews with aged relatives and friends as well as press clippings and journals of the era form the basis for Rich's informative biography of Coleman.

COMDEN, BETTY (1919–)
Librettist   Brooklyn, New York

Betty Comden is an award-winning librettist. She was born Elizabeth Cohen on May 3, 1919, to a lawyer and a schoolteacher. After graduating from New York University with a degree in drama, she formed a cabaret act with **Judy Holliday** and Adolph Green. Five years later, she and Green wrote the book and lyrics for the Broadway hit *On the Town*, in which she also acted. In 1947, she and Green made their screenwriting debut with *Good News*, and in 1952, they wrote *Singin' in the Rain*. Other projects include *Bells Are Ringing*, *A Party with Betty Comden and Adolph Green*, *What a Way to Go*, *Applause*, *All About Eve*, *Follies in Concert*, *Auntie Mame*, and *The Will Rogers Follies*. Single songs for which they are well known include "Take Me Out to the Ballgame." Although Comden and Green have remained working partners, both married others, and Comden raised two children while continuing her career. Among her awards are five Tony Awards, a Grammy Award, a National Board of Review Special Award for Career Achievement, and the Kennedy Center Honors Lifetime Achievement Award.

BIBLIOGRAPHY

Comden, Betty. *Off Stage*. New York: Simon and Schuster, 1995. 0–671–70579–2, 272p. Comden recalls her Brooklyn childhood, her friends, and her son's drug addiction and subsequent death from AIDS.

Robinson, Alice M. *Betty Comden and Adolph Green: A Bio-Bibliography*. Westport, CT: Greenwood Press, 1994. 0–313–27659–5, 360p. Robinson's biography of Comden precedes information about her collaborations on Broadway musicals, radio, television, and film.

COOLIDGE, ELIZABETH SPRAGUE (1864–1953)
Music Patron   Chicago, Illinois

Elizabeth Penn Sprague Coolidge was a music patron. She was born on October 30, 1864, the only child to reach maturity of a wholesale grocer and his wife. During her youth she studied piano and played with the Chicago Symphony of which her father was a sponsor, became a watercolorist, and traveled abroad. Following her marriage in 1891, she studied piano in Vienna, Austria. After her father died, she and her mother gave Sprague Memorial Hall to Yale University, and after her mother's death, she endowed a pension fund for the Chicago Symphony in memory of her parents. She sponsored the Berkshire Quartet and established the Berkshire Chamber Music Festival in Pittsfield, Massachusetts. In 1923, she funded a festival in Rome, and in 1925, she built an auditorium at the Library of Congress and established the Elizabeth Sprague Coolidge Foundation. She also privately aided composers such as Samuel Barber, Béla Bartók, Benjamin Britten, Maurice Ravel, Arnold Schoenberg, and Hector Villa-Lobos. She assisted modern dance by commissioning composers, including Igor Stravinsky, Aaron Copland, and Paul Hindemith to create works for **Martha Graham** and others. Performers who received her beneficence included *Myra Hess and Rudolf Serkin. Although she avoided publicity, she received honors in England, Belgium, Germany, and France. Following her death, a two-day memorial festival honored her in her Pittsfield building, the Temple of Music.

BIBLIOGRAPHY

Barr, Cyrilla. *Elizabeth Sprague Coolidge: Portrait of a Patron.* New York: Schirmer, 1998. 0–02–864888–9, 436p. Barr used private family papers to uncover Coolidge's private life and how she created a career for herself as an American philanthropist.

COOPER, ANNA JULIA (1858–1964)
Educator   Raleigh, North Carolina

Anna Julia Cooper believed that African American women could fulfill themselves intellectually through study and vocation. She was born on August 10, 1858, the daughter of a slave and her master. Cooper's mother worked as a nursemaid for another man's child, and in this home, Cooper developed her love of learning. In later life, she said that she owed her father nothing other than her procreation. At age nine, she entered St. Augustine's Normal School in Raleigh, North Carolina, where she began to coach and tutor older students. She met her husband, a Greek teacher from Nassau, and for two years, until he died, they worked to improve the school. As a young widow, Cooper went to Oberlin, where she studied with **Mary Eliza Church Terrell**. Cooper became concerned about the inequities for African American women and clearly argued her views before joining the faculty of the M Street High School in Washington, DC. As its principal, she helped students gain acceptance to such colleges as Amherst, Brown, Cornell, Harvard, and Yale. She continued to lecture and became the only woman elected to membership in the American Negro Academy, founded in 1897. In 1900, she went to London and addressed the international gathering at the Pan-American Conference on "The Negro Problem in America." After difficulties and setbacks in her work, Cooper decided to obtain her Ph.D., and in her fifties, she attended the Sorbonne in Paris, where she became the fourth African American woman to earn a Ph.D. for which she wrote in French a dissertation titled "The Attitude of France Toward Slavery During the Revolution." When she returned to America, she became a college president. In 1992, the Anna Julia

Cooper Professorship in Women's Studies was endowed at Spelman College in Atlanta.

BIBLIOGRAPHY

Baker-Fletcher, Karen. *A Singing Something: Womanist Reflections on Anna Julia Cooper*. New York: Crossroad, 1994. 0-8245-1399-1, 215p. Baker-Fletcher's scholarly, carefully researched, and documented text examines Cooper's theological themes in her work.

Cooper, Anna J. *A Voice from the South, by a Black Woman of the South*. 1892. New York: Negro Universities Press, 1969. 0-8371-1384-9, 304p. Cooper examines American history from her own perspective, offering insight into her thoughts about womanhood in relation to God and Western culture.

Gabel, Leona C. *From Slavery to the Sorbonne and Beyond: The Life and Writings of Anna J. Cooper*. Northampton, MA: Smith College, 1982. 0-87391-028-1, 104p. This readable, carefully researched and documented biography is based on archives of the family with whom Cooper lived.

Hutchinson, Louise Daniel. *Anna J. Cooper, a Voice from the South*. Washington, DC: Smithsonian Institution Press, 1981. 0-87474-528-4, 201p. In her carefully researched biography, Hutchinson includes over 200 photographs, maps, letters, official documents, and papers covering Cooper's life.

COPPIN, FANNY JACKSON (1837-1913)
Educator and Missionary   **Washington, District of Columbia**

Fanny Jackson Coppin was both an influential African American educator and a missionary to Africa. She was born a slave in 1837, but after an aunt purchased Coppin when she was a child, she lived with relatives in New England and worked as a domestic. With money she earned, Coppin hired a tutor for three hours each week, and after six years, attended public school and then the Rhode Island State Normal School. With financial assistance from her aunt and from the African Methodist Episcopal Church, she enrolled at Oberlin College in 1860, and five years later, after opening a school for migrating freedpeople and an evening school, she graduated as the second African American woman with an A.B. degree. Subsequently, she took an appointment as principal of the female department of the Institute for Colored Youth in Philadelphia, and when the principal of the institute left, she became the first African American woman to head an institution of higher learning in the United States. She married in 1881, and her minister husband eventually moved to Philadelphia to be with her. When she retired from the Institute in 1902, she and her husband went to Cape Town, South Africa, where she developed missions around the country. Among her honors was having Coppin State College in Baltimore, Maryland, named for her.

BIBLIOGRAPHY

Coppin, Fanny Jackson. *Reminiscences of School Life and Hints on Teaching*. New York: Hall, 1995. 0-8161-1633-4, 191p. This text includes Coppin's autobiography, written in 1913, educational views, her travel experiences, and a discussion of her missionary work in South Africa.

Perkins, Linda Marie. *Fanny Jackson Coppin and the Institute for Colored Youth, 1865–1902.* New York: Garland, 1987. 0-8240-6847-5, 347p. This scholarly study and dissertation examines Coppin's achievements.

CORNELL, KATHARINE (1893–1974)
Actor   Berlin, Germany

Katharine Cornell was a celebrated actor often called the first lady of the American theater. She was born on February 16, 1893, the only daughter of a timid mother unhappily married to a doctor from Buffalo, New York, who, disinterested in medicine, became a theater manager after returning from Berlin. At his theater, Cornell saw **Maude Adams** play Peter Pan and decided to become an actor. Cornell attended a finishing school, and after traveling abroad, returned to the school to teach dramatics and coach athletics. When her mother died in 1915, Cornell took her sizeable inheritance to New York. When an actor she was understudying with the Washington Square Players became ill, she took the part and remained with the company for two years. In 1921, she married the Garrick Theater's director, Guthrie McClintic, and three years later received positive reviews for her portrayal of George Bernard Shaw's Candida. Cornell and her husband then formed Cornell and McClintic Productions in 1930, a company in which she had all the lead roles and her husband did all the directing. They made $12 million with an initial investment of $30,000. Among their most renowned plays were *The Barretts of Wimpole Street* and *Romeo and Juliet,* for which Cornell won the New York Drama League Award. Cornell's Saint Joan in Shaw's play was a highlight of her career as well. Cornell especially enjoyed performing for the troops in Europe during World War II at camps and hospitals. She brought culture and professionalism to the American stage until her retirement in 1961.

BIBLIOGRAPHY

Cornell, Katharine. *I Wanted to Be an Actress: The Autobiography of Katharine Cornell.* New York: Random, 1939. No ISBN, 361p. Cornell's autobiography recounts her stage career.

Mosel, Tad. *Leading Lady: The World and Theatre of Katharine Cornell.* Boston: Little, Brown, 1978. 0-316-58537-8, 534p. Mosel's readable, well-researched, and authoritative biography, almost psychobiography, dwells on Cornell's relationship with her husband and her father.

Pederson, Lucille M. *Katharine Cornell: A Bio-Bibliography.* Westport, CT: Greenwood Press, 1994. 0-313-27718-4, 231p. Pederson's biography precedes a discussion of Cornell's appearances on radio, television, the stage, and film.

CRAFT, ELLEN (1826–1897)
Slave and Reformer   Clinton, Georgia

Ellen Craft was an escaped slave who tried to help others gain an education. She was born in 1826 to a slaveholder and his house slave, and her father gave Craft to her half-sister. She met and married a fellow slave in 1846, and in 1848, they attempted to escape. The light-skinned Craft dressed as a slave master traveling to Philadelphia for medical reasons, and her husband William pretended to be her valet. They reached Boston, and Craft became a seamstress. In 1850, with the passage of the Fugitive Slave Act, they feared slave catchers and went to England for 19 years. In England, they attended an agricultural school and purchased a home with proceeds from lecturing on the antislavery circuit. They also raised funds for southern freedpeople and to establish a school for girls in Sierra Leone. After their five children were born, they returned to the United States and purchased a plantation in Georgia. While raising cotton and rice, Craft ran a school for local children.

BIBLIOGRAPHY
Craft, William, and Ellen Craft. *Running a Thousand Miles for Freedom.* 1860. New York: Arno Press, 1969. No ISBN, 111p. This biography of Craft and her husband discloses that her mistress gave her away as a wedding present so that people would not think Craft was her daughter.

Sterling, Dorothy. *Black Foremothers: Three Lives.* 1979. New York: Feminist Press, 1988. 0-935312-89-7, 174p. This readable collective biography for young adults tells Craft's story and discusses the special problems of slave children born to white masters.

CRANDALL, PRUDENCE (1803–1890)
Educator   Hopkinton, Rhode Island

Prudence Crandall, a teacher and abolitionist, attempted to open a boarding school for African American girls in the 1830s. She was born on September 3, 1803, as the eldest daughter of four children to a Quaker farmer and his wife. After Crandall attended boarding school and later taught, wealthy families asked her to open a school for their daughters in Canterbury, Connecticut, during 1831. When the daughter of an African American farmer requested admission and Crandall accepted her, white students attending the school threatened to withdraw. She closed her school and reopened it as a boarding and teacher-training school for African American girls living in the nearby cities of Boston, Providence, and New York. A Connecticut politician neighbor of Crandall's lobbied the state legislature to pass the "Black Law" so that African American students living outside the state could only be educated inside the state with the approval of town authorities. Crandall was arrested and jailed under this act. Abolitionist supporters left her in jail for the night to publicize her case. The jury that heard her first trial did not convict her, but the second jury did. When a higher court reversed the decision, the citizens of Canterbury insidiously attacked and destroyed the school. Crandall married and moved to Illinois with her husband, where she held a school in her home. Near the end of her life, Connecticut voted to give her a small pension, but it could never adequately right the wrongs done to her or those she wanted to help.

BIBLIOGRAPHY

Foner, Philip Sheldon. *Three Who Dared: Prudence Crandall, Margaret Douglass, Myrtilla Miner*. Westport, CT: Greenwood Press, 1984. 0-313-23584-8, 234p. In a collective biography, Foner gives an overview of Crandall's life.

Fuller, Edmund. *Prudence Crandall: An Incident of Racism in Nineteenth-Century Connecticut*. Middletown, CT: Wesleyan University Press, 1971. 0-8195-4030-7, 113p. Fuller uses surviving documents in a critical study of Crandall's determination to open a school for African American girls.

Strane, Susan. *A Whole-Souled Woman: Prudence Crandall and the Education of Black Women*. New York: Norton, 1990. 0-393-02826-7, 278p. In addition to an account of Crandall's life, this accessible biography is also a history of the racial tension in the antebellum North.

Welch, Marvis Olive. *Prudence Crandall: A Biography*. Manchester, CT: Jason, 1983. 0-9613180-0-7, 234p. Using diaries, documents, letters, and legends for a well-researched scholarly biography, Welch has recreated Crandall's life.

CRAWFORD, JOAN (1904-1977)
Actor   San Antonio, Texas

Joan Crawford was an award-winning actor. She was born Lucille Le Sueur on March 23, 1904, into a poor family. She attended a private school where her mother worked, but when her own part-time job interfered with her study, the headmaster's wife falsified her records so that Stephens College would admit her. Since Crawford was not academically prepared for Stephens, she had to withdraw. In 1923, she won an amateur dance contest and joined a chorus line in New York. A Metro-Goldwyn-Mayer studio producer spotted her and offered her a screen test, but not until her twenty-first film, *Our Dancing Daughters*, did she become a star. She successfully transferred her talents to sound films, but MGM refused to give her challenging roles. With Warner Brothers, she performed in *Mildred Pierce*, a role for which she won an Academy Award and other honors. She also earned additional Academy Award nominations. Most of her other films in the 1960s, except for *Whatever Happened to Baby Jane?*, were undistinguished horror films. In 1969, she received the Cecil B. De Mille Award for lifetime achievement. Off-stage, she married four times and adopted four children, and after her affiliation with Christian Science, she refused treatment when she fell ill in the 1970s, a decision that subsequently killed her.

BIBLIOGRAPHY

Guiles, Fred Lawrence. *Joan Crawford: The Last Word*. Secaucus, NJ: Carol, 1995. 1-55972-269-X, 233p. Guiles posits that Crawford was not the greatest but that she was the most successful actress in film.

Quirk, Lawrence J. *The Complete Films of Joan Crawford*. Secaucus, NJ: Citadel, 1988. 0-8065-1078-1, 224p. After a brief biography of Crawford, Quirk summarizes each of her films and adds anecdotal information.

Thomas, Bob. *Joan Crawford: A Biography*. New York: Simon and Schuster, 1978. 0-671-24033-1, 315p. Thomas's popular biography of Crawford, although without depth, reveals her eccentricities and her obsessive personality.

Walker, Alexander. *Joan Crawford, the Ultimate Star*. New York: Harper and Row, 1983. 0-06-015123-4, 192p. Alexander's detailed biography, with over 250 photographs, reveals Crawford at all the stages of her career in Hollywood's studio system.

Wayne, Jane Ellen. *Crawford's Men*. New York: Prentice-Hall, 1998. 0-13-188665-7, 256p. In a candid, popular biography based on interviews with Crawford, Wayne investigates her theories about life and her relationships with the men she knew.

CRAWFORD-SEEGER, RUTH. *See* SEEGER, RUTH CRAWFORD

CROSBY, FANNY (1820–1915)
Hymn Writer   **Southeast Putnam, New York**

Fanny Crosby wrote over 5,500 hymns, many of which church congregations continue to sing. She was born on March 24, 1820, as an only child, but her father died before she was one, and her mother remarried and had three more children. Crosby lost her eyesight at six weeks when a doctor prescribed hot poultices for an eye infection. But as a child, she rode horses, climbed trees, and led neighborhood antics. She memorized passages from the Bible that her mother read to her, and since she wanted to study formally, eagerly enrolled at the New York Institution for the Blind in New York City when she was 15, remaining for eight years. She often traveled to promote education for the blind, and she addressed joint sessions of Congress and President Polk. After a phrenologist suggested that she compose poetry, her poems appeared in the *New York Herald*, the *Saturday Evening Post*, and other publications beginning in the 1840s. Grover Cleveland, brother of the superintendent at the school, often served as her secretary. In 1864, William B. Bradbury, the "father of popular Sunday School music in America," suggested that she write hymns. Through the years, she wrote between 5,500 and 9,000 hymns, often using pseudonyms. She varied her methods of composition using poems, words for a melody, verses for an existing hymn, or revisions of verses by other writers. In 1858, she married a blind man who insisted that she continue publishing under her own name. Among her most famous hymns, "Safe in the Arms of Jesus," "Rescue the Perishing," and "Blessed Assurance" reflect the sentimental attitudes of her day. She also spoke at Chautauqua meetings, for the Bowery Mission, and at railroad branches of the YMCA.

BIBLIOGRAPHY
Dengler, Sandy. *Fanny Crosby, Writer of 8,000 Songs*. Chicago: Moody, 1985. 0-8024-2529-1, 140p. This fictional biography, suitable for young adults, gives an overview of Crosby's life and accomplishments.

Ruffin, Bernard. *Fanny Crosby*. Chicago: United Church, 1976. 0-8298-0290-8, 257p. In a well-documented biography focusing on Crosby's achievements, Ruffin notes that she was well known during her life.

CUNNINGHAM, IMOGEN (1883-1976)
Photographer   Portland, Oregon

Imogen Cunningham was an experimental photographer known for her portraits of plants and people. She was born April 12, 1883, and began taking pictures in 1901 after enrolling in a photography correspondence course. Her earliest prints, imitations of academic painting at the turn of the century in the Romantic Pictorialism style, were softly focused sentimental photography. After studying photographic chemistry in Germany, she opened a gallery in Seattle and established her reputation with both realistic and allegorical prints. She moved to San Francisco after her marriage to another photographer and met Edward Weston. He helped her place 10 photographs in the Deutsche Werkbund's 1929 Film und Foto exhibition. After her association with these German designers and architects, she joined a group of West Coast photographers, Group F.64, who liked sharply focused prints. While Cunningham managed a portrait gallery, she also taught at the San Francisco Art Institute. Later, she became a fellow of the American Academy of Arts and Sciences, and when 87, she received a Guggenheim Foundation fellowship. Her last work was a collection of portraits of old people that she called *After Ninety*.

BIBLIOGRAPHY
Cunningham, Imogen. *Imogen Cunningham: Selected Texts and Biography*. Ed. Amy Rule. Boston: Hall, 1992. 0-8161-0575-8, 194p. The editor's introduction to Cunningham's life includes a chronology, a critical essay, personal letters, diary entries, photographs, and articles.
Dater, Judy. *Imogen Cunningham: A Portrait*. Boston: New York Graphic Society, 1979. 0-8212-0751-2, 126p. Anecdotes from 40 people who knew Cunningham in the last 20 years of her life reveal her as an extraordinary woman.
Lorenz, Richard. *Imogen Cunningham: Flora*. Boston: Little, Brown, 1996. 0-8212-2221-X, 160p. Cunningham's photographs, isolating her botanical subjects with closeups, complement the text about her style.
———. *Imogen Cunningham: Ideas Without End, A Life in Photographs*. San Francisco: Chronicle, 1993. 0-8118-0390-2, 180p. Lorenz's carefully researched and documented biography, with photographs, utilizes the archives of the Imogen Cunningham Trust to capture her personality.

CUSHMAN, CHARLOTTE (1816-1876)
Actor   Boston, Massachusetts

Charlotte Saunders Cushman was the first native-born actor to become a star on the American stage. She was born on July 23, 1816, the first of five children of a merchant and his second wife. Cushman's mother supported the family by taking in boarders after the collapse of her father's business and his health. Cushman became a domestic at age 13 to help support the family but studied singing when she could. She went on tour singing the role of Countess Almaviva in Mozart's opera *The Marriage of Figaro* after a debut at 19, but her voice failed from straining to sing in the wrong register. She then made her debut as an actor in New Orleans in 1836 as Lady Macbeth. In 1842, she became manager of the Walnut Street Theatre in Philadelphia, alternating nights playing in Philadelphia and New York. In 1844, she sailed to London with recommendations but no contacts. She eventually secured a part, and rave reviews made her a star overnight. Critics hailed her as the successor to Mrs. *Sarah Kemble Siddons. She toured in England and performed in London playing Romeo, Lady Macbeth, Queen Katharine in *Henry VIII*, and Meg Merrilies in *Guy Mannering*. With her new wealth, she brought her family to London and secured roles for her sister. In 1848, she played a command performance for Queen Victoria, and the next year, she successfully toured the United States. Three years later, she announced her retirement, moved to Rome, and accepted only benefit performances in Europe or in America. She never married, although her constant companion after 1857 was American sculptor Emma Stebbins. The two returned to the United States to live in 1870, and four years later, at Cushman's final performance, 25,000 people waited outside her New York hotel. In 1915, she was elected to New York University's Hall of Fame, and clubs with her name still existed after World War II.

BIBLIOGRAPHY

Leach, Joseph. *Bright Particular Star: The Life and Times of Charlotte Cushman*. New Haven, CT: Yale University Press, 1970. 0-300-01205-5, 453p. Letters, theatrical archives, and trade papers helped Leach re-create Cushman's life and career.

$\mathscr{D}$

DANDRIDGE, DOROTHY JEAN (1923–1965)
Singer and Actor   Cleveland, Ohio

African American Dorothy Dandridge was an award-winning actor. She was born November 9, 1923, to a cabinetmaker and minister father and a mother who wanted to act. Her parents separated before her birth, and Dandridge and her sister helped support the family by performing as children in Baptist churches. After answering silly questions at the end of each performance, Dandridge hated interviews the remainder of her life. In Los Angeles, Dandridge and her sister added another female to their act, named themselves the Dandridge Sisters, and left for New York's Cotton Club. In 1942, Dandridge married and stayed home for six years until her brain-damaged child had to be institutionalized. Her marriage ended and she returned to the stage as a singer. Her subsequent performance in the film *Carmen Jones* won her an Academy Award nomination, the first received by an African American female for best actor. Although she was an international star, she did not work in films for another three years. In 1959, she won the Golden Globe Award for best actress in a musical for her work in *Porgy and Bess*. She was offered the part of Cleopatra, but she knew that the film industry would not allow an African American to play the part, and **Elizabeth Taylor** was eventually cast. While still performing, she died from an antidepressant overdose. In 1977, she was inducted into the Black Filmmakers Hall of Fame.

BIBLIOGRAPHY

Bogle, Donald. *Dorothy Dandridge: A Biography*. New York: St. Martin's, 1997. 1-56743-034-1, 613p. Bogle's biography suggests that Dandridge secured work as an actor because she avoided alienating people who could ruin her career.

Dandridge, Dorothy, and Earl Conrad. *Everything and Nothing: The Dorothy Dandridge Tragedy*. New York: Abelard-Schuman, 1970. 0-200-71690-5, 215p. Dandridge taped her autobiography before she died, and Conrad transcribed her notes.

DAVIS, BETTE (1908–1989)
Actor   Lowell, Massachusetts

Bette Davis was an award-winning actor. She was born Ruth Elizabeth Davis on April 5, 1908, one of two daughters of a lawyer and his wife who were later divorced. Davis's mother supported her daughters by working as a governess and as a photographer. Davis adopted the name Bette from Balzac's character in *La Cousine Bette* and began pursuing a career in acting when she was still a teenager. In New York, she studied at the Robert Milton–John Murray Anderson School of the Theater and danced with **Martha Graham** before making her Broadway debut in 1929. In 1930, Universal hired her, and after an inauspicious start, she won acclaim in *The Man Who Played God* and *Of Human Bondage*. After 1935, she won two Academy Awards for her roles in the movies *Dangerous* and *Jezebel*. Critical acclaim and stardom led to her election as the first woman president of the Academy of Motion Picture Arts and Sciences. In 1950, she won a third Academy Award for *All About Eve*, and in 1962, she won her tenth nomination for *What Ever Happened to Baby Jane?* In 1977, the American Film Institute gave her a Lifetime Achievement Award, and in 1979, she received an Emmy Award. Her intense characterizations of strong women solidified her place in cinema history.

BIBLIOGRAPHY

Davis, Bette. *This 'N That*. New York: Putnam, 1987. 0-399-13246-5, 207p. Davis reminisces about her career and colleagues in this autobiography.

Hadleigh, Boze. *Bette Davis Speaks*. New York: Barricade Books, 1996. 1-56980-066-9, 256p. Hadleigh's interviews with Davis from 1975 to 1989 appear in a question and answer format.

Leaming, Barbara. *Bette Davis: A Biography*. New York: Simon and Schuster, 1992. 0-671-70955-0, 397p. This well-researched definitive biography, based on Davis's personal papers and diaries as well as interviews with her friends, examines her life.

Quirk, Lawrence J. *Fasten Your Seat Belts: The Passionate Life of Bette Davis*. New York: Morrow, 1990. 0-688-08427-3, 464p. Quirk collected materials for his biography of Davis for 43 years, and he reports many details about her personal life, especially her sexual exploits.

Spada, James. *More than a Woman: An Intimate Biography of Bette Davis*. New York: Bantam, 1993. 0-553-09512-9, 514p. This carefully researched and documented biography of Davis, based on over 150 interviews with friends, family, co-workers, and acquaintances during three years, presents a readable view of her life.

DAVIS, FRANCES ELLIOTT (1882–1965)
Nurse   Knoxville, Tennessee

Frances Elliott Davis became the first African American nurse acknowledged by the American Red Cross. At Davis's birth in 1882, her white mother's family ousted her because Davis's father was mixed Cherokee and African American. When Davis was five, her mother died from tuberculosis, and Davis lived in an orphanage and with several foster families. Her last family treated her like a servant and took her to Pittsburgh, Pennsylvania, where she met a wealthy jewelry store owner who financed her education at Knoxville College for professional training as a nurse. Davis eventually graduated from the Freedmen's Hospital Training School in Washington, DC, in 1910, and worked as a private duty nurse before applying to the Red Cross. When told she would need public health training, she attended Columbia University and applied to the Red Cross after finishing her study in 1917. When the Red Cross sent her a nursing pin, it had written "1A" on the back to signify that Davis was African American, and therefore without the same status as other Red Cross nurses. Davis married in 1921 but continued her vocation by organizing the first training school for African American nurses in Michigan. She died before receiving belated recognition from the Red Cross in 1965 as a full member of the organization.

BIBLIOGRAPHY
Pitrone, Jean Maddern. *Trailblazer: Negro Nurse in the American Red Cross*. San Diego: Harcourt, 1969. No ISBN, 191p. Pitrone's young adult biography of Davis recounts her experiences.

DAY, DOROTHY (1897–1980)
Reformer   Brooklyn, New York

Dorothy Day was a social reformer and editor who co-founded the Catholic Worker Movement. She was born on November 8, 1897, to a sportswriter who forced his family to move around the country and live in poverty. Day received a scholarship to the University of Illinois from the Hearst newspapers but often skipped classes to chat with a Jewish friend who later became a communist. After two years, Day went to New York and lived in Greenwich Village, where she met Leon Trotsky and John Reed. She worked on radical papers, and after the *Masses* closed in 1917, she marched with the suffragists and was arrested for the first of eight times in her life. A bad marriage led her to alcohol, but royalties from a novel saved her from self-destruction. During another marriage and the birth of a daughter, she became interested in the Catholic Church. Her atheist husband made her choose between him and the church, and they separated. She supported her daughter by writing articles on poverty in Mexico for *Commonweal*. She met Peter Maurin, a French Catholic intellectual, and they started the *Catholic Worker* and the Catholic Worker Movement, which advocated feeding the hungry, sheltering the homeless, communal living, and pacifism, using Catholic rather than communist answers to the problems. Thomas Merton claimed that the *Catholic Worker* influenced his decision to become a monk, and the president of Notre Dame gave Day the Laetare Medal.

BIBLIOGRAPHY

Coles, Robert. *Dorothy Day: A Radical Devotion*. Reading, MA: Addison-Wesley, 1987. 0-201-02829-8, 182p. After corresponding and conversing with Day for over 10 years, Cole recounted her early life and work.

Day, Dorothy. *Loaves and Fishes*. 1963. Maryknoll, NY: Orbis, 1997. 1-57075-156-0, 221p. Day's straightforward autobiography examines her own motivations for her work.

———. *The Long Loneliness: The Autobiography of Dorothy Day*. 1952. New York: Curtis, 1972. No ISBN, 320p. This autobiography describes Day's early life and her conversion to Catholicism.

Forest, James H. *Love Is the Measure: A Biography of Dorothy Day*. 1986. Maryknoll, NY: Orbis, 1994. 0-88344-942-0, 166p. Forest used Day's personal papers, speeches, personal anecdotes, and correspondence to recreate her spirituality and commitment to her cause.

Merriman, Brigid O. *Searching for Christ: The Spirituality of Dorothy Day*. Notre Dame, IN: University of Notre Dame Press, 1994. 0-268-01750-6, 333p. Archival sources, interviews, and Day's letters are the basis for Merriman's scholarly biography.

DE MILLE, AGNES (1905–1993)
Dancer and Choreographer   New York, New York

Agnes de Mille was an author, dancer, and choreographer who used American and folk dance themes in her work. She was born on September 18, 1905, the daughter of a playwright and his wife. Film director Cecil B. De Mille was her uncle. When her family went to California, de Mille saw **Ruth St. Denis, Isadora Duncan**, and *Anna Pavlova perform. She decided to dance, but when allowed to take lessons, she was too old to begin ballet. She worked hard at other styles before and while attending the University of California at Los Angeles, where she majored in English. In Europe at 19 with her mother, de Mille gave concerts of character sketches in mime-dance but had more success as a choreographer when she created her first major roles with the Ballet Rambert. She returned to America permanently before World War II, where she became the American Ballet Theater's first choreographer. In 1943, she choreographed the play *Oklahoma!* using American themes of the West. Other successes included *Carousel, Brigadoon, Gentlemen Prefer Blondes*, and *Paint Your Wagon*. Throughout her career, de Mille lobbied for federal arts funding while writing 12 books and many articles. Among the numerous awards she received were the Kennedy Center Honors Lifetime Achievement Award, a National Medal for the Arts, and a Tony Award.

BIBLIOGRAPHY

de Mille, Agnes. *Dance to the Piper and Promenade Home: A Two-Part Autobiography*. New York: Da Capo Press, 1979. 0-306-80161-2, 301p. De Mille recalls the first 50 years of her life and the revolution and art of dance in this dual autobiography.

————. *Reprieve: A Memoir*. Garden City, NY: Doubleday, 1981. 0–385–15721–5, 288p. De Mille discusses her life after she sustained and recovered from a cerebral hemorrhage.

————. *Speak to Me, Dance with Me*. Boston: Little, Brown, 1973. 0–316–18038–6, 404p. As part of her autobiography, de Mille uses letters written to her mother from 1933 to 1934 and describes personal relationships with family and acquaintances.

————. *Where the Wings Grow*. Garden City, NY: Doubleday, 1978. 0–385–12106–7, 268p. De Mille's memoir recalls the pleasure of summers in Sullivan County, New York.

Easton, Carol. *No Intermissions: The Life of Agnes de Mille*. Boston: Little, Brown, 1996. 0–316–19970–2, 548p. In a carefully and thoroughly researched look at a writer who danced and a dancer who wrote, Easton examines de Mille's life.

DE WOLFE, ELSIE (1865–1950)
Interior Decorator   New York, New York

Elsie de Wolfe was an actor and interior decorator. She was born Ella Anderson de Wolfe on December 20, 1865, as the only daughter of five children to a physician and his austere wife. De Wolfe attended private schools in New York, and at age 14, she went to Edinburgh to complete her education. At 17, she was presented at Queen Victoria's court and entered London society. After returning to America, she made her professional acting debut in 1891. She left the stage in 1905, and at the urging of friends, entered the previously masculine field of interior decoration. Rejecting the heavy Victorian interiors of the past, de Wolfe used light colors, chintz instead of velvet, mirrors, wall brackets, table lamps, and outlets with cords concealed in the walls. Articles about her style appeared in 1912 and 1913 in the *Delineator* and *Good Housekeeping*. A later book, *The House in Good Taste*, sold well. In five years, she made enough money so that she could devote time to charities. In World War I, she went to France to work in hospitals and won the Croix de Guerre and the ribbon of the Legion of Honor. At 60, she married a British lord, and as Lady Mendl, became an internationally known hostess.

BIBLIOGRAPHY

Campbell, Nina, and Caroline Seebohm. *Elsie de Wolfe: A Decorative Life*. New York: C. Potter, 1992. 0–517–58467–0, 143p. A collection of photographs and a well-researched, readable text present de Wolfe's life and career.

de Wolfe, Elsie. *After All*. 1935. New York: Arno Press, 1974. 0–405–06085–8, 278p. De Wolfe wrote her autobiography after she became Lady Mendl, and in it she focuses on her friendships and her career.

Smith, Jane S. *Elsie de Wolfe: A Life in the High Style*. New York: Atheneum, 1982. 0–689–11141–X, 366p. Smith carefully researched de Wolfe's life to uncover the many firsts credited to her, including being the first woman to dye her hair blue.

DENNETT, MARY WARE (1872–1947)
Reformer and Activist   Worcester, Massachusetts

Mary Dennett was a suffragist, pacifist, and advocate of birth control and sex education. She was born Mary Coffin Ware on April 4, 1872, as the second of four children to a wool merchant and his wife. After her father's death when she was 10, the family moved to Boston, and she attended local schools before graduating from the Boston Museum of Fine Arts. She first taught at the Drexel Institute in Philadelphia, but after traveling with her sister to Spain in 1898, she opened a cooperative handicraft shop to revive the lost art of Cordovan leather gilding. In 1900, after marriage to an architect, she became concerned about woman suffrage, and in 1910 moved to New York City to become the corresponding secretary of the National American Woman Suffrage Association. She divorced and retained custody of her children as she developed interest in the Intercollegiate Socialist Society. During this time, when the post office ruled **Margaret Sanger**'s magazine, *Woman Rebel*, obscene, Dennett merged the National Birth Control League with the Voluntary Parenthood League. She supported a peaceful rather than militant approach to changing the laws. When Sanger returned from hiding in Europe, however, she formed a competing organization. Dennett lobbied in Washington to eliminate all legal restraints on birth control, saying that such laws violated civil liberties. She linked birth control and sex education in her pamphlet "The Sex Side of Life," but the postmaster general's obscenity ruling convicted her for continuing to send it via first-class mail. A federal court of appeals reversed the decision. During World War II, Dennett served in an organization advocating peace through world government and international law.

BIBLIOGRAPHY
Chen, Constance M. *The Sex Side of Life*. New York: New Press, 1996. 1-56584-132-8, 374p. In a carefully researched work using Dennett's letters and other sources, Chen reveals her importance at the forefront of America's birth control movement.

DEREN, MAYA (1917–1961)
Film Director and Producer   Kiev, Russia

Maya Deren was an author and filmmaker, known as the "mother of the underground film." She was born Eleanora Derenkowsky on April 29, 1917, to a Russian medical corps officer and his educated wife. In 1922 the family immigrated to the United States, where her father retrained and her mother taught. Deren attended several schools in Switzerland and the United States before receiving her M.A. in literature from Smith College in 1939. She became interested in socialism during her college years and joined the Young People's Socialist League. In 1940, she began working with **Katherine Dunham** and wrote her first article focusing on dance in the Haitian culture. During this period, she married and divorced a second husband who introduced her to the techniques of filmmaking. She produced her first film, *Meshes of the Afternoon*, with him. After several more films, she became the first person to receive a Guggenheim Foundation fellowship to work on motion pictures. In 1946, she wrote her theory of film, *An Anagram of Ideas on Art, Form and Film*. The next year, she became the first woman and first American to receive the Cannes Grand Prix Internationale for Avant-Garde Film, an award for her first four films. In the early 1950s, while continuing to create art films, she traveled to Haiti several times to study the voodoo culture. In 1955, she founded the Creative Film Foundation to recognize other independent filmmakers and began collaborating with composer Teiji Ito, whom she married in 1960.

BIBLIOGRAPHY

Clark, VeVe A., et al. *The Legend of Maya Deren*. New York: Anthology Film Archives, 1984. 0–911689–14–1. The authors of this documentary biography use interviews, photographs, articles, unpublished documents, and Deren's writing to re-create her life and career.

Rabinovitz, Lauren. *Points of Resistance: Women, Power and Politics in the New York Avant-Garde Cinema*. Urbana: University of Illinois Press, 1991. 0–252–06139–X, 250p. In this collective biography, Rabinovitz thoroughly discusses Deren's career as a filmmaker.

DICKINSON, EMILY (1830–1886)
Poet   Amherst, Massachusetts

Emily Dickinson, a lyric poet often called the "New England mystic," wrote with originality of both content and style. She was born on December 10, 1830, the second of three children of a lawyer who served one term in the United States Congress and his sickly wife. While Dickinson attended Mount Holyoke Female Seminary, she investigated nature but refused to profess as a Christian, leading the headmistress to think her doomed. After she left the school, she remained unmarried in the family home and began writing poetry around 1850. Only a few poems, however, can be dated prior to 1858, when she began to collect them in small, handsewn booklets. Among her mentors were Benjamin Newton, her father's law clerk; Samuel Bowles, an editor of the *Springfield Republican*; and Thomas Wentworth Higginson. When she sent Higginson four of her poems, he recognized their originality but advised her not to publish. Based on Higginson's advice, Dickinson also refused to let any of her friends publish her work, and only seven of her poems were published during her lifetime. In 1860, her poems became more experimental, and she adapted the quatrain of three iambic feet, much like hymn writing at the time. She used off-rhymes, cut extra words from the text, and experimented with syntax. During the Civil War years, she wrote over 800 poems, although none mentions the war. She mainly investigated her relationship with God but never overcame her skepticism. After 1865, she never left home, and by 1870 dressed only in white and refused to entertain guests face-to-face. Higginson and Mabel Loomis Todd, the mistress of Dickinson's brother, edited and published her poems after her death, but not until 1955, when Thomas H. Johnson published his edition of her 1,775 poems, were they published as she wrote them. She was elected to The National Women's Hall of Fame.

BIBLIOGRAPHY

Knapp, Bettina Liebowitz. *Emily Dickinson*. New York: Continuum, 1989. 0–8264–0441–3, 204p. Knapp uses Dickinson's letters and poems to create a scholarly and thoughtful picture of an independent thinker, a "protest-ant."

Loving, Jerome. *Emily Dickinson: The Poet on the Second Story*. New York: Cambridge University Press, 1986. 0–521–32781–4, 128p. In a psychobiography, Loving sees the second story of the house where Dickinson wrote her poetry as the underlying meaning in her life.

McNeil, Helen. *Emily Dickinson*. New York: Pantheon, 1986. 0–394–74766–6, 208p. McNeil examines Dickinson's letters, poetry, and life through modern literary theories.

Sewall, Richard Benson. *The Life of Emily Dickinson*. 1974. Cambridge, MA: Harvard University Press, 1994. 0–674–53080–2, 821p. Sewall's meticulously researched and documented biography of Dickinson examines all aspects of her life. National Book Award.

Wolff, Cynthia Griffin. *Emily Dickinson*. New York: Knopf, 1986. 0–394–54418–8, 641p. Wolff relates Dickinson's life to her poetry and the times in which she lived to conclude that Dickinson remained very lonely.

DIDRIKSON ZAHARIAS, BABE. *See* ZAHARIAS, BABE DIDRIKSON

DIX, DOROTHEA (LYNDE) (1802–1887)
Reformer and Humanitarian   Hampden, Maine

Dorothea Dix was a social reformer and humanitarian. She was born on April 4, 1802, the eldest of three children of a Harvard dropout, who followed a variety of occupations including the Methodist ministry, and his older, uneducated wife. Dix disliked having to care for the younger children, and visits to her grandparents made her want an education. At 14, Dix opened a school for children, meanwhile continuing her own education through private study and public lectures. Intermittent bouts of tuberculosis eventually stopped her teaching career, but she found a new vocation while teaching a Sunday school class for women in the East Cambridge jail. She became furious on discovering the insensitive incarceration of criminals with women who were merely insane, in unheated cells. She complained to the local court, and although jail administrators denied her claims, they renovated the women's quarters. She discovered that others agreed that the insane should not be in jail. With help from friends, she visited every jail, almshouse, and house of correction in Massachusetts and assessed their conditions. Her report forced the state to expand and renovate the state mental institution. Dix took her crusade to other states, succeeding in both New York and Rhode Island. For three years, she traveled 30,000 miles to prepare "memorials" in other states on the needs of their insane populations. During the Civil War, she volunteered and became the superintendent of army nurses, but her stern ways and arbitrary rules alienated many who wanted to help the war effort. After the war, she tried to correct other social problems. Her work increased the number of mental hospitals in the United States from 13 in 1843 to 123 in 1880 and directly influenced the founding of 32 state mental hospitals. For her achievements, she was elected into The National Women's Hall of Fame.

BIBLIOGRAPHY

Brown, Thomas J. *Dorothea Dix: New England Reformer.* Cambridge, MA: Harvard University Press, 1998. 0–674–21488–9, 432p. Although well researched, Brown's unbalanced biography of Dix posits that her reputation is undeserved.

Gollaher, David. *Voice for the Mad: The Life of Dorothea Dix.* New York: Free Press, 1995. 0–02–912399–2, 538p. This thorough scholarly biography follows Dix in her pursuits for the mentally ill.

Schlaifer, Charles. *Heart's Work: Civil War Heroine and Champion of the Mentally Ill, Dorothea Lynde Dix.* New York: Paragon House, 1991. 1–55778–419–1, 175p. This examination of Dix's life and career, suitable for young adults, gives insight into her character and her motivations.

Wilson, Dorothy Clarke. *Stranger and Traveler: The Story of Dorothea Dix, American Reformer.* Boston: Little, Brown, 1975. 0–316–54496–3, 360p. This fictional biography, suitable for young adults, uses quotes from friends and colleagues as well as Dix's letters tell the story of her crusade.

DODGE, MARY MAPES (1831–1905)
Author and Editor   **New York, New York**

Mary Mapes Dodge was an author of children's books and the editor of *St. Nicholas* magazine. She was born on January 26, 1831, one of five surviving children of a scientist and inventor and his wife. As a young girl, she was an avid reader and met many intellectuals who visited her father. Dodge began her editorial experience on her father's journal, *The Working Farmer,* before marrying and moving to New York. Dodge's husband died seven years later, and to support herself and her two sons, she returned to her father's farm and began writing. Critics liked her first publication, *Irvington Stories,* and at her editor's request, she wrote *Hans Brinker; or the Silver Skates.* Over 100 editions appeared in her lifetime, and the French Academy awarded it the Montyon literary prize in 1869. She returned to New York to become an editor for *Hearth and Home,* and in 1873 accepted an offer to edit the children's magazine *St. Nicholas,* focusing the contents on the interests of children rather than those of miniature adults. Leading authors and artists contributed, and it was immediately successful. Later writers included Rudyard Kipling, *Frances Hodgson Burnett, Mark Twain, **Louisa May Alcott,** and Jack London. Illustrators included Frederic Remington and Howard Pyle. To recover after her son's unexpected death, she turned to writing essays and verse for *Atlantic Monthly, Century,* and *Harper's.* She led juvenile literature for 30 years.

BIBLIOGRAPHY

Gannon, Susan R., and Ruth Anne Thompson. *Mary Mapes Dodge*. New York: Twayne, 1992. 0–8057–3956–4, 181p. Thompson and Gannon used memoirs, manuscripts, family documents, photographs, and personal correspondence in their documented critical study of Dodge's life and work.

Wright, Catharine Morris. *Lady of the Silver Skates: The Life and Correspondence of Mary Mapes Dodge*. Jamestown, RI: Clingstone Press, 1979. 0–9602454–1–3, 251p. This readable and well-documented biography, based on Dodge's papers, photographs, and correspondence with writers whom she published, reveals her many contacts in the literary world.

DOLE, ELIZABETH (1936–)
Attorney and Cabinet Member   **Salisbury, North Carolina**

Elizabeth Dole, a lawyer, has served as secretary of transportation, secretary of labor, and president of the American Red Cross. She was born on July 29, 1936, the daughter of a flower wholesaler. After being May Queen and Leader of the Year for both the men's and women's campuses, she graduated Phi Beta Kappa from Duke University and attended Harvard Law School. She worked for the government, and in 1967 began practicing privately in Washington as a defender of indigents and transvestite street walkers. In 1972, she met her husband when she went to his office to lobby for President Nixon's Office of Consumer Affairs, and the same year, she won the Arthur S. Flemming Award for outstanding government service. The next year, she joined the Federal Trade Commission, and two years later, she married. In 1983, she became the seventh woman to serve in a presidential cabinet and the first female to head an armed service, the Coast Guard, when she became the secretary of transportation, focusing on automobile and air safety. In 1989, she became the secretary of labor but resigned the next year to serve as president of the American Red Cross. She has continued her service career, stopping only when campaigning for her husband's presidential nominations. Other awards she has won include the North Carolinian of the Year Award, the Radcliffe Medal, the Raoul Wallenberg Award for Humanitarian Service, and election to The National Women's Hall of Fame.

BIBLIOGRAPHY

Dole, Robert J., and Elizabeth Dole. *The Doles: Unlimited Partners*. New York: Simon and Schuster, 1988. 0–671–60202–0, 287p. In this dual autobiography, Dole shares some of her background and the surprise of her mother to discover that her daughter wanted to go to law school.

Mulford, Carolyn. *Elizabeth Dole, Public Servant*. Hillside, NJ: Enslow, 1992. 0–89490–331–4, 144p. This researched and documented biography for young adults covers Dole's career.

DOOLITTLE, HILDA (H.D.) (1886–1961)
Poet   Bethlehem, Pennsylvania

Hilda Doolittle, known as H.D., became a translator and Imagist poet. She was born on September 10, 1886, the daughter of an astronomer, who already had three children, and his second wife, a musician and painter. She attended Quaker schools in Philadelphia, and at 15, she met the 16-year-old Ezra Pound at the home of friends, and they became engaged. She attended Bryn Mawr College for two years, but failed and studied at home before her first poem's publication in 1910. The next year, she sailed to Europe to join Pound, but they broke their engagement, and she married translator Richard Aldington. Her poetry at this time reflected the concreteness of the Imagist movement, and she adopted the name H.D. Although they had a daughter, World War I separated Doolittle and her husband. After her divorce, Doolittle's friend, *Bryher, legally adopted her daughter, and Doolittle often stayed in Bryher's home. She continued to live in Europe with intermittent trips to America while writing, publishing, reviewing films, and studying the occult in Western and Eastern religions. Among experiences in her life, she credited psychoanalysis with Sigmund Freud as one of the most significant. In 1960, she traveled to America for the last time to accept the Award of Merit Medal for Poetry from the American Academy of Arts and Letters.

BIBLIOGRAPHY

King, Michael, ed. *H.D., Woman and Poet.* Orono, ME: National Poetry Foundation, 1986.
    0–915032–68–6, 522p. This scholarly, critical look at H.D. discloses her abilities as poet,
    novelist, memorist, critic, essayist, correspondent, actor, and filmmaker.
Robinson, Janice S. *H.D.: The Life and Work of an American Poet.* Boston: Houghton
    Mifflin, 1982. 0–395–31855–6, 490p. Robinson's well-documented critical study of
    H.D. and her life dwells on her prose and poetry.

DRESSLER, MARIE (1869–1934)
Actor   Cobourg, Canada

Marie Dressler was an actor on stage and in film. She was born Leila Marie Koerber on November 9, 1869, the younger of two daughters of a piano teacher and his wife. Dressler's mother kept the family together by taking in boarders and sometimes finding her husband jobs as a church organist. Dressler hated both her father's temper and his inability to provide for the family, and when she was 14, she and her sister left home to become actors. She worked in traveling stock before joining the Bennett-Moulton Opera Company, where she experienced the rigors of learning a new comic opera every week while performing another. Dressler made her New York debut in 1892 as a brigand in the comic opera *The Robber of the Rhine,* but also sang at a Bowery beer hall and a music hall. In 1893 and 1894, she supported **Lillian Russell** before establishing herself as a musical comedienne with the play *The Lady Slavey,* which ran for 128 performances in New York and for four years on the road. She then appeared in many musicals and in vaudeville during the next 10 years before making her London debut in 1907. London audiences loved her, but disliked the plays, and she returned to New York bankrupt. Her greatest success occurred the following year with *Tillie's Nightmare*. In 1914, she began her film career, starring with Mack Sennett and an unknown, Charlie Chaplin, whom she selected for the cast. During World War I, she sold millions of dollars in Liberty Bonds, and after the war sang in veterans' hospitals and helped found the Chorus Equity Association. Considered too old for the stage, she was out of work for several years before being cast in the film version of Eugene O'Neill's *Anna Christie*. Her superb performance began a second career, and she won an Academy Award in 1931 for *Min and Bill*, following it the next year with a nomination for her work in *Emma*. She mastered slapstick and improvisation before showing her power as a serious actress.

BIBLIOGRAPHY

Lee, Betty. *Marie Dressler: The Unlikeliest Star*. Lexington: University Press of Kentucky, 1997. 0–8131–2036–5, 318p. In her well-researched biography, Lee illuminates Dressler's interests, but declares that Dressler's success came from her ability to make her audiences think she was one of them.

DREXEL, KATHARINE MARY (1858–1955)
Religious   Philadelphia, Pennsylvania

Katharine Mary Drexel founded the Blessed Sacrament Sisters for Indians and Colored People (renamed Sisters of the Blessed Sacrament) out of concern for the welfare of Native and African Americans. She was born on November 26, 1858, the daughter of a financier and philanthropist. Her mother died five weeks after her birth, and her father remarried when Drexel was two. Her new mother distributed aid to the poor three times a week, and the family regularly contributed to mission work among Native and African Americans. After the death of her mother in 1883 and her father in 1885, Drexel and her sister inherited $14 million. They determined to continue the family's philanthropy, and Drexel went west to aid mission schools. When she went to Rome to plead for extra nuns, Pope Leo XIII suggested that she become a missionary. She eventually agreed and received her training at the Sisters of Mercy in Pittsburgh in preparation for establishing her own order. On February 12, 1891, she became the first of the Sisters of the Blessed Sacrament for Indians and Colored People. Her novitiate and motherhouse started in 1892, and in 1894, four missionary sisters left for Sante Fe, New Mexico, to teach in a school for Pueblo Indians. For 40 years, Mother Katharine directed all aspects of the order's work, including establishing schools combining religious instruction with vocational skills, liberal arts, and native culture. In 1925, she chartered Xavier University, the only Catholic college for African Americans in America. When she died, Mother Drexel had placed 501 sisters in 51 convents and 61 schools, one university, a study house, and three social service houses. In 1988, Pope John Paul II beatified her.

BIBLIOGRAPHY

Burton, Katherine. *The Door of Hope: The Story of Katharine Drexel*. New York: Hawthorn, 1963. No ISBN, 187p. Burton's biography of Drexel recounts her remarkable achievements without pursuing her motivations.

Duffy, Consuela Marie. *Katharine Drexel: A Biography*. Philadelphia: Reilly, 1966. No ISBN, 434p. Duffy's definitive biography of Drexel, based on original source material, is recommended.

O'Brien, Felicity. *Treasure in Heaven: Katharine Drexel*. New York: State Mutual, 1990. 0-85439-323-4, 120p. This biography of Drexel discusses her generosity and her accomplishments.

Tarry, Ellen. *Katharine Drexel: Friend of the Neglected*. Nashville, TN: Winston–Derek, 1990. 1-55523-345-7, 100p. Tarry's biography covers Drexel's life and her contributions to the Native and African American communities.

DUNBAR-NELSON, ALICE MOORE (1875–1935)
Author, Educator, and Activist   **New Orleans, Louisiana**

African American Alice Dunbar-Nelson was both a writer and an activist. She was born Alice Ruth Moore on July 19, 1875, to an ex-slave seamstress and a partially white seaman father. Her light skin and auburn hair elevated her in Creole society and allowed her to sometimes pass for white and see operas and visit museums not open to African Americans. She finished a two-year teachers' program in 1892, and while teaching, was also a bookkeeper and stenographer for an African American printing firm. She studied art, played both the piano and cello, acted in amateur theater, wrote for a newspaper, and participated in church activities. She published her first book in 1895 before moving to Brooklyn to teach in the slums, depending on her six-foot height to protect her. In 1898, she married Paul Laurence Dunbar, who liked her poems, but his alcohol and heroin habits and her need to control dissolved their three-year marriage. Although they separated, when he died in 1906, Dunbar-Nelson gained visibility by being known as his widow. In her fiction, she explored the motifs of "passing" and "the color line" about people who could move between races without detection. She remarried in 1916, and she and her husband published the *Wilmington Advocate* from 1920 to 1922 while participating in Delaware politics. She became a voice in the Harlem Renaissance, and her legacy may lie in the full-length diaries she kept in 1921 and from 1926 to 1931.

BIBLIOGRAPHY

Dunbar-Nelson, Alice Moore. *Give Us Each Day: The Diary of Alice Dunbar-Nelson*. New York: Norton, 1984. 0-393-01893-8, 480p. The diary that Dunbar-Nelson kept between 1921 and 1931 illuminates aspects of the Harlem Renaissance.

Hull, Gloria T. *Color, Sex and Poetry: Three Women Writers of the Harlem Renaissance*. Bloomington: Indiana University Press, 1987. 0-253-34974-5, 240. Hull posits in her collective study of Dunbar-Nelson that she exhibited her sexuality in less well known poems but was uncomfortable about mixing race with belles lettres.

DUNCAN, ISADORA (1877–1927)
Dancer   San Francisco, California

Isadora Duncan made dancing a creative art and influenced its twentieth-century development. She was born Angela Duncan on May 26, 1877, as the youngest of four children, to a gambler and adventurer whom her music teacher mother divorced soon after Duncan's birth. Her mother often had to move the family when she had no money for overdue rent, and Duncan acquired her mother's opposition to material possessions. She began dancing early, and by the age of six began teaching other children, using any money she earned to help support the family. At age 10, she left school to work with her dance classes, and at 11, she and her sister's classes had attracted children from some of San Francisco's wealthier families. After going to New York, she performed first with her uncle's troupe but soon started her own studio and began performing privately. She made her London debut in 1900, crediting her innovations to American dancer **Loie Fuller.** She rejected classical ballet movements, preferring motion beginning in the solar plexus rather than the spine. Her first successes on the Continent occurred in 1902, and after the birth of a child, she toured America, but few embraced her style as had her European audiences. She reached the high point of her professional career in Paris during 1909 and formed a liaison with the wealthy Paris E. Singer, son of the sewing machine inventor and manufacturer, by whom she had a second child. In 1913, however, both of her sons drowned in an automobile that rolled into the Seine. Duncan never fully recovered, although she continued to dance in Europe and America, paying more attention to her accompaniment, preferring music of great composers rather than traditional dance music. After World War I, she opened a school in Moscow, but the new Soviet government withdrew its support. A bad marriage and other frustrations filled the next years, and in 1927, her long scarf caught in the spoke of a sportscar as she drove away, breaking her neck.

BIBLIOGRAPHY
Blair, Fredrika. *Isadora: Portrait of the Artist as a Woman.* New York: McGraw-Hill, 1986. 0–07–005598–X, 470p. This carefully and thoroughly documented biography, with photographs of Duncan, presents details about her life and career.

Daly, Ann. *Done into Dance: Isadora Duncan in America.* Bloomington: Indiana University Press, 1995. 0–253–32924–8, 266p. This well-researched and carefully documented biography examines Duncan's dancing and attempts to reconstruct her processes, structures, and techniques.

Loewenthal, Lillian. *The Search for Isadora: the Legend and Legacy of Isadora Duncan.* Pennington, NJ: Princeton Book, 1993. 0–87127–179–6, 225p. Loewenthal collected materials on Duncan for 30 years, gleaning information from her disciples, those who saw her dance, and French archives.

Rosemont, Franklin, ed. *Isadora Speaks.* San Francisco: City Lights Books, 1981. 0–87286–134–1, 147p. Rosemont has arranged this collection of Duncan's speeches, interviews, essays, letters to the editor, and press releases to reveal her defiant and definitive attitude.

Splatt, Cynthia. *Life into Art: Isadora Duncan and Her World.* New York: Norton, 1993. 0-393-03507-7, 199p. The text looks at Duncan's career and her life through photographs and accompanying text.

DUNHAM, KATHERINE (1910-)
Dancer, Choreographer, and Anthropologist   Glen Ellyn, Illinois

Katherine Dunham, dancer, choreographer, and anthropologist, created unique interpretations of ethnic dances and organized the first concert-caliber African American dance troupe. She was born on June 22, 1910, to a father of Malagasy and West African descent and a mother who was mixed French-Canadian and Native American. Her mother died when Dunham was young, and while her father traveled as a salesman, Dunham and her brother stayed with aunts in Chicago. While attending Joliet Junior College, she took dance lessons, and after transferring to the University of Chicago, she supported herself by teaching dance and working as a librarian. She joined the Chicago Civic Opera Company and established a dance troupe that performed in 1931. After taking a course in anthropology with a professor who stressed the connection between dance and culture, she went to the Caribbean to do field work. She received funding for her research, and her Ph.D. dissertation, "Dances of Haiti," was later translated into French and Spanish. Her husband designed costumes and sets for her productions until his death. In addition to performing, Dunham gave lectures and demonstrations at universities and raised an adopted daughter. She established a second troupe in the 1940s and choreographed Broadway stage productions, films, and opera, including *Aïda* for the New York Metropolitan Opera. In 1943, the Katherine Dunham School of Arts and Research opened in New York. In 1965, Dunham went to Senegal to train the National Ballet of Senegal, and when she returned in 1967, she developed the Performing Arts Training Center of Southern Illinois University, where she retired as professor emeritus. Among her awards are the Kennedy Center Honors Lifetime Achievement Award, the Albert Schweitzer Music Award, and the Distinguished Service Award of the American Anthropological Society.

BIBLIOGRAPHY
Beckford, Ruth. *Katherine Dunham: A Biography.* New York: Dekker, 1979. 0-8247-6828-0, 146p. Beckford's biased biography reflects Dunham's determination to gain recognition for African American artists.
Donloe, Darlene. *Katherine Dunham.* Los Angeles: Melrose Square, 1993. 0-87067-775-6, 187p. This undocumented biography, suitable for young adults, relates Dunham's life and career.
Dunham, Katherine. *A Touch of Innocence: Memoirs of Childhood.* 1959. Chicago: University of Chicago Press, 1994. 0-226-17112-4, 312p. In her autobiography, Dunham discusses both her life and the times in which she lived.

DUNIWAY, ABIGAIL (1834–1915)
Pioneer, Journalist, and Businesswoman   Groveland, Illinois

Abigail Jane Scott Duniway was a pioneer and suffrage leader. She was born on October 22, 1834, to a farmer and his wife, the second of their nine children to survive infancy. She worked on the farm while growing up and attended a nearby school when she could. In 1852, she traveled with the family on the Overland Trail to Oregon, a trip during which her frail mother and her young son died of cholera. Duniway, 17 at the time, recorded the 2,400-mile ordeal in a journal. After arrival, Duniway began teaching school and soon married a farmer. In 1862, her husband lost the farm in a bad business deal about which he had not informed her and then became disabled in an accident. To support him and their six children, Duniway ran a boarding school, taught in a private school, and opened a millinery shop. In 1871, after her sons had grown and could assist the family financially, she began publishing a weekly newspaper, *New Northwest*, and for the next 16 years, she trumpeted divorce reform, property rights, temperance, economic and educational equality, and women's rights. After she heard **Susan B. Anthony** speak in 1871, Duniway began lecturing and founded the Oregon Equal Suffrage Association. She openly disagreed with suffragists advocating prohibition because she opposed outlawing alcohol. Duniway then edited a new weekly magazine, *Pacific Empire*, to which she contributed articles on women's rights and serialized fiction. When women won the vote in Oregon, she and the governor signed the suffrage proclamation, and she became Oregon's first registered female voter. Among the honors garnered in her final years were an invitation to address the Congress of Women at the Columbian Exposition in Chicago.

BIBLIOGRAPHY

Duniway, Abigail Scott. *Path Breaking: An Autobiographical History of the Equal Suffrage Movement in Pacific Coast States*. New York: Schocken, 1971. 0-8052-0322-2, 297p. In her autobiography, Duniway imparts her belief that for a mother to build character in her children, she must first have her own freedom.

Morrison, Dorothy Nafus. *Ladies Were Not Expected: Abigail Scott Duniway and Women's Rights*. Portland, OR: Western Imprints, 1985. 0-87595-168-6, 146p. Using interviews, family papers, pictures, and Duniway's Trail Diary, Morrison recounts Duniway's achievements after her mother's lament, "I wept bitterly when you were born," in a biography for young adults.

Moynihan, Ruth Barnes. *Rebel for Rights, Abigail Scott Duniway*. New Haven, CT: Yale University Press, 1983. 0-300-02952-7, 273p. This scholarly and balanced biography, based on Duniway's serialized fiction, letters, and autobiography, emphasizes the feminist aspects of her life.

DYER, MARY   (d. 1660)
Reformer   England

Mary Barrett Dyer was a Quaker martyr whose self-sacrifice for religious freedom benefitted all Americans. Little is known of her early life although she may have been the daughter of James I's cousin, Lady Arabella Stuart. On October 27, 1633, she was married at St. Martin's-in-the-Fields in London to William Dyer, a Puritan milliner. They immigrated to Massachusetts in 1635 and were admitted to a Boston church, where they sided with **Anne Hutchinson** against their pastor. Dyer delivered a stillborn child soon after, and John Winthrop declared it her punishment. When Hutchinson was excommunicated, Dyer accompanied her and was also banished. After they settled in Newport, Rhode Island, Dyer's husband held civic offices until they returned to England with Roger Williams. During her five years in England, Dyer heard George Fox speak about his Society of Friends, and after she returned to Boston in 1657, she was imprisoned for being a heretic Quaker. Connecticut also expelled her for preaching Quakerism, and on October 19, 1658, the Massachusetts government passed a law by a one-vote majority saying that Quakers would be banished under pain of death. The next year, Dyer was banished again from Boston, but she returned, and on October 27, she was led through the streets to her death, but Winthrop reprieved her at the last minute. She returned to Boston in 1660 to again defy the terrible law and went to the gallows on June 1, dying for her belief in freedom of conscience. In 1959, 300 years later, Massachusetts erected a statue in her memory at the Boston State House.

BIBLIOGRAPHY
Crawford, Deborah. *Four Women in a Violent Time*. New York: Crown, 1970. 0-517-50313-1, 191p. Using journals, letters, and family papers, Crawford relates Dyer's story in a collective biography for young adults.
Plimpton, Ruth Talbot. *Mary Dyer: Biography of a Rebel Quaker*. Boston: Branden, 1994. 0-8283-1964-2, 247p. Since Dyer left only two letters, Plimpton had few primary sources for her biography.
White, Ethel. *Bear His Mild Yoke: The Story of Mary Dyer, a Quaker Martyr in Early New England*. Nashville, TN: Abingdon Press, 1966. No ISBN, 251p. White used diaries and journals of early Quakers who knew Dyer to recount her bravery.

EARHART, AMELIA (1897-1937)
Aviator   Atchison, Kansas

Amelia Earhart was an aviator who became the first woman to fly alone across the
Atlantic Ocean. She was born on July 24, 1897, as the first of two daughters to an
attorney and railroad claim agent and his socially prominent wife. The family's
moves and poverty interrupted Earhart's education until her mother took Earhart
and her sister to Chicago for high school. As a hospital volunteer in Canada, she
began admiring the daring Royal Flying Corps members, and after World War I,
she had her first airplane ride and began taking lessons. In June 1921, she made her
first solo flight, and the next year, she earned money to buy her first plane. In it,
she set a women's altitude record of 14,000 feet. She moved to Boston in 1926 and
continued flying as a demonstration pilot. In 1928, George Putnam selected her to
fly across the Atlantic. Earhart merely kept the log on the flight, but she gained
fame overnight when the plane in which she flew started in Trepassey Bay,
Newfoundland, and landed near Burry Port, Wales, the next day. People called her
"Lady Lindy," "First Lady of the Air," and "A.E." As she continued setting records
as a pilot, she and Putnam married, and he promoted her work. She became the
first woman to fly across the Atlantic alone in 1932 and flew solo from Hawaii to
the U.S. mainland and from Mexico City to Newark, New Jersey. In 1937, she and
her pilot, Frederick Noonan, disappeared in the Pacific, and the plane was never
found. Her efforts helped the airline industry gain the public's approval. She was
later elected into The National Women's Hall of Fame.

BIBLIOGRAPHY

Butler, Susan. *East to the Dawn: The Life of Amelia Earhart*. Reading, MA: Addison-Wesley, 1997. 0-201-31144-5, 489p. Butler used family diaries and an unpublished biography by one of Earhart's friends for her balanced, recommended biography.

Goldstein, Donald M., and Katherine V. Dillon. *Amelia: The Centennial Biography of an Aviation Pioneer*. Washington, DC: Brassey's, 1997. 1-57488-134-5, 321p. This well-documented, well-researched, and recommended biography relies on contemporary newspapers and unpublished materials to cover Earhart's life and career.

Rich, Doris L. *Amelia Earhart: A Biography*. Washington, DC: Smithsonian Institution, 1989. 0-87474-836-4, 321p. Rich carefully describes Earhart's goals and sense of pioneering in this thoroughly researched biography.

Roessler, Walter. *Amelia Earhart: Case Closed*. Hummelstown, PA: Aviation Publishers, 1996. 0-938716-24-7, 206p. This documented and researched biography of Earhart, with technical information about flying, emphasizes her position as one who accomplished her goals at great risk.

Ware, Susan. *Still Missing: Amelia Earhart and the Search for Modern Feminism*. New York: Norton, 1993. 0-393-03551-4, 304p. Earhart lectured that women could do what they wanted, and Ware examines Earhart's life from this thesis in her scholarly, well-researched biography.

EDDY, MARY BAKER (1821–1910)
Religious Leader   Bow, New Hampshire

Mary Baker Eddy founded the Christian Science Church. She was born on July 16, 1821, as the youngest of six children to a strict Congregationalist farmer and his wife. While Eddy was growing up, religious discussions between her and her father caused her to develop convulsions and fevers. A doctor's orders ended their talks, with the family adjusting to her illnesses. Eddy married in 1843, but her husband died before their son was born, and her subsequent ailments made her incapable of parenting. Family servants became her son's foster parents, and a second marriage debilitated her completely. After her husband was captured as a prisoner during the Civil War, a mesmerist convinced her that her illnesses had evolved from a separation of mind and body. She was completely invigorated until she fell and hurt herself on the ice. Three days later, she randomly opened her Bible and read about Jesus's healing of a palsied man, became well, and at 45, changed her life. For the next nine years, she taught, gathered disciples in New England, and recorded her ideas. She published the work in 1875 as *Science and Health*. She taught that the Eternal Mind of God and Truth was the source of all being, and healers were to unite body and mind and destroy the idea of their separateness. Christian Science saw God as both male and female and emphasized health and religion. On June 6, 1875, the first Christian Science service was held. Within 15 years, the denomination included 20 churches and 33 teaching centers. Eddy went into seclusion to retain her power and to hide the state of her own health. When Joseph Pulitzer's *New York World* condemned her, she started her own newspaper in 1908 called the *Christian Science Monitor*. She was later elected to The National Women's Hall of Fame.

BIBLIOGRAPHY

Cather, Willa. *The Life of Mary Baker G. Eddy and the History of Christian Science*. 1909. Lincoln: University of Nebraska Press, 1993. 0-8032-1453-7, 501p. Cather's biography, written near the end of Eddy's life, depicts her as vindictive and forceful.

Nenneman, Richard A. *Persistent Pilgrim: The Life of Mary Baker Eddy*. Etna, NH: Nebbadoon Press, 1997. 1-891331-02-7, 366p. Nenneman used the archives of the church and several thousand letters that Eddy wrote in his thoroughly researched and balanced biography.

Silberger, Julius. *Mary Baker Eddy: An Interpretive Biography of the Founder of Christian Science*. Boston: Little, Brown, 1980. 0-316-79090-7, 274p. Both biography and psychobiography, this recommended look at Eddy's life tries to explain her strengths and weaknesses.

Thomas, Robert David. *With Bleeding Footsteps: Mary Baker Eddy's Path to Religious Leadership*. New York: Knopf, 1994. 0-679-41495-9, 363p. Using Christian Science Church archives as well as Eddy's journals and poetry, Thomas's psychoanalytic approach to Eddy's life shows her early health problems and her religious tendencies.

Tomlinson, Irving Clinton. *Twelve Years with Mary Baker Eddy*. Boston: Christian Science Publication Society, 1996. 0-87510-311-1, 308p. Tomlinson fondly recounts his 12 years with Eddy when serving her and her cause of Christian Science.

EDELMAN, MARIAN WRIGHT (1939-)
Reformer   **Bennettsville, South Carolina**

African American Marian Wright Edelman has worked to redefine and to defend rights of children. One of five children, she was born on June 6, 1939, into a family espousing community service. She attended Spelman College and traveled abroad while a student, an opportunity that changed her world view and made her refuse to accept the segregated life of her past. She returned to the United States in 1960 as the civil rights demonstrations were beginning, and after participating, she decided to become a lawyer rather than a Russian specialist. She graduated from Spelman as valedictorian in 1960 and entered Yale University Law School. She returned to the South and became the first African American woman to pass the Mississippi bar. In 1968, she began the Washington, DC, Research Project before marrying and moving to Boston, where she became director of the Harvard University Center for Law and Education. She often returned to Washington, however, to direct her project, which evolved into the Children's Defense Fund. In 1980, she became chair of Spelman's board of trustees, the first African American and the second woman to hold the position. She was also elected to the Yale University Corporation. She has served on many boards and written books. In 1985, she received a MacArthur Foundation Fellowship, and through the years, 30 universities have bestowed honorary degrees on her. She was also elected into The National Women's Hall of Fame.

BIBLIOGRAPHY

Old, Wendie C. *Marian Wright Edelman: Fighting for Children's Rights*. Springfield, NJ: Enslow, 1995. 0–89490–623–2, 128p. In this well-researched biography for young adults, Old sees Edelman as a strong woman.

Siegel, Beatrice. *Marian Wright Edelman: The Making of a Crusader*. New York: Simon and Schuster, 1995. 0–02–782629–5, 159p. Based on primary sources, including interviews with Edelman herself, Siegel focuses on Edelman's political work and her connection to the civil rights movement in this biography for young adults.

EDMONDS, SARAH EMMA EVELYN (1841–1898)
Soldier   New Brunswick, Canada

Sarah Emma Evelyn Edmonds was a Civil War soldier. She was born in December 1841, the sixth child of a farmer and his Irish immigrant wife. To escape her father's severity, Edmonds left home, dressed like a man, and sold bibles using the name Frank Thompson. Living in Michigan when the Civil War began, she joined her friend's volunteer company, the Flint Union Greys. She went with the company to Virginia and participated in Blackburn's Ford, the first Bull Run, and the first Peninsular campaign. She also did hospital duty and served as a mail carrier. At least twice, she volunteered to be a spy, once dressed as a woman. Although some of her acquaintances learned her identity, others never knew. In 1863, Edmonds deserted her company, saying that she had a high fever, and went to Oberlin, Ohio, to enter the hospital as a woman. Afterward, she served as a nurse for the United States Christian Commission. In Oberlin, she wrote of her experiences, pretending that she had participated in the war as a female nurse instead of a male soldier. Her book, *Nurse and Spy in the Union Army*, published by the firm for which she had peddled Bibles, sold over 175,000 copies before being reprinted under various titles. She married after the war and moved often, once taking charge of a Freedmen's Bureau orphanage for freed slave children. Not until 1882 did her story become known, and Edmonds then decided to apply for a veteran's pension, asking her former army friends to help. They invited her to their 1884 reunion and testified to her service and behavior, many asserting that they had no idea she was a woman. The same year, her name went on the pension role, and she received 12 dollars a month for her Union service. Before her death, she also served in the Grand Army of the Republic in Houston.

BIBLIOGRAPHY

Reit, Seymour. *Behind Rebel Lines: The Incredible Story of Emma Edmonds, Civil War Spy*. San Diego: Harcourt, 1988. 0–15–200587–0, 102p. For his juvenile biography, Reit uses Edmonds's memoirs.

Stevens, Bryna. *Frank Thompson: Her Civil War Story*. New York: Macmillan, 1992. 0–02–788185–7, 144p. Edmonds's own account of her life, *Nurse and Spy*, is the basis of Stevens's biography for juveniles.

ELDRIDGE, ELLEANOR (1784–1865)
Businesswoman   Warwick, Rhode Island

Elleanor Eldridge was a respected African American businesswoman and amateur lawyer in her community. She was born on March 27, 1784, as the youngest of seven girls to an African father, whose family was brought to America on a slave ship, and a Native American mother. Because of a Rhode Island bill enacted in 1784 calling for gradual emancipation, Eldridge was born free. Her father gained his freedom by fighting in the American Revolution, but because he had been paid in worthless Old Continental currency, he could not take the land he had been promised. Eldridge's mother died when she was 10, and after she began boarding with the family for whom her mother had worked, she learned arithmetic and became an accomplished weaver. When her father died, she and her sister went into business weaving, nursing, and soap making, activities at which they earned enough money to buy a lot and build a house, which Eldridge rented to others. She continued to start businesses and buy land, and when her land was once sold without her knowledge to pay off a loan, she was able to reclaim it when she paid the note because the land had not been legally advertised.

BIBLIOGRAPHY
McDougall, Frances Harriet. *Memoirs of Elleanor Eldridge.* 1843. Freeport, NY: Books for Libraries, 1977. 0-8369-8748-9, 127p. The text, written for Eldridge by a friend, includes letters and information about her life.

ENTERS, ANGNA (1907–1989)
Dancer, Choreographer, and Pantomimist   New York, New York

Angna Enters was a dancer, choreographer, and mime. She was born on April 28, 1907, to an Austrian father and a French mother. She spent her childhood in Milwaukee, where she studied ballet and piano, and in Europe. In 1922, she enrolled in the Art Students' League and studied with John Sloan at night while working for an advertising agency during the day. When she became interested in dance, she studied with Michio Ito in 1922 and performed as his partner in a series of recitals in 1923. That same year she choreographed and performed her first piece, *Ecclesiastique,* which evolved into *Moyen Age.* Her first solo program in 1924 led her to her individual style of dance-mime and her specialization of character vignettes or wordless monologues. She debuted in London in 1928 and in Paris the following year. She held her first New York exhibition as a sculptor and artist in 1933. After her Theater of Angna Enters began touring in 1928, she developed and performed nearly 300 separate characters over the next 30 years. She created all of her costumes and props, illustrated several books that she wrote, and composed the scores for some of her pieces. She received fellowships, lectured, and taught, and in the early 1960s was an artist-in-residence at the Dallas Theater Center and Baylor University.

BIBLIOGRAPHY

Enters, Angna. *Artist's Life*. New York: Coward-McCann, 1958. No ISBN, 447p.
Enters reflects on her careers in painting, writing, and theater.

———. *First Person Plural*. 1937. New York: Da Capo Press, 1978. 0-306-77594-8, 386p.
Enters used her diary notes to describe her life and the evolution of the figures in her
repertory.

Mandel, Dorothy. *Uncommon Eloquence: A Biography of Angna Enters*. Denver: Arden
Press, 1986. 0-912869-07-0, 366p.   A readable, thoroughly researched, and
documented scholarly biography presents Enters as performer, writer, designer,
musician, and painter.

ESTEFAN, GLORIA (1958–)
Entertainer   Havana, Cuba

Gloria Estefan, a Latina American, has won both artistic and humanitarian awards.
She was born Gloria Maria Fajardo on September 1, 1958, daughter of a
schoolteacher and a soldier serving the Cuban dictator Fulgencio Batista Zaldivar's
security guard. After Fidel Castro overthrew the regime in 1958, the Fajardo
family left Cuba for the United States. Her father became an invalid in Vietnam,
and Estefan had to nurse him while attending high school in Miami. She
entertained herself with music, but not until she met Emilio Estefan, also a Cuban
refugee, while attending the University of Miami did she begin singing with a
band. After she graduated from college with a B.A. in 1978, she married Estefan,
and his band, the Miami Sound Machine, recorded its first album of
Spanish-language ballads. Over the next two years, the band recorded Estefan
singing English songs. The band gained renown in South and Central America,
and when it recorded an all-English-language album in 1985, it gained popularity in
the United States. Seriously injured in an accident involving the band's tour bus in
1990, Estefan began a difficult rehabilitation before resuming appearances the next
year. She won a Grammy Award and performed for Cuban refugees at the naval
base in Guantanamo, Cuba, in 1995. Among her other awards are the Top Pop
Singles Artist, Songwriter of the Year, Crossover Artist of the Year, and B'nai
B'rith's Humanitarian of the Year.

BIBLIOGRAPHY

Catalano, Grace. *Gloria Estefan*. New York: St. Martin's, 1991. 0-312-92586-7, 188p.
Catalano's biography of Estefan for young adults overviews her life and career.

DeStefano, Anthony M. *Gloria Estefan: The Pop Superstar from Tragedy to Triumph*.
New York: Signet, 1997. 0-451-19417-9, 158p.   This carefully researched and
recommended biography, also in Spanish, covers Estefan's life and career.

Stefoff, Rebecca. *Gloria Estefan*. New York: Chelsea House, 1991. 0-7910-1244-1,
103p. Stefoff begins her young adult biography in 1990 when Estevan's back was
broken in a bus accident.

EVANS, ALICE CATHERINE (1881–1975)
Microbiologist   Neath, Pennsylvania

Alice Catherine Evans was a microbiologist who discovered the basis of the disease brucellosis. She was born on January 29, 1881, as the younger of two children to a Civil War veteran and farmer and his wife. Evans attended Susquehanna Collegiate Institute, taught, and then enrolled in Cornell University for a two-year nature study course. Her interest in science bloomed, and a scholarship helped her obtain a degree in bacteriology. She then attended the University of Wisconsin on another scholarship for her master's degree but decided to work as a researcher for the government rather than pursue her Ph.D. She started identifying bacteria in milk products and followed this research with work on brucellosis and the discovery that a common origin existed for both the human and cattle diseases. She reported the results of her research in 1917 at the Society of American Bacteriologists and published them in 1918 in the *Journal of Infectious Diseases*. Her assertion that raw cow's milk might endanger humans infuriated dairymen, but fellow scientists replicated her work and confirmed her conclusion. In 1922, she became infected with the disease, suffering chronic bouts for the remainder of her life. The illness then became recognized as hazardous for anyone in close contact with domestic animals, and the diary industry was forced to begin pasteurizing milk. The Society of American Bacteriologists recognized Evans's work in 1928 by electing her its first woman president. She then became the U.S. delegate to the First International Congress of Microbiology in Paris in 1930 and to the second in London in 1936. After she retired, she was elected honorary president of the Inter-American Committee on Brucellosis, an honorary member of the American Society for Microbiology, and into The National Women's Hall of Fame.

BIBLIOGRAPHY
Burns, Virginia. *Gentle Hunter: A Biography of Alice Evans, Bacteriologist*. Laingsburg, MI: Enterprise Press, 1993. 0-9604726-5-7, 214p. This well-researched biography, suitable for young adults, is the only in-depth look at Evans's life.

EVERT, CHRIS (1954–)
Athlete   Fort Lauderdale, Florida

Chris Evert won many major titles as a professional tennis player. The second of five children, she was born on December 21, 1954, to a tennis center manager and his wife. She showed an aptitude for tennis as a child, and to give her strokes added strength, her father taught her to use two hands for her backhand shots. Her accurate ground strokes hit from the baseline then kept her opponents off balance. In 1970, she beat Margaret Court Smith, a winner of the Grand Slam in the previous year. The next year, she continued to beat accomplished players and was selected to play for the American Wightman Cup's competition against Great Britain. The same year, she reached the semifinals at the United States Open, where **Billie Jean King** defeated her. Between 1971 and 1983, she entered 34 Grand

Slam tournaments and reached the semifinals in all of them. She never lost on clay courts between August 1973 and May 1979, winning 125 consecutive matches. Her lowest world ranking was fourth while she won 1,309 singles matches, losing only 146 times. Between 1974 and 1978, she won the United States Open every year and added two more titles there in 1980 and 1982. She entered the Australian Open five times, reached the finals all five, and won twice. She won the French Open seven times. Preferring clay to grass, she won at Wimbledon only three times. Since her retirement at the end of 1989, she has offered leadership to the Women's Tennis Association and sponsored pro-celebrity charity tournaments and other fund-raising tennis programs.

BIBLIOGRAPHY

Evert, Chris. *Chrissie: My Own Story*. New York: Simon and Schuster, 1982. 0-671-44376-3, 238p. Evert's autobiography recounts her life in tennis between 1974 and 1981.

Phillips, Betty Lou. *Chris Evert, First Lady of Tennis*. New York: Messner, 1977. 0-671-32890-5, 189p. This undocumented biography for young adults, based on news sources, covers Evert's success through 1977.

F

FARRAND, BEATRIX (1872–1959)
Landscape Architect   New York, New York

Beatrix Farrand was the first female landscape architect in the United States. She was born on June 19, 1872, the only child of wealthy parents whose English ancestors had loved gardens. Tutored at home, she traveled abroad with her family and with her aunt, **Edith Wharton**. In the late 1880s, Farrand studied horticulture with Charles Sprague Sargent, and she followed his advice to make "the plan fit the ground rather than the ground fit the plan" as she developed her own style. In 1897, she began to take private commissions, and her list of clients soon included **Abby Aldrich Rockefeller**. In 1899, she joined Frederick Law Olmsted and others to form the American Society of Landscape Architects, and in 1913 Farrand married a Yale history professor who championed her work. Farrand admired *Gertrude Jekyll's use of wild plants, and she incorporated some of Jekyll's ideas into her designs for Princeton University's gardens in 1916 and gardens at Yale in 1923. Farrand's finest gardens were those at Dumbarton Oaks in Washington, DC, which evolved over 20 years, and they remain the only gardens retaining her design. Among her awards were the Garden Club of America Medal of Achievement and the New York Botanical Garden Distinguished Service Award. She devoted the last two decades of her life to a test garden, a library, and a herbarium at her Maine home that she eventually transferred to the department of landscape architecture at the University of California at Berkeley.

BIBLIOGRAPHY

Balmori, Diana, et al. *Beatrix Farrand's American Landscapes: Her Gardens and Campuses*. Millwood, NY: Kraus, 1985. 0-89831-003-2, 215p. The carefully researched and documented text includes biographical information on Farrand and photographs of her gardens.

Brown, Jane. *Beatrix: The Gardening Life of Beatrix Jones Farrand*. New York: Viking, 1995. 0-670-83217-0, 252p. Brown analyzed Farrand's journals and correspondence as well as photographs and drawings to re-create her life and work in a recommended biography.

McGuire, Diane Kostial, and Lois Fern, eds. *Beatrix Jones Farrand (1872-1959): Fifty Years of American Landscape Architecture*. Washington, DC: Dumbarton Oaks Trustees, 1982. 0-88402-106-8, 142p. Essays on Farrand's life and work give an overview of her 50 years as an American landscape architect.

FARRAR, GERALDINE (1882-1967)
Opera Singer   Melrose, Massachusetts

Geraldine Farrar was an opera singer known for her dramatic talent and vocal timbre. She was born on February 28, 1882, as the only child of a storekeeper and his wife, both of whom were amateur singers. Farrar began taking music lessons at age five, and she went to New York to study at twelve. By the age of 14, after studying with **Emma Thursby**, she was giving recitals. When *Nellie Melba heard her and recommended European training, the family borrowed money to live in Paris for a year while she studied. In 1901, she made her debut as Marguerite in Gounod's *Faust* at the Berlin Court Opera. The opera company allowed her to sing her first three roles in Italian while she mastered German, and the renowned *Lilli Lehmann accepted her as a student. Farrar sang in Europe for three years before debuting at the Metropolitan Opera on opening night in 1906. The same season, she began singing with Enrico Caruso. She also worked with Gustav Mahler and Arturo Toscanini. In New York, she sang 493 performances of 29 roles, 95 times as Butterfly. The strain of her study under different teachers became apparent when her voice broke during a performance in 1913. She rested, but it was never the same. She retired from opera in 1921, although she sang concert repertoire from 1924 to 1931. Her performances of operas including Mascagni's *Amica*, Saint-Saëns's *L'Ancêtre*, and Puccini's *Suor Angelica* remain highlights of opera history. She wrote poetry and composed songs during retirement, and in World War II served as a Red Cross volunteer, frequently corresponding with servicemen abroad.

BIBLIOGRAPHY

Farrar, Geraldine. *Such Sweet Compulsion: The Autobiography of Geraldine Farrar*. 1938. Freeport, NY: Books for Libraries Press, 1970. 0-8369-5205-7, 303p. Farrar credits her mother's spirit with guiding the writing of her autobiography.

Nash, Elizabeth. *Always First Class: The Career of Geraldine Farrar*. Washington, DC: University Press of America, 1981. 0-8191-1882-6, 281p. Nash emphasizes Farrar's excellence in her carefully researched, documented, scholarly, and recommended biography.

FARRELL, SUZANNE (1945–)
Ballerina   Cincinnati, Ohio

Suzanne Farrell is a world-renowned ballerina. She was born Roberta Sue Ficker on August 16, 1945, one of three daughters. She began dancing at the age of eight and attended the Cincinnati Conservatory of Music before going to New York and the School of American Ballet on scholarship. She began dancing with the New York City Ballet in 1961 and became a principal dancer in 1965, with George Balanchine creating roles especially for her. After her marriage to Paul Mejia, a fellow dancer, they went to the Bejart Ballet of the Twentieth Century, in Brussels, Belgium, in 1970, and returned to the New York City Ballet in 1975. By the time Farrell retired in 1989, she had a repertory of over 110 ballets, more than any other single dancer, with her major roles including that of Dulcinea in Balanchine's *Don Quixote* and the lead in Balanchine's *Mozartiana*. She has also appeared on television and in films and has taught at the School of American Ballet. Among her awards are a *Dance* Magazine Award, an Emmy Award, and honorary degrees.

BIBLIOGRAPHY
Farrell, Suzanne. *Holding on to the Air: An Autobiography*. New York: Penguin, 1990. 0–14–015722–0, 322p. Farrell tells the story of her career as a ballerina.
Swope, Martha. *Suzanne Farrell*. Brooklyn, NY: Dance Horizons, 1975. No ISBN, 17p. This brief monograph, including photographs, covers Farrell's career up to the age of 30.

FAUSET, JESSIE REDMON (1882–1961)
Author   Camden County, New Jersey

Jessie Redmon Fauset wrote about the condition of other African Americans in her novels during the Harlem Renaissance in the 1920s. She was born on April 26, 1882, as the youngest of seven children to a cultured but never wealthy African Methodist Episcopal minister and his wife. After high school, her college choice, Bryn Mawr, was not prepared to admit an African American woman, and its officials helped her get a scholarship to Cornell University. There she studied classical languages and graduated Phi Beta Kappa. She had difficulty finding work but went to Washington, DC, to teach Latin and French at the M Street High School while completing an M.A. in French at the University of Pennsylvania. She then became the literary editor of *Crisis* in New York at the recommendation of W.E.B. Du Bois. Emphasizing poetry and fiction, she published young writers including Claude McKay, Jean Toomer, Countee Cullen, Arna Bontemps, and Langston Hughes. In 1922, she began writing novels herself. After returning from European travel, she could not secure employment in the white publishing world, even with her impeccable credentials, and she returned to teaching. In her work, she wanted to show how passing for white made the racial constructions in the United States both destructive and arbitrary.

BIBLIOGRAPHY

Allen, Carol. *Black Women Intellectuals*. New York: Garland, 1998. 0-8153-3112-6, 169p. In this collective biography, Allen posits that critics should include Fauset's work as a journalist in their assessments of her legacy.

McLendon, Jacquelyn Y. *The Politics of Color in the Fiction of Jessie Fauset and Nella Larsen*. Charlottesville: University Press of Virginia, 1995. 0-8139-1553-8, 142p. In her scholarly collective study, McLendon opines that Fauset blames the whites rather than the blacks for attitudes toward mulattoes.

Sylvander, Carolyn Wedin. *Jessie Redmon Fauset, Black American Writer*. Troy, NY: Whitston, 1981. 0-87875-196-3, 275p. Sylvander used letters, office memos, and interviews along with published sources to create a carefully documented, scholarly biography of Fauset.

Wall, Cheryl A. *Women of the Harlem Renaissance*. Bloomington: Indiana University Press, 1995. 0-253-32908-6, 246p. Wall looks at Fauset's work, its historical context, and her success in this collective biography.

FAY, AMY (1844–1928)
Pianist

Bayou Goula, Louisiana

Amy Fay was a professional pianist. She was born on May 21, 1844, as the fifth of nine children to a Harvard-educated minister and his wife. When Fay was four, she exhibited her musical abilities through playing the piano by ear and improvising. Her mother, a self-taught musician, supervised Fay until her death when Fay was 12. Fay's father taught her French, Latin, German, Greek, and mathematics. When 17, Fay began studying music seriously at the New England Conservatory. Seeing the German influence on music, Fay went to Germany in 1869 to study in Berlin with a student of Franz Liszt. While in Germany, she wrote many letters home carefully describing her experiences, including hearing pianists such as *Clara Schumann and Liszt himself. She later studied with Liszt, and he remembered her in a list of his best students. Fay made her debut in Frankfurt in 1875, and a few weeks later she returned to New York, where she made her debut with the Mendelssohn Glee Club. In the Cambridge and Worcester music festivals, she was the first pianist to play a full-length concerto, and in Chicago, she began "piano conversations" while founding the Artists' Concert Club. When she returned to New York in the 1890s, she became president of the Women's Philharmonic Society, sponsoring a women's orchestra and helping young musicians.

BIBLIOGRAPHY

Fay, Amy. *More Letters of Amy Fay: The American Years, 1879–1916*. Ed. Margaret William McCarthy. Detroit: Information Coordinators, 1986. 0-89990-028-3,

168p. The text includes Fay's correspondence after she returned to the United States from Germany.

―――. *Music-Study in Germany: The Classic Memoir of the Romantic Era.* 1880. New York: Dover, 1991. 0-486-26562-5, 352p. This collection of Fay's letters includes her observations from 1869 to 1875.

McCarthy, Margaret William. *Amy Fay: America's Notable Woman of Music.* Warren, MI: Harmonie Park Press, 1995. 0-89990-074-7, 196p. McCarthy collected Fay's letters, written mainly in the United States, and with them traces her career.

FEARING, MARIA (1838–1937)
Slave and Missionary   Gainesville, Alabama

African American Maria Fearing wanted to be a missionary all of her life, and when she was 56 in 1894, she sailed to the Congo Free State. Born a slave on July 26, 1838, Fearing completed ninth grade and taught in a rural school. In 1894, she heard a missionary on furlough from the Presbyterian Congo Mission appeal for volunteers. When refused funds because of her age, she sold her home and, using her savings along with $100 donated by the women in her church, paid her own way for two years. Then the Southern Presbyterian Church appointed her and paid her salary for her work founding and directing the Pantops Home for Girls. She taught in the mission school and Sunday school until she took a furlough in 1915.

BIBLIOGRAPHY
Sammon, Patricia. *Maria Fearing: A Woman Whose Dreams Crossed an Ocean.* Huntsville, AL: Writers Consortium, 1989. No ISBN, 127p. This biography for juveniles is the only available story of Fearing's life and work.

FERBER, EDNA (1887–1968)
Author   Kalamazoo, Michigan

Edna Ferber was a novelist and short story writer who wrote about the middle class in the Midwest. She was born on August 15, 1887, the second daughter of nonpracticing Jews. Her Hungarian immigrant father lost his eyesight when Ferber was young, and her mother had to manage the family store to support them. Ferber read a book a day during her childhood, and on regular family excursions to the theater, dreamed of becoming an actor. She wanted to attend college, but her family could not pay for it, so she became the first woman reporter for the *Appleton Daily Crescent.* After a second newspaper job in Wisconsin, Ferber began to publish short stories, including ones about Emma McChesney, a traveling saleswoman who needed assertiveness to succeed. In 1914, Ferber traveled to Europe, happy to have visited before the destruction of World War I. Her career as a playwright began in 1919, but she did not become successful until she collaborated with George S. Kaufman. Among their works were *Royal Family*, *Dinner at Eight, Stage Door,* and *Show Boat,* a play that has been in production since

1927. In 1924, she won a Pulitzer Prize for her novel *So Big*. Later novels were *Saratoga Trunk* and *Giant*, both of which became successful movies. Ferber was a best-selling author whom the critics ignored, but her strong women characters refused to allow men to ruin them.

BIBLIOGRAPHY

Gilbert, Julie Goldsmith. *Ferber: A Biography*. Garden City, NY: Doubleday, 1978. 0-385-03960-3, 445p. Ferber's grandniece used Ferber's diaries and notebooks for a balanced, readable biography.

Shaughnessy, Mary Rose. *Women and Success in American Society in the Works of Edna Ferber*. New York: Gordon, 1977. 0-87968-454-2, 356p. This scholarly dissertation examines Ferber's life and major works.

FERN, FANNY (1811–1872)
Journalist   Boston, Massachusetts

Fanny Fern was a novelist, columnist, and children's author. She was born Sara Payson on July 9, 1811, to an upper-class Boston deacon and his wife. She was educated at the Hartford Female Seminary, the best American school for women at the time, and when she married at 25, she expected a traditional life. Ten years later, however, she became a widow with two children who needed financial support. Her family offered no help, and after her writing prospered, she refused to forget those who had ignored her needs. She chose the pseudonym "Fanny Fern," and in her first novel, she satirized members of her family with transparent disguises. Her newspaper columns for small magazines were both sentimental, as was expected during her time, and satirical, with their popularity leading to newspaper reprints. Three collections of Fern's writing quickly sold over 132,000 copies, and she earned royalties of $10,000 in two years. The owner of the *New York Ledger* hired her for the shockingly high sum of $100 a week to write a column in which she discussed women's rights, prostitution, venereal disease, birth control, male dominance, and prison conditions. She stayed with the newspaper until the end of her life, never missing an issue and reaching an audience of 500,000 each week. Her work clearly depicts American life during the time in which she lived.

BIBLIOGRAPHY

Walker, Nancy A. *Fanny Fern*. New York: Twayne, 1993. 0-8057-3981-5, 135p. This critical biography, based on primary sources and critical studies, reveals the life of Sara Payson Willis Parton or Fanny Fern.

Warren, Joyce W. *Fanny Fern: An Independent Woman*. New Brunswick, NJ: Rutgers University Press, 1992. 0-8135-1763-X, 374p. In her well-researched and well-written academic recreation of Fern, Warren reveals Fern's aggressive writing.

FERRARO, GERALDINE ANNE (1935-)
Attorney and Congresswoman   Newburgh, New York

Geraldine Ferraro was the first woman nominated for vice president of the United States by a major political party. She was born on August 26, 1935, to Italian immigrant parents. Ferraro was eight when her father died, and her mother had to support the family. Ferraro won a scholarship to and graduated from Marymount College before teaching in New York City and attending Fordham University law classes at night, earning her degree in 1960. After practicing privately, in 1974, she became the assistant United States district attorney for Queens County. Concerned about treatment of women, she helped create a bureau for abused or raped women and changed her political views from conservative to liberal. In 1978, she won election as the representative from New York's Ninth District, and after earning a reputation for hard work, she chaired the 1984 Democratic Platform Committee, helping to establish the party's agenda for the presidential campaign. Her skills impressed Walter Mondale, and he chose her to run with him on the ticket as his vice president. Although they lost the election, Ferraro made political history and was elected to The National Women's Hall of Fame.

BIBLIOGRAPHY
Breslin, Rosemary, and Joshua Hammer. *Gerry! A Woman Making History*. New York: Pinnacle, 1984. 0–523–42444–2, 162p. This in-depth examination of Ferraro notes that Mario Cuomo called her the "Queen of Queens."
Ferraro, Geraldine. *Ferraro: My Story*. New York: Bantam, 1985. 0–553–05110–5, 340p. Ferraro tells the story of her campaign in 1984 as the first female candidate for vice president.
Katz, Lee Michael. *My Name Is Geraldine Ferraro*. New York: New American Library, 1984. 0–451–13506–7, 224p. This popular unauthorized biography examines Ferraro's life.

FERRÉ, ROSARIO (1942-)
Author   Ponce, Puerto Rico

Rosario Ferré is a Latina American writer and publisher. She was born on July 28, 1942, to a financier and governor of Puerto Rico and his wife. As a young girl, she attended a Jesuit school with her brothers, and at the Catholic school for girls to which she transferred, she experienced typically inferior female education. She then attended Manhattanville College in New York before returning to Puerto Rico. While Ferré worked on her M.A. at the University of Puerto Rico, her mother died, and she assumed the position of official hostess for her governor father. She briefly published a literary magazine for new Puerto Rican literature before moving to Mexico, where she published her first collection of short stories, *Papeles de Pandora (The Youngest Doll)*. In the 1980s, she returned to the United States to enter the University of Maryland for her Ph.D. Having avidly read fairy tales as a child, she started recording some of her nanny's stories and used these traditional themes and structures in her own work. In her fiction, she examines the roles of women in a male-dominated culture and reflects on the act of writing for women. She has been one of Puerto Rico's strongest feminist spokespersons since her first publication and since her return to the island in 1990. Among her honors is the National Book Critics Circle Award.

BIBLIOGRAPHY

Hintz, Suzanne S. *Rosario Ferré: A Search for Identity.* New York: Lang, 1995. 0–8204–2691–1, 275p. The scholarly text, based on Ferré's personal papers and writings, is a critical biography of her life and work.

FIELD, SALLY (1946–)
Actor   Pasadena, California

Sally Field is an award-winning actor. She was born on November 6, 1946, as one of two children to a drug salesman and his actor wife. They divorced when Field was four. Field's mother remarried, and Field attended acting classes with her and participated in drama clubs at school. After Field graduated, an old family friend suggested that she screen test for a television series, and she won the lead role in *Gidget.* She then won the starring role in another television series, *The Flying Nun.* Not until 1976, however, did she gain recognition for serious acting. Her role in the NBC television movie *Sybil* won her an Emmy Award. In 1979, she won many honors, including an Academy Award for her performance in *Norma Rae.* Wanting more control over her roles, Field formed a production company in 1981. In 1984, she won the Golden Globe Award and another Academy Award for *Places in the Heart.* In 1991, she produced her first film, *Dying Young.* Other films have included *Steel Magnolias, Mrs. Doubtfire,* and *Forrest Gump,* and she has continued to work in television and film, starring, producing, and most recently, directing.

BIBLIOGRAPHY

Bonderoff, Jason. *Sally Field.* New York: St. Martin's, 1987. 0–312–01086–9, 169p. This popular biography of Field gives an overview of her life.

FIELDS, ANNIE (1834–1915)
Author and Hostess   Boston, Massachusetts

Annie Fields was an author and literary hostess. She was born Ann West on June 6, 1834, as one of seven children to a physician and his wife. She received her education mainly at home, although she briefly attended school. When she was 20, she married James Thomas Fields, a man 17 years her senior whom she had known since childhood. During their happy marriage, after her husband became editor of the *Atlantic* and senior partner in the publishing house of Ticknor & Fields, her home became a literary salon for such regular visitors as **Harriet Beecher Stowe,**

Louis Agassiz, Oliver Wendell Holmes, and Nathaniel Hawthorne. Charles Dickens, William Makepeace Thackeray, Charles Reade, and Anthony Trollope also enjoyed her hospitality. Between European tours, she started to write, and her husband published her 11 undistinguished books of fiction and poetry. After his death in 1881, she wrote biographies of persons she had known. Concurrently, **Sarah Orne Jewett** moved into Fields's home at 148 Charles Street and co-hosted her salons for 20 years. As Fields aged, she became interested in social welfare work and aided tenement dwellers after the 1872 Boston fire. She then founded the Co-operative Society of Visitors Among the Poor in 1875 and the Associated Charities of Boston in 1879. She also wrote a handbook for charity workers which sold 22,000 copies in two years. At her death, she left her largest donation to the Associated Charities.

BIBLIOGRAPHY

Howe, M. A. De Wolfe. *Memories of a Hostess.* 1922. New York: Arno Press, 1974. 0-405-06103-X, 312p. Howe has collected information on Fields from her diaries during the 1860s and 1870s to reveal her charm and generosity.

Roman, Judith. *Annie Adams Fields: The Spirit of Charles Street.* Bloomington: Indiana University Press, 1990. 0-253-35022-0, 191p. Roman used Fields's journals and other materials to reveal her life and service.

FIELDS, DOROTHY (1905–1974)
Librettist   Allenhurst, New Jersey

Dorothy Fields was regarded by her colleagues as one of the best lyricists in the music business. She was born on July 15, 1905, as one of four children to second generation Polish immigrant parents. Her father was a vaudeville and music hall manager who disapproved of a stage career for his children. During the 1920s, when songs became integral to the plays in which they appeared, Fields started writing for revues and African American entertainers at Harlem's Cotton Club. Her first collaborative Broadway show, *Blackbirds of 1928,* included the songs "I Can't Give You Anything But Love" and "On the Sunny Side of the Street." In 1936, the film *Swing Time*, with her song "The Way You Look Tonight," won her an Academy Award. Through the years, she continued to write lyrics for Broadway successes such as *Annie Get Your Gun, Sweet Charity,* and *Seesaw.* In 1959, her collaboration on *Redhead* won her a Grammy and a Tony Award for best lyrics. Her songs projected aspects of the characters who sang them, and she said before her death of a heart attack that she still had songs waiting to be written.

BIBLIOGRAPHY

Winer, Deborah Grace. *On the Sunny Side of the Street: The Life and Lyrics of Dorothy Fields.* New York: Schirmer, 1997. 0-02-864730-0, 267p. Winer has written a thoroughly researched and documented biography on Fields's life.

FISHER, DOROTHY CANFIELD (1879–1958)
Author   Lawrence, Kansas

Dorothy Canfield Fisher was an author. She was born on February 17, 1879, as the second child of a professor and his artist wife. Both of Fisher's parents were feminists, and when she was 11, Fisher attended school in Paris for a year while her mother studied art. When they returned to America, the family moved to Nebraska where Fisher became friends with **Willa Cather**. After Fisher's father became president of Ohio State University, she enrolled there, graduating with a degree in French in 1899. She returned to Paris to study at the Sorbonne, and at Columbia she finished her Ph.D. in French literature. While working as an administrator at New York's experimental Horace Mann School, she began to write short stories and published in popular magazines using a pseudonym before marrying in 1907. She moved with her husband to Vermont and continued writing while raising two children and remaining active in civic affairs as the first woman appointed to the Vermont state board of education. After a trip to Europe, where she saw some of *Maria Montessori's schools, Fisher helped popularize the Montessori method in the United States. In World War I, the family went to France, where Fisher printed books in braille for the war blind and established a refugee camp in southern France for Parisian children while her husband served in the ambulance corps. In 1926, Fisher became a member of the first board of selection of the Book-of-the-Month Club, serving as its only woman for 25 years and helping to establish the reputations of such authors as **Pearl Buck**, *Isak Dinesen, and Richard Wright. She also served on other boards. In World War II, she organized the Children's Crusade to encourage American children to help young victims of war abroad. She is best remembered for the blend of idealism and realism in her fiction.

BIBLIOGRAPHY

Washington, Ida H. *Dorothy Canfield Fisher: A Biography.* Shelburne, VT: New England Press, 1982. 0–933050–08–9, 258p. Washington uses evidence in her carefully researched and documented biography to show that Fisher's writing was timeless.
Yates, Elizabeth. *The Lady from Vermont: Dorothy Canfield Fisher's Life and World.* 1958. Brattleboro, VT: S. Greene Press, 1971. 0–8289–0127–9, 290p. Yates interviewed Fisher and her husband and used other resources to create her readable biography.

FISHER, MARY FRANCES KENNEDY (1908–1992)
Author   Albion, Michigan

M.F.K. Fisher, a writer, explored the relationship between food and life. She was born July 3, 1908, one of four children of a journalist father and an antisocial mother who took her to California two years after her birth. As a child, she admitted to being an insatiable reader and scribbler. She attended several colleges before marrying a doctoral student in 1929 and moving to Dijon, France. After her first divorce in 1937, she married twice more and raised two daughters. During her 60-year career, she wrote hundreds of stories for the *New Yorker*, 15 books of essays and reminiscences, dozens of travelogues, a novel, a screenplay, a book for children, and an English translation of Brillat-Savarin's book *The Physiology of Taste*. She thought that Americans should learn to enjoy new foods rather than to eat the same things, and repeatedly treated food as a metaphor of culture.

BIBLIIOGRAPHY

Ferrary, Jeannette. *Between Friends: M.F.K. Fisher and Me*. New York: Atlantic Monthly Press, 1991. 0-87113-450-0, 237p. Ferrary's biography is a memoir of Fisher's friendship.

Fisher, M.F.K. *Long Ago in France: The Years in Dijon*. New York: Prentice-Hall, 1991. 0-13-929548-8, 159p. Fisher describes her experience in France in a combination memoir, travelogue, and gastronomical experience.

———. *Stay Me, Oh Comfort Me: Journals and Stories, 1933–1941*. New York: Pantheon, 1993. 0-679-42725-2, 349p. Diary entries, letters, and notes form the core of Fisher's account of her life.

———. *To Begin Again: Stories and Memoirs, 1908–1929*. San Francisco: Pantheon, 1992. 0-679-41576-9, 179p. Fisher recalls her endurance of a pompous father and a grandmother who denied all things that heightened the senses.

Reardon, Joan. *M.F.K. Fisher, Julia Child, and Alice Waters: Celebrating the Pleasures of the Table*. New York: Harmony, 1994. 0-517-57748-8, 302p. In a collective biography, Reardon discusses Fisher's role in changing American ideas about food.

FISKE, MINNIE MADDERN (1865–1932)
Actor   New Orleans, Louisiana

Minnie Maddern Fiske was an actor. She was born on December 19, 1865, the only child of a stage manager who had come to America from Wales and his actor wife. By the age of three, she occasionally acted in her father's troupe, but he left the family, and Fiske and her mother continued their careers in New York, with Fiske touring widely as a child prodigy and having little opportunity for formal education. Her mother died when Fiske was 13, and after living with her aunt, she returned to touring at 16. In her second marriage, Fiske worked with her husband and decided to play only roles that she liked. She preferred Ibsen, with her portrayals of his characters bringing a new naturalism to American theater. She also liked plays adapted from novels, such as *Tess of the d'Urbervilles* and *Becky Sharpe*, a play she often revived. During her career, she opposed the Theatrical Trust, a monopoly of producers who tried to gain control of what played and who starred in major theaters. Fiske refused to capitulate because she believed in artistic freedom, but in the 12 years before the Trust allowed independent bookings, Fiske and her husband used most of their financial resources to pay for their productions. Her last performance in 1930 was as Mrs. Malaprop. During her career, she took her adopted child on tour and encouraged young actors and playwrights. She received honorary degrees and was twice named one of the 12 greatest living American women.

BIBLIOGRAPHY

Binns, Archie. *Mrs. Fiske and the American Theatre.* New York: Crown, 1955. No ISBN, 436p. Binns's thoroughly researched biography of Fiske, based on letters and manuscripts, reveals her importance to the American theater.

Fiske, Minnie Maddern. *Mrs. Fiske: Her Views on the Stage.* 1917. New York: B. Blom, 1968. No ISBN, 229p. In these conversations between Fiske and Alexander Wolcott, Fiske explores her theory of the theater.

FITZGERALD, ELLA (1918–1996)
Entertainer   **Newport News, Virginia**

African American Ella Fitzgerald, the "First Lady of Jazz," became known for her sweetness of voice and her style of singing, called "scat." Born on April 25, 1918, she was orphaned early and grew up in Yonkers, New York, before winning an amateur contest at the Apollo Theater. Her performance won her a job with big-band drummer William Chick Webb, and after his death in 1939, she directed his band for three years before establishing her own solo career and performing around the world with musicians such as Louis Armstrong, Duke Ellington, Oscar Peterson, and Count Basie. Among the composers she recorded were Richard Rodgers, Cole Porter, George Gershwin, Duke Ellington, Jerome Kern, Irving Berlin, and Johnny Mercer. During her career, she received 14 Grammy Awards, more than any other jazz singer. She was also elected to The National Women's Hall of Fame.

BIBLIOGRAPHY

Colin, Sid. *Ella: The Life and Times of Ella Fitzgerald.* London: Elm Tree, 1986. 0-241-11754-2, 151p. Colin used interviews and research for this overview of Fitzgerald's life and career.

Fidelman, Geoffrey Mark. *First Lady of Song: Ella Fitzgerald for the Record.* Secaucus, NJ: Carol, 1994. 1-55972-240-1, 379p. Fidelman examines Fitzgerald's career in this biography.

Kliment, Bud. *Ella Fitzgerald.* New York: Chelsea House, 1988. 1-55546-586-2, 112p. Kliment's biography of Fitzgerald for young adults emphasizes her enormous talent, technical control, and pleasant personality.

Nicholson, Stuart. *Ella Fitzgerald: A Biography of the First Lady of Jazz.* New York: Scribner, 1994. 0-684-19699-9, 334p. Nicholson used written accounts of Fitzgerald's life and interviews with her friends for his exhaustive, thoroughly researched biography.

FLANAGAN, HALLIE (1890–1969)
Theatrical Producer and Dramatist   Redfield, South Dakota

Hallie Mae Ferguson Flanagan was a theater educator and administrator. She was born on August 27, 1890, as the eldest of three children to a homemaker and a father who became involved in a series of unsuccessful business ventures but who taught her that every new thing had intriguing possibilities. Flanagan attended public schools, and after graduating from Grinnell College in 1911, married a fellow student. He died of tuberculosis in 1919, and she began teaching to support her children. A professor with whom she worked suggested that she start acting, but she preferred to write plays so that she could stay at home. After one of her sons died, she took the other one with her to Cambridge while working on a Radcliffe degree. She then directed plays at Grinnell, visited European theaters on a Guggenheim Foundation fellowship, and became a director, teacher, and playwright at Vassar, creating productions at the recently founded Vassar Experimental Theatre. In 1935, she became the director of Roosevelt's Federal Theatre Project established to employ theater workers on relief during the Great Depression. In the first year, over 12,000 people went to work, and during its four years, over 1,200 productions allowed 25 million people to enjoy the theater, many of whom had never before attended a play. Flanagan helped build an innovative national network of regional theaters before the project's demise in 1939. In 1940, her second husband died, and for financial security, she became the dean of Smith College and established a theater department on Smith's campus, integrating theater into the liberal arts curriculum. Her honors included the first annual citation of the National Theatre Conference and her name on theaters at both Smith and Vassar.

BIBLIOGRAPHY
Bentley, Joanne. *Hallie Flanagan: A Life in the American Theatre.* New York: Knopf, 1988. 0-394-57041-3, 436p. Bentley's carefully researched and balanced biography relies on interviews and Flanagan's personal papers.

FLANNER, JANET (1892–1978)
Author   Indianapolis, Indiana

Janet Flanner reported from Paris between 1925 and 1975 for the *New Yorker* magazine. She was born on March 13, 1892, the daughter of a prosperous Quaker businessman and his wife. She attended private school, spent time in Germany, and, after her father's suicide, studied at the University of Chicago until 1914. During World War I, she worked for the *Indianapolis Star* as its art and drama critic and in Philadelphia at a reformatory school. After the war, she married, went to New York, and met the love of her life, Solita Solano. Flanner left with Solano for Paris and stayed until World War II began. In 1925, Flanner's friend Harold Ross hired her to write "Letter from Paris" for his new magazine, the *New Yorker*. In articles signed "Genêt," she wrote about politics, art, theater, and French life.

Among her expatriate friends were Ernest Hemingway, Kay Boyle, **Gertrude Stein**, and Djuna Barnes. In the 1930s, she sometimes wrote "Letter from London," and during World War II, while living in New York, she translated *Colette's novels. Among her awards were the French Legion of Honor and the National Book Award.

BIBLIOGRAPHY

Flanner, Janet. *Darlinghissima: Letters to a Friend.* San Diego: Harcourt Brace Jovanovich, 1986. 0–15–623937–X, 507p. Flanner's letters span 1944 to 1975 in this collection.

Wineapple, Brenda. *Genêt: A Biography of Janet Flanner.* Lincoln: University of Nebraska Press, 1989. 0–8032–974–0, 361p. Wineapple's well-researched biography of Flanner describes expatriate life in Paris.

FLETCHER, ALICE CUNNINGHAM (1838–1923)
Anthropologist   Havana, Cuba

Alice Cunningham Fletcher was an ethnologist. She was born on March 15, 1838, the only child of a lawyer and his second wife. Her father died from consumption when she was one, and her mother then remarried a man who refused to let Fletcher read fiction, although he permitted her to study. After education in New York City's best schools, she met Frederic Ward Putnam, director of Harvard's Peabody Museum, who suggested she read archaeology and ethnology. She also began field work, joined the Archaeological Institute of America in 1879, and raised funds to preserve the prehistoric Serpent Mound in Ohio. She then became interested in the welfare of Native Americans when Bright Eyes (**Susette La Flesche Tibbles**) and her husband toured the East asking for help. Fletcher listened, visited the Omaha, and vowed to save their lands. She lobbied for the Dawes Act, and when it eventually passed, she managed the apportionment process. The Omaha began to trust her enough to send their children east to school and to reveal some of their tribal secrets. Among her publications, both academic and government, were *Indian Education and Civilization, The Omaha Tribe, Indian Story and Song from North America,* and *The Hako: A Pawnee Ceremony.* She formed a mother-son relationship with Tibbles's younger brother, Francis La Flesche, leaving her estate to him at her death, although never officially adopting him. Based on Fletcher's influence, the Archaeological Institute of America established a school in Santa Fe to study Native American ruins. She sat on the editorial board of the *American Anthropologist* and received many awards, including the presidencies of the American Folk-Lore Society and the Anthropological Society of Washington.

BIBLIOGRAPHY

Gay, E. Jane. *With the Nez Perces: Alice Fletcher in the Field.* Ed. Frederick E. Hoxie and Joan T. Mark. Lincoln: University of Nebraska Press, 1981. 0–8032–3062–1, 188p.

Gay wrote letters and took photographs of her travels with Fletcher to the Nez Perce reservation in Idaho during the summers between 1889 and 1892.

Mark, Joan T. *A Stranger in Her Native Land: Alice Fletcher and the American Indians.* Lincoln: University of Nebraska Press, 1988. 0–8032–3128–8, 428p. In this biography, Mark empathizes with Fletcher's frustrations while working with male-dominated institutions.

FLYNN, ELIZABETH GURLEY (1890–1964)
Labor Leader   Concord, New Hampshire

Elizabeth Gurley Flynn was a labor organizer, radical, and communist. She was born on August 7, 1890, as the eldest of four to a stonecutter and engineer who worked intermittently and his Irish nationalist and feminist wife. Influenced by poverty before meeting *Emma Goldman and Alexander Berkman, Flynn entertained anarchism before choosing communism. When she was 16, she spoke to the Harlem Socialist Club about women under socialism, and by the end of the summer, her success as a soapbox speaker led to her arrest for blocking traffic. The same year, she joined the Industrial Workers of the World, and the next year, she participated in the strike against American Tube and Stamping Company as well as in the textile strikes in the East. When she went west on a speaking tour, she met a miner and married him but soon regretted her decision. After the war, Flynn helped found the Workers' Defense Union and the American Civil Liberties Union (ACLU). In 1926, she became chairman of the International Labor Defense, an organization of lawyers and civil libertarians connected to the Communist Party. Recovering from an illness in Oregon took 10 years, but she returned to New York, joined the Communist Party, and began advocating equality of pay and employment opportunity and protection for women in the *Daily Worker.* In 1941, the political bureau elected her into the Communist Party hierarchy. In 1942, she based a campaign for congressman-at-large in New York on women's issues and received 50,000 votes. After the war, when she returned from the socialist Women's Congress in Paris, the government indicted, tried, convicted, and imprisoned her under the Smith Act for conspiring to teach and advocate the overthrow of the United States government by force and violence. After prison, she became the first woman to be elected the American Communist Party national chairman. The State Department revoked her passport, but she won an appeal in the Supreme Court. At her death, the Soviet Union gave her a state funeral in Moscow's Red Square.

BIBLIOGRAPHY
Baxandall, Rosalyn Fraad, ed. *Words on Fire: The Life and Writing of Elizabeth Gurley Flynn.* New Brunswick, NJ: Rutgers University Press, 1987. 0–8135–1240–9, 302p. A thoroughly researched and documented introduction precedes excerpts from Flynn's writings, especially unpublished poems and letters.

Camp, Helen C. *Iron in Her Soul: Elizabeth Gurley Flynn and the American Left.* Pullman: Washington State University Press, 1995. 0–87422–105–6, 396p. Camp uses primary and secondary sources in her thoroughly researched and balanced biography of Flynn.

Flynn, Elizabeth Gurley. *The Rebel Girl: An Autobiography, My First Life (1906–1926)*. 1955. New York: International Publishers, 1973. 0–7178–0367–8, 351p. The autobiography reveals Flynn's political involvements.

FONDA, JANE (1937–)
Actor and Activist   New York, New York

Jane Fonda is an actor, political activist, and fitness expert. She was born on December 21, 1937, as one of two children to an actor and his wife. Her mother committed suicide when Fonda was 12. Fonda attended Vassar College for two years before studying at the Actors Studio. She worked as a model before opening on Broadway, and in the 1960s, her film career began. She earned her first Academy Award nomination for *They Shoot Horses, Don't They?* and then won the award for *Klute*. After *Klute*, Fonda's radical politics, including public statements from Hanoi, distressed soldiers in Vietnam and their families; critics named her "Hanoi Jane." After her second husband became a politician, she campaigned for him. Within five years, she performed in *Julia* and produced and starred in *Coming Home* (a second Academy Award), *The China Syndrome*, *9 to 5*, and *On Golden Pond*, in which she starred with her father, Henry Fonda. During the 1980s, she began her fitness business by making and selling videotapes for different types of exercise and ability levels. She continued to act and received another Academy Award nomination for *The Morning After* (1986). In 1991, Fonda married Ted Turner and retired from films. Recently Fonda created the Georgia Campaign for Adolescent Pregnancy Prevention. In her career, she won over 20 major performance awards.

BIBLIOGRAPHY

Andersen, Christopher P. *Citizen Jane: The Turbulent Life of Jane Fonda*. New York: Henry Holt, 1990. 0–8050–0959–0, 389p. In a well-researched, documented, and readable biography, Andersen examines Fonda's life and career.

Davidson, Bill. *Jane Fonda: An Intimate Biography*. New York: Dutton, 1990. 0–525–24888–9, 245p. This readable, researched popular biography focuses on Fonda's complexities of character.

Freedland, Michael. *Jane Fonda: A Biography*. New York: St. Martin's, 1988. 0–312–01048–6, 247p. Based mainly on interviews, Freedland's popular biography of Fonda overviews her life and career.

Guiles, Fred Lawrence. *Jane Fonda: The Actress in Her Time*. Garden City, NY: Doubleday, 1982. 0–385–15920–X, 298p. Although unauthorized, this biography of Fonda somewhat erratically examines her career.

Spada, James. *Fonda: Her Life in Pictures*. Garden City, NY: Doubleday, 1985. 0–385–18827–7, 225p. This biography of Fonda focuses on photographs of her performing various roles and as a private citizen.

FORCE, JULIANA (1876–1948)
Art Patron   Doylestown, Pennsylvania

Juliana Rieser Force was an art museum director. She was born on December 25, 1876, as one of nine children to a hatter and his wife. She attended an evangelical girls' boarding school but left to become a secretary and later managed a secretarial school. When she moved to New York City, Helen Hay Whitney hired her as a secretary, and when 35, Force married a Manhattan dentist. Whitney introduced Force to **Gertrude Vanderbilt Whitney,** a sculptor and art patron, who asked Force to help administer the Whitney Studio, a gallery she had opened to show works by young American artists. They established the Friends of the Young Artists in 1915, which held exhibitions and purchased paintings instead of giving prizes. From this grew the Whitney Studio Club, a social and exhibiting center, with Force as director. Among those who exhibited here were John Sloan, Edward Hopper, and Joseph Stella. In January 1930, Whitney announced the opening of the Whitney Museum of American Art with Force as director. Whitney donated her collection and the buildings, but Force created the interior with her excellent taste and managed the museum with hospitality. She also donated her own collection of American primitives and began producing monographs on living artists along with full-length biographies of Thomas Eakins and Winslow Homer. Her care forged the Whitney Museum into a prestigious institution. Force also helped organize the federal PublicWorks of Art Project during the Great Depression, and as Region 2 manager, employed 900 artists. In 1945, she headed a New York State Art Program and was one of the first women to serve as trustee and officer on three museum boards.

BIBLIOGRAPHY
Berman, Avis. *Rebels on Eighth Street: Juliana Force and the Whitney Museum of American Art.* New York: Atheneum, 1990. 0-689-12086-9, 572p. According to Berman, Force supplied the energy to make the Whitney Museum successful.

FORD, BETTY (1918–)
First Lady   Chicago, Illinois

Betty Ford was First Lady of the United States and co-founder of the Betty Ford Center. She was born on April 8, 1918, as Elizabeth Anne Bloomer, the daughter of a salesman and his wife. She attended Bennington College for two years before her first marriage and was a model and a dancer with the **Martha Graham** Concert Group. After marrying Gerald Ford and raising her family, she followed Ford to Washington, where he served in Congress, became vice president, and then president when Richard Nixon resigned. Shortly after becoming First Lady, Ford discovered that she had breast cancer. She underwent a radical mastectomy and chemotherapy, but because of her frankness in facing cancer and telling about it, she probably saved many other women from the disease. While later suffering a pinched nerve and spinal arthritis, she began to depend on medication and alcohol for pain relief. She discussed this trauma in her second autobiography, the proceeds of which supported the Betty Ford Center for chemical dependency recovery. She has received both credit and reproach in public life for saying what she thinks appropriate rather than using prepared, politically proper texts. Among her honors are the *Newsweek* and *Ladies' Home Journal* woman of the year, the Media Award for Communication of Hope from the American Cancer Society, and the Alfred P. Sloan, Jr., Memorial Award.

BIBLIOGRAPHY

Cassiday, Bruce. *Betty Ford: Woman of Courage.* New York: Dale, 1978. 0–89559–116–2, 162p. This popular biography of Ford views her courage both privately and publicly.
Ford, Betty. *The Times of My Life.* New York: Harper and Row, 1978. 0–06–011298–0, 302p. Ford's readable autobiography is an honest account of her personal life.

FORNÉS, MARÍA IRENE (1930–)
Dramatist   Havana, Cuba

Latina American María Fornés is one of America's leading contemporary playwrights and producers. She was born on May 14, 1930, to a Cuban government employee who believed his six daughters should be educated. He tutored them at home but died when Fornés was 15, and her mother took the family to New York, where Fornés began working in a factory to help support them. She learned English well enough to translate, and in 1951, she became a naturalized citizen. She began to pursue painting in Europe, but after she returned to New York as a fabric designer, she realized that her interest was writing. For her first published play, she received a John Hay Whitney Foundation fellowship in 1961. Her first work to be produced on stage debuted in San Francisco during 1963, and in 1965, she won her first of six Obie Awards (off-Broadway theater award). While writing nearly 40 plays, including several musicals, she has also taught and tried to help young Latino writers find a place in the theater. Many of her plays contain feminist themes and strong advocacy for the rights of women. She has received other honors including the American Academy and Institute of Arts and Letters Award.

BIBLIOGRAPHY

Kent, Assunta Bartolomucci. *María Irene Fornés and Her Critics.* Westport, CT: Greenwood Press, 1996. 0–313–29735–5, 230p. Kent emphasizes the key themes that Fornés repeats in her work and overviews her life.
Moroff, Diane Lynn. *Fornés: Theater in the Present Tense.* Ann Arbor: University of Michigan Press, 1996. 0–472–10726–7, 155p. Moroff's critical biography analyzes Fornés's 30 years in the theater.

FORTEN (GRIMKÉ), CHARLOTTE L. (1837–1914)
Educator and Activist   Philadelphia, Pennsylvania

African American Charlotte Grimké was a poet, educator, and civil rights advocate. She was born on August 17, 1837, into a wealthy family of abolitionists. After attending a school where she was the only nonwhite among 200 students, she continued her education at Salem's Normal School, where her antislavery activities increased. Among the speakers she heard were Ralph Waldo Emerson, Henry Ward Beecher, and William Lloyd Garrison. Although she accepted a position teaching at Epes Grammar School, her recurring tuberculosis caused her to return to Philadelphia, where she developed her poetic skills. Her writing began to appear in antislavery periodicals, although she published elsewhere on other subjects. In her desire to help slaves during the Civil War, she took a post teaching in Georgia's Sea Islands for two years. She also wrote about these experiences, and her work revealed to skeptical Northerners that the people she taught were eager to learn and to work. Among her posts during the war was clerk at the U.S. Treasury Department, one of 15 selected from 500 applicants. After marriage in 1878, she lived with her minister husband first in Jacksonville, Florida, and then in Washington, DC, while persistently advocating African American civil rights.

BIBLIOGRAPHY

Douty, Esther. *Charlotte Forten, Free Black Teacher.* Champaign, IL: Garrard, 1971. 0-8116-4512-6, 144p. This biography for young adults gives an overview of Forten Grimké's life and career.
Forten, Charlotte L. *The Journals of Charlotte Forten Grimké.* Ed. Brenda Stevenson. New York: Oxford University Press, 1988. 0-19-505238-2, 609p. Forten Grimké kept five journals which reveal her life and thoughts.
Longsworth, Polly. *I, Charlotte Forten, Black and Free.* 1953. New York: Crowell, 1970. No ISBN, 288p. This biography for young adults presents Forten Grimké and her work.

FOSSEY, DIAN (1932–1985)
Primatologist   San Francisco, California

Dian Fossey was a zoologist who became the leading authority on mountain gorillas. She was born January 16, 1932, as the only child of an insurance agent and a fashion model who divorced when Fossey was six. Her stepfather showed little affection and allowed Fossey to have only a goldfish as a pet. At San Jose State University, she became a prize-winning equestrian, and after graduation went to Kentucky to be near horses. George Schaller's book *The Mountain Gorilla: Ecology and Behavior* enticed Fossey to Africa to see the animals in their homeland. She met Louis Leakey, and three years later, he and the National Geographic Society began funding her study of the mountain gorilla. After visiting *Jane Goodall to learn some of her techniques, Fossey set up camp in Zaire. A civil war erupted, and when she reassembled her camp in Rwanda, she discovered that the government did not enforce laws against poachers. While trying to protect the gorillas from extinction, she studied 51 gorillas in four family groups, learning their sounds and behavior. She felt successful when one of the gorillas eventually touched her hand. To secure future research funding, Fossey earned a Ph.D. in zoology from Cambridge University in 1974. A national news broadcast brought her donations, but health problems intervened. As a visiting associate professor at Cornell University for three years, she completed her book, *Gorillas in the Mist*. When she returned to the Karisoke Research Center in Rwanda in 1983, she actively battled the poachers, and people speculate that they murdered her.

BIBLIOGRAPHY

Hayes, Harold. *The Dark Romance of Dian Fossey*. New York: Simon and Schuster, 1990. 0-671-63339-2, 351p. Hayes's biography of Fossey shows the heroic and the fanatic in her personality.

Montgomery, Sy. *Walking with the Great Apes: Jane Goodall, Dian Fossey, Birute Galdikas*. Boston: Houghton Mifflin, 1991. 0-395-51597-1, 280p. In a collective biography, Montgomery discusses Fossey's contribution to science.

Mowat, Farley. *Woman in the Mists: The Story of Dian Fossey and the Mountain Gorillas of Africa*. New York: Warner, 1987. 0-446-51360-1, 380p. Using Fossey's diaries and personal archives, Mowat re-creates her life.

FOSTER, ABBY KELLEY (1810–1887)
Reformer   Pelham, Massachusetts

Abby Kelley Foster was a feminist, abolitionist, and lecturer. She was born on January 15, 1810, as one of six girls in a family of seven to a yeoman Quaker and his second wife. She early developed her independence, and after attending a Friends School, she began teaching in Lynn, Massachusetts. There she read about abolitionism in William Lloyd Garrison's *Liberator* and shared with **Angelina Emily** and **Sarah Moore Grimké** a commitment to abolition and a belief in helping others. In 1838, she made her first public address before a mixed audience, and she was so successful that Theodore Weld encouraged her to become an abolitionist lecturer. She thoughtfully agreed and spoke on nonresistance, the role of women, abusive language, and political action. For 15 years, she traveled and lectured constantly, influencing such people as **Lucy Stone** and **Susan B. Anthony**. Others abhorred her message, calling her "Jezebel" and pelting her with rotten eggs. In the 1840s, she met Stephen Foster, a New Hampshire radical who wanted to destroy all proslavery churches; they married and lectured together. After the birth of a child, Foster at first stayed home but soon returned to the lecture circuit, advocating temperance and women's rights. After the Civil War, Foster and her husband refused to pay taxes on their farm, but friends purchased it at public auction and returned it to them.

BIBLIOGRAPHY

Bacon, Margaret Hope. *I Speak for My Slave Sister: The Life of Abby Kelley Foster*. New York: Crowell, 1974. 0-690-00515-6, 235p. This well-researched, documented, balanced biography of Foster, based on letters and other primary sources, emphasizes her renown during her lifetime.

Morin, Isobel V. *Women Who Reformed Politics*. Minneapolis: Oliver Press, 1994. 1-88150-816-1, 160p. In a collective biography for young adults, Morin examines Foster's work to overcome inequities.

Sterling, Dorothy. *Ahead of Her Time: Abby Kelley and the Politics of Anti-Slavery*. 1991. New York: Norton, 1994. 0-393-31131-7, 436p. Careful research from original sources helps Sterling reveal the contributions that Foster made to the abolitionist and woman suffrage movements.

FOSTER JODIE (1962–)
Actor, Film Director, and Producer   Los Angeles, California

Jodie Foster is an award-winning actor, film director, and producer. She was born Alicia Christian Foster on November 19, 1962, the youngest of four children, and was raised by her divorced mother. She began reading at age three, and at four, she made her professional acting debut in a Coppertone suntan oil commercial. She continued working in television, and after beginning films in 1972, she played an impressive role as a young prostitute in *Taxi Driver* for which she received several awards. Determined that Foster would be bilingual, her mother sent her to the Lycée Français in Los Angeles where she graduated as class valedictorian before attending Yale and graduating magna cum laude in literature in 1985. In 1986, she co-produced a film, and in 1988, she won an Academy Award, the National Board of Review Award for Best Actress, and the Golden Globe Award for *The Accused*. In 1991, she made her directing debut in *Little Man Tate*. The same year, she won an Academy Award and several other awards for *The Silence of the Lambs*. In 1992, her company, Egg Pictures, made a deal for her to choose her own projects, and the first, *Nell*, won her a fourth Academy Award nomination and the Screen Actors Guild Award. Other awards include the first annual Arthur Knight Excellence in Filmmaking Award for Special Achievement in Directing and Acting and an honorary degree from Yale.

BIBLIOGRAPHY

Chunovic, Louis. *Jodie: A Biography*. Chicago: Contemporary, 1995. 0-8092-3404-1, 200p. In this balanced researched and documented biography of Foster, Chunovic covers her life and career.

Foster, Buddy. *Foster Child: A Biography of Jodie Foster*. New York: Dutton, 1997. 0-525-94143-6, 278p. Foster's brother has written a biography trying to correct media stories about her.

Kennedy, Philippa. *Jodie Foster: A Life on Screen*. New York: Carol, 1996. 1-55972-348-3, 211p. This undocumented popular biography of Foster covers her achievements in film.

FRANKENTHALER, HELEN (1928–)
Artist   New York, New York

Helen Frankenthaler is an artist. She was born on December 12, 1928, the third daughter of an affluent New York State Supreme Court justice and his wife. She enjoyed many cultural advantages, and at the age of nine, won her first prize in an art contest. Frankenthaler's father died when she was 11, but she continued her art work, studying with the Mexican painter Rufino Tamayo in high school, and then graduating from Bennington College in 1949. She admired the work of Arshile Gorky and Jackson Pollock and joined a group of Abstract Expressionists. After her first one-woman show in 1951, she began using thinned oils soaked into raw canvas. Critics call her work using this medium, *Mountains and Sea*, one of the landmark paintings in contemporary art. Her method became known as the stain technique, and it signaled the beginning of color field painting. Frankenthaler began to exhibit frequently in the 1950s and 1960s when she shifted to acrylics and experimented with the rectangular shape of the canvas, sometimes creating borders. While married to painter Robert Motherwell in the 1960s and 1970s, she began overlapping layers of color and using Cubist ideas of space. To create her texture and unusual color combinations with the paint on large canvases, Frankenthaler uses sponges, mops, and squeegees. Although other techniques have developed in color field painting, Frankenthaler has retained her own style, and critics have admired her canvases for their emotional and lyrical quality.

BIBLIOGRAPHY
Elderfield, John. *Frankenthaler*. New York: Abrams, 1989. 0–8109–0916–2, 448p. Elderfield interviewed Frankenthaler and analyzed her work for his critical study.
Harrison, Pegram. *Frankenthaler: A Catalogue Raisonné*. New York: Abrams, 1996. 0–8109–3332–2, 510p. After an explanation of Frankenthaler's printmaking technique, Harrison examines her work from 1961 to 1994 in a thoroughly researched and documented text with plates and notes on 235 of her prints.
Rose, Barbara. *Frankenthaler*. New York: Abrams, 1971. 0–8109–0126–9, 272p. In this carefully researched and documented look at Frankenthaler's life and work, Rose has included 205 plates and photographs.

FRANKLIN, ARETHA (1942–)
Entertainer   Memphis, Tennessee

Aretha Franklin, a gospel and blues singer-composer, has been called the "Queen of Soul." She was born on March 25, 1942, to a well-known revivalist preacher who attracted many African American singers to his Detroit church, including **Mahalia Jackson**. Franklin's mother was also a gospel singer, but she left the family when Franklin was young and died soon after. Instead of studying piano, Franklin listened to records and taught herself. She made her first recording at age 12, but when she had a child at 15 and another two years later, her career almost ended. Franklin's grandmother, however, helped her with the children while she performed on the gospel and "chitlin" circuits, singing a combination of gospel, jazz, and blues. Franklin initially recorded for Columbia in 1960, but not until 1967, with the release of "I Never Loved a Man," "Baby, I Love You," and "Respect," did she become a major singer. She performed at the funeral of Martin Luther King, Jr., in 1968 and at the inaugurations of President Jimmy Carter in 1977 and President Bill Clinton in 1993. She appeared in the film *The Blues Brothers* in 1980 and has made several television specials. She has 15 Grammy Awards, won every year between 1967 and 1974, and a Lifetime Achievement Award. Other awards include induction into the Rock and Roll Hall of Fame and a declaration as one of Michigan's "natural resources."

BIBLIOGRAPHY

Bego, Mark. *Aretha Franklin, the Queen of Soul.* New York: St. Martin's, 1989. 0-312-02863-6, 340p. Bego interviewed Franklin and others in preparation for his thorough and balanced but undocumented biography.

Sheafer, Silvia Anne. *Aretha Franklin: Motown Superstar.* Springfield, NJ: Enslow, 1996. 0-89490-686-0, 128p. Sheafer's young adult biography of Franklin relies on critical reviews.

FREEMAN, MARY WILKINS (1852–1930)
Author   **Randolph, Massachusetts**

Mary Eleanor Wilkins Freeman, a writer, described life in New England. She was born on October 31, 1852, as one of four children to a housewright who failed at a dry goods business that his wife encouraged him to pursue. The family lived in near poverty, but Freeman attended Mount Holyoke Female Seminary, leaving after a year because she disliked it. In her twenties, she began to write verse and children's stories. After the deaths of her parents in 1880 and 1883, she began writing seriously to support herself. *Harper's Bazaar* published several of her adult stories and helped establish her reputation in the United States, England, and Europe. To escape the intensity of a small-town social code, she often visited friends and relatives, and on one of these trips she met and married a man seven years younger than herself. In 1902, they moved to New Jersey where Freeman wrote for the next 21 years. Her husband became an alcoholic in the later years of their marriage, and Freeman obtained a legal separation from him. Her awards include the Howells Medal of the American Academy of Arts and Letters.

BIBLIOGRAPHY

Glasser, Leah Blatt. *In a Closet Hidden: The Life and Work of Mary E. Wilkins Freeman.* Amherst: University of Massachusetts Press, 1996. 1-55849-027-2, 266p. In her literary biography, Glasser analyzes Freeman's life and work.

FRÉMONT, JESSIE BENTON (1824–1902)
Author   Cherry Grove, Virginia

Jessie Benton Frémont, an author, helped write reports of the West that encouraged expansionism in the United States. Born on May 31, 1824, she was one of five children of a senator from Missouri and his wife. Educated first by private tutors, she learned French and Spanish, played the piano, and studied the classics before briefly attending a finishing school. Growing up in Washington's political climate and often serving as her father's hostess during her mother's illnesses, Frémont understood the diversity of politics at a young age. She fell in love with an impoverished and illegitimate explorer, a guest in her father's home, and secretly married him when only 17, although he was 11 years older. Frémont's father blessed the marriage, however, and she encouraged her husband's exploration of the West that the government supported. She edited his first expedition report in 1842 , and its lively, readable text made him and his guide, Kit Carson, heroes. Readers compared their exploits to those of Defoe's Robinson Crusoe. The Senate published 10,000 copies of a second report, and when commercially released, it became an important influence for western settlement. Frémont's husband was then elected senator from California. When his term ended, they visited England to raise money for gold mine development, finding that the British, having read their reports, clamored to meet them. In 1856 Frémont bolstered her husband's unsuccessful campaign as the first Republican candidate for president. During the Civil War, she helped establish the sanitary commission, raised funds, and recruited volunteers for hospitals in the West. In the 1870s, when Frémont's husband went bankrupt, she supported the family by publishing articles in *Harper's*, the *Century*, *New York Ledger*, and *Wide Awake*. Later she collected her best work for several books and worked on her husband's memoirs. Not until her husband began receiving military retiree pay two months before his death did they regain financial security. Frémont spent the remainder of her life in Los Angeles writing articles and her memoirs.

BIBLIOGRAPHY

Herr, Pamela. *Jessie Benton Frémont: A Biography*. New York: Franklin Watts, 1987. 0-531-15011-9, 496p. Herr's thoroughly researched, readable, and balanced biography of Frémont examines the Victorian constraints on her life.

Herr, Pamela, and Mary Lee, eds. *The Letters of Jessie Benton Frémont*. Urbana: University of Illinois Press, 1993. 0-252-01942-3, 595p. The editors have identified seven key periods in Frémont's life and grouped 271 letters accordingly.

Morrison, Dorothy Nafus. *Under a Strong Wind: The Adventures of Jessie Benton Frémont*. New York: Atheneum, 1983. 0-689-31004-8, 176p. In a readable, researched biography for young adults, Morrison discusses Frémont's life.

Phillips, Catherine Coffin. *Jessie Benton Frémont: A Woman Who Made History*. Ed. Christine Bold. Lincoln: University of Nebraska Press, 1995. 0-8032-8740-2, 361p. Phillips knew Frémont when she lived in Los Angeles, and she used private letters, newspaper clippings, and interviews with confidantes to illuminate her life.

Rather, Lois. *Jessie Frémont at Black Point.* Oakland, CA: Rather Press, 1974. No ISBN, 108p. A brief overview of Frémont's life precedes an examination of the time she lived at Black Point in San Francisco.

FRIEDAN, BETTY (1921–)
Activist and Author   Peoria, Illinois

Betty Friedan published *The Feminine Mystique* in 1963, exploring the frustrations of modern women remaining in traditional roles. She was born Naomi Goldstein on February 4, 1921, one of three children of an uneducated but wealthy businessman father whose younger wife had given up a career in journalism. Friedan graduated Phi Beta Kappa from Smith College in 1942 and attended graduate school at the University of California at Berkeley until marrying in 1947 and moving to New York City's suburbs to raise her three children. When she was fired as a newspaper reporter in the early 1960s after requesting a second maternity leave, she realized that male editors wanted women's lives to seem idyllic, and Friedan reported these attitudes and others in *The Feminine Mystique*. She showed women that their feelings of uselessness as housewives trying to fulfill their husband's desires were not unique, and her book's success rocketed the feminist movement into the public eye. As an instant leader of the women's movement, Friedan founded the National Organization for Women (NOW) and served as its president until 1970. After her divorce, she began teaching, lecturing, and writing columns and articles. In 1973, she helped to organize the First Women's Bank, and in 1974, the Economic Think Tank for Women. She wrote *The Second Stage* in 1981, and in 1983, she published *The Fountain of Age,* in which she challenges stereotypes of aging in America. Among the awards and honorary degrees she has received are the Humanist of the Year, the **Eleanor Roosevelt** Leadership Award, and election to The National Women's Hall of Fame.

BIBLIOGRAPHY
Henry, Sondra, and Emily Taitz. *Betty Friedan, Fighter for Women's Rights.* Hillside, NJ: Enslow, 1990. 0-89490-292-X, 128p. Henry and Taitz discuss Friedan's early life and subsequent career.

FULLER, LOIE (1862–1928)
Dancer   Fullersburg, Illinois

Loie Fuller was a dancer who won international acclaim for her lighting techniques and her invention of the serpentine dance. She was born Marie Louise on January 15, 1862, to a farmer and fiddler at public dances and his wife. Fuller gave her first performance at age two and a half at a Spiritualist Sunday School that the family attended. She made a debut with a Chicago stock company when a child, and at 15, she toured as a Shakespearean reader and actor. By 1883, she had been cast in a Broadway play, and in 1886, she appeared in the title role of a burlesque at the Bijou Theater. She organized her own tour, but it collapsed, placing her and her backer in debt. Her first appearance as a dancer occurred in 1891. When she needed a costume for a scene involving hypnotism, she ran through a green light in a skirt of flowing transparent china silk. Realizing that the audience appreciated the effect, she experimented with different colors and created a dance scene to correspond to the changes of light. The "serpentine dance" became a hit, and she took her act to Berlin and then to Paris, where she engaged the Folies Bergère in October 1892. Among the artists who wanted to paint or sculpt her movements were Toulouse-Lautrec, Auguste Rodin, and Jules Cheret. When she danced at the Paris Exposition of 1900, her use of draperies and lighting influenced **Ruth St. Denis** and interested **Isadora Duncan**. Fuller remained in Europe, continuing to expand her use of light, including luminous phosphorescent materials on a dark stage, in such creations as *Fire Dance* and *Shadow Ballet*. Fuller performed for the Allied troops during World War I and won decorations from the French, Belgian, and Rumanian governments. Her last appearance was in London in 1927.

BIBLIOGRAPHY

Current, Richard Nelson, and Marcia Ewing Current. *Loie Fuller, Goddess of Light*. Boston: Northeastern University Press, 1997. 1–55553–309–4, 400p. The authors reveal Fuller's life and career in their carefully researched, definitive biography.
Fuller, Loie. *Fifteen Years of a Dancer's Life*. 1913. New York: Dance Horizons, 1978. 0–87127–066–8, 288p. In her autobiography, Fuller discusses the people she knew.

FULLER (OSSOLI), MARGARET (1810–1850)
Activist and Author   Cambridgeport, Massachusetts

Margaret Fuller (Ossoli) was a social activist, critic, and author. She was born on May 23, 1810, as Sarah Margaret, the first of nine children of a Harvard-educated lawyer and politician and a mother who had been a teacher. Disappointed that Fuller was not a male, her father educated her as he would a son and had her reading English at five, and Latin and Greek at six. At 12, she read French and Italian, in addition to Shakespeare, Cervantes, and Molière. The effort of such study almost wrecked her health, and she attended a school with males including Oliver Wendell Holmes and Richard Henry Dana. At 22, she studied German and was soon translating Goethe and Schiller. After her father's death, Fuller started teaching, first at Bronson Alcott's Temple Street School, and then in Providence, Rhode Island. She began conducting conversations for women on a variety of topics, and from 1840 to 1842, she edited *The Dial*. In 1845, she published *Woman in the Nineteenth Century*, condemning women's social roles, and men lampooned her ideas, with Edgar Allan Poe saying that the world could be divided into three categories, "men, women, and Margaret Fuller." Fuller began to mistrust the benefits of American government when she saw Native American horrors and poverty, and she went to Europe where she embraced socialism and its endorsement of equality for all. There she met the younger Marchese Giovanni

Angelo Ossoli and had his son before secretly marrying him. They died in a shipwreck while returning to the United States. She was elected to The National Women's Hall of Fame.

BIBLIOGRAPHY

Balducci, Carolyn. *Margaret Fuller: A Life of Passion and Defiance.* New York: Bantam, 1991. 0-553-08123-3, 209p. Balducci's young adult biography reveals the unconventional Fuller.

Capper, Charles. *Margaret Fuller: An American Romantic Life.* New York: Oxford University Press, 1992. 0-19-504579-3, 2 vols. Capper's definitive two-volume biography uses letters, diaries, and journals to re-create Fuller's life.

Dickenson, Donna. *Margaret Fuller: Writing a Woman's Life.* New York: St. Martin's, 1993. 0-312-09145-1, 247p. This biography, based on letters, shows that Fuller's interpretation of her life differed greatly from that of males who wrote about her.

Kornfeld, Eve. *Margaret Fuller: A Brief Biography with Documents.* Boston: Bedford, 1997. 0-312-16387-8, 252p. Kornfeld's well-researched and carefully documented biography of Fuller employs feminist and poststructuralist theory.

Von Mehren, Joan. *Minerva and the Muse: A Life of Margaret Fuller.* Amherst: University of Massachusetts Press, 1994. 0-8702-3941-4, 398p. Von Mehren's scholarly, well-researched biography reveals Fuller's intelligence.

FURBISH, KATE (1834–1931)
Botanist **Exeter, New Hampshire**

While gathering flora specimens throughout the state of Maine and painting them, Kate Furbish discovered several plants, two of which were named for her. She was born Catharine Furbish on May 19, 1834, as the oldest of six children to a hardware store owner and his wife. The family moved to Maine when Furbish was one, and while attending schools near her home, she began to study plants under her father's tutelage. She later attended art schools in Portland and Boston and briefly studied in Paris but returned to Brunswick, Maine, to spend her life. After attending botany lectures in the 1860s, she began to collect and classify Maine's flora, and to create watercolor drawings of them. She traveled by hay wagon, mail stage, and boat over mountains and through bogs to gather and record plant specimens. During her career, she published articles in the *American Naturalist* and lectured, but the main display of her "children" occurred in her 14-volume work, *Flora of Maine.* For it, Furbish collected over 4,000 plant specimens, including 182 ferns, and produced approximately 1,300 sketches. She was technically an amateur, but her scientific approach made her the botanist for whom the *Pedicularis furbishiae* and *Aster cordifolius*, variation *furbishiae*, were named. She worked throughout her life, refining her paintings and donating specimens and drawings to Bowdoin College and the New England Botanical Club, now housed at Harvard.

BIBLIOGRAPHY

Graham, Ada. *Kate Furbish and the Flora of Maine.* Gardiner, ME: Tilbury House, 1995. 0-88448-175-1, 161p. Furbish's journals, correspondence, and watercolors of Maine's flowers helped Graham create a carefully researched and readable biography.

G

GARLAND, JUDY (1922–1969)
Entertainer and Actor   **Grand Rapids, Minnesota**

Judy Garland was a singer and actor. She was born Frances Gumm on June 10, 1922, the daughter of vaudeville performers. At three, she made her stage debut and toured with her siblings, the Gumm Sisters, before she made her first film in 1936. In 1937, she began a partnership with Mickey Rooney, appearing in several films with him. Her role in *The Wizard of Oz* won her international fame and a special Academy Award. Musical roles followed including *For Me and My Gal* (1942), *Meet Me in St. Louis* (1944), and *Easter Parade* (1948). During the last 15 years of her life, Garland had serious mental health problems, although she played to full houses when she returned to the stage several times. Her performances in *A Star Is Born*, for which she received the Golden Globe Award, and in *A Child Is Waiting* won critical acclaim. In 1961, she received the Cecil B. De Mille Award for her career achievement, and in 1997 a posthumous Grammy for Lifetime Achievement Award. She married five times and had three children; one was entertainer **Liza Minnelli.**

BIBLIOGRAPHY
Fricke, John. *Judy Garland: World's Greatest Entertainer*. New York: Holt, 1992. 0–8050–1738–0, 256p. Fricke bases his laudatory biography of Garland on her colleagues' reminiscences and contemporary critiques.
Meyer, John. *Heartbreaker*. Garden City, NY: Doubleday, 1983. 0–385–18421–2, 322p. As Garland's lover before she died, Meyer remembers the many imbalances in her life.

Nestor, Basil. *Judy*. New York: MetroBooks, 1997. 1-56799-436-9, 96p. While exploring the vulnerability of Garland's persona, Nestor also examines her distaste for restrictions.

Shipman, David. *Judy Garland: The Secret Life of an American Legend*. New York: Hyperion, 1993. 1-56282-846-0, 540p. Shipman used other biographies and information to expand on Garland's supposed bisexuality.

Vare, Ethlie Ann, ed. *Icon: The Myth Life of Judy Garland*. New York: Boulevard Books, 1998. 1-57297-334-X, 221p. Vare's collection of essays provides a readable overview of Garland's life.

GIBSON, ALTHEA (1927-)
Athlete   Silver, South Carolina

Althea Gibson was the first African American to win either the Wimbledon or the United States singles championship in tennis. She was born August 25, 1927, the oldest of five children. Her father moved the family to Harlem when Gibson was three, but she fled from her family when a teenager. After her athletic ability surfaced when she won Police Athletic League and Parks Department competitions, musician Buddy Walker gave her a tennis racket and took her to play on local courts. She won her first tennis tournament in 1942 and played the season without a loss until the girls' singles finals of the American Tennis Association (ATA). For 10 years, from 1947 to 1956, she won the ATA women's singles titles and established herself as the best African American tennis player. During this time, she attended and graduated from Florida Agricultural and Mechanical University. Among those who helped her were Sugar Ray Robinson and Alice Marble, who thought that Gibson should be allowed to play tennis in the United States Open tournament regardless of her skin color. In 1950, Gibson competed at Forest Hills, and the next year she became the first African American woman to play at Wimbledon, winning in 1957 and 1958. In 1957, she also won at Forest Hills. She retired in 1959, and after four years returned to professional sports, playing golf until 1967. In 1975, she became the athletic director of the state of New Jersey. Among her honors were being named the Associated Press Woman Athlete of the Year and induction into the Lawn Tennis Hall of Fame and the Black Athletes Hall of Fame.

BIBLIOGRAPHY

Biracree, Tom. *Althea Gibson*. New York: Chelsea House, 1989. 1-55546-654-0, 107p. Biracree used Gibson's journal as a source to illuminate her life and career in his biography for young adults.

Davidson, Sue. *Changing the Game: The Stories of Tennis Champions Alice Marble and Althea Gibson*. Seattle: Seal Press, 1997. 1-878067-88-5, 180p. In a dual biography for young adults, Davidson emphasizes Gibson's achievements and Marble's encouragement.

Gibson, Althea. *So Much to Live For*. New York: Putnam, 1968. No ISBN, 160p. Gibson discusses her life and reasons for retiring from tennis in an autobiography suitable for young adults.

GILBRETH, LILLIAN (1878–1972)
Industrial Engineer   Oakland, California

Lillian Evelyn Moller Gilbreth was a pioneer in the field of time and motion studies. Born on May 24, 1878, she was the first of eight children to survive of a wealthy hardware business owner and his wife. Gilbreth grew up in Oakland, California, where her family moved soon after her birth, and tutors educated her before she entered Oakland schools. Her mother's illnesses added the burden of childcare to Gilbreth's day, but she still had opportunities to travel and to pursue her interests of poetry and music. Her parents at first opposed her enrolling at the University of California at Berkeley, but they acquiesced, and she became the first female to deliver the commencement address when she graduated. She attended Columbia briefly but returned to California to finish her M.A. En route to Europe, Gilbreth met her chaperone's cousin, one of Boston's leading building contractors, and after they married in 1904, she helped him study the attributes of motion. In the next 17 years, Gilbreth had 12 children, edited her husband's publications, completed a Ph.D. in psychology at Brown University, and published her book, *Psychology of Management*. The Gilbreths tried to find the best way to accomplish a task with the least exertion by studying each part of the process using motion pictures. They lectured widely, established a laboratory in their home, and wrote several books. When her husband died in 1924, Gilbreth applied their techniques to the home and reported her research in *Good Housekeeping*, *Better Homes & Gardens*, and two books. She accepted a professional appointment to Purdue University and helped establish a time and motion laboratory on campus. She also developed a model kitchen at the New York University Medical Center's Institute of Rehabilitation. Her volunteer work included the Girl Scouts, her church, her library, and several national committees. The Society of Industrial Engineers created the Gilbreth Medal in 1931 (named for her husband) and selected her as the first recipient. Among many other awards were honorary membership (not open to women) in the Society of Industrial Engineers, the Hoover Medal, and election to The National Women's Hall of Fame.

BIBLIOGRAPHY
Gilbreth, Frank B., and Ernestine Gilbreth Carey. *Belles on Their Toes*. New York: Crowell, 1950. No ISBN, 237p. Gilbreth's children wrote this loving biography.
Gilbreth, Lillian Moller. *As I Remember*. Norcross, GA: Engineering and Management Press, 1998. 0–89806–186–5, 256p. Gilbreth remembers the people and experiences that influenced her life.
Graham, Laurel. *Managing on Her Own: Dr. Lillian Gilbreth and Women's Work in the Interwar Era*. Norcross, GA: Engineering and Management Press, 1998. 0–89806–185–7, 288p. Graham used primary sources to examine Gilbreth's life after the death of her husband.
Yost, Edna. *Frank and Lillian Gilbreth, Partners for Life*. New Brunswick, NJ: Rutgers University Press, 1949. No ISBN, 372p. Yost knew the Gilbreths, and in her

biography, she tries to offer a balanced account of their unusual but complementary partnership.

GILMAN, CHARLOTTE PERKINS (1860–1935)
Author   Hartford, Connecticut

Charlotte Anna Perkins Stetson Gilman was a theorist for the women's movement and an author. She was born on July 3, 1860, as one of four children to a librarian and magazine editor who left his wife soon after Gilman's birth. He provided little support for the children, and Gilman lived in poverty, moving 19 times in 18 years, while her mother worked and sought refuge with relatives. Gilman had limited schooling but supported herself while a teenager as a commercial artist and governess. She eschewed traditional roles for women by exercising, practicing self-denial, and engaging in private philosophical arguments. In 1884, she married, but became depressed and moved to California without her husband in 1888. She began writing to support herself, her daughter, and her mother. In 1892, she published "The Yellow Wall-Paper," a story in which the female protagonist becomes mentally unstable after her physician husband confines her to the bedroom. Two years later, Gilman briefly edited a woman's journal. Lecture fees speaking to various groups on labor reform, women's rights, and social organization were her main income. In 1896, she went to London as a delegate to the International Socialist and Labor Congress, meeting *Beatrice Webb and George Bernard Shaw. In 1898, she published *Women and Economics*, a feminist tract that argued for female economic independence, a condition more radical than suffrage. She married her first cousin in 1900, and a friend kept house while Gilman actively supported women's rights and pacifism. Gilman gained the reputation of being the most intellectual member of the woman's movement during her lifetime. She was elected to The National Women's Hall of Fame.

BIBLIOGRAPHY

Ceplair, Larry, ed. *Charlotte Perkins Gilman: A Nonfiction Reader*. New York: Columbia University Press, 1991. 0-231-07616-9, 345p. Ceplair reveals Gilman as a radical thinker on many subjects.

Gilman, Charlotte Perkins. *The Living of Charlotte Perkins Gilman: An Autobiography*. 1935. Madison: University of Wisconsin Press, 1991. 0-299-12740-0, 341p. In her autobiography, Gilman discusses her unhappy childhood, her failure as a mother and wife, and her social activism.

Hill, Mary Armfield. *Charlotte Perkins Gilman: The Making of a Radical Feminist, 1860–1896*. Philadelphia: Temple University Press, 1980. 0-87722-160-X, 362p. Using Gilman's unpublished diaries and letters, Hill reveals her early life.

Kessler, Carol Farley. *Charlotte Perkins Gilman: Her Progress Toward Utopia*. New York: Syracuse University Press, 1995. 0-8156-2644-4, 316p. Kessler examines Gilman's writing and life in terms of utopia.

Lane, Ann J. *To Herland and Beyond: The Life and Work of Charlotte Perkins Gilman*. New York: Pantheon, 1990. 0-394-50559-X, 413p. Lane illuminates Gilman's life through her relationships in a carefully researched biography.

GILPIN, LAURA (1891–1979)
Photographer and Author   Aurora Bluffs, Colorado

Laura Gilpin was the most acclaimed female photographer of Native Americans and Southwestern landscapes. She was born on April 22, 1891, one of two surviving children of an unsuccessful rancher father and an intellectual mother. Her parents gave her a Brownie camera when she was 12, and the next year she became the "eyes" for her mother's blind friend at the St. Louis World's Fair, learning the value of detail as she described the scenes both verbally and visually with her camera. In 1905, Gilpin's mother took her and her brother to New York, where **Gertrude Käsebier** photographed them, and Gilpin's early style emulated Käsebier's pictorialist mode. Gilpin attended boarding schools in Connecticut and Pennsylvania and studied violin at the New England Conservatory of Music. She then won an award from *American Photographer* magazine, and to earn money for training at the Clarence H. White School of Photography, she managed a poultry business. In Colorado following the 1918–1919 influenza pandemic, she opened a studio for portrait commissions and began exhibiting her work. Her western landscapes, revealing her belief that "design is the fundamental of everything," earned her a solid reputation. In the mid-1920s, she began using clearer focus on her images and started photographing the Navahos in some of her best work. Before World War II, when she supported the war effort by working with Boeing as a public relations photographer, she began composing her photographic books. To capture the best lighting for her images, she often camped outside, continuing the practice until her death. Her books include *The Pueblos: A Camera Chronicle*; *Temples in Yucatan: A Camera Chronicle of Chichen Itza*; *The Rio Grande: River of Destiny, an Interpretation of the River, the Land, and the People*; and *The Enduring Navaho*. In 1972, the New Mexico Museum of Fine Arts honored her with a major retrospective of her work.

BIBLIOGRAPHY
Sandweiss, Martha A. *Laura Gilpin: An Enduring Grace*. Fort Worth, TX: Amon Carter Museum, 1986. 0–88360–077–3, 339p. Sandweiss includes a thoughtful biographical essay and 127 reproductions in her retrospective of Gilpin's life and career.

GINSBURG, RUTH BADER (1933–)
Supreme Court Justice and Attorney   Brooklyn, New York

Ruth Bader Ginsburg is a Supreme Court justice. She was born on March 15, 1933, into a middle-class family. Her mother wished her to have advantages previously unavailable to females, and after high school, Ginsburg entered Cornell University and graduated Phi Beta Kappa before attending Harvard Law School, where she served on the *Law Review*. She transferred to Columbia Law School when her husband took a job in New York. Although she graduated at the top of her class, law firms refused to hire her, and she served as a law clerk before teaching at Rutgers University Law School and Harvard. When Harvard denied her tenure, she became Columbia's first tenured female professor. During the next years, she won five of the six cases that she argued before the Supreme Court and established the unconstitutionality of unequal treatment for men and women. In 1980, President Jimmy Carter named her to a judgeship on the United States Court of Appeals for the District of Columbia and in 1993, President Bill Clinton appointed her as a justice to the Supreme Court. Among her awards are many honorary degrees.

BIBLIOGRAPHY

Ayer, Eleanor H. *Ruth Bader Ginsburg: Fire and Steel on the Supreme Court*. New York: Dillon, 1994. 0-87518-651-3, 128p. In a biography for young adults, Ayer focuses on Ginsburg's life and career.

Bredeson, Carmen. *Ruth Bader Ginsburg: Supreme Court Justice*. Springfield, NJ: Enslow, 1995. 0-89490-621-6, 128p. In this biography for young adults, Bredeson discusses Ginsburg's law career.

GIOVANNI, NIKKI (1943-)
Poet
                                                                            Knoxville, Tennessee

Nikki Giovanni is an African American poet. She was born Yolande Cornelia Giovanni, Jr., on June 7, 1943, the daughter of a probation officer and a social worker. She says that her grandfather, a Latin scholar, and her mother gave her a sense of storytelling and of pride in her race. She graduated with honors from Fisk University and completed postgraduate study at the University of Pennsylvania and Columbia University. While at Fisk, she worked to reinstate the Student Non-Violent Coordinating Committee (SNCC). She has served as co-chair of the Literary Arts Festival for the State of Tennessee Homecoming, the Ohio Humanities Council, the Virginia Foundation for the Humanities and Public Policy, the Appalachian Community Fund, and the Volunteer Action Center. In 1991, she was the featured poet at the International Poetry Festival in Utrecht, Holland. She has given numerous poetry readings and lectures at universities in the United States and Europe, including at the University of Warsaw, Poland, and has appeared numerous times on television and stage. Among her many awards are grants, a Woman of the Year citation from *Mademoiselle*, and election to the Ohio Women's Hall of Fame.

BIBLIOGRAPHY

Fowler, Virginia C., ed. *Conversations with Nikki Giovanni*. Jackson: University Press of Mississippi, 1992. 0-87805-586-X, 220p. This collection of 27 interviews, spanning 20 years, reveals the evolution of Giovanni's poetry.

Giovanni, Nikki. *Gemini: An Extended Autobiographical Statement on My First Twenty-Five Years of Being a Black Poet*. Indianapolis: Bobbs-Merrill, 1972. No ISBN, 149p. In a collection of essays suitable for young adults Giovanni discusses her poetry and militant attitudes.

————. *A Poetic Equation: Conversations Between Nikki Giovanni and Margaret Walker.* 1974. Washington, DC: Howard University Press, 1983. 0–88258–003–5, 148p. Giovanni discusses her views on various topics with Margaret Walker.

GLASGOW, ELLEN (1873–1945)
Author   Richmond, Virginia

Ellen Anderson Gholson Glasgow was an author whose novels realistically depicted life in Virginia. She was born on April 22, 1873, as the eighth of ten children into a wealthy and socially prominent Virginia family. Her mother influenced her greatly, but Glasgow discounted her father as merely a boorish Calvinist. She wrote her first stories and poems at age seven while in poor health. Her wide reading included the classics, political economy, and social reform, and especially Charles Darwin's *On the Origin of Species*, all of which prepared her to write her own books. She refused a formal debut in Richmond, and after her mother's death when Glasgow was 20, she moved to New York City. When her father died in 1916, she returned to Richmond to enjoy the independence her inheritance made possible. Her first two novels were unsuccessful, and she began writing about a young girl carefully groomed for a society in which she needed little intelligence. Glasgow wanted to describe the society around her—all ages, races, and occupations. In 1925, she gained critical acclaim with *Barren Ground*, and within 10 years, she was considered the "first lady of American fiction." She received several honorary degrees and was elected to the National Institute of Arts and Letters before reaching the pinnacle of the American Academy of Arts and Letters in 1938. In 1940, she received the Howells Medal, and the next year, she won the Pulitzer Prize for *In This Our Life*.

BIBLIOGRAPHY
Glasgow, Ellen Anderson Gholson. *The Woman Within: An Autobiography.* 1954. Charlottesville: University Press of Virginia, 1994. 0–8139–1563–5, 314p. Glasgow's recommended autobiography, first published nine years after her death, reveals her innermost thoughts.

Godbold, E. Stanly. *Ellen Glasgow and the Woman Within.* Baton Rouge: Louisiana State University Press, 1972. 0–8071–0040–4, 322p. Godbold's critical biography of Glasgow, based on letters, documents, interviews, records, and notes, carefully and thoroughly examines her life and work.

Goodman, Susan. *Ellen Glasgow: A Biography.* Baltimore: Johns Hopkins University Press, 1998. 0–8018–5728–7, 328p. Goodman explores Glasgow's life and writing in a well-researched biography.

GOLDBERG, WHOOPI (1950–)
Actor   New York, New York

African American Whoopi Goldberg denies that she is a comedienne, caring instead to be known for her accomplished acting skills. In 1950, she was born in a housing project. She began acting at eight, watched old movies while growing up, and left high school to participate in civil rights demonstrations and to perform in choruses of musicals such as *Hair*, *Jesus Christ Superstar*, and *Pippin*. A brief marriage produced a daughter. In 1974, Goldberg went to San Diego where she helped found the San Diego Repertory Theater, joined an improvisational troupe, and changed her name (which she has since refused to reveal). She supported herself and her daughter working as either a bricklayer or a cosmetician and with public assistance. She developed *The Spook Show*, a one-woman social satire involving four characterizations with which she toured in the United States and Europe. When Mike Nichols saw it, he asked to produce it on Broadway, and the show received mixed reviews. However, her subsequent work in *The Color Purple* gained her an Academy Award nomination, and for the film *Ghost* in 1990 she received an Academy Award, the first African American to win since **Hattie McDaniel** in 1939. Goldberg has also voluntarily founded the Comic Relief benefit shows on television's Home Box Office to help the homeless.

BIBLIOGRAPHY

Goldberg, Whoopi. *Book*. New York: R. Weisbach, 1997. 0–688–15252–X, 240p. Rather than a standard autobiography, Goldberg has written her thoughts on a variety of topics.

GRABLE, BETTY (1916–1973)
Actor   St. Louis, Missouri

Betty Grable was an actor and pinup girl. She was born Elizabeth Ruth Grable on December 18, 1916, to an accountant and stockbroker and his wife. Grable's mother decided that her daughter would be an actor and made her take dancing, singing, acting, and music lessons from the age of four, punishing her for missing a single lesson. After her mother took her to Hollywood without her father, Grable got a small part in a film in 1930 by claiming to be 15, and in 1934, she obtained a small part in *The Gay Divorcee* with Fred Astaire, winning a movie studio contract with her performance. While appearing on Broadway with **Ethel Merman** in 1939, she became a star. When she returned to film, Fox Studios promoted her legs, and when World War II started, men wanted her photograph. Over 3 million men requested pictures, and the studio had to mail over 60,000 in one week alone. Grable's color musicals cast her as an innocent but alluring young woman, like many of the girlfriends soldiers had left behind. Women also liked her because she appeared average and unthreatening. After the war, Grable raised her two daughters (she married and divorced twice), demonstrated her professionalism, and in 1953, starred with **Marilyn Monroe** and **Lauren Bacall** in *How to Marry a Millionaire*. She made one other film and then performed only on stage.

BIBLIOGRAPHY

Billman, Larry. *Betty Grable: A Bio-Bibliography*. Westport, CT: Greenwood Press, 1993. 0–313–28156–4, 306p. Billman's extensive research and interviews with

Grable's friends and co-workers helped him document all phases of her life and career.

McGee, Tom. *Betty Grable: The Girl with the Million Dollar Legs.* Vestal, NY: Vestal Press, 1995. 1-879511-15-0, 416p. McGee's biography reveals Grable as a hard worker who had a sense of humor.

Pastos, Spero. *Pin-up: The Tragedy of Betty Grable.* New York: Putnam, 1986. 0-399-13189-2, 175p. Pastos has carefully researched Grable's life to create a balanced biography.

Warren, Doug. *Betty Grable, the Reluctant Movie Queen.* New York: St. Martin's, 1981. 0-312-07732-7, 237p. A popular but undocumented biography of Grable gives an overview of her life.

GRAHAM, KATHARINE (1917-)
Newspaper Publisher and Businesswoman   **New York, New York**

Katharine Meyer Graham is the owner and publisher of the *Washington Post* and *Newsweek*. She was born on June 16, 1917, the daughter of a publisher and an educator. After living in a wealthy home, she attended Vassar for two years and graduated from the University of Chicago in 1938. She worked for the *San Francisco News* before joining the editorial staff at the *Washington Post* in 1939 and marrying Philip Graham, a law clerk, the next year. Her husband became an associate publisher at the *Post* when he returned from World War II. After he became publisher, Graham's father sold them the newspaper. In 1961, they added *Newsweek* to their company. When Graham's husband committed suicide two years later, she became president of the company, and under her leadership the newspaper's circulation increased. It became an influential national paper, and in 1973, when Graham became chairman of the board and chief executive officer of the *Washington Post* Company, it had achieved even greater prestige. In 1998, Graham won a Pulitzer Prize for her autobiography.

BIBLIOGRAPHY
Davis, Deborah. *Katharine the Great: Katharine Graham and Her Washington Post Empire.* 1979. New York: Sheridan Square Press, 1991. 0-941781-14-3, 344p. After researching for three years, Davis wrote a biography in which she suggested that Graham had a role in controlling government because of her position with the *Washington Post*.

Felsenthal, Carol. *Power, Privilege, and the Post: The Katharine Graham Story.* New York: Putnam, 1993. 0-399-13732-7, 511p. Felsenthal thoroughly examines the background from which Graham came and contrasts it to the woman she became after her husband's suicide.

Graham, Katharine. *Personal History.* New York: Knopf, 1997. 0-394-58585-2, 642p. Graham discusses her unhappy childhood, her marriage to Phil Graham, and her career. Pulitzer Prize.

GRAHAM, MARTHA (1894–1991)
Dancer and Choreographer   Pittsburgh, Pennsylvania

Martha Graham was a dancer, teacher, and choreographer of modern dance. She was born on May 11, 1894, one of three daughters of a physician interested in the bodily expression of human behavior. When the family moved to California, Graham discovered the sea and its rhythms along with Oriental art, and both influenced her choreography. She began her professional career in 1916 at **Ruth St. Denis** and Ted Shawn's school and dance company, Denishawn. Exploring dances from different American cultures and styles and studying dancers such as *Mary Wigman and **Isadora Duncan** prepared her to dance Shawn's Aztec ballet, *Xochitl*, and become a star. She debuted as an independent artist in 1926, with critics first liking her and later condemning her when she used avant-garde music by composers such as Arthur Honegger to stage social protest dances. In 1935, after she began using pieces of sculpture or three-dimensional properties on stage instead of backdrops, the critics became more receptive to her work probing the spiritual and emotional essence of a human being. Near the end of the 1930s, Graham added men to her company, and Erick Hawkins appeared in her *American Document*, a work based on history. Graham also used literature to portray her message in *Letter to the World*, based on **Emily Dickinson**'s letters. One of Graham's most famous works is *Appalachian Spring* (1944), choreographed to the music of Aaron Copland. Her dance technique was the first significant alternative to classical ballet because she expressed universal feelings using forceful movements with muscular contraction rather than merely displaying graceful gestures. She has received numerous awards including the Medal of Freedom and the French Legion of Honor.

BIBLIOGRAPHY
de Mille, Agnes. *Martha: The Life and Work of Martha Graham*. New York: Random, 1991. 0-394-55643-7, 509p. De Mille, Graham's friend for over 60 years, recalls Graham's techniques and imaginative approach to dance as a religious celebration.

Graham, Martha. *Blood Memory*. New York: Doubleday, 1991. 0-385-26503-4, 279p. Graham dwells on the influences in her childhood.

Probosz, Kathilyn Solomon. *Martha Graham*. New York: Dillon Press, 1995. 0-87518-568-1, 184p. Using secondary source materials in her biography for young adults, Probosz describes Graham's youth and influences.

Stodelle, Ernestine. *Deep Song: The Dance Story of Martha Graham*. New York: Schirmer, 1984. 0-02-872520-4, 329p. Stodelle's definitive biography, based on interviews and letters, presents Graham's life and work.

Tracy, Robert. *Goddess: Martha Graham's Dancers Remember*. New York: Limelight Editions, 1997. 0-87910-086-9, 339p. Tracy interviewed 31 dancers who worked with Martha Graham in analyzing her achievements.

GRATZ, REBECCA (1781–1869)
Charity Worker   Lancaster, Pennsylvania

Rebecca Gratz, a charity worker, was considered the "foremost American Jewess of her day." She was born on March 4, 1781, the seventh of twelve children of a Jewish merchant and his wife. Gratz's father supported the Patriots during the American Revolution Gratz attended female academies and read widely in her father's library, including the work of *Grace Aguilar. She also contributed several articles to *Port Folio*, the country's most highly regarded literary magazine at the time. Gratz early showed her interest in charity work when, at the age of 20, she helped found a relief organization for women and children. She also helped found the Philadelphia Orphan Asylum, and she established the Female Hebrew Benevolent Society. Also concerned about religious education for Jewish children, she taught 11 children in her home. After the death of her sister Rachel in 1823, Gratz raised her sister's nine children, and in 1838, she started a Hebrew Sunday School Society of Philadelphia based on the model of the Christian Sunday school and served as its president for over 25 years. In 1855, she helped found the Jewish Foster Home and Orphan Asylum. Washington Irving was a family friend, and when he visited Sir Walter Scott in England, he supposedly told him about Gratz's kindnesses. Based on this information, Scott may have modeled his Rebecca in *Ivanhoe* on Gratz's life.

BIBLIOGRAPHY
Ashton, Dianne. *Rebecca Gratz: Women and Judaism in Antebellum America*. Detroit: Wayne State University Press, 1997. 0-8143-2666-8, 329p. Ashton's carefully researched, documented, and recommended scholarly biography thoroughly examines Gratz's life.
Philipson, David, ed. *Letters of Rebecca Gratz*. 1969. New York: Arno Press, 1975. 0-405-06714-3, 454p. Gratz's letters reveal her everyday life and her attitudes on a variety of subjects.

GREEN, ANNA KATHARINE (1846–1935)
Author   Brooklyn, New York

Anna Katharine Green was a detective fiction writer whose work made the genre popular in the United States. She was born on November 11, 1846, as one of five children to a prominent defense lawyer and his wife, who died when Green was only three. When her father remarried, Green became close to her stepmother, giving her credit for encouraging her own literary career. Green attended public schools before entering Ripley Female College and earning a degree in 1866. She wanted to write romantic verse, but her first work was a detective story called *The Leavenworth Case* with the character Ebenezer Gryce. Her understanding of the law from observing her father in the courtroom and her technical skill made the novel immediately popular, and it sold more than 500,000 copies. She wrote over 35 more novels, each with a tightly constructed, carefully developed plot containing an unusual twist and an exciting climax. Among her readers were Presidents Theodore Roosevelt and Woodrow Wilson. Sir Arthur Conan Doyle and Wilkie Collins, both master mystery writers, also praised her work.

BIBLIOGRAPHY

Maida, Patricia D. *Mother of Detective Fiction: The Life and Works of Anna Katharine Green*. Bowling Green, OH: Bowling Green State University Press, 1989. 0–87972–445–5, 120p. Maida's well-researched and documented study of Green reveals her as a hard-working, dedicated woman.

GRIMKÉ, ANGELINA EMILY (1805–1879)
Activist   Charleston, South Carolina

Angelina Emily Grimké was an antislavery crusader and women's rights advocate. The youngest of 14 children, she was born as on February 20, 1805, to an aristocratic slaveholder. She hated the slavery system and went to Philadelphia to live with her older sister, **Sarah Moore Grimké**. There she helped with charitable deeds and planned to become a teacher, but her suitor's disapproval changed her mind. She decided to support the abolitionists, and in 1835, she joined the Philadelphia Female Anti-Slavery Society. William Lloyd Garrison printed one of her letters in his newspaper, the *Liberator*, and the family name, Grimké, was publicly tied to the cause of antislavery. When she wrote *An Appeal to the Christian Women of the South* in 1836, her southern family name attracted immediate interest. By lecturing to "mixed audiences" containing both men and women, Grimké irritated her church, and a pastoral letter warned her of "unwomanly" behavior. She then realized that she had to address issues of women's rights before she could successfully argue for abolition. She wrote a series of letters to the *Liberator* noting that all women should have a voice in making laws, and in 1838, she was the first woman allowed to testify before the Massachusetts legislature. The same year, she joined her sister for a lecture series in Boston that drew thousands of spectators. Soon she married Theodore Weld, an antislavery orator whom she had met two years earlier. She, her sister, and Weld started a school called Eagleswood in 1848. When they later moved to Massachusetts, Grimké's belief in equality was tested when she discovered that her brother's sons by a slave were attending Lincoln University. Both sisters welcomed the boys into their home, however, and they helped one graduate from Harvard Law School and the other from Princeton Theological Seminary. As one of the first generation of feminist leaders, Grimké always based her arguments on biblical texts. She was elected to The National Women's Hall of Fame.

BIBLIOGRAPHY

Birney, Catherine H. *The Grimké Sisters: Sarah and Angelina Grimké*. 1885. St. Clair Shores, MI: Scholarly Press, 1970. 0–403–00230–3, 319p. Birney used diaries and letters in her recreation of the story of the Grimké sisters.

Ceplair, Larry, ed. *The Public Years of Sarah and Angelina Grimké: Selected Writings,*
1835–1839. New York: Columbia University Press, 1989. 0–231–06801–8, 380p.
Ceplair has chosen letters from original manuscripts that the Grimkés wrote during
their public years.

Lerner, Gerda. *The Grimké Sisters from South Carolina.* New York: Oxford University
Press, 1997. 0–19–510603–2, 368p. For her documented collective biography of the
Grimké sisters, Lerner consulted manuscripts, unpublished letters and documents,
and diaries.

Lumpkin, Katharine Du Pre. *The Emancipation of Angelina Grimké.* Chapel Hill:
University of North Carolina Press, 1974. 0–8078–1232–3, 265p. Lumpkin used
manuscript materials from the Grimké sisters and Theodore Weld along with
contemporary documents and periodicals to create a readable, well-researched, and
carefully documented biography.

GRIMKÉ, ANGELINA WELD (1880–1958)
Dramatist and Poet   Boston, Massachusetts

Angelina Weld Grimké's play *Rachel* was the first staged play by an African
American woman. She was born on February 27, 1880, into a wealthy family with
a biracial father and a white mother. When Grimké was three, her mother left
Grimké's father and took her along. When Grimké was seven, her mother
relinquished her to her father and never returned. Grimké's father was the
executive director of the NAACP, and because of his status and that of her aunt,
Angelina Emily Grimké (Weld), she was able to attend excellent schools in
Massachusetts before moving to Washington to work. While teaching at her
second school, Dunbar High School, she wrote and staged her first play, *Rachel,* in
which the African American heroine vows never to raise children who will suffer
from discrimination. With this play, staged African American theater began.
Grimké also wrote poetry heavily influenced by romanticism and revealing her
feelings of isolation and abandonment.

BIBLIOGRAPHY
Hull, Gloria T. *Color, Sex, and Poetry: Three Women Writers of the Harlem Renaissance.*
Bloomington: Indiana University Press, 1987. 0–253–34974–5, 240p. In her
collective study of the life and writings of Grimké, Hull posits that she dealt with
the confinements of sex.

GRIMKÉ, CHARLOTTE FORTEN. *See* FORTEN (GRIMKÉ), CHARLOTTE L.

GRIMKÉ, SARAH MOORE (1792–1873)
Activist   Charleston, South Carolina

Sarah Moore Grimké was an antislavery crusader and women's rights advocate.
She was born on November 26, 1792, as the sixth of 14 children to an aristocratic

slaveholder. Educated by private tutors, she complained when not allowed to study Greek, Latin, and philosophy like her brothers, and she learned what she could from the males in her family. She outwardly conformed to her genteel society, but inwardly, she rebelled against slavery and religion. In 1819, she visited Philadelphia with her father, and when she met Quakers, she felt comfortable with their simplicity and their antislavery stance because she had broken the law to teach her own maid to read. When she was 28, she moved to Philadelphia, renounced her Episcopalian upbringing, and joined the Quakers. In 1836, she went to New York to join her younger sister, **Angelina Emily Grimké**. At a course for abolitionist workers, noted orator Theodore Weld inspired her to write *Epistle to the Clergy of the Southern States*, refuting the argument that the Bible supported slavery. In 1838, she wrote a pamphlet, *Letters of Equality of the Sexes, and the Condition of Women*, in which she, like her sister, recognized that before women could support abolitionism, they had to have a voice in deciding the laws. Also in 1838, she joined her sister at a lecture series in Boston that drew thousands of spectators. She then accompanied her sister and her sister's husband, Weld, to New Jersey, where in 1848, they started a school called Eagleswood. Grimké later moved with the Welds to Massachusetts and taught in another school, where she met her brother's sons by a slave who were attending Lincoln University. She and her sister welcomed them and helped the two finish the professional schools of their choice, one at Harvard Law School and the other at Princeton Theological Seminary. Grimké always based her arguments for women's rights or for abolition on the Scriptures. She has been elected into The National Women's Hall of Fame.

BIBLIOGRAPHY

Birney, Catherine H. *The Grimké Sisters: Sarah and Angelina Grimké*. 1885. St. Clair Shores, MI: Scholarly Press, 1970. 0–403–00230–3, 319p. Birney used diaries and letters in her biography of the Grimké sisters.

Ceplair, Larry, ed. *The Public Years of Sarah and Angelina Grimké: Selected Writings, 1835–1839*. New York: Columbia University Press, 1989. 0–231–06801–8, 380p. An attempt to reveal the Grimké sisters' public statements and private struggles led Ceplair to carefully research materials, including original manuscripts of letters, and document them.

Lerner, Gerda. *The Grimké Sisters from South Carolina*. New York: Oxford University Press, 1997. 0–19–510603–2, 368p. For her collective biography of the Grimké sisters, Lerner consulted manuscripts, unpublished letters and documents, and diaries.

———, ed. *The Feminist Thought of Sarah Grimké*. New York: Oxford University Press, 1998. 0–19–510604–0, 193p. A carefully documented and researched scholarly biography precedes a collection of documents that illustrate Grimké's feminist beliefs.

GUGGENHEIM, PEGGY (1898–1980)
Art Patron   New York, New York

Peggy Guggenheim was an art collector and patron for the New York school of artists. She was born on August 26, 1898, as Marguerite Guggenheim, to a copper-mining heir who died in the sinking of the *Titanic*. She gained control of her fortune in 1919 before marrying and changing her lifestyle. In London, she met Marcel Duchamp, who taught her the difference between Surrealism, Cubism, and abstract art while introducing her to artists from whom she bought many paintings. After her divorce in 1930, she moved to Paris until the beginning of World War II, having shipped her paintings to Switzerland and then to the United States as "household goods." She returned to the United States, married Max Ernst, and opened her second gallery, Art of This Century, in which she exhibited artists for whom she served as patron, including Jackson Pollock, Alberto Giacometti, and Pablo Picasso. Her gallery played a major role in making New York the capital of modern art. Of the fifty exhibitions during the gallery's five-year history, two were devoted solely to women artists, and Jackson Pollock, who had been working at the Guggenheim museum as a carpenter, had four. She thought Pollock was the greatest painter since Picasso. She gave away 20 Jackson Pollock paintings, and although the University of Iowa complained about a shipping and insurance charge of $100 in 1948 for a mural 23 feet long and 6 feet wide, it refused to exchange the painting for a Braque still life 13 years later. After World War II, she moved to Venice, settled on the Grand Canal, and began displaying her art collection to the public as the first and prime patron of the Abstract Expressionist movement. Guggenheim also gave art to many other museums. Her support of American artists greatly influenced the understanding, acceptance, and success of twentieth-century modern art.

BIBLIOGRAPHY

Guggenheim, Peggy. *Confessions of an Art Addict.* 1960. Hopewell, NJ: Ecco Press, 1997. 0-88001-576-4, 176p. Guggenheim's lively autobiography recalls her childhood and her eccentric relatives.

Tacou-Rumney, Laurence. *Peggy Guggenheim: A Collector's Album.* Trans. Ralph Runney. New York: Abbeville, 1996. 2-08-013610-0, 175p. The author, Guggenheim's granddaughter-in-law, uses photographs not previously published along with her text about Guggenheim's bohemian life.

Vail, Karole, and Thomas Messer. *Peggy Guggenheim: A Celebration.* New York: Harry N. Abrams, 1998. 0-8019-4914-9, 160p. Vail, Guggenheim's granddaughter, provides an intimate account of her life.

Weld, Jacqueline Bograd. *Peggy, the Wayward Guggenheim.* New York: Dutton, 1986. 0-525-24380-1, 493p. Weld interviewed Guggenheim and had access to her private papers to write her authorized biography.

H

HALE, SARAH JOSEPHA (1788–1879)
Editor   **Newport, New Hampshire**

Sarah Josepha Hale became the first female editor of a magazine. She was born Sarah Buell on October 24, 1788, one of four children of a property owner and his wife. After her mother educated her at home and her brother shared his reading course from Dartmouth with her, she opened a school in 1806 for children in the community. When she married a lawyer in 1813, she depended on him for intellectual stimulation while raising their five children, but he died of pneumonia four days before their youngest child was born in 1822. To support her family, she opened a millinery shop with her sister-in-law and started writing. Her first book of poetry, published in 1823, revealed her feelings of intense loss, and she followed it with a novel in 1827 and another book of poetry in 1830 in which she published "Mary's Lamb." In 1827, Rev. John Lauris Blake recognized her talent by asking her to become the editor of his new woman's magazine. In 1828, the first issue of the *Ladies' Magazine* appeared, and Hale moved to Boston for her work. Employing rigorous editorial standards, her goal was to improve the female intellectually by publishing only original works and editorials. She disapproved of women openly entering public affairs, even as philanthropists, thinking that women should retain their "meekness." In 1836, Louis Antoine Godey purchased the magazine, enlarged it, and invited Hale to edit the new publication, called *Godey's Lady's Book*. Under her editorship, it broke records, with circulation reaching 150,000 by 1860. She also published over 50 books under her name on a variety of topics, one of them *Women's Record*, containing 2,500 entries on women who had contributed to society. She finally retired at the age of 90. Throughout her life, she supported charities and raised funds for causes including the establishment of Thanksgiving Day as a national holiday.

BIBLIOGRAPHY

Finley, Ruth E. *The Lady of Godey's: Sarah Josepha Hale*. 1931. New York: Arno Press, 1974. 0-405-06095-5, 318p. In this dated biography, Finley emphasizes Hale's publishing career.

Fryatt, Norma R. *Sarah Josepha Hale: The Life and Times of a Nineteenth-Century Career Woman*. New York: Hawthorn, 1975. 0-8015-6568-5, 152p. Using primary sources, Fryatt looks at Hale and nineteenth-century publishing.

Okker, Patricia. *Our Sister Editors*. Athens: University of Georgia Press, 1995. 0-8203-1686-5, 264p. Okker's biography examines Hale's career as writer and editor.

Rogers, Sherbrooke. *Sarah Josepha Hale: A New England Pioneer, 1788-1879*. Grantham, NH: Tompson and Rutter, 1985. 0-936988-10-X, 135p. Rogers used Hale's writings to investigate her private and public life in a researched biography.

HAMER, FANNIE LOU (1917–1977)
Activist   Montgomery County, Mississippi

Fannie Lou Hamer, a sharecropper, became an African American orator and political activist in support of civil rights. She was born on October 6, 1917, to parents who eventually had 19 children. At age six, Hamer began working in the cotton fields, but when her employer discovered that she could read and write, she became his time and record keeper. In 1945, she married, and she and her husband continued to work on the plantation for the next 18 years. When she tried to vote in 1962, her life changed. Gunshots threatened her and her friends, but instead of returning quietly to the plantation, she became an active member of the Student Non-Violent Coordinating Committee (SNCC). Hamer recognized the connection between the lack of political power and the low economic status of African Americans and remained active in civic life, running for office and becoming a delegate to the Democratic National Convention. In 1969, she founded the Freedom Farm Corporation to help needy families raise food and keep livestock. She won several awards and honorary degrees including the **Sojourner Truth** Meritorious Service Award and election into The National Women's Hall of Fame.

BIBLIOGRAPHY

Mills, Kay. *This Little Light of Mine: The Life of Fannie Lou Hamer*. New York: Dutton, 1993. 0-525-93501-0, 390p. In a thorough and carefully documented young adult biography based on interviews with Hamer, her friends, and colleagues, Mills reveals Hamer's strength.

Rubel, David. *Fannie Lou Hamer: From Sharecropping to Politics*. Englewood Cliffs, NJ: Silver Burdett, 1990. 0-382-09923-0, 130p. This researched biography for young adults gives an overview of Hamer's life and career in civil rights.

HAMILTON, ALICE (1869–1970)
Physician   New York, New York

Alice Hamilton was a pathologist who researched industrial diseases. She was born on February 27, 1869, one of five children of a Princeton graduate and his wife. Her father owned a wholesale grocery store but later retreated from public life when his store failed. Hamilton was educated at home, where she learned languages and literature before attending Miss Porter's School in Farmington, Connecticut. Knowing that her mother treasured personal liberty and that she would need to support herself, Hamilton decided to study medicine. Her father objected, but when she made up educational deficiencies, he supported her entrance to the University of Michigan in 1892. She decided that she preferred research to patient care and interned at the Northwestern Hospital for Women and Children in Minneapolis and at the New England Hospital for Women and Children in Boston. In 1895, she returned to Michigan to work in a bacteriology laboratory, but wanting more information, she went to Germany to study. She hated the anti-Semitic attitudes encountered there and returned for study at Johns Hopkins before becoming a professor of pathology at the Woman's Medical School of Northwestern University. While in Chicago, she became a resident at Hull-House, taught evening classes, gave a well-baby clinic, and took immigrant children on outings. After more research and study in Paris, she read Thomas Oliver's *Dangerous Trades* about industrial diseases. The discovery that workers had no protective laws of occupational safety and no union support gave her life purpose. In 1911, she became a special investigator for the Bureau of Labor, and in five years, she had become the American authority on lead poisoning and one of the few experts on industrial poisoning. In 1919, she became Harvard University's first woman professor but continued her field work. In 1925, her book, *Industrial Poisons in the United States*, was the first American text on the topic, and in it she named two new poisons, tetraethyl lead and radium. She received numerous honorary degrees and awards for her pioneering work, including election into The National Women's Hall of Fame.

BIBLIOGRAPHY

Grant, Madeleine P. *Alice Hamilton: Pioneer Doctor in Industrial Medicine*. New York: Abelard-Schuman, 1967. No ISBN, 223p. For this fictional biography, suitable for young adults, Grant used Hamilton's autobiography and interviewed Hamilton, her sister, and friends.

Hamilton, Alice. *Exploring the Dangerous Trades: The Autobiography of Alice Hamilton, M.D.* 1943. Boston: Northeastern University Press, 1985. 0–930350–81–2, 433p. In her autobiography, Hamilton discusses her life and work.

Sicherman, Barbara. *Alice Hamilton: A Life in Letters*. Cambridge, MA: Harvard University Press, 1994. 0–674–01553–3, 460p. Hamilton wrote the 1,311 letters in the text over 76 years.

HAMILTON, GRACE TOWNS (1907–1992)
Government Official and Activist   Atlanta, Georgia

Grace Towns Hamilton became Georgia's first African American female legislator. She was born on February 10, 1907, as the eldest of four children in a family that supported her college aspirations and her graduate school achievement of an M.A. in psychology. After marrying the dean and professor of education at Memphis's LeMoyne College, she began teaching at the college before joining the Works Progress Administration and then the Young Women's Christian Association to develop interracial programs on college campuses. She returned to Atlanta with her husband in 1943 and became executive director of the Atlanta Urban League, actively supporting school children and registering African American citizens to vote. In 1966, she was elected to the Georgia legislature, and in this position, she advocated fair housing, more jobs for African American workers, and hospital integration. In her honor, Emory University began the Grace Towns Hamilton Lectureship in 1989, the first lecture series named for an African American woman, and endowed a distinguished chair in her name.

BIBLIOGRAPHY

Spritzer, Lorraine Nelson, and Jean B. Bergmark. *Grace Towns Hamilton and the Politics of Southern Change.* Athens: University of Georgia Press, 1997. 0-8203-1889-2, 266p. The authors used oral history and archival materials to place Hamilton within her times.

HAMILTON, VIRGINIA (1936–)
Author   Yellow Springs, Ohio

African American Virginia Hamilton is a prize-winning author. She was born March 12, 1936, as the youngest of five children to parents who offered her a cultured background. She received a scholarship to Antioch College and obtained her B.A. degree before attending Ohio State University and the New School for Social Research. In New York City, where she spent summers while in college and went to live afterward, she met Jewish teacher Arnold Adoff and married him. In 1974, she published *M. C. Higgins, the Great*, and became the only author to receive the Newbery Medal, the Boston Globe–Horn Book Magazine Award, the National Book Award, the Lewis Carroll Shelf Award, and the International Board on Books for Young People Award for the same book. Since then, she has worked in several genres, including realistic fiction, historical fiction, biography, folktales, and fantasy. Other awards for subsequent books include the Hans Christian Andersen Award and the **Laura Ingalls Wilder** Award. In 1995, she received a MacArthur Foundation grant. She believes that a writer must first tell a good story and then must provide the reader with a deeper and different understanding of the world.

BIBLIOGRAPHY

Mikkelsen, Nina. *Virginia Hamilton*. New York: Twayne, 1994. 0–8057–4010–4, 169p.
 After looking at Hamilton's life, Mikkelsen discusses her work in detail.

HANSBERRY, LORRAINE (1930–1965)
Dramatist   Chicago, Illinois

Lorraine Vivian Hansberry's *A Raisin in the Sun* was the first play by an African
American woman produced on Broadway. She was born on May 19, 1930, as the
youngest of four children, to a real estate broker and a college-educated mother.
Her father fought for African Americans to have rights to move out of the ghetto,
and when her family moved into a white neighborhood, Hansberry daily faced
hostility as she went to school. She attended the University of Wisconsin for two
years before studying painting in Chicago and Mexico. When she realized that she
had little talent as an artist, she went to New York in 1950 to support herself while
she wrote. She married Robert Nemiroff, a Jewish intellectual who was also a civil
rights activist, and he supported her literary efforts before they divorced. *A Raisin
in the Sun* won the New York Drama Critics' Circle Award (the first play by an
African American to win) and a special Cannes Festival award. Other plays were
less successful. Hansberry died from cancer very early in her career.

BIBLIOGRAPHY

Cheney, Anne. *Lorraine Hansberry*. Boston: Twayne, 1984. 0–8057–7365–7, 174p.
 Interviews with Hansberry's executor and former husband aided Cheney in this
 biography.
Nemiroff, Robert, ed. *To Be Young, Gifted, and Black*. New York: Vintage, 1995.
 0–679–76415–1, 261p. This collection of Hansberry's writings, including plays,
 essays, and letters, shows her achievements.
Scheader, Catherine. *Lorraine Hansberry: Playwright and Voice of Justice*. Springfield,
 NJ: Enslow, 1998. 0–89490–945–2, 128p. Scheader interviewed members of
 Hansberry's family and used Hansberry's papers and writings to re-create her life in
 this well-documented biography for young adults.
Tripp, Janet. *Lorraine Hansberry*. San Diego: Lucent, 1998. 1–56006–081–6, 112p. This
 recommended, researched, and documented biography for young adults is a
 thorough view of Hansberry's life and work.

HARKNESS, GEORGIA ELMA (1891–1974)
Theologian and Religious Leader   Harkness, New York

Georgia (Elma) Harkness was a theologian and religious educator. She was the
youngest of four children, born on April 21, 1891, to a well-to-do farmer and his
wife. She attended a one-room schoolhouse in the local Methodist church to which
her family belonged. After her religious conversion at 14 and her graduation from
high school, she attended Cornell University on a scholarship. After graduation as
a Phi Beta Kappa, however, she returned home to help her parents and began

teaching in local schools. She then entered Boston University and received her religious education master's degree before completing her Ph.D. in 1923. The same year, she became a philosophy instructor at Elmira College. Three years later, her Methodist church ordained her as a local deacon and then as a local elder, the highest position available to a Methodist woman at the time, but the rank gave her no vote at the annual conference. She began preaching, continued teaching, and published both poetry and books on the philosophy of religion and ethics. Her interest shifted to theology, however, and she wrote her remaining 38 books from the perspective of evangelical liberalism. In the later days of her career, she argued that theologians needed to make Christianity meaningful to the layperson, and she accepted an invitation from the Pacific School of Religion in Berkeley to teach applied theology. She worked for international ecumenism through the World Council of Churches, supported civil rights, and disapproved of American policy in Vietnam. Among her many honorary degrees and awards were the General Federation of Women's Clubs Award and Garrett-Evangelical Theological Seminary's establishment of a chair in her name for a woman theologian.

BIBLIOGRAPHY

Keller, Rosemary Skinner. *Georgia Harkness: For Such a Time as This*. Nashville, TN: Abingdon Press, 1992. 0–687–13276–2, 336p. Keller's carefully researched and documented scholarly biography shows Harkness as a feminist in a male world of theology.

HARPER, FRANCES E. W. (1825–1911)
Author   Baltimore, Maryland

Frances Ellen Watkins Harper was an African American author, orator, and social reformer. She was born on September 24, 1825, the only child of free African Americans, but was orphaned before age three. Her uncle, a shoemaker by trade, raised and educated her. While in his home, she learned to sew, worked for a bookseller after school, and read voraciously. In 1845, she published a book of poetry. Five years later, she left for Columbus, Ohio, to become a sewing teacher at the Union Seminary. Strongly supporting abolition like her uncle, she delivered her first antislavery lecture in 1854, with impressively strong oratory ability, and proceeded to lecture in several states through 1860. Her writing was conventional but honest, and when her book, *Poems on Miscellaneous Subjects*, sold 12,000 copies, she became the best-known African American poet since **Phillis Wheatley**. Her short story, "The Two Offers," became the first short story published by an African American. She married before the Civil War began, but her husband died in 1864. Harper recruited African Americans into the National Woman's Christian Temperance Union and established Sunday schools in Philadelphia for African Americans to help local ministers curb juvenile delinquency. In 1894, she became director of the American Association of Education of Colored Youth, and two years later, she helped found the National Association of Colored Women.

BIBLIOGRAPHY

Boyd, Melba Joyce. *Discarded Legacy: Politics and Poetics in the Life of Frances E.W. Harper.* Detroit: Wayne State University Press, 1994. 0-8143-2488-6, 260p. Boyd examines Harper's life and her poetry, speeches, and letters.

HARRISON, HAZEL (1883–1969)
Pianist   La Porte, Indiana

African American Hazel Harrison was a superb pianist and an inspiring teacher. Born on May 12, 1883, to supportive parents, she began to study piano before she was five, soon performing for friends. After completing high school in 1904, she went to Europe, where critics lauded her Berlin debut. Another European tour six years later lasted until 1914. She performed works by African Americans and by the avant-garde composers Igor Stravinsky and Maurice Ravel before joining the staff of Pauline James Lee's Chicago University of Music. In 1930, she again visited Europe and returned to perform in New York City's Town Hall and Boston's Jordan Hall. The next year, she began teaching at Tuskegee Institute, and five years later, she moved to Howard University. In 1955, she toured for three more years and then ended her career by teaching at Alabama State College. She received a number of awards, including the Young Women's Christian Association recognition of her as a model for young people in the arts.

BIBLIOGRAPHY

Cazort, Jean E., and Constance Tibbs Hobson. *Born to Play: The Life and Career of Hazel Harrison.* Westport, CT: Greenwood Press, 1983. 0-313-23643-7, 171p. This recommended, documented biography of Harrison, based on careful research and interviews, emphasizes her greatness as a performer.

HAUGHERY, MARGARET (1813–1882)
Philanthropist and Businesswoman   Killeshandra, County Cavan, Ireland

Margaret Gaffney Haughery was a businesswoman and philanthropist who became known as "the Bread Woman of New Orleans." She was born in 1813, as one of six children, to an Irish tenant farmer and his wife. She emigrated with her parents when she was five, but their deaths in the yellow fever epidemic of 1822 orphaned her. A neighbor and a priest cared for her, but neither taught her to read or write. She worked as a domestic until going to New Orleans with her husband, where both he and her young daughter died in 1836. While supporting herself as a hotel laundress, she began to help the Sisters of Charity in the Poydras Orphan Asylum. With her savings, she bought cows and started a dairy, selling milk along the streets and giving it away to those in need. She helped the Sisters of Charity open the New Orleans Female Orphan Asylum in 1840, the first of 11 that she helped to found and maintain with the proceeds from her dairy. She also helped stranded families along the flooded Mississippi River and looked after yellow fever victims during several epidemics. In 1858, she assumed ownership of a bakery in payment for a debt, relinquished the dairy, and enlarged the bakery to employ 40 men. With her shrewd business sense, she established the first steam bakery in the South and was the first to package crackers for export. During the Civil War, she organized sewing and knitting groups, assisted with "free markets," secretly donated to those too proud to ask for help, and cared for sick soldiers on both sides. In the 1870s, she gave $9,000 in three years for repairs on the Home for the Aged, and in her will, she gave large amounts to 10 institutions. At her death, mourners lined the streets, and city offices closed. The city collected funds for a statue of her which stands in the park bearing her name, and February 9 in New Orleans is Margaret Haughery Day.

BIBLIOGRAPHY

Widmer, Mary Lou. *Margaret, Friend of Orphans*. Gretna, LA: Pelican, 1996. 1-56554-251-7, 176p. Although fictional, the text is the only available biography revealing Haughery's generosity.

HAWES, ELIZABETH (1903–1971)
Fashion Designer and Author   **Ridgewood, New Jersey**

Elizabeth Hawes was a fashion designer and author. She was born on December 16, 1903, as one of four children to a general freight manager of the Southern Pacific steamship line and his activist wife. Hawes began making her own clothes when she was 10, and she sold her first product to a store in Haverford, Pennsylvania, when she was 12. After graduation from Vassar with a degree in economics, she went to Paris to study couture. Back in New York, she began designing clothes and writing articles on Paris fashion for newspapers. In 1930, she married a sculptor she had met in Paris, and he taught her to think of clothes as architecture, made to fit the body and its curves. She developed softly fitting bias-cut dresses and showed her collection in Paris the next year. When clothing manufacturers changed her fabrics and designs, she broke with the garment district and wrote her book, *Fashion Is Spinach* (1938). In it, she attacked the industry for wanting constant change in order to improve sales. She closed her store, wrote a weekly newspaper column, and began to promote childcare centers in New York during World War II while working the night shift at an aeronautical plant. After the war, she continued writing and tried to reestablish her fashion designing, but the industry had changed. In 1967, the Fashion Institute of Technology recognized her contribution with a retrospective of her work.

BIBLIOGRAPHY

Berch, Bettina. *Radical by Design: The Life and Style of Elizabeth Hawes*. New York: Dutton, 1988. 0-525-24715-7, 214p. This readable, carefully researched, and documented biography, based on interviews with Hawes's friends, presents an account of her life and career.

HAWES, HARRIET BOYD (1871–1945)
Archaeologist   Boston, Massachusetts

Harriet Ann Boyd Hawes was a classical archaeologist. She was born on October 11, 1871, the youngest of five children. Hawes's father owned a leather business and was a civic leader. Her mother died in 1872 when Hawes was one. Hawes's older brother shared his interest in and knowledge of ancient history with her before she attended boarding schools and graduated from Smith College in 1892. She taught briefly before going to Athens for graduate work at the American School of Classical Studies. In 1897, she served as a volunteer nurse in Thessaly during the Greco-Turkish War, and Greece awarded her a Red Cross decoration. She volunteered the following year in Florida, helping Spanish-American War soldiers. In 1900, she went to Crete and explored the island on muleback with another woman before digging at Kavousi as Sir Arthur Evans had suggested and finding several Iron Age tomb sites. She described them in the M.A. thesis she wrote at Smith, where she later taught Greek archaeology and modern Greek. She returned to Kavousi and became the first archaeologist to discover and excavate Gournia, a Minoan town inhabited during the Early Bronze Age. After Hawes married an anthropologist, she raised her family and continued her volunteer work by nursing cholera and typhoid victims on Corfu during World War I and encouraging Smith College to establish a relief unit before going to France to help as a hospital volunteer near Paris. In 1920, she resumed teaching, and in 1922, her college class created a graduate scholarship in her name. She received an honorary degree from Smith.

BIBLIOGRAPHY
Allsebrook, Mary. *Born to Rebel: The Life of Harriet Boyd Hawes*. Bloomington, IN: D. Brown, 1992. 0–946897–40–9, 236p. Written by Hawes's daughter, this thorough and loving biography explores the many facets of a mother's life and career.

HAWN, GOLDIE (1945–)
Actor   Washington, District of Columbia

Goldie Hawn is an actor. She was born on November 21, 1945, as one of two daughters to a musician father and a Jewish mother who was a jewelry wholesaler and dance school owner-administrator. At age three, she began taking ballet and tap dance lessons, and at ten, she appeared in the chorus of the Ballets Russes de Monte Carlo production of *The Nutcracker*. At 16, she made her stage debut as Juliet in *Romeo and Juliet*. While in college at American University, where she planned to major in drama, she ran a ballet school but left college early to make her professional dance debut in New York. In 1967, she made her television debut, and the following year had a small role in a film as a dancer. When she joined *Rowan and Martin's Laugh-In* in 1968, she earned two Emmy Awards for her work as a comedienne, and opposite Walther Matthau in *Cactus Flower*, she won a Golden Globe Award and an Academy Award. After her first television special in 1970, she hosted several more and served as the master of ceremonies for the 48th annual Academy Awards presentation. In 1980, she was executive producer of *Private Benjamin*, and for her portrayal of a Jewish girl who serves in the army, she received an Academy Award nomination. In 1997, she made her debut as a director for the television movie *Hope*. The same year, she became the first female actor and producer to be honored by the American Museum of the Moving Image.

BIBLIOGRAPHY

Berman, Connie. *Solid Goldie: An Illustrated Biography of Goldie Hawn*. New York: Simon and Schuster, 1981. 0–671–43994–4, 125p. This biography overviews Hawn's movies and her life with appropriate photographs.

Shapiro, Marc. *Pure Goldie: The Life and Career of Goldie Hawn*. Secaucus, NJ: Carol, 1998. 1–55972–467–6, 210p. Shapiro recounts Hawn's life and career straightforwardly with photographs.

HAYES, HELEN (1900–1993)
Actor   Washington, District of Columbia

Helen Hayes, an actor, was often called "First Lady of the American Theater." She was born on October 10, 1900, the daughter of a traveling salesman and his wife, a stock company actor, but her paternal grandmother raised her. At the age of five, Hayes made her stage debut in Washington, DC. She attended Holy Cross Academy and Sacred Heart Academy before she starred at 17 in James Barrie's *Dear Brutus*. Other roles followed in plays such as George Bernard Shaw's *Caesar and Cleopatra* in 1925 and Barrie's *What Every Woman Knows* the next year. Her most famous role was as Queen Victoria in Laurence Housman's *Victoria Regina*, which she first performed in 1935 and repeated throughout her old age. In 1955, the Fulton Theater in New York City was renamed the Helen Hayes Theater, and then in 1983, a year after that building was razed, Broadway's Little Theater took her name. In addition to stage performances, Hayes also played on radio and television and in films. She received an Academy Award for *The Sin of Madelon Claudet* in 1931 and another for *Airport* in 1969. She was married to Charles MacArthur, a playwright, for 30 years; after their daughter died of polio, her son became the center of her life. In memory of her child and for others, she established the MacArthur Fund to help children dying from polio and convinced Nyack Hospital in New York to offer treatment and therapy for paralyzed survivors; in the 1970s, it was renamed the Helen Hayes MacArthur Hospital. She served as president of the American National Theatre and Academy and chaired the women's activities for the National Foundation for Infantile Paralysis. She received honorary degrees and over 20 other major awards including the Medal of Freedom Award, the Kennedy Center Honors Lifetime Achievement Award, and election into The National Women's Hall of Fame.

BIBLIOGRAPHY

Barrow, Kenneth. *Helen Hayes, First Lady of the American Theater*. Garden City, NY: Doubleday, 1985. 0-385-23196-2, 216p. Barrow knew and interviewed Hayes as well as others for his thorough, recommended biography of her life and career.

Hayes, Helen. *Loving Life*. Garden City, NY: Doubleday, 1987. 0-385-23903-3, 178p. Hayes discusses diverse topics in this autobiography.

———. *My Life in Three Acts*. San Diego: Harcourt Brace Jovanovich, 1990. 0-15-163695-8, 266p. Hayes describes the hard work and difficult decisions that accompany a life in the theater.

Murphy, Donn B., and Stephen Moore. *Helen Hayes: A Bio-Bibliography*. Westport, CT: Greenwood Press, 1993. 0-313-27793-1, 354p. This scholarly look at Hayes's life and work includes a brief biography and a thorough analysis of her career.

Robbins, Jhan. *Front Page Marriage*. New York: Putnam, 1982. 0-399-12691-0, 224p. In a carefully researched biography, Robbins recounts Hayes's life and career.

HAYWORTH, RITA (1918-1987)
Actor   Brooklyn, New York

Latina American Rita Hayworth became a film star in the 1940s, with fans calling her the "Great American Love Goddess." Margarita Carmen Cansino was born October 17, 1918, the daughter of a Spanish-born dancer and his partner. After the family moved to Los Angeles, Hayworth began appearing in her father's nightclub act across the border in Tijuana, Mexico, when she was 12. She later performed as the Spanish dancer "Rita Cansino" in films during the late 1930s before the first of five husbands suggested that she change her name and dye her hair auburn. Films with Cary Grant, James Cagney, Tyrone Power, Fred Astaire, and Gene Kelly led her to stardom and to becoming a pinup girl for American servicemen during World War II. Her second husband was Orson Welles, the director. Throughout her life, she never seemed to recover from a longing to return to her Spanish heritage as "Margarita" or from the strong, dictatorial influence of her father, choosing husbands with similar personalities. She suffered from Alzheimer's disease for 15 years prior to her death.

BIBLIOGRAPHY

Kobal, John. *Rita Hayworth: The Time, the Place and the Woman*. New York: Norton, 1978. 0-393-07526-5, 328p. Kobal's biography of Hayworth relies on anecdotal information.

Leaming, Barbara. *If This Was Happiness: A Biography of Rita Hayworth*. New York: Viking, 1989. 0-670-81978-6, 404p. This well-researched and documented biography of Hayworth is a balanced account of her life and career.

Morella, Joe. *Rita: The Life of Rita Hayworth*. New York: Delacorte, 1983. 0-385-29265-1, 261p. Morella's popular biography of Hayworth emphasizes the role that her father played in her career.

Ringgold, Gene. *The Films of Rita Hayworth*. Secaucus, NJ: Citadel, 1974. 0-8065-0439-0, 256p. The text includes a brief biography of Hayworth followed by photographs from her roles.

H.D. *See* DOOLITTLE, HILDA (H.D.)

HELLMAN, LILLIAN (1905–1984)
Dramatist   New Orleans, Louisiana

Lillian Hellman was a playwright and screenwriter whose dramas helped shape a golden age of American theater. She was born on June 20, 1905, to a businessman and his cultured wife. She attended New York public schools, New York University, and Columbia University before becoming a manuscript reader for a New York City publisher. After marrying a press agent, she went with him to Paris and, on excursions into Germany, saw the emerging anti-Semitism of the Nazis, a topic she pursued in her plays *Watch on the Rhine* and *The Searching Wind*. In 1930, they moved to Hollywood, where Hellman met the mystery novelist and screenwriter Dashiell Hammett, who encouraged her first produced play, *The Children's Hour*, in 1933. In the 1940s, Hellman wrote *The Little Foxes*, perhaps her best known work, and also directed plays in New York City after World War II. Her credible dialogue gave her characters life in her well-made but sometimes didactic plays. In the 1950s, Joseph McCarthy's House Un-American Activities Committee summoned her to testify because of radical themes in her work. She also translated French works and assisted in the adaptation of Voltaire's *Candide* to music. In the 1960s, after completing *Toys in the Attic*, she taught writing at Yale University, Massachusetts Institute of Technology, and Harvard University. When she died, she had had five long-running Broadway dramas, more than Tennessee Williams, Edward Albee, or Thornton Wilder. She was a member of the American Academy of Arts and Letters and a fellow of the American Academy of Arts and Sciences. She received numerous honorary degrees and awards, including a National Book Award.

BIBLIOGRAPHY
Feibleman, Peter S. *Lilly: Reminiscences of Lillian Hellman.* New York: Morrow, 1988. 0-688-06188-5, 364p. Feibleman, 25 years younger than Hellman, reconstructed conversations with her during the time he knew her.
Hellman, Lillian. *Maybe: A Story.* Boston: Little, Brown, 1980. 0-316-35509-7, 106p. Hellman uses a persona in this third-person autobiography.
Lederer, Katherine. *Lillian Hellman.* Boston: Twayne, 1979. 0-8057-7275-8, 169p. In a critical examination of Hellman's life and work, Lederer includes a brief biography.
Newman, Robert P. *The Cold War Romance of Lillian Hellman and John Melby.* Chapel Hill: University of North Carolina Press, 1989. 0-8078-1815-1, 375p. Government papers, letters between Hellman and John Melby, and transcripts of Melby's testimony during the McCarthy era form the basis of this account of the Hellman-Melby affair.
Wright, William. *Lillian Hellman: The Image, the Woman.* New York: Simon and Schuster, 1986. 0-671-52687-1, 507p. After examining Hellman's life and work, Wright concluded that the best character Hellman created was herself.

HEPBURN, KATHARINE (1909-)
Actor   Hartford, Connecticut

Katharine Hepburn is an award-winning stage and screen actor. She was born on May 12, 1909, as one of six children. Her father was a urologist who risked his career by honestly informing the public about venereal disease, and her mother was a suffragette who championed birth control. By age 12, Hepburn had begun appearing in amateur stage productions, and at Bryn Mawr College, she majored in drama and performed in college theater before graduating in 1928. The same year, she made her professional debut in Baltimore, and soon she became a well-known Broadway performer. Although she did not plan to make films, a studio agreed to pay her the huge sum of $1,500 a week, and she accepted. In 1932, she starred in her first motion picture, and for her second, *Morning Glory*, in 1933, she won her first Academy Award. In 1967, she won her second Academy Award for *Guess Who's Coming to Dinner*. *The Lion in Winter* earned her a third, and *On Golden Pond* won her a fourth. In 1942, she began starring with Spencer Tracy, making nine films with him before his death. She won 11 more Academy Award nominations for films and, in 1969, received a Tony nomination for *Coco*. Four years later, she received an Emmy nomination for the television adaptation of Tennessee Williams's *The Glass Menagerie*. In 1957, she won an Emmy for *Love Among the Ruins*. Her last performance was in 1994 in the television movie *One Christmas*. Among additional memorable films are *The Philadelphia Story*, *The African Queen*, and *Long Day's Journey into Night*. Other awards include the Kennedy Center Lifetime Achievement Award.

BIBLIOGRAPHY
Bergan, Ronald. *Katharine Hepburn: An Independent Woman*. Boston: Little, Brown, 1996. 1-55970-351-2, 192p. Bergan interviewed Hepburn for this biography.

Britton, Andrew. *Katharine Hepburn: A Portrait of the Actress as Feminist*. New York: Continuum, 1995. 0-8264-0801-X, 256p. This updated version of Britton's biography has new photographs.

Hepburn, Katharine. *Me: Stories of My Life*. New York: Knopf, 1991. 0-679-40051-6, 420p. Hepburn treats everyone she has known positively in her autobiography, suitable for young adults and augmented with over 160 photographs.

Leaming, Barbara. *Katharine Hepburn*. New York: Crown, 1995. 0-517-59284-3, 549p. Leaming uses family papers to show Hepburn and other women in her family in a psychobiography.

Prideaux, James. *Knowing Hepburn and Other Curious Experiences*. Boston: Faber and Faber, 1996. 0-571-19892-9, 319p. Prideaux created three television projects for Hepburn and bases his biography on her personal account.

HESSE, EVA   (1936–1970)
Sculptor and Artist   Hamburg, Germany

Eva Hesse was a sculptor. One of two daughters, she was born on January 11, 1936. Her father was a criminal lawyer who began a new career as an insurance broker after escaping from the Nazis to New York in 1939; her depressed mother committed suicide when Hesse was 10. When her parents divorced, Hesse chose to live with her father and his second wife, becoming a naturalized citizen in 1945. Hesse attended schools in New York before graduating from the School of Industrial Arts in 1952. She wanted to become an artist, and after attending Pratt Institute and the Art Students' League, she enrolled in Cooper Union. In 1957, she entered Yale School of Art and Architecture, and the conflict she felt between expressionism and formalism began. After receiving a B.F.A. from Yale in 1959, she returned to New York to find her place in the art world but instead found herself in Germany with her sculptor husband. She discovered that she preferred to experiment with string and to create small reliefs and sculptures which expanded her work with geometrical forms and other substances including latex and fiberglass. She held her first one-woman show in 1968, and after the Museum of Modern Art purchased her work the next year, doctors discovered that she had a brain tumor. While undergoing three unsuccessful operations, she worked prodigiously, synthesizing opposites of texture and material to reconcile her concern about emotion and intellect. The Guggenheim Museum's retrospective of her work in 1972, its first such show for a woman artist, acknowledged her important contribution to Minimalist Art.

BIBLIOGRAPHY

Lippard, Lucy R. *Eva Hesse*. 1976. New York: Da Capo Press, 1992. 0–306–80484–0, 249p. Lippard knew Hesse well, and her readable but scholarly biography utilizes Hesse's own workbooks and diaries.

Wagner, Anne Middleton. *Three Artists (Three Women): Modernism and the Art of Hesse, Krasner, and O'Keeffe*. Berkeley: University of California Press, 1996. 0–520–20608–8, 346p. Wagner examines the work of Hesse in a collective biography to see how she coped with life as both professional artist and wife.

HIGGINS, MARGUERITE (1920–1966)
Journalist   Hong Kong, China

Marguerite Higgins was the first woman to win a Pulitzer Prize for journalism. She was born on September 3, 1920, the only child of a steamship company freight manager and his French wife. When the family returned to California, she attended the Anna Head School in Berkeley before graduating with honors from the University of California in 1941. The next year, she received her M.S. in journalism from Columbia University while working as campus correspondent for the *New York Herald Tribune*. The newspaper hired her as a reporter when she graduated, and in 1944, she asked the paper's publisher, Helen Rogers Reid, to send her to the London bureau of the paper. She moved to Paris and then became the Berlin bureau chief in 1945; there she covered the capture of Munich and Berchtesgaden, and the liberation of both Buchenwald and Dachau. Her stories of the concentration camps won her the New York Newspaper Women's Club Award for best foreign correspondent in 1945. She later reported on Marshal Henri Pétain's treason trial, the Nuremberg war trials, and the Berlin blockade. In 1950, she went to Tokyo as the Far East bureau chief and began covering the Korean War. As the best known woman correspondent reporting the war, she won over 50 awards during the next few years. She then went to Washington, where she covered the State Department, and in 1962 warned of Soviet military activity in Cuba. The next year, she made two trips to Vietnam and suggested that the self-burnings by the Buddhists were political methods of bringing down Ngo Dinh Diem's regime. On a trip to Vietnam, India, and Pakistan, she contracted a tropical infection, leishmaniasis, and died from the complications.

BIBLIOGRAPHY

May, Antoinette. *Witness to War: A Biography of Marguerite Higgins.* New York: Beaufort, 1983. 0-8253-0161-0, 274p.   This biography recounts Higgins's achievements.

HOLIDAY, BILLIE (1915-1959)
Entertainer   Baltimore, Maryland

African American Billie Holiday, known as "Lady Day," was, according to jazz critics, the greatest jazz singer from the 1930s to the 1950s. She was born Eleanora Fagan on April 7, 1915, to an itinerant guitarist and his teenage wife. Her father never lived with the family, and Holiday learned about jazz from the local brothel manager's recordings of **Bessie Smith** and Louis Armstrong. As a teenager, she moved with her mother to New York City, where she was a truant from school and probably a prostitute before beginning her professional career in Harlem nightclubs during 1931. By 1935, when she was 20, she was performing regularly at Harlem's Apollo Theater and recording under her own name. In 1947, despite her attempts to stop taking drugs, she was arrested for possession and incarcerated. Her cabaret license revoked in New York City, she spent the next 10 years performing in other cities and recording her unique style with impeccable diction and phrasing. She never overcame her addiction and died when she was only 44. Thousands attended her high requiem mass.

BIBLIOGRAPHY

Chilton, John. *Billie's Blues: The Billie Holiday Story, 1933-1959.* New York: Da Capo Press, 1975. 0-306-80363-1, 264p.   Chilton used reviews, articles, previous biographies, and interviews with Holiday's friends in his recommended biography.
Clarke, Donald. *Wishing on the Moon: The Life and Times of Billie Holiday.* New York: Viking, 1994. 0-670-83771-7, 468p.   Clarke based his balanced biography of Holiday on interviews with people who knew her.

Holiday, Billie. *Lady Sings the Blues*. 1956. New York: Penguin, 1984. 0–14–006762–0, 199p. Holiday's autobiography reveals the sad and sordid facts of her life.

Nicholson, Stuart. *Billie Holiday*. Boston: Northeastern University Press, 1995. 1–55553–248–9, 311p. In a thoroughly researched, scholarly biography of Holiday based on interviews, court records, police files, and newspaper accounts, Nicholson looks at the two main stages in her life.

O'Meally, Robert G. *Lady Day: The Many Faces of Billie Holiday*. New York: Arcade, 1991. 1–55970–147–1, 207p. O'Meally concentrates on Holiday's music in this biography.

HOLLEY, MARIETTA (1836–1926)
Author   Jefferson County, New York

Marietta Holley, an author, used her humorous columns to advocate women's rights and temperance. She was born on July 16, 1836, as the youngest of seven children to a farmer and his wife. She began writing verse as a child, but when her brothers laughed at her attempts, she hid her work. She attended area schools until the family's financial plight kept her at home, but an uncle supported piano study, and eventually she began to give music lessons. She also began publishing her poems under a pseudonym in a local newspaper. In 1871, under the name "Josiah Allen's Wife," she submitted a comic narrative of a practical woman and a completely sentimental stereotypical spinster named Betsy Bobbet. The president of the American Publishing Company, Elijah Bliss, asked her to write more sketches to publish in a book. Her first book, *My Opinions and Betsy Bobbet's*, which Bliss published in 1873 at his own expense, became an immediate success. In total, Holley published 20 books as Josiah Allen's Wife, in which the opinions of Samantha Allen, a farmer's mate, revealed her support of women's rights and temperance, along with a distaste for affectation, white slave traffic, the double standard, imperialism, capitalist exploitation of labor, and race problems. Her foil, Betsy Bobbet, wanted to marry any man available. Other women, including **Frances Willard** and **Susan B. Anthony**, appreciated Holley's efforts and asked her to support their causes. In 1893, Holley's writing commanded advances of $15,000, and her royalties secured her a comfortable old age.

BIBLIOGRAPHY
Curry, Jane. *Marietta Holley*. New York: Twayne, 1996. 0–8057–4020–1, 114p. In a well-researched and documented text, Curry shows Holley's use of humor to espouse political and social equality.

Morris, Linda. *Women Vernacular Humorists in Nineteenth-Century America*. New York: Garland, 1988. 0–8240–0184–2, 288p. In a carefully researched and documented scholarly dissertation and collective biography, Morris gives an overview of Holley's life and work.

Winter, Kate H. *Marietta Holley: Life with Josiah Allen's Wife*. Syracuse, NY: University of Syracuse, 1984. 0–8156–2324–0, 182p. Winter used Holley's reminiscences, correspondence, and newspaper reports to examine her life and work.

HOLLIDAY, JUDY (1921–1965)
Actor   New York, New York

Judy Holliday was what her colleagues called an "actor's actor." She was born Judith Tuvim on June 21, 1921, the only child of a fund-raiser for Jewish organizations and his wife, a piano teacher. When Holliday's parents separated, she was six, and the situation distressed her. She lived with her mother and a grandmother who had escaped the Russian czar during a pogrom, and after graduating from high school, she worked briefly as a theater switchboard operator. Although she never furthered her education, her IQ was reported to have been 172. She soon joined **Betty Comden** and Adolph Green in "The Revuers," a topical nightclub act. Holliday's stage debut in a small role as a silly female won her the Clarence Derwent and the Theatre World Awards. In 1945, she replaced the ill star of *Born Yesterday* and played the role of Billie Dawn for 1,600 performances, missing the play only for contracted work. Later she filmed the role and won an Academy Award. Jack Benny supposedly studied her performances to improve his timing on stage, and others thought she was Charlie Chaplin's peer as a great comedian. In the early 1950s, however, the Senate Internal Security Subcommittee of Joseph McCarthy summoned her to testify, and although she had supported many of the organizations connected to communists, she pretended to be a "dumb blonde" to protect her friends. In 1956, after colleagues helped free her from blacklisting, she played in Comden and Green's *Bells Are Ringing*. When Holliday died from cancer at a young age, she had starred in only seven films and several stage plays but had taken the roles that Hollywood gave her and imbued them with her own intelligence.

BIBLIOGRAPHY
Carey, Gary. *Judy Holliday: An Intimate Life Story*. New York: Seaview, 1982. 0-87223-757-5, 271p. Carey's popular biography, based on interviews and research, focuses on Holliday's life and ability.

Holtzman, Will. *Judy Holliday: Only Child*. New York: Putnam, 1982. 0-399-12647-3, 306p. For his popular biography of Holliday, Holtzman's interviews with family members made him focus on her intelligence and vulnerability.

HOLLINGWORTH, LETA STETTER (1886–1939)
Psychologist   Chadron, Nebraska

Leta Anna Stetter Hollingworth was an educational psychologist. She was born in a dugout on May 25, 1886, as the oldest of three daughters to a gregarious father with little purpose in life and his well-educated wife. When her mother died in 1890, Hollingworth went to live with her maternal grandparents until she had to return to her hostile stepmother. At the University of Nebraska, she majored in literature and education, graduating in 1906. After she taught for two years, she married a classmate, but New York law forbade married women to teach. She pursued graduate study in sociology, obtaining a degree that qualified her to administer clinical tests for persons with mental problems. The next year, she became New York City's first civil service psychologist and worked at Bellevue Hospital in the new field of clinical psychology. When she received her Ph.D. from Columbia in 1916, she helped found the American Association of Clinical Psychology and began teaching educational psychology at Teachers' College. In her research on women, she tested the differences between the sexes to see if physical or psychological reasons limited women's intellectual and career possibilities, but she found no evidence of impairment either in or out of the menstrual cycle. She claimed that differences between male and female intellectual abilities were based on sociological rather than biological factors. In the 1920s and 1930s, she studied the "exceptional" child and the social isolation that highly intelligent children often endure, developed experimental programs for gifted children, and in New York, established and directed the experimental Speyer School. She received honorary degrees and other awards.

BIBLIOGRAPHY

Hollingworth, Harry L. *Leta Stetter Hollingworth: A Biography.* 1942. Bolton, MA: Anker, 1990. 0–9627042–0–2, 168p.   This loving biography of Hollingworth, written by her husband, includes her mother's memoir of her early childhood and excerpts from letters.

HOLM, HANYA (1893–1992)
Dancer and Choreographer   Worms am Rhein, Germany

Hanya Holm was a dancer and a choreographer of modern dance and Broadway musicals. She was born Johanna Eckert sometime during 1893 to German parents and studied at the Hoch Conservatory and the Dalcroze Institute before receiving her dance diploma from the *Mary Wigman Central Institute in Dresden. In 1931, she came to the United States to open a Mary Wigman Studio in New York City, but changed the name to the Hanya Holm Studio in 1936, emphasizing the importance of both technical expertise and emotional expression. The *New York Times* named *Trend,* her large-scale dance of social protest presented in 1937, the best dance composition of the year, and a work of social commentary, *Tragic Exodus* (1939), won *Dance* magazine's award for best group choreography. In 1939, the same year she became a naturalized citizen, she became the first concert dancer to appear on television. In 1941, she established the Center of Dance in the West in Colorado Springs, Colorado, and taught summer courses there for more than 25 years. While teaching at Juilliard, Holm choreographed more than a dozen Broadway musicals, including *Kiss Me, Kate, Out of This World, My Fair Lady,* and *Camelot.* The first choreographer to copyright a dance, she submitted a written Labanotation score of her choreography for *Kiss Me, Kate* in 1952. She also copyrighted *My Darlin' Aida* and *My Fair Lady.* Among honorary degrees and awards were a New York Drama Critics Award and an Astaire Award for lifetime achievement.

BIBLIOGRAPHY

Sorell, Walter. *Hanya Holm: The Biography of an Artist.* Middletown, CT: Wesleyan University Press, 1969. No ISBN, 226p. Sorell approaches Holm's life and contributions to modern dance chronologically in his recommended biography.

HOMER, LOUISE (1871–1947)
Opera Singer   Pittsburgh, Pennsylvania

Louise Homer was a leading operatic contralto during the first quarter of the twentieth century. She was born Louise Dilworth Beatty on April 30, 1871, as one of eight children in the musical family of a minister. After her father's death when she was 11, her mother moved the family to West Chester, Pennsylvania, where Homer made her first public appearance. She worked as a stenographer for several years to help the family while continuing her voice lessons and singing in a professional church quartet. In 1893, she went to Boston, where her teacher of theory and harmony became a major influence in her life. He took her to her first opera, an entertainment her Calvinist family had condemned, and married her. They borrowed money for her to study in Paris, and in 1898, Homer made her debut in Vichy, France, as Leonora in Donizetti's *La Favorita.* Other European engagements at Covent Garden and the Royal Opera in Brussels followed in the operas *Samson and Dalila* and *Aïda.* When the manager of the Metropolitan Opera heard Homer in Paris, he hired her for three years, and she returned to make her debut in 1900 and remained until 1919, showing as early as her second season a facility for rapidly learning her roles. She sang under the baton of Arturo Toscanini and with **Geraldine Farrar** and with Enrico Caruso on the night of his debut. In addition to traditional opera roles, Homer supported contemporary opera, singing Ignace Paderewski, Frederick Converse, and Horatio Parker. After 1919, she appeared in other houses and maintained an active schedule of recitals in which she always sang her husband's compositions until her retirement in 1929. She made many records of diverse styles of music, but when she was offstage, she preferred to live quietly with her husband and six children. She received several honorary degrees and was named one of the twelve greatest living American women.

BIBLIOGRAPHY

Homer, Anne. *Louise Homer and the Golden Age of Opera.* New York: Morrow, 1974. 0–688–00208–8, 439p. Homer's daughter communicates her mother's courage and perseverance.

Homer, Sidney. *My Wife and I: The Story of Louise and Sidney Homer.* 1939. New York: Da Capo Press, 1978. 0–306–77526–3, 269. This recommended biography of Homer, written by her husband, reveals her many roles in life.

HOOKS, JULIA BRITTON (1852–1942)
Educator   Frankfort, Kentucky

African American Julia Hooks gained the name "the Angel of Beale Street" for trying to help poor African Americans who migrated from the South during the late nineteenth century to more easily integrate into their new environments. She was born in 1852 to a musically talented mother freed by her mistress in 1848 and a free carpenter father. Her parents enrolled her in interracial Berea College, and in 1870, she began teaching there, making her one of the first African American professors to teach white students in Kentucky. After she married in 1872 and moved to Mississippi with her husband, they both taught, but her husband died a year later in the yellow fever epidemic. When Hooks then moved to Memphis to teach, she married a former slave. In 1883, Hooks and a wealthy friend started the Liszt-Mullard Club, probably the first African American organization devoted to music. The group raised money for scholarships for music students, and several years later Hooks established the Hooks School of Music, which taught students including W. C. Handy, Sidney Woodward, and Nell Hunter. In 1892, she opened a private kindergarten and elementary school to combat education problems for African Americans. An article she wrote in 1887 about the government's duty toward its children and how it was failing became so popular that it was published in the 1895 edition of the *African-American Encyclopedia*. Also concerned about orphans and the aged, she established the Colored Old Folks and Orphans Home Club in 1891, giving concerts to pay the debt. She became a charter member of the NAACP in Memphis and actively supported the needy until her death.

BIBLIOGRAPHY
Lewis, Selma S., and Marjean G. Kremer. *The Angel of Beale Street: A Biography of Julia Ann Hooks*. Memphis, TN: St. Luke's, 1986. 0-918518-39-3. In the absence of extant biographical material, the authors use conjecture to re-create some of Hooks's life.

HOPE, LUGENIA BURNS (1871–1947)
Reformer   Natchez, Mississippi

African American Lugenia Burns Hope worked as a dedicated social reformer in the South. Born on February 19, 1871, the last of seven children, Burns attended school until her family's economic situation deteriorated and she had to work full time. Charitable groups with which she volunteered included the Kings Daughters and Hull-House, and these experiences increased her interest in public service and communities. She met her husband, a theological student at Brown University, and married him in 1897. They moved to Nashville, and then to Atlanta when he accepted a position at Atlanta Baptist College (later Morehouse). Hope and a group of women organized kindergartens and daycare facilities for working mothers and built a playground on donated land. For 25 years, she led the Neighborhood Union which helped communities with services not offered by the government, including classes. Hope became widely known as a competent social reformer and leader in her challenges of racism. She also helped create African American Young Women's Christian Association branches and fostered an antilynching movement in which she accused **Jessie Ames** of ignoring the consequences of lynching.

BIBLIOGRAPHY

Rouse, Jacqueline Anne. *Lugenia Burns Hope, Black Southern Reformer*. Athens: University of Georgia Press, 1989. 0–8203–1082–4, 182p. Using manuscripts, archives, and interviews with family, friends, and colleagues, Rouse presents Hope's personal and social contributions in a recommended biography.

HOPPER, GRACE (1906–1992)
Computer Engineer and Military Official   New York, New York

Grace Hopper, mathematician and rear admiral in the United States Navy, was a pioneer in computer technology. Known as "Amazing Grace" and "the First Lady of Software," she was born Grace Brewster Murray on December 9, 1906, into a supportive family. After graduating Phi Beta Kappa from Vassar, she received her M.A. and Ph.D. degrees at Yale before returning to Vassar to teach mathematics. She became an associate professor and studied further at New York University before entering the United States Naval Reserve as a lieutenant. In 1944, she went to the Bureau of Ordnance's Computation Project at Harvard University to work on Mark I, the first large-scale automatic calculator and a precursor of electronic computers. She remained at Harvard as a civilian research fellow while maintaining her naval career as a reservist. After a moth infiltrated the circuits of Mark I, she coined the term "bug" to refer to unexplained computer failures. Later, she worked on the first commercial computer for Sperry Rand, and published the first paper on compilers in 1952. In her career, she published over 50 papers on software and programming languages. In1957, her division developed Flow-Matic, the first English-language data-processing compiler, and she created COBOL, the first user-friendly business software program. She retired from the navy with the rank of commander in 1966, but she was recalled to active duty the following year to help standardize the navy's computer languages. She contributed over $34,000 to the Navy Relief Society from honoraria earned by lecturing around the world about computers. She was elected a fellow of the Institute of Electrical and Electronic Engineers in 1962, was named the first computer science Man of the Year by the Data Processing Management Association in 1969, and was awarded the National Medal of Technology in 1991. She was the oldest officer on active U.S. naval duty when she retired again in 1986 at 79. She also received numerous honorary degrees and other awards, including election to The National Women's Hall of Fame.

BIBLIOGRAPHY

Billings, Charlene W. *Grace Hopper: Navy Admiral and Computer Pioneer*. Hillside, NJ: Enslow, 1989. 0–89490–194–X, 128p. Billings's standard biography for young adults emphasizes Hopper's importance to computer science.

HORNE, LENA (1917–)
Entertainer   Brooklyn, New York

African American Lena Horne became a symbol of achievement for African American women by using her talent and her dignity to become a major American entertainer. She was born on June 30, 1917, to a gambler and a struggling actress who gave her a middle-class background before divorcing when Horne was three. While still young, she often attended activist meetings with her grandmother. Horne traveled with her mother, facing Jim Crow laws, before returning to Brooklyn and then the Bronx, where she had to quit high school when her mother became ill. Horne's beauty got her a job at the Cotton Club, and she began taking music lessons. At 17, when she joined Noble Sissle's Society Orchestra as a singer in Philadelphia, she became reacquainted with her father and married his friend. After having two children, they divorced, and she returned to New York. Walter White and Paul Robeson encouraged her to go to Hollywood to become a film star. During World War II, she entertained the troops around the country, and after the war, she commanded up to $60,000 a week at various New York clubs and appeared on Ed Sullivan's television program in 1950. When she supported friends blacklisted in the McCarthy era, she herself was blacklisted, and no one hired her for television until nine years later. In 1963, she joined the March on Washington and began speaking around the country to African American women before reappearing on Broadway in 1974. In 1981, her one-woman show won a Tony Award and several others. She was also honored with the Spingarn Medal.

BIBLIOGRAPHY

Haskins, James. *Lena: A Biography of Lena Horne*. Chelsea, MI: Scarborough House, 1991. 0–8128–8524–4, 230p. Haskins has carefully researched Horne's life for a balanced biography suitable for young adults.

———. *Lena Horne*. New York: Coward-McCann, 1983. 0–698–20586–3, 160p. Haskins notes that Horne did not begin to accept herself until in her mid-50s in his straightforward, undocumented biography.

Horne, Lena. *Lena*. 1965. New York: Limelight, 1986. 0–879–10066–4, 300p. Horne's autobiography focuses on her life as a celebrity.

Howard, Brett. *Lena Horne*. 1981. Los Angeles: Melrose Square, 1991. 0–87076–757–2, 222p. Howard examines the complexity apparent in Horne's character in his undocumented, popular biography.

HOSMER, HARRIET (1830-1908)
Sculptor   Watertown, Massachusetts

Harriet Goodhue Hosmer was a sculptor. Born on October 9, 1830, she was one of four children, of a physician and his wife, who died from tuberculosis when Hosmer was four. After Hosmer's sister died at 13 from the same disease, her father determined that she should have outdoor exercise to avoid the same fate. Hosmer became an independent and active young woman. During her three years at Mrs. Charles Sedgwick's school in Lenox, she met other liberal women, including novelist **Catharine Maria Sedgwick** and the British actor *Fanny Kemble, who suggested that Hosmer turn her interest in mechanics into clay modeling. At home, Hosmer started a studio, studied with a Boston sculptor, and later pursued anatomy with a family friend's physician at a local medical school. In 1852, when she went to Rome to work, actor **Charlotte Cushman** chaperoned her. Hosmer worked with British sculptor John Gibson to create a bust of Daphne as a present for the friend who had located an anatomy teacher for her. When Hosmer heard in 1854 that her father had lost money, she decided to sell her work in order finance more time in Rome. She began creating full-length figures and other pieces. Her humorous "Puck" sitting on a toadstool sold 50 copies at $1,000 each. In 1860, the state of Missouri gave her a commission to create a statue of Senator Thomas Hart Benton. She exhibited her work in London in 1862 and in New York and Boston in 1864. She retained her independence and continued to fulfill public commissions as well as private ones. She was the first American female sculptor, and of all the nineteenth-century women who pursued the career, the most successful.

BIBLIOGRAPHY
Sherwood, Dolly. *Harriet Hosmer, American Sculptor, 1830–1908.* Columbia: University of Missouri Press, 1991. 0-8262-0766-9, 378p. Careful research using contemporary letters and literary works as well as other sources helped Sherwood capture Hosmer's personality and artistic success.

HOWE, JULIA WARD (1819-1910)
Author   New York, New York

Julia Ward Howe, woman's club and suffrage leader, wrote "Battle Hymn of the Republic." She was born on May 27, 1819, as the fourth of seven children to a partner in a Wall Street banking firm and his wife, who died when Howe was five. Governesses and a young ladies' school educated her, while her exposure to her witty aunt embellished her social ability, a constant conflict to her father's Calvinism throughout her life. Howe enjoyed parties, but she was also intelligent and wrote essays on Goethe, Schiller, and Lamartine, which she published in the *New York Review* and *Theological Review* before she married in 1843. Her husband, 19 years her senior and whom she at first deemed noble, refused to let her engage in public life. In Boston society, Howe was an outsider who hated housekeeping and rarely contained her caustic comments. Additionally, she had an inheritance, a source of money that both irritated and appealed to her husband. Howe entertained herself through reading and writing, and her first play, *Leonora, or the World's Own*, was produced but closed after one week. Her poems and plays, exploring the motifs of violent love and betrayal, dismayed readers who knew her. Her work appeared in *Atlantic Monthly* and the *New York Tribune* but had little impact until the publication of her poem "Battle Hymn of the Republic" in 1862. When someone set it to the tune of "John Brown's Body," it became instantly recognizable, and Boston society decided to accept her. In 1868, she helped **Lucy Stone** start the New England Women's Club and the New England Woman Suffrage Association, began lecturing, and helped found the weekly *Woman's Journal*. In 1874, she edited *Sex and Education* in defense of coeducation, and in 1883, she published a biography of **Margaret Fuller**. In her many lectures, she advocated the values of American life. As she aged, she became known as the "Dearest Old Lady in America" while sustaining her husband's interest in Europe by founding the American Friends of Russian Freedom in 1891 and by becoming the first president of the United Friends of Armenia in 1894. In 1908, she was the first woman elected to the American Academy of Arts and Letters, and hundreds had to remain outside during her memorial service. She was later elected to The National Women's Hall of Fame.

BIBLIOGRAPHY

Clifford, Deborah Pickman. *Mine Eyes Have Seen the Glory: A Biography of Julia Ward Howe*. Boston: Little, Brown, 1979. 0-316-14747-8, 313p. This well-researched and documented scholarly study of Howe notes that she was one of the most renowned women of her time.

Grant, Mary Hetherington. *Private Woman, Public Person: An Account of the Life of Julia Ward Howe*. Brooklyn, NY: Carlson, 1994. 0-926019-66-X, 268p. Grant's biography posits that Howe's husband imprisoned her with pregnancies and frequent moves.

Hall, Florence Howe. *Julia Ward Howe and the Woman Suffrage Movement*. 1913. New York: Arno Press, 1969. No ISBN, 241p. Howe's daughter has written a memoir of her, now dated but still of historical interest.

Richards, Laura Elizabeth Howe, and Maud Elliot. *Julia Ward Howe*. 1915. Atlanta: Cherokee, 1990. 0-87797-196-X, 2 vols. Howe's daughters used letters and recollections about her to thoroughly examine her private and public life. Pulitzer Prize.

HOWLAND, EMILY (1827–1929)
Educator and Reformer   Cayuga County, New York

Emily Howland was an educator, social reformer, and philanthropist. She was born on November 20, 1827, as the only daughter of three children to a merchant and landowner and his strict but loving wife. Howland's maternal grandparents greatly influenced her with their Quaker beliefs, and her grandfather taught her to read before she attended schools and the Poplar Ridge Seminary for two years. In the 1850s, her abolitionist father made their house a way station on the Underground Railroad, and after attending abolitionist conventions, Howland realized that she had to contribute something to the cause. She went to Washington, DC, to substitute for **Myrtilla Miner** at her school in 1857, and she stayed for two years, working only with an assistant. In 1863, when slaves needed help on their way north, she volunteered as a teacher in the freedmen's camps and also helped nurse the needy. In 1867, she convinced her father to purchase 400 acres near the mouth of the Potomac in Heathsville, Virginia, and she began to settle slave families, giving them an opportunity to purchase land. After returning home to nurse her ailing mother, she financed an enlargement of the Sherwood Select School and became interested in women's education, offering interest-free loans and suggesting that Ezra Cornell make his university coeducational. She also donated money to the women's rights, temperance, and peace movements, but her main concern was the education of African Americans. At the age of 99, she went to Albany to accept an honorary degree from the University of the State of New York.

BIBLIOGRAPHY

Breault, Judith Colucci. *The World of Emily Howland: Odyssey of a Humanitarian*. Millbrae, CA: Les Femmes, 1976. 0-89087-987-7, 173p. Based on journals and correspondence, Breault's balanced biography of Howland reveals her contributions to those less fortunate than she.

HOXIE, VINNIE REAM. *See* REAM, VINNIE

HUERTA, DOLORES FERNANDEZ (1930–)
Labor Leader   **Dawson, New Mexico**

Latina American Dolores Fernandez Huerta, a believer in nonviolence and unionism, is the founder, vice president, and chief negotiator of the United Farm Workers union. She was born on April 10, 1930, to parents who divorced while she was still small. Her mother moved Huerta and her two siblings to Stockton, California, saved money from working in a cannery and as a waitress, and opened a restaurant and then a hotel where Huerta and her brothers worked. After Huerta graduated from high school and had several jobs, she realized the need for more schooling, graduated from a junior college, and obtained a provisional teaching certificate. Her positive interaction with students and war veterans incited her to become a social activist and a labor organizer. After marrying another community activist, she met Cesar Chavez and became a spokesperson and negotiator for the United Farm Workers, striving to improve the lives of field workers by organizing them. After suffering an injury at a peaceful demonstration in San Francisco during the 1988 presidential election, she received a large financial award. While recovering, she added immigration reform, pesticide use, and encouraging women to run for public office to her civic concerns. She has been elected into The National Women's Hall of Fame.

BIBLIOGRAPHY

de Ruiz, Dana Catharine, and Richard Larios. *La Causa: The Migrant Farmworkers' Story*. Austin, TX: Raintree Steck-Vaugh, 1993. 0–8114–7231–0, 92p. Using interviews with colleagues and comments by co-workers, de Ruiz and Larios present Huerta's life in a biography for young adults.

Rountree, Cathleen. *On Women Turning 50*. San Francisco: HarperSanFrancisco, 1993. 0–81147–231–0, 214p. Rountree profiles Huerta's career as an older woman pursuing her beliefs.

Telgen, Diane. *Latinas! Women of Achievement*. Detroit: Visible Ink, 1995. 0–7876–0883–1, 405p. This collective biography discusses Huerta's contributions.

HUMPHREY, DORIS (1895–1958)
Dancer   Oak Park, Illinois

Doris Humphrey was a choreographer and a dancer. She was born on October 17, 1895, the only child of a hotel manager and a trained musician. She began dancing lessons at an early age, and when she graduated from school, she wanted to perform. Since the family needed money, Humphrey taught social dancing in local schools while her mother played accompaniment. In 1917, Humphrey finally enrolled in the Denishawn School in Los Angeles and went on its tour to Asia in 1925. Here she began to choreograph, but when the company discouraged her new movement forms, she resigned in 1928. The same year, she opened a New York studio where she used tuition received for dance technique classes to pay for concerts of her new choreography. Humphrey conceived of her dances as "moving from the inside out." She started with feelings and then created the movements and the vocabulary to fit them. Two of her earliest works, *Water Study* (1928) and *Life of the Bee* (1929), focused on natural movement. In 1931, she created *The Shakers*, with its roots in American history. Unable to afford scenery, she used a set of rectangular boxes which she rearranged to create the scene or mood. During the 1930s, her Humphrey-Weidman company toured the "gymnasium circuit" and performed at colleges across the country. By 1944, Humphrey, crippled with arthritis, choreographed for her former student, José Limón, and critics applauded these works as some of her best. At Juilliard after 1950, she founded the Juilliard Dance Theater. She won several honors including the Capezio Award.

BIBLIOGRAPHY

Humphrey, Doris. *Doris Humphrey, an Artist First: An Autobiography*. 1972. Ed. Selma Jeanne Cohen. Pennington, NJ: Princeton, 1995. 0–87127–201–6, 305p. Cohen edited Humphrey's unfinished autobiography and added comments from letters and documents.

Siegel, Marcia B. *Days on Earth: The Dance of Doris Humphrey*. 1988. Durham, NC: Duke University Press, 1993. 0–8223–1346–4, 333p. Siegel's critical biography examines Humphrey as an American dance pioneer.

HUNTER, ALBERTA (1895–1984)
Singer and Composer   Memphis, Tennessee

African American Alberta Hunter achieved international fame as a blues singer during the 1930s. She was born on April 1, 1895, and her career began in Chicago, where she moved when she was 11. In 1921, she went to New York and continued to sing in clubs while recording with such figures as Louis Armstrong and Fats Waller. From 1927 until 1953, Hunter sang throughout Europe and the United States while also performing on USO tours during World War II and the Korean War. In London, she acted in *Show Boat* with Paul Robeson. In 1954, she became a nurse and retired from the stage, although in 1961 she made several recordings. In 1977, she resumed her musical career and continued singing until her death. In addition to performing, Hunter also composed music, including at least one classic composition, "Downhearted Blues," which **Bessie Smith** recorded.

BIBLIOGRAPHY
Taylor, Frank C. *Alberta Hunter: A Celebration in Blues*. New York: McGraw-Hill, 1987. 0–07–063171–9, 311p. Reminiscences, interviews, letters, and reviews form the basis of Taylor's balanced biography.

HUNTER, CLEMENTINE (1886–1988)
Artist   Cloutierville, Louisiana

Clementine Hunter became known internationally for her folk paintings of African Americans in the Cane River region of northern Louisiana. She was born in December 1886. Her mother was a slave, and her father was of mixed Irish and Native American descent, which led Hunter to think of herself as a Creole. The father of Hunter's first two children died, and when she married again 10 years later, she had five children. Only one of her children outlived her. After Hunter created her first painting in 1939, she painted over 5,000 more on any type of surface available. Her work depicts five general subjects: plantation workers, recreation, religious scenes, flowers and birds, and abstract concepts. Her first exhibit was in New Orleans during 1949, and although it received little attention, it garnered fame for Hunter when it reappeared at the Museum of American Folk Art in New York City during 1973 and in the Los Angeles County Museum of Art during 1976. After this time, she held one-woman exhibits and was the subject of oral history projects and television shows. She received an honorary doctor of fine arts degree from Northwestern State University of Louisiana.

BIBLIOGRAPHY
Lyons, Mary, ed. *Talking with Tebe: Clementine Hunter, Memory Artist*. Boston: Houghton Mifflin, 1998. 0–395–72031–1, 48p. Lyons's biography of Hunter for

young adults tells the story of the first self-taught African American artist to receive widespread recognition.

Wilson, James L. *Clementine Hunter, American Folk Artist*. Gretna, LA: Pelican, 1988. 0-88289-658-X, 160p. Wilson records Hunter's life, personality, and work.

HUNTER, JANE EDNA (1882-1971)
Reformer   **Pendleton, South Carolina**

Jane Edna Hunter devoted herself to obtaining better conditions for African American women, believing, like Booker T. Washington, that a person who could do something well would be self-sufficient. Born as the granddaughter of a slave woman and her plantation overseer on December 13, 1882, Hunter was given the name of her paternal English grandmother. She attended school until her father's death when she was 10, and when she was 14, missionaries invited her to attend school in Abbeville, South Carolina, in exchange for working. She became a nurse after attending Dixie Hospital and Training School at Hampton Institute. In Cleveland in 1905, she found that African American nurses could only get private duty jobs and that housing was almost nonexistent. She determined that she would help other young African American women avoid similar problems, and when she asked the YWCA to help her open a separate home for African American women, its leaders agreed. She opened the **Phillis Wheatley** Home in 1913 and maintained cordial relationships with white leaders in order to obtain regular donations. She remained executive director until 1946 while founding other groups for African American women, attending classes at the Cleveland School of Law, and passing the bar in 1926. After her retirement, she established the Phillis Wheatley Foundation, a scholarship fund, from the nearly half million dollars she saved from investments made from a salary that never exceeded $3,000 per year. Her light skin had alienated Hunter from her dark-skinned mother, and after years of fighting her race, Hunter embraced it and successfully improved its conditions.

BIBLIOGRAPHY

Jones, Adrienne Lash. *Jane Edna Hunter: A Case Study of Black Leadership*. Brooklyn, NY: Carlson, 1990. 0-926019-18-X, 189p. In this biography, Jones emphasizes Hunter's willingness to work.

HURSTON, ZORA NEALE (1903-1960)
Author and Anthropologist   **Eatonville, Florida**

Zora Neale Hurston, an anthropologist by training, used folklore as a basis for exploring the African American culture during the Harlem Renaissance. She was born on January 17, 1903, the fifth of eight children. Her mother died when Hurston was three, and her father later sent her to boarding school, with his remarriage a few months later destroying the family. Hurston began living with family members or strangers and working to support herself. An employer gave her financial help for school, and she was able to attend Howard University and Barnard College, finishing her study at Columbia in anthropology with Franz Boas. She published her first short stories in 1924, and in 1926 began collaborating with Langston Hughes as editor for the magazine *Fire!*, in which one of her stories appeared. In 1930, the two wrote *Mule Bone*, a play. In the 1930s, she traveled in the American South and the West Indies to collect local myths and legends about African Americans, and near the end of the decade, she published her masterpiece, *Their Eyes Were Watching God*. As the most published female author of her day, she wrote about characters dealing with their gender while trying to understand their spiritual struggles. Later, when Hurston had difficulty getting her work published, she returned to Florida and died in poverty. Critics have recently realized her literary value, and her work has been either reissued or published for the first time. She has also been elected to The National Women's Hall of Fame.

BIBLIOGRAPHY

Hemenway, Robert E. *Zora Neale Hurston: A Literary Biography*. Urbana: University of Illinois Press, 1977. 0-252-00652-6, 371p. Hemenway reveals Hurston's complexities through his carefully documented, recommended biography.

Howard, Lillie P. *Zora Neale Hurston*. Boston: Twayne, 1980. 0-8057-7296-0, 192p. Carefully documented, this critical study offers insight on Hurston's life and work.

Lyons, Mary E. *Sorrow's Kitchen: The Life and Folklore of Zora Neale Hurston*. New York: Scribner, 1990. 0-684-19198-9, 144p. Lyons uses excerpts from Hurston's writing in her young adult biography.

Nathiri, N. Y. *Zora! Zora Neale Hurston, a Woman and Her Community*. Orlando, FL: Sentinel, 1991. 0-941263-21-5, 134p. Although not a scholarly biography, the text presents Hurston from the perspective of her friends, relatives, and other authors.

Witcover, Paul. *Zora Neale Hurston*. New York: Chelsea House, 1991. 0-7910-1129-1, 119p. Witcover's young adult biography is also suitable for adults since he examines not only Hurston's life but also the problems of African American identity.

HUTCHINSON, ANNE MARBURY (1591–1643)
Religious Leader   **Alford, England**

Anne Hutchinson led the first organized dissension to Puritan orthodoxy in the Massachusetts Bay Colony. She was born in 1591 as the second of 13 children to a censured clergyman and his wife. Hutchinson learned the Scriptures as a child and inherited some of her father's willfulness. In 1612, she married a businessman, and between 1613 and 1630, bore 12 children. She heard John Cotton's teachings in which he espoused the Covenant of Grace in addition to the Covenant of Works, and she interpreted his view to mean that God's spirit dwelled within the elect, uniting them directly to God, and making the evidence of sanctification, as required by the Covenant of Works, unnecessary. When Anglican authorities sent Cotton to the Massachusetts Bay Colony, Hutchinson told her family that God had said to follow him. The family left the next year for Boston, where her husband entered the cloth trade and gained a place of status in Boston society.

Hutchinson's nursing skills for both sickness and childbirth introduced her to many of the women, but hearing most of them profess a Covenant of Works concerned her, and she began lecturing on a Covenant of Grace. Boston's leaders began to follow her, but after the Reverend John Wilson replaced Cotton in the pulpit, Wilson emphasized the necessity of sanctification. The government decided that Hutchinson's way was dangerous when the males following her refused to fight the Pequot Indians, and thereby jeopardized public safety. John Winthrop, as the new governor, worked to unseat her supporters on the General Court, and in 1637 brought Hutchinson to trial. She almost succeeded in her case until she said that God would destroy those who disagreed with her. Although immediately banished from the colony, she had to wait until spring before she could leave, and in March 1638, she joined her husband in a new settlement on the Narragansett Bay. After his death in 1642, Hutchinson and her six youngest children went to the Dutch colony of New Netherland, near Pelham Bay Park in the Bronx, and the following year, Indians massacred all but her youngest daughter. Hutchinson's efforts and sacrifice made religious difference possible in the colonies. She has been elected to The National Women's Hall of Fame.

BIBLIOGRAPHY

Dunlea, William. *Anne Hutchinson and the Puritans*. Pittsburgh: Dorrance, 1993. 0-8059-3434-0, 286p. Dunlea's researched but undocumented biography of Hutchinson declares her the "mother of all Americans."

IlgenFritz, Elizabeth. *Anne Hutchinson*. New York: Chelsea House, 1991. 1-555-46660-5, 111p. IlgenFritz's researched biography of Hutchinson for young adults covers her life.

Lang, Amy Schrager. *Prophetic Woman: Anne Hutchinson and the Problem of Dissent in the Literature of New England*. Berkeley: University of California Press, 1987. 0-520-05598-5, 237p. Lang used Puritan tracts and histories to trace Hutchinson's life.

Leonardo, Bianca, and Winnifred K. Rugg. *Anne Hutchinson: Unsung Heroine of History*. Joshua Tree, CA: Tree of Life, 1995. 0-930852-30-3, 347p. In this biography for young adults, Leonardo sees Hutchinson as a feminist.

Williams, Selma R. *Divine Rebel: The Life of Anne Marbury Hutchinson*. New York: Holt, Rinehart and Winston, 1981. 0-03-055846-8, 246p. Williams examines Hutchinson's life in terms of her seventeenth-century world, in a carefully researched and documented biography.

J

JACKSON, HELEN HUNT (1830–1885)
Author and Reformer   **Amherst, Massachusetts**

Helen Hunt Jackson was a poet and author. Born Helen Fiske on October 13, 1830, she was one of four children of whom only two survived, of a Greek and Latin professor and his Calvinist wife. When Jackson was 14, her mother died of tuberculosis, and her father died three years later. During Jackson's sporadic schooling, her charm attracted an army engineer, whom she married in 1852, as well as **Emily Dickinson**, who remained her lifelong friend. After a happy but nomadic life, she lost her husband and two sons within three years. To escape her subsequent despondency, she began writing verse under the mentorship of Thomas Wentworth Higginson. Through him, she discovered the poetic formula that magazine editors would purchase, and her poetry and prose began appearing in many leading magazines of the time. In the 1870s, even Ralph Waldo Emerson thought she was America's best female poet. (Dickinson was not yet widely known.) Jackson remarried in 1875, and the financial stability her marriage provided freed her from constantly having to write. In 1879, after hearing Bright Eyes (**Susette La Flesche Tibbles**) talk about the plight of the Ponca Indians, Jackson contacted the secretary of the interior, and her tirade over the government's treatment of Native Americans gained national attention. In 1881, she published her rage in the book *A Century of Dishonor*, and sent a copy at her own expense to every official who had a connection to the problem. The following year, the Interior Department asked her to survey the needs of the Mission Indians on the West Coast, but after a well-documented report caused no response from Washington, Jackson wrote a novel, *Ramona*, in which she described how the

Spanish society in California and other whites had victimized the Indians. The book was reprinted over 300 times and remains the work for which Jackson is remembered.

BIBLIOGRAPHY

Banning, Evelyn I. *Helen Hunt Jackson*. New York: Vanguard Press, 1973. 0-8149-0735-0, 248p. Banning indicates in her biography that Jackson will be remembered for her concerns about Native American rights.

Jackson, Helen Hunt. *Helen Hunt Jackson's Colorado*. Colorado Springs: Colorado College, 1989. 0-935052-20-8, 83p. Jackson wrote the essays selected for the text when she first went to Colorado in 1873.

Mathes, Valerie Sherer. *Helen Hunt Jackson and Her Indian Reform Legacy*. Norman: University of Oklahoma Press, 1997. 0-8061-2963-8, 235p. Mathes's well-researched intellectual history of Jackson concludes that her actions hindered rather than helped Native Americans.

May, Antoinette. *Helen Hunt Jackson: A Lonely Voice of Conscience*. San Francisco: Chronicle, 1987. 0-87701-376-4, 146p. May used Hunt's writings, including books, poems, and letters, as her primary source for this biography.

JACKSON, MAHALIA (1911–1972)
Singer   **New Orleans, Louisiana**

African American Mahalia Jackson's singing earned her the name "Queen of Gospel Song." She was born on October 26, 1911, the third of six children. Her stevedore, barber, and preacher father died when she was four. The same year, she began to sing in the children's choir, and after her mother's early death, she lived with her mother's sisters and heard the music of **Bessie Smith** and **Ma Rainey** in her friends' homes. She began performing in churches and at religious meetings before going at age 16 to Chicago, where the mixture of New Orleans jazz and sacred music attracted her to the gospel style. She had several jobs in Chicago, and when she joined a church choir, the director immediately chose her as a soloist. Her singing gained the attention of Thomas A. Dorsey, the "Father of Gospel Music," who asked her to record his songs and to sing them around the country at religious meetings. Her style offended some who thought her hand-clapping was irreverent, and others wanted her to sing in clubs, but she refused, saying that gospel music offered hope, while blues music did not. She recorded over 30 albums with such songs as "He's Got the Whole World in His Hands," and had among her single records 12 gold ones. After World War II, she appeared in movies and traveled to Europe, performing for thousands. She sang in Carnegie Hall, supported Martin Luther King, Jr.'s March on Washington, and established the Mahalia Jackson Scholarship Fund to help poor youth attend college even though she had only completed the eighth grade. At one of her several funeral service memorials, **Aretha Franklin** sang one of the Dorsey songs Jackson recorded, "Precious Lord, Take My Hand."

BIBLIOGRAPHY

Donloe, Darlene. *Mahalia Jackson*. Los Angeles: Melrose Square, 1992. 0-87067-585-0, 172p. In this biography for young adults, Donloe gives an overview of Jackson's life and career.

Goreau, Laurraine. *Just Mahalia, Baby*. Waco, TX: Word, 1975. No ISBN, 611p. Goreau's readable and recommended biography of Jackson re-creates her life and her music.

Gourse, Leslie. *Mahalia Jackson: Queen of Gospel Song*. New York: Franklin Watts, 1996. 0-531-11228-4, 128p. In this balanced young adult biography, based mainly on Jackson's autobiography, Gourse shows the importance of religion in her choice of music.

Schwerin, Jules Victor. *Got to Tell It: Mahalia Jackson, Queen of Gospel*. New York: Oxford University Press, 1992. 0-19-507144-1, 204p. The author met Jackson in the 1950s, and he recalls their friendship.

Wolfe, Charles K. *Mahalia Jackson*. New York: Chelsea House, 1990. 1-55546-661-3, 111p. Wolfe's biography for young adults presents Jackson's life.

JACKSON, REBECCA (1795-1871)
Religious Leader   Horntown, Philadelphia

Rebecca Cox Jackson, an itinerant African American preacher, founded a religious communal family in Philadelphia. Born into a free African American family in 1795, she lived with her maternal grandmother and her mother, who died when Jackson was 13. She married but remained childless, and while she and her husband lived with her brother, she helped raise his four children. Jackson had a religious experience during a storm in 1830, and during the Holiness movement became a preacher. By being a woman who announced that only celibates could lead holy lives, she caused consternation. Her beliefs separated her from her family, and she joined the Shakers in Watervliet, New York. Since the Shakers would not take their message to African Americans, Jackson broke with the group and went to Philadelphia, where she and her friend Rebecca Perot founded an African American female Shaker family which survived her for 25 years.

BIBLIOGRAPHY

Williams, Richard E. *Called and Chosen: The Story of Mother Rebecca Jackson and the Philadelphia Shakers*. Metuchen, NJ: Scarecrow Press, 1981. 0-8108-1382-3, 179p. Using the journals that Jackson kept from 1830 to 1876 and journals of those who knew her, Williams places her in both Shaker and American history.

JACOBI, MARY PUTNAM (1842-1906)
Physician   London, England

Mary Putnam Jacobi was a physician and suffragist. The oldest of 11 children, she was born to the founder of the Putnam Publishing firm and his wife, who were enjoying London at the time of her birth on August 31, 1842. Educated mainly at home by her mother, Putnam also commuted to New York City to study at a public school and to take Greek with a tutor. When she was 18, her first published essay appeared in the *Atlantic Monthly*, and even though she enjoyed writing, she expected to study medicine. Her father did not understand her choices, but he never opposed her, and in 1864, she received her M.D. from the Female Medical College of Pennsylvania before working in **Marie Zakrzewska**'s hospital in Boston. During the Civil War, she went to Louisiana to nurse her brother, who had malaria, and to South Carolina to help a sister with typhoid. In 1866, she went to Paris for more training, and while there, she decided that she preferred medical practice to research. She also decided that she wanted to enter the École de Médecine, a school that had never enrolled women. She gained admission in 1868 and graduated with high honors in 1871. When she returned to New York, she became the first woman to deliver a paper at the Medical Library and Journal Association and wrote hundreds more on pathology, neurology, pediatrics, and physiology. In 1872, she organized the Advancement of the Medical Education of Women and served as its president for 31 years, and in 1873, she married another physician renowned as a pediatrician. The same year, she took the rank of professor of materia medica and therapeutics at *Elizabeth Blackwell's New York Infirmary for Women and Children, remaining until 1889. In 1876, she won Harvard's Boylston Prize for her essay "The Question of Rest for Women During Menstruation." Jacobi supported high educational standards and demanded much of her female medical students. She has been elected to The National Women's Hall of Fame.

BIBLIOGRAPHY
Truax, Rhoda. *The Doctors Jacobi*. Boston: Little, Brown, 1952. No ISBN, 270p. This fictional biography of Jacobi and her husband presents her achievements as the first woman admitted to the École de Médecine in Paris.

JACOBS, HARRIET A. (1813–1897)
Slave, Reformer, and Activist   Edenton, North Carolina

Harriet Ann Jacobs became an abolitionist, wrote a slave narrative, and helped African American Civil War refugees. She was born a slave in 1813 with a white paternal grandfather. After her mother died when she was six, Jacobs went to live with her grandmother, and in 1825, when Jacobs's mistress died, she was not freed as had been anticipated but bequeathed to her mistress's three-year-old niece. To stop her master from turning her into a concubine, she became sexually involved with a white attorney who lived nearby and with whom she had two children. She escaped at 21, but to keep her children safe, Jacobs spent seven years in a tiny crawl space seven feet by nine feet by three feet above a porch in her grandmother and uncle's home. In 1842, she finally escaped to the North and was reunited with her children, who had already left. Fearing for her life after the passage of the Fugitive Slave Law in 1850, she went to Massachusetts, and unknown to her, the family for whom she had worked in New York City bought her and her children and gave them their freedom. She then wrote the story about the sexual abuse she had endured, and it made her famous. As a celebrity, she asked Northern women supporters of abolition for money, and she and her daughter established a school and provided emergency health care for African American refugees in Alexandria, Virginia, and then in Savannah, Georgia. She also helped others in Massachusetts and Washington, DC, until her death.

BIBLIOGRAPHY

Jacobs, Harriet A. *Incidents in the Life of a Slave Girl*. Ed. Jean Fagan Yellin. New York: Oxford University Press, 1988. 0-19-505243-9, 306p. Yellin attempts to demonstrate that Jacobs wrote her autobiography herself by using Jacobs's handwritten manuscript, Chowan County records, plantation records, and contemporary newspapers.

JAMISON, JUDITH (1943-)
Dancer   Philadelphia, Pennsylvania

Judith Jamison is an African American dancer, choreographer, and artistic director. She was born on May 19, 1943, as one of two children to parents she credits with her love of dance and her pride in being African American. To help her expend her boundless energy, they enrolled Jamison in the Judimar School of Dance, where she gave her first dance recital at the age of six. She attended for 11 years, studying ballet, tap, acrobatics, jazz, and primitive dance, while also attending public school. After enrolling at Fisk University on a physical education scholarship, Jamison left three semesters later for the Philadelphia Dance Academy. In 1965, she first danced professionally in **Agnes de Mille**'s *Four Marys* at the American Ballet Theatre. Alvin Ailey invited her to dance with his troupe the same year, and until 1980, she was a lead dancer on tours around the world. Learning more than 70 ballets, she also performed as a guest with other companies. Vienna Opera choreographers created lead roles for her, and she choreographed her own ballets for companies including that of Maurice Bejart in Paris. She also starred on Broadway in *Sophisticated Ladies*. In the 1980s, she choreographed, established a dance troupe, and became artistic director of Ailey's dance company, merging it with hers. Among her honorary degrees and awards are the *Dance Magazine Award* and a Candace Award.

BIBLIOGRAPHY

Jamison, Judith. *Dancing Spirit: An Autobiography*. New York: Doubleday, 1993. 0-385-42557-0, 272p. In her autobiography, suitable for young adults, Jamison discusses her life.
Maynard, Olga. *Judith Jamison: Aspects of a Dancer*. Garden City, NY: Doubleday, 1982. 0-385-12985-8, 294p. The two parts of Maynard's well-documented biography present both Jamison's career and life.

JEMISON, MAE (1956–)
Astronaut   Decatur, Alabama

Mae C. Jemison became the first African American female astronaut in the National Aeronautics and Space Administration (NASA). She was born on October 17, 1956, to a carpenter and roofer and his wife, an elementary school teacher. Her parents moved to Chicago when she was three, and in elementary school, she began working on serious science projects. At 16, she graduated from high school, where she had been a cheerleader, and accepted a National Achievement Scholarship to Stanford University, where she received a B.S. in chemical engineering and completed requirements for a B.A. in African and Afro-American studies. She then attended Cornell University Medical School and received her M.D. in 1981. While attending school, she also worked in a Thai refugee camp and studied in Kenya. Afterward, she served as a Peace Corps medical officer in Sierra Leone and Liberia, researching hepatitis B, schistosomiasis, and rabies. In 1987, she became an astronaut candidate, and in 1988, she qualified as a mission specialist. She went into space for a week on September 12, 1992, and studied the effects of zero gravity on people and animals. Afterward, she resigned from NASA to form her own company to adapt technology for use in underdeveloped nations. She was recently elected to The National Women's Hall of Fame.

BIBLIOGRAPHY
Yannuzzi, Della A. *Mae Jemison: A Space Biography*. Springfield, NJ: Enslow, 1998. 0–89490–813–8, 48p. This researched and documented biography for young adults discusses Jemison's life and career.

JEMISON, MARY (1743–1833)
Pioneer and Indian Captive   On the Atlantic Ocean

Mary Jemison was an Indian captive known as the "white woman of the Genesee." She was born on shipboard in 1743, the fourth of six children, while her parents traveled to America. Her farming family was wealthy, and she received some schooling and religious training. In 1758, during the French and Indian War, a raiding party of Shawnee and French captured and killed her family except for her and two brothers. A Seneca family adopted her and took her with them to the Ohio River, where two years later she married a Delaware Indian named Sheninjee. Jemison retained her tribal and family affiliation after her marriage, the Iroquois custom, but her husband died soon after the death of a daughter and the birth of a son, and Jemison went to the Genesee Valley with her Seneca family. There she married a Seneca warrior named Hiokatoo in 1765 and bore six children who kept her surname. During the American Revolution, Jemison's husband fought with his tribe for England, and a war party destroyed their community. After the war, she refused to leave because she knew that the white community would not accept her children. Throughout her life, she lived in a log cabin, but she became owner of a huge area of land when the government granted the tribe more territory. In 1817, Jemison was naturalized as a citizen of New York State. She lived like the other Seneca women and remained known for her kindness to both whites and Native Americans.

BIBLIOGRAPHY

Merrill, Arch. *The White Woman and Her Valley*. Interlaken, NY: Empire State, 1987. 0-932334-88-1, 207p. In a biography suitable for young adults, Merrill includes background on Jemison's life.

Seaver, James E. *A Narrative of the Life of Mrs. Mary Jemison*. Norman: University of Oklahoma Press, 1993. 0-8061-2381-8, 192p. Appropriate for young adults, this edition of Jemison's story reveals her positive views of the people with whom she lived.

JEWETT, SARAH ORNE (1849–1909)
Author   **South Berwick, Maine**

Sarah Orne Jewett was an author who set her stories in the state of Maine. She was born on September 3, 1849, the daughter of a physician and his wife. Her poor health as a child interfered with her schooling, and her father often took her on his rounds. She said that his tales of life and people in the region became the content of her stories. She also read constantly to prepare herself for her work. Beginning in 1868, she published three stories before "The Shore House," published in *Atlantic*, gained her acclaim. Jewett used her father's advice to write not *about* things but to "write the things themselves just as they are." After her father's death in 1878, Jewett became close friends with **Annie Fields**, wife of the publisher James T. Fields. She lived part of each year with Fields in Boston after the death of Fields's husband and visited Europe with her. During this period, Jewett never married but devoted herself to the hard work of her craft, planning her stories carefully and keeping the discipline to create them. Critics consider *The Country of the Pointed Firs*, published in 1896, her best work. Among her awards were honorary degrees.

BIBLIOGRAPHY

Blanchard, Paula. *Sarah Orne Jewett: Her World and Her Work*. Reading, MA: Addison-Wesley, 1994. 0-201-51810-4, 397p. Blanchard examines Jewett's life in her balanced, definitive biography.

Keyworth, C. L. *Master Smart Woman: A Portrait of Sarah Orne Jewett*. Unity, ME: North Country Press, 1988. 0-945980-02-7, 179p. In a brief text for a film, accompanied by thoughtful photographs of interest to researchers, Keyworth gives a general overview of Jewett's life and work.

Silverthorne, Elizabeth. *Sarah Orne Jewett: A Writer's Life*. Woodstock, NY: Overlook Press, 1993. 0-87951-484-1, 238p. Unpublished letters and diaries helped Silverthorne to create this well-researched biography of Jewett.

JONES, LOÏS MAILOU (1905-1998)
Artist   Boston, Massachusetts

African American Loïs Mailou Jones, a professor of art, has emphasized technique, skill, elegance, and design in her art. Her beautician mother and her lawyer father influenced her greatly after her birth on November 3, 1905, by instilling in her the need for both ambition and beauty. She studied art while attending high school, and in 1923 entered the Boston Museum of Fine Arts, where she won the Susan Minot Lane Scholarship in Design for each of her four years. She continued graduate study in Boston and at Harvard before going south to help other African Americans. After developing the art department at Palmer Memorial Institute for **Charlotte Hawkins Brown,** Jones went to Howard University in 1930 and remained there until 1977. In 1937, she took her first sabbatical in Paris, and on her return, she began to exhibit throughout the United States. She married a Haitian graphic artist and designer in 1953, and on her first visit to Haiti fell in love with the people and the culture. In 1969, Howard University funded her research trip to 11 African countries, where she photographed the work of contemporary artists. Among her awards are the National Thayer Prize and the Honneur et Mérité au Grade de Chevalier from Haiti. When the *Washington Post* interviewed her at age 90 in 1995, she said that to live long, one had to have "passion" for one's work.

BIBLIOGRAPHY
Benjamin, Tritobia H. *The Life and Art of Loïs Mailou Jones.* San Francisco: Pomegranate
    Artbooks, 1994. 0-87654-105-8, 142p. Benjamin, one of Jones's former students,
    has written a historical and biographical review of her work.

JONES, MARGO (1912-1955)
Theatrical Producer and Director   Livingston, Texas

Margo Jones was an advocate of regional theater and theater-in-the-round. She was born Margaret Virginia Jones on December 12, 1912, as one of four children to a lawyer and a teacher. She first planned to be a lawyer because she enjoyed courtroom action, but realizing that it was the same as a play, she decided to stage plays instead, using the more theatrical name of Margo. At 11, she organized her siblings and staged plays in their barn, but she did not see her first professional production until she was 15. That same year, she enrolled in the College of Industrial Arts (Texas Woman's University), where she earned her M.A. in psychology, writing her thesis on psychological conflict in Henrik Ibsen's drama. Jones began reading a play a day, acted in several plays in order to understand the actor's problems, and took her first directing job in 1933 at the Ojai Community Players in California. In Houston in 1936, she started the adult Houston Community Players, which became self-supporting and expanded from 9 members to 600. She first saw theater-in-the-round in 1939 and took the concept to Houston. In 1944, she used a grant from the Rockefeller Foundation to start a professional repertory company in Dallas. After success in 1947, she produced 57 new plays out of 85 before her accidental death in 1955 from spilled cleaning fluid fumes. Her influence enabled other innovators to continue regional theater work.

BIBLIOGRAPHY

Sheehy, Helen. *Margo: The Life and Theatre of Margo Jones*. Dallas: Southern Methodist University Press, 1989. 0-87074-296-5, 316p. Sheehy's well-researched biography examines Jones and her work.

JONES, MARY (MOTHER) (1830?–1930)
Labor Leader   Cork, Ireland

"Mother Jones" was a labor agitator who helped mine workers form unions. She was born on May 1, 1830, as Mary Harris, daughter of an Irishman who immigrated to America when she was five, with the rest of the family eventually following. She attended school in Canada, but her first job was teaching in Michigan. While teaching in Memphis, Tennessee, at a later time, she met her husband, an iron-molder. In 1867, her husband and her four children died in the yellow fever epidemic, during which she served as a volunteer nurse. When she returned to Chicago to become a dressmaker, sewing for the wealthy, she began to resent the differences among economic classes. In 1871, she lost everything she owned in the Chicago Fire. While the Kings of Labor harbored her, she saw how the group tried to improve wages, working hours, and poor working conditions. She joined them. By the end of the 1870s, she had gone to Pittsburgh to aid striking railroad workers and found her life's mission. She traveled to areas undergoing strikes caused by economic depression, and in the 1890s, she began to help the coal miners by founding the Social Democratic Party and organizing the anthracite strikes of 1900 and 1902. She decided that the sight of children marching to a textile mill owner's home in Oyster Bay, New York, would attract national attention to the horrors of child labor, and she was right. After going west to help miners, machinists, and those suffering from the Mexican Revolution, she returned to West Virginia in 1913, and was arrested, tried, and convicted of conspiracy to commit murder for aiding strikers. The newly elected governor of the state freed her, and during the next few years, she participated in streetcar, garment, and steel strikes. In her labor negotiations, she refused to compromise, always supporting the downtrodden worker. For her achievements, she was elected to The National Women's Hall of Fame.

BIBLIOGRAPHY

Atkinson, Linda. *Mother Jones, the Most Dangerous Woman in America*. New York: Crown, 1978. 0-517-53201-8, 246p. This carefully researched and readable young adult biography of Mother Jones places her within her times.
Fetherling, Dale. *Mother Jones, the Miners' Angel*. Carbondale: Southern Illinois University Press, 1974. 0-8093-0643-3, 263p. With little information available about Mother Jones's earlier years, Fetherling's well-documented text reveals a tireless agitator.

Jones, Mary (Mother). *The Autobiography of Mother Jones.* Ed. Mary Field Parton. Chicago: Kerr, 1990. 0-88286-167-0, 302p. This edition of Mother Jones's autobiography is preceded by a foreword by Meridel Le Sueur, who has never forgotten seeing Mother Jones at work.

Josephson, Judith Pinkerton. *Mother Jones: Fierce Fighter for Workers' Rights.* Minneapolis: Lerner, 1997. 0-8225-4924-7, 144p. Josephson's carefully researched and documented biography for young adults relies on Mother Jones's autobiography and the writing of labor historians.

JOPLIN, JANIS (1943–1970)
Entertainer   Port Arthur, Texas

Janis Joplin was a singer known as the "first female superstar of rock music." She was born as the older of two children on January 19, 1943, to an engineer for Texaco and the registrar of a local business college. She took art lessons as a child but also performed in the church choir and the glee club at school. She and her friends listened to jazz, and Joplin memorized songs from records by **Bessie Smith**, Odetta, and Leadbelly. Her first chance to sing occurred in Austin, Texas, where she had returned to school as an art student at the University of Texas. In 1966, she met a Texan who suggested that she sing with the rock group Big Brother and the Holding Company in San Francisco. When she sang "Love Is Like a Ball and Chain" with the group at the first Monterey International Pop Festival in 1967, she was immediately successful. The same summer, she signed a management contract for over $150,000 a year. In 1968, she made her New York debut and appeared at the Newport, Rhode Island, Folk Festival. Her first album, *Cheap Thrills*, sold over 1 million copies. After she toured the country and successfully debuted in London, she began singing with the Full Tilt Boogie Band, a group able to capture the excitement of live concerts on an album. Although she loved performing for audiences, she also drank heavily and took drugs. In her performances, she wore whatever she wanted and sang the songs of past African American blues singers. Her refusal to follow convention changed contemporary music. Those who saw her in concert thought that she could hold an audience with a charisma similar to that of Elvis Presley. But as her fame was rising, she died of acute heroin-morphine intoxication.

BIBLIOGRAPHY
Amburn, Ellis. *Pearl: The Obsessions and Passions of Janis Joplin.* New York: Warner, 1992. 0-446-51640-6, 340p. Amburn's recommended biography of Joplin, based on interviews and earlier biographies, places Joplin in her times.

Dalton, David. *Piece of My Heart: The Life, Times, and Legend of Janis Joplin.* New York: St. Martin's, 1985. 0-312-61055-6, 284p. Dalton's biography of Joplin is a researched examination of her life and career.

Friedman, Myra. *Buried Alive: The Biography of Janis Joplin.* New York: Harmony, 1992. 0-517-58650-9, 353p. Friedman, Joplin's publicist and best friend, reveals her complexity in this researched and recommended biography.

Joplin, Laura. *Love, Janis*. New York: Villard, 1992. 0-679-41605-6, 342p. The author uses her older sister's unpublished letters home to describe Joplin's life in a biography suitable for young adults.

Landau, Deborah. *Janis Joplin, Her Life and Times*. New York: Paperback, 1971. No ISBN, 160p. Landau tries to find the "real" Joplin in her popular biography.

JORDAN, BARBARA (1936–1996)
Attorney and Congresswoman   Houston, Texas

Barbara Jordan was a lawyer and educator who became the first African American Congresswoman from Texas. She was born on February 21, 1936, as the youngest of three girls to a Baptist minister and a domestic worker. Jordan graduated near the top of her high school class and magna cum laude from Texas Southern University with degrees in political science and history. She earned her J.D. from Boston University in 1959 and returned to Texas to practice law. Elected to the Texas State Senate in 1966, she was the first African American to serve since 1883. Her success led her to run for Congress, and in 1972, she won. Her main concerns were the poor and disadvantaged, especially African Americans, and she helped pass the Workman's Compensation Act to increase benefits for injured workers. In 1974, she became nationally known as a member of the House Judiciary Committee during the Watergate hearings. In 1976, as the first African American woman to deliver the keynote address at the Democratic National Convention, she astounded people throughout the country with her articulate and insightful delivery. Among her many awards were the Democratic Woman of the Year, the Spingarn Medal, and election to The National Women's Hall of Fame. She retired to the classroom in 1978, suffering from multiple sclerosis.

BIBLIOGRAPHY

Haskins, James. *Barbara Jordan*. New York: Dial, 1977. 0-8037-0452-6, 215p. Haskins's young adult biography of Jordan covers her life and career.

Jeffrey, Laura S. *Barbara Jordan: Congresswoman, Lawyer, Educator*. Springfield, NJ: Enslow, 1997. 0-89490-692-5, 112p. Jeffrey used primary sources and background on the historical times in her young adult biography of Jordan.

Jordan, Barbara. *Barbara Jordan: A Self-Portrait*. Garden City, NY: Doubleday, 1979. 0-385-13599-8, 269p. Jordan dwells mainly on her family and other people who influenced her in this intellectual autobiography.

Kelin, Norman, and Sabra-Anne Kelin. *Barbara Jordan*. Los Angeles: Melrose Square, 1993. 0-87067-598-2, 187p. This biography for young adults traces Jordan's life.

Rogers, Mary Beth. *Barbara Jordan: American Hero*. New York: Bantam, 1998. 0-553-10603-1, 432p. Rogers received cooperation from the Jordan estate for her biography.

JOYNER-KERSEE, JACQUELINE (1962–)
Athlete   East St. Louis, Illinois

Jackie Joyner-Kersee has won Olympic Gold medals in several events and broken world records in the heptathlon. Born to teenage parents on March 3, 1962, Joyner-Kersee entered her first track competition when she was nine. At 14, she won her first National Junior Pentathlon Championship. She played basketball at UCLA and qualified for the 1980 Moscow Olympics, but the United States boycott kept her at home. When assistant track coach Bob Kersee saw her perform, he received permission to coach her and suggested that she begin heptathlon training. She set collegiate records before qualifying for the 1984 Olympics, and in Los Angeles became the first American woman to win any multievent medal by winning the silver medal in the heptathlon. She married Kersee in 1986 and prepared for Seoul where she collected over 7,000 points, a feat equal to a four-minute mile for heptathlon competitors. For this performance, she won the Sullivan Award and the Jesse Owens Award. At the age of 30, in the 1992 Barcelona Olympics, she won the gold for the second time. Although an injury forced her withdrawal from heptathlon competition at the 1996 Atlanta Olympics, she was able to win a bronze medal in the long jump. In 1998, she retired after winning the heptathlon at the Goodwill Games.

BIBLIOGRAPHY
Cohen, Neil. *Jackie Joyner-Kersee*. Boston: Little, Brown, 1992. 0–316–15047–9, 124p. In a biography for young adults, Cohen discusses Joyner-Kersee's career.
Joyner-Kersee, Jacqueline. *A Kind of Grace*. New York: Warner, 1997. 0–446–52248–1, 310p. Joyner-Kersee's autobiography recounts her life and career.

K

KAAHUMANU (1777?–1832)
Ruler and Regent   Hana, Maui

Kaahumanu was co-ruler of the Hawaiian people after her husband's death.
The date of her birth is disputed, having been reported as 1768, 1773, or 1777.
As the daughter of warrior Keeaumoku and Namahana, widow of the king of
Maui, she may have been born in a cave while Hawaiian chiefs were at war. Her
father promised her in marriage while a child to the much older Kamehameha,
and she became one of his several wives when only a teenager. One of the most
beautiful women on the island according to cultural standards, at six feet and
300 pounds, Kaahumanu quickly became his favorite. She encouraged her
husband to unite the islands and become the absolute monarch, and she helped
him rule the new state. When he died in 1819, she created a new position,
kohina nui (co-ruler), with the new king, Kamehamela II, until he left for
England and died. She then served as regent for the boy king, Kamehamela III.
During this period in Hawaii's history, while many explorers were visiting the
islands, Kaahumanu exerted great influence. She disliked religious and social
taboos for women, and she and another widow persuaded Kamehamela II to be
the first man to eat with the women. She refused to practice the old religion,
and when missionaries arrived soon after, she was ready to listen to their ideas.
They taught her to read and write, and after four years, she accepted
Christianity, taking the name Elizabeth. Her new religious zeal included
disdain for Christian church icons because they reminded her of old Hawaiian
idols. In 1824, she proclaimed the first code of laws in Hawaii to forbid murder,
fighting, and theft. She proclaimed that all should observe the Sabbath and that

everyone should learn to read and write as soon as schools were available. The next year, she established trial by jury. Toward the end of her life, she traveled throughout the islands to assure that people observed her dictates, especially regarding school attendance and religious observance.

BIBLIOGRAPHY

Silverman, Jane L. *Kaahumanu: Molder of Change*. Honolulu: Friends of the Judiciary Historical Society, 1987. 0-96192340-7, 181p. Silverman's carefully researched and documented biography gives a thorough account of Kaahumanu's contributions.

KÄSEBIER, GERTRUDE (1852-1934)
Photographer   Des Moines, Iowa

Gertrude Käsebier was the first American female professional photographer. She was the elder of two children, born Gertrude Stanton on May 18, 1852, to Quakers who took her in a covered wagon to Leadville, Colorado, for her father to become a silver miner. After her father's death, she returned east to live with her grandmother in New York City. There she met her husband, a shellac importer, and after their marriage, she raised her children instead of becoming an artist. In 1888, however, she entered Brooklyn's Pratt Institute. She studied for six years to become a portrait painter, but after using a camera, she decided to take it with her to Paris in 1893. She forgot painting, and when she returned to New York, she worked in a studio to learn how to photograph people. After establishing her own studio on Fifth Avenue, she soon gained renown with her exhibits at the Camera Club and in Alfred Stieglitz's *Camera Work* magazine. She founded Photo-Secession with Stieglitz in 1902 and was a member of the English Linked Ring group. She won many awards for her work and her portraits of such people as Robert Henry, John Sloan, George Luks, and Stanford White. Her photographs appeared in magazines including *Scribner's, McClure's, Munsey's, Photographic Art*, and *Photographic Times*. Her work was most influential between 1898 and 1910, before the innovative Armory Show in 1913 outdated her soft-focus effect. She maintained her studio until 1926, gaining international recognition as a professional photographer and commanding commensurate fees.

BIBLIOGRAPHY

Homer, William Innes. *A Pictorial Heritage: The Photographs of Gertrude Käsebier*. Newark: University of Delaware, 1979. No ISBN, 63p. Homer's biography on Käsebier identifies her as one of the world's best portrait photographers.
Michaels, Barbara L. *Gertrude Käsebier: The Photographer and Her Photographs*. New York: Abrams, 1992. 0-8109-3505-8, 192p. This recommended, carefully researched and documented biography of Käsebier explores her life and career.

KECKLEY, ELIZABETH (1818–1907)
Slave and Dressmaker   Dinwiddie, Virginia

Elizabeth Keckley served as a domestic in the Lincoln White House, became a family confidante, and wrote her memoirs about the experience. She was born Elizabeth Hobbs in 1818 as the daughter of slaves. After her owners sold her to a North Carolina plantation master, she had a son by him. She was repurchased and taken to St. Louis, where she began her career as a dressmaker to support her new owners and their five daughters. She married James Keckley, believing him to be free and trustworthy, and when she discovered that he was neither, she separated from him. Customers bought her and her son's freedom, and Keckley kept her dressmaking business while learning to read and write. In 1860, she went to Baltimore and then Washington, where her customers included the wife of Jefferson Davis. When the Lincolns had been in Washington for two weeks, Mary Todd Lincoln sent for Keckley and asked her to make her dresses and become her traveling companion. In 1862, Keckley helped to found the Contraband Relief Association, a group of African American women who provided assistance to slaves arriving in the District of Columbia. After Lincoln was assassinated, Mary Todd Lincoln could no longer afford to pay Keckley, but they remained friends, and Keckley helped Lincoln sell her wardrobe at auction in New York. Keckley admired Lincoln and planned to use proceeds from her book about the White House to help her, but Lincoln's son, angry at the book, had the publisher withdraw it. In reduced circumstances herself, Keckley survived on a pension she received after her son's death as a Union soldier. She eventually died at the Home for Destitute Women and Children, a place she had helped found.

BIBLIOGRAPHY
Keckley, Elizabeth. *Behind the Scenes, or, Thirty Years a Slave and Four Years in the White House.* 1843. New York: Oxford University Press, 1988. 0–19–505259–5, 371p. In her memoirs, Keckley discusses her life as a slave.
Rutberg, Becky. *Mary Lincoln's Dressmaker.* New York: Walker, 1995. 0–8027–8224–8, 166p. Rutberg's young adult biography draws on Keckley's autobiography.

KEENE, LAURA (1820–1873)
Actor, Theatrical Producer, and Director   London, England

Laura Keene, an actor, was the first female theater manager in the United States. She was born Mary Moss around 1820 (some sources record 1826) as one of four children to a builder and his wife. As a child, she played in Joseph Turner's studio and heard the melodious voice of the French actor *Rachel outside a theater's open window. After Keene married and her husband was banished to Australia for a felony, she began acting to support herself and her two daughters. She made her London debut in 1851, and in six months joined the company of *Madame Vestris. An American actor-manager saw her perform and engaged her to come to New York. She met John Lutz after her arrival, and he persuaded her to manage the Charles Street Theatre in Baltimore. On December 24, 1853, she became the first female manager of an American theater. In November 1856, she opened her own theater in New York City, and for the next seven years enjoyed major success. She mounted comedies and extravaganzas, personally painting scenery, training actors, making costumes, and managing publicity. She played all of the leading female roles, her most successful part being Florence Trenchard in *Our American Cousin*. Displaying her dignity and reserve to best effect, the play lasted from October 18, 1858, until March 1859, the longest run in New York to that date, and she often revived it. She relinquished her theater in 1863 and began touring. In 1865, Lincoln was attending her performance in Ford's Theater the night he was shot. After heavy losses at her second husband's death, she gave public lectures, but her own health soon failed. She encouraged young actors, set high standards, introduced the matinee, started long runs of plays in the theater, and made New York City the theater capital of the country.

BIBLIOGRAPHY

Bryan, Vernanne. *Laura Keene*. Jefferson, NC: McFarland, 1992. 0–7864–0075–7, 222p. Bryan's thoroughly researched and documented biography of Keene examines her life.

Henneke, Ben Graf. *Laura Keene: A Biography*. Tulsa, OK: Council Oak, 1990. 0–933031–31–9, 317p. Henneke details changes that Keene made to the American theater.

KELLER, HELEN (1880–1968)
Author   Tuscumbia, Alabama

Helen Keller overcame her disabilities of deafness and blindness to become an author and lecturer. She was born on June 27, 1880, as the oldest of three children to a Confederate veteran who published a country weekly and his second wife. At 19 months, acute congestion of the stomach and brain (probably scarlet fever) left Keller deaf, blind, and mute. She became destructive, and her parents heard of Alexander Graham Bell, to whom they brought her when she was six. He introduced the family to **Anne Sullivan (Macy)**, a graduate of the Perkins Institution in Boston, and she became Keller's teacher and governess in 1887. In a few months, Keller learned 300 words, and by the end of the year, the world knew about Keller's achievements when the head of Perkins made news reports. When Keller's father and her patron died, Sullivan Macy convinced a group of Keller's friends to create a fund for her education. In 1896, Keller entered the Cambridge School for Young Ladies to prepare for Radcliffe. In college, she carried a full schedule, with Sullivan Macy attending every class with her and spelling the lectures in her hand. After her graduation, *Ladies' Home Journal* persuaded Keller to write her autobiography. With the money from this venture, she and Sullivan Macy bought land. Among the causes that Keller supported as an adult were ophthalmia neonatorum (blindness of newborn infants); abolition of child labor; birth control; socialism; and suffrage, preferring the militant version to moderation. In 1924, she became a spokesperson for the American Foundation for the Blind and, after Sullivan Macy's death, went abroad to make appeals. **Katharine Cornell**, a close friend, created a documentary on Keller's life, and she received several honorary degrees and the Presidential Medal of Freedom.

BIBLIOGRAPHY

Herrmann, Dorothy. *Helen Keller: A Life*. New York: Knopf, 1998. 0-679-44354-1, 400p. For a balanced, recommended biography, Herrmann used Keller archives and unpublished memoirs.

Keller, Helen. *The Story of My Life*. 1903. Mineola, NY: Dover, 1996. 0-486-29249-5, 75p. Keller recalls the experiences with her teacher, Anne Sullivan Macy.

Lash, Joseph P. *Helen and Teacher: The Story of Helen Keller and Anne Sullivan Macy*. New York: Delacorte, 1980. 0-440-03654-2, 811p. This readable and carefully researched biography used Keller's archived materials, including her correspondence.

Nicholson, Lois. *Helen Keller: Humanitarian*. New York: Chelsea House, 1996. 0-7910-2086-X, 111p. Nicholson's biography of Keller for young adults examines her life and her accomplishments.

KELLEY, FLORENCE (1859-1932)
Reformer   Philadelphia, Pennsylvania

Florence Kelley was a social reformer. She was born on September 12, 1859, the third of eight children, to a self-educated lawyer and judge who opposed slavery and his Quaker wife. That her aunt refused to use cotton and sugar produced through slave labor impressed Kelley as she was growing up. Five of Kelley's sisters died in infancy, and Kelley was often ill as a child, so most of her schooling took place at home, with her reading in her father's library. Her father encouraged her to attend Cornell University, and when the University of Pennsylvania refused her admission to graduate school because of her sex, she took evening classes at the women's New Century Club in Philadelphia. In Europe with her brother in 1883, she heard that the University of Zurich admitted women. She enrolled, and while there, she discovered socialism and translated Engels's *The Condition of the Working Class in England in 1844*, which New York socialists published in 1887. She married a Russian medical student and socialist, but after children and debt problems, they divorced. In 1891, she went to live at Hull-House and became close friends with **Jane Addams, Julia Lathrop,** and **Alice Hamilton**. Her crusade against child labor caused the Illinois legislature to pass a law in 1893 limiting hours of work for women, prohibiting child labor, and regulating sweatshops. As the chief factory inspector, Kelley had trouble getting the infractions prosecuted, so she decided to attend law school. She earned her law degree from Northwestern University in 1894 and renewed her attacks. She became the secretary of the

National Consumers' League in 1899, and while living in **Lillian Wald**'s Henry Street Settlement in New York, made thousands of speeches about the problems. She wrote *Some Ethical Gains Through Legislation* in 1905, and organized the National Child Labor Committee. Her idea led Congress to create the Children's Bureau in 1912 with **Julia Lathrop** as its head. In 1909, Kelley helped organize the National Association for the Advancement of Colored People, and in 1919, she was a founding member of the Women's International League for Peace and Freedom, while keeping her socialist loyalties.

BIBLIOGRAPHY

Goldmark, Josephine Clara. *Impatient Crusader: Florence Kelley's Life Story.* 1953. Westport, CT: Greenwood Press, 1976. 0-8371-9011-8, 217p. Goldmark's balanced biography of Kelley focuses on her concerns and achievements.

Sklar, Kathryn Kish. *Florence Kelley and the Nation's Work.* New Haven, CT: Yale University Press, 1995. 0-300-05912-4, vol 1. The first volume of Sklar's biography of Kelley's focuses on her public life.

KENNEDY, JACQUELINE. *See* ONASSIS, JACQUELINE KENNEDY

KING, BILLIE JEAN (1943–)
Athlete   Long Beach, California

Billie Jean King was a professional tennis player who changed women's tennis. She was born Billie Jean Moffitt on November 22, 1943, one of two children of a fire department engineer and his wife. Both parents encouraged her to participate in sports, but since no professional baseball teams for women existed, they suggested tennis. When King was 11, she enrolled in a city recreation program and saved money to buy her own racket, practicing constantly. She also began walking three miles to school to improve her stamina. When she started playing at the junior-tournament level in southern California, she overcame the elitism of her wealthy opponents to win her first juniors' championship at the age of 14. During the 1950s, while a teenager, she carefully balanced school with tennis practice and competition. When King was 15, Alice Marble, a former tennis champion, offered to teach her. King qualified for the women's rounds at England's renowned Wimbledon tournament and, with her partner Karen Hantze, won the women's doubles title, becoming part of the youngest winning team in Wimbledon history. While attending Los Angeles State College of Applied Arts and Sciences, she married a fellow student, and the next year, she won Wimbledons, receiving as her prize a gift certificate for tennis clothing. When she won a third title in 1968, she joined men's tennis champion Rod Laver and other well-known players to force the United States Lawn Tennis Association to offer prize money at tournaments. Men, however, received sometimes nearly eight times more money than women, and King complained about the discrepancy even though she was the first female athlete in history to earn $100,000. Tournaments she won include six Wimbletons; four U.S. Opens; three South African Opens; the Italian, the West German, the Australian, and the French Opens; 29 Virginia Slims singles; and many doubles championships. She played on the Wightman Cup Team 10 times and was a World Tennis Team All-Star. One of her most interesting matches was a well-publicized match against a former tennis professional, Bobby Riggs, who at 55 in 1973, challenged her when she was the world's leading female tennis player; she won in straight sets. She helped found *WomenSports* magazine, the Women's Tennis Association, and World Team Tennis. After becoming the first female television commentator in professional sports history, she coached the Federation Cup Women's Tennis Team and the USA Olympic Women's Tennis Team. She has also served as the national spokesperson for Literacy Volunteers of America. Awards include Woman of the Year, one of 100 Most Important Americans of the Twentieth Century, and election into The National Women's Hall of Fame.

BIBLIOGRAPHY

Baker, Jim. *Billie Jean King*. New York: Grosset and Dunlap, 1973. No ISBN, 90p. Baker's simple biography of King for juveniles and young adults relates her tennis career through 1973.

King, Billie Jean. *Billie Jean*. New York: Viking, 1982. 0-670-47843-1, 220p. In a personable and forthright autobiography, King tells why she left tennis.

KING, CAROL WEISS (1895-1952)
Attorney   **New York, New York**

Carol Weiss King was a civil libertarian and an authority on immigration law. She was born on August 24, 1895, as one of four children to two German immigrants, a lawyer and his wife. King early in her life developed an interest in art and culture and had exposure to the power associated with the law. She graduated from Horace Mann School and attended Barnard College. While researching for the American Association of Labor Legislation after graduation, she realized that she could be more effective if she were an attorney. She entered the New York University Law School in 1917 (the same year she married) and graduated in 1920, but could not find a job. She rented an office in a law firm involved with foreign-born workers and began defending immigrants and those whose civil liberties had been abused. Among her clients were workers, labor unions, African Americans, counterfeiters, and Jehovah's Witnesses. After her husband died suddenly and after a trip to the Soviet Union in 1932, King traveled through Germany and saw fascism functioning. She returned and founded a journal on human rights, the *International Juridical Association Bulletin* (later *Lawyers Guild Review*), which offered a forum for attorneys to discuss immigration, labor, poverty, and landlord-tenant relations. One law school dean termed it the best legal publication in the country. She defended nine young African Americans in Scottsboro, Alabama, argued for the inclusion of African Americans on juries trying African American defendants, saved Harry Bridges from deportation, and retained the U.S. citizenship of Communist Party leader William Schneiderman. In 1948, the Supreme Court accepted her interpretation of legal rights of aliens, and the Immigration Service's illegal deportations stopped. In 1951, after deportations resumed, she lost her one argument before the Supreme Court. Although she never joined the Communist Party, detractors accused her of sympathizing with them. Throughout her career, however, she intelligently and effectively defended those whom others would not help.

BIBLIOGRAPHY

Ginger, Ann Fagan. *Carol Weiss King, Human Rights Lawyer*. Niwot: University Press of Colorado, 1993. 0-87081-285-8, 599p. This thoroughly researched and carefully documented biography of King, based on notes, documents, files the FBI kept on her, and interviews with King and those who knew her, investigates her life and career.

KING, CORETTA SCOTT (1927-)
Activist   Heilberger, Alabama

Coretta Scott King is an African American social activist. She was born on April 27, 1927, the second of three children. Her father was a landowning farmer and later a country store proprietor who became the first African American in his community to purchase a truck. King was educated in a one-room schoolhouse five miles from her home to which she walked every day until she attended a private missionary high school, leaving home early on Monday morning and returning after school on Friday. In 1945, King enrolled at Antioch College in Ohio. During her schooling, King took music lessons, and after college, she attended the New England Conservatory of Music in Boston on scholarships to prepare for a vocal concert career. Another student at the conservatory introduced her to Martin Luther King, Jr., who proposed soon after. They married in 1953, returned to Boston to finish their educations, and went to Montgomery, Alabama, in 1954, where King's husband became pastor of the Dexter Avenue Baptist Church. The next year, the civil rights movement began with **Rosa Parks**'s refusal to move to the back of a bus, and they became deeply involved. When the family moved to Atlanta in 1960, King began teaching voice at Morris Brown College, and two years later she was a delegate for the Women's Strike for Peace to the Disarmament Conference in Geneva. She continued her activism in the civil rights movement after her husband's death in 1968 by forming the Center for Non-Violent Social Change in Atlanta and lecturing around the world on the subject.

BIBLIOGRAPHY

King, Coretta Scott. *My Life with Martin Luther King, Jr.* New York: Henry Holt, 1993. 0-8050-2445-X, 335p. King's autobiography clearly reveals her beliefs.

Patrick, Diane. *Coretta Scott King.* New York: Franklin Watts, 1991. 0-531-13005-3, 128p. Patrick's well-researched and informative biography for young adults covers King's life.

Schraff, Anne E. *Coretta Scott King: Striving for Civil Rights.* Springfield, NJ: Enslow, 1997. 0-89490-811-1, 128p. Schraff's scholarly biography for young adults about King is well researched, based on recent sources.

Turk, Ruth. *Coretta Scott King: Fighter for Justice.* Boston: Branden, 1997. 0-8283-2028-4, 108p. Turk's undocumented biography of King for young adults presents an overview of her life.

KINGSTON, MAXINE HONG (1940-)
Author **Stockton, California**

Maxine Hong Kingston is an award-winning Asian American author. She was born on October 27, 1940, the daughter of first-generation immigrants from China. She graduated from the University of California at Berkeley in 1962 and married one of her classmates. She then taught high school in California and Hawaii. After her book *The Woman Warrior* (1976) won awards, she became a visiting associate professor at the University of Hawaii in Honolulu. In the 1980s, she began teaching at Berkeley before serving as the Thelma McCandless Distinguished Professor in the Humanities at Eastern Michigan University. In 1981, she published *China Men.* The first two autobiographical books also incorporated aspects of Chinese mythology. Her first novel in 1989 was *Tripmaster Monkey.* Her articles and poems have appeared in major magazines and newspapers throughout the country. Among her awards are the *Mademoiselle* Magazine Award, the National Education Association Award, and several honorary degrees.

BIBLIOGRAPHY

Kingston, Maxine Hong. *China Men.* 1979. New York: Vintage, 1989. 0-679-72328-5, 308p. Kingston's story of her Chinese male ancestors gives insight into her own character.

———. *Hawai'i One Summer.* 1987. Honolulu: University of Hawai'i Press, 1998. 0-8248-1887-3, 64p. Kingston relates her experiences living in Hawaii.

———. *The Woman Warrior: Memoirs of a Girlhood Among Ghosts.* New York: Knopf, 1976. 0-394-40067-4, 209p. Kingston's autobiographical narrative presents a young Chinese American woman trying to reconcile her life. Anisfield-Wolf Book Award.

Skenazy, Paul, and Tera Martin, eds. *Conversations with Maxine Hong Kingston.* Jackson: University Press of Mississippi, 1998. 1-57806-058-3, 237p. In this collection of interviews, Kingston talks about her life, her writing, and her goals.

KRASNER, LEE (1908–1984)
Artist   Brooklyn, New York

Lee Krasner (Pollock) was an Abstract Expressionist painter. She was born Lenore Krassner in Brooklyn on October 27, 1908, to Jewish emigrants from Odessa, Russia. She was the sixth of seven children, and the first one born in the United States. At the age of 13, she decided to become an artist. She studied the classical curriculum at the Women's Art School of Cooper Union, and from 1929 to 1932, at the National Academy of Design. From 1936 to 1940, she studied with Hans Hofmann, an Abstract Expressionist, who taught her about Cubism as well as the seriousness and commitment needed by a painter. After Krasner began exhibiting with American avant-garde abstract artists in 1940, she met Jackon Pollock and married him in 1945. Her work was more advanced than his at the time, and during the next 12 years, while he produced his major works, Krasner had her first one-woman show. In it and other shows, she showed her mastery of bulbous shapes and lines cutting across pictorial fields. Although seen as merely a connection to Pollock after his death in 1956, Krasner had her own unrelated style and talent. In the early 1960s, her large paintings such as *Charred Landscape* and *Another Storm* revealed the stormlike force of her line and color. In the 1980s, she gained deserved recognition when her work was exhibited with that of Pollock in a New York show demonstrating their influence on each other. In 1983, a retrospective of her work at the Museum of Fine Arts in Houston showed her to be a superb draftsman, with her strong sense of color expressing aggression and violence. She received several awards and honorary degrees.

BIBLIOGRAPHY

Hobbs, Robert Carleton. *Lee Krasner*. New York: Abbeville, 1993. 1–55859–651–8, 127p. In this critical-biographical study based on interviews with Krasner in the 1980s and other sources, Hobbs examines influences on the artist.

Rose, Barbara. *Lee Krasner: A Retrospective*. Houston, TX: Museum of Fine Arts, 1983. 0–87070–415–X, 184p. Rose discloses Krasner's changes in artistic direction in a chronological examination of her life and work.

Wagner, Anne Middleton. *Three Artists (Three Women): Modernism and the Art of Hesse, Krasner, and O'Keeffe*. Berkeley: University of California Press, 1996. 0–520–20608–8, 346p. In this collective biography, Wagner examines Krasner's work and life.

KUHLMAN, KATHRYN (1907–1976)
Evangelist and Healer   Concordia, Missouri

Kathryn Kuhlman was a "faith healer" and evangelist. She was born May 9, 1907, the daughter of a Baptist mayor and his wife. She felt called to religion at 13, and at that time began her life's work. She established the Kathryn Kuhlman Foundation in 1954 with daily radio broadcasts, and in 1966, she expanded to weekly broadcasts on television lasting for eight years. By the 1960s, she was one of the foremost "faith healers," and had thousands attending her "miracle services." Much controversy surrounded her supposed healings, but she objected to the term "faith healer" because she said that God did the healing; she did not. Her foundation established 22 missions in Asia, South America, Africa, and Europe. Among her awards are the Medal of Honor from the Vietnamese military and honorary degrees. Her book, *I Believe in Miracles*, is still an important document in Pentecostal and charismatic churches.

BIBLIOGRAPHY

Buckingham, Jamie. *Daughter of Destiny: Kathryn Kuhlman, Her Story.* Plainfield, NJ: Logos International, 1976. 0-8827-0078-2, 309p. Buckingham knew Kuhlman well, and his undocumented biography is a balanced account of her life.

Kuhlman, Kathryn. *Nothing Is Impossible with God.* Englewood Cliffs, NJ: Prentice-Hall, 1974. 0-13-625293-1, 305p. In this autobiography, Kuhlman reflects on the bounty of her miracles.

McDonald, Jimmie. *The Kathryn Kuhlman I Knew.* Shippensburg, PA: Treasure House, 1996. 1-56043-272-1, 193p. McDonald, an African American singer for Kuhlman's services, recounts their 15 years together.

Roberts, Liardon. *Kathryn Kuhlman: A Spiritual Biography.* Tulsa, OK: Harrison House, 1990. 0-89274-562-2, 154p. Liardon's brief biography of Kuhlman precedes six of her radio messages.

Warner, Wayne E. *Kathryn Kuhlman: The Woman Behind the Miracles.* Ann Arbor, MI: Servant, 1993. 0-89283-794-2, 283p. For this researched and documented biography of Kuhlman, based mainly on secondary sources, Warner contacted people whom Kuhlman supposedly healed.

L

LA FLESCHE (PICOTTE), SUSAN (1865–1915)
Physician   Thurston County, Nebraska

Susan La Flesche (Picotte), a Native American physician, probably treated every member of the Omaha tribe, saving many lives with her efforts. She was born on June 17, 1865, as the youngest of five children to the Omaha chief Joseph La Flesche (Iron Eye) and his wife Mary (One Woman). La Flesche learned no English until she went to mission and government schools on the reservation. At 14, she went to Elizabeth, New Jersey, as had her sister, **Susette La Flesche (Tibbles)**, to attend the Institute for Young Ladies for three years. She spent two more years at Hampton Institute, graduating as salutatorian in 1886. La Flesche then received money from the Women's National Indian Association to attend the Woman's Medical College of Pennsylvania. She completed the three-year course in two years, receiving her M.D. degree in 1889 at the head of her class. After her internship, she returned to the reservation, serving first as a medical missionary and then in a private medical practice serving her tribe. After marriage to a half-Sioux and French man, she raised two children and nursed her husband through a long terminal illness. When the town of Walthill was founded on the reservation, La Flesche took her knowledge of alcoholism to Washington to ask that every deed for property in new towns forbid the sale of liquor. In her professional as well as charity work, she was an Omaha leader, although the tribe never traditionally followed women. In 1913, as a medical missionary for the Presbyterian Board of Home Missions, she established a hospital at Walthill, renamed for her after her death.

BIBLIOGRAPHY

Brown, Marion Marsh. *Homeward the Arrow's Flight: The Story of Susan La Flesche (Dr. Susan La Flesche Picotte)*. 1980. Grand Island, NE: Field Mouse, 1995. 0–96475860–1, 185p. In an undocumented biography for young adults, Brown discusses La Flesche Picotte's unusual achievements.

Ferris, Jeri. *Native American Doctor: The Story of Susan La Flesche Picotte*. Minneapolis: Carolrhoda, 1991. 0–87614–443–1, 88p. This readable researched and documented biography for young readers, with endnotes of interest to young adults, covers La Flesche Picotte's life and career.

LA FLESCHE (TIBBLES), SUSETTE (1854–1903)
Activist and Author   Bellevue, Nebraska

Susette La Flesche (Tibbles) was an activist. She was born in 1854 as the second of five children to Omaha chief Joseph La Flesche (Iron Eye) and his wife Mary (One Woman). When La Flesche's father realized that white men would always threaten his land, he became a Christian. His daughter began attending a Presbyterian mission school and then entered the Institute for Young Ladies in Elizabeth, New Jersey. After La Flesche returned to the Omaha reservation in 1873, she became a teacher. In 1877, the federal government mistakenly assigned the lands of the Poncas to the Sioux, and forcibly removed the Poncas from their land. Over one-third of the tribe died on the new reservation. When the Ponca chief, Standing Bear, and his followers returned to their homeland, the government arrested them. A Nebraska newspaperman, Thomas Henry Tibbles, arranged Standing Bear's release by having the court acknowledge that in the eyes of the law, a Native American was a person. Tibbles then went east to lecture on the government's unfair policy, taking with him Standing Bear and La Flesche, Standing Bear's interpreter. La Flesche, using her Native American name, Inshta Theumba (Bright Eyes), also lectured. As a result of their speeches, the Dawes Severalty Act of 1887 became law. After their marriage in 1881, La Flesche and Tibbles testified before Congressional committees and lectured in England for ten months. La Flesche also wrote articles and books that revealed the Native American plight. For her work, she was elected to The National Women's Hall of Fame.

BIBLIOGRAPHY

Brown, Marion Marsh. *Susette La Flesche: Advocate for Native American Rights*. Chicago: Childrens Press, 1992. 0–516–03277–1, 117p. This undocumented biography for juveniles places La Flesche Tibbles in the context of her Native American Omaha heritage.

Crary, Margaret. *Susette La Flesche: Voice of the Omaha Indians*. New York: Hawthorn, 1978. No ISBN, 173p. This well-written fictional biography for young adults gives insight about La Flesche Tibbles overcoming her shyness to speak for her people.

Wilson, Dorothy Clarke. *Bright Eyes: The Story of Susette La Flesche, an Omaha Indian*. New York: McGraw-Hill, 1974. 0–07–070752–9, 396p. This researched fictional biography, suitable for young adults, is a readable account of the life of Bright Eyes.

LA FOLLETTE, BELLE CASE   (1859–1931)
Journalist and Activist   Baraboo, Wisconsin

Belle Case La Follette was a journalist and political advisor. She was born in a log cabin on April 21, 1859, as one of three surviving children of six to a Unitarian farmer and his wife. After attending public schools, she entered the University of Wisconsin in 1875 and won academic awards, including the prize for best commencement oration. She taught for two years before marrying a lawyer (dropping the word "obey" from the ceremony) whom she helped review law books. She then entered the University of Wisconsin Law School, graduating as its first woman in 1885, and gained admittance to both the bar and the Wisconsin supreme court. Although she never actively practiced, she advised her husband and participated actively in numerous reform movements including public welfare reform and consumer legislation, where she interacted with **Jane Addams**, **Florence Kelley**, and **Julia Lathrop**. She helped her Wisconsin governor husband develop a series of reforms soon known as Wisconsin Progressivism. In Washington, after her husband's election to the Senate, La Follette and her husband established *La Follette's Weekly* Magazine, a political education publication for which La Follette edited a "Women and Education Department" and wrote articles on education, child welfare, health, and Washington life. By 1911, she was writing a syndicated column for the North American Press. She testified before the Senate Committee on Suffrage, asking, "Are not women people?" and addressed President Woodrow Wilson about improving race relations. She also helped organize the Women's International League for Peace and Freedom, and her march in Washington to inform women that their votes could accomplish disarmament produced the Naval Arms Limitation Conference, the first of its kind. In 1921, she helped found the National Council for the Prevention of War. In 1924, La Follette campaigned actively for her husband's unsuccessful presidential race, and after his defeat and his death the next year, people petitioned her to finish his unexpired Senate term, but she refused. The *New York Times* noted that La Follette was one of the most influential women in American public affairs.

BIBLIOGRAPHY

Freeman, Lucy, Sherry La Follette, and George A. Za. *Belle: The Biography of Belle Case La Follette*. New York: Beaufort, 1986. 0-8253-0314-1, 253p. This documented, researched, and readable biography based on family papers and family interviews presents the view of one of La Follette's grandchildren that her grandfather had undiagnosed manic depression.

Weisberger, Bernard A. *The La Follettes of Wisconsin*. Madison: University of Wisconsin Press, 1994. 0-299-14130-6, 384p. This well-researched and readable collective biography of La Follette and her family discloses the complexity of balancing politics with privacy.

LANGE, DOROTHEA (1895–1965)
Photographer   Hoboken, New Jersey

Dorothea Lange's photographs remain an important document of the human condition. She was born on May 26, 1895, as one of two children to a father who abandoned the family after Lange contracted polio and began limping at age seven. She, her mother, and her brother went to live with her German immigrant grandmother in New York City. As Lange grew up, she preferred wandering around the city to attending school. When she graduated from high school, she knew that she wanted to photograph what she saw. Her mother made Lange enroll in the New York Training School for Teachers in 1914, but simultaneously, she apprenticed herself to photographers and attended Clarence H. White's photography class at Columbia University. She moved to San Francisco, married a painter, and had children, with her portraits of wealthy patrons supporting the family. As the Great Depression became worse, Lange saw people in the streets, and during this time, she photographed her famous *White Angel Breadline*, a line of well-dressed men standing in a food line. This picture received immediate recognition from the photographers of Group F.64, and she and the social economist Paul Taylor began documenting the lives of California's migrant workers. The Farm Security Administration saw the reports and hired her in 1937 to photograph destitute farmers in the Dust Bowl. In 1941, she went to California and photographed the Japanese leaving their homes to be interned in camps. Because of her sympathy with the Japanese, the government withheld her photographs for 30 years. In the 1950s, she worked in Asia, South America, and northern Africa. After a diagnosis of cancer of the esophagus in 1964, Lange designed a final retrospective of her work for the Museum of Modern Art in New York, creating a sequence of photographs on the country woman.

BIBLIOGRAPHY

Heyman, Therese Thau. *Dorothea Lange: American Photographs*. San Francisco: Chronicle, 1994. 0–8118–0725–8, 192p. Carefully documented essays on Lange and her relationship with Paul Taylor precede a collection of her photographs.

Meltzer, Milton. *Dorothea Lange: A Photographer's Life*. New York: Farrar, Straus and Giroux, 1978. 0–374–14323–4, 399p. Meltzer used letters, recorded interviews, Lange's notes about her work, and others' comments to create a carefully researched, recommended biography.

Ohrn, Karin Becker. *Dorothea Lange and the Documentary Tradition*. Baton Rouge: Louisiana State University Press, 1980. 0–8071–0551–1, 277p. Based on interviews with Lange near the end of her life, correspondence, photographs, and her notes, Ohrn's carefully researched, documented, and recommended biography also includes a collection of Lange's photographs.

Partridge, Elizabeth. *Restless Spirit: The Life and Work of Dorothea Lange*. New York: Viking, 1998. 0–670–87888–X, 128p. This biography of Lange includes 80 photographs and examines her life and her role as a documentary photographer.

————, ed. *Dorothea Lange—A Visual Life*. Washington, DC: Smithsonian Institution Press, 1994. 1–56098–350–7, 168p. Six scholarly essays by those who knew or worked with Lange and one interview introduce her and her photographs.

LANSBURY, ANGELA (1925–)
Actor   London, England

Angela Lansbury is an actor. One of three children of a lumber merchant and his actor wife, she was born on October 16, 1925. She came to the United States at the beginning of World War II and attended the Webber-Douglas Academy of Dramatic Art and the Feagin School of Dramatic Art. In 1944, she made her film debut in *Gaslight* and followed it the next year with the lead in *The Picture of Dorian Gray*, a role for which she won her first Golden Globe. Three other films, *The Manchurian Candidate*, *All Fall Down*, and *Death on the Nile*, all earned her the National Board of Review's Best Supporting Actess Award. Two years after her naturalization, she debuted in television. Her Broadway 1957 debut in *Hotel Paradiso* preceded *Dear World*, *Anyone Can Whistle*, *Mame*, *Gypsy*, and *Sweeney Todd*. In 1984, she began the television series *Murder, She Wrote* and performed in it until 1996. She has won many accolades including more Golden Globe Awards, Tony Awards, *Sarah Siddons Awards, the Screen Actors Guild Life Achievement Award, and the National Medal of Arts. She was also inducted into both the Theatre Hall of Fame and the Academy of Television Arts and Sciences' Hall of Fame.

BIBLIOGRAPHY
Bonanno, Margaret Wander. *Angela Lansbury: A Biography*. New York: St. Martin's, 1987. 0–312–00561–X, 225p. Bonanno's popular, undocumented biography of Lansbury gives an overview of her life and career.
Edelman, Rob, and Audrey E. Kupferberg. *Angela Lansbury: A Life on Stage and Screen*. Secaucus, NJ: Carol, 1996. 1–55972–327–0, 287p. In their popular, researched biography of Lansbury, Edelman and Kupferberg discuss her career, emphasizing her refusal to allow herself to be impressed by the reviews of her work.

LARCOM, LUCY (1824–1893)
Mill Girl and Poet   Beverly, Massachusetts

Lucy Larcom, a worker in the Lowell, Massachusetts, textile mills, was also an author. She was born on May 5, 1824, as the ninth of ten children to a merchant and sea captain who died when she was young, and his wife, who became supervisor of one of the Lowell female dormitories. Larcom had little schooling, although she started writing verse before going to work in the mills when she was 11. She enjoyed the other mill girls, and in her book *A New England Girlhood*, she told of her experiences during 10 years at the mills. Throughout her life, Larcom studied independently and read all types of literature. In 1846, she went west with her sister and taught in Illinois for three years before attending the Monticello

Seminary for college training. When she returned to the East, she painted, studied French, and won a prize for poetry encouraging settlers to go to Kansas. During her eight years teaching at Wheaton Seminary, she continued to write seriously and began editing a children's magazine, *Our Young Folks*. She also published regularly in other magazines and worked on poetry collections. She saw her writing as an extension of her strong religious beliefs.

BIBLIOGRAPHY

Addison, Daniel Dulany. *Lucy Larcom: Life, Letters, and Diary*. 1894. Freeport, NY: Books for Libraries, 1971. 0-8369-5759-8, 295p. Addison used Larcom's personal papers, letters, diary, and the outline that she had sketched for a sequel to *A New England Girlhood* as a basis for his scholarly examination of her life.

Larcom, Lucy. *A New England Girlhood: Outlined from Memory*. 1889. Boston: Northeastern University Press, 1986. 0-930350-82-0, 274p. Larcom recalls her enjoyment of childhood and her life in Lowell, Massachusetts, working in the mills.

Marchalonis, Shirley. *The Worlds of Lucy Larcom, 1824-1893*. Athens: University of Georgia Press, 1989. 0-8203-1113-8, 326p. In this carefully documented, researched, and recommended biography on Larcom's life and work, Marchalonis used over 2,000 letters.

Selden, Bernice. *The Mill Girls: Lucy Larcom, Harriet Hanson Robinson, Sarah G. Bagley*. New York: Atheneum, 1983. 0-689-31005-6, 191p. In a collective biography for young adults, Selden describes Larcom's life in the mills from a historical context.

LARSEN, NELLA (1891-1964)
Author   Chicago, Illinois

Nella Larsen was the first African American woman to win a creative writing award from the Guggenheim Foundation. She was born on April 13, 1891, to a Danish mother and a West Indian father who died when she was two. Her mother then remarried a white man and had a second daughter. Larsen attended a private school with her white half-sister before attending all-African American Fisk University. After a year at Fisk, Larsen went to Copenhagen to study for two years before finishing her education at Lincoln Hospital in New York City. She became assistant superintendent of nurses at Tuskegee Institute and married a physicist in 1919. She began working in a library, started reading everything, and decided to become a writer. As part of the African American elite, she met Harlem Renaissance authors including James Weldon Johnson, **Jessie Fauset**, Jean Toomer, and Langston Hughes, who encouraged her work. Then Carl Van Vechten, a white patron of new African American authors, published her first novel in 1928; in this book and others Larsen explored the difficulties of children from mixed parentage whom both races reject. The success of this novel and of her second, *Passing*, earned her the Guggenheim Foundation honor, but an accusation of plagiarism in one of her short stories and reports of her husband's affair so distressed her that she never completed another novel. After 1941, she worked as a nurse.

BIBLIOGRAPHY

Davis, Thadious M. *Nella Larsen, Novelist of the Harlem Renaissance*. Baton Rouge: Louisiana State University Press, 1994. 0-8071-1866-4, 429p. Davis's carefully researched biography of Larsen discusses her heartbreak as a child of mixed racial parentage whose mother denied her.

Larson, Charles R. *Invisible Darkness: Jean Toomer and Nella Larsen*. Iowa City: University of Iowa Press, 1993. 0-87745-425-6, 241p. Larson critically examines Larsen's works for autobiographical elements and decides that she hid details of her life, creating fictive biography.

McLendon, Jacquelyn Y. *The Politics of Color in the Fiction of Jessie Fauset and Nella Larsen*. Charlottesville: University Press of Virginia, 1995. 0-8139-1553-8, 142p. McLendon discusses Larsen's life in this collective work, and sees that Larsen used the "mulatto" theme both politically and artistically.

Wall, Cheryl A. *Women of the Harlem Renaissance*. Bloomington: Indiana University Press, 1995. 0-253-32908-6, 246p. Wall looks at Larsen's treatment of race, class, and gender during the Harlem Renaissance.

LATHROP, JULIA (1858–1932)
Reformer   Rockford, Illinois

Julia Clifford Lathrop was a social welfare worker and the first director of the federal Children's Bureau. She was born on June 29, 1858, the oldest of five children. Her father was a lawyer who later served in Congress, and her mother was valedictorian of her class at Rockford Seminary. After attending high school, Lathrop enrolled at Rockford and then received her degree from Vassar in 1880. While spending the next 10 years as a secretary in her father's office, women's rights, civil service reform, and treatment of the insane began to concern her. In 1890, she joined **Jane Addams** at Hull-House and entered welfare work three years later to investigate nearby relief applicants. The Illinois Board of Charities then appointed her to visit all relief sites in the state. In her report, she opposed grouping of young and old with the sick and insane in the same institutions. She then traveled to Europe in 1898 to study its relief conditions and solutions. In 1909, as a charter member of the National Committee for Mental Hygiene to disseminate information about mental illness, she called for training the staffs of mental institutions and helped begin courses which became part of the Chicago School of Civics and Philanthropy. She then established the school's research department and created occupational therapy classes for those who worked with the insane. Her campaign for separate courts led Chicago to establish the first juvenile court in 1909. In 1912, President Theodore Roosevelt appointed Lathrop head of the newly created federal Children's Bureau, and with her staff, she began investigating infant mortality. During World War I, she lobbied for aid to dependents of enlisted men and for protection of mothers and infants. As the president of the National Conference of Social Work, she supported the repatriation of children in Poland, and among her awards was the Order of the White Lion from Czechoslovakia.

BIBLIOGRAPHY

Addams, Jane. *My Friend, Julia Lathrop*. 1935. New York: Arno Press, 1974. 0-405-05942-6, 228p. Addams recounts her work with Lathrop in Chicago and emphasizes many details of Lathrop's ideals and devotion to her friends.

Lathrop, Julia. *Selected Writings*. Ed. Culbertson, Diana. New York: Paulist, 1993. 0-8091-0463-6, 242p. This collection of Lathrop's letters and personal papers includes a lengthy introduction in which Culbertson examines Lathrop's life and faith.

LATHROP, ROSE HAWTHORNE (1851–1926)
Religious   Lenox, Massachusetts

Mother Mary Alphonsa Lathrop was both the founder of the Dominican Congregation of St. Rose of Lima and a writer. She was born Rose Hawthorne on May 20, 1851, one of three children of the author Nathaniel Hawthorne and his wife. While still young, Mother Mary Alphonsa went to Europe with her family, where governesses educated her. They returned to America in 1860 and after her father's death three years later, her mother took the children to Germany and London, where Mother Mary Alphonsa studied art. She married in London, but moved to Boston with her husband and began publishing short stories in *St. Nicholas* magazine and *Atlantic Monthly*. After she and her husband joined the Catholic Church, they separated with the Church's approval in 1895; her husband died three years later. Mother Mary Alphonsa began working with cancer sufferers in 1896, emulating St. Rose of Lima, about whom she had read. Father Damien's work with lepers on the island of Molokai also influenced her, as did the death of her good friend, **Emma Lazarus**, in 1887. She took a nursing course for three months at the New York Cancer Hospital and opened three rooms in Manhattan's Lower East Side slums for people dying of the disease. She used her maiden name, Hawthorne, to solicit contributions, and when Alice Huber joined her the next year, they called their work Servants of Relief for Incurable Cancer. In 1899, the archbishop allowed them to become lay sisters of the Dominican third order, to take vows, and to wear the Dominican habit. Their community became the Dominican Congregation of St. Rose of Lima in 1909. In 1912, they moved to a new building with 75 beds, and by the end of the year, they had ministered to 1,045 patients from all denominations.

BIBLIOGRAPHY

Valenti, Patricia Dunlavy. *To Myself a Stranger: A Biography of Rose Hawthorne Lathrop*. Baton Rouge: Louisiana State University Press, 1991. 0-8071-1612-2, 192p. Valenti's well-researched biography reveals Lathrop's early life and her family relationships.

LAZARUS, EMMA (1849–1887)
Poet   New York, New York

Emma Lazarus's poem "The New Colossus" became the inscription on the pedestal of the Statue of Liberty. She was born on July 22, 1849, as one of seven children to a sugar refiner and his wife, descendants of Sephardic Jews. Isolated as a child, Lazarus received a private education of languages and classics but began to write poetry as a teenager, publishing her first collection at age 18. She won critical praise in England and the United States for a second volume of poems in 1871 and a novel in 1874. During the 1870s, her poems appeared in *Scribner's* and *Lippincott's*. Ralph Waldo Emerson encouraged her, but he omitted her work from an 1874 anthology. Although Lazarus did not attend religious services, she read the Hebrew poetry of medieval Spain in German translation, and after Czar Alexander II of Russia was assassinated, she became interested in her Jewish heritage. When Jews escaping from Russian pogroms began arriving in New York, she worked with the Hebrew Emigrant Aid Society and began writing about the emigrants' problems in both poetry and prose. Her articles published in *American Hebrew*, beginning in 1882, anticipated the Zionist movement by advocating a homeland for the Jews in Palestine. She stressed training and farming opportunities for arriving emigrants, and her ideas developed into New York's Hebrew Technical Institute. Although always shy, she freely expressed her beliefs in writing before her early death at 38 from Hodgkin's disease.

BIBLIOGRAPHY
Vogel, Dan. *Emma Lazarus*. Boston: Twayne, 1980. 0–8057–7233–2, 183p. In a carefully researched and documented critical biography, Vogel traces Lazarus's life and career.

Young, Bette Roth. *Emma Lazarus in Her World: Life and Letters*. Philadelphia: Jewish Publication Society, 1995. 0–8276–0516–1, 298p. Young discovered 60 original letters that revealed Lazarus as an active member of Victorian literary and intellectual life for her biography.

LE SUEUR, MERIDEL (1900–1996)
Author   Murray, Iowa

Meridel Le Sueur, an author blacklisted by Senator Joseph McCarthy's Un-American Activities Committee, remained unpublished for 30 years. She was born on February 22, 1900, the daughter of a man from whom her mother escaped with her children after slavish treatment. When her mother remarried, Le Sueur's stepfather adopted her. Both parents were ardent socialists who imbued her with lasting idealism. She attended high school in Kansas and the American Academy of Dramatic Art, staying with *Emma Goldman while living in New York. Among others she knew with similar politics were John Reed, Theodore Dreiser, and **Edna St. Vincent Millay**. After a brief career in Hollywood as a stunt woman and actor, she published her first story, "Persephone," in 1927, winning acclaim for it as well as for her novella *The Horse*. As a journalist, she reported on the bread lines, unemployment offices, deserted mining towns, and uninhabited farms during the Great Depression, and in 1945, she published *North Star Country* about the settling of Minnesota and Wisconsin. She wrote books for children during her blacklisting, receiving acclaim for such works as *Little Brother of the Wilderness*, *Nancy Hanks of Wilderness Road*, *Sparrow Hawk*, and *Chanticleer of Wilderness Road*. In the 1970s, collections of her prose began to appear, and *Ripening: Selected Work, 1927–1980* included stories of immigrants and Native American women that she had heard since her childhood. In 1991, she published *The Dread Road*, a novel about a mining strike in Colorado. She has taught writing courses and won several awards, including a Bush Foundation grant after she was 80.

BIBLIOGRAPHY

Boehnlein, James M. *The Sociocognitive Rhetoric of Meridel Le Sueur: Feminist Discourse and Reportage of the Thirties*. Lewiston, NY: E. Mellen Press, 1994. 0–773491–36–8, 159p. Boehnlein examines Le Sueur's "reportage," a literary genre emphasizing sociocognitive rhetoric as a way to relate the difficulties of workers and farmers.

Coiner, Constance. *Better Red: The Writing and Resistance of Tillie Olsen and Meridel Le Sueur*. New York: Oxford University Press, 1995. 0–19–505695–7, 282p. With a mixture of literary criticism and oral history, Coiner's biography examines Le Sueur as a working-class writer.

Roberts, Nora Ruth. *Three Radical Women Writers: Class and Gender in Meridel Le Sueur, Tillie Olsen, and Josephine Herbst*. New York: Garland, 1996. 0–81530–330–0, 209p. Roberts used journals and unpublished materials in this collective critical examination of Le Sueur's writing.

Schleuning, Neala. *America, Song We Sang Without Knowing: The Life and Ideas of Meridel Le Sueur*. Minneapolis: Little Red Hen Press, 1983. 0–9612892–0–1, 171p. Schleuning used published and unpublished work, letters, personal conversations, interviews with Le Sueur, and excerpts from Le Sueur's 120 unpublished journals in her carefully researched, documented, and recommended biography.

LEASE, MARY (1850–1933)
Politician   Ridgway, Pennsylvania

Mary Lease was an orator. She was the sixth of eight children, born on September 11, 1850, to native Irish farmers. Her father died in the Civil War, and family friends helped her attend St. Elizabeth's Academy in Allegany, New York. After her graduation, she taught for two years before moving to Kansas in 1870 to teach at a Catholic girls' school and marrying the local pharmacist. Unsuccessful at farming, they moved to the city where she formed Hypatia, a society for women to discuss current issues. In 1885, she began lecturing for the Irish National League about frustrated Kansas farmers laboring under huge debts. She also spoke for the Farmers' Alliance, the Knights of Labor, and the Union Labor Party, whose journal she edited. In 1889, she helped found the *Colorado Workman*. For her oratory, her friends called her "Our Queen Mary," but her enemies saw her as "the Kansas Pythoness." In 1893, the governor appointed her president of the Kansas

State Board of Charities, but quarreling with him lost her this position. The next year, she wrote *The Problem of Civilization Solved*, in which she advocated a strong leader who could help people learn to legislate and gain their rights. Among the changes she suggested were annexation of Cuba, Canada, and the West Indies; free trade within the hemispheric Americas; and high tariffs on foreign products. Her other interests included woman suffrage and prohibition. When she returned to the East in 1896, she devoted herself to her children, although she served briefly as president of the National Society for Birth Control.

BIBLIOGRAPHY

Stiller, Richard. *Queen of Populists: The Story of Mary Elizabeth Lease.* New York: Crowell, 1970. No ISBN, 245p. Stiller's young adult biography of Lease shows her Populist movement leadership.

LEE, MOTHER ANN (1736–1784)
Evangelist   Manchester, England

Mother Ann Lee was religious leader of the Shakers. She was born on February 29, 1736, as one of eight children to a blacksmith and his wife. She had no schooling and worked as a young girl in a textile mill. In 1758 she joined James and Jane Wardley's society, a group of Quakers known as the "Shakers" who had added singing, shouting, dancing, and shaking to their worship. In 1762, her parents married her, against her wishes, to a blacksmith. After her four children all died in infancy, she refused to sleep and eat, wasting herself "into the spiritual kingdom." No one sympathized with her plight, and she decided that cohabitation of the sexes caused all evil. In 1770, she began to take leadership in the Shakers and, arrested twice for breaching the Sabbath, was imprisoned in Bedlam. There she received her revelation to take up God's work in America. In 1774, her brother, her husband, and seven others left England and acquired land at Watervliet, New York, where she began to teach the gospel. People came to hear "the woman clothed with the sun" who preached of the millennium. She opposed slavery, taking oaths, and bearing arms, and supported neatness, economy, and help for the poor. Later she agreed to marriage, but only on a higher plane, without lust. She also advocated equal rights and responsibilities within the group, which made her religious community one of the most successful experiments in America's history. By her death in 1784, she had begun 11 Shaker communities, teaching that confession and celibacy were the way to salvation.

BIBLIOGRAPHY

Campion, Nardi Reeder. *Mother Ann Lee: Morning Star of the Shakers.* 1976. Hanover, NH: University Press of New England, 1990. 0-87451-527-0, 179p. Carefully documented, this biography of Lee discusses her role as the female Christ in the Shaker faith.
Shakers. *Testimonies of the Life, Character, Revelations, and Doctrines of Mother Ann Lee.* 1888. New York: AMS Press, 1975. 0-404-10756-7, 302p. Shakers who knew

Mother Ann Lee share their knowledge of her life in England and in the United States and the importance of her Shaker ministry.

LEWIS, (MARY) EDMONIA (1845?–1909?)
Artist   Greenbush, New York

Edmonia Lewis was the first major sculptor of mixed African American and Native American background. She was born to an African American father and a Chippewa mother in either 1843 or 1845 (although Lewis claimed 1854). Orphaned at four, Lewis remained with the Chippewa, who called her Wildfire, and learned to make and sell crafts as the tribe moved throughout New York State. She left the tribe in the 1850s when her brother arranged for her to attend school near Albany and then entered Oberlin College in 1859, where two white female students accused her of poisoning them and vigilantes beat her before a prominent lawyer with a similar lineage became her protector. The next year, when others accused her of stealing art supplies, the college refused to graduate her. In Boston, the abolitionist William Lloyd Garrison introduced her to a sculptor who helped her establish a reputation. After the Civil War, when she was 20, she moved to Europe, finally choosing to live in Rome. While carving in marble, she ignored the local custom of hiring someone to finish the work, a decision that limited her production to only 46 documented compositions of subjects depicting racial discrimination and slavery. After returning to the United States, she converted to Catholicism, and her last commission was for a Baltimore church in 1883. Since the last years of her life are undocumented, no one knows when or where she died although someone reported seeing her in Rome in 1909.

BIBLIOGRAPHY
Wolfe, Rinna. *Edmonia Lewis: Wildfire in Marble*. Parsippany, NJ: Dillon, 1998. 0–382–39713–4, 128p. This well-researched biography for young adults reveals the importance of Lewis's contribution to African American heritage.

LILI'UOKALANI (1838–1917)
Ruler   Honolulu, Hawaii

Lili'uokalani was the first and only queen of Hawaii. She was born Lydia Kamakaeha (or Paki) on September 2, 1838, the third of 10 children of the chief Kapaakea and the chiefess Keohokalole. A counselor of King Kamehameha III and his wife adopted her at birth as part of traditional tribal unity, and she became closer to her foster sister than to any of her biological siblings. Educated in American missionary schools, she learned English and actively participated in the Congregational Church. In 1862, she married the son of a Boston sea captain, but their marriage was both childless and unhappy. Lili'uokalani's brother, Kalakaua, became king when Lunalilo died without an heir, and he, in turn, designated Lili'uokalani his heir. After that time, she was known by her royal name,

Lili'uokalani, and prepared for her role by serving as regent and visiting all of the islands. She also helped create and supervise a school for boys and girls of Hawaiian blood and organized a society to properly train young women. In 1887, she and her husband accompanied Kapiolani, her brother's wife, to meet Queen Victoria, and on their journey, President Cleveland graciously received them in the United States. When her brother died in 1891, Lili'uokalani inherited a weakened government constitution in which Americans had forced him to assign major power to his American cabinet ministers. When the McKinley Tariff of 1890 placed sugar on the free list, it removed Hawaii's trading advantage, and economic depression engulfed the islands. In 1893, the Americans set up a provisional government, applied for annexation to the United States, and arrested Lili'uokalani. In 1898, Congress annexed Hawaii. Lili'uokalani remained in Honolulu, receiving an annual pension. There she wrote "Aloha Oe," a song now symbolic of her islands.

BIBLIOGRAPHY

Allen, Helena G. *The Betrayal of Liliuokalani, Last Queen of Hawaii, 1838-1917.* Glendale, CA: Clark, 1982. 0-87062-144-0, 432p. This biased, undocumented biography catalogs wrongs against Lili'uokalani.
Lowe, Ruby Hasegawa. *Lili'uokalani.* Honolulu: Kamehameha Schools, 1993. 0-87336-018-4, 101p. This brief biography of Lili'uokalani for juveniles presents an overview of her life.

LIN, MAYA YING (1959-)
Architect   Athens, Ohio

Maya Lin, an Asian American architect, designed the Vietnam Memorial in Washington, DC. She was born on October 5, 1959, the daughter of emigrés who had left China in the late 1940s. Her father became the dean of fine arts at Ohio University, and her mother was a professor of Asian and English literature. After growing up in Ohio, Lin attended Yale University, receiving both her B.A. and M.A. In 1980, while still a Yale student, she submitted a design proposal to create a Vietnam veterans' memorial in Washington, DC. Her entry, one of 1,421, won the award for its plan to name all of the 58,000 American men and women killed in the war on huge granite slabs shaped like a V, one end pointing toward the Lincoln Memorial and the other toward the Washington Monument. To prepare her design, Lin visited the site, studied funerary art to see how people had approached death through the centuries, and read journals of soldiers who had served in World War I. The resulting design focused on people rather than politics, but some war veterans opposed it. Others expressed distress that the designer was Asian American. When planners decided to place a statue of several soldiers near the wall, Lin objected. After a compromise to move the sculpture away from the wall, the memorial was dedicated in 1982. Lin tried to separate herself from the turmoil, but in the next years, the public's strong emotional response to the names of loved ones and friends visible for all to see confirmed her initial composition. (A

Plexiglass replica tours the United States for those who are unable to travel to Washington.) In 1988, Lin created a memorial to the civil rights movement in Montgomery, Alabama, a project for which she used water as a motif, just as Martin Luther King, Jr., had done in his "I Have a Dream" speech. She also designed the Museum for African Art in New York City. In her continuing work as an architect and artist away from the public's eye, she has served on art commissions and received awards.

BIBLIOGRAPHY

Malone, Mary. *Maya Lin: Architect and Artist.* Springfield, NJ: Enslow, 1995. 0–89490–499–X, 112p. In a biography for young adults, Malone gives insight into Lin's life as an Asian American female architect.

LINDBERGH, ANNE MORROW (1906–1993)
Author   Englewood, New Jersey

Anne Morrow Lindbergh was an author and aviator. She was born in June 22, 1906, the daughter of an ambassador to Mexico and his wife, a poet who supported woman suffrage. Her wealth allowed Lindbergh to travel widely, and she graduated from Smith College in 1928. In her senior year, she met Charles Lindbergh at the ambassador's home in Mexico, and after their marriage, she learned how to co-pilot, navigate, and operate the radio in order to fly with him. In 1932, they left the country after the kidnapping and subsequent death of their son, but they had to face the publicity a second time when the kidnapper was brought to trial. Lindbergh's husband, a source of comfort throughout the ordeal, encouraged her to write about their 1931 survey flight to the Orient via the Arctic Circle in *North to the Orient* to divert her thoughts. He also convinced her to join him on a five-month flight exploring the Atlantic for commercial air routes. Simultaneously, she pursued her M.A. at Smith. Prior to World War II, Lindbergh and her husband voiced support for the Nazi regime, which she later acknowledged as a mistake. Another book, *Listen! The Wind*, solidified Lindbergh's reputation for writing beautiful prose because it transformed technical achievement into a story rather than merely a sequence of facts. Her most enduring work, *Gift from the Sea*, remains in print after 30 years. Among her awards were the Hubbard Medal of the National Geographic Society and two honorary degrees. She was also inducted into the Aviation Hall of Fame and elected to The National Women's Hall of Fame.

BIBLIOGRAPHY

Herrmann, Dorothy. *Anne Morrow Lindbergh: A Gift for Life.* New York: Ticknor and Fields, 1993. 0–395–56114–0, 382p. Herrmann relies on Lindbergh's published diaries and letters to interpret her relationship with her husband.
Lindbergh, Anne Morrow. *The Flower and the Nettle.* 1976. New York: Harcourt Brace Jovanovich, 1994. 0–15–631942–X, 605p. Lindbergh decided to document a

collection of her letters and diaries for the years 1936 to 1939 rather than write an autobiography.

———. *Locked Rooms and Open Doors*. 1974. New York: Harcourt Brace Jovanovich, 1993. 0-15-652956-4, 352p. Lindbergh discloses that during her early marriage, her child's kidnaping and murder, and her early flying days with her husband, she kept her sanity by keeping a diary.

Milton, Joyce. *Loss of Eden: A Biography of Charles and Anne Morrow Lindbergh*. New York: HarperCollins, 1993. 0-06-016503-0, 520p. Milton's well-researched and detailed biography looks at the Lindbergh marriage with compassion.

Vaughan, David Kirk. *Anne Morrow Lindbergh*. Boston: Twayne, 1988. 0-8057-7520-X, 138p. Vaughan's critical biography of Lindbergh's life and work shows her desire to understand how one should live one's life.

LLOYD, ALICE (1876-1962)
Educator   Athol, Massachusetts

Alice Lloyd established a college and a community center in Appalachia which she supported throughout her life. She was born on November 13, 1876, the only child of a wealthy merchant and his wife. After her graduation from a Boston preparatory school, she entered Radcliffe but had to leave when her family's financial situation worsened. While living with her grandmother in Boston, she began publishing the *Cambridge Press*. After a brief marriage ended, Lloyd and her mother moved to a climate more favorable for Lloyd's pain and partial paralysis from spinal meningitis. After they settled in eastern Kentucky's Knott County, an isolated spot with only one college graduate and few other literate citizens, a resident offered Lloyd 50 acres of land to educate his children. With additional funds solicited from friends remaining in the North, she constructed a schoolhouse and purchased the rest of the farm for a community center. Her mission was to train the youth of the area to become community leaders. She opened her school in 1919 with two students, and in five years, she had secured accreditation for the Knott County High School at Pippa Passes, the Caney Creek community in which she lived. In five years, Lloyd opened seven other high schools and recruited college graduates to teach without salary. In 1922, she founded Caney Junior College, and it relied on contributions rather than tuition charges, with students who wore uniforms working and maintaining the buildings. Students left the area to solicit funds, and over 200 graduates transferred to universities on scholarships, while another 1,200 taught in the community. Lloyd worked constantly throughout her life to support the school although her right arm never functioned and she walked with pain. In 1951, when she visited California, expecting to raise funds, she found herself the subject of the television show *This Is Your Life*. Although she was displeased at the ruse, the publicity earned $50,000 for the school. After her death, Caney was renamed Alice Lloyd College and continued to function as Lloyd had planned.

BIBLIOGRAPHY

Searles, P. David. *A College for Appalachia: Alice Lloyd on Caney Creek*. Lexington: University Press of Kentucky, 1995. 0-8131-1883-2, 216p. In his critical biography, Searles concludes that Lloyd came to Appalachia not for her health, but to help others.

Sloane, Robert W. *Alice Lloyd—Boston's Gift to Caney Creek*. Lexington: Thoroughbred Press, 1982. No ISBN, 241p. Sloane was seven when Lloyd arrived in his Appalachian community, and he recalls her attention with admiration and love.

LOCKWOOD, BELVA (1830–1917)
Attorney   Royalton, New York

Belva Lockwood was a social activist and the first female lawyer to practice law before the Supreme Court. She was born Belva Bennett on October 24, 1830, as the second of five children to a farmer. She attended school until age 15, and since her father opposed her further education, she began teaching. Lockwood's husband died five years after their marriage, and she supported her child and herself. She began attending Genesee College, later Syracuse University, and graduated in 1857 with honors. Elected preceptress of the Lockport, New York, Union School, she advocated gymnastics, public speaking, and skating for women students. After meeting **Susan B. Anthony**, Lockwood's interest in woman suffrage escalated. In 1866, Lockwood moved to Washington, DC, opened her own school, and married a Baptist minister who was also a dentist. When George Washington University rejected her for admission to law school on grounds of her sex, she attended the National University Law School, which issued her diploma only after she appealed to President Grant. Although the District of Columbia had passed a law allowing women to practice, the federal court of claims in the city denied her the right to plead a case. The Supreme Court refused her first application. She lobbied Congress, and in 1879, she became the first woman admitted to the Supreme Court. The following year, she sponsored a southern African American for the same right. Lockwood campaigned for suffrage, equal pay for women government workers, and work and property rights for married women. One of her cases gained a $5 million settlement for the Cherokee. When Lockwood realized the importance of publicity, she decided to support **Victoria Woodhull**'s candidacy for president on the independent women's ticket, and in 1884, Lockwood herself was nominated. Her platform espoused equal rights for all, limited prohibition, uniform marriage and divorce laws, and universal peace. As she aged, she focused on world peace, serving on the committee for the Nobel Peace Prize nomination. Today, the Belva Lockwood Awards honor young female lawyers for outstanding contributions to women, the community, and the legal profession. Lockwood herself was elected to The National Women's Hall of Fame.

BIBLIOGRAPHY

Dunnahoo, Terry. *Before the Supreme Court: The Story of Belva Ann Lockwood*. Boston: Houghton Mifflin, 1974. 0-395-18520-3, 186p. This straightforward account of Lockwood's life for young adults illuminates her achievements.

Fox, Mary Virginia. *Lady for the Defense: A Biography of Belva Lockwood*. New York: Harcourt Brace Jovanovich, 1975. 0-15-243400-3, 158p. Although a fictional biography for juveniles, the text clearly presents Lockwood's commitment to reform.

LOOS, ANITA   (1888–1981)
Author   Mount Shasta, California

Anita Loos was a novelist and screenwriter known for her satirical intertitles and cynical dialogue. She was born on April 26, 1888, to a theater manager and his wife. Her father featured her on his stage as a child, and her success led to other roles in San Francisco and Los Angeles, with her income eventually supporting the family. Although educated intermittently, she read any book she could find, collecting extraneous facts later used in her scripts. At age 13, she started selling humorous anecdotes to a theatrical newspaper, the *New York Morning Telegraph*. When watching a movie, she realized that someone wrote the plots, and she composed *The New York Hat*, sent it to the American Biograph Company, and received $25. **Mary Pickford** and Lionel Barrymore starred in the film, and festivals still screen it. D. W. Griffith hired her as a screenwriter when she was not yet 20, and she began work on the more than 60 silent films created in her early career. Critics consider her subtitles for *Intolerance,* in 1916, to be classic. In 1925, her novel, *Gentlemen Prefer Blondes*, brought her international fame and made the "dumb blonde" of the book, Lorelei Lee, famous as well. Loos was one of the first screenwriters to mock sex, and her defensible logic led George Santayana to call it the "best philosophical work by an American." The stage adaptation began on Broadway in 1926 followed by the musical version in 1949 and the film version in 1953, starring **Marilyn Monroe**. During Loos's lifetime, the novel had 85 editions and was translated into 14 languages. After the Great Depression, she wrote *Happy Birthday* for **Helen Hayes** and adapted *Gigi* for *Colette. In her later career, she also wrote novels and autobiography.

BIBLIOGRAPHY

Carey, Gary. *Anita Loos: A Biography*. New York: Knopf, 1988. 0-394-53127-2, 331p. Carey's readable biography, is based on interviews with Loos and those who knew her.

Loos, Anita. *Cast of Thousands*. New York: Grosset and Dunlap, 1977. 0-448-12264-2, 280p. Loos's chatty autobiography includes anecdotes about famous people she knew, illustrations, photographs, and copies of personal letters.

———. *Kiss Hollywood Good-by*. New York: Viking, 1974. 0-670-41374-7, 213p. Loos discusses relationships and her husband's jealousy over her success.

LOPEZ, NANCY (1957–)
Athlete   Torrance, California

Latina American Nancy Lopez is an accomplished professional golfer. After her birth on January 6, 1957, her family moved to Roswell, New Mexico, where her father began an automobile repair business. Both parents enjoyed golf, and when Lopez accompanied them on the greens, her father let her hit the ball. Although she played other sports, her father realized her skill at golf, and he started coaching her seriously. Lopez won her first competition at age 9, and at twelve, she won the Women's State Amateur tournament. In high school, she played the number one spot on the previously all-male golf team. Although she had a scholarship to Oklahoma's University of Tulsa, she decided at the end of her sophomore year that joining the women's professional tour would be more beneficial. After her impressive string of victories, the Ladies Professional Golf Association (LPGA) named her Rookie of the Year and Player of the Year, and the Associated Press named her Female Athlete of the Year. After a brief marriage, Lopez divorced, but she remarried and took her two-month-old daughter on tour. Lopez won over 35 official tournaments, and in 1987 became the youngest woman to be inducted into the LPGA Hall of Fame. She interrupted her career for additional children but returned to competition in 1996.

BIBLIOGRAPHY
Lopez, Nancy. *The Education of a Woman Golfer*. New York: Simon and Schuster, 1979. 0–671–24756–5, 191p. Lopez describes her life on the professional golf tour, her perception of winning, and the differences between men and women golfers.

LORD, BETTE BAO (1938–)
Author   Shanghai, China

Bette Bao Lord is an Asian American author. She was born November 3, 1938, as one of two daughters to a Nationalist Chinese government official, and when the Cultural Revolution began, she and her family immigrated to the United States, leaving her infant sister behind with foster parents. Lord graduated from Tufts University and received an M.A. from the Fletcher School of Law and Diplomacy. Her novels include *Spring Moon* and *In the Year of the Boar and Jackie Robinson*. Her book *Legacies* is a nonfiction account of the Cultural Revolution's repressions of the Chinese based on oral histories that Lord collected while living with her husband in Beijing from 1985 to 1989 during his service as the ambassador to China. Her other occupations have been teaching and performing modern dance; serving as a program officer for the Fulbright Exchange Program, selector of White House Fellows, and trustee for the Asia Foundation and the Committee of 100; and television news consultant. Among her honors are a National Graphic Arts Award, a Distinguished Americans of Foreign Birth Award, membership in the International Women's Hall of Fame, and honorary degrees from six universities and colleges.

BIBLIOGRAPHY

Fox, Mary Virginia. *Bette Bao Lord: Novelist and Chinese Voice for Change*. Chicago: Childrens Press, 1993. 0–516–03291–7, 107p. This biography for young adults covers Lord's life and career.

LORDE, AUDRE (1934–1992)
Poet   New York, New York

Audre Lorde was an African American lesbian poet. Her immigrant parents expected to return to Grenada, but after Lorde's birth on February 18, 1934, near the end of the Great Depression, they adapted to the United States. Lorde hated her family's strict control, so she left after high school but eventually went to college. She began working as a librarian and briefly joined the Harlem Writers Guild, an organization to which Langston Hughes also belonged. She received her B.A. from Hunter College in 1959, and in 1960 Columbia University awarded her an M.L.S. She was married and had two children when her first book of poetry appeared in 1968. She left her family that same year for Tougaloo College in Mississippi as the poet-in-residence and enjoyed, for the first time, the experience of teaching African American students. She also fell in love with another female and left her husband. Lorde returned to New York, and in 1974, her book *From a Land Where Other People Live* was nominated for a National Book Award. A subsequent book, *The Black Unicorn*, examined the effects of European and African cultures on each other, and at its publication, critics reviewed it carefully. During the 1970s, Lorde traveled widely, and in 1980 she published *The Cancer Journals*, in which she described her experience with breast cancer, the disease that eventually killed her after she relocated her home to St. Croix. She received honorary doctorates from three colleges and other awards including the Walt Whitman Citation of Merit.

BIBLIOGRAPHY

Keating, AnaLouise. *Women Reading Women Writing: Self-Invention in Paula Gunn Allen, Gloria Anzaldua, and Audre Lorde*. Philadelphia: Temple University Press, 1996. 1–56639–419–8, 240p. In a collective critical examination, Keating identifies ways, including biographical ones, to make Lorde's poetry more accessible.

Lorde, Audre. *A Burst of Light*. Ithaca, NY: Firebrand, 1988. 0–932379–40–0, 134p. Lorde reacts to life and her second bout with cancer up to 1987.

———. *The Cancer Journals*. San Francisco: Aunt Lute, 1997. 1–879960–51–6, 99p. In this two-part volume, Lorde describes her experiences as a cancer patient and a post-mastectomy female.

LOVEJOY, ESTHER POHL (1869–1967)
Physician   Seabeck, Washington

Esther Pohl Lovejoy was a physician and social activist. She was born Esther Clayson, the third of six children, on November 16, 1869, to a seaman in the navy and the daughter of a tailor. She attended school at a lumber camp and took a few lessons in Latin and history from a needy professor. After a woman delivered her mother's youngest child, she decided to become a physician and worked in a department store to save money. She became the University of Oregon Medical School's second woman graduate in 1894, married a surgeon, and established a joint practice with obstetrics as her specialty. Lovejoy's brothers persuaded the couple to move to Alaska as the area's first physicians. After her brother was mysteriously murdered, Lovejoy returned to Portland, visited her husband in Alaska during the summer, and left her son in her mother's care while she pursued her career. As director of the Portland Board of Health, the first woman to hold such a position in a large American city, she had laws passed to regulate the supply of milk, provide funds for school nurses, and keep the city sanitary. After her son died in 1908 and her husband in 1911, she married a businessman. He used her name to promote projects with which she disagreed, and she divorced him. During World War I, after unsuccessfully trying to secure permission for female physicians to serve abroad in the armed forces, she went to France to help the Red Cross, volunteering at night in a charity hospital. In 1919, after lecturing to raise money for the American Women's Hospitals, she visited troubled areas in Europe and solicited funds from the United States while helping to found the Medical Women's International Association. In 1920, after losing a Congressional campaign, she devoted herself to helping impoverished European refugees. To encourage women to enter medicine, she established the Pohl Scholarships at the University of Oregon, designating one-third of the awards for women. Among the honors she received were the Legion of Honor from France, the Gold Cross of Saint Sava from Yugoslavia, the Gold Cross of the Holy Sepulcher from Jerusalem, the Gold Cross of the Order of George I (Greece), and, twice, the *Elizabeth Blackwell Medal.

BIBLIOGRAPHY

Burt, Olive Woolley. *Physician to the World: Esther Pohl Lovejoy*. New York: Messner, 1973. 0–671–32587–6, 189p. This researched fictional biography for young adults follows Lovejoy's life and career.

LOW, JULIETTE GORDON (1860–1927)
Reformer   Savannah, Georgia

Juliette Magill Kinzie Gordon Low founded the Girl Scouts of America. She was born on October 31, 1860, the second of six children of a cotton broker, who later served in the Confederate Army and the Spanish-American War, and his wife. Low studied painting, wrote plays, and performed in New York City amateur productions while attending private schools. She also began to sculpt and travel abroad. In England, she met her husband, but the unhappy marriage led them to agree on divorce, although he died before it was final. Also in England, Low met Sir Robert Baden-Powell, founder of the Boy Scouts. Based on his organization, she began the Girl Guides during 1912 in Savannah, Georgia. The movement grew, and in 1915, Low founded the Girl Scouts of America. In 1919, the first International Council of Girl Guides and Girl Scouts met in London with Low as the American representative. By 1922, she had contracted cancer, but she used her remaining energy to prepare for the international Girl Scout Camp held in the United States during the summer of 1926. By the time of her death in 1927, over 140,000 Girl Scouts had joined troops in every state. She was elected to The National Women's Hall of Fame.

BIBLIOGRAPHY

Pace, Mildred Mastin. *Juliette Low*. Ashland, KY: Jesse Stuart, 1997. 0-945084-61-7, 202p. Pace used family letters, diaries, records, and photographs of Low and her family in this biography for young adults.

Shultz, Gladys Denny, and Daisy Gordon Lawrence. *Lady from Savannah: The Life of Juliette Low*. New York: Girl Scouts of America, 1988. 0-88441-147-8, 383p. Lawrence, Low's niece and the first registered Girl Scout, has written a carefully researched but undocumented biography on Low's life and work.

LOWELL, JOSEPHINE SHAW (1843–1905)
Philanthropist and Reformer   **West Roxbury, Massachusetts**

Josephine Shaw Lowell was an influential charity worker and social reformer. She was born on December 26, 1843, to wealthy Bostonian parents as the fourth of their five children. As a young girl, she traveled abroad with her family for five years, attending school in Rome and in Paris. She became a linguist and a poet before returning to America and Miss Gibson's School in New York. Lowell's radical abolitionist parents supported the Union and Emancipation, and her brother commanded the first African American regiment during the Civil War before dying in 1863. Lowell and her sister joined the Woman's Central Association of Relief in New York, her first experience in charity work. She married, but her husband's death six weeks before their daughter was born made her a widow at 20. She decided to support her father's and brother's charities, and in New York, volunteered in the Charities Aid Association to make periodic inspections of state charitable institutions. Her reports realistically revealed the abominable condition of jails and almshouses. In 1875, she conducted a statewide study of paupers who were capable of working, and as she inspected hospitals, asylums, orphanages, jails, and poorhouses, she exposed the politics and inequities of these institutions. In 1881, she investigated waste and duplication in privately financed charities, and her report led to the beginning of the New York Charity Organization Society, for which she served as director for 25 years. Her book *Public Relief and Private Charities* stated that charity should not relieve suffering but help the recipient become a productive member of society, and she advocated rehabilitation programs as integral to public charity. In 1890, she shifted to labor and founded the Consumers' League of New York to improve wages and working conditions. In 1893, she organized a committee including **Lillian Wald** to provide work relief for the unemployed, and two years later she worked for civil service reform. Her insistence on intellectual bases for laws and goals and efficient, professional management improved charitable organizations.

BIBLIOGRAPHY

Waugh, Joan. *Unsentimental Reformer: The Life of Josephine Shaw Lowell*. Cambridge, MA: Harvard University Press, 1997. 0-674-93036-3, 296p. In this carefully researched, thoughtful, and documented biography, Waugh reveals Lowell's public life.

LUCE, CLARE BOOTHE (1903–1987)
Dramatist, Ambassador, and Congresswoman   New York, New York

Clare Boothe Luce was a playwright and politician. She was born on April 10, 1903, the daughter of a pit orchestra violinist and sometime businessman and his former chorus girl wife. Her parents separated when Luce was eight, and she lived in genteel poverty, although her mother took her to France to have her privately educated for a year. Luce's first husband was wealthy, and at their divorce after six years of marriage, she received a large settlement but decided to return to work. In 1930, she became the associate editor of *Vogue* and then the managing editor of *Vanity Fair*. In 1935, she married magazine publisher Henry R. Luce, and the next year, her comedy *The Women* ran on Broadway for 657 performances. *Kiss the Boys Goodbye* and *Margin for Error*, an anti-Nazi play, followed its success. During World War II, she was elected to the United States House of Representatives as a Republican from Connecticut, serving for four years. In 1946, after the death of her daughter, she converted to Catholicism. In 1953, she went to Italy as President Dwight Eisenhower's ambassador, but after her term, she left politics until her husband's death. At that time, she joined President Ronald Reagan's Foreign Intelligence Advisory Board, and in 1983, Reagan presented her with the Presidential Medal of Freedom.

BIBLIOGRAPHY

Martin, Ralph G. *Henry and Clare: An Intimate Portrait of the Luces*. New York: Putnam, 1991. 0-399-13652-5, 463p. Martin's recommended biography, suitable for young adults, details Luce's marriage to the founder of the Time-Life magazine company, revealing their relationship as a social rather than sexual union.

Morris, Sylvia Jukes. *Rage for Fame: The Ascent of Clare Boothe Luce*. New York: Random, 1997. 0-394-57555-5, 561p. Using Luce's papers for a thorough and balanced biography, Morris thinks that Luce decided to create a persona after being born illegitimate and spent her life building success and status.

Sheed, Wilfrid. *Clare Boothe Luce*. New York: Dutton, 1982. 0-525-03055-7, 183p. Sheed knew Luce and her family, and in his biased biography, she emerges as an intelligent, complex, and entertaining woman.

LYON, MARY   (1797–1849)
Missionary and Educator   Buckland, Massachusetts

Mary Lyon, an educator, founded the Mount Holyoke Female Seminary. She was born on February 28, 1797, the sixth of eight children of a veteran of the Revolution who died when she was five. She lived on the family's farm and attended one-room schools, remaining on the farm after her mother's remarriage and departure in 1810. Lyon's brother paid her for keeping house so that she could afford an education. In 1814, she started teaching summer school, and in 1817, she enrolled in the new Sanderson Academy, alternating her teaching with study. In 1824, she opened a school during the winter where her students discussed ideas from current periodicals, and in the summer she joined Zilpah Grant at the new Adams Female Academy in East Derry, New Hampshire. After recovering from typhoid fever in 1828, she stayed with Grant in her new school, Ipswich Female Academy. In 1834, Lyon decided to found a residential seminary for young women with its own property and finances in the hands of unpaid trustees. She raised the money, and in 1836, Mount Holyoke Female Seminary was chartered. It opened in 1837 with 80 students aged 17 and older. The next year, it had 116 students. For 12 years, she served as principal and organizer of the domestic work system in which the girls worked together for the good of the school. The relentless work, however, weakened Lyon, but her school and legacy remained after her death, and she was elected into The National Women's Hall of Fame.

BIBLIOGRAPHY

Green, Elizabeth Alden. *Mary Lyon and Mount Holyoke: Opening the Gates*. Hanover, NH: University Press of New England, 1979. 0-87451-172-0, 406p. Reproductions of letters, school pamphlets, and diary excerpts help to re-create Lyon's achievement at a time when women rarely attended college.

Porterfield, Amanda. *Mary Lyon and the Mount Holyoke Missionaries*. New York: Oxford University Press, 1977. 0-19-511301-2, 179p. Porterfield attended Mount Holyoke, and her carefully documented research on Lyon as the school's founder focuses on Lyon's life and goals.

M

MACLAINE, SHIRLEY (1934–)
Actor   Richmond, Virginia

Shirley MacLaine is an actor. One of two children, she was born Shirley MacLean Beaty on April 24, 1934, to parents who encouraged her dancing at age two. She appeared in public as a dancer at age four and made her professional dance debut with the National Symphony Orchestra in Washington at age twelve. After attending high school in Arlington, Virginia, she went to New York and changed her name. In 1954 her successful replacement of the star of *The Pajama Game* on Broadway led to her film debut the next year in Alfred Hitchcock's *The Trouble with Harry*. Her first Academy Award nomination was for her performance in *Some Came Running*, and she won an Academy Award and several other awards for her role in *Terms of Endearment*. She has starred in film, on Broadway, and in television. Other interests have ranged from politics to reincarnation, and in the 1980s, she wrote several books discussing her spiritual beliefs. Among other honors are British Film Academy Awards, a Film Society of Lincoln Center Career Achievement Award, and a Cecil B. De Mille Lifetime Achievement Award.

BIBLIOGRAPHY
Denis, Christopher. *The Films of Shirley MacLaine*. Secaucus, NJ: Citadel, 1987. 0–80650–693–8, 217p. A brief biography of MacLaine precedes a synopsis of each of her films, the cast, and short quotes from critics.

MacLaine, Shirley. *Dance While You Can*. New York: Bantam, 1991. 0-553-07607-8, 303p. MacLaine's autobiography is a lively overview of her life with comments from her parents interspersed throughout.

————. *Dancing in the Light*. New York: Bantam, 1985. 0-553-05094-X, 421p. While pursuing the spiritual meaning of her life, MacLaine discloses her attitudes on reincarnation as well as the past lives she might have had.

————. *It's All in the Playing*. New York: Bantam, 1987. 0-553-05217-9, 338p. In this autobiography, MacLaine begins with her exultation of mountaintops while in Peru's Andes mountains and then makes a transition from prior years with background on the reception of her autobiography, *Out on a Limb*.

————. *My Lucky Stars: A Hollywood Memoir*. New York: Bantam, 1995. 0-553-09717-2, 381p. In this autobiography, MacLaine discusses the complexities of life as an actor and recalls the men and women who influenced her.

MACY, ANNE SULLIVAN. *See* SULLIVAN (MACY), ANNE

MADISON, DOLLEY (1768-1849)
First Lady   Guilford County, North Carolina

Dolley Payne Madison was First Lady of the United States. She was born on May 20, 1768, the third of nine children of a Quaker and his wife. Her father freed his slaves, sold his plantation, and moved to Philadelphia in 1783. In 1790, Madison married a Quaker lawyer, but he died in the yellow fever epidemic of 1793, and her younger son died two weeks later; one child survived. In 1794, she married James Madison, a Virginia Congressional leader who was 17 years older than she. Madison shed her Quaker background, and her gaiety and ability to entertain complemented her husband's reserve during the 42 years of their marriage. When President Thomas Jefferson appointed Madison's husband secretary of state, they moved to Washington, and she became the hostess for Jefferson and Vice President Aaron Burr, both widowers. When her own husband became president, Madison restored formality to White House dinners and made guests feel so welcome that even her husband's enemies remained pleasant. In August 1814, the British captured Washington and burned the public buildings, including the White House. As Madison escaped to Virginia, she grabbed a Gilbert Stuart portrait of George Washington, important state papers, and other treasures. Her foresight made history. After her husband's death, Madison continued to entertain, but to support herself and her spendthrift son she had to sell her husband's papers.

BIBLIOGRAPHY
Arnett, Ethel Stephens. *Mrs. James Madison: The Incomparable Dolley*. Greensboro, NC: Piedmont Press, 1972. No ISBN, 520p. Arnett chose topics from Madison's letters, diaries, and other primary sources to reveal her as she appeared from the written records of her day.

Hunt-Jones, Conover. *Dolley and the Great Little Madison*. Washington, DC: American Institute of Architects, 1977. No ISBN, 148p. The text about Madison alone and with her husband accompanies plates of artifacts that belonged to them before her son dispersed their estate.

Moore, Virginia. *The Madisons: A Biography*. New York: McGraw-Hill, 1979. 0-07-042903-0, 568p. In a well-researched and readable biography, Moore posits that Madison changed during her marriage.

Thane, Elswyth. *Dolley Madison, Her Life and Times*. New York: Crowell-Collier, 1970. No ISBN, 184p. Thane's researched biography for young adults, based on letters and documents without citations, is a straightforward examination of Madison's life.

MADONNA (1958–)
Entertainer and Actor   Bay City, Michigan

Madonna is an entertainer who has managed her business with acumen. She was born Madonna Louise Ciccone on August 16, 1958, the third of eight children and the oldest daughter of an engineer. When her mother died, Madonna and her siblings lived with relatives until her father married the family's housekeeper. In high school, she studied dance and prepared herself academically to attend the University of Michigan. She left college after two years to enter show business, and eventually Alvin Ailey's American Dance Theater hired her. After leaving this group, she began working at New York City clubs before a partnership with a New York club disc jockey helped her obtain a record contract. Her second album, *Like a Virgin*, with her song "Material Girl," "went platinum." She made her first concert tour in 1985, married, and began acting. She starred in several films, including *Evita*, mostly with positive reviews. A business arrangement lasting through the end of the twentieth century gives her artistic control over all her music or movie releases, but she continues to take risks by changing her performance style. Among her honors are Grammy Awards and a Golden Globe Award.

BIBLIOGRAPHY
Bego, Mark. *Madonna: Blonde Ambition*. New York: Harmony, 1992. 0-517-58242-2, 308p. Using interviews with Madonna's friends, Bego discusses her childhood and early career as well as her life as a major entertainer.

Claro, Nicole. *Madonna*. New York: Chelsea House, 1994. 0-7910-2330-3, 127p. The accessible text, written for young adults, addresses both the positive and negative aspects of Madonna's personal and professional choices through 1993.

Gulick, Rebecca. *Madonna: Portrait of a Material Girl*. Philadelphia: Courage, 1993. 1-56138-236-1, 71p. This brief biography of Madonna covers the diversity of her career with photographs accompanied by concise explanations of their significance.

King, Norman. *Madonna: The Book*. New York: Morrow, 1991. 0-688-10389-8, 256p. King interviewed Madonna, and he uses her words to describe her life.

MANKILLER, WILMA (1945-)
Tribal Leader   Stilwell, Oklahoma

Wilma Mankiller is the first woman to have served as the head of a major Native American tribe in North America. She was born on November 18, 1945, one of eleven children of a poor full-blooded Cherokee farmer and his Dutch-Irish wife. ("Mankiller" was originally a Cherokee military title that one of Mankiller's relatives adopted as his own name.) When drought struck in the 1950s, a government assistance program helped the family move to San Francisco, and Mankiller's father became a union organizer. In the 1960s, Mankiller studied sociology and became a social worker before marrying a wealthy Ecuadoran accountant. Not until 1969, when Native Americans held the former Alcatraz prison complex for 18 months, did she develop an interest in the American Native Rights movement. In 1975, she divorced and took her daughters back to Oklahoma to reclaim her ancestral land. As the economic stimulus coordinator for the Cherokee Nation, she developed self-help programs. After a serious automobile accident in 1979 for which rehabilitation took one year, she founded the Community Development Department and served as its first director, her goals being provide water for all Cherokees and to improve housing standards. Her ability to raise funds impressed tribal leaders, and in 1983, a conservative Republican asked her, a liberal Democrat, to campaign as his deputy chief of the nation. When he resigned as the principal chief two years later, she became the first female Cherokee leader. In 1987, she ran her own campaign for principal chief, and after persuading some of the tribal men that voting for a woman was acceptable, she won. She reinstated the role of women as tribal leaders, which had disappeared with the acceptance of white men's sexism. After helping her Oklahoma tribe of over 70,000 members gain both economic independence and a sense of cultural pride, she was named *Ms.* magazine's Woman of the Year and elected to The National Women's Hall of Fame.

BIBLIOGRAPHY
Mankiller, Wilma Pearl. *Mankiller: A Chief and Her People*. New York: St. Martin's, 1993. 0-312-09868-5, 292p. Within Mankiller's powerful autobiography is a story of the government's mistreatment of the Cherokee Nation as well as her personal trials.
Schwarz, Melissa. *Wilma Mankiller: Principal Chief of the Cherokees*. New York: Chelsea House, 1994. 0-7910-1715-X, 111p. This biography of Mankiller for young adults gives an overview of her life and her major achievements.

MARION, FRANCES (1888-1973)
Film Director and Author   San Francisco, California

Frances Marion, an acclaimed Hollywood scriptwriter known for her generosity and kindness, won two Academy Awards. She was born Marion Benson Owens on November 18, 1888, the daughter of an advertising executive and his society wife, an accomplished musician. Marion's parents divorced when she was 12, and she responded to her father's remarriage by drawing cartoons of teachers on a blackboard and getting herself expelled from all the system's schools. She attended a private school before entering the University of California at Berkeley and then transferring to Mark Hopkins School of Art. At 18, she married her 19-year-old art teacher, but they soon divorced. She worked as an illustrator for a theater manager, and as a reporter on the *San Francisco Examiner* she wrangled an exclusive interview with **Marie Dressler**. In 1914, she started her career in film, working with **Lois Weber**. Her first original screenplay, *The Foundling*, starred **Mary Pickford**, later one her best friends. In one year, Marion collected credits from several studios for writing and directing. In 1920, she married a Princeton-educated equestrian and made 68 westerns with him for which he received $10,000 a week in 1925. They had two children, but after his death in 1928, she remarried. With her fourth husband, she made award-winning films including *The Big House*, *Min and Bill*, and *The Secret Six* (making $17,000 a week). For *The Big House* and another script, *The Champ*, Marion won Academy Awards. In her career, she wrote over 100 scripts and was a script consultant on many other projects, innately understanding what would work visually on the screen. Her careful research made her movies authentic, but she never allowed audiences to leave the theater depressed. Disillusioned with Hollywood's changes, she left in 1937 to write novels and short stories and to create sculpture.

BIBLIOGRAPHY

Beauchamp, Cari. *Without Lying Down: Frances Marion and the Powerful Women of Early Hollywood*. New York: Scribner, 1997. 0–684–80213–9, 475p. This carefully researched and documented biography of Marion covers the contributions she made to Hollywood films and her personal life.

Marion, Frances. *Off with Their Heads: A Serio-Comic Tale of Hollywood*. New York: Macmillan, 1972. No ISBN, 356p. Marion learned at age 10 to listen to people without revealing her thoughts, an attribute that served her well during her Hollywood collaboration with egotistical or insecure colleagues.

MARSHALL, PAULE (1929–)
Author   Brooklyn, New York

Paule Marshall writes about the experiences of African Americans in North and South America. Born Valenza Pauline Burke on April 9, 1929, to emigrants from Barbados, she grew up in a sheltered community. At nine, she visited Barbados and wrote poems about the visit. Later she adapted the speech patterns of women from Barbados talking around the kitchen table for her other work. She graduated cum laude and Phi Beta Kappa from Brooklyn College in 1954. She began writing her fiction after working as a researcher and staff writer for *Our World* in New York City and as an English professor at Virginia Commonwealth University. Her works include "To Da-duh, in Memoriam"; *Brown Girl, Brownstones*; *Soul Clap Hands and Sing*; *The Chosen Place, the Timeless People*; and *Praisesong for a Widow*.

Among her many awards are several grants, the Before Columbus Foundation American Book Award, and a MacArthur Fellowship.

BIBLIOGRAPHY

Coser, Stelamaris. *Bridging the Americas: The Literature of Paule Marshall, Toni Morrison, and Gayl Jones*. Philadelphia: Temple University Press, 1995. 1–56639–266–7, 227p. Coser examines Marshall's work in this collective critique and concludes that her writing reflects the Latin American storytelling tradition of Gabriel Garcia Marquez.

DeLamotte, Eugenia C. *Places of Silence, Journeys of Freedom: The Fiction of Paule Marshall*. Philadelphia: University of Pennsylvania Press, 1998. 0–8122–3437–5, 240p. This critical text analyzes Marshall's contribution to feminism in her fiction through her techniques of "superimposition" or "double exposure."

Denniston, Dorothy Hamer. *The Fiction of Paule Marshall*. Nashville: University of Tennessee Press, 1995. 0–87049–839–8, 187p. Using connections between Marshall's life and work, Denniston critiques her writing and her dependence on African storytelling traditions such as oral narrative, proverbs, and nonlinear plot progression.

Melchior, Bernhard. *"Re/visioning" the Self away from Home: Autobiographical and Cross-Cultural Dimensions in the Works of Paule Marshall*. New York: Peter Lang, 1998. 0–8204–3523–6, 358p. Melchior's critical biography examines Marshall's autobiographical content in her four novels, noting especially the importance of her cross-cultural experiences transformed into fiction.

Pettis, Joyce Owens. *Toward Wholeness in Paule Marshall's Fiction*. Charlottesville: University Press of Virginia, 1995. 0–8139–1614–3, 173p. Pettis uses African American feminist criticism to examine concepts of race, class, and gender in Marshall's fiction.

MARTIN, ANNE (1875–1951)
Politician and Activist   Empire City, Nevada

Anne Henrietta Martin, a political activist, was the first woman to run for the United States Senate. She was born on September 30, 1875, the second of seven children of a politician and banker and his wife. Martin attended private schools and entered the University of Nevada, graduating in 1894. She received a second degree from Stanford University in history, and in 1897 established a history department at the University of Nevada. She then studied at Columbia University's Chase Art School and at universities in Leipzig and London for training to lecture in art. After her father died in 1901, Martin took her inheritance and left for England, where as a feminist, she joined Emmeline Pankhurst's militant suffragettes and began writing on social issues under the name Anne O'Hara. When she returned to Nevada in 1911, she successfully crusaded for ratification of a state suffrage amendment. She turned to national suffrage concerns, establishing the National American Woman Suffrage Association and the militant Congressional Union before becoming chairman of the National Woman's Party. In 1918, she ran for the U.S. Senate, asking women to support her by filling her platform with concerns of welfare for mothers and infants, land controls to protect farmers and other laborers, prohibition, amnesty for political prisoners, and opposition to the League of Nations, but she received only 20 percent of the vote. She then wrote for both American and British magazines advocating the Women's International League for Peace and Freedom, serving on its board, and attending its world conferences in Dublin (1926) and Prague (1929). After the group lost power, she joined the People's Mandate to Governments to End War in 1936.

BIBLIOGRAPHY

Howard, Anne Bail. *The Long Campaign: A Biography of Anne Martin*. Reno: University of Nevada Press, 1985. 0-87417-092-3, 220p. In this balanced biography, Howard shows Martin's courage as a crusader for woman suffrage and as a candidate for the United States Senate.

MAYNOR, DOROTHY (1910-1996)
Singer   Norfolk, Virginia

In addition to performing as a concert singer, African American Dorothy Maynor established a school for aspiring African American musicians. She was born Dorothy Leigh Mainor on September 3, 1910, and remained in Virginia to study at Hampton Institute, completing a home economics degree in 1933. She then decided to pursue vocal study at Westminster Choir College and gained critical acclaim in a performance at the Berkshire Music Festival. She began to sing spirituals, *lieder*, operatic arias, and oratorios around the world, gaining international recognition for her exceptional talent. She never appeared on the opera stage because of her race, and this lack of exposure in opera kept her from becoming widely known in the United States. In 1963, she retired from performing to found and direct the Harlem School of the Arts for children to study ballet, music, modern dance, drama, and art, most often for free. Using her two degrees, she taught; conducted church, college, and community choirs; wrote articles; and made speeches. In 1975, she joined the Metropolitan Opera board of directors, and in the ensuing years, she received honorary degrees from five colleges and universities.

BIBLIOGRAPHY

Rogers, William Forrest. *Dorothy Maynor and the Harlem School of the Arts: The Diva and the Dream*. Lewiston, NY: Mellen Press, 1993. 0-7734-9377-8, 286p. This scholarly biography of Maynor, carefully researched and documented with interviews and print materials, records her life and career.

MCAULIFFE, CHRISTA (1948–1986)
Educator   Framingham, Massachusetts

Christa McAuliffe, a social studies teacher chosen to be America's first private citizen in space, died when the space shuttle *Challenger* exploded on January 28, 1986. She was born on September 2, 1948, as the oldest of five children to a college student who became a businessman and his wife. As a teenager, she played sports and worked part-time. She married a high school boyfriend after graduating from Framingham State College, and in 1978, while teaching in Maryland, completed her M.A. Later, while teaching social studies in Concord, New Hampshire, McAuliffe applied to become the first teacher in space and was chosen from among 11,000 candidates for the honor of becoming a teacher-astronaut. During five months of training at the Johnson Space Center in Houston, Texas, she said she was not afraid because everyday life had as many risks as taking a space shuttle. She equated her mission to frontier settlement in the West, going on a space shuttle instead of a wagon into the unknown. McAuliffe had planned to conduct history lessons via television from space while the astronauts completed scientific experiments, but the death of all aboard shocked the nation.

BIBLIOGRAPHY
Corrigan, Grace George. *A Journal for Christa: Christa McAuliffe, Teacher in Space.* Lincoln: University of Nebraska Press, 1993. 0–8032–1459–6, 191p. McAuliffe's mother recalls her daughter's hard work and community involvement before being chosen over 11,000 other applicants to become the Teacher in Space.
Hohler, Robert T. *I Touch the Future: The Story of Christa McAuliffe.* New York: Random, 1986. 0–394–55721–2, 262p. Interviews and personal recollections form the nucleus of Hohler's biography of McAuliffe, also appropriate for young adults. Hohler followed McAuliffe during the seven months after her selection for the space shuttle ride.

MCCARDELL, CLAIRE (1905–1958)
Fashion Designer   Frederick, Maryland

Claire McCardell, a fashion designer, initiated sportswear styles for women. She was born on May 24, 1905, as the only daughter of four children to a bank president and state senator and his southern belle wife. McCardell enjoyed sewing for her dolls and creating patterns from magazine pictures at an early age, and by the time she entered high school, she had consulted with the family dressmaker and learned to pattern all of her own clothes. She briefly attended Hood College before persuading her father to let her enroll at the New York School of Fine and Applied Arts (Parsons School of Design). She spent the second year in Paris, dismantling the shopworn dress models of famous designers to learn their construction. Her idol, *Madeleine Vionnet, invented the bias cut. After graduating from Parsons in 1928, the only job McCardell could find was painting rosebuds on lampshades, but two years later, she joined the sportswear firm of

Townley and remained until her death. She created the first "separates," a bare and a covered top, a long and a short skirt, and a culotte in black wool jersey to wear either formally or informally. When she wore a Moroccan robe to a Beaux Arts ball, many wanted a copy, and the monastic dress, cut completely from bias with no difference from back to front, became popular. During World War II, she designed the "popover," a denim wraparound for women to wear for cleaning at home, and the "body suit." The loose fit and easy adjustments of her designs made ready-to-wear clothes popular. She also introduced wool jersey for evening wear and used cotton for all types of clothes. During her career, she earned all of the fashion industry awards including the most prestigious, the American Fashion Critics Award and the Neiman-Marcus Award. She was the first fashion designer chosen as one of America's Women of Achievement by the National Women's Press Club. In 1953, a retrospective of her work was the first show of dress designs exhibited like other works of art.

BIBLIOGRAPHY

Yohannan, Kohle, and Nancy Nolf. *Claire McCardell: Redefining Modernism*. New York: Harry N. Abrams, 1998. 0-8109-4375-1, 152p. In their biography of McCardell, which includes 103 illustrations of her designs, Yohannan and Nolf emphasize her role in changing American fashion.

MCCARTHY, MARY (1912–1989)
Author   Seattle, Washington

Mary McCarthy was an author and critic whose satire about marriage, sexual expression, impotent intellectuals, and women tried to expose institutional deceit. She was born on June 21, 1912, the daughter of a lawyer and his wife. Before graduating Phi Beta Kappa from Vassar, she founded a literary magazine to protest Vassar's existing magazine. Wanting to be an actor but having no talent, she became a book reviewer for the *Nation* and the *New Republic* and a ghostwriter. Her affiliation with the *Partisan Review* began in 1937, and she remained its drama critic until 1962. Her second husband, Edmund Wilson, encouraged her to write fiction, and her popular novel *The Group* was later made into a movie. In the 1960s, she became concerned about the war in Vietnam, and when she visited the country, she saw decay in the American system. She objected to pollution of the jungles, the sordid refugee camps, and the war's inefficiency as well as its purpose. When she visited North Vietnam in 1968, she became certain that the United States should withdraw. In 1971, she used her observations of the trial of the captain accused of the My Lai massacre for her third book of essays on the Vietnam War. Among her many awards were the Edward MacDowell Medal, a National Medal for Literature, and six honorary degrees. She was a member of the American Academy of Arts and Letters and of the National Institute of Arts and Letters.

BIBLIOGRAPHY

Brightman, Carol. *Writing Dangerously: Mary McCarthy and Her World.* New York: Potter, 1992. 0–517–56400–9, 714p. Brightman discusses McCarthy's life and her displeasure with her own fiction in a thoroughly detailed and definitive biography based on McCarthy's papers and interviews with people who knew her. National Book Critics Circle Award.

Grumbach, Doris. *The Company She Kept.* New York: Coward-McCann, 1967. No ISBN, 218p. In an undocumented, readable biography, based on previously unpublished material and an interview with McCarthy, Grumbach posits that McCarthy's fiction is autobiographical.

McCarthy, Mary. *How I Grew.* San Diego: Harcourt Brace Jovanovich, 1987. 0–15–142193–5, 278p. McCarthy traces her intellectual development from ages 13 to 21, remembering herself as somewhat anti-Semitic and generally insensitive to the conditions of others.

———. *Intellectual Memoirs: New York, 1936–1938.* San Diego: Harcourt Brace, 1993. 0–15–644787–8, 134p. McCarthy describes the birth of her writing career when she was in her twenties and the ways she hurt others with her irresponsible behavior.

McCLINTOCK, BARBARA (1902–1992)
Geneticist   Hartford, Connecticut

Barbara McClintock was a geneticist who won the Nobel Prize for her research on corn reproduction. She was born on June 16, 1902, a doctor's daughter, and grew up in Brooklyn, where she attended Erasmus Hall High School. At Cornell University, she studied plant genetics while working on her B.A., M.A., and Ph.D. degrees. In the 1930s, she discovered that chromosomes break and recombine to create genetic changes in a process known as "crossing over," a discovery that explained puzzling patterns of inheritance. She also discovered a structure called the nucleolar organizer of the chromosome, which seemed to order genetic material during cell division. She spent her professional life working on corn, using patterns of colored kernels to disclose the breaking, joining, and rearranging of genes and chromosomes inside the cells. Because the kernels inherit pigments, McClintock could trace genes through the changes in the kernels. In 1941, she began working at the Cold Spring Harbor Laboratory, and she remained there for the rest of her career. Since genetics was such a new science when she made her first discoveries, scientists ignored her work, but her findings were so profound that she began to garner honors and prizes, including membership in the National Academy of Sciences in 1944, president of the Genetics Society in 1945, the National Medal of Science in 1970, and the first MacArthur Laureate Award to support her for the rest of her life at $60,000 a year in 1981. She was also elected to The National Women's Hall of Fame. In 1983, when the significance of her work 40 years before was finally recognized, she became the first woman to win an unshared Nobel Prize in physiology or medicine and the third woman to win an unshared Nobel Prize in science. James Watson, director of the Cold Spring Harbor Laboratory and co-discoverer of the structure of DNA, nominated

McClintock as one of the three most important figures in the history of genetics, one of "the three M's," the other two being Gregor Mendel and Thomas Hunt Morgan.

BIBLIOGRAPHY

Fedoroff, Nina, and David Botstein. *The Dynamic Genome: Barbara McClintock's Ideas in the Century of Genetics.* Cold Spring Harbor, ME: Cold Spring Harbor Laboratory, 1992. 0-87969-422-X, 422p. This critical collection of recommended and scholarly essays on McClintock's life and work includes some of her scientific papers and essays by people who knew her.

Fine, Edith Hope. *Barbara McClintock, Nobel Prize Geneticist.* Springfield, NJ: Enslow, 1998. 0-89490-983-5, 128p. This biography for young adults presents McClintock's life and career.

Keller, Evelyn Fox. *A Feeling for the Organism: The Life and Work of Barbara McClintock.* San Francisco: W. H. Freeman, 1983. 0-7167-1433-7, 235p. Keller interviewed McClintock and others to create a strong picture of her life and work.

Kittredge, Mary. *Barbara McClintock.* New York: Chelsea House, 1991. 1-55546-666-4, 103p. This balanced biography for young adults relates McClintock's achievements and the importance of transposable genetic elements in disease prevention.

McCULLERS, CARSON (1917-1967)
Author   Columbus, Georgia

Carson McCullers was an author concerned with loneliness. She was born Lula Carson Smith on February 19, 1917, as the eldest of three children to a watch repairman and jewelry store owner and his wife. She was introverted as a child, preferring to play the piano. At six, she could pick out songs, and by ten, she was an accomplished pianist. In addition to practicing her music, she read all the books she could find. At 15, an attack of rheumatic fever sapped her stamina, and she began to write. She went to New York after graduation from high school to attend Juilliard, but her tuition money disappeared, either lost or stolen, and she enrolled in writing courses at Columbia University. Her rheumatic fever recurred, and she returned to Columbus to recuperate. While there, she continued to write and married Reeves McCullers, but the marriage dissolved as a result of her disinterest in domestic activities and her enchantment with other writers and their world. In 1940, she published *The Heart Is a Lonely Hunter,* which became an immediate success. In the next four years, she received several fellowships, allowing her to complete *Reflections in a Golden Eye* and *The Member of the Wedding.* In 1945, she remarried McCullers, but two years later, she suffered two strokes and tried to commit suicide. In 1950, however, her play *The Member of the Wedding* opened in New York to critical acclaim, and in 1952, she was elected to membership in the National Institute of Arts and Letters. She moved to Paris with her husband, but her later work did not match her earlier creations since illness seemed to undermine her concentration.

BIBLIOGRAPHY

Carr, Virginia Spencer. *The Lonely Hunter: A Biography of Carson McCullers*. Garden City, NY: Doubleday, 1975. 0-385-04028-8, 600p. Based on 500 interviews, Carr's definitive and balanced biography of McCullers's complex character and her work also pictures the 1940s literary scene.

McDowell, Margaret B. *Carson McCullers*. Boston: Twayne, 1980. 0-8057-7297-7, 158p. McDowell's critical study of McCullers includes a brief biography and a discussion of her theory of fiction and of the thematic content in her five novels.

McDANIEL, HATTIE (1895–1952)
Actor   Wichita, Kansas

Hattie McDaniel was the first African American actor to win an Academy Award, for her role in *Gone with the Wind*. She was born on June 10, 1895, to former slaves and moved to Denver, Colorado, where she lived for most of her life. She attended white public schools but left before graduating to perform in minstrel shows with her brothers and father. She began entertaining as a solo performer in 1916 and eventually sang on the radio. In the late 1920s, after her first husband died from a gunshot wound soon after their marriage, her father died, and the Great Depression left her unemployed. She went to Los Angeles with her brothers and supported herself as a maid between small film roles. Before she appeared in *Gone with the Wind*, she had over 50 film credits. After her success, she helped other African Americans, and responded to derogatory comments about her stereotypical roles that she would rather play a maid than be one. The National Association for the Advancement of Colored People (NAACP) continued to verbally attack her because of her visibility in the white community. This hostility and the difficulties of her several marriages plagued her last decade, although she continued to work throughout her life.

BIBLIOGRAPHY

Jackson, Carlton. *Hattie: The Life of Hattie McDaniel*. Lanham, MD: Madison, 1990. 0-8191-7295-2, 220p. Jackson extrapolates from McDaniel's life the struggles of African American entertainers who needed to work but were chastised by their own people for accepting roles as stereotypes.

McMEIN, NEYSA (1888–1949)
Artist   Quincy, Illinois

Neysa McMein was an illustrator. She was born Isabelle Lee Parker on January 24, 1888, the only child of a newspaper editor and his wife. While growing up, she spent most of her time drawing or practicing piano, and after high school, her parents sent her to the Art Institute of Chicago. For extra support, she played the piano in nickelodeons, worked as a church organist, and occasionally sold songs. In 1913, she left Chicago and her music for New York to become an artist. After consulting a numerologist, she changed her name to Neysa and enrolled in the Art

Students' League, selling her first drawing within a few months. Butterick's *Designer* bought her drawings, and in 1915, she sold her first cover to the *Saturday Evening Post*. Her career was at its peak between 1923 and 1937 while she worked under contract to design *McCall's* magazine covers, first for $25,000, and then for $30,000 a year. She created covers in pastel for other major magazines including the *Saturday Evening Post* and *Woman's Home Companion* while illustrating advertisements for Palmolive soap, Lucky Strike cigarettes, and Betty Crocker foods. She also sold some of her songs, wrote a filmscript, and published articles. For charities of her choice, she donated posters, and during World War I, she went to France to lecture and entertain the troops. She traveled widely to Egypt, India, and the Near East, but managed to marry happily in 1923 without changing her lifestyle. In the mid-1930s, interest in pastel illustrations decreased, and she changed to oil portraits, painting well-known persons of the day including Presidents Harding and Hoover, **Edna St. Vincent Millay**, **Anne Lindbergh**, and Dorothy Parker.

BIBLIOGRAPHY

Gallagher, Brian. *Anything Goes*. New York: Times, 1987. 0–8129–1215–2, 241p. This carefully researched and readable biography of McMein captures her personality and the unconventional life that she led.

McPHERSON, AIMEE SEMPLE (1890–1944)
Evangelist   Ingersoll, Ontario, Canada

Aimee Semple McPherson, evangelist and founder of the International Church of the Foursquare Gospel, preached personal salvation and reform rather than a social gospel. Born on October 9, 1890, she was the only child of a wealthy farmer who led the choir in the Methodist Church and of his second wife, an orphan raised by a Salvation Army captain. The year after McPherson converted at a Pentecostal revival in 1907, she married the evangelist who converted her. She began preaching in 1909, with a Pentecostal ceremony her only ordination. She and her husband went to China, where he died unexpectedly, and when her daughter was born a month later, McPherson returned to America. Work as a Salvation Army lecturer preceded a second unhappy marriage. In 1915, she began conducting revival services, and in June 1916 led her first tent revival. McPherson soon adopted a white dress and shoes with a blue cape, a uniform she wore throughout her preaching career. Between 1918 and 1923, she crossed the United States eight times and visited Australia. In Denver, for a month in both 1921 and 1922, she filled the Coliseum with 12,000 people every night. In 1921, she began construction of Angelus Temple in Los Angeles, and in 1922 delivered the first radio sermon by a woman. From 1923 to 1927, she preached every night and three times on Sunday to over 5,000 people each time. In 1927, she incorporated her church as the International Church of the Foursquare Gospel, a new Pentecostal denomination. She asked attendees to bring food or clothing for the needy, and within the church, she established a free employment bureau, a parole committee, summer camps, Bible conferences, and a radio station. She also published a weekly and a monthly magazine and founded a Bible college. Reaching many people searching for something basic in their lives, she was one of the best known women in America during the 1930s.

BIBLIOGRAPHY

Bahr, Robert. *Least of All Saints: The Story of Aimee Semple McPherson*. Englewood Cliffs, NJ: Prentice-Hall, 1979. 0–13–527978–X, 308p. Bahr's biography of McPherson omits the last 14 years of her life.

Blumhofer, Edith Waldvogel. *Aimee Semple McPherson: Everybody's Sister*. Grand Rapids, MI: Eerdmans, 1993. 0–8028–3752–2, 431p. This objective and scholarly text focuses on McPherson's family and her relationship with the Salvation Army before she established the Church of the Foursquare Gospel.

Epstein, Daniel Mark. *Sister Aimee: The Life of Aimee Semple McPherson*. San Diego: Harcourt Brace Jovanovich, 1993. 0–15–600093–8, 475p. In this balanced, well-researched, documented, and readable biography, Epstein defuses accusations that McPherson was a fraud.

McPherson, Aimee Semple. *This Is That*. 1919. New York: Garland, 1985. 0–8240–6428–3, 685p. In a thorough autobiography, McPherson discusses her spiritual choices.

MEAD, LUCIA AMES (1856–1936)
Activist   Boscawen, New Hampshire

Lucia True Ames Mead was a pacificist who worked throughout her life for world peace. She was born on May 5, 1856, as one of four children to a businessman farmer and his wife. After her mother died when she was five, she lived with her father in Chicago until she was 14 and then attended high school in Boston, living with her brother. After additional tutoring from her uncle, she studied music and lectured to women's clubs that educated women had the responsibility to correct social problems rather than remain at leisure. She also served as president of the Massachusetts Woman Suffrage Association and supported many other groups. After her marriage to a man with similar ideals, she began writing. Among her books were *Great Thoughts from Little Thinkers*, *Memoirs of a Millionaire*, and *To Whom Much Is Given*. Unsatisfied with literary achievements, however, she developed into an ardent pacificist who suggested an international police force and a world legislature to create world law. In 1915, she participated in the Women's Peace Party, and after World War I, she wanted the United States to join the League of Nations and spoke against armaments. She served as an officer in several organizations, including the National Council for the Prevention of War, the American Peace Society, and the League for Permanent Peace. As a logical, intelligent speaker whose strong faith propelled her tireless efforts, she influenced those who heard her lecture until she was past 70.

BIBLIOGRAPHY
Craig, John M. *Lucia Ames Mead and the American Peace Movement*. Lewiston, NY: Mellen Press, 1990. 0–88946–094–9, 223p. Personal papers, diaries, correspondence, and published works helped Craig recreate Mead's life and work.

MEAD, MARGARET (1901–1978)
Anthropologist   Philadelphia, Pennsylvania

Margaret Mead was an anthropologist. She was born on December 16, 1901, as the oldest of four children to an economics professor and a sociologist who finished her college work when Mead was a child. Mead's mother believed that women should have their own careers and take responsibility to right the ills of society, and she first introduced her daughter to anthropology through her field work with Italian Americans living in New Jersey. Mead's grandmother, who lived with the family, also influenced her by teaching her subjects such as algebra. Mead attended several Quaker schools before entering DePauw University as an English major. Disliking the Midwest, she enrolled in Barnard to study psychology, but classes with Franz Boas and **Ruth Benedict** propelled her to anthropology. Boas supervised her Ph.D. work when she studied adolescent behavior in Samoa. Her field work on the sexual behavior, natural character, and the effects of culture change on the nonliterate peoples of Oceana became one of her best-known studies. She joined the American Museum of Natural History in New York City in 1926, and advanced from assistant curator to curator of ethnology and, finally, to curator emeritus. After her daughter's birth by her third husband in 1939, Mead served on the United States Committee on Food Habits and participated in a national character study examining British and American relations during World War II. She also taught at Columbia and New York universities, and outside of her professional capacities, she lectured and wrote on women's rights, childrearing, sexual morality, nuclear proliferation, race relations, drug abuse, population control, environmental pollution, and world hunger. When she was 72, she was elected to the presidency of the American Association for the Advancement of Science, and in 1979, she was posthumously awarded the Presidential Medal of Freedom. She was also elected to The National Women's Hall of Fame.

BIBLIOGRAPHY
Bateson, Mary Catherine. *With a Daughter's Eye: A Memoir of Margaret Mead and Gregory Bateson*. New York: Morrow, 1984. 0–688–03962–6, 242p. Bateson, Mead's daughter, offers in her memoir new insight about her mother's work and fondly remembers loving parents and a happy childhood.
Howard, Jane. *Margaret Mead: A Life*. New York: Simon and Schuster, 1984. 0–671–25225–9, 527p. Howard interviewed over 300 people for her balanced biography of Mead, collecting much information unavailable elsewhere about her life after 1945.

Mark, Joan T. *Margaret Mead, Anthropologist: Coming of Age in America.* New York: Oxford University Press, 1998. 0–19–511679–8, 144p. In this biography for young adults, Mark traces Mead's life and her achievements.

Mead, Margaret. *Blackberry Winter: My Earlier Years.* 1972. New York: Kodansha International, 1995. 1–56836–069–X, 305p. Mead describes her childhood, her family, college years, marriages, field trips, and experiences as mother and grandmother to expand the point that generations in a family remain important and should be nurtured.

Tilton, Rafael. *Margaret Mead.* San Diego: Lucent, 1995. 1–56006–039–5, 112p. Using Mead's writings and other sources, Tilton presents a chronological view of her public and private life in an objective biography for young adults.

MEARS, HELEN FARNSWORTH (1872–1916)
Sculptor and Artist   Oshkosh, Wisconsin

Helen Farnsworth Mears was a sculptor who instilled each piece of her work with a sense of honest emotion. She was born on December 21, 1872, one of three daughters. Her father was a surgeon who became a miner and an inventor, and her mother was a poet known as "Wisconsin's first poet." Mears attended local schools, and when she decided to sculpt, her father provided her with an understanding of anatomy, tools, and a workshop. At 20, Mears received a commission for the Wisconsin Building at the World's Columbian Exposition of 1893, went to Chicago to chisel the nine-foot marble piece, and used her fees for study in New York. Further aid from a wealthy Milwaukee woman supported her in France and Italy for two years. In 1899, she returned to New York and opened a studio with her sister where she continued to create large pieces in both bronze and marble. Her full-length statue of **Frances Willard** stands in the Statuary Hall of the United States Capitol. Although she won awards and exhibited, she worked within the accepted styles of her time, without noticeable innovation.

BIBLIOGRAPHY
Green, Susan Porter. *Helen Farnsworth Mears.* Oshkosh, WI: Castle-Pierce, 1972. No ISBN, 177p. This carefully researched, documented, and readable biography of Mears includes photographs of some of her major sculptures.

Mears, Helen. *Year of the Wild Boar: An American Woman in Japan.* 1942. Westport, CT: Greenwood Press, 1973. 0–8371–6936–4, 346p. Mears gives an account of her year in Tokyo during 1935, with a balanced report of Japanese culture and attitudes.

MENDOZA, LYDIA (1916–)
Singer   Houston, Texas

Latina American Lydia Mendoza, "Lark of the Border," has been the foremost singer of *tejano* music since the early 1930s. She was born in 1916, the second child of Mexican parents. Her uneducated father disapproved of education for women, and neither Mendoza nor her sisters could speak or write English. Her mother taught her music, and by the time Mendoza was 12, she could play the guitar and mandolin. After her father quit his job, the family members supported themselves by playing and singing anywhere they could. They also went to Michigan to work in the fields but, unaccustomed to the hard work, returned to Texas, where they had difficulty surviving during the Great Depression. In San Antonio, when Mendoza started singing solo, a radio announcer encouraged her to enter his amateur radio contest. She won and began to sing regularly, becoming known along the southern border of Texas by 1934. During World War II, she retired to become a mother while her husband served in the military. In the early 1950s, she restarted her career by playing and singing different styles of music. She started a third career in the 1970s when she began performing folk music. Because of her contribution to the folk heritage of the nation, she received a National Heritage Fellowship from the National Endowment for the Arts. In the 1980s, she was inducted into the Tejano Music Hall of Fame and the Texas Women's Hall of Fame, and in 1991, the Conjunto Music Hall of Fame.

BIBLIOGRAPHY

Strachwitz, Chris. *Lydia Mendoza: A Family Autobiography*. Houston, TX: Arte Publico, 1993. 1-55885-065-1, 432p. Using interviews with Mendoza, her family, and her associates, collected over 10 years, Strachwitz discusses her career.

MERMAN, ETHEL (1909–1984)
Entertainer   **Astoria, New York**

Ethel Merman was an entertainer. She was born Ethel Agnes Zimmerman on January 16, 1909, and attended William Cullen Bryant High School in Queens. After her graduation, she became a stenographer, and her employer gave her a letter of introduction to a producer in 1926 who offered her a chorus role, which she declined. The next year, she contracted with an agent who then attached her to Warner Brothers studio for six months. In 1929, she adopted the name Merman and prepared for her Broadway debut in *Girl Crazy*, a musical play in which she sang "I Got Rhythm." She then added film and radio to her venues, with her own radio show beginning in 1935. Other Broadway appearances were *Anything Goes*, *Annie Get Your Gun*, *Call Me Madam*, and *Gypsy*. She also made the films for *Anything Goes* and *Call Me Madam*. Her last film was a cameo appearance in *Airplane* (1980). Merman's rendition of "There's No Business Like Show Business" has become the anthem of the entertainment industry. Among her honors are two Tony Awards, a Golden Globe Award, and a Drama Desk Award.

BIBLIOGRAPHY

Bryan, George B. *Ethel Merman: A Bio-Bibliography*. Westport, CT: Greenwood Press, 1992. 0-313-27975-6, 298p. In his critical study of Merman's career, Bryan includes a biographical essay and sections discussing her work.

Merman, Ethel. *Merman*. New York: Simon and Schuster, 1978. 0–671–22712–2, 320p. Merman's autobiography recounts her successes and her tragedies but does not reveal why she made certain choices in her life.

Thomas, Bob. *I Got Rhythm! The Ethel Merman Story*. New York: Putnam, 1985. 0–399–13041–1, 239p. This undocumented but readable, recommended, and balanced biography of Merman is based on over 60 interviews and additional print materials.

MERRY, ANN BRUNTON (1769–1808)
Actor   London, England

Ann Brunton Merry was an actor. She was born on May 30, 1769, the oldest of seven children of a grocer and tea dealer and his wife. Her father had wanted to be an actor, and Merry early showed her aptitude for the stage, making her first appearance in 1785 with immediate success. She married an older man in 1791, and when his family opposed their marriage, Merry had to retire from the stage. But after her husband accrued more debt, he happily accepted an opportunity for Merry to go to America to act in the new Chestnut Street Theatre in Philadelphia. Merry was instantly recognized as America's finest tragedienne, and she remained with the Chestnut Street company until her death. She has been compared to Mrs. *Sarah Siddons, but critics think that her demeanor was more gentle on stage than that of Siddons. Merry would not play the role of Lady Macbeth because she thought she could never equal Mrs. Siddons's own stellar performance in the role. Merry died at 39 after the birth of a stillborn child.

BIBLIOGRAPHY
Doty, Gresdna A. *The Career of Mrs. Ann Brunton Merry in the American Theatre*. Baton Rouge: Louisiana State University Press, 1971. 0–8071–0947–9, 170p. Doty traces Merry's career in a thoroughly documented, chronological biography, from 1796 to 1808, noting her importance in early American theater history.

MEYER, LUCY RIDER (1849–1922)
Physician and Religious Leader   New Haven, Connecticut

Lucy Jane Rider Meyer was a social worker and a leader in the Methodist deaconess movement. She was born on September 9, 1849, as the oldest of three children to a farmer and his second wife. She had six older half-siblings. Her family read the Bible daily and sang hymns, and at 13, Meyer was converted during a Methodist revival. She attended local schools and graduated in 1867 from the New Hampton Literary Institution in Fairfax, Vermont. She then entered Oberlin College and graduated in two years. After her fiancé died in 1875, she became principal of a school, studied chemistry at Massachusetts Institute of Technology, and took an appointment at McKendree College in Illinois as professor of chemistry. She resigned, however, in 1881 to become the field secretary of the Illinois State Sunday School Association. While traveling extensively to lecture and write, she met a businessman interested in church social work whom she married. In 1885, she and her husband began the Chicago Training School for City, Home, and Foreign Missions with students attending for two years while visiting and serving the poor. After the birth of a son in 1887, she received her M.D. degree at Woman's Medical College of Chicago. She was simultaneously interested in the deaconess idea of women organizing for social services as they had in Germany in the 1830s. Meyer opened the first American "deaconess" home with **Isabella Thoburn** as its director. The women served without salary or taking vows, adopting a uniform of black with white collar and cuffs. Meyer also edited the *Deaconess Advocate* and the *Message* while writing a history, *Deaconesses: Biblical, Early Church, European, American*. When she and her husband resigned in 1917, they had trained over 5,000 students and had assets of $500,000. Methodist Episcopal Church records credited Meyer with the creation of 40 other institutions after her initial school and thought that she had done more in the field of social service for women and their training than any other woman in any denomination.

BIBLIOGRAPHY

Horton, Isabelle. *High Adventure: Life of Lucy Rider Meyer*. 1928. New York: Garland, 1987. 0-8240-0665-8, 359p. This balanced biography of Meyer is undocumented, but it covers her life and work in the church.

MIDLER, BETTE (1945–)
Entertainer   Honolulu, Hawaii

Bette Midler is a singer and entertainer. She was born on December 1, 1945, to a dictatorial housepainter and his wife as one of four children. While attending high school in Honolulu, Hawaii, she performed with a folk trio that toured army bases and was senior class president before graduating as valedictorian. Although she attended the University of Hawaii, she left after a year to go to Hollywood to complete her small part in the film *Hawaii*. In 1966, she went to New York, worked as a go-go dancer, hat check girl, glove saleswoman, and typist before enrolling in the Herbert Berghof Studio. In 1966, she sang in the chorus of the Broadway production of *Fiddler on the Roof* and then played the role of Tzeitel for three years. In 1970, she began appearing in a gay nightclub with Barry Manilow as her accompanist. The next year, she signed a contract with Atlantic Records and performed in *Tommy* with the Seattle Opera Company. During this period, she also began her film career and debuted on television. She formed her own production company, All Girl Productions, and in 1989, her first number one hit on the popular charts was "Wind Beneath My Wings." In 1993, her first concert tour in 10 years, titled "Experience the Divine," played for 30 nights to a sold-out house at New York's Radio City Music Hall. Among her films are *Ruthless People* and *Beaches*, and her honors include Golden Globe Awards, Grammy Awards, Emmy Awards, and a Tony Award.

BIBLIOGRAPHY

Bego, Mark. *Bette Midler, Outrageously Divine.* New York: New American Library, 1987. 0–451–14814–2, 190p. Bego's readable and recommended biography of Midler is undocumented.

Collins, Ace. *Bette Midler.* New York: St. Martin's, 1989. 0–312–02869–5, 164p. In this straightforward but undocumented biography of Midler, Collins attempts to identify her real personality as opposed to her stage persona.

Mair, George. *Bette: An Intimate Biography of Bette Midler.* Secaucus, NJ: Carol, 1996. 1–55972–272–X, 312p. Mair's adulatory biography of Midler refuses to probe her decisions, either psychologically or critically.

Midler, Bette. *A View from a Broad.* New York: Simon and Schuster, 1980. 0–671–24780–8, 150p. Using letters, songs, gags, and anecdotes, Midler recounts her world tour of 1978 in a popular biography suitable for young adults.

Spada, James. *The Divine Bette Midler.* New York: Collier, 1984. 0–02–612590–0, 214p. Spada presents Midler's life and career in his popular biography which includes photographs.

MILLAY, EDNA ST. VINCENT (1892–1950)
Poet   Rockland, Maine

Edna St. Vincent Millay was a poet and playwright. She was born on February 22, 1892, as one of three daughters to a gambling insurance salesman and school superintendent and his wife. They divorced when Millay was eight, and her mother supported the family by working as a practical nurse. Millay had wanted to become a concert pianist, but small hands made her focus on poetry. Her mother had taught Millay how to write verse at the age of four, and *St. Nicholas* magazine published her first poems when she was fourteen. In 1909, she graduated from high school, and with college financially unavailable, stayed at home, doing housework for her mother. In 1911, she entered a literary anthology contest, and although she did not win first place, her poem "Renascence" won acclaim. Millay met Caroline B. Dow, who arranged for her to enter Vassar College. Older than the other students, Millay at first rebelled at the rules, but she soon enjoyed the intellectual stimulation and wrote a play in which she starred before graduating. She moved to Greenwich Village with her mother and sisters and joined the Provincetown Players, but supported herself by writing formulaic stories for magazines under a pseudonym. In 1921, *Vanity Fair* hired her to become its foreign correspondent in Paris, and during her time abroad, she wrote three books of verse. In 1923, her book *Ballad of the Harp-Weaver* won the Pulitzer Prize. She married and soon began a series of international reading tours. In 1927, while becoming embroiled in the Sacco and Vanzetti affair, she wrote the libretto for Deems Taylor's opera *The King's Henchman*, which opened at the Metropolitan Opera House. In the 1930s, she actively participated in the Writers' War Board, the Red Cross, and the *New York Times* Conference of Women. In World War II she used her poetry as propaganda. She received several honorary degrees in addition to the Pulitzer Prize.

BIBLIOGRAPHY

Cheney, Anne. *Millay in Greenwich Village*. Tuscaloosa: University of Alabama Press, 1975. 0-8173-7161-3, 160p. Cheney's psychobiography of Millay illuminates those who influenced her and her poetry during her years in Greenwich Village between 1918 and 1925.

Gould, Jean. *The Poet and Her Book: A Biography of Edna St. Vincent Millay*. New York: Dodd, Mead, 1969. No ISBN, 308p. Gould's biography, based on letters, gives information unavailable elsewhere on Millay's relationship with Arthur Ficke.

Gurko, Miriam. *Restless Spirit: The Life of Edna St. Vincent Millay*. New York: Crowell, 1962. No ISBN, 271p. In her biography of Millay, suitable for young adults, Gurko adds new information about Millay's childhood and her mother's positive influence.

Sheean, Vincent. *The Indigo Bunting: A Memoir of Edna St. Vincent Millay*. 1951. New York: Schocken, 1973. 0-8052-3518-3, 131p. Sheean met Millay, and in his memoir, he describes his enjoyment of her eccentricities and foibles while she lived at Steepletop in New York State.

MINER, MYRTILLA (1815–1864)
Educator and Reformer   **Brookfield, New York**

Myrtilla Miner was a pioneer in teacher education for African Americans. She was born on March 4, 1815, one of many children of a farmer and his wife. Miner attended her aunt's school in their home and decided to become a teacher. After working at several schools, she went to the Newton Female Institute in Whitesville, Mississippi, where her request to teach the slaves was refused. She left, and two abolitionists encouraged her to start a school for African American women in Washington, DC. In 1851, the Colored Girls School opened, and its enrollment rapidly jumped from six to forty young women from moderately wealthy families. Among the school's supporters were Senator William Seward, President Pierce, **Harriet Beecher Stowe**, and the Society of Friends. Miner's major emphasis was training teachers, and by 1858, six former students had opened their own schools. Miner also wanted her students to cultivate flower gardens, study the stars, and practice composition. She invited scholars to lecture, built a library, and encouraged her students to become physically fit, but her main purpose in founding the school was to help abolish slavery. In the years before the Civil War began, however, Miner's health deteriorated, and **Emily Howland** substituted while Miner recuperated. In 1860, when war was imminent, Miner had to close the school, but she died before the war ended. After the war, Miner Normal School functioned intermittently until 1879, when it became part of the local school system. In 1929, it was renamed Miner Teachers College. When the Supreme Court outlawed segregation in 1954, the school merged with another to become the District of Columbia Teachers College.

BIBLIOGRAPHY

Foner, Philip Sheldon, and Josephine F. Pacheco. *Three Who Dared*. Westport, CT: Greenwood Press, 1984. 0-313-23584-8, 234p. This well-documented and well-researched collective biography recounts Miner's suffering and struggle as a white woman supporting African American advancement.

O'Connor, Ellen M. *Myrtilla Miner: A Memoir*. Miami: Mnemosyne, 1969. No ISBN, 129p. This memoir, suitable for young adults, is a recollection of Miner's life by persons who knew her, and although undocumented, offers insight about her endeavors.

MINNELLI, LIZA (1946–)
Entertainer and Actor   Los Angeles, California

Liza Minnelli is an entertainer and actor. She was born on March 12, 1946, the daughter of a movie director and an actor and singer mother, **Judy Garland**. She attended both public day and private boarding schools in New York and California. After enrolling at the Sorbonne in Paris, she decided to return to New York and study at the Herbert Berghof Studio. She appeared in her first film at age three and acted in several others before making her stage debut in 1961. In 1963, she joined her mother on television, released her first solo album, and won a Tony Award for her work in *Flora, the Red Menace*. Two years later, she made her Broadway debut, and two more years passed before her film debut in a starring role. In 1969, she received an Academy Award nomination for *The Sterile Cuckoo*, and in 1972, when she played Sally Bowles in *Cabaret*, she won an Academy Award. The same year, she won an Emmy Award for a television special. Other honors include Golden Globe Awards and a British Film Academy Award.

BIBLIOGRAPHY

Leigh, Wendy. *Liza: Born a Star*. New York: Dutton, 1993. 0–525–93515–0, 298p. This biography of Minnelli discusses her life and her relationship with her parents, other actors, drugs, and her husbands and lovers.

Mair, George. *Under the Rainbow: The Real Liza Minnelli*. Secaucus, NJ: Carol, 1996. 1-55972-312-2, 248p. Mair's popular, undocumented biography of Minnelli suggests that the one performance that she made with her mother, Judy Garland, was when her own stardom began.

Parish, James Robert. *Liza! An Unauthorized Biography*. New York: Pocket, 1975. 0–671–78946–5, 176p. This unauthorized popular biography, without documentation, traces Minnelli's life and career.

Petrucelli, Alan W. *Liza! Liza! An Unauthorized Biography of Liza Minnelli*. New York: Karz-Coh, 1983. 0–94382–857–0, 174p. This popular researched biography, written by one of Minnelli's fans, gives an overview of her life and career with accompanying photographs.

Spada, James. *Judy and Liza*. Garden City, NY: Doubleday, 1983. 0–385–18202–3, 216p. Spada examines the relationship between Minnelli and her mother, Judy Garland, as Minnelli began her own career, and Garland's dependence on people and substances increased.

MITCHELL, LUCY SPRAGUE (1878–1967)
Educator   Chicago, Illinois

Lucy Sprague Mitchell was an educator and author. She was born on July 2, 1878, as the fourth of six children to a wealthy wholesale grocer and his musically artistic wife. As a child, Mitchell kept secret notebooks of her creative writing in which she told stories of herself in an imaginary family. She felt as if she were split into two—the young girl who participated in activities and the person who hid in the corner. Since she hated classrooms, her chief education became her father's library. In 1893, when Mitchell's family suffered severe health problems, she went with them for recovery in California, nursing those who survived. In 1894, when Mitchell agreed with **Jane Addams**'s support of the Pullman strike, her father disapproved, and the two severed their relationship. Mitchell had earlier met **Alice Freeman Palmer**, and Palmer arranged for Mitchell to attend Radcliffe, where she graduated with honors in philosophy in 1900. Palmer then took her to Europe, but when Palmer died in London, Mitchell kept house for Palmer's widower before going to the University of California to work with women students in 1906. There, she improved housing for women, started sex education courses, and urged social action in the San Francisco area. In 1912, she resigned and married an economist who agreed to let her follow her interests. In New York, after Mitchell took courses at Teachers College of Columbia University with John Dewey, her cousin, **Elizabeth Sprague Coolidge**, helped her start the Bureau of Educational Experiments to teach and research progressive education. Mitchell thought that public education, with learning an active process of discovery, was the best way to combat social problems, and she guided the bureau for many years. She also founded the Cooperative School for Teachers and the Writers Workshop for children's book writers.

BIBLIOGRAPHY
Antler, Joyce. *Lucy Sprague Mitchell: The Making of a Modern Woman*. New Haven, CT: Yale University Press, 1987. 0–300–03665–5, 436p. In this biography, Mitchell's letters, journals, and published writings, along with words of her family and friends, show the difficulties she experienced in balancing the professional and the personal.

MITCHELL, MARGARET (1900–1949)
Author   Atlanta, Georgia

Margaret Munnerlyn Mitchell wrote the best-selling novel *Gone with the Wind*. She was born on November 8, 1900, one of two children of a lawyer and his wife. The family members enjoyed southern history and had supported the Confederacy during the Civil War. After attending public schools in Atlanta, Mitchell went to Smith College, but at her mother's death in the influenza epidemic of 1919, she returned to keep house for her father. She married twice in the next few years, and with her second husband entertained Atlanta's elite. In 1922, Mitchell began her career by becoming a popular reporter for the *Atlantic*

Journal Sunday Magazine. When an ankle injury forced her resignation, she began her novel. She finished most of it by 1929, but not until 1935, when a friend told a visiting Macmillan editor of its existence, did she think about publication. Just before the editor left, she took the manuscript of 1,057 pages to his hotel, and in 1936, the book appeared. The next year, it received the Pulitzer Prize. It remained at the head of the best-seller list for two years with the largest sale in a single day of 50,000. By 1965, it had sold over 12 million copies. After it was translated into 25 languages, Mitchell won a suit in a Dutch court over an unauthorized edition, establishing a legal precedent for writers. In 1939, the book became a movie. Although Mitchell only wrote one book, she discovered that answering thousands of fan letters was a full-time job. She remained active in community affairs, serving in the Women's Defense Corps, the American Red Cross, and the war bond campaign during World War II. She died after being struck by an automobile when she was only 48.

BIBLIOGRAPHY

Edwards, Anne. *Road to Tara: The Life of Margaret Mitchell*. New Haven, CT: Ticknor and Fields, 1983. 0-89919-169-X, 369p. Edwards compares the people in Mitchell's life to her characters in *Gone with the Wind* and discovers possible resemblances between her own loves and the two male protagonists of her novel.

Farr, Finis. *Margaret Mitchell of Atlanta, the Author of "Gone with the Wind."* New York: Morrow, 1965. No ISBN, 244p. Farr's biography of Mitchell is a factual account of her life and of the phenomenal success of *Gone with the Wind*.

Hanson, Elizabeth I. *Margaret Mitchell*. Boston: Twayne, 1990. 0-8057-7608-7, 122p. Hanson focuses on Mitchell's life, devoting chapters to its various periods, including the making of the film *Gone with the Wind*.

Pyron, Darden Asbury. *Southern Daughter: The Life of Margaret Mitchell*. New York: Oxford University Press, 1991. 0-19-505276-5, 533p. Pyron uses unpublished material from archives and interviews in a carefully documented scholarly and definitive biography of Mitchell.

MITCHELL, MARIA (1818–1889)
Astronomer   Nantucket, Massachusetts

Maria Mitchell was an astronomer. She was born the third of ten children, to the master of the first free school in Nantucket and a stern mother on August 1, 1818. Her father became interested in astronomy and began to rate chronometers for the Nantucket whaling fleet, checking them through stellar observations. In 1831, when Mitchell was 12, she helped her father record the time of a solar eclipse, and she said later that she became an astronomer because people who grew up in a place where ships needed to navigate knew about the stars. Mitchell became the librarian of the Nantucket Atheneum and stayed for 20 years, reading all of the books that interested her, including Bowditch's *Practical Navigator*. At night, she worked in her father's observatory on the roof of a bank making myriad observations with an altitude and azimuth circle, a four-inch equatorial telescope, and a two-inch

Dollond telescope. On October 1, 1847, Mitchell discovered a new comet, and when it was named for her, she received a gold medal. The next year, she became the first woman elected to the American Academy of Arts and Sciences and was the only woman so named for almost 100 years. In 1849, she became one of the computers of the new *American Ephemeris and Nautical Almanac*, and the next year was elected to the American Association for the Advancement of Science. In 1857, she went abroad and met European scientists including *Mary Somerville, and when she returned, **Elizabeth Peabody** and others gave her a five-inch Alvan Clark telescope. In 1861, Matthew Vassar asked her to become the professor of astronomy at his woman's college, and when he offered to build her an observatory with a 12-inch telescope, the third largest in the country, she accepted. Among her students who became scientists, 25 appeared in *Who's Who in America*, including **Ellen Swallow Richards**. In 1873, Mitchell helped found the Association for the Advancement of Women and proselytized for women in science. Her interest in experiment and research led to her election to the American Philosophical Society in 1869 and then as vice president of the American Social Science Association. After her death, Vassar alumnae created an endowment fund in her honor, and in 1922, her statue was erected in New York University's Hall of Fame. She was later elected to The National Women's Hall of Fame.

BIBLIOGRAPHY

Gormley, Beatrice. *Maria Mitchell: The Soul of an Astronomer*. Grand Rapids, MI: Eerdmans, 1995. 0-8028-5116-9, 123p. Gormley's recommended young adult biography of Mitchell, based on primary sources, includes photographs.

Morgan, Helen L. *Maria Mitchell, First Lady of American Astronomy*. Philadelphia: Westminster, 1977. 0-664-32614-5, 141p. This overview of Mitchell for young adults recounts her life and career.

Wright, Helen. *Sweeper in the Sky: The Life of Maria Mitchell*. 1949. Clinton Corners, NY: College Avenue Press, 1997. 1-88355-170-6, 288p. This lightly fictionalized biography, although for young adults, is a recommended examination of Mitchell and her accomplishments as an astronomer and teacher.

MOHR, NICHOLASA (1938-)
Artist and Author New York, New York

Latina American Nicholasa Mohr has achieved recognition in both graphics and literature for her portrayal of life in the barrio. She was born November 1, 1938, as Nicholasa Rivera-Golpe, the youngest of seven and the only daughter of Puerto Rican immigrants. Her father died when she was eight, and with her mother often ill, Mohr had to help at home, although her mother continually encouraged her artistic interests. At school, a counselor refused to let her attend a high school that would prepare her for college, saying that she needed a trade instead, and sent her to fashion illustration school. After her mother's death when Mohr was 14, she continued to work on her art, eventually attending the Art Students' League. She saved money while working as a graphic artist to study in Mexico City, and while there, she became impressed with the work of Diego Rivera and *Frida Kahlo. When she returned to New York, she began hunting for her own ethnic roots and married a fellow student at the New School for Social Research. She and her husband moved to New Jersey, where she taught; to New Hampshire; and then back to New York City, where she became artist-in-residence for the New York City public schools. At that time, she discovered that she could communicate through words as well as pictures. She began writing, and her first book, *Nilda*, received several important juvenile fiction awards. Other books, including *Felita* and *Going Home*, have also received awards. Additional honors include the Lifetime Achievement Award of the National Conference of Puerto Rican Women and the Hispanic Heritage Award from the Hispanic Heritage Foundation as well as honorary degrees.

BIBLIOGRAPHY

Mohr, Nicholasa. *Growing Up in the Sanctuary of My Imagination*. New York: Messner, 1994. 0-671-74171-3, 118p. Mohr's memoir, suitable for young adults, covers the years of her childhood until her mother's death when Mohr was 14. She examines the impact of her own imagination on her behavior and development.

MONROE, HARRIET (1860–1936)
Poet and Editor   Chicago, Illinois

Harriet Monroe was a poet, and her establishment of *Poetry* made her one of the most influential literary editors in American history. She was born on December 23, 1860, as one of four children to a lawyer and his wife. She began reading the books in her father's superb library while a child before attending Visitation Convent in Washington, DC. One of the sisters encouraged her literary interests, and when she returned to Chicago in 1879, she began working as a journalist, becoming a critic of art, drama, and other subjects for the next 20 years. She also won several awards for her poetry. After a court case against the *New York World* for publishing her "Ode" without permission, she used the judgment money to make an extended European tour, where she met members of literary circles in London, Paris, and Rome. Not until she was 50 did her life focus, however, and she decided to found a magazine for poets. Her Chicago friends eventually guaranteed five years of publication for *Poetry: A Magazine of Verse*. The first number appeared in 1912, and in its time, it published work by Vachel Lindsay, Carl Sandburg, Edgar Lee Masters, Robert Frost, Wallace Stevens, **Marianne Moore**, T. S. Eliot, and others. The first modern verse journal, it was also the first to make awards and give writers a place to discuss their differences. Monroe edited the journal for 24 years. During that time, she continued her trips abroad, and at 76, she served as the American delegate to the International Association of Poets, Playwrights, Editors, Essayists, and Novelists.

BIBLIOGRAPHY

Cahill, Daniel J. *Harriet Monroe*. New York: Twayne, 1973. 0-8057-0515-5, 148p. Many facts about Monroe's life appear in this critical biography which recounts her youthful aspirations and discusses her poetry. An important chapter covers her magazine, *Poetry*.

Monroe, Harriet. *A Poet's Life: Seventy Years in a Changing World*. 1938. New York: AMS Press, 1969. No ISBN, 488p. Monroe tends to emphasize, in rather dry text, the poets who found recognition in her magazine, *Poetry*, rather than to reveal her own personality and character.

Williams, Ellen. *Harriet Monroe and the Poetry Renaissance*. Urbana: University of Illinois Press, 1977. 0-252-00478-7, 312p. Williams suggests that poets communicating to Monroe while she was editor of *Poetry* revealed themselves in unexpectedly personal ways, and by studying Monroe's letters, letters from the poets, and other papers, Williams takes a biographical look at her influence.

MONROE, MARILYN (1926-1962)

Actor   Los Angeles, California

Marilyn Monroe was an actor. She was born on June 1, 1926, as Norma Jean Mortenson (or Baker), the daughter of a film splicer whose husband and Monroe's biological father had left before Monroe's birth. Monroe grew up thinking her mother's close friend was her father. Since her mother had to work to support her, Monroe stayed in foster homes, and when she was seven, her schizophrenic mother entered a state mental hospital. Afterward, Monroe spent her years from nine to eleven in the Los Angeles Orphan's Home Society. She attended high school but married before she graduated, and after her husband went to sea in 1944, an army photographer chose her as a model for an article on women workers for *Yanks* magazine. Other photographers saw his work, and Monroe began modeling for various publications. She divorced her husband in Nevada, and in 1946 signed a contract with Fox Studios and changed her name to Marilyn Monroe. After two films, while out of work she posed for the nude calendar photograph for which she remained famous. She eventually secured work in the movies *Gentlemen Prefer Blondes* and *How to Marry a Millionaire*. In 1953, she met Joe DiMaggio; after they married, her tour of army posts in South Korea, during which she earned a reputation as a sex symbol, displeased her husband, and their marriage ended the same year it began. In 1955, she made *The Seven Year Itch*, but she wanted to star in serious films. Her own company, Marilyn Monroe Productions, allowed her to control her movies, and after studying acting with Lee Strasberg, she starred in *Bus Stop*, *The Prince and the Showgirl* (with Laurence Olivier), *Some Like It Hot*, and *The Misfits*. In 1956, Monroe married Arthur Miller, a playwright, suffered two miscarriages, and converted to Judaism, Miller's religion. Erratic behavior, however, interrupted both her private and professional lives, and they divorced in 1961. After a short stay in a mental hospital and failure to report for a film in which she was to star, she took an overdose of sleeping pills in June 1962. Although she received three Golden Globe Awards for her work, she embodied the exploitation of women in the mass media, a role from which she never escaped.

BIBLIOGRAPHY

Brown, Peter H., and Patte B. Barham. *Marilyn: The Last Take*. New York: Dutton, 1992. 0-525-93485-5, 452p. The biography looks at Monroe's life with special emphasis on her last days.

Haspiel, James. *Marilyn: The Ultimate Look at the Legend*. New York: Henry Holt, 1991. 0-8050-1856-5, 207p. Haspiel remembers his friendship with Monroe as a photographer and highlights the text with his photographs.

Leaming, Barbara. *Marilyn Monroe*. New York: Crown, 1998. 0-517-70260-6, 448p. Leaming's well-researched and fully documented biography, based on previously unpublished letters and documents as well as interviews with stagehands, explores Monroe's relationships.

Miracle, Berniece Baker. *My Sister Marilyn: A Memoir of Marilyn Monroe*. Chapel Hill, NC: Algonquin, 1994. 1-56512-070-1, 238p. Monroe's half-sister, Miracle, writes about Monroe's life as Norma Jean Baker, revealing much that has previously been omitted about her early life. Because Miracle lived with her father, the two did not meet until Monroe was 12 and Miracle 19.

Spoto, Donald. *Marilyn Monroe: The Biography*. New York: HarperCollins, 1993. 0-06-017987-2, 698p. Spoto consulted Monroe's archives of personal documents, tapes and letters, and production and legal papers, and held interviews to write his carefully documented and recommended biography of her.

MOON, LOTTIE (1840-1912)
Missionary   Scottsville, Virginia

Lottie Moon served in China as a Southern Baptist missionary. She was born on December 12, 1840, as the third of seven children to a merchant and planter and his wife. She was educated at home and at a boarding school before attending Valley Union Seminary (Hollins College) and graduating with a B.A. in 1857. She enrolled at Albemarle Institute in Charlottesville for her M.A., graduating with five others in 1861 as the first southern women to receive graduate degrees. While in Charlottesville, she converted and decided to serve in China as a missionary, but the Southern Baptists would not accept single women. After the Civil War, she started a school in Georgia, and when the Southern Baptists changed their policies, she joined her sister, one of the first two women to go to China, in Tengchow, Shantung Province. She remained in China for the rest of her life except for three short trips abroad in 1892, during the Boxer Uprising of 1900, and in1903. Chinese resistance to education for women closed her school, so instead, Moon worked as an evangelist with the women and their daughters in the villages. She wrote many articles for Southern Baptist periodicals promoting missions, and when she campaigned for women in the church to organize, they formed the Woman's Missionary Union. Moon suggested that a week of prayer ending with a special Christmas offering be the method of supporting the organization, and the first offering provided money for three additional missionaries to work in Pingtu with her. During the 1911 famine, Moon received no money from the Mission Board, and she gave most of her salary for the victims, starving herself. While returning home in ill health, she died on the ship, and the offering was renamed the Lottie Moon Christmas Offering, a continuing collection in the Southern Baptist Church that earns millions each year for foreign missions.

BIBLIOGRAPHY

Allen, Catherine B. *The New Lottie Moon Story*. 1980. Birmingham, AL: Woman's Missionary Union, 1998. 1-56309-225-5, 320p. Allen's carefully researched and well-documented, but biased, biography re-creates Moon's life and work, with accompanying photographs.

Hyatt, Irwin T. *Our Ordered Lives Confess: Three Nineteenth-Century American Missionaries in East Shantung*. Cambridge, MA: Harvard University Press, 1976. 0-674-64735-1, 323p. Hyatt, in his collective biography including Moon, discusses her Christian witnessing adapted for the Chinese.

Rankin, Jerry. *A Journey of Faith and Sacrifice: Retracing the Steps of Lottie Moon*. Birmingham, AL: New Hope, 1996. 1-56309-188-7, 110p. The documented text, with accompanying photographs of Moon, other missionaries, and places in China where Moon lived, recounts her life and work.

MOORE, MARIANNE (1887–1972)
Poet   St. Louis, Missouri

Marianne Craig Moore reflected her sense of privacy and her strong belief, expressed in careful poetical detail, that beauty, of all things, lasts. She was born on November 15, 1887, as one of two children to a father whose financial and physical breakdown caused his wife to take the children to her own father's home. Moore's father died when she was seven, and her mother began teaching. In 1905, Moore entered Bryn Mawr, where she published stories and poems in the literary monthly. After graduation in biology, a study reflecting her love of nature, she learned shorthand and typing in order to work, and in her first job, she helped a librarian revise the Dewey Decimal Index, a lesson in categorizing she never forgot. In 1911, Moore joined the business department faculty at the United States Indian School in Carlisle, Pennsylvania, but after her brother graduated from Princeton Theological Seminary, Moore and her mother went to live with him at his pastorate in Chatham, New Jersey. He married, and Moore and her mother moved to New York's Greenwich Village. There Moore published in **Harriet Monroe**'s *Poetry* in 1915, and the same year, the London magazine *The Egoist* published two of her poems. The Egoist Press in London published a booklet with 24 of her poems without her knowledge, and the collection, *Observations*, won her the *Dial* Award of 1924, an award T. S. Eliot had received for "The Wasteland" in 1922. Moore then edited the *Dial* for seven years. Other volumes of poetry followed in 1935 and 1936. In 1946, she received a grant from the American Academy of Arts and Letters which gave her time to work on a translation of La Fontaine. Other honors included election to the National Institute of Arts and

Letters, the Bollingen Prize, the National Book Award, the Pulitzer Prize, and the Gold Medal for Poetry from the National Institute of Arts and Letters. In 1955, she was elected to the American Academy of Arts and Letters.

BIBLIOGRAPHY

Hadas, Pamela White. *Marianne Moore, Poet of Affection.* Syracuse, NY: Syracuse University Press, 1977. 0-8156-2162-0, 243p. Although meticulously documented, this scholarly but unrecommended biography of Moore places little emphasis on her poems.

Molesworth, Charles. *Marianne Moore: A Literary Life.* New York: Atheneum, 1990. 0-689-11815-5, 472p. Molesworth's biography relies on Moore's archives and previous research. Moore's executors forbade his use of direct quotes, so he paraphrases in his examination of her personality and work.

Stapleton, Laurence. *Marianne Moore: The Poet's Advance.* Princeton, NJ: Princeton University Press, 1978. 0-691-06373-7, 282p. Stapleton used Moore's poems, notebooks, and other unpublished sources in this scholarly biography focusing on family relationships, fellow poets, publisher negotiations, and Moore's work.

MOORE, MARY TYLER (1936-)
Entertainer   Brooklyn, New York

Mary Tyler Moore is an actor and producer. She was born on December 29, 1936, as one of three children to a utilities company clerk and his wife. She made her professional show busines debut as a dancing elf in commercials for Hotpoint appliances. When she was 22, she began appearing on television in minor roles, but three years later, she began playing Laura Petrie on *The Dick Van Dyke Show* television series, staying for the show's five-year duration. The same year she made her film debut, but she did not return to film until 1967 with *Thoroughly Modern Millie.* In 1969, she and Grant Tinker formed MTM Studios, and in 1970, she began a seven-year run as Mary Richards on *The Mary Tyler Moore Show.* After other Broadway and film roles including *First You Cry* and *Whose Life Is It, Anyway?*, she starred in Robert Redford's *Ordinary People* (1980), for which she received an Academy Award nomination. She has continued to accept serious roles while simultaneously appearing in other shows, with some critics considering her the peer of two other television comediennes, **Lucille Ball** and **Carol Burnett**. Her volunteer work has included international chairperson for the Juvenile Diabetes Foundation and board memberships for the American Society for the Prevention of Cruelty to Animals, the Juilliard School of Drama, and the New York City Opera. Among her honors are Emmy Awards, Golden Globe Awards, a Tony Award, and induction into the Television Academy Hall of Fame.

BIBLIOGRAPHY

Bonderoff, Jason. *Mary Tyler Moore.* New York: St. Martin's, 1986. 0-312-51887-0, 200p. This popular biography of Moore recounts her life in television and film as well as her personal difficulties.

Finn, Margaret L. *Mary Tyler Moore*. New York: Chelsea House, 1997. 0–7910–2416–4, 127p. In a researched and documented biography for young adults, Finn discusses Moore's life and career, including personal tragedies and problems with alcohol abuse.

Moore, Mary Tyler. *After All*. New York: Putnam, 1995. 0–399–14091–3, 332p. Moore reveals many of the unpleasant aspects of her life hidden behind a public smile and a seemingly positive attitude.

MOOREHEAD, AGNES (1900–1974)
Actor   Clinton, Massachusetts

Agnes Moorehead was an award-winning actor. As the older of two daughters, she was born on December 6, 1900, to a Presbyterian minister and his wife, formerly a professional singer. Her father's religious and educational views greatly influenced her, as did her mother's love of the arts. Moorehead, a public school student, first performed on stage at 12. She wanted to be an actor, but her father demanded education, and after she graduated from Muskingum College in 1928, she briefly taught school. In 1929, after study at the American Academy of Dramatic Arts, she began playing minor roles in Theatre Guild productions, but the Great Depression forced her into radio. Her sonorous voice, however, was an asset on radio, and sometimes she did six shows in one day. Her thousands of performances included *Calvacade of America, The Shadow*, and *March of Time*, where she was the only person ever allowed to portray **Eleanor Roosevelt**. After screaming in the background of *War of the Worlds*, she got a job with Orson Welles and John Houseman in the Mercury Players. She then moved to films in Hollywood and took the role of Kane's mother in *Citizen Kane* (1941). In 1942, she won awards for *The Magnificent Ambersons*. She especially enjoyed performing with the First Drama Quartet in *Don Juan in Hell*, a work often revived until 1972. When Moorehead moved to television, she became Endora in *Bewitched*, a series that lasted for eight years. Married twice, Moorehead rarely discussed her private life, and as she grew older, she reverted to the religious faith of her youth. Among her honors were an Emmy Award and four Academy Award nominations.

BIBLIOGRAPHY
Kear, Lynn. *Agnes Moorehead: A Bio-Bibliography*. Westport, CT: Greenwood Press, 1992. 0–313–28155–6, 276p. Kear's scholarly text includes a brief biography followed by a comprehensive assessment of Moorehead's career.

Sherk, Warren. *Agnes Moorehead: A Very Private Person*. Philadelphia: Dorrance, 1976. 0–8059–2317–9, 137p. Sherk, who knew Moorehead, has written a selective biography based on his own knowledge and interviews.

MORA, PAT (1942-)
Educator   El Paso, Texas

Patricia Mora is a Latina American poet and educator. She was born January 19, 1942, to an optician father and his wife. Educated at Texas Western University and the University of Texas at El Paso, where she received an M.A., Mora became a teacher and then director of the El Paso Independent School District before instructing at El Paso Community College and the University of Texas at El Paso. She has served as a judge for the Texas Institute of Letters and on the literary advisory council for the Texas Commission on the Arts. For National Public Radio, she has hosted a radio show, *Voices: The Mexican-American in Perspective.* Her poetry books, *Chants* and *Borders*, received many awards, including a Kellogg National Fellowship and a Chicano/Hispanic Faculty and Professional Staff Association Award. She is also a member of the *El Paso Herald-Post* Writers Hall of Fame.

BIBLIOGRAPHY

Mora, Pat. *House of Houses.* Boston: Beacon Press, 1997. 0-8070-7200-1, 296p. Mora writes about 12 extended family members and their effect on her own life.
———. *Nepantla: Essays from the Land in the Middle.* Albuquerque: University of New Mexico Press, 1993. 0-8263-1454-6, 181p. Mora's writings in a variety of genres illuminate her feelings about being half-Latina and Anglo-American, a person *nepantla* ("in the middle" in the Nahuatl language), emphasizing the importance of her heritage.

MORENO, RITA (1931-)
Actor   Humacao, Puerto Rico

Latina American Rita Moreno is the world's only entertainer to have won all four of the most important show business awards—an Academy Award (film), a Grammy Award (recording), a Tony Award (Broadway), and two Emmy Awards (television). After her birth as Rosa Dolores Alverio on December 11, 1931, her parents divorced, and her mother went to New York City, returning to Puerto Rico for Moreno when the child was five. In New York, Moreno began taking dancing lessons from **Rita Hayworth**'s uncle and began helping to support her family with performances in children's theater and at weddings. She changed her name first to Rosita Cosio, then Rosita Moreno, and finally Rita Moreno. She worked in films briefly, but after losing contracts or playing demeaning stereotypical roles, she attempted suicide. During her recovery, her attitude changed, and afterward, she won a part in the film *West Side Story*, doing her own singing and dancing. For it, she won an Academy Award. When she returned to Broadway, she performed as a superb actor rather than as a Latina stereotype, and three years later, she won a Tony Award for her performance in *The Ritz*. For a vocal performance on the *Electric Company Album*, she won a Grammy Award, and individual appearances on *The Muppets* and on *The Rockford Files* each won her an Emmy Award. In 1989, she received the Hispanic Woman of the Year award for her commitment to the community from which she came.

BIBLIOGRAPHY

Suntree, Susan. *Rita Moreno*. New York: Chelsea House, 1993. 0–7910–1247–6, 111p. This biography for young adults covers Moreno's life and accomplishments in theater, television, and film with accompanying photographs.

MORGAN, JULIA (1872–1957)
Architect   San Francisco, California

Julia Morgan was an architect known especially for her design of William Randolph Hearst's castle at San Simeon, California. She was born on January 26, 1872, the second in a family of five, to a dilettante father and a mother with a large inheritance. After a sickly childhood, Morgan graduated from public high school and attended the University of California at Berkeley, becoming the first female student in the College of Engineering. After graduation, she decided to attend the École des Beaux-Arts in Paris. In 1898, she became the first woman admitted to its architectural section and the first woman to graduate four years later. When she returned to California, she became the state's first licensed female architect. Her initial projects were helping build two University of California structures funded by Phoebe Apperson Hearst. Hearst liked Morgan and commissioned her to remodel her own residence and to design a castle with a "dependent village." Hearst also encouraged Morgan to open her own office in San Francisco. Among Morgan's other commissions were a bell tower for Mills College and the Fairmont Hotel restoration after the San Francisco earthquake. That building solidified her reputation, and she had many jobs for which she adapted a variety of architectural styles. She hired a number of women and, during the same time, gave anonymous financial aid to women students. In the late 1920s, she had a mastoid operation but continued working. At the beginning of World War II, she had such skill with steel-reinforced concrete that she attracted many requests for institutional work. By the end of her career, she had designed and erected more than 800 structures, each expressing its function and its location architecturally. She used all styles and combined them creatively in original compositions.

BIBLIOGRAPHY

Boutelle, Sara Holmes. *Julia Morgan, Architect*. New York: Abbeville Press, 1988. 0–8965–9792–X, 271p. Boutelle draws from letters, photographs, blueprints, sketches, and reminiscences to follow Morgan and her career as the most important female architect in the first half of the twentieth century.
James, Cary. *Julia Morgan*. New York: Chelsea House, 1990. 1–55546–669–9, 111p. This documented and researched biography for young adults re-creates Morgan's life and career.

MORRISON, TONI (1931-)
Author   Lorain, Ohio

Tony Morrison received the Nobel Prize for Literature in 1993 for a body of work in which she tries to record the past so that no one will forget what has constituted the African American community. She was born Chloe Anthony Wofford on February 18, 1931, as the second of four children to parents who had migrated from the South, where her grandparents had been sharecroppers. Morrison learned that loyalty to community was extremely important and that great writers including Fyodor Dostoyevsky, *Jane Austen, and Leo Tolstoy had written in detail about their own cultures. She graduated from high school with honors and attended Howard University, where she began to write seriously before receiving her M.A. from Cornell University. After college, she married a Jamaican and had two children, but when she and her husband realized that their cultural expectations were too different, they separated. She moved to Syracuse to help Random House revise its textbooks, and there she began working on *The Bluest Eye*. Novels to follow were *Sula*, *Song of Solomon*, and *Tar Baby*. The State University of New York at Albany offered her its Albert Schweitzer Chair in the Humanities, and there she finished *Beloved*, winner of the Pulitzer Prize. Morrison then moved to Princeton and the Robert F. Goheen professorship. She has delivered the Massey Lectures in American Civilization at Harvard University and the Clark Lectures at Trinity College, Cambridge. She is a member of the American Academy and Institute of Arts and Letters and of the American Academy of Arts and Sciences. Honorary degrees have also come from many universities and colleges.

BIBLIOGRAPHY
Century, Douglas. *Toni Morrison*. New York: Chelsea House, 1994. 0–7910–1877–6, 103p. Century includes information about Morrison's development of her works in this thorough young adult biography.
Kramer, Barbara. *Toni Morrison, Nobel Prize–Winning Author*. Springfield, NJ: Enslow, 1996. 0–89490–688–7, 112p. Kramer examines Morrison from several aspects in this biography for young adults—her life, her hard work, the themes in her books, and her strengths as a writer.
Samuels, Wilfred D., and Clenora Hudson-Weems. *Toni Morrison*. New York: Twayne, 1990. 0–8057–7601–X, 160p. After a brief biography of Morrison, commentaries on her novels dwell on her characters as outside the mainstream.

MOSES, ANNA (GRANDMA MOSES) (1860–1961)
Artist   Greenwich, New York

Grandma Moses (Anna Mary Robertson Moses) was an artist known for her primitive style. She was born on September 7, 1860, as one of ten children to a farmer and inventor (who also liked to paint and encouraged his children to draw on the paper he purchased for a penny) and his wife. At 12, she left home to earn money as a hired girl, and in 1887, she married a farmer and worked with him while bearing ten children, five of whom survived. Her husband died when she was 67, and she relinquished the farm work to her son while she began oil painting in her bedroom on an old kitchen table under one light bulb. As she became more experienced, she shifted to painting on hard wood, which she prepared with linseed oil and three coats of flat white paint. When her pictures went on sale at the Woman's Exchange in Thomas's Drug Store in Hoosick Falls, New York, an art collector saw her work in 1938. He bought those pictures, went to her house, and purchased 15 more. Three appeared in an exhibit entitled "Contemporary Unknown American Painters" at the Museum of Modern Art in 1939. The next year, the Galerie St. Etienne gave her a one-woman show. At 80 years of age, Grandma Moses became a major success. Her first paintings had been copies of pictures within her possession, but she had quickly moved to original subjects, including scenes from her childhood such as apple picking, maple sugaring, and Christmas tree cutting. She taught herself, having never seen other painters at work, and continued painting through her nineties, gaining confidence with each of her nearly 1,000 pictures.

BIBLIOGRAPHY

Biracree, Tom. *Grandma Moses*. New York: Chelsea House, 1989. 1-55546-670-2, 111p. Biracree's biography for young adults about Grandma Moses illuminates her life and career and includes photographs.

Hickok, Beth Moses. *Remembering Grandma Moses*. Bennington, VT: Seal Press, 1994. 1-88459-201-5, 63p. This memoir, written by her daughter-in-law, recounts the life of Grandma Moses when her family casually handled her paintings before they knew of their value and after she became famous.

Kallir, Jane. *Grandma Moses, the Artist Behind the Myth*. New York: Potter, 1982. 0-517-54748-1, 160p. This researched, documented history of Grandma Moses covers her life and career and includes illustrations of her work, personal photographs, and facsimiles of her writings.

Kallir, Otto. *Grandma Moses*. New York: Henry N. Abrams, 1973. 0-8109-0166-8, 357p. Plates of Grandma Moses's paintings accompany Kallir's thoughtful biography, in which he discusses her methods of work and analyzes her subjects.

Ketchum, William C. *Grandma Moses: An American Original*. New York: Smithmark, 1996. 0-8317-8085-1, 80p. In a study appropriate for young adults, Ketchum examines Grandma Moses's life and her place in the American artistic canon with discussion of her nature and everyday life themes.

MOSKOWITZ, BELLE (1877–1933)
Social Worker and Political Consultant   New York, New York

Belle Moskowitz was a social worker who became a trusted political advisor to the governor of New York. She was born Belle Lindner Israels on October 5, 1877, to a prosperous Polish-Jewish immigrant watchmaker and his wife. She attended public schools, graduating from Horace Mann High School and studying at Teachers College of Columbia University for a year. At the same time, she began volunteering with the Educational Alliance to provide recreational services to young Jewish immigrants, easing their assimilation process, and soon became a member of the paid staff. After marrying in 1903, while raising three children, her concern about the inner city continued, and she served part-time on *Survey*, a publication analyzing social problems. To aid unmarried women arriving alone in New York, she helped organize the New York Travelers Aid Society. Moskowitz's husband died unexpectedly in 1911, leaving her to support the family, and she took a variety of jobs, including secretary of the Mayor's Committee of Women on National Defense. In 1917, she and her second husband established themselves as public relations counselors, a new profession, and began serving many clients. Moskowitz simultaneously suggested to Alfred E. Smith, the Democratic candidate for governor, that he campaign to women voting for the first time; he followed her advice and won. Smith, an Irish Catholic, then began to rely on her suggestions, research, and diplomatic skills with the press and other politicians and continued to do so during his long political career. Moskowitz suggested reform of the state government administration, modernization, protection for working girls, public housing and aid for the poor, regulation of charities, defense of free speech, and promotion of industrial peace. After Smith's defeat in 1928, Moskowitz served as a director of the Council of Jewish Women and as vice president of the Association to Promote Proper Housing for Girls before dying at the age of 55 from a heart attack after a fall.

BIBLIOGRAPHY

Perry, Elisabeth Israels. *Belle Moskowitz: Feminine Politics and the Exercise of Power in the Age of Alfred E. Smith*. New York: Routledge, 1992. 0-415-90545-1, 280p. Since Moskowitz's son discarded much of her memorabilia, Perry, Moskowitz's granddaughter, had to unearth other sources to compose her scholarly biography.

MOTT, LUCRETIA (1793–1880)
Reformer   **Nantucket, Massachusetts**

Lucretia Mott was a social reformer and minister who helped found the women's rights movement. She was born Lucretia Coffin on January 3, 1793, as one of seven children to a sea captain and his wife, who kept a shop of the East India goods her husband collected on his trips. When the family moved to Boston, Mott attended both public and private schools. At 13, she went to a Quaker boarding school, soon becoming a teacher there for half the salary of the males. Her interest in women's rights began, and in 1811, she married a man who supported this and her other causes and went with her on speaking engagements. After her firstborn son died, Mott began to think about religion, and the next year, in 1818, she made her first "appearance in the ministry" at a Quaker meeting. She soon began speaking publicly about her opposition to slavery and her refusal to use cotton cloth, cane sugar, or any other product slaves produced. Her husband even changed his livelihood from the cotton trade to the wool commission business. Mott became an active member of the American Anti-Slavery Society after women were allowed to join, and she followed William Lloyd Garrison's radical approach to the subject, demanding immediate emancipation. In 1840, she attended the World's Anti-Slavery Convention in London as a delegate, and although being a woman, she was not allowed to speak, she was described as the "lioness of the convention." Eight years later, the women's rights movement began when she and **Elizabeth Cady Stanton** realized that half of the world's population had been denied a vote in the London convention because of their sex. However, Mott was more concerned with the inequalities in education, labor, wages, employment, and political rights in general than with suffrage. After the Thirteenth Amendment passed, Mott was further distressed about African American suffrage and higher education for the freed slaves. Throughout her life, she dedicated herself to emancipation for everyone from all restrictions. For her work, she was elected to The National Women's Hall of Fame.

BIBLIOGRAPHY

Bacon, Margaret Hope. *Valiant Friend: The Life of Lucretia Mott.* New York: Walker, 1980. 0-8027-7190-4, 265p. Well-researched with many details, Bacon's biography of Mott, suitable for young adults, emphasizes her relationships with family and other reformers, her abolitionist work, and her crusade for women's rights.

Bryant, Jennifer. *Lucretia Mott: A Guiding Light.* Grand Rapids, MI: Eerdmans, 1996. 0-8028-5115-0, 188p. Bryant examines Mott's fight for abolition by examining both her personal life and the time in which she lived in a thorough young adult biography.

Cromwell, Otelia. *Lucretia Mott.* 1958. New York: Russell and Russell, 1971. No ISBN, 241p. Cromwell's carefully researched and documented biography of Mott thoughtfully illuminates her life and the causes she espoused.

MUSGROVE, MARY (1700-1765)
Businesswoman and Tribal Leader   Coweta, Georgia

Mary Musgrove was a Native American leader. She was born about 1700 as Coosaponakeesa to an unnamed English trader and his Creek wife. When Musgrove was seven, her father took her to Charles Town, South Carolina, where she remained to learn English in a school with 27 whites, 2 Native Americans, and 1 African American. In 1716, Musgrove returned to the Creek tribe, and soon after, when the government sent a prominent South Carolinian to negotiate with the Creeks, his accompanying son met and married her. With him she ran a business trading Charleston merchandise for Creek deerskins. When James Oglethorpe arrived to found the colony of Georgia, Musgrove was one of the first persons he met, and she became his interpreter. Because of her influence, the Creeks remained friendly with the English. Musgrove's husband died in 1739, and she remarried before helping the Creeks in their war with Spain—the War of Jenkins' Ear—which lasted from 1739 until 1744. When Oglethorpe left, he gave Musgrove money and a diamond, and she continued serving the colony during the War of the Austrian Succession, which countered French influence in the area.

After the British ignored Musgrove's claims for compensation for her services, she brought warriors to Savannah and terrorized the town for a month. When she and her husband went to England, the English government took five years to give her St. Catherines Island and 2,000 pounds for her services. They returned to the island, with Musgrove as the largest landowner and richest colonist in Georgia, to build a home, but Musgrove only lived a short while to enjoy her riches.

BIBLIOGRAPHY

Todd, Helen. *Mary Musgrove, Georgia Indian Princess.* Savannah, GA: Seven Oaks, 1981. 0–96055–140–9, 148p. This straightforward researched and documented biography, suitable for young adults, presents Musgrove's life and the circumstances that surrounded her childhood and marriage.

$\mathcal{N}$

NAVRATILOVA, MARTINA (1956-)
Athlete   Prague, Czechoslovakia

Martina Navratilova has broken many records as a professional tennis player. She
was born on October 18, 1956, to Czechoslovakian citizens who had to work at
menial jobs and were never promoted because they had spoken against the
government and refused to join the Communist Party. While a teenager,
Navratilova won the Czechoslovakian National singles titles each year from 1972
to 1974. She came to the United States in 1975 and continued her winnings. She
holds 167 singles titles and 165 doubles titles, and in 1991, she became the overall
leader in number of singles-match wins at 1,309. Among the tournaments she has
won are the Virginia Slims, Wimbledon, and the French, Australian, and Italian
Opens. Since her naturalization as a citizen of the United States in 1981, she has
supported charitable causes including Mi Casa, recycling, and selective animal
rights. She is also politically active for homosexual and human rights. Among the
awards she has received are the Women's Sports Foundation Flo Hyman Award,
the Female Athlete of the Decade, Women's Tennis Association Player of Year,
and the Women's Sports Foundation Sportswoman of the Year. She has been
inducted into the Chicago Hall of Fame and received an honorary degree.

BIBLIOGRAPHY
Blue, Adrianne. *Martina: The Lives and Times of Martina Navratilova.* Secaucus, NJ:
    Birch Lane, 1995. 1-559-72300-9, 240p. Although Blue's balanced biography is
    unauthorized, she received access to Navratilova's friends and family.

NAYLOR, GLORIA (1950-)
Author   New York, New York

Gloria Naylor is an African American author. She was born on January 25, 1950, the daughter of a transit worker and a telephone operator. Very early in Naylor's life, her mother encouraged her to read, although obtaining books in rural Mississippi was especially difficult because African Americans were restricted from using public libraries. In New York, Naylor got her first library card at four and, as an introverted child, began reading constantly. Her mother also gave her a diary. After Naylor finished her advanced classes in high school, she responded to her intense reaction at the death of Martin Luther King, Jr., by becoming a missionary for the Jehovah's Witnesses in New York, North Carolina, and Florida for the next seven years. She then earned a B.A. in English from Brooklyn College and followed it with an M.A. from Yale University in Afro-American Studies, graduating in 1983. In school, she discovered **Toni Morrison**'s work, and then that of **Zora Neale Hurston** and **Alice Walker**, and realized for the first time that African American women were a growing force in the literary world. In 1980, *Essence* published one of her short stories, and Viking offered her a contract. While still attending college, she published her first novel, *The Women of Brewster Place*. After graduation, she wrote, lectured, and worked for the United States Information Agency in India. She founded an independent film production company, One Way Productions, while contributing to *Southern Review*, *Essence*, *Ms.*, *Life*, *Ontario Review*, and *People*. She has become a major figure in the African American feminist literary movement but has avoided some criticisms by refusing to depict African American males as negative stereotypes. Among her honors are the American Book Award, a National Endowment for the Arts Fellowship, a Guggenheim Foundation Fellowship, and a Lillian Smith Award.

BIBLIOGRAPHY
Fowler, Virginia C. *Gloria Naylor: In Search of Sanctuary.* New York: Twayne, 1996. 0–8057–4025–2, 181p. For this well-researched critical biography, Fowler consulted Naylor as well as others about her life and ideas.

NEVELSON, LOUISE (1899–1988)
Sculptor   Kiev, Ukraine

Louise Nevelson was a sculptor. She was born on September 23, 1899 (some sources say 1900, but Nevelson has never clarified this), into a family that moved from the Ukraine to Maine in 1905. When 20, Nevelson married and had a child, but she later left both of them to pursue her art. In 1929, she began studying at New York's Art Students' League, and in 1931, she went to Munich to study with Hans Hofmann. Her first one-woman exhibit in New York in 1941 showed her interest in masses of wood, terra-cotta, bronze, and plaster which resembled sculpture of Central America. Later, she worked with found objects (*objets trouvés*) such as stylized features and appendages. At first ignored by the public, Nevelson continued to work, but in the 1950s, critics became attracted to her almost totally abstract sculptures consisting of one-color, open-faced wooden boxes stacked as freestanding walls and holding collections of abstract-shaped objects beside chair legs, pieces of balustrades, and other found objects or pieces of bric-a-brac. Among her works are *Sky Cathedral*, *Silent Music II*, and *Sky Gate—New York*. Later pieces include her work in aluminum, Plexiglas, and Lucite, and a large wall sculpture, *World Trade Center, New York City*. In the late 1950s, museums started purchasing her wall sculptures, and in 1967, the Whitney Museum of American Art in New York presented the first major retrospective of her work.

BIBLIOGRAPHY

Bober, Natalie. *Breaking Tradition: The Story of Louise Nevelson*. New York: Atheneum, 1984. 0-689-31036-6, 166p.   In a young adult biography, Bober describes Nevelson's life as a sculptor.

Cain, Michael. *Louise Nevelson*. New York: Chelsea House, 1989. 1-55546-671-0, 111p. Nevelson once burned an entire exhibit after no one purchased a piece of her work, and Cain captures her volatile personality in his biography for young adults.

Lipman, Jean. *Nevelson's World*. New York: Hudson Hills, 1983. 0-933920-33-4, 244p. Over 100 photographs of Nevelson's graphic art and sculptures with her commentary give insight into the woman's devotion to her work.

Lisle, Laurie. *Louise Nevelson: A Passionate Life*. New York: Summit, 1990. 0-671-67516-8, 352p.   For this well-researched and balanced biography, Lisle interviewed Nevelson, her family, and her friends.

Nevelson, Louise. *Dawns + Dusks: Taped Conversations with Diana MacKown*. New York: Scribner, 1976. 0-684-14781-5, 190p.   In conversations, Nevelson recalls her childhood and career.

NEY, ELISABET (1833–1907)
Sculptor   Münster, Prussia

Elisabet Ney was a sculptor. She was one of two surviving children born to a stonecutter and his Polish refugee wife. By the age of eight, Ney decided to become a sculptor. She persuaded her parents to let her take drawing lessons, and after attending Catholic schools, she enrolled in the Royal Bavarian Academy of Fine Arts in Munich as the only female. Two years later, she went to Berlin to study with Christian Rauch during the last two years of his professional work. Among the people she met, and often sculpted, were Alexander von Humboldt, Hans von Bülow, Franz Liszt, and *Cosima Wagner. Intensely feminist, she refused at first to marry a medical student when they fell in love, and she agreed only after she had become famous and because she could keep her name. Pretending to be "living in sin" rather than married, Ney and her husband went to Rome where she sculpted Garibaldi and Bismarck. When Bismarck tried to unify Germany, they immigrated to the United States, settling in Texas, where they bought a plantation. Her husband began writing philosophy, and Ney raised their child according to her own unusual tastes. Ney's first Texas commissions, statues of Sam Houston and Stephen F. Austin, appeared in the Texas exhibit at the World's Columbian Exposition in Chicago during 1893. The following year, she opened a studio in Austin and successfully secured many more commissions of famous Texans, including a statue of Houston for Statuary Hall in the United States Capitol. Two major goals were to publish her husband's philosophical books and to create a statue of her favorite character, Lady Macbeth, and with the fees she earned, she was able to complete both projects before her death.

BIBLIOGRAPHY

Cutrer, Emily Fourmy. *The Art of the Woman: The Life and Work of Elisabet Ney.* Lincoln: University of Nebraska Press, 1988. 0-8032-1438-3, 278p. Cutrer uses original and unpublished material in her well-documented biography of Ney.

Goar, Marjory. *Marble Dust: The Life of Elisabet Ney.* Austin, TX: Eakin Press, 1984. 0-89015-430-9, 309p. Goar's researched and documented fictional biography explores Ney's unconventional life as wife and artist.

Ney, Elisabet. *Sursum! Elisabet Ney in Texas.* Ed. Willie B. Rutland. Austin, TX: Hart Graphics, 1977. No ISBN, 200p. This collection of Ney's letters reveals her Texas life and her participation in her community.

NUTTING, MARY ADELAIDE (1858–1948)
Nurse and Educator   Waterloo, Quebec, Canada

Mary Adelaide Nutting was one of nursing education's most important influences. She was born on November 1, 1858, the fourth of five children. Her father was a Methodist clerk of the circuit court, and her intellectual mother helped support the family with her beautiful needlework. Nutting attended local schools and a private school in Montreal, where she became a gifted musician. Nutting chose to enter the new Johns Hopkins Hospital Training School for Nurses. She graduated as one of seventeen students in the first class and remained to become a head nurse and then assistant superintendent of nurses. After visiting other training schools, she returned to improve course content, personnel, working conditions, living quarters, and teaching facilities. Realizing that nursing instruction should be independent from hospitals and that schools should be professional, she created a preparatory course and a library with materials covering the history of nursing. An experimental program began at Teachers College, Columbia University, supporting Nutting's conviction that universities should educate nurses. Nutting became the first nurse to be appointed to a university chair when she accepted a full-time professorship at Columbia in institutional management with the charge to establish a department of household administration with a section on hospital economics. She set up the department of nursing and health three years later, served as its chair until her retirement, and published *Educational Status of Nursing*, one of the "seven historic publications" to measure nursing education. During World War I, she served as chair of the committee on nursing of the General Medical Board of the Council of National Defense. She also headed a project that created the *Standard Curriculum for Schools of Nursing.* Another committee produced *Nursing and Nursing Education in the United States.* She was also active in civic clubs. Her book, *History of Nursing,* co-authored with Lavinia L. Dock was a standard work documenting nursing's early years. Among her awards were the Liberty Service Medal of the National Institute of Social Sciences, the Mary Adelaide Nutting Medal, established in 1944 by the National League of Nursing Education, and an honorary degree from Yale. **Cecilia Beaux**'s portrait of Nutting hangs in the Johns Hopkins Hospital.

BIBLIOGRAPHY

Marshall, Helen E. *Mary Adelaide Nutting, Pioneer of Modern Nursing.* Baltimore, MD: Johns Hopkins University Press, 1972. 0-8018-1365-4, 396p. From notebooks, lecture notes, drafts of her writing, and correspondence, Marshall has created a thoroughly researched, documented, and scholarly biography of Nutting.

$\mathcal{O}$

OAKLEY, ANNIE (1860–1926)
Entertainer
Woodland, Ohio

Annie Oakley was an entertainer often called "Little Sure Shot." She was born Phoebe Anne Oakley Moses on August 13, 1860, as the fifth of eight children to Quakers. Her father died when she was four, and after her mother became the district nurse, she and her siblings lived in foster homes, with Oakley going to an orphanage at nine. When other children taunted her by forming rhymes on her name, she eliminated the "Moses" and changed her name in the family Bible as well. At 10, Oakley joined a farm family that used her as a laborer, but she ran away and found her mother, with whom she lived for the next four years. During this time, she learned to shoot with her father's old cap-and-ball rifle and discovered that she was a superb marksperson. She sold game and used the proceeds to pay off the mortgage on the family home. After she out-shot a professional marksman, he married her, taught her to read, and honed her stagecraft. He arranged for her to work with Buffalo Bill's Wild West Show in 1885, and she remained for 16 years, becoming a feature of the production. One of her tricks was to shoot holes in a playing card as it flew through the air, and for many years "Annie Oakley" designated a complimentary ticket with a hole punched in it. Offstage, Sitting Bull named her "Little Sure Shot," treating her like a daughter, and Oakley stitched needlework. In 1887, she went to London and met Queen Victoria, but when Buffalo Bill became irritated that she was more famous than he, she left but rejoined for a four-year tour of Europe. In 1901, a train wreck injury ended her career in the arena, but she played on the stage for several years, and during World War I toured army camps to demonstrate her shooting skills. In

1922, she was partially paralyzed in an automobile accident which ended all performances. She was later elected to The National Women's Hall of Fame.

BIBLIOGRAPHY

Flynn, Jean. *Annie Oakley: Legendary Sharpshooter*. Springfield, NJ: Enslow, 1998. 0-7660-1012-0, 128p. This well-researched and documented biography for young adults overviews Oakley's life and includes photographs.

Havighurst, Walter. *Annie Oakley of the Wild West*. 1954. Norman: University of Oklahoma Press, 1992. 0-8032-7253-7, 246p. Havighurst's researched and documented biography of Oakley describes her life and her place in the Wild West Show.

Kasper, Shirl. *Annie Oakley*. Norman: University of Oklahoma Press, 1992. 0-8061-2418-0, 288p. Kasper's balanced biography depicts Oakley as one who would not align with the women's rights movement, preferring to be known as a lady.

Riley, Glenda. *The Life and Legacy of Annie Oakley*. Norman: University of Oklahoma Press, 1994. 0-8061-2656-6, 252p. In a well-researched text, Riley interprets Oakley's dilemma of promoting herself as an athletic western woman when she privately considered herself a genteel Victorian.

Sayers, Isabelle S. *Annie Oakley and Buffalo Bill's Wild West*. New York: Dover, 1981. 0-486-24120-3, 89p. In a descriptive biography based mainly on newspaper clippings, Sayers chronicles Oakley's life and career with text and photographs.

OATES, JOYCE CAROL (1938-)
Author   Lockport, New York

Joyce Carol Oates is an author. She was born on June 16, 1938, to a sign painter and his poorly educated but pleasant wife. After a childhood of poverty, Oates attended Syracuse University for her B.A. and the University of Wisconsin for her M.A. Her first collection of short stories, *By the North Gate*, was published in 1963, and her first novel, *With Shuddering Fall*, appeared in 1964. Since then, she has published an average of two books a year. Her most critically acclaimed works include *A Garden of Earthly Delights*, *Them*, *Do with Me What You Will*, *Bellefleur*, *A Bloodsmoor Romance*, and *Mysteries of Winterthurn*. She has published other works under the pseudonym Rosamond Smith. She has also written plays, essays, poetry, and literary criticism. She has taught English at the universities of Detroit, Windsor, and Princeton, where she is the Roger S. Berlind Distinguished Professor of English. The characters in her novels and short stories reveal their intensity and their self-destructiveness as well as an inability to cope with forces beyond their control. Among the awards she has received are the National Book Award, the O. Henry Award, the Rosenthal Award from the National Institute of Arts and Letters, and the Alan Swallow Award. She is a member of the American Academy and Institute of Arts and Letters.

BIBLIOGRAPHY

Johnson, Greg. *Invisible Writer: A Biography of Joyce Carol Oates*. New York: Dutton, 1998. 0-452-94163-0, 235p. In a thoroughly researched and documented scholarly biography, Johnson traces myriad facets of Oates's life and makes connections in her writings to reveal autobiographical strains.

O'CONNOR, FLANNERY (1925-1964)
Author											Savannah, Georgia

Flannery O'Connor was an author who set her works in the rural South. She was born on March 25, 1925, as the only child in her family. She enjoyed her parents' company and raising chickens, especially unusual ones with strange markings or odd habits. At the onset of her father's lupus, when she was 12, they moved to her mother's family home. The three-year ordeal of her father's illness led O'Connor to religion, and her strong Catholic faith guided her life. After graduation from public high school, she attended Georgia State College for Women in Milledgeville, and then went to the University of Iowa to study creative writing at the Writers' Workshop. She had begun writing as a child, and her first published work, a short story, appeared in *Accent* in 1946. During her second year at Iowa, she won the Rinehart-Iowa Prize for her novel *Wise Blood*. In 1950, when she felt unwell and almost died, she was diagnosed with hereditary lupus. She settled in Georgia to write and steadily produced short stories revealing her mastery of the form. In her work, she examined human alienation and the relationship of the individual to God, "religious consciousness without a religion," which often gave her strange and sometimes violent characters dignity and importance. During her physical deterioration, a Ford Foundation grant helped support her. Other honors she received included a National Institute of Arts and Letters grant, O. Henry Memorial Awards, a National Book Award, and honorary degrees.

BIBLIOGRAPHY

Balee, Susan. *Flannery O'Connor: Literary Prophet of the South*. New York: Chelsea House, 1994. 0-7910-2418-0, 111p. In this balanced biography for young adults based on diaries and letters, Balee describes O'Connor's life and work.

Coles, Robert. *Flannery O'Connor's South*. 1980. Athens: University of Georgia Press, 1993. 0-8203-1536-2, 166p. Coles reflects on O'Connor's life and her view of the South in her work.

Fickett, Harold, and Douglas R. Gilbert. *Flannery O'Connor: Images of Grace*. Grand Rapids, MI: Eerdmans, 1986. 0-8028-0187-0, 151p. The authors trace O'Connor's life and work, including critical analyses reflecting her spirituality.

Getz, Lorine M. *Flannery O'Connor, Her Life, Library, and Book Reviews*. New York: Mellen Press, 1980. 0-88946-997-0, 223p. Using previously unavailable papers and other sources, Getz discusses O'Connor's life and heritage in a carefully researched and documented scholarly biography.

Paulson, Suzanne Morrow. *Flannery O'Connor: A Study of the Short Fiction*. New York: Twayne, 1988. 0-8057-8301-6, 238p. In a critical study of O'Connor, Paulson analyzes themes in her life and work.

O'CONNOR, SANDRA DAY (1930–)
Supreme Court Justice and Attorney   El Paso, Texas

Sandra Day O'Connor was the first woman to become a Supreme Court justice of the United States. She was born on March 26, 1930, and grew up on her family's 160,000 acre ranch in Arizona. She graduated from Stanford University in 1950 and from its law school in 1952. Marrying after graduation, she returned with her husband to Arizona. Since she could only find work as a secretary in the legal field because of her sex, she decided to work for the government. She eventually became assistant attorney general for the state in 1965, serving for four years, and then a Republican member of the Arizona senate for the next five years, becoming the first woman in the United States to hold the position of majority leader in a state legislature. In 1974, she left the senate when elected a superior court judge in Maricopa County. In 1979, she was appointed to the Arizona Court of Appeals. Two years later, President Ronald Reagan chose her as his first appointee to the United States Supreme Court, and she was sworn in as an associate justice on September 25, 1981. She is both conservative and pragmatic, sometimes liberal on social issues, but known for carefully researched opinions. For her achievements, she was elected to The National Women's Hall of Fame.

BIBLIOGRAPHY
Herda, D. J. *Sandra Day O'Connor: Independent Thinker*. Springfield, NJ: Enslow, 1995. 0–89490–558–9, 104p. This biography for young adults is a straightforward account of O'Connor's life and career.
Huber, Peter W. *Sandra Day O'Connor*. New York: Chelsea House, 1990. 1–55546–672–9, 111p. Huber's introduction to O'Connor's life for young adults clarifies the functions of the judiciary system and details her balancing of career and family.
Van Sickel, Robert W. *Not a Particularly Different Voice: The Jurisprudence of Sandra Day O'Connor*. New York: P. Lang, 1998. 0–8204–3914–2, 216p. Van Sickel examines all of O'Connor's opinions, speeches, articles, and work on the Arizona Court of Appeals to show that she has had consistent values in her decisions over the last 15 years.

O'KEEFFE, GEORGIA (1887–1986)
Artist   Sun Prairie, Wisconsin

Georgia O'Keeffe was an artist. She was born on November 15, 1887, and lived on the family farm where she decided that she wanted to be an artist. First taking lessons from an artist boarding with the family, she then studied at the Art Institute of Chicago in 1904 and at the Art Students' League of New York in 1907. She supported herself with commercial art and then taught at various schools and colleges in the South from 1912 to 1916 before photographer Alfred Stieglitz discovered her work and exhibited it. His praise, promotion, and photographs of her wooed O'Keeffe, and they married in 1924. In the 1920s, she began to develop her individual style and content using subjects including enlarged skulls and other animal bones, flowers and plant organs, shells, rocks, mountains, and varied natural forms. She painted these objects with clear color, setting them against an open space without perspective. Although she completed her best-known paintings before 1950, she continued working until the 1980s. Later works highlight the skies and deserts in New Mexico, her home for many years. The Whitney Museum of American Art held a retrospective exhibition of her work in 1970. She has been elected to The National Women's Hall of Fame.

BIBLIOGRAPHY

Castro, Jan Garden. *The Art and Life of Georgia O'Keeffe*. New York: Crown, 1995. 0-517-88387-2, 192p. To write this scholarly critical biography of O'Keeffe's life and work, Castro consulted unpublished materials and many of O'Keeffe's original works in both private and public collections.

Hogrefe, Jeffrey. *O'Keeffe: The Life of an American Legend*. New York: Bantam, 1992. 0-553-08116-0, 376p. As he traces O'Keeffe's career and themes in an in-depth biography, Hogrefe posits that O'Keeffe rebelled against social expectations.

Peters, Sarah Whitaker. *Becoming O'Keeffe: The Early Years*. New York: Abbeville, 1991. 0-89659-907-8, 397p. Peters examines O'Keeffe's early work between 1915 and 1930 with its traces of Art Nouveau and Symbolism in a carefully researched text with photographs.

Pollitzer, Anita. *A Woman on Paper: Georgia O'Keeffe*. New York: Simon and Schuster, 1988. 0-671-66431-X, 290p. Pollitzer and O'Keeffe became friends at Columbia in 1914, and their correspondence forms part of this memoir.

Robinson, Roxana. *Georgia O'Keeffe: A Life*. New York: HarperCollins, 1989. 0-06-015965-0, 639p. O'Keeffe's family granted Robinson permission to use sources unavailable during O'Keeffe's lifetime, and the resulting biography acknowledges her important contributions as both a feminist and an artist.

OLSEN, TILLIE (1913-)
Author   Omaha, Nebraska

Tillie Olsen is an author who writes about the dreams and failures of people who have been unable to express themselves because of class, sex, or race. She was born on January 14, 1913, as the second of six children to a Russian immigrant and his wife. Her father became the Nebraska Socialist Party state secretary. Olsen grew up on their farm, and after leaving high school, got jobs working in industry, but was jailed in 1930 after trying to organize packinghouse workers. She also started writing *Yonnondio* in 1932, publishing the first chapter in *Partisan Review* along with two essays on her involvment in the San Francisco Maritime Strike in 1934. In 1936, she met her husband and then worked as a typist-transcriber, abandoning her writing until 1953 while raising her four children in California. In 1955, she enrolled in a writing course, and the next year she received a Stanford University Stegner fellowship in creative writing. She began winning awards for her work and serving as a visiting writer at several colleges and universities. Among her honors are the O. Henry Award, an award from the American Academy and National Institute of Arts and Letters, and honorary degrees.

BIBLIOGRAPHY

Coiner, Constance. *Better Red: The Writing and Resistance of Tillie Olsen and Meridel Le Sueur*. New York: Oxford University Press, 1995. 0-19-505695-7, 282p. With a mixture of literary criticism, biographical information, and oral history, Coiner's collective biography examines Olsen as a working-class writer.

Martin, Abigail. *Tillie Olsen*. Boise, ID: Boise State University Press, 1984. 0-88430-039-0, 48p. This brief overview of Olsen's life and writings places her in the western writers' tradition.

Orr, Elaine Neil. *Tillie Olsen and a Feminist Spiritual Vision*. Jackson: University Press of Mississippi, 1987. 0-87805-300-X, 193p. Orr's researched and documented scholarly critical biography of Olsen examines her place in American letters.

Pearlman, Mickey, and Abby Werlock. *Tillie Olsen*. Boston: Twayne, 1991. 0-8057-7632-X, 159p. This critical biography of Olsen includes a lengthy interview with her.

Roberts, Nora Ruth. *Three Radical Women Writers: Class and Gender in Meridel Le Sueur, Tillie Olsen, and Josephine Herbst*. New York: Garland, 1996. 0-81530-330-0, 209p. Roberts used journals and unpublished materials in this collective critical examination, placing Olsen in the American radical movement during the 1930s.

ONASSIS, JACQUELINE KENNEDY (1929-1994)
First Lady and Editor   **Southampton, New York**

Jacqueline Lee Bouvier Kennedy Onassis was First Lady of the United States. She was born on July 28, 1929, one of two daughters of an alcoholic stockbroker and his wife. Her parents divorced when she was 11, and her mother remarried. She remained a privileged child, later attending George Washington University, Vassar, and the Sorbonne in Paris. She could speak French, Spanish, and German and was the 1947 Queen Deb of the Year before becoming a reporter and photographer for the *Washington Times-Herald*, where she drove around town in a dented car, interviewing people on the street. In 1951, she met Jack Kennedy, a congressman 11 years her senior, who told her he planned to be president. Two years later, she married him in a major social event uniting two Roman Catholic families. When he became president, she created a White House fine arts commission, hired a White House curator, and redecorated the building with early nineteenth-century furnishings, museum quality paintings and objets d'art, about which she gave a guided tour for the three television networks in 1961. When she was only 34, in 1963, she planned the funeral for her husband after his assassination. In 1968, she married Aristotle Onassis, a Greek shipping magnate, and his death in 1975 left her again a widow. The same year, she began working at Viking Publishing, and three years later became an associate editor at Doubleday, editing 10 to 12 books a year on performing arts and other cultural subjects. Kennedy Onassis refused to give personal interviews, preferring a privacy she had been previously denied, for the last 30 years of her life.

BIBLIOGRAPHY

Andersen, Christopher P. *Jackie After Jack: A Portrait of the Lady.* 1996. New York: Morrow, 1998. 0-688-15312-7, 400p. Andersen's biography of Kennedy Onassis and her husband, John Kennedy, borders on the sensational, with information from sometimes unidentified sources.

Davis, John H. *Jacqueline Bouvier: An Intimate Memoir.* New York: Wiley, 1996. 0-471-12945-3, 208p. In this biography of Kennedy Onassis's years until her marriage to John Kennedy, Davis (her first cousin) used family papers and his memories of summers with Kennedy Onassis to relate the difficulties and the delights of developing social graces in a wealthy society.

Heymann, C. David. *A Woman Named Jackie: An Intimate Biography of Jacqueline Bouvier Kennedy Onassis.* New York: Carol, 1994. 1-55972-266-5, 766p. This readable carefully researched, documented, and recommended biography of Kennedy Onassis covers her life.

Klein, Edward. *All Too Human: The Love Story of Jack and Jackie Kennedy.* New York: Pocket, 1996. 0-671-50187-9, 406p. Klein quotes from over 200 people who knew the Kennedys and reveals a marriage between two strong-willed people.

Ladowsky, Ellen. *Jacqueline Kennedy Onassis.* New York: Park Lane Press, 1997. 0-517-20077-5, 184p. Ladowsky's documented, popular biography of Kennedy Onassis, based mainly on secondary sources, overviews her life.

O'NEILL, ROSE CECIL (1874–1944)
Artist and Dollmaker   Wilkes-Barre, Pennsylvania

Rose Cecil O'Neill was an illustrator and author. She was born on June 25, 1874, as the second of six children to a bookdealer and a musical mother who had once been a teacher. Her father wanted her to be an actor, but she won a children's art contest at 13, and the *Omaha World Herald* hired her to do a weekly cartoon series. In 1893, she went to New York to find a market for her drawings and stayed at the convent of the Sisters of Saint Regis, with one of the sisters accompanying her on rounds to sell her illustrations. After marrying in 1896, she continued to sell her pictures while working as an illustrator on the staff of *Puck*, a humor magazine. When well established, with drawings in publications including *Life* and *Good Housekeeping*, she divorced her husband, and in 1909, encouraged by the editor of *Ladies' Home Journal*, began creating her first kewpie figures. O'Neill first used these cupids with tiny wings and heads sprouting tufts of hair to illustrate stories of their adventures waking flowers and protecting babies. Soon the figures adorned a variety of objects, and in 1912, kewpie dolls became popular. O'Neill had them manufactured in Germany until World War I, and with her sister, sold them in a Madison Avenue shop in New York. Royalties from these kewpies reached over $1.5 million, and O'Neill used the money to live in Europe for six years. When she returned to the United States, friends often stayed on her Connecticut estate. In 1921, O'Neill exhibited a different style of work, with drawings somewhat like the visionary art of William Blake. The next year, she was elected to the Société des Beaux Arts. She then began writing and publishing poetry and novels in which she explored Celtic mythology and romanticism. For the last decade of her life, she lived quietly with her sister.

BIBLIOGRAPHY

Armitage, Shelley. *Kewpies and Beyond: The World of Rose O'Neill*. Jackson: University Press of Mississippi, 1994. 0-87805-710-2, 227p. O'Neill, according to Armitage, was a serious artist, although without formal training.

Axe, John. *Kewpies: Dolls and Art of Rose O'Neill and Joseph L. Kallus*. Cumberland, MD: Hobby House Press, 1987. 0-87588-297-8, 181p. A biography of O'Neill precedes revealing photographs of her kewpies in whatever form they were produced and of her other art as collectible items.

Formanek-Brunell, Miriam, ed. *The Story of Rose O'Neill: An Autobiography*. Columbia: University of Missouri Press, 1997. 0-8262-1106-2, 154p. This autobiography of O'Neill includes an introductory chapter with information about her life and career.

McCanse, Ralph Alan. *Titans and Kewpies: The Life and Art of Rose O'Neill*. New York: Vantage, 1968. No ISBN, 220p. Interviews with friends who admired O'Neill's work form the basis of this readable memoir emphasizing her wide fame during her lifetime.

Ruggles, Rowena Fay. *The One Rose, Mother of the Immortal Kewpies*. Albany, CA: Ruggles, 1972. No ISBN, 96p. This carefully researched and recommended biography of O'Neill is based on a variety of unpublished sources and interviews and includes photographs of her drawings, kewpies, and people that she knew.

ORTIZ COFER, JUDITH. *See* COFER, JUDITH ORTIZ

OSSOLI, MARGARET FULLER. *See* FULLER (OSSOLI), MARGARET

OZICK, CYNTHIA (1928-)
Author   New York, New York

Cynthia Ozick is an author who focuses on Jewish culture. She was born on April 17, 1928, the daughter of a pharmacist and his wife. Since Ozick's parents were often working in their store during her childhood, Ozick's grandmother influenced her with stories about growing up in Russia. Ozick graduated from New York University as a member of Phi Beta Kappa and received her M.A. from Ohio State University. She has worked as an advertising copywriter as well as a college instructor. Of her short stories, essays, and critical works, she is known best for her fiction, concerned with careful phrasing and an underlying morality. Subjects about which she writes include mysticism and Judaic law and history. Her first book, *Trust*, was published in 1966, and she followed it with three award-winning collections of short stories and novellas. She is a member of the American Academy of Arts and Sciences. Her many honors include the B'nai B'rith Jewish Heritage Award, the Edward Lewis Wallant Memorial Award, an

American Academy of Arts Award for Literature, O. Henry Awards, induction into the American Academy and Institute of Arts and Letters, and several honorary degrees.

BIBLIOGRAPHY

Bloom, Harold, ed. *Cynthia Ozick*. New York: Chelsea House, 1986. 0–87754–713–0, 175p. In a series of essays on Ozick's fiction, the authors analyze her life and her work.

Friedman, Lawrence S. *Understanding Cynthia Ozick*. Columbia: University of South Carolina Press, 1991. 0–87249–772–0, 182p. This researched, documented, and recommended critical biography of Ozick gives an overview of her life and ideas.

Lowin, Joseph. *Cynthia Ozick*. Boston: Twayne, 1988. 0–8057–7526–9, 188p. In this critical biography, researched and documented, Lowin includes aspects of the Jewish aesthetic and Ozick's adaptations of the Jewish technique of rewriting.

$\mathscr{P}$

PAGE, RUTH (1899–1991)
Dancer and Choreographer   Indianapolis, Indiana

Ruth Page was a dancer. She was born on March 22, 1899, the daughter of a brain surgeon and a pianist. Her parents supported her dance study with local teachers, and when Page was 15, Anna Pavlova visited and encouraged her to make a career of dancing. Page then moved to Chicago to study with Adolph Bolm, a former member of Diaghilev's Ballets Russes. In 1919, Bolm choreographed *The Birthday of the Infanta* for Page, one of the first twentieth-century ballets with a score by an American composer (John Alden Carpenter) and scenery by an American designer (Robert Edmond Jones). They made history again in 1928 when Page played Terpsichore in the world premiere of Stravinsky's *Apollo*, choreographed by Bolm in Washington. Page married a wealthy lawyer in 1925, and on her honeymoon in Europe, she danced with Diaghilev's company. While she was performing with the Ballets Russes, George Balanchine choreographed two divertissements for her, *Etude* and *Polka Melancolique*, which may have been his first works created for an American. Page studied with Mary Wigman, the great German Expressionist choreographer in 1930, and in 1933, she toured with German modern dancer Harald Kreutzberg. During the 1940s, she began staging works in Chicago and for the Ballet Russe de Monte Carlo. She also began choreographing, and in 1956 her successes encouraged her to form the Chicago Opera Ballet, a group dedicated to performing ballets inspired by operas and operettas as well as internationally known stars, including Rudolf Nureyev. She first staged *The Nutcracker* in Chicago in 1965 (an annual event) and directed the Ruth Page Foundation School of the

Dance, still in existence. Among her honors were the *Dance* Magazine Award, the Illinois Gubernatorial Award, and several honorary degrees.

BIBLIOGRAPHY

Martin, John Joseph. *Ruth Page: An Intimate Biography.* New York: Dekker, 1977. 0-8247-6490-0, 342p. This chatty biography relies on interviews with Page and those who knew her during her pioneering career in ballet.

Page, Ruth. *Page by Page.* Brooklyn, NY: Dance Horizons, 1978. 0-87127-102-8, 224p. The text, composed of 47 essays by Page, presents her ideas on a variety of topics.

PALMER, ALICE FREEMAN (1855–1902)
Educator   Colesville, New York

Alice Elvira Freeman Palmer was an educator. She was born on February 21, 1855, as the oldest of four children to a physician and a former teacher. Palmer learned to read at three, and her parents' constant concern for self-improvement influenced her achievements. She attended the University of Michigan and was one of the first two women chosen to speak at commencement. She then taught, using part of her salary to pay her sister's tuition while taking her own graduate courses. After having had to refuse two teaching jobs at Wellesley because of family difficulties, she accepted the third to become head of the history department. When the president of Wellesley resigned, Palmer was appointed vice president, and then in 1882, at the age of 27, she became the president, a job she kept for six years. Encouraging educated women of her era to organize, she and 16 other women from eight colleges formed the Association of Collegiate Alumnae, later the American Association of University Women. Also in 1882, Michigan awarded her an honorary degree because after summers working on her Ph.D. there, she was unable to remain and complete her dissertation. In 1884, she went abroad for the first time as one of three delegates to the International Conference on Education in London. Three years later, she married a Harvard professor and became a member of both Wellesley's board of trustees and the Massachusetts State Board of Education. In 1892 she became the first dean of women at the University of Chicago. Throughout her life, she remained active in the Congregational Church, teaching Sunday school, and serving on the American Board of Commissioners for Foreign Missions and as president of the Woman's Home Missionary Association. She gave several women financial support to attend college, including **Charlotte Hawkins Brown**, an African American who named her own school the Palmer Memorial Institute.

BIBLIOGRAPHY

Bordin, Ruth Birgitta Anderson. *Alice Freeman Palmer: The Evolution of a New Woman.* Ann Arbor: University of Michigan Press, 1993. 0-472-10392-X, 314p. Letters, archives, and literature about women's education helped Bordin decide that Palmer represented the independent New Woman.

Linenthal, Arthur J. *Two Academic Lives: George Herbert Palmer and Alice Freeman Palmer*. Boston: Arthur J. Linenthal, 1995. 0-9626606-1-2, 630p. This scholarly, carefully documented text covers the lives and works of Palmer and her husband.

PALMER, PHOEBE (1807–1874)
Evangelist   New York, New York

Phoebe Worrall Palmer was an evangelist and author. She was born on December 18, 1807, as the fourth of ten children to an iron foundry and machine shop owner and his wife. Her father had been converted by John Wesley as a boy in England, and the family held daily family worship services. Palmer enjoyed writing as a child and composed poems by the age of 10. At 19, she married a physician and fellow Methodist who, like Palmer, had been converted at age 13. After the deaths of her two sons soon after birth, Palmer concentrated on her religion, thinking that their deaths had directed her, and she established weekly afternoon prayer in her home. After several years of these meetings, at which attendance continued to grow, she began to include men in her group, started writing, and fulfilled lecture requests. Her first book, *The Way of Holiness* (1845), about her own religious experience, sold over 24,000 copies in six years, and she wrote seven more books to popularize the perfectionist movement. In 1850, she and her husband began to travel to revivals half the year, and the same year, she helped found Five Points Mission in one of New York's poorest neighborhoods. She remained publicly neutral, however, concerning slavery and women's rights. In 1859, she wrote *Promise of the Father*, a book in which she cited biblical authority for women to be involved in church work. She and her husband then went to England to conduct tent revivals. In 1862, her husband purchased the monthly *Guide to Holiness*, and she became its editor, increasing circulation from 13,000 to 30,000. Her role in religion reveals the growth of the doctrine of perfectionism and the increased role of women as religious leaders.

BIBLIOGRAPHY
Raser, Harold E. *Phoebe Palmer, Her Life and Thought*. Lewiston, NY: Mellen, 1987. 0-88946-527-4, 389p. Raser places Palmer within a theological context and examines her rejection of John Wesley's belief that emotion was the sign of sanctification.

Wheatley, Richard. *The Life and Letters of Mrs. Phoebe Palmer*. 1881. New York: Garland, 1984. 0-8240-6432-1, 636p. Wheatley knew Palmer, and he edited her journals and letters to create a biography of her that is stylistically dated but historically relevant.

White, Charles Edward. *The Beauty of Holiness: Phoebe Palmer as Theologian, Revivalist, Feminist, and Humanitarian*. Grand Rapids, MI: F. Asbury, 1986. 0-310-46250-9, 330p. In his detailed biography, White posits that Palmer was one of John Wesley's major theological heirs.

PARKS, ROSA (1913-)
Reformer   Tuskegee, Alabama

Rosa Parks refused to ride at the back of a Montgomery, Alabama, bus, which led to the Supreme Court ruling that segregation on city buses was unconstitutional. She was born on February 4, 1913, and her mother raised her with the expectation that she would attend college at Alabama State Teachers College, which she did for a time. Parks married a barber, and they became active in the local chapter of the National Asssociation for the Advancement of Colored People (NAACP), with her husband volunteering to help free defendants in the Scottsboro cases of the 1930s. Parks became a youth advisor while working as a tailor's assistant in a department store. A white activist interested in the plight of African Americans who were denied seats on buses or whom bus drivers left standing on the curb encouraged Parks to train as a labor organizer at the Highlander Folk School; this experience prepared her to withstand the loss of her job during the bus boycott. For her sacrifice, Parks received other job offers and awards, including the Spingarn Medal, the Martin Luther King, Jr., Nonviolent Peace Prize, and election to The National Women's Hall of Fame. In 1987, she founded the Rosa and Raymond Parks Institute for Self Development in Detroit, which offers career training to youth.

BIBLIOGRAPHY
Friese, Kai. *Rosa Parks: The Movement Organizes*. Englewood Cliffs, NJ: Silver Burdett, 1990. 0-382-09927-3, 128p. This biography of Parks for young adults covers her life and her contributions to the civil rights movement.

Hull, Mary. *Rosa Parks*. New York: Chelsea House, 1994. 0-7910-1881-4, 111p. Hull's biography for young adults covers Parks's part in the fight for civil rights and includes photographs.

Parks, Rosa. *Rosa Parks: My Story*. New York: Dial, 1992. 0-8037-0673-1, 192p. With a background of the difficult times in which she lived, Parks reveals her strength and perseverance in an autobiography for young adults.

PARSONS, ELSIE CLEWS (1875-1941)
Anthropologist   New York, New York

Elsie Worthington Clews Parsons was a sociologist and anthropologist. She was born on November 27, 1875, as the oldest of three children to a banker and his wife, who was 25 years his junior. Parsons studied with private tutors and at Miss Ruel's school in New York before entering Barnard College. She continued her education at Columbia University and completed her Ph.D. in 1899. In 1900, she married a lawyer but continued her professional life as a Harley House Fellow at Barnard, also teaching a course at Columbia on the family in which students had to work with underprivileged families. From this course came her first book, *The Family*, in which she said that to be fit wives, women had to have the same opportunities to develop themselves as men. The book advocated trial marriages and caused ministers and her husband's political opponents for Congressional office to take notice. Later books also looked at age, sex, class, and locale as ways with which to control personality. Parsons refused to submit to social mores and meaningless entertainments but published two books under the pseudonym "John Main" to save her husband political embarrassment. In 1915, when Parsons went west with him, she saw Native Americans in their own environment for the first time, and she began extended field trips in the area, interviewing and living with tribes including the Zuñi, Hopi, Taos, Tewa, and Laguna. Out of this research came several books, including *Pueblo Indian Religion* (1939); an interest in how folktales revealed tribal views; and concern about Spanish influence remaining in twentieth-century Native American cultures. Her work gained her professional prestige, and she was elected president of the American Folklore Society, the American Ethnological Association, and the American Anthropological Association. She also supported these groups with financial contributions for young scholars who needed field experience, as well as helping Native American artists who lived in the field. Throughout her life, she held to her convictions, refusing to let others dictate her thinking.

BIBLIOGRAPHY

Deacon, Desley. *Elsie Clews Parsons: Inventing Modern Life.* Chicago: University of Chicago Press, 1997. 0-226-13907-7, 520p. That Deacon thoroughly researched Parsons's life is clear from the personal and professional papers quoted, but the biography of her unusual life is slightly biased in her favor.

Hare, Peter H. *A Woman's Quest for Science: Portrait of Anthropologist Elsie Clews Parsons.* Buffalo, NY: Prometheus, 1985. 0-87975-274-2, 192p. In this biography of Parsons, Hare pursues the themes of pacificism, romanticism, feminism, and anti-conventionalism.

Zumwalt, Rosemary Levy. *Wealth and Rebellion: Elsie Clews Parsons, Anthropologist and Folklorist.* Urbana: University of Illinois Press, 1992. 0-252-01909-1, 360p. Zumwalt used interviews, Parsons's personal papers, correspondence, and publications as the basis of her readable biography disclosing Parsons's many achievements.

PARTON, DOLLY (1946–)
Entertainer and Actor   Sevierville, Tennessee

Dolly Parton is an entertainer and actor. She was born on January 19, 1946, as the fourth of 11 children to a dirt farmer and his wife. She supposedly began composing her own songs before she was five, and she continued to use autobiographical material in her songs through the beginning of her career. In 1964, she left home for Nashville, Tennessee, and sang with country groups until she began performing alone in 1974. She made her television debut on the *Porter Wagoner Show* and appeared many times afterward in that medium. In 1977, she entered the pop-rock music field. Three years later, she made her film debut in *9 to 5*, a film in which she acted and for which she wrote the title song, which received both an Academy Award nomination and a Grammy Award. She wrote a music score for the film *Rhinestone* in 1984, but her best performance was in *Steel Magnolias* five years later. She owns her own production company and her own theme park, Dollywood, two indications of her astute business sense. She has won three other Grammy Awards, and the Country Music Association named her best female singer in both 1975 and 1976.

BIBLIOGRAPHY
James, Otis. *Dolly Parton*. New York: Quick Fox, 1978. 0-8256-3922-0, 95p. After a critical examination of Parton's albums, James includes photographs with his text for young adults on her life and career.

Nash, Alanna. *Dolly*. Los Angeles: Reed, 1978. 0-89169-523-0, 275p. Nash emphasizes Parton's determination and sense of self-preservation in her thorough, although undocumented, recommended biography.

Parton, Dolly. *Dolly: My Life and Other Unfinished Business*. New York: HarperCollins, 1994. 0-06-017720-9, 338p. This chatty and entertaining autobiography reveals anecdotes about the famous people that Parton has known.

Pasternak, Judith Mahoney. *Dolly*. New York: MetroBooks, 1998. 1-56799-557-8, 128p. Seemingly based on Parton's autobiography, this biography, with photographs, follows her career and her marriage.

PARTON, SARA PAYSON WILLIS. *See* **FERN, FANNY**

PAUL, ALICE (1885-1977)
Activist   Moorestown, New Jersey

Alice Paul was a political activist. She was born on January 11, 1885, into a Quaker family. After attending Swarthmore College and serving as a social worker in the College Settlement House in New York City, she entered the University of Pennsylvania for her M.A. and Ph.D. When she went to England for graduate work in 1907, she met *Emmeline Pankhurst and began supporting Pankhurst's militant tactics. In Washington, DC, in 1913, Paul and Lucy Burns organized the first major suffrage parade and established the Congressional Union for Woman Suffrage (later the National Woman's Party), with Paul as chairman. Paul wanted to secure woman suffrage through an amendment to the Constitution rather than state by state. After the Nineteenth Amendment was ratified, Paul wanted equal rights for women, and she wrote the Equal Rights Amendment (the "**Lucretia Mott**" amendment) in 1923, after receiving her law degree. Not all women agreed with her, fearing that equal rights would destroy laws already in place that protected women in the workplace. Paul, however, spent the rest of her life lobbying for the Equal Rights Amendment while also organizing the World Party for Equal Rights for Women (World Woman's Party) and successfully lobbying for references to sex equality in the preamble to the United Nations Charter and in the 1964 United States Civil Rights Act. She never wavered from her commitment to equal rights for all and was elected to The National Women's Hall of Fame.

BIBLIOGRAPHY

Gillmore, Inez Haynes. *Up Hill with Banners Flying*. 1921. Penobscot, ME: Traversity, 1964. No ISBN, 501p. In this biography, Gillmore pursues Paul's character and training.

Lunardini, Christine A. *From Equal Suffrage to Equal Rights: Alice Paul and the National Woman's Party, 1910–1928*. New York: New York University Press, 1986. 0-8147-5022-2, 230p. Lunardini used personal papers, written and oral histories, and organizational records to show the importance of Paul's barely acknowledged National Woman's Party in feminist history.

PEABODY, ELIZABETH PALMER (1804–1894)
Educator   Billerica, Massachusetts

Elizabeth Palmer Peabody was an author and educational reformer. She was born on May 16, 1804, the oldest of seven children of a dentist and his educator wife. Her father, who taught her Latin, inspired her to learn ten languages, and she had private tutoring and instruction at her mother's school. After teaching several years, Peabody and her sister opened their own school in 1820, allowing her to become independent from the family. When she became the secretary to William Ellery Channing, an early leader of Unitarianism, he exposed her to international writers and conversed with her about her reading. In 1834, she began a two-year association with Bronson Alcott in his Temple School, about which she wrote in *Record of a School* (1835). Her intellectual preparation with Channing allowed her to join **Margaret Fuller** as a female charter member of the Transcendentalist Club in 1837. Two years later, she opened a bookstore in her West Street home, a place to purchase or borrow foreign books and for intellectuals to gather. Fuller held Conversations there on Wednesday nights, and Peabody published Fuller's three German translations and three of Nathaniel Hawthorne's earliest books. For two years, she published and wrote articles for the *Dial*, the monthly publication of the Transcendental movement, while also writing for other periodicals. Peabody's main concern, however, was the true education of children. She produced 10 books and 50 articles between 1850 and 1884 in which she discussed how education should proceed. She also organized the first kindergarten in the United States based on Friedrich Froebel's German model. Late in life, she became concerned about the Native Americans, and gave much money to **Sarah Winnemucca** and the Piutes. Peabody's most important contribution was her ability to recognize and expose the attributes of others, including Channing, Alcott, Hawthorne, and Froebel.

BIBLIOGRAPHY

Peabody, Elizabeth Palmer. *Letters of Elizabeth Palmer Peabody, American Renaissance Woman*. Ed. Bruce A. Ronda. Middletown, CT: Wesleyan University Press, 1984. 0-8195-5093-0, 477p. Ronda wanted to give insight into Peabody's personality and to illuminate the movements with which she was involved, and his editing and commentary on this collection of letters achieve his goal.

Tharp, Louise Hall. *The Peabody Sisters of Salem*. 1950. Boston: Little, Brown, 1988. 0–316–83920–5, 372p. In this carefully researched and documented collective biography suitable for young adults, based on letters and diaries, Tharp presents Peabody as "grandmother of Boston."

PERKINS, FRANCES (1882–1965)
Government Official   Boston, Massachusetts

Frances Perkins was the first woman to serve in a cabinet post for the federal government. She was born Fannie Coralie on April 10, 1882, the older of two daughters of a wholesale-retail stationer and his wife. She attended Worcester Classical High School and Mount Holyoke College, where she majored in chemistry and physics. As a senior, she heard **Florence Kelley** speak and realized that women could work to improve welfare for the needy. She taught several years, and in Chicago spent free time at Hull-House to help workers who had been cheated collect wages. In Philadelphia, she served as general secretary of the Research and Protective Association and joined the Socialist Party. She surveyed Hell's Kitchen in preparation for her M.A. from Columbia in 1910, and the same year, she became secretary of the New York Consumers' League, where she exposed sweatshop conditions in bakeries and lobbied for industrial reform. In 1912, she worked for passage of the 50-hour work week, and with the Committee on Safety of the City of New York, exposed employers who did not protect their workers. When she married in 1913, she kept her maiden name and legally changed her first name to Frances. Perkins was appointed to the New York State Industrial Commission, becoming the highest paid state employee in the nation. After becoming chair of the Industrial Board, she rose to commissioner for the state of New York, where she administered the Workmen's Compensation Act. When Franklin Roosevelt was elected president, he appointed her secretary of labor, and she worked on the New Deal, advocating a minimum wage and a maximum work week, encouraging a limit on employment of children under 16, creating the Civilian Conservation Corps, and supporting unemployment compensation. In the late 1930s, she strengthened the Bureau of Labor Statistics. Although she resigned when Roosevelt died, Harry S. Truman asked her to become a Civil Service commissioner. When she left government in 1953, she continued to lecture on problems in labor and industry until her death. She has been elected to The National Women's Hall of Fame.

BIBLIOGRAPHY
Martin, George Whitney. *Madam Secretary, Frances Perkins*. Boston: Houghton Mifflin, 1976. 0–395–24293–2, 589p. Martin's biography, based on Perkins's oral history and available papers, reveals her inestimable importance for American workers.

Mohr, Lillian Holmen. *Frances Perkins, That Woman in FDR's Cabinet!* Croton-on-Hudson, NY: North River Press, 1979. 0–88427–010–X, 328p. Mohr's readable biography discusses Perkins's private and personal life.

Severn, Bill. *Frances Perkins: A Member of the Cabinet.* New York: Hawthorn, 1976. 0-8015-2816-X, 256p. In a biography suitable for young adults, Severn briefly discusses Perkins's childhood and personal life before focusing on her public life.

PESOTTA, ROSE (1896–1965)
Reformer and Labor Leader   Derazhnya, Ukraine

Rose Pesotta was a labor organizer and leader. She was born on November 20, 1896, one of eight children of a Jewish grain merchant and his wife. At home she learned Hebrew and Russian before attending a private school. Instead of marrying at 17 as her parents wished, she went to New York, where her sister was already working in a shirtwaist factory, and took a similar job. She joined Local 25 of the International Ladies' Garment Workers' Union (ILGWU), and within two years helped the union set up its first education department. In five years, she rose to membership on the executive board. In 1922, she attended the Bryn Mawr Summer School for Women Workers and then studied at Brookwood Labor College. In the late 1920s, she helped the ILGWU organize the women garment workers and became a paid staff member in 1933, going to Los Angeles to organize workers. She followed this success by organizing workers in other cities, and her popularity with the workers earned her autonomy within the ILGWU. However, as the only woman on the General Executive Board, she felt isolated, and in 1942 returned to her own shop to operate a sewing machine. She complained at the next convention about the governing board having only one woman when its membership was 85 percent female. Her own contribution, however, left the union stronger than when she entered it.

BIBLIOGRAPHY
Leeder, Elaine J. *The Gentle General: Rose Pesotta, Anarchist and Labor Organizer.* Albany: State University of New York Press, 1993. 0-7914-1671-2, 212p. Leeder explores Pesotta's life in an attempt to understand her and her background.
Pesotta, Rose. *Bread upon the Waters.* 1944. Ithaca, NY: ILR Press, 1987. 0-87546-127-1, 435p. Pesotta's lively autobiography covers her career involvement in the labor movement.

PETRY, ANN (1908–1997)
Author   Old Saybrook, Connecticut

African American Ann Lane Petry trained as a pharmacist but became a novelist. She was born on October 12, 1908, into an educated family to the only African American pharmacist in town and his businesswoman wife. Petry graduated from the Connecticut College of Pharmacy in 1931 and began working in her father's drugstore. After her marriage, however, she moved to New York and looked for a job in journalism. While working for the New York Foundation, a group studying the effects of segregation on African American children, she gained insights about their plight. She included these as well as other experiences as a Harlem reporter in

her first book, *The Street* (1946), which won her a Houghton Mifflin Literary
Fellowship Award. When later adult books did not receive the same favorable
reviews, she began writing children's books. She won a distinguished writer award
in 1994 and was inducted into the Connecticut Women's Hall of Fame that same
year. She also received several honorary degrees.

BIBLIOGRAPHY

Ervin, Hazel Arnett. *Ann Petry: A Bio-Bibliography*. New York: Hall, 1993.
0-8161-7278-1, 115p. Ervin includes a brief biographical essay on Petry, who is
considered to have influenced Toni Morrison and Gloria Naylor, along with a
chronological bibliography of her works.
Holladay, Hilary. *Ann Petry*. New York: Twayne, 1996. 0-8057-7842-X, 149p. This
carefully researched and documented critical biography examines Petry's literary
career.

PHILLIPS, LENA MADESIN (1881–1955)
Attorney   Nicholasville, Kentucky

Lena Madesin Phillips founded the National and International Federations of
Business and Professional Women's Clubs. She was born on September 15, 1881,
the only child of a county judge and his second wife, a musician. Phillips also had
four half-siblings. Her mother taught her music, and desiring to become a concert
pianist, Phillips first attended Woman's College of Baltimore (later Goucher
College) and then transferred to the Peabody Conservatory of Music. A fall
damaged nerves in her arm, however, and ended hopes of a career as a performer.
Instead she taught music for several years before having a nervous breakdown in
1915. She recovered and entered the University of Kentucky Law School,
receiving honors as the first woman graduate in 1917. As she began her law
practice, she agreed to do a national survey of business and professional women in
1918, and she became the executive secretary of the YWCA's National Business
Women's Committee. The next year, she founded the National Federation of
Business and Professional Women's Clubs (NFBPWC), established its executive
offices as its first executive secretary, and began publishing the journal *Independent
Woman*. In 1922, she received a master's degree in law from New York University
Law School and began living with Marjory Lacey-Baker, her life companion.
Although she set up her own practice, she spent more time with the NFBPWC,
trying to get it to support child labor laws, equal pay for women, and equal rights.
In 1928, she went to Europe to establish an international federation, and in 1930
was elected its president. Phillips also contributed frequently to *Independent
Woman* and gave up her law practice to be associate editor of *Pictorial Review*. She
ran unsuccessfully for political office several times. In 1955, when on her way to
Lebanon to study the organization of professional women in the Middle East, she
died of a perforated ulcer.

BIBLIOGRAPHY
Sergio, Lisa. *A Measure Filled: The Life of Lena Madesin Phillips*. New York: Luce, 1972.
    No ISBN, 246. Sergio knew and worked with Phillips, and this undocumented
    biography is based on her unpublished papers.

PICKFORD, MARY (1893–1979)
Actor   Toronto, Canada

Mary Pickford was an actor often called "America's Sweetheart"; she was also a
businesswoman. Born Gladys Smith on April 8, 1893, she was one of three
children to an alcoholic father who died when she was four, and his wife. Pickford
began acting in melodramas at age six and supported the family. In 1909, she began
working in movies, with her first big hit in 1910, *The Little Teacher*. In her roles,
"Little Mary" moved only when appropriate, and her stillness attracted the
viewers' eyes. By 1916, she was earning $10,000 a week plus her profits. Three
years later, she co-founded United Artists with Douglas Fairbanks, D. W. Griffith,
and Charlie Chaplin. In 1929, she acted in her first talking film, *Coquette*, for
which she won an Academy Award. The same year, in answer to public requests
for "King Doug and Queen Mary," she starred with her husband, Douglas
Fairbanks, in *The Taming of the Shrew*, but the movie was a failure. Her
competition from other actresses was much stronger in these types of roles, and
she decided that *Secrets* would be her last film. She made a vaudeville appearance,
broadcast frequently on the radio, and wrote two books in the 1930s. She also
divorced and remarried. As the first and perhaps the only female movie mogul, she
retained her business sense by joining Chaplin to buy United Artists, and they
later sold the studio for a large profit. Pickford received a special Academy Award
in 1976 for her contribution to the artistry of the film industry.

BIBLIOGRAPHY
Carey, Gary. *Doug and Mary: A Biography of Douglas Fairbanks and Mary Pickford*. New
    York: Dutton, 1977. 0–525–09512–8, 248p. In this dual biography, focusing on
    Pickford and her husband Douglas Fairbanks from 1916 to 1933, Carey examines
    their influence on the movie industry and on the American public.
Eyman, Scott. *Mary Pickford, America's Sweetheart*. New York: Donald I. Fine, 1990.
    1–55611–147–9, 342p. Using interviews between Pickford and her contemporaries,
    Eyman posits that she was 70 years ahead of her time as a Hollywood icon.
Herndon, Booton. *Mary Pickford and Douglas Fairbanks: The Most Popular Couple the
    World Has Ever Known*. New York: Norton, 1977. 0–393–07508–7, 324p. In this
    recommended biography of Pickford and Douglas Fairbanks, Herndon carefully
    documents his thorough research to reveal Pickford's influence.
Whitfield, Eileen. *Pickford: The Woman Who Made Hollywood*. Lexington: University
    Press of Kentucky, 1997. 0–8131–2045–4, 441p. In a definitive biography, Whitfield
    recounts Pickford's early career and describes the period in which she lived to show
    the acclaim of her adoring public.
Windeler, Robert. *Sweetheart: The Story of Mary Pickford*. New York: Praeger, 1974.
    0–275–51410–5, 226p. This researched and recommended biography of Pickford

examines her life and reveals that for 20 years she was one of the best known women in the world.

PICOTTE, SUSAN LA FLESCHE. *See* LA FLESCHE (PICOTTE), SUSAN

PINCKNEY, ELIZA (1722–1793)
Horticulturist and Businesswoman   **Antigua, West Indies**

Eliza Pinckney was a plantation manager who first successfully cultivated indigo in the United States. She was born Eliza Lucas on December 28, 1722, in Antigua, as the oldest of four children to a British army officer stationed on the island and his wife. To help his ill wife, her father brought her to South Carolina to live on a plantation he had inherited. When he had to return to Antigua during the War of Jenkins' Ear between Spain and England, he left the plantation in the care of Pinckney, who had spent several years studying in England, where she enjoyed music, read widely, and learned French. She tutored her sisters, taught two African American girl slaves to read, and in 1741 sighted a comet that Sir Isaac Newton had predicted. At her father's suggestion, Pinckney tried growing ginger, cotton, indigo, and alfalfa on the plantation but concentrated on indigo, a crop that the British disliked buying from French islands. She experimented with the proper season to grow the crop and how to produce the dye from freshly cut plants. The first dyemaker sent to the plantation by her father sabotaged the endeavor because he feared competition, but a second helped her succeed. In 1744, she exported six pounds of dye from her plantation, and seeds from this crop went to other planters. Two years later, 40,000 pounds went to England, and the next year, the planters exported over 100,000 pounds. The indigo trade supported the economy of South Carolina until the American Revolution severed it. In 1744, Pinckney married, and on her own plantation she cultured silkworms and privately manufactured silk. Her husband became a commissioner to London, and Pinckney enjoyed their social life until war with France began. Her sons remained in England for their education, but her husband died, and she managed his seven landholdings. When she died, President Washington requested to serve as one of her pallbearers.

BIBLIOGRAPHY

Pinckney, Eliza Lucas. *The Letterbook of Eliza Lucas Pinckney*. 1972. Ed. Elise Pinckney. Columbia: University of South Carolina Press, 1997. 1–57003–186–X, 195p. This valuable view of Pinckney's daily life and letters includes a documented introduction with an overview of her life and notes on the letterbook.

Williams, Frances Leigh. *Plantation Patriot: A Biography of Eliza Lucas Pinckney*. New York: Harcourt, Brace, 1967. No ISBN, 181p. This fictional biography of Pinckney, based on contemporary sources, reveals her life and describes the plantation society in which she lived.

PINKHAM, LYDIA (1819–1883)
Businesswoman   Lynn, Massachusetts

Lydia Estes Pinkham was a patent-medicine proprietor. She was born on February 9, 1819, as the tenth of 12 children to a cordwainer and farmer and his second wife. Her parents were excluded from the Quakers in a conflict over slavery, and after her graduation from Lynn Academy, Pinkham helped organize the Freeman's Institute, a place where people could openly discuss all social issues. Abolition was a major concern, and those who attended included **Abby Kelley Foster**, **Sarah Grimké**, and **Angelina Grimké Weld**. Other causes Pinkham supported included temperance, Grahamism, and phrenology. After teaching school for a few years, Pinkham married, and for 30 years she tried to support her family of five according to her husband's wishes, but they became destitute during the panic of 1873. Pinkham's sons suggested that she bottle one of her botanical home remedies for sale. Adapted from John King's *The American Dispensatory*, her remedy for female reproductive system problems contained unicorn root and pleurisy root, and many of her neighbors had used it. Pinkham added 18 percent alcohol to the mixture as a solvent and preservative, selling the first batch in 1875. Her sons marketed the product by distributing flyers and advertising in the *Boston Herald*. Pinkham's face graced the label, and her dignified expression made her one of the best-known American females in the nineteenth century. Her customers, including temperance leaders, loved the product and endorsed it without reserve. Pinkham let her sons sell the product while she created the advertising copy, using sayings such as "Only a woman can understand a woman's ills," and supervised its production. She answered every letter by suggesting additional medicinal cures and advocating exercise, careful diet, and cleanliness as beneficial to her Vegetable Compound. A tasteful pamphlet about sex and reproduction which she wrote also received wide sales. After her death, her daughters continued the advice department. Her company, incorporated shortly before her death in 1883, grossed nearly $300,000 each year, and even with muckrakers' exposure of patent medicines in the early 1900s, it continued to grow through the 1920s.

BIBLIOGRAPHY
Stage, Sarah. *Female Complaints: Lydia Pinkham and the Business of Women's Medicine*. New York: Norton, 1979. 0–393–01178–X, 304p. Not only a biography of Pinkham but also a study of patent medicine and doctors, the well-documented text, based on the Pinkham family papers, reveals an independent woman.

Washburn, Robert Collyer. *The Life and Times of Lydia E. Pinkham*. 1931. New York: Arno Press, 1976. 0–405–08055–7, 221p. Washburn recounts Pinkham's achievements in establishing the basis for modern advertising in a well-researched and documented biography.

PLATH, SYLVIA (1932–1963)
Poet   Boston, Massachusetts

Sylvia Plath was a poet and author. She was born on October 27, 1932, as the older of two children to a German entomologist and a former student 21 years his junior. Her father died when Plath was eight, and she spent the rest of her life dealing with this loss. Plath, always a disciplined student, determined to do well, and after graduating from high school, she received a scholarship from Olive Higgins Prouty (a novelist) to Smith College. While working the summer of 1953 as an intern for *Mademoiselle* magazine in New York, she became severely depressed and had to undergo electroshock treatments at her patron's expense. She graduated in 1955 and received a Fulbright fellowship to Cambridge University in England. There she met Ted Hughes, a working-class poet, and married him the next year when they imagined themselves as dedicated to poetry and complementary to each other in their backgrounds and tastes. They returned to the United States after she graduated but went back to London in 1960. Plath published her first book of poems, *The Colossus*, which critics liked, and, in 1961 received a grant to work on her novel, *The Bell Jar*, recalling her breakdown in 1953. After her second child was born in 1962, she discovered that Hughes was having an affair. She asked for a divorce, and unexpectedly, he agreed. During the next few months, she finished a remarkable amount of work, delving into her themes concerning opposites of various kinds. Her poems showed a desire to escape from the past, for a rebirth, and ultimately, to transcend the ego itself. In 1963, six months after her suicide, 10 poems appeared in *Encounter* magazine and elicited a strong positive response. Other work was also published posthumously. Women of her era considered her a voice of liberation, but her poetry speaks to other times and needs as well.

BIBLIOGRAPHY

Alexander, Paul. *Rough Magic: A Biography of Sylvia Plath*. New York: Viking, 1991. 0-670-81812-7, 402p. Alexander refused to ask Plath's executor, Olwyn Hughes, for permission to quote directly from her work, so he paraphrased much of the material in his detailed look at Plath's early life and her publications.

Bundtzen, Lynda K. *Plath's Incarnations: Woman and the Creative Process*. Ann Arbor: University of Michigan Press, 1983. 0-472-10033-5, 284p. Bundtzen places Plath in the context of women who have had to face the difficulties of being female before they developed their writing careers. Hamilton Prize in the Women and Culture Series of the University of Michigan Press.

Malcolm, Janet. *The Silent Woman: Sylvia Plath and Ted Hughes*. New York: Knopf, 1994. 0-679-43158-6, 207p. In a readable and carefully researched detective biography, Malcolm uses letters, fiction, journals, and poems, in tracing Plath's life and suggests that Plath's former husband and his sister deliberately misplaced her journals after her death.

Stevenson, Anne. *Bitter Fame: A Life of Sylvia Plath*. Boston: Houghton Mifflin, 1989. 0-395-45374-7, 413p. In her critical biography, Stevenson opines that Plath decided her own fate and was not the victim of her husband's supposed infidelities.

Wagner-Martin, Linda. *Sylvia Plath: A Biography*. New York: Simon and Schuster, 1987. 0–671–60404–X, 282p. Wagner-Martin has thoroughly researched Plath's life but does not quote her work since her executor, Olwyn Hughes, refused to grant permission.

POCAHONTAS (d. 1617)
Princess   Tidewater, Virginia

Pocahontas was a Native American woman who served as a mediator between the English settlers and her Powhatan tribe. She was born as Matoaka around 1595, the daughter of Powhatan, the great chief of the Tidewater, Virginia, area. She first appears in recorded history when she intervened with her father for Captain John Smith, founder of the new colony of Jamestown, on December 30, 1607. She kept the tribe from killing Smith, and after Smith returned to Jamestown, the tribe began sending food via Pocahontas. In 1609, she probably warned Smith that Powhatan was planning an attack. Several years later, after Smith had returned to England, Samuel Argall lured Pocahontas aboard his ship, saying that he would take her to see her Jamestown friends, but held her hostage in return for release of English prisoners and goods. Jamestown received her kindly and treated her as a guest. While in the town, Pocahontas learned English ways, and in 1613, she met John Rolfe, an older widower who wanted to marry her. He requested her hand from the marshal of Virginia, Sir Thomas Dale, by saying that he would make a Christian of her. In 1614, she was baptized Rebecca and married to Rolfe. After her father gave them land, the English and the Native Americans lived peacefully for a time. Two years later, Pocahontas and her husband took their son to England, and she was presented to King James I and Queen Anne in 1617. The next spring, when Rolfe had to return to Virginia, Pocahontas, who had wanted to remain in England, died on shipboard while waiting for favorable winds to allow their departure. Through the years, many legends about her contributions have arisen, but she seems to have helped both her own people and the colonists while alive.

BIBLIOGRAPHY

Holler, Anne. *Pocahontas: Powhatan Peacemaker*. New York: Chelsea House, 1993. 0–7910–1705–2, 103p. Holler's biography for young adults is a researched overview of Pocahontas and the times in which she lived.
Mossiker, Frances. *Pocahontas: The Life and the Legend*. 1976. New York: Da Capo Press, 1996. 0–306–80699–1, 383p.   This carefully researched, documented, and recommended scholarly biography of Pocahontas shows her relationships to both her tribe and to the settlers.
Woodward, Grace Steele. *Pocahontas*. Norman: University of Oklahoma Press, 1969. No ISBN, 227p.   Woodward's carefully researched and readable biography of Pocahontas reveals what is known about her life and the times in which she lived.

PONCE, MARY HELEN (1938-)
Author   San Fernando Valley, California

Latina American Mary Helen Ponce is a writer who investigates everyday experiences and universalizes them. She was born on January 24, 1938, as the youngest of 10 children in a first- and second-generation family of Mexican Americans who came to Southern California in the 1940s. Her father never passed fourth grade, but he avidly read the newspaper every day, and as a young girl, she never realized that her family was poor. She earned a B.A. and an M.A. from California State University at Northridge, starting college after her son had entered first grade, and another M.A. from the University of California at Los Angeles. The Chicano movement in the early 1970s showed her that people she knew had valuable experiences, but the only role model she had for women writing was her sister. In her work, including *Hoyt Street: An Autobiography*, Ponce explores bilingualism and biculturalism as she recreates the lives of those like her family who came to California in the 1940s and 1950s. She teaches Chicano studies and creative writing at the University of Southern California in both Los Angeles and Santa Barbara.

BIBLIOGRAPHY
Ponce, Mary Helen. *Hoyt Street: An Autobiography*. Albuquerque: University of New Mexico Press, 1993. 0-8263-1446-5, 338p. In this autobiography, Ponce describes her happy Catholic Latina childhood in Pacoima, California (23 miles northeast of Los Angeles), a disreputable area that she remembers with fondness.

PONSELLE, ROSA (1897-1981)
Opera Singer   Meriden, Connecticut

Rosa Ponselle was an opera singer known for her vocal range and expression. She was born Rosa Melba Ponzillo on January 22, 1897, the daughter of a baker and grocery-store owner who had emigrated from Naples and his musician wife. As a child listening to her mother sing, Ponselle often stood near the window, pretending that the windowsill was a piano, to accompany her own songs. At 10, she had become a church soloist, and her piano training prepared her to play for silent movies while still a teenager. At 16, she began singing in vaudeville, performing with her sister. Although she had never taken voice lessons, she made her first operatic appearance at the Metropolitan Opera in New York City after Enrico Caruso heard her, perhaps in vaudeville, in the role of Leonora in Giuseppe Verdi's *La Forza del Destino*. She began her association with her voice coach, Romano Romani, who remained with her throughout her career. Ponselle remained at the Met for 19 seasons and sang 22 different dramatic and coloratura roles, with appearances in London and Florence before retiring from the stage in 1937. She made many recordings, and in the 1950s, she made additional private recordings. She then taught and served as artistic director for the Civic Opera of Baltimore, where she encouraged young singers. As one of the greatest operatic talents to have been born in America, her dramatic soprano moved effortlessly from the low notes of a contralto to a dazzling high C. She had coloratura flexibility, control over volume and tone, and ability to interpret her roles with emotion.

BIBLIOGRAPHY
Aloi, Enrico. *Rosa Ponselle: A Pictorial History.* New York: Vantage, 1996. No ISBN, 171p. Following a biographical essay suitable for young adults, Aloi has included photographs of Ponselle during her career, many of them autographed, and copies of concert programs.
Drake, James A. *Rosa Ponselle: A Centenary Biography.* Portland, OR: Amadeus, 1997. 1-57467-019-0, 494p. Drake interviewed Ponselle, and in this recommended biography, he follows each chapter of interviews with a section including remarks from her letters and from reviewers about her performances.
Phillips-Matz, Mary Jane. *Rosa Ponselle: American Diva.* Boston: Northeastern University Press, 1997. 1-55553-317-5, 357p. Since Phillips-Matz focuses on details of Ponselle's career, Drake's biography gives more insight into Ponselle, the private woman.
Ponselle, Rosa. *Ponselle: A Singer's Life.* Garden City, NY: Doubleday, 1982. 0-385-15641-3, 328p. Ponselle relates her childhood and career with much information about the opera world and her colleagues.

PORTER, KATHERINE ANNE (1890–1980)
Author   Indian Creek, Texas

Katherine Anne Porter was an author. She was born Katherine Anne Maria Veronica Callista Russel Porter on May 15, 1890, the fourth of five children in a family of storytellers. Her mother died when she was two, and her grandmother raised the children. Porter became interested in music, dance, and theater during her education in private and convent schools. She then married at 16, worked on the *Rocky Mountain News* in Denver during World War I, and divorced at 19. The next year, she went to Mexico to study the renascence of Mexican art, but the Obregon Revolution and her revolutionary, artist, and composer friends stimulated her writing instead of her art. In 1923, at the age of 33, she sold her first story, "Maria Concepcion," to *Century* magazine. Later, she worked as a ghostwriter and joined Boston demonstrations in support of Sacco and Vanzetti. In the years between 1948 and 1961, she was writer in residence or a member of the faculty of English at several universities. In 1962, her award-winning novel, *Ship of Fools*, won her popular and financial success, becoming a Book-of-the-Month Club selection and scoring an immediate $500,000 movie sale. She served as vice president of the National Institute of Arts and Letters, and in 1966 was elected to its 50-member "inner circle," the American Academy of Arts and Letters. Other awards included the first annual gold medal of the Society of the Libraries of New York University, an O. Henry Memorial Award, the Emerson-Thoreau Bronze Medal for Literature from the American Academy of Arts and Sciences, a Pulitzer

Prize, two National Book Awards, a gold medal of the National Institute of Arts and Letters, and several honorary degrees.

BIBLIOGRAPHY

Givner, Joan. *Katherine Anne Porter: A Life*. 1982. Athens: University of Georgia Press, 1991. 0–8203–1348–3, 576p. Based on Porter's papers, Givner posits in her carefully researched biography that Porter's reputation rests on three collections of novellas and short stories.

Stout, Janis P. *Katherine Anne Porter: A Sense of the Times*. Charlottesville: University Press of Virginia, 1995. 0–8139–1568–6, 381p. Stout's carefully researched and balanced scholarly biography based on Porter's letters examines her ideas on pacifism, feminism, communism, and the freedom of expression necessary for an artist.

Tanner, James T. F. *The Texas Legacy of Katherine Anne Porter*. Denton: University of North Texas Press, 1991. 0–929398–22–X, 237p. Tanner's critical study of Porter's relationship to Texas, researched and documented, offers an examination of some of her works in terms of their Texas background.

Walsh, Thomas F. *Katherine Anne Porter and Mexico: The Illusion of Eden*. Austin: University of Texas Press, 1992. 0–292–74311–4, 269p. After an interview with Porter and research in her Mexican friend Mary Louise Doherty's papers, Walsh examines Porter's life in Mexico.

POST, MARJORIE MERRIWEATHER (1887–1973)
Philanthropist   **Springfield, Illinois**

Marjorie Merriweather Post was a philanthropist and businesswoman. She was born on March 15, 1887, the only child of Charles William Post, founder of Postum Cereal Company, and his wife. She attended public schools and Mount Vernon Seminary, where she learned business management and techniques. Post's father knew that she would inherit his business, so he trained her for the position. She frequented his business meetings, toured his factories, and answered his questions about what she had learned. After she married and had a family, her father committed suicide, and she took over the business. Her lawyer husband represented her on the company board since women were not welcome, but consulted her about major decisions. After she divorced her first husband, she married the stockbroker E. F. Hutton. After he became chairman of the board, she convinced the board to purchase the food freezing equipment of Clarence Birdseye, against his wishes. With its name changed to General Foods Corporation, the company grew into the largest food industry in the United States. Her husband further opposed her interest in charity, and she divorced him. Her third husband became the ambassador to the Soviet Union, and after enjoying the opportunity to entertain abroad, she divorced him and again remarried. Throughout her life, Post contributed to causes, making certain that her money helped other people. During World War I, she provided Red Cross funds to build, equip, and run a 2,000-bed hospital in Savenay, France. In 1929, she provided funds for a New York City Salvation Army food kitchen and was known as "Lady

Bountiful of Hell's Kitchen." She became the principal benefactor of Mount Vernon College and helped build a service center for the Boy Scouts in Washington, DC. She also contributed generously to the building of the John F. Kennedy Center for the Performing Arts and to the National Symphony Orchestra.

BIBLIOGRAPHY

Rubin, Nancy. *American Empress: The Life and Times of Marjorie Merriweather Post.* New York: Villard, 1995. 0-679-41347-2, 445p. Rubin's balanced biography follows Post as she learned the family business from her father and became a philanthropist who quietly helped those in need.

Wright, William. *Heiress: The Rich Life of Marjorie Merriweather.* New York: Simon and Schuster, 1978. 0-915220-36-9, 256p. This popular biography of Post reveals a strong woman who got what she wanted but who also gave plenty of it away.

POWELL, MAUD (1867–1920)
Violinist   Peru, Illinois

Maud Powell was a violinist with large tone and breadth of style. She was born on August 22, 1867, the older of two children of a superintendent of schools and his Hungarian immigrant wife, an accomplished musician. Powell's mother taught her music when she showed an aptitude at age four, and at eight, Powell played Mozart sonata duets on the violin with her mother. On Saturdays, she traveled 40 miles to Chicago to study both violin and piano, and while still a child, went on a six-week tour of the Midwest with the Chicago Ladies' Quartet. When she was 12, she went to Europe to study, using funds contributed by her townspeople. In 1833, she went to London from Paris to play in the provinces and before the royal family. She also met Joseph Joachim, and he invited her to study at the Royal High School of Music in Berlin. She later said that the French taught her to become an artist and that the Germans taught her to be a musician. She made her debut with the Berlin Philharmonic in 1885 and returned to make her American debut with the New York Philharmonic the same year. At 17, she was probably the only female professional concert violinist. Later, she was the first violinist to record with the Victor Talking Machine Company. She played in many cities, and in 1894 formed the Maud Powell String Quartet to perform chamber music. After it disbanded in 1898, she returned to Europe for touring, revealing her interest in contemporary music through program choices such as Camille Saint-Saëns, Harry Rowe Shelley, Antonin Dvorák, Max Bruch, and Jean Sibelius. At first, she played on a Joseph Guarnerius instrument, but in 1907, she shifted to a large-model Giovanni Battista Guadagnini. She felt that a musician needed musical surroundings as well as talent, and in later years, she took her music to colleges and small towns. Powell entertained troops during World War I with performances and monologues about the music she played, and served in the Music Service of America to provide institutions with phonographs and records. She also spent time trying to encourage young musicians with their careers. Before performances, however, she suffered acute nervousness, a problem that she never overcame.

BIBLIOGRAPHY

Shaffer, Karen A., and Neva Garner Greenwood. *Maud Powell, Pioneer American Violinist*. Ames: Iowa State University Press, 1988. 0-8138-0989-4, 530p. This well-researched, adulatory biography of Powell dwells on her importance musically.

PRICE, (MARY) LEONTYNE (1927-)
Opera Singer   Laurel, Mississippi

African American Leontyne Price has been called *la diva di tutte le dive* (the diva of divas) and *la prima donna assoluta* (the best of the prima donnas) in her career as an international opera singer. She was born on February 10, 1927, as one of two children to a laborer and a midwife. She started studying piano when only three and one-half and sang in her Methodist preacher grandfather's churches as a girl. Although she decided to become a musician after hearing **Marian Anderson** in 1936, not until she graduated from Central State College in Ohio did she decide to become a singer. Financial aid from a friend helped support her during four years at New York's Juilliard School of Music, where her performance in Verdi's *Falstaff* won her the attention of Virgil Thomson, who was preparing an opera for an all–African American cast. He selected her to sing *Porgy and Bess* throughout Europe during 1954. The same year, she made her New York debut at Town Hall, and the following year, she sang on television in Puccini's *Tosca* and three other operas. She made debuts in Chicago, London, Verona, and Vienna before coming to the Metropolitan Opera in 1961, where she received 42 minutes of cheering from the audience after her performance in Verdi's *Il Trovatore*. She won more than 20 Grammy Awards for her recordings and had spent more than 30 years on stage when she concluded her career as Aïda in a 1985 Metropolitan Opera production. She received the Presidential Medal of Freedom and the National Medal of the Arts.

BIBLIOGRAPHY

Lyon, Hugh Lee. *Leontyne Price: Highlights of a Prima Donna*. New York: Vantage, 1972. 0-533-00606-6, 218p. Lyon used newspapers, magazine articles, and interviews in his readable, thorough, and recommended biography of Price and her development as an opera singer.

$\mathscr{R}$

RAINER, YVONNE (1934-)
Filmmaker
San Francisco, California

Yvonne Rainer has been a director, screenwriter, and choreographer. She was born in 1934 and began studying modern dance in 1957. Three years later she began choreographing her own pieces, and in 1962, she was a co-founder of the Judson Dance Theater in New York with dancers performing her works in the United States and in Europe. In 1968, she began to integrate short films into dance pieces and, the next year, made her Broadway debut using this technique. In 1975, she turned exclusively to avant-garde filmmaking and appeared in Rosa Von Praunheim's *Underground and Emigrants*. Her first film released to general theaters was *The Man Who Envied Women* in 1985. Her films try to break Hollywood illusions by relying on verbal language and emphasizing relationships of fluctuating power, especially between the sexes. Rainer uses Bertolt Brecht's techniques to create distance, including voice-overs and documentary combined with acting. *Privilege* (1990) focuses on a group of women facing menopause, while *Fast Trip, Long Drop* (1993) profiles an HIV-positive activist during the AIDS crisis. In 1996, Rainer directed *Murder and Murder*, a film examining an affair between two older women. Among her awards are the **Maya Deren** Award, the Sundance Film Festival Filmmaker's Trophy, and a MacArthur Foundation award.

BIBLIOGRAPHY
Green, Shelley. *Radical Juxtaposition: The Films of Yvonne Rainer*. Metuchen, NJ: Scarecrow, 1994. 0-8108-2863-4, 144p. Green's carefully researched and documented critical study of Rainer's films includes interviews with her.

Rainer, Yvonne. *The Films of Yvonne Rainer*. Bloomington: Indiana University Press, 1989. 0–253–34906–0, 225p. This researched and documented look at Rainer's films and life includes essays by critics, an interview with Rainer, and excerpts from film scripts.

RAINEY, MA (1886–1939)
Entertainer   Columbus, Georgia

Ma Rainey was the first great African American professional blues artist, the "mother of the blues." Born Gertrude Malissa Pridgett on April 26, 1886, she was the second of five children. At 14, she sang in a review at the Springer Opera House in Columbus. She also performed in southern minstrel shows before marrying William "Pa" Rainey in 1904 and joining him in performance. She soon starred in her own show although she briefly worked with **Bessie Smith**. In 1923, she separated from her husband, and her recordings began to gain national recognition, often backed by Louis Armstrong. She also toured with her arranger and band director, Thomas A. Dorsey, the composer whose songs **Mahalia Jackson** often sang. After Rainey recorded more than 90 songs, deaths in her family brought her back to Columbus, where she purchased and managed theaters. When she died at 53, no one reported it, but in the 1940s, blues poets and musicians began to acknowledge her enormous contribution to their craft.

BIBLIOGRAPHY
Lieb, Sandra R. *Mother of the Blues: A Study of Ma Rainey*. Amherst: University of Massachusetts Press, 1981. 0–87023–334–3, 226p. Using available facts about Rainey's life and career, Lieb's scholarly and readable biographical study also examines her style.
Stewart-Baxter, Derrick. *Ma Rainey and the Classic Blues Singers*. New York: Stein and Day, 1970. 0–8128–1317–0, 112p. Stewart-Baxter includes other blues singers in his carefully researched study of Rainey.

RANKIN, JEANNETTE (1880–1973)
Congresswoman   Missoula, Montana

Jeanette Pickering Rankin was the first woman to be elected to Congress, and the only member of Congress to vote against entering both world wars. She was born on June 11, 1880, as the oldest of seven children to a rancher and lumber merchant and his teacher wife. Rankin attended public schools before graduating from the University of Montana in 1902 with a B.S. in biology. She taught briefly, but after her father's death in 1904 and her mother's withdrawal, she had to care for the family. She then attended both the New York School of Philanthropy and the University of Washington before campaigning for woman suffrage. After deciding that peace and suffrage should go together, she returned to Montana to urge the state legislature to give women the vote and decided to run for Congress. Her platform called for woman suffrage, tariff revision, prohibition, child labor laws, and peace. She won, and in 1917, four days after becoming a congresswoman, she voted against entering World War I. She continued lobbying for the same causes, and in the 1920s joined the National Council for the Prevention of War. After 10 years, she again ran for Congress and won. After she voted against intervention in World War II, she lost her seat, and traveled abroad to expound her pacifist views. She subsequently opposed the Cold War, American involvement with Korea, and the Vietnam War, leading the Jeannette Rankin Brigade demonstration against that war on January 15, 1968. She was later elected to The National Women's Hall of Fame.

BIBLIOGRAPHY

Davidson, Sue. *A Heart in Politics: Jeannette Rankin and Patsy T. Mink.* Seattle: Seal Press, 1994. 1-87806-753-2, 183p. Davidson's collective undocumented biography of Rankin for young adults notes her achievements.

Giles, Kevin S. *Flight of the Dove: The Story of Jeannette Rankin.* Beaverton, OR: Touchstone, 1980. 0-918688-03-5, 256p. Giles's biography of Rankin explores her career.

Josephson, Hannah. *Jeannette Rankin, First Lady in Congress: A Biography.* Indianapolis: Bobbs-Merrill, 1974. 0-672-51921-6, 227p. Josephson, a friend of Rankin's for 20 years, in this recommended biography examines her desire for human equality.

RAY, DIXY LEE (1914–1994)
Zoologist and Government Official   Tacoma, Washington

Dixy Lee Ray was a zoologist who in 1976 was elected Washington State's first female governor. She was born on September 3, 1914, one of five girls, and was christened Margaret, although her family called her Dick as a child, short for "that little Dickens." She renamed herself after her favorite region and a Civil War general. Athletic as a child, she was, at 12, the youngest girl to climb Mt. Rainier. After graduating Phi Beta Kappa from Mills College, she earned a doctorate in zoology at Stanford University, was an associate professor of zoology at the University of Washington for 27 years, and directed the Pacific Science Center for 9 years. She spoke in support of the nuclear industry, heading the Atomic Energy Commission from 1973 to 1975. When the commission ended, she became an assistant secretary of state, overseeing the Bureau of Oceans, International Environment and Scientific Affairs. In 1986, Ray became a director of American Ecology Corporation, a toxic waste management firm. She also served as a consultant to the United States Department of Energy and the Los Alamos National Laboratory in New Mexico. She was outspoken, disliking waste and misinformation, and her candor cost her reelection to a second term as governor. In 1990, she published a book on the environment, *Trashing the Planet: How Science Can Help Us Deal with Acid Rain, Depletion of the Ozone and Nuclear Waste.* Among her citations were 20 honorary degrees and numerous awards.

BIBLIOGRAPHY

Guzzo, Louis R. *Is It True What They Say about Dixy?* Mercer Island, WA: Writing Works, 1980. 0–916076–26–1, 234p. Guzzo knew Ray and says that her honesty compromised her political power.

Williams, Barbara. *Breakthrough, Women in Politics.* New York: Walker, 1979. 0–8027–6366–9, 186p. This collective biography emphasizes that Ray's election as an unmarried governor was one of the first times a woman had been elected as a governor without the influence of her husband.

REAM, VINNIE (1847–1914)
Sculptor   Madison, Wisconsin

Vinnie Ream was a sculptor. She was born on September 25, 1847, as one of three children to a government surveyor and recorder of deeds and his wife. Her family moved to Missouri when she was 10, and she briefly attended school, showing abilities in music and art. When the Civil War began, the family moved to Washington, DC, and Ream visited Clark Mills's sculpture studio in the Capitol Building in 1863, where she modeled a medallion of a Native American chief's head. Mills accepted her as a student, and by 1864, friends arranged for her to make a bust of Lincoln. Because she was young, he posed each day for one-half hour for the next five months. In 1866, the government gave her a contract for $10,000 to create a full-size statue of Lincoln to stand in the Capitol rotunda, making her the first female to win such a large federal commission. Many condemned Ream's selection since she was only 18, but her parents went with her to Rome, where she sculpted the statue into marble, and its unveiling in 1871 won her further acclaim. In 1875, she won another large commission, $20,000, for a statue of Admiral David G. Farragut. She married in 1878, and after bearing one son, she relinquished her professional career at her husband's request and instead worked for charities, especially those aiding the blind. After his death, she created another statue for Statuary Hall, one of Iowa's governor, Samuel Kirkwood. She completed a statue of Sequoyah, commissioned by the state of Oklahoma, shortly before her death from uremic poisoning.

BIBLIOGRAPHY

Sherwood, Glenn V. *A Labor of Love: The Life and Art of Vinnie Ream.* Hygiene, CO: SunShine Press, 1997. 0–9615743–6–4, 440p. Sherwood overviews Ream's life and career.

RENO, JANET (1938–)
Attorney and Cabinet Member   Miami, Florida

Janet Reno was the first female attorney general of the United States. She was born on July 21, 1938, as one of four children, to a Danish immigrant police reporter and his wife. She attended Dade County public schools and became a state debating champion. She earned a degree in chemistry from Cornell University, where she served as president of the Women's Student Government. In 1963, she graduated from Harvard University Law School as 1 of 16 women in a class of 500. She then worked in private law firms until she shifted to a political post in 1971, the Judiciary Committee of the Florida House of Representatives. She served in several different capacities in Florida, rising to state's attorney, where she supported legal aid for the poor and advocated children's rights. She then served on the Governor's Council for Prosecution of Organized Crime. In 1993, she became attorney general of the United States. Among her awards are the Herbert Harley Award, Public Administrator of the Year, and a Medal of Honor Award from the Florida Bar Association.

BIBLIOGRAPHY

Anderson, Paul. *Janet Reno: Doing the Right Thing*. New York: Wiley, 1994. 0-471-01858-9, 328p. Anderson discusses Reno's altruistic motives, showing her as a woman of great integrity.

Meachum, Virginia. *Janet Reno: United States Attorney General*. Springfield, NJ: Enslow, 1995. 0-89490-549-X, 128p. In a young adult biography, Meachum discusses Reno's childhood and the influence of an independent mother who built the family home alone.

RICH, ADRIENNE (1929-)
Poet   Baltimore Maryland

Adrienne Rich is a poet, translator, and author. She was born on May 16, 1929, to a physician and his wife. Her father encouraged her intellectual development, and she published a play and poems at age 10 and another play at 12. The year that she graduated Phi Beta Kappa from Radcliffe College, she published her first book of poetry. She married in 1953 and had three sons in six years while continuing to write and publish. In 1966, when the family moved to New York, she began teaching at colleges and universities including Swarthmore and Cornell. Her husband died in 1970, and in 1976, she began living with writer and historian Michelle Cliff. Rich has published nine volumes of poetry and much nonfiction. Her early poetry suggests that people cope with frustration by controlling the mind, but later work incorporated the manipulation of language as a tool of destruction. Her many awards include the Yale Series of Younger Poets Prize, a National Institute of Arts and Letters Award, the National Book Award, and several honorary degrees.

BIBLIOGRAPHY

Keyes, Claire. *The Aesthetics of Power: The Poetry of Adrienne Rich*. Athens: University of Georgia Press, 1986. 0-8203-0803-X, 216p. In her critical biography, Keyes suggests that after Rich began writing, she realized the value of the feminine voice.

Rich, Adrienne Cecile. *What Is Found There: Notebooks on Poetry and Politics*. New York: Norton, 1993. 0-393-03565-4, 304p. Rich sees the writing of poetry as a social responsibility in this collection.

Templeton, Alice. *The Dream and the Dialogue*. Nashville: University of Tennessee, 1994. 0-87049-859-2, 192p. Templeton examines Rich's poetry for the influence of feminist thinking.

Werner, Craig Hansen. *Adrienne Rich: The Poet and Her Critics*. Chicago: American Library Association, 1988. 0-8389-0487-4, 199p. Werner illuminates the political and aesthetic values in Rich's life and work.

RICHARDS, ANN (1933-)
Government Official   Lakeview, Texas

Ann Richards was the governor of Texas. She was born Dorothy Ann Willis on September 1, 1933, as the only child of a truck driver and his wife. Her parents gave her piano and elocution lessons and told her that she could do whatever she wanted but that she should always seek justice. In high school, she dropped her first name and began debating, earning the privilege of representing the school at Girls State, and then as the Texas representative to meet with President Harry S. Truman. She attended Baylor University on a debating scholarship, and after graduation, enrolled at the University of Texas at Austin to earn a teaching certificate. She became an active Democrat when she and her husband moved to Dallas, and in 1974 helped Wilhemina Delco become the first African American woman elected to the Texas legislature. Local Democrats encouraged Richards to run for county commissioner the next year, and in this job, Richards initiated the Infant Parent Training program for families with children afflicted with Down's syndrome, a rape crisis center, and a center for battered women. In 1980, as her marriage failed, Richards became alcohol dependent, but friends encouraged her attempts to rehabilitate. In 1981, the Texas Women's Political Caucus named her woman of the year. In 1982, Richards was elected state treasurer, becoming the first woman to hold statewide office in Texas since "Ma" Ferguson. She actively recruited minorities and was inducted into the Texas Women's Hall of Fame. In 1984, national Democratic leaders asked her to second the presidential nomination of former vice president Walter F. Mondale, and in 1988, she was the keynote speaker at the Democratic National Convention in Atlanta. She won the governorship of Texas in 1990 but was defeated for reelection in 1994.

BIBLIOGRAPHY
Richards, Ann. *Straight from the Heart: My Life in Politics and Other Places*. New York: Simon and Schuster, 1989. 0-671-68073-0, 256p. Richards recalls her life in Texas before and after politics.

Shropshire, Mike, and Frank Schaefer. *The Thorny Rose of Texas: An Intimate Portrait of Governor Ann Richards*. Secaucus, NJ: Carol, 1994. 1-55972-232-0, 271p. The authors have based their balanced biography of Richards on interviews with friends, family, and colleagues.

RICHARDS, ELLEN SWALLOW (1842–1911)
Chemist   Dunstable, Massachusetts

Ellen Henrietta Swallow Richards was a chemist and founder of the home economics movement. She was born on December 3, 1842, the only child of a farmer who taught school and his teacher wife. Richards won prizes at a state fair when 13 for her embroidery and her bread. In high school, Richards helped her father and studied Latin and French. She tried to save money for college by teaching, but her mother's illnesses delayed her efforts. At 25, Richards finally entered Vassar, financing herself by tutoring younger students in mathematics and Latin, and earned an A.B. in chemistry in only two years. Then she became the first woman to enter the Massachusetts Institute of Technology (MIT), graduating with a B.S. in chemistry in 1873, and the same year receiving an M.A. from Vassar. She studied for two additional years, but the MIT faculty never awarded her a doctorate because it did not want a woman to receive the first doctorate in chemistry. She and her engineering professor husband devoted themselves to science. In 1876, she developed a women's science laboratory at MIT, and in 1882 became one of the founding members of the Association of Collegiate Alumnae (later the American Association of University Women). In 1884, she set up a chemical laboratory at MIT to study sanitation, eventually taking charge of the experimentation, with her text, *Air, Water, and Food for Colleges*, evolving from the research. Around 1890, she opened the New England Kitchen, modeled on the public kitchens in Europe, offering for sale cooked foods scientifically prepared. At the Chicago World's Fair in 1893, she set up the Rumford kitchen and listed the nutritional values of 30-cent lunches on the menu. Her work revealed how research impacted home management, and at a series of conferences, beginning in 1899, she created a curriculum for the new field of "home economics." In 1908, she was chosen first president of the American Home Economics Association. She has been elected to The National Women's Hall of Fame.

BIBLIOGRAPHY
Clarke, Robert. *Ellen Swallow: The Woman Who Founded Ecology.* Chicago: Follett, 1973. 0-695-80388-3, 276p. Clarke's researched biography of Swallow, suitable for young adults, discusses her achievements.

Hunt, Caroline Louisa. *The Life of Ellen H. Richards, 1842–1911.* Washington, DC: American Home Economics Association, 1980. 0-8461-5043-3, 175p. Although undocumented, this biography of Richards includes some of her letters.

RICHARDS, LINDA (1841–1903)
Nurse and Educator   Potsdam, New York

Linda Richards was an educator and nurse. She was born Melinda Ann Judson Reynolds on July 27, 1841, as the youngest of four girls to a father who hoped she would be a missionary. The family moved to Wisconsin when Richards was four, but her father died within weeks, and Richards and her sisters returned to Vermont to live with her grandfather, a major influence on her life. Neighbors contacted Richards, a "born nurse," when ill, and since she had to support herself, she began thinking about nursing as an occupation during the Civil War. In 1877, she fulfilled her dream by going to England to study with Florence Nightingale and became the first student at Boston's recently founded New England Hospital for Women and Children. One year later, she received the first diploma from the first American nursing school. At the Boston Training School (Massachusetts General Hospital of Nursing), she developed regular classroom instruction with hospital wards opened to the pupils, the first Nightingale school in America associated with a hospital, and used her diplomatic skills to make the endeavor a success. In 1886, Richards went to Japan, and after intensive language study, opened a training school for nurses in Kyoto, the first to offer an American two-year program. She remained five years, teaching and serving as an evangelist. For the 20 years after she returned from Japan, she held several supervisory positions and became known as "America's First Trained Nurse." In 1962, the National League for Nursing started the Linda Richards Award for an outstanding practicing nurse. She was later elected to The National Women's Hall of Fame.

BIBLIOGRAPHY

Baker, Rachel. *America's First Trained Nurse, Linda Richards.* New York: Julian Messner, 1959. No ISBN, 191p. This fictional biography of Richards for young adults is carefully researched from letters and archives.

Wayne, Bennett. *Four Women of Courage.* Champaign, IL: Garrard, 1975. 0–811–64911–3, 167p. In this collective biography, Wayne discusses Richards's contributions to nursing.

RIDE, SALLY KRISTEN (1951–)
Astronaut   Encino, California

Sally Kristen Ride was the first American woman to fly into outer space as an astronaut. She was born on May 26, 1951, as one of two daughters to an American government professor and his talented wife. Ride and the family went abroad when she was 10, and her parents' tutoring placed her half a grade ahead of her class. Although Ride's parents did not influence her career, they did suggest that she become a professional tennis player rather than a football player when she was 12, and she became a teenage tennis champion before starting college at Swarthmore and transferring to Stanford. She earned bachelor's degrees in English and physics and stayed at Stanford for her Ph.D. in astrophysics. In 1978, she began training as an astronaut with the National Aeronautics and Space Administration (NASA), and she later married an astronaut. On June 18, 1983, Ride and four other astronauts took the *Challenger* space shuttle on its seventh mission, during which she helped deploy two satellites, served as the flight engineer, and recaptured a satellite using the shuttle's mechanical arm. In October 1984, she flew an eight-day *Challenger* mission, but her third scheduled shuttle flight was canceled after the in 1989, she became director of the Space Science Institute at the University of California at San Diego. She has been elected to The National Women's Hall of Fame.

BIBLIOGRAPHY

Camp, Carole Ann. *Sally Ride: First American Woman in Space.* Springfield, NJ: Enslow, 1997. 0-89490-829-4, 104p. Camp's documented biography of Ride for young adults discusses her life and career.

Hurwitz, Jane, and Sue Hurwitz. *Sally Ride: Shooting for the Stars.* New York: Fawcett Columbine, 1989. 0-449-90394-X, 115p. This biography for young adults focuses on Ride's early life and career.

RINCON DE GAUTIER, FELISA (1897–1994)
Government Official   Ceiba, Puerto Rico

Latina American Felisa Rincon de Gautier served as mayor of San Juan, Puerto Rico, for almost 25 years. She was born in Ceiba, Puerto Rico, on January 9, 1897, one of eight children of an attorney and a schoolteacher. At her mother's death when Rincon de Gautier was 12, she took over the household duties and listened to her father's guests discuss the politics and philosophy of the day. She became aware of discrimination when her friend, a black, was not allowed to attend a party at a social club, and Rincon de Gautier refused to go to the party herself. On the family farm, she worked with the field hands and saw that their low social status did not stifle their innate kindness. After visiting New York, she returned to San Juan and opened a dress boutique that catered to the elite, but she kept her interest in the poor. Her father wanted his children to avoid public life, but when Rincon de Gautier began voting, she joined the Liberal Party and then led it for several years before switching to the Popular Democratic Party of Luis Muñoz Marín. She married in 1940, and with her husband encouraging her political interests, she became mayor of San Juan in 1946. She created neighborhood medical facilities, found jobs for the poor, and helped medical students obtain scholarships to study in America. Because she had once wanted to be a physician, she emphasized the importance of modernized medical centers. She became the best known Latin American woman, receiving awards from Spain, the Vatican, France, Israel, and the United States. She received seven honorary doctorates and was named the Woman of the Americas in 1954.

BIBLIOGRAPHY

Gruber, Ruth. *Felisa Rincon de Gautier: The Mayor of San Juan.* New York: Crowell, 1972. 0-690-29475-1, 238p. A well-documented biography, suitable for young adults, reveals Rincon de Gautier's personal as well as public life.

ROBERTS, LYDIA JANE (1879–1965)
Educator and Nutritionist   Hope Township, Michigan

Lydia Jane Roberts was an educator and a specialist in nutrition for children. She was born on June 30, 1879, as one of four children to a carpenter and his wife. She attended community schools before entering Mt. Pleasant Normal School (later Central Michigan University) and teaching. At 36, she entered the University of Chicago as an advanced student. Roberts realized that most children attending school missed the main family meal at noon, and her college work focused on feeding the appropriate foods to children. She majored in home economics and completed an M.S. in 1919 with her thesis exploring the causes of malnutrition. The same year, she became an assistant professor of home economics at the University of Chicago. She and her students gathered information that became a book, *Nutrition Work with Children*, and the subject of Roberts's dissertation for her Ph.D. in home economics. In two years, she rose to chair and full professor, while researching caloric, protein, vitamin, and mineral requirements in the diet of children. On national committees, she advocated the addition of vitamins and minerals to flour and bread during the war. After her mandatory retirement, Roberts went to the University of Puerto Rico at the invitation of its chancellor. She chaired the home economics department and continued her research on food habits, which she published in *Patterns of Living in Puerto Rican Families*. Her insight that economic assistance and nutrition should be united in the Doña Elena project helped to improve rural roads, sanitary facilities, and electricity access on the island. Roberts received many awards, including Exemplary Citizen of Puerto Rico and honorary degrees. The universities of Puerto Rico and of Chicago also established the Lydia Jane Roberts Memorial Lectures.

BIBLIOGRAPHY
Doyle, Margaret D. *Lydia Jane Roberts: Nutrition Scientist, Educator, and Humanitarian.* Chicago: American Dietetic Association, 1989. 0–88091–047–X, 167p. Doyle, one of Roberts's students, notes that few documents contain information on her childhood because she retained no memorabilia and her family was unaware of her valuable research.

ROBINS, MARGARET DREIER (1868–1945)
Reformer and Philanthropist   Brooklyn, New York

Margaret Dreier Robins was a labor reformer. She was born on September 6, 1868, as the oldest of five surviving children to a wealthy businessman and his wife. She had a disciplined childhood, a good education, and a sense of responsibility learned from her parents, loyal supporters of the German Evangelical Church. Although she did not attend college, she read history and philosophy under the tutelage of a minister. When she was 19, she joined the women's auxiliary at Brooklyn Hospital and saw the conditions of the poor for the first time. She joined charity groups, and married a settlement worker with the same goals. Robins lived in a cold-water apartment in a Chicago tenement even though she was independently wealthy, meeting the settlement workers in the area, including **Jane Addams**. She made the Women's Trade Union League (WTUL) a viable force in labor reform by supporting garment workers' strikes, raising money, gaining legal advice, organizing relief, and contributing her own money. She also edited *Life and Labor*, the organization's magazine. Her sincerity won over both the workers and the middle-class women helping them, and in 1915, the governor of Illinois appointed her to the state unemployment commission. She led a protest when labor leaders were falsely accused of murder, and she marched in suffrage parades because she thought that women must participate in politics. After resigning from the WTUL, she devoted herself to the International Federation of Working Women, organizing two congresses, one in Washington and another in Geneva. After retirement, she contributed to other charitable organizations.

BIBLIOGRAPHY

Payne, Elizabeth Anne. *Reform, Labor, and Feminism: Margaret Dreier Robins and the Women's Trade Union League.* Urbana: University of Illinois Press, 1988. 0–252–01445–6, 218p. This critical biography of Robins includes an introduction to the WTUL.

ROBINSON, HARRIET HANSON (1825–1911)
Mill Girl and Activist   Boston, Massachusetts

Harriet Jane Hanson Robinson was a mill girl, social activist, and an author. She was born on February 8, 1825, the daughter of a carpenter and his wife. Her father died when she was six, and her mother supported the family by boarding mill workers in Lowell, Massachusetts. Robinson started working in the mills at age 10 as a bobbin doffer, where between duties she had time to read. The mill management provided schools, churches, and libraries, and Robinson contributed poems to the *Lowell Offering*, a monthly literary magazine. One of her journalist readers married her, and she began her struggle as wife, mother, and editorial assistant for her husband's militant antislavery columns. While they lived in Concord from 1854 to 1857, Robinson met other abolitionists including Ralph Waldo Emerson and Henry Thoreau. After the war, she began campaigning for woman suffrage, and in 1881, she wrote *Massachusetts in the Woman Suffrage Movement* to separate from **Lucy Stone** and join **Susan B. Anthony**'s broader interpretation of the movement. Robinson and her daughter helped organize the National Woman Suffrage Association of Massachusetts and spoke before a Senate committee in Washington. Robinson also promoted **Julia Ward Howe**'s women's clubs, helping her form the New England Women's Clubs in 1868 and serving on the first board of directors of the General Federation of Women's Clubs in the 1890s. In 1898, Robinson published a recollection of her years in the mills, *Loom and Spindle*, a valuable document of the times.

BIBLIOGRAPHY

Bushman, Claudia L. *A Good Poor Man's Wife: Being a Chronicle of Harriet Hanson Robinson.* Hanover, NH: University Press of New England, 1981. 0-87451-193-3, 276p. Diaries, scrapbooks, and correspondence are the core of Bushman's detailed biography of Robinson.

Selden, Bernice. *The Mill Girls: Lucy Larcom, Harriet Hanson Robinson, Sarah G. Bagley.* New York: Atheneum, 1983. 0-689-31005-6, 191p. Selden's collective, researched biography for young adults examines Robinson's life and career.

ROBINSON, JULIA (1919–1985)
Mathematician   St. Louis, Missouri

Julia Robinson was a mathematician who researched number theory. Born on December 8, 1919, Robinson missed much school as a child because of scarlet and rheumatic fever, scoring below average on an IQ test in junior high school. In high school, however, she began winning awards in advanced mathematics and physics classes in which she was the only female. While in college, she read E. T. Bell's *Men of Mathematics* to find out what mathematicians do, and after deciding to become one, earned her Ph.D. at Berkeley. She married a mathematics professor and began work at the Rand Corporation in 1948. David Hilbert's list of unsolved problems fascinated her, and after concentrating on the tenth problem, she wrote several articles about her conclusions. In 1970, a young Russian solved the problem using Fibonacci numbers and her prior articles as a basis. She later collaborated with him, and the two, along with another mathematician, were credited with the solution to which all three contributed. Not until 1976, after she was the first female mathematician to be elected to the National Academy of Science, was she offered a professorship at Berkeley. In 1982, she became president of the American Mathematical Society, a job in which she tried to encourage young women to study mathematics. In 1983, she received a MacArthur Foundation award, but two years later she died of leukemia.

BIBLIOGRAPHY

Reid, Constance. *Julia: A Life in Mathematics.* Washington, DC: Mathematical Association of America, 1996. 0-88385-520-8, 123p. Reid, Robinson's sister, based her "autobiography" of her on interviews and articles by three of Robinson's colleagues.

ROBINSON, RUBYE DORIS SMITH (1942–1967)
Activist   Atlanta, Georgia

Rubye Doris Smith Robinson was an African American civil rights activist and reformer. She was born on April 24, 1942, as the second of seven children to a self-employed mover and a beautician. Robinson started first grade at four, staying ahead of her age group throughout elementary school. She entered Spelman College at 16, and the next year, when the lunch-counter sit-in in Greensboro,

North Carolina, occurred, she joined fellow students in a local sit-in. Later that spring, she helped form the Student Non-Violent Coordinating Committee (SNCC). She supported other sit-ins and spent time in jail, sometimes serving a full sentence to emphasize the importance of civil rights. In 1961, she participated in Alabama Freedom Rides sponsored by the Congress of Racial Equality (CORE). When she was arrested for trying to use white-only restrooms and refusing to obey police officers, she returned to jail. SNCC began to separate from Martin Luther King, Jr., thinking that nonviolence was only one way to work rather than the only way. In 1963, Robinson became a full-time staff member of SNCC, working with James Forman, and for the next four years kept the organization functioning efficiently. She recruited African American volunteers, believing they should lead civil rights efforts in the South rather than whites. After visiting Africa in 1964, she felt a strong nationalism and demanded that more women have responsibility in SNCC. In 1966, Robinson succeeded Forman as executive secretary, and under chairman Stokely Carmichael, the group began the transition to African American nationalism. At the same time, Robinson contracted cancer, but she kept working until a few months before her death.

BIBLIOGRAPHY

Fleming, Cynthia Griggs. *Soon We Will Not Cry: The Liberation of Rubye Doris Smith Robinson*. Lanham, MD: Rowman and Littlefield, 1998. 0–8476–8971–9, 224p. Fleming interviewed former members of SNCC and members of Robinson's family for a readable, researched, and documented biography.

ROCKEFELLER, ABBY ALDRICH (1874–1948)
Philanthropist   Providence, Rhode Island

Abby Aldrich Rockefeller was a philanthropist and art patron. She was born on October 26, 1874, as the third of eight children to a self-made businessman and future United States senator and his wife. Her father's eclectic interests dominated the family, and Rockefeller received private instruction. As a socialite and debutante, she made her first trip to Europe at 20. In 1901, she married the oil heir John Davison Rockefeller, Jr., and their happy union produced six children. She enjoyed her role as hostess but spent much time with her philanthropies. She founded a neighborhood association including representatives from immigrant and minority groups, and supported the YWCA, the Girl Scouts, the American Red Cross, Riverside Church, and her husband's projects for the Rockefeller Foundation and the Rockefeller Institute for Medical Research. The two also became active in the restoration of colonial Williamsburg in Virginia. In 1919, her interest in conditions for workmen at her husband's company led her to have a workman's model house constructed. This project developed into a community center with a baby clinic, a Mothers' Club, and sponsorship of athletic and social activities. Rockefeller actively entertained servicemen and planned veterans' centers during both world wars. Her father had instilled within her a love of art, and in 1929 she helped found the Museum of Modern Art, to which she donated more than 2,000 art objects and for which she set up an unrestricted purchase fund. She commissioned works from artists during the Great Depression and enjoyed American folk art. Rockefeller tried to overcome the barriers of wealth by sharing her money with others.

BIBLIOGRAPHY

Kert, Bernice. *Abby Aldrich Rockefeller: The Woman in the Family*. New York: Random, 1993. 0-394-56975-X, 537p.   In her thoroughly researched biography of Rockefeller, Kert suggests that her warmth and intelligence humanized her husband.

ROGERS, GINGER (1911–1995)
Dancer and Actor   Independence, Missouri

Ginger Rogers was a dancer and an actor. She was born Virginia Katherine McMath on July 16, 1911, as the only surviving child of three to an electrical engineer who kidnapped her from her screenwriter and agent mother after their separation when Rogers was six. In Texas, after her father died when she was 11, she participated in high school dramatics and studied dancing. She made her professional debut at 14 and began working regularly in vaudeville at 15. At 18, she played a supporting role in the musical *Top Speed* and won a contract for *Young Man of Manhattan*. At 19, she returned to Broadway as the female lead in George and Ira Gershwin's successful *Girl Crazy*, earning $1,000 per week. In 1933, at 22, she first danced with Fred Astaire in the film *Flying Down to Rio*, and in 1936, she made her radio debut. She starred in the first color film in 1944, *Lady in the Dark*, wearing a mink and sequin gown costing over $30,000, later donated to the Smithsonian Institution. By 1945, she was the highest paid woman, and the eighth highest paid overall, in the United States, earning over $250,000. In 1952, she made her television debut, and in 1959, she debuted in Las Vegas. In the early 1960s, she toured and performed *Hello, Dolly!* 1,116 times. In her 1969 London debut, as the highest paid performer ever to appear on London stage, she earned $12,000 per week for a 56-week run in *Mame*. In 1987, she directed her first play, *Babes in Arms*. She made over 70 films and won many honorary degrees and awards including an Academy Award and a Kennedy Center Honors Award for Lifetime Achievement.

BIBLIOGRAPHY

Dickens, Homer. *The Films of Ginger Rogers*. Secaucus, NJ: Citadel, 1975. 0-8065-0496-X, 256p. A brief biographical essay precedes photographs, synopses, and reviews from each of Rogers's films.
Faris, Jocelyn. *Ginger Rogers: A Bio-Bibliography*. Westport, CT: Greenwood Press, 1994. 0-313-29177-2, 299p. Faris's biography of Rogers includes a thorough accounting of her career.

McGilligan, Patrick. *Ginger Rogers.* New York: Pyramid, 1975. 0–515–03894–6, 158p. McGilligan's biography of Rogers includes details about her career and her partnership with Fred Astaire.

Morley, Sheridan. *Shall We Dance? The Life of Ginger Rogers.* New York: St. Martin's, 1995. 0–312–14149–1, 96p. Morley's biography of Rogers is an overview of her life, with photographs.

Rogers, Ginger. *Ginger: My Story.* New York: HarperCollins, 1991. 0–06–018308–X, 450p. Rogers fondly remembers her colleagues and her career dancing with Fred Astaire.

RONSTADT, LINDA (1946–)
Singer   Tucson, Arizona

Linda Ronstadt is an award-winning Latina American vocalist. She was born on July 15, 1946. Her father, a German-Mexican businessman, wanted to be a singer and exposed her to a variety of musical styles. Ronstadt also listened to **Billie Holiday** and **Ella Fitzgerald** records, absorbing their techniques. She began her career at 14, after always planning to be a singer, when she sang with her sister and brother as part of the Stone Poneys at parties and restaurants. She entered the University of Arizona but soon left for Los Angeles and joined tours where she opened concerts for established stars. Although she had recorded with the Stone Poneys in 1967, not until 1974, when she combined rock and roll with country music, did she have a success. That album sold over a million copies. Since then, she has produced 17 gold and 12 platinum albums. She also expanded her interest to politics by fund-raising for the Democrats. In her career, she has performed rock, Mexican folk, country and western, ballads, and opera, and she has also acted on stage and in film. Although never wanting to marry, she has adopted two children with whom she spends much time at home in Tucson. Among her honors are Grammy Awards.

BIBLIOGRAPHY

Amdur, Melissa. *Linda Ronstadt.* New York: Chelsea House, 1993. 0–7910–1781–8, 111p. Amdur's young adult biography of Ronstadt objectively catalogs her life and career.

Bego, Mark. *Linda Ronstadt: It's So Easy.* Austin, TX: Eakin Press, 1990. 0–89015–775–8, 212p. Bego based his researched and recommended biography of Ronstadt, suitable for young adults, on interviews and printed material.

Berman, Connie. *Linda Ronstadt: An Illustrated Biography.* Carson City, NE: Proteus, 1979. 0–906071–08–9, 117p. This undocumented popular biography, suitable for young adults, covers Ronstadt's career.

Claire, Vivian. *Linda Ronstadt.* New York: Flash, 1978. 0–8256–3918–2, 72p. In her biography of Ronstadt for young adults, Claire quotes newspaper interviews and prior biographies.

Moore, Mary Ellen. *The Linda Ronstadt Scrapbook.* New York: Sunridge Press, 1978. 0–441–48410–7, 121p. Moore's undocumented biography, suitable for young adults, contains many photographs.

ROOSEVELT, ELEANOR (1884–1962)
First Lady and Ambassador   New York, New York

Anna Eleanor Roosevelt was a First Lady of the United States, a diplomat, and a humanitarian. She was born on October 11, 1884, one of two surviving children in a wealthy family. By the time she was 10, both parents and a brother had died. She lived with her unemotional grandmother until attending boarding school in England, where the headmistress, Marie Souvestra, gave her confidence in herself and her abilities. When she returned to the United States, she married her second cousin, Franklin D. Roosevelt, and raised their five children while simultaneously helping him in his political campaigns. During World War I, while they lived in Washington, she rose early to serve at the train station canteen and directed Red Cross activities. In 1921, her husband became crippled with polio, and she later went on speaking tours, although very shy, to help his campaigns, starting with his quest for governor of New York in 1928. She joined the Women's Trade Union League and actively participated in the New York Democratic Party. After her husband's election as president in 1932, she supported several liberal causes, which shocked the nation but earned her enormous popularity. Her emphasis on education gained women's votes for her husband's 1936 reelection. The same year, her newspaper column, "My Day," began, and she spoke on radio and lectured across the country. She helped farmers reclaim their lands and supported both antilynching laws and civil rights. After resigning from the Daughters of the American Revolution when the group refused to let African American **Marian Anderson** sing in their Washington hall, she arranged for Anderson to sing at the Lincoln Memorial. After her husband's death in 1945, she served as United States delegate to the United Nations for Harry Truman, persuading the General Assembly to pass the Universal Declaration of Human Rights. In the 1950s, she supported Israel and decried Joseph McCarthy's "witch hunts." Her last official position was to chair President John F. Kennedy's Commission on the Status of Women in 1961. Later, she was elected to The National Women's Hall of Fame because she was one of the most influential women of her own or any time.

BIBLIOGRAPHY
Cook, Blanche Wiesen. *Eleanor Roosevelt*. New York: Viking, 1992. 0–670–80486–X. Vol.1. Cook used archives, government documents, and letters for a well-researched first volume of a feminist biography on Roosevelt.
Goodwin, Doris Kearns. *No Ordinary Time: Franklin and Eleanor Roosevelt. The Home Front in World War II*. New York: Simon and Schuster, 1994. 0–671–64240–5, 759p. Goodwin covers the life of Eleanor and Franklin Roosevelt from 1940 to 1945, during World War II, using primary sources and interviews.
Hershan, Stella K. *The Candles She Lit: The Legacy of Eleanor Roosevelt*. Westport, CT: Praeger, 1993. 0–275–94366–6, 106p. Hershan's brief biography includes anecdotes and testimonies from Roosevelt's staff, Holocaust survivors, and others.
Scharf, Lois. *Eleanor Roosevelt: First Lady of American Liberalism*. New York: Twayne, 1987. 0–8057–7769–5, 202p. In a well-researched biography suitable for young adults, Scharf emphasizes Roosevelt's accomplishments.

Somerville, Mollie D. *Eleanor Roosevelt as I Knew Her*. McLean, VA: EPM, 1996.
0-939009-96-X, 176p. Somerville was Roosevelt's secretary, and she used her own
diary, jottings, memoranda, and invitations for her unique view in which she notes
that she did not know about FDR's affair until after Eleanor Roosevelt's death.

ROSE, ERNESTINE L. (1810–1892)
Activist   Piotrkow, Poland

Ernestine Rose was a feminist, reformer, and freethinker. She was born in a Jewish
ghetto on January 13, 1810, as Ernestine Louise Siismondi Potowski, the only
child of a rabbi. Her father, who taught her Hebrew, gave her more education and
freedom than was usual for Jewish girls. She began questioning the Torah at age
five, and by fourteen, she had rejected all Jewish teaching about the inferiority of
women. Her mother's death when Rose was 16 left her with a substantial amount
of property, but when her father arranged a marriage contract, Rose obtained her
rights in court. The next year, she gave the inheritance to her father and left home.
She lived in Berlin, Holland, Paris, and England, where she met other reformers
including *Elisabeth Fry before marrying a silversmith and coming to the United
States. In 1840, Rose supported **Elizabeth Cady Stanton**'s married women's
property bill before the New York legislature. At the same time, she lectured for
the free-thought movement, and began contributing to the *Boston Investigator*, an
activity which she continued for 50 years. In the 1850s, Rose devoted her energy to
women's rights, wanting political, legal, and social equality. Often called "Queen
of the Platform," she lectured in more than 20 states and addressed legislative
bodies on antislavery, temperance, freedom of thought, and equality. In 1869, she
helped change the Equal Rights Association into the National Woman Suffrage
Association, and her last speech was to this group in 1873 before returning to
England, where she died. She was elected to The National Women's Hall of Fame.

BIBLIOGRAPHY
Eiseman, Alberta. *Rebels and Reformers: Biographies of Four Jewish Americans*. Garden
    City, NY: Zenith, 1976. 0-385-01588-7, 131p. In this collective biography for
    young adults, Eiseman includes a concise profile of Rose.
Kolmerten, Carol A. *The American Life of Ernestine L. Rose*. Syracuse NY: Syracuse
    University Press, 1998. 0-8156-0528-5, 272p. Kolmerten includes Rose's speeches
    and letters to suggest that Rose's atheism, Jewish heritage, and foreign background
    led to her exclusion from history books.
Suhl, Yuri. *Ernestine L. Rose: Women's Rights Pioneer*. 1958. New York: Biblio Press,
    1990. 0-930395-09-3, 314p. The lack of personal papers led Suhl to use Rose's
    speeches and letters to recount her life.

ROSS, DIANA (1944-)
Entertainer   Detroit, Michigan

Diana Ross is a versatile performer who has had success on stage and in films as an African American singer, actor, and entertainer. A clerk mistakenly recorded Diane as Diana when she was born on March 26, 1944, and after her happy but poor childhood in a Detroit neighborhood, Ross chose "Diana" when she joined two other women she met in her church choir to form the Supremes. The group sang backup to Marvin Gaye and Mary Wells before recording their first gold record, "Where Did Our Love Go?" in 1964. They followed this success with 11 more number-one hits before Ross began performing solo in 1970. After 1971, she married twice, had six children, earned an Academy Award nomination for her portrayal of **Billie Holiday** in *Lady Sings the Blues*, took concert tours across country, and performed at the Newport Jazz Festival. Among her honors are a Grammy Award, a Tony Award, and a Golden Globe Award. In 1988, she was inducted into the Rock and Roll Hall of Fame, and in 1994, she received the French Commander of Arts and Letters medal.

BIBLIOGRAPHY
Brown, Geoff. *Diana Ross*. New York: St. Martin's, 1981. 0–312–19932–5, 144p. In a popular biography, Brown discusses Ross's life and career.
Ross, Diana. *Secrets of a Sparrow: Memoirs*. New York: Villard, 1993. 0–679–42874–7, 299p. Ross's adulatory autobiography offers little insight about her life.
Taraborrelli, J. Randy. *Call Her Miss Ross: The Unauthorized Biography of Diana Ross*. New York: Ballantine, 1991. 0–345–36925–4, 566p. This is a poorly written, hostile biography of Ross.
Wyeth, John, Jr. *Diana Ross*. New York: Chelsea House, 1996. 0–7910–1882–2, 102p. In this researched biography for young adults, Wyeth discusses Ross's career.

ROWSON, SUSANNA HASWELL (c. 1762–1824)
Author and Actor   Portsmouth, England

Susanna Haswell Rowson was an author and actor. She was born around 1762, the only child of a Royal Navy lieutenant and his first wife, who died when Rowson was born. When Rowson was six, her father came to Massachusetts and remarried. Her voyage from England ended in shipwreck, and life in Massachusetts seemed a peaceful change. She studied and read widely, but during the American Revolution, her father's property was seized and his family interned at Hingham for two years. They eventually went to England, where they lived in poverty while waiting for her father's pension. Rowson searched for a job and became governess to a wealthy family who took her to the Continent. In 1786, she published her first novel, and the next year she married. In 1791, she wrote her popular novel *Charlotte Temple*, probably based on her husband's intemperate ways. The two became actors and settled in Boston. During her five years in the theater, Rowson performed 129 different roles in 126 diverse productions, some of which she wrote.

Her most successful was *Slaves in Algiers*. She based another, *The Volunteers*, on the Whiskey Rebellion. In 1797, she opened a Young Ladies Academy in Boston which was one of the first in the United States to offer educational study above the elementary level for females. She wrote some of her own textbooks, instructed her students in public speaking, and hired European-trained instructors to teach music. Rowson and her husband both performed and organized concerts in Boston, and in 1802, she began contributing to *Boston Weekly Magazine*. Of all her works, her most famous novel remained *Charlotte Temple*, the first American best-seller, with over 200 editions after its 1794 publication in the United States.

BIBLIOGRAPHY

Brandt, Ellen B. *Susanna Haswell Rowson, America's First Best-Selling Novelist*. Chicago: Serbra Press, 1975. No ISBN, 251p. Brandt carefully researched and documented her readable critical biography of Rowson.

Parker, Patricia L. *Susanna Rowson*. New York: Twayne, 1986. 0–8057–7458–0, 146p. Parker prefaces her discussion of Rowson's career with a brief overview of her times.

Stern, Julia A. *The Plight of Feeling: Sympathy and Dissent in the Early American Novel*. Chicago: University of Chicago Press, 1997. 0–226–77310–8, 306p. In a critical and scholarly text, Stern's analysis of *Charlotte Temple* includes biographical information on Rowson.

Weil, Dorothy. *In Defense of Women: Susanna Rowson*. University Park: Pennsylvania State University, 1976. 0–271–01205–6, 204p. Weil's carefully researched, documented, and scholarly biography of Rowson identifies her as a serious writer.

ROYALL, ANNE NEWPORT (1769–1854)
Journalist   **Baltimore, Maryland**

Anne Newport Royall was an author and probably America's first female journalist. She was born on June 11, 1769, as the older of two daughters to a farmer and his wife. The family moved to western Pennsylvania after her birth. Her father, who died when she was six, taught her to read. After her mother's second husband died, Royall went with her to West Virginia, where her mother secured employment as a servant. The library in this wealthy home was one of the largest in Virginia, and when her mother's employer recognized Royall's intelligence, he invited her to read his books. Then he married her when she was 28 and he was nearly 50. After his death, his family had his will voided and made her penniless. She demanded a widow's pension, but her case lagged in court. Not for 25 years did she receive compensation, but after her husband's legal heirs took half of the money and she paid court fees, she cleared only 10 dollars. To support herself while waiting, she traveled to almost every settlement in the United States and published 10 volumes of her experiences. When she returned to Washington in 1829, she publicly abused a group of Presbyterians worshiping near her house, and they had her convicted as a common scold. Because of her age, she received a fine instead of a ducking, and Andrew Jackson's secretary of war, a witness for her defense, paid the fine. In 1830, she started publishing pamphlets, sheets, and books before beginning a newspaper, *Paul Pry*. This first newspaper lasted six years, and a second, *The Huntress*, was published for nineteen more. She defended Sunday transportation of the mails, states' rights, and tolerance for Catholics. She despised graft, ministers, and missionaries, who, according to her, wanted to seize the government. She had enemies and admirers, but all recognized her sincerity and her courage.

BIBLIOGRAPHY

James, Bessie. *Anne Royall's U.S.A.* New Brunswick, NJ: Rutgers University Press, 1972. 0–8135–0732–4, 447p. James traced Royall's travels and activities in her records, journals, and letters for a scholarly, carefully annotated biography.

Maxwell, Alice S. *Virago! The Story of Anne Newport Royall.* Jefferson, NC: McFarland, 1985. 0–89950–133–8, 305p. Maxwell examines Royall's life in terms of Jacksonian politics.

Porter, Sarah Harvey. *The Life and Times of Anne Royall.* 1908. New York: Arno Press, 1972. 0–405–04472–0, 298p. Porter's researched and balanced biography of Royall presents both her achievements and accusations against her.

RUDOLPH, WILMA (1940–1994)
Athlete
St. Bethlehem, Tennessee

African American Wilma Glodean Rudolph became the first American woman to ever win three track and field gold medals in a single Olympics (in Rome during 1960). She was born on June 23, 1940, as the twentieth of 22 children. At four, she contracted polio, and no one thought she would walk again. But her family helped her, and by 12, she had discarded her brace, and by 16, she was an All-State basketball player and a bronze medal winner at the Olympics. At 18, she got pregnant and feared her dreams were over, but with the support of a coach and a full track scholarship, she attended Tennessee State University. She returned to the Olympics in 1960 and won gold medals in the 100-meter dash, the 200-meter dash, and the 4 x 100-meter relay. When she retired in 1962, she held world records in all three events. She married and raised four children while teaching, coaching, and directing youth foundations, including the Wilma Rudolph Foundation. Among her awards were the Sullivan Award; the Babe Didrikson Zaharias Award; election to The National Women's Hall of Fame, and selection for the Black Sports, Women's Sports, and United States Olympic Halls of Fame. In 1984, she was one of five chosen as America's Greatest Women Athletes.

BIBLIOGRAPHY

Biracree, Tom. *Wilma Rudolph.* New York: Chelsea House, 1988. 1–55546–675–3, 111p. Biracree's researched biography of Rudolph traces her career development.

RUKEYSER, MURIEL (1913–1980)
Poet and Activist   New York, New York

Muriel Rukeyser was a poet and author. She was born December 13, 1913, a third generation Ashkenazi Jew, to a concrete salesman and a bookkeeper. Her family had servants, but she always identified with children in working-class neighborhoods. Rukeyser loved to read and learned to appreciate music and opera from her parents while attending private Jewish religious schools. She began writing poetry in high school, and at Vassar College was the literary editor of the leftist journal, *Student Review.* After her father's bankruptcy, she had to leave Vassar, but in her job, she traveled to Scottsboro, Alabama, to report on the conviction of nine young African Americans for raping two white women. She was arrested for talking to African American journalists, and during her time in jail, she contracted typhoid fever, an illness that continued to affect her health throughout her life. In 1935, at 21, Rukeyser won the Yale Series of Younger Poets Award for her first book of poetry, *Theory of Flight.* After evacuation to London when the Spanish Civil War began, she became interested in the influence of biography and culture. In the 1940s, Rukeyser went to San Francisco and married, but had her marriage annulled after three months, and her son, born in 1947, never knew his father. The same year, a wealthy woman anonymously donated an annual stipend to Rukeyser which she forfeited in 1954 to teach. Joseph McCarthy's committee investigated her political activities, but she was not blacklisted. At 50, in 1964, she had her first stroke, and as she struggled to relearn language skills, she became a feminist. Her activism continued when she traveled on an unofficial peace mission to Hanoi and was arrested in an anti–Vietnam War demonstration. She also protested in South Korea. Rukeyser's complex poetic message often baffled critics since she refused to espouse any specific political view or to fulfill their expectations. Among her honorary degrees and awards were the Oscar Blumental Prize, the **Harriet Monroe** Poetry Award, an American Academy of Arts and Letters prize, and a National Institute of Arts and Letters prize.

BIBLIOGRAPHY
Kertesz, Louise. *The Poetic Vision of Muriel Rukeyser.* Baton Rouge: Louisiana State University Press, 1980. 0–8071–0552–X, 412p. In a carefully researched critical work, Kertesz evaluates images and themes in each of Rukeyser's works.
Rukeyser, Muriel. *The Life of Poetry.* 1974. Williamsburg, MA: Paris Press, 1996. 0–9638183–3–3, 223p. In this group of essays, Rukeyser posits that poetry is a medium through which to heal spiritually and mentally.

RUSSELL, LILLIAN (1861–1922)
Entertainer   Clinton, Iowa

Lillian Russell was an actor. She was christened Helen Louise Leonard after her birth on December 4, 1861, as the youngest of five children of a newspaper owner and his feminist wife. Russell attended private schools, took voice lessons, and sang in the church choir. After moving with her mother and her siblings to New York City, Russell began training for an operatic career, but after joining an operetta cast, she married the director. After her divorce, a Broadway variety producer heard her sing at her boardinghouse and cast her in a variety theater, changing her name to Lillian Russell. She eventually won recognition, and in 1882, she became a star. She then made her debut in London's Gaiety Theater. In 1888, she received an offer of $20,000 a season to appear at the Casino, New York's leading light opera theater. As a feminine symbol of her time, with lovely voice and great beauty, she became the first person to speak over long-distance telephone in 1890. The next year, she starred in The Lillian Russell Opera Company, but during the decade, her fame faded, and she returned to music halls and vaudeville companies. After her fourth marriage, she began writing a syndicated newspaper column, recruited for the Marine Corps, and during World War I, spoke for bond drives. After the war, she raised money for the American Legion. In 1922, President Warren G. Harding asked her to tour Europe to investigate immigration, and when she returned, she urged tighter laws and isolationism. Even though scandal often surrounded her name, she remained loyal to her family, and although she never developed her talent to the fullest, her fans remembered her beauty.

BIBLIOGRAPHY

Burke, John. *Duet in Diamonds.* New York: Putnam, 1972. No ISBN, 286p. Burke's carefully researched biography of Russell discusses her relationship with Diamond Jim Brady.

Schwartz, Donald Ray. *Lillian Russell: A Bio-Bibliography.* Westport, CT: Greenwood Press, 1997. 0–313–27764–8, 303p. This recommended, well-researched, and carefully documented biography of Russell elaborates on her fame as a singer and entertainer.

RUSSELL, ROSALIND (1912–1976)
Actor   Waterbury, Connecticut

Rosalind Russell was an actor. She was born on June 4, 1912, as the daughter of an attorney and a magazine fashion editor. She attended both Marymount College and the American Academy of Dramatic Arts in New York City, from which she graduated in 1929. She made her film debut in 1934, with her role in The Women making her a star. In 1941, she made films for all of the major studios, and in 1946, she was the co-founder of Independent Artists, a motion picture and play production company. Russell also wrote articles for magazines including Reader's Digest, Saturday Evening Post, and Ladies' Home Journal. Her most famous stage and screen role was in Auntie Mame, for which she received her fourth Academy Award nomination. She continued making films into the early 1970s, but when overcome with rheumatoid arthritis in her later years, she stopped performing in 1972. She devoted much of her time to charity work, with her many causes including the Sister Kenny Institute and Foundation, the Arthritis and

Rheumatism Foundation, and the Motion Picture and Television Relief Fund and Country Home. Among the boards on which she served were the National Council of the Arts, the Los Angeles International Film Exposition, and the Center Theatre Group. She was awarded a Jean Hersholt Humanitarian Award by the Academy of Motion Picture Arts and Sciences for her commitments. Russell was long married to producer Frederick Brisson, who helped manage her career. Her personality and talent garnered her honorary degrees and almost every award from the theater community, including Golden Globe Awards, a Tony Award, and the Screen Actors Guild Life Achievement Award.

BIBLIOGRAPHY

Russell, Rosalind. *Life Is a Banquet*. New York: Random, 1977. 0-394-42134-5, 260p.
    Russell's autobiography, published after her death, gives insights into a life with physical rather than emotional trials.
Yanni, Nicholas. *Rosalind Russell*. New York: Pyramid, 1975. 0-515-03737-0, 160p.
    Yanni's biography of Russell includes details about each stage in her career.

$\mathcal{S}$

SABIN, FLORENCE (1871-1953)
Physician   **Central City, Colorado**

Florence Rena Sabin was a physician. She was born on November 9, 1871, as the second of two children to an engineer and his wife. Her mother died when Sabin was seven, and she went to Chicago and Vermont to live with relatives. In 1889, when she entered Smith College, she became aware of women's rights issues. To earn money to attend medical school, she taught, and in 1896, she gained admittance to Johns Hopkins Medical School's fourth class. After she completed her M.D., she won one of the four highly competitive internships in internal medicine at Johns Hopkins where she constructed a three-dimensional model of the mid- and lower brain. Her book, *An Atlas of the Medulla and Mid-Brain*, was published in 1901 and adopted as a textbook. After choosing to work on anatomical and histological research, she became an assistant in the department of anatomy in 1902, the first woman on the Hopkins medical faculty. She was also the first female full professor by 1917. While at Hopkins until 1925, she discovered that lymphatic vessels arose from the embryo in a series of small buds from the veins. She often visited Germany to find new ideas and techniques to use in the research that she thought lifted teaching to a "high plane." In 1924, she was elected the first female president of the American Association of Anatomists and, in 1925, was the first woman elected to membership in the National Academy of Sciences. She was also the first woman with full membership at the Rockefeller Institute of New York, where she headed a study of the cellular aspects of immunity for 13 years. In 1944, she went to Colorado to assess the state's health needs and found poorly trained staff, insufficient funds, and ineffective laws. Her crusade for public health reform in Colorado became a model for other states. She received numerous awards from the scientific community and many honorary degrees. After her death, buildings were named for her at the University of Colorado School of Medicine and Smith College. She was also elected to The National Women's Hall of Fame. She is one of two persons from Colorado with statues in the United States Capitol's Statuary Hall.

BIBLIOGRAPHY

Kronstadt, Janet. *Florence Sabin*. New York: Chelsea House, 1990. 1-55546-676-1, 110p. Kronstadt emphasizes Sabin's many interests in this well-written biography for young adults.

Phelan, Mary Kay. *Probing the Unknown: The Story of Dr. Florence Sabin*. New York: Crowell, 1969. No ISBN, 176p. Phelan's readable biography of Sabin for young adults is based on an earlier biography and other sources.

SACAJAWEA   (1786–1884)
Translator and Guide   Lemhi, Idaho

Sacagawea, also called "Bird Woman," was the translator for Lewis and Clark's expedition to the Pacific Northwest. She was born around 1786 into the Lemhi band of the Shoshoni Indians. By 1804, after an enemy tribe captured her and sold her into slavery, she had become the property of a French-Canadian fur trader, Toussaint Charbonneau, who married her. When Meriwether Lewis and William Clark met Charbonneau, they hired him to go on the expedition as an interpreter, and his wife and child went with him. When the expedition neared Armsted, Montana, it encountered a band of Shoshoni led by Sacajawea's brother, Cameahwait, and their reunion positively affected negotiations for horses and guides. Sacajawea's presence with her son on the journey also helped facilitate meetings with other Native Americans. In their journals, Lewis and Clark recorded Sacajawea's ability to cope with the adverse situations they encountered along the trail. Because of her courage and contributions to the expedition, many legends and memorials honor her.

BIBLIOGRAPHY

Clark, Ella Elizabeth, and Margot Edmonds. *Sacagawea of the Lewis and Clark Expedition*. Berkeley: University of California Press, 1979. 0-520-03822-3, 171p. The text recounts Sacagawea's role in the Lewis and Clark expedition and her life afterward.

Howard, Harold P. *Sacajawea*. Norman: University of Oklahoma Press, 1971. 0-8061-0967-X, 218p. Facts about Sacajawea are few, and Howard expands his biography of her to include background on the Lewis and Clark expedition.

Kessler, Donna J. *The Making of Sacagawea: A Euro-American Legend*. Tuscaloosa: University of Alabama Press, 1996. 0-8173-0777-X, 258p. Kessler looks at Sacajawea by examining her myth as it has evolved from 1805 to the present.

St. George, Judith. *Sacagawea*. New York: Putnam, 1997. 0-399-23161-7, 115p. In this
    young adult biography, St. George re-creates scenes, but not dialogue, from
    Sacajawea's life, based on Lewis and Clark's journals.
White, Alana. *Sacagawea: Westward with Lewis and Clark*. Springfield, NJ: Enslow,
    1997. 0-89490-867-7, 128p. In a young adult biography, White tells the life of
    Sacajawea using known sources, especially the Lewis and Clark journals.

SAGE, KAY (1898–1963)
Artist   Albany, New York

Kay Sage was an artist and a poet. She was born on June 25, 1898, as one of two
daughters to a wealthy business owner and his unconventional wife. Sage's mother
often took her to France, and Sage loved Paris, learning to speak fluent French.
When her parents divorced, she also lived in Italy and learned Italian. Her
education was erratic, but in 1911, she entered the Brearley School in New York
and stayed, except for one European trip, until 1914. During World War I, she
enrolled in the Corcoran Art School in Washington, DC. After the war, she
returned to Rome to study art at the Scuolo Libera delle Belli Arti, and met
Onorato Carlandi, an artist who taught her to view objects differently. She began
painting landscapes and portraits, but in the 1930s, she shifted to abstracts. When
World War II started, she returned to Paris to help those caught in the German
occupation. After coming to the United States with her second husband, she held
her first solo exhibition, but when her husband died in 1955, she no longer
appeared in public. At her death, she bequeathed more than 100 works of art from
her collection to the Museum of Modern Art and left the largest legacy of
unrestricted funds that it had received until that time. She never talked about her
paintings, thinking that they spoke for themselves. In them, she reveals space and
obstacle, with her objects juxtaposed in the surrealist style.

BIBLIOGRAPHY
Suther, Judith D. *A House of Her Own: Kay Sage, Solitary Surrealist*. Lincoln: University
    of Nebraska Press, 1997. 0-8032-4234-4, 288p.   This carefully researched,
    documented, and recommended critical biography relies on unpublished writings,
    letters, and poems that Sage wrote.

ST. DENIS, RUTH (1877–1968)
Dancer   Newark, New Jersey

Ruth St. Denis was a dancer. She was born Ruth Dennis on January 20, 1877, as the
oldest of three children to an intermittently employed machinist and his
common-law wife. St. Denis, always athletic, defended herself when others
insulted her because of her parents' low economic status. After studying dance as a
young girl, she spent a term at Dwight Moody's Northfield Seminary in
Massachusetts, but he failed to dissuade her from wanting to perform. St. Denis
made her debut as a skirt dancer in New York's Worth's Museum in early 1894,

and for the next 10 years appeared in variety shows to help support her separated parents. In 1896, she entered Packer Collegiate Institute in Brooklyn to study French, although still wanting to act and dance on the legitimate stage. She adapted an Oriental theme for her dancing style in 1904, studied ancient religions, and two years later danced *Radha*, the dance-drama that made her famous. Using her new stage name, St. Denis, she successfully toured Europe for three years. When she opened a New York studio in 1914, Ted Shawn, a former divinity student, came for dance lessons. They married the same year and moved to Los Angeles, where they founded the Denishawn Company, with their students including **Martha Graham** and **Doris Humphrey**. St. Denis broke from the company in 1919 to perform "music visualizations" but returned when she could not support herself. In 1925, the company toured the Orient, and in 1931, the couple separated, with Shawn forming his own company of males and St. Denis forming the Society of Spiritual Arts to promote dance as a form of worship. In 1938, she became dance director of Adelphi College, and two years later, she revived *Radha*. With her additional efforts to bring the art of dance to small American towns, she earned the name "First Lady of American Dance."

BIBLIOGRAPHY

St. Denis, Ruth. *Ruth St. Denis, an Unfinished Life: An Autobiography.* 1939. Brooklyn, NY: Dance Horizons, 1969. 0–87127–030–7, 391p. In her autobiography, St. Denis relates both a record of her important public work and her quest for fulfillment through spiritual connections in her dance.

Shelton, Suzanne. *Divine Dancer: A Biography of Ruth St. Denis.* Garden City, NY: Doubleday, 1981. 0–385–14159–9, 338p. In a well-researched readable and scholarly biography, based mainly on St. Denis's unpublished journals, Shelton discusses her life and career. De la Torre Bueno Prize

Terry, Walter. *Miss Ruth: The More Living Life of Ruth St. Denis.* New York: Dodd, Mead, 1969. No ISBN, 206p. Terry knew and admired St. Denis, or "Miss Ruth," as her friends called her, and his biography of her, based on unpublished material, discusses her life in detail.

SAMPSON (GANNETT), DEBORAH (1760–1827)
Soldier and Lecturer   **Plympton, Massachusetts**

Deborah Sampson was a United States soldier and a lecturer. She was born on December 17, 1760, as the oldest of six children to a farmer and his wife. Her father abandoned the family, and the children had to find work elsewhere. At 10, Deborah was bound out as a servant to Jeremiah Thomas. She remained until she was 18, attending school part-time and learning from the family children before teaching herself. In 1782, Sampson disappeared and entered the Continental Army to participate in the American Revolution. She assumed the male identity of "Robert Shurtleff" in the Fourth Massachusetts Regiment. The other soldiers nicknamed her "Molly" because she had no beard, but she fought in several skirmishes, receiving both sword and musket wounds. When a fever forced her to enter the hospital, a doctor discovered her disguise, and in 1783, she was discharged from the military. The next year she married a farmer and won a small pension from Congress. She began to lecture on her experiences in 1802 because her family needed money, ending her presentations by dressing in a soldier's uniform and performing the manual of arms. She was most likely the first woman to lecture professionally in the United States. In 1838, Congress passed an act providing a full military pension to her heirs.

BIBLIOGRAPHY

Freeman, Lucy, and Alma Halbert Bond. *America's First Woman Warrior: The Courage of Deborah Sampson.* New York: Paragon House, 1992. 1-55778-514-7, 224p. The authors picture Sampson's achievements as soldier and speaker in modern terms.

Mann, Herman. *The Female Review: Life of Deborah Sampson; the Female Soldier in the War of Revolution.* 1866. New York: Arno Press, 1972. 0-405-04476-3, 267p. In this edited edition, new information enhances a scholarly text about Sampson's life in the American Revolution.

SANDOZ, MARI (1896–1966)
Author   Sheridan, Nebraska

Mari Sandoz was an author. She was born Marie Susette Sandoz on May 11, 1896, as the oldest of six children to a medical student who had emigrated from Switzerland to homestead and his German-Swiss wife. She learned how to survive on the frontier, walking to school six miles a day at nine years old, and heard the storytellers relate their experiences. She quickly learned to read, and although her father objected to fiction, she read as many novels as she could find. At 10, she published a story in the *Omaha Daily News* but had only four years of schooling before passing the rural teachers' examination at 16. For the next seven years, she taught. In 1922, she entered the University of Nebraska as an "adult special," and studied intermittently for 10 years while writing and working at a variety of jobs to support herself. Although her father hated fiction, he suggested before his death in 1928 that she write about his struggles as a settler. She happily devoted herself to his story and incorporated the endeavors of her family and the history of Nebraska in *Old Jules.* In 1933, dejected at its rejection, she burned 75 stories, but the next year, she resubmitted *Old Jules* to *Atlantic Monthly,* and won its $5,000 prize for the best work of nonfiction; the Book-of-the-Month Club also selected it. The book became the first of a series examining human occupation in the region between the Missouri River and the Rocky Mountains. Others in her series are *Crazy Horse, Cheyenne Autumn, The Buffalo Hunters, The Cattlemen,* and *The Beaver Men.* In her books, unromanticized stories about the West, Sandoz emphasizes the importance of social justice and her understanding of the Plains Indians. Among her honorary degrees and awards were the Oppie Award, a Western Heritage Award, a Western Writers of America Spur Award, and the Levi Straus Award.

BIBLIOGRAPHY

Sandoz, Mari. *The Christmas of the Phonograph Records*. Lincoln: University of Nebraska Press, 1996. 0–8032–9242–2, 31p. Sandoz's brief memoir recounts a family Christmas on the Plains.

———. *Letters of Mari Sandoz*. Lincoln: University of Nebraska Press, 1992. 0–8032–4206–9, 493p. These letters written by Sandoz to presidents, friends, and other authors show her concern with accuracy and truth in her own writing and in Hollywood's depiction of Native Americans.

Stauffer, Helen Winter. *Mari Sandoz, Story Catcher of the Plains*. Lincoln: University of Nebraska Press, 1982. 0–8032–9134–5, 322p. In her thoroughly researched biography of Sandoz, Stauffer reveals both strengths and weaknesses.

SANGER, MARGARET (1879–1966)
Reformer   Corning, New York

Margaret Sanger was the founder of the birth control movement. She was born Margaret Higgins on September 14, 1879, as the sixth of 11 children to the owner of a stone monument shop and his Catholic wife. Sanger watched her mother's health deteriorate with the births of her children and became convinced that women needed control over their reproduction. Sanger's two older sisters paid her tuition to Claverack College while she worked for room and board. After finishing college, she taught immigrant children for three years, reluctantly kept house for her father, and attended a new nursing school. Operations on her tubercular glands interrupted her studies, but she returned. She then married an architect, and difficulty with her first child almost ruined her health. She hated housework, and when she and her husband moved to New York, she joined the International Workers of the World to organize textile workers, using the tactic of evacuating the strikers' children from their towns to arouse national sympathy. In her concern for personal liberty, she refused to remain faithful to her husband. After realizing that women from all classes needed information on birth control, sex, and venereal disease, she published a series of articles on female sexuality in *The Call*, but the post office would not deliver the issue containing her article on syphilis. It also banned information on contraception and abortion, but Sanger had witnessed a horrible death caused by a self-inflicted abortion and determined to change attitudes. In 1914, she visited Europe, and when she returned, she began a militant feminist journal, *The Woman Rebel*, which the post office refused to mail. She escaped arrest by fleeing to Europe but left behind an informative pamphlet. In 1916, she and her sister opened a Brooklyn clinic, but the police closed it 10 days later. The judge did not free her, but he agreed that doctors could dispense information on contraceptives. Then Sanger lobbied for "doctors only" bills to remove legal prohibition to medical advice, breaking with **Mary Ware Dennett**. In 1921, she organized the American Birth Control League. In 1923, the first doctor-staffed birth control clinic opened and gave instruction to hundreds of physicians on contraceptive techniques, and by 1938, over 300 birth control clinics existed. Sanger also organized the first World Population Conference in Geneva, Switzerland, in 1927. She was elected to The National Women's Hall of Fame.

BIBLIOGRAPHY

Chesler, Ellen. *Woman of Valor: Margaret Sanger and the Birth Control Movement in America*. New York: Simon and Schuster, 1992. 0–671–60088–5, 639p. Chesler's carefully researched, documented, and recommended biography discusses Sanger's complex personality.

Douglas, Emily Taft. *Margaret Sanger, Pioneer of the Future*. Garrett Park, MD: Garrett Park, 1975. 0–912048–75–1, 298p. Sanger's personality and spirit become apparent in Douglas's detailed, researched biography.

Gray, Madeline. *Margaret Sanger: A Biography of the Champion of Birth Control*. New York: Marek, 1979. 0–399–90019–5, 494p. Gray incorporates much previously unpublished material in her biography, revealing both the public and the private Sanger.

Kennedy, David M. *Birth Control in America: The Career of Margaret Sanger*. New Haven, CT: Yale University Press, 1970. 0–300–01202–0, 320p. Kennedy's scholarly, well-researched, and balanced biography asserts that Sanger's approach to birth control both helped and hindered the movement.

Sanger, Margaret. *Margaret Sanger: An Autobiography*. 1937. New York: Dover, 1971. 0–486–20470–7, 504p. In her autobiography, Sanger discusses the social change during her 25 years of work.

SARTON, MAY (1912–1995)
Poet and Author   Wondelgem, Belgium

May Sarton was a poet and author who incorporated the subjects of feminism and lesbianism in her 45 works. She was born Eleanor Sarton on May 3, 1912, the daughter of a science historian and his artist wife. The family came to the United States when Sarton was four, and 10 years later, she became a naturalized citizen. She began writing poetry at nine, and attended both public and private schools before being offered a Vassar scholarship. She decided instead to work as an apprentice at ˚Eva Le Gallienne's Civic Repertory Theatre and later founded the Associated Actors Theatre. In 1937, her first book of poetry, *Encounter in April,* appeared to generally favorable critical reviews. After publishing another book of poetry, *Inner Landscape*, and a novel, *The Single Hound*, she became a creative writing instructor in Boston. In 1943, she joined the Overseas Film Unit as a scriptwriter, and in 1949, she became the Briggs-Copeland Instructor in English Composition at Harvard University. During the next several years, she lectured at several colleges and gave poetry readings throughout the United States. Her many awards included a Johns Hopkins University Poetry Festival Award, the Emily Clark Balch Prize, and the American Book Award. She also received many honorary degrees.

BIBLIOGRAPHY

Peters, Margot. *May Sarton: A Biography.* New York: Knopf, 1997. 0–679–41521–1, 474p. Peters based her carefully researched, recommended literary biography on interviews with Sarton.

Sarton, May. *At Eighty-Two: A Journal.* New York: Norton, 1996. 0–393–03889–0, 350p. Sarton writes during her eighty-second year about her daily life and frail body.

———. *Endgame: A Journal of the Seventy-Ninth Year.* New York: Norton, 1992. 0–393–03346–5, 345p. In this journal series, Sarton becomes frustrated with her loss of independence resulting from ill health.

SCHOFIELD, MARTHA (1839–1916)
Educator   Newton, Pennsylvania

Martha Schofield was an educator who devoted her life to furthering African American education in the South. She was one of five children born to a Quaker farmer and his wife, who often harbored escaped slaves. Schofield attended a private school run by her uncle before teaching at a Friends' school and a Philadelphia school for African Americans. At the end of the Civil War, she volunteered to serve with the Pennsylvania Freedmen's Relief Association and went to South Carolina's Sea Islands. She immediately founded a school and then taught at several others before vocally condemning the incompetence of Freedmen's Bureau agents and the ineffectiveness of southern whites. Soon ill with tuberculosis, however, she moved to a small town away from the coast. She persuaded the Freedmen's Bureau to replace the school building on land she donated, recruited funds from Pennsylvania Quakers, and through the ensuing years developed the Schofield Normal and Industrial School. By 1900, it was one of the most widely known schools for African Americans in the South, offering traditional subjects plus farming, carpentry, sewing, cooking, and printing. Schofield emphasized cleanliness and diet, believing, as did Booker T. Washington, that education would improve living conditions. For the last 30 years of her life, she also served as the school's business manager.

BIBLIOGRAPHY

Smedley, Katherine. *Martha Schofield and the Re-education of the South.* Lewiston, NY: Mellen Press, 1987. 0–88946–525–8, 320p. Letters, correspondence, journals, and articles in newspapers and periodicals form the basis for Smedley's researched, documented, and readable scholarly biography of Schofield.

SCHUMANN-HEINK, ERNESTINE (1861–1936)
Opera Singer   Lieben, Bohemia

Ernestine Schumann-Heink was an internationally famous contralto, known especially for her Wagnerian opera interpretations. She was born on June 15, 1861, as the oldest of four children to an army lieutenant and his wife. The family moved often and rarely had money, but her grandmother and a nun in a convent school recognized her talent. Rejected first by the Court Opera in Vienna for being too poor and too unattractive, Schumann-Heink secured a position with the Dresden Royal Opera, where she made her debut in 1878 as Azucena in *Il Trovatore*. She was relegated to minor roles, and not until she had married, had four children, and divorced did she have a better opportunity. A disagreement between a prima donna and the director of the Hamburg Opera gave her a last-minute opportunity to perform Carmen without even an orchestra rehearsal. Other roles solidified her status as a major singer with a range of nearly three octaves, from D below middle C to high C, including invitations to Bayreuth from *Cosima Wagner. After Schumann-Heink spent several years with the Hamburg Opera and remarried, Maurice Grau of the Metropolitan Opera pursued her and agreed to offer her husband the position of stage consultant. Her husband's unexpected death in 1904 and her subsequent remarriage to an American led to her naturalization in 1905. After unsuccessfully trying light opera, she then devoted herself to performing throughout America. During World War I, she gave Red Cross concerts, entertained servicemen in her home, and toured army camps, where soldiers called her "Mother of the A.E.F." In 1926, the fiftieth anniversary of her Graz debut, she gave a concert at Carnegie Hall and followed it with a 20,000-mile "farewell" tour. Her final performance at the Metropolitan Opera, in 1932, followed a *Good Housekeeping* poll in which she was chosen as one of America's 12 greatest living women. When Schumann-Heink died, her train cortege took eight hours to travel between Los Angeles and San Diego, stopping at crossings for services, and United States Army planes flew low over her home to drop flowers.

BIBLIOGRAPHY

Howard, Joseph L. *Madame Ernestine Schumann-Heink: Her Life and Times.* San Diego: San Diego Historical Society, 1990. 1-881591-04-2, 409p. Based on 48 professional clipping books and 700 photographs, this carefully researched and documented biography of Schumann-Heink, suitable for young adults, illuminates her family and career.

Lawton, Mary. *Schumann-Heink, the Last of the Titans.* 1928. New York: Arno Press, 1977. 0-405-09687-9, 390p. This biography, from the first person point of view, gives an enlightening view of Schumann-Heink's life.

SCHUYLER, PHILIPPA (1931-1967)
Pianist and Composer   New York, New York

African American Philippa Schuyler was a pianist and composer. She was born on August 2, 1931, the daughter of an African American writer and his wealthy white wife, who was from a Texas ranching family. Schuyler's mother fed her raw foods and claimed they aided her daughter's genius. Schuyler read by age two and played piano at three, performing her own compositions on the radio a year later. At seven, she went on tour. With an IQ measured at 180, she finished elementary school at 10, and when she was 13, the New York Philharmonic performed one of her 100 compositions. She toured the world with command performances in Belgium, Ethiopia, and Haiti where she received the Haitian Order of Honor and Merit for her composition written for the inauguration of the Haitian president, Paul Magloire. Schuyler was fluent in several languages and wrote five books before her death in a helicopter crash in Da Nang during the Vietnam War, where she had gone to evacuate Catholic schoolchildren during the fighting.

BIBLIOGRAPHY

Talalay, Kathryn M. *Composition in Black and White: The Life of Philippa Schuyler*. New York: Oxford University Press, 1995. 0-19-509608-8, 368p. Talalay's biography of Schuyler reveals her difficulties as the talented prodigy of mixed parentage.

SEAMAN, ELIZABETH. *See* BLY, NELLIE

SEDGWICK, CATHARINE MARIA (1789–1867)
Author   Stockbridge, Massachusetts

Catharine Maria Sedgwick was an author whose readers appreciated her didacticism. She was born on December 28, 1789, the sixth of seven surviving children, to a government servant and his second wife. Sedgwick's mother had brief periods of insanity, and an African American servant raised Sedgwick and her siblings. She enrolled in private schools sporadically, but her father tutored her at home and encouraged her to read the classics. After her mother's death when Sedgwick was 17 and her father's remarriage, she lived with her brothers in New York. When her father died in 1813, she began to question the strict Calvinism of her youth and eventually joined the Unitarian Meeting House in New York. She had become a disciple of William Ellery Channing, and he convinced her to publish her first novel, *A New-England Tale*, in 1822. That and two other books firmly established her reputation as the best female writer in America. She wrote three more novels and over 100 stories in which she challenged the social and political mores of the country. She advocated reforms in tenement conditions, the end of dueling, and religious toleration. Although she hated slavery, she refused to join the abolitionists and avoided the early women's rights movement. Her later activism focused on prison reform, and she served as the first director of the Women's Prison Association of New York. She received several marriage proposals but refused all of them, preferring to focus on her writing.

BIBLIOGRAPHY

Foster, Edward Halsey. *Catharine Maria Sedgwick*. New York: Twayne, 1974. 0-8057-0658-5, 171p. Foster explores influences on Sedgwick in a carefully researched, documented, and recommended biography.

Sedgwick, Catharine Maria. *The Power of Her Sympathy: The Autobiography and Journal of Catharine Maria Sedgwick*. Ed. Mary Kelley. Boston: Massachusetts Historical Society, 1993. 0-934909-35-0, 165p. The critical and carefully documented introduction to this edition of Sedgwick's journals and autobiography reveals her literary influence.

SEEGER, RUTH CRAWFORD (1901–1953)
Composer   East Liverpool, Ohio

Ruth Crawford Seeger was a composer, folk music scholar, and educator. She was born on July 3, 1901, as the younger of two children to a Methodist minister and a teacher. Her father died when Seeger was 13, and her mother supported the family by operating a boardinghouse. Seeger's mother taught her piano, and Seeger taught after her graduation from high school to earn fees for one year of composition and theory study at the American Conservatory in Chicago. In 1921, she decided to work as a theater usher and teach piano so she could finish school, and in 1929, she completed her master's degree. At Elmhurst College of Music, she met Carl Sandburg's children and wrote some of the accompaniments for songs in his *American Songbag* (1927). In 1930, she received a Guggenheim Foundation fellowship to study in Europe; met many leading composers including Béla Bartók, Alban Berg, and Maurice Ravel; and created some of her best work. In 1932, she married Charles Seeger after forming with him and other composers the Composers' Collective, a group exploring the connection between music and political views. While in the group, she composed "Chinaman, Laundryman" "Sacco, Vanzetti," and "Prayers of Steel" as her *Three Songs*, chosen for performance at the International Society for Contemporary Music in Amsterdam. Later, in Washington, DC, where her husband worked, she taught and published collections of folk music. Even though she composed few works, she investigated the treatment of dynamics, nondirectional harmonies, and parallel progressions, influencing American composers who followed her.

BIBLIOGRAPHY
Gaume, Matilda. *Ruth Crawford Seeger: Memoirs, Memories, Music.* Metuchen, NJ: Scarecrow, 1986. 0-8108-1917-1, 268p. Gaume's critical biography, based on diaries, correspondence, random notes, published and unpublished writings, music manuscripts, printed editions, and recordings, examines Seeger's contributions to American music.

Tick, Judith. *Ruth Crawford Seeger: A Composer's Search for American Music.* New York: Oxford University Press, 1997. 0-19-506509-3, 457p. Using interviews and new sources, Tick analyzes Seeger's musical compositions and her varied personas in a scholarly biography.

SETON, ELIZABETH ANN (1774–1821)
Religious   New York, New York

Elizabeth Ann Bayley Seton was the founder of the Sisters of Charity, the first American religious society, and the first native-born American to be canonized by the Roman Catholic Church. She was born on August 28, 1774, as the second of three daughters to a physician and his first wife. Her mother died when Seton was only three, but her father's second wife gave Seton religious training while raising her own seven children. At school in New York City, Seton learned to play the piano and to speak French. At 19, she married and became active in charity work, forming a society for destitute widowed mothers. After her husband's series of health problems, Seton went with him to Italy for recuperation, but he died there in 1803. While she was waiting to return to the United States, Italian friends told Seton about Roman Catholicism, and in 1805, she became Catholic. Eventually she moved to Baltimore, where society was more accepting of her new faith, and to support her five children she started a Catholic girls' school for daughters of prominent families. Her desire to found a religious community came nearer to fruition when she was offered land in Emmitsburg, Maryland. On December 7, 1808, her first recruit joined her, and on March 25, 1809, Seton took her initial vows before Archbishop John Carroll. In June, she and four other candidates appeared in public for the first time wearing the order's habit. The sisters cared for the sick and poor, but St. Joseph's School was their main activity and financial support. Soon Mother Seton offered free schooling to the needy, and she became known as the foundress of the parochial school system in the United States. Mother Seton's community spread in the East after her death. Her cause for canonization was proposed in 1907, and the process ended in 1975 when she was canonized. She has also been elected to The National Women's Hall of Fame.

BIBLIOGRAPHY

Dirvin, Joseph I. *Mrs. Seton, Foundress of the American Sisters of Charity.* 1962. New York: Farrar, Straus and Giroux, 1975. 0-374-51255-8, 498p. Dirvin used Seton's own writings as a basis for his thorough and carefully documented biography.
―――. *The Soul of Elizabeth Seton.* San Francisco: Ignatius Press, 1990. 0-89870-269-0, 232p. Dirvin researched Seton's life for over 30 years to write a biography of her soul.
Feeney, Leonard. *Mother Seton: Saint Elizabeth of New York.* 1947. Cambridge, MA: Ravengate Press, 1975. 0-911218-06-8, 212p. Feeney's biography of Seton, written for Catholics, gives insight into her life and work.
Marie Celeste, Sister. *Intimate Friendships of Elizabeth Ann Bayley Seton, First Native-Born American Saint.* New York: Alba House, 1989. 0-8189-0555-7, 212p. This well-researched and carefully documented biography, based on Seton's letters and diaries, illuminates the two phases of her life.
Melville, Annabelle M. *Elizabeth Bayley Seton, 1774-1821.* 1951. New York: Scribner, 1975. 0-684-14735-1, 411p. Melville's biography scrutinizes Seton's life and work.

SEXTON, ANNE (1928-1974)
Poet   Newton, Massachusetts

Anne Sexton was a poet of autobiographical and confessional poetry, concentrating especially on her own suffering. She was born November 9, 1928, the daughter of a salesman and his wife. She graduated from Garland Junior

College in 1948, married a salesman, and worked as a fashion model for a year. She had repeated battles with mental illness, spending years in psychoanalysis, including several extended stays in mental hospitals. Her writing began as therapy for her, but throughout her life, she remained dependent on her daughters during bouts of depression. She published her first book, *To Bedlam and Part Way Back*, in 1960. After studying with Robert Lowell, her book *Live or Die* won the Pulitzer Prize. In 1967, she began teaching and lecturing in creative writing while also reading her poetry at colleges and universities around the country. Among her honorary degrees and awards were the Audience Poetry Prize, the Levinson Prize, and the Shelley Memorial Award. Sexton committed suicide.

BIBLIOGRAPHY

Hall, Caroline King Barnard. *Anne Sexton*. Boston: Twayne, 1989. 0–8057–7538–2, 192p. Hall's researched and well-documented critical biography of Sexton examines her life and the themes in her poetry.

Middlebrook, Diane Wood. *Anne Sexton: A Biography*. Boston: Houghton Mifflin, 1991. 0–395–35362–9, 488p. Middlebrook used tapes from Sexton's therapy sessions and talked to members of her family to research this balanced and thorough biography.

Sexton, Linda Gray. *Searching for Mercy Street: My Journey Back to My Mother, Anne Sexton*. Boston: Little, Brown, 1994. 0–316–78207–6, 307p. Sexton reveals her mother's dependency as a troubled woman in an unhealthy marriage who mistreated her children.

Sexton, Linda Gray, and Lois Ames, eds. *Anne Sexon: A Self-Portrait in Letters*. Boston: Houghton Mifflin, 1977. 0–395–25727–1, 433p. The editors sorted through 50,000 pieces of writing, including letters written on carbon copies, to focus on the years 1959 to 1974 after Sexton began writing poetry as a therapy.

SHAW, ANNA (1847–1919)
Physician, Clergy, and Activist   **Newcastle-upon-Tyne, England**

Anna Howard Shaw was a minister, lecturer, and suffragist. She was born on February 14, 1847, as the sixth of seven surviving children, to a skilled wallpaper maker and his wife. Three years after Shaw was born, her father lost his new grain business, and the family immigrated to America, where their house became a way station on the Underground Railroad. When Shaw was 12, family circumstances left her and her younger brother in charge of the family's survival. They worked constantly, and Shaw developed a poor opinion of the abilities of males to support their families. At 15, she began teaching, and at 23, she delivered her first sermon. The next year, she received her license as a Methodist preacher. From 1873 to 1875 she studied at Albion College in Michigan and, in 1878, she graduated from the divinity school of Boston University, the only woman in her class. When she requested a permanent appointment, the New England Conference of the Methodist Episcopal Church refused and revoked her license to preach. The Methodist Protestant Church then ordained her as its first woman minister in

1880, and in the next few years she preached, lectured on temperance and woman suffrage, and secured an M.D. from Boston University (1886). When she met **Susan B. Anthony**, she resigned her pastorate positions to help found the National Woman Suffrage Association, serving eight years as vice president, and as president for 11 more years after it merged into the National American Woman Suffrage Association. She also joined **Frances Willard** in the leadership of the Woman's Christian Temperance Union, serving for four years. She participated in demonstrations, conferences, and Congressional hearings while lecturing in every state of the Union. During World War I, she coordinated women's contributions to the war effort and received the Distinguished Service Medal in return. She lived long enough to find out that woman suffrage had passed in both houses of Congress.

BIBLIOGRAPHY

Linkugel, Wil A. *Anna Howard Shaw: Suffrage Orator and Social Reformer*. Westport, CT: Greenwood Press, 1991. 0-313-26345-0, 238p. This carefully researched and documented biography traces Shaw's life.
Pellauer, Mary D. *Toward a Tradition of Feminist Theology: The Religious Social Thought of Elizabeth Cady Stanton, Susan B. Anthony, and Anna Howard Shaw*. Brooklyn, NY: Carlson, 1991. 0-926019-51-1, 427p. In this collective critical biography, Pellauer gives a brief overview of Shaw's life and theological contribution.
Shaw, Anna Howard. *Anna Howard Shaw: The Story of a Pioneer*. 1915. Cleveland: Pilgrim Press, 1994. 0-8298-1018-8, 337p. Shaw's autobiography relates her experiences as a pioneer of the woman suffrage movement.

SILKO, LESLIE (1948–)
Poet and Author   **Albuquerque, New Mexico**

Leslie Marmon Silko is a Native American author. She was born on March 5, 1948, to a Laguna and Plains Indian and his part Cherokee wife. She grew up on the nearby Laguna reservation and has remained in the Southwest all of her life. She said that as a child she could never orally tell stories as well as the other Lagunas and that her comfort was writing the words on paper, especially at the public school in Albuquerque to which she transferred from the reservation in the fifth grade. She later attended the University of New Mexico and earned her degree summa cum laude. She then taught at the universities of New Mexico and Arizona. While living in Tucson, she has shared her home with a welcome rattlesnake, a sacred symbol in Native American and African mythology. Her novel *Ceremony*, published in 1977, received critical acclaim for its depiction of life on a Native American reservation and its examination of philosophical issues. Earlier stories and poetry earned her recognition for her ability to unite the profound with everyday events. Her novel *Almanac of the Dead* indicts the European destroyers of Native American culture and predicts their own demise, based on old Mayan almanacs. Her awards include a National Endowment for the Arts grant, a poetry award from *Chicago Review*, the Pushcart Prize, and MacArthur Foundation grant.

BIBLIOGRAPHY

Jaskoski, Helen. *Leslie Marmon Silko: A Study of the Short Fiction*. New York: Twayne, 1998. 0-8057-0868-5, 198p. Jaskoski includes background information about Silko's life, excerpting from interviews since 1976.

Salyer, Gregory. *Leslie Marmon Silko*. New York: Twayne, 1997. 0-8057-1624-6, 151p. Salyer's critical biography discusses Silko's life and work.

Seyersted, Per. *Leslie Marmon Silko*. Boise, ID: Boise State University, 1980. 0-88430-069-2, 50p. Seyersted's monograph on Silko includes information about her life and writing.

Silko, Leslie. *Sacred Water: Narratives and Pictures*. Tucson, AZ: Flood Plain Press, 1993. 0-9636554-4-2, 77p. Silko's brief biographical essay, suitable for young adults, reflects on the importance of water in her life.

SILLS, BEVERLY (1929–)
Opera Singer   Brooklyn, New York

Beverly Sills has performed as an opera singer and as an opera house manager. She was born Belle Miriam Silverman on May 25, 1929, the daughter of Russian-Jewish immigrants. Her parents immediately nicknamed her "Bubbles," a name to which she still answers. She was only three when she sang a song and won a "Miss Beautiful Baby of 1932" contest, and by six, she had begun performing regularly on a New York radio station. Her parents had opera recordings, and Sills memorized arias in Italian before she was seven. She studied privately, and after high school, joined a national touring company performing Gilbert and Sullivan operettas. In 1947, she made her debut with the Philadelphia Civic Opera, singing the part of Frasquita in Bizet's *Carmen*. She returned to touring but enjoyed opportunities to sing opera at houses around the country. She continued to audition with the New York City Opera until she finally secured a position in 1955 as Rosalinde in Johann Strauss's *Die Fledermaus*. After her marriage to a newspaperman, she commuted from Cleveland and Boston to appear on the New York stage. In 1959, her daughter was born with progressive deafness, and two years later, her son was born autistic. After spending time raising her children, she returned to the stage in the mid-1960s for Mozart's *The Magic Flute* in Boston. In 1966, she rejoined the New York City Opera as Cleopatra in Handel's *Julius Caesar* at Lincoln Center. By 1969, Sills had earned recognition as one of America's best coloratura sopranos and debuted in Milan at La Scala, where fans called her "La Fenomena" (the phenomenon) and "Il Mostro" (the prodigy). Nearly 40 at the peak of her stardom, Sills pushed her voice to record and perform before her debut at New York's Metropolitan Opera in 1975 to an 18-minute ovation. She achieved fame from her public television appearances but decided to retire from singing when she realized that her vocal ability was suffering. She then became manager of the New York City Opera when it was in debt and having artistic problems, and her work reversed the company's fortunes. Sills resigned in 1989, and in 1994, she became chair of the Lincoln Center for the Performing Arts, making her the first performing artist ever to serve on its board. She has also served as chair of the board of the March of Dimes Foundation and as national chair of the Mothers' March on Birth Defects. Awards and honorary degrees include an Emmy Award, the Presidential Medal of Freedom, a Kennedy Center Honors Award for Lifetime Achievement, and election to The National Women's Hall of Fame.

BIBLIOGRAPHY

Paolucci, Bridget. *Beverly Sills*. New York: Chelsea House, 1990. 1-55546-677-X, 111p. In this adulatory biography for young adults, Paolucci depicts Sills as a cheerful opera singer rather than a prima donna.

Sills, Beverly. *Beverly: An Autobiography*. New York: Bantam, 1987. 0-553-05173-3, 356p. In this autobiography, Sills speaks openly about the opera world, anti-Semitism, and raising disabled children.

———. *Bubbles: An Encore*. New York: Grosset and Dunlap, 1981. 0-448-12044-5, 280p. Sills recalls her early life and her struggle to gain recognition.

SLYE, MAUD   (1869–1954)
Pathologist   Minneapolis, Minnesota

Maud Caroline Slye was a pathologist known for her cancer research. She was born on February 8, 1869, as one of three children to a lawyer and his wife, a poetry lover. Although Slye's mother wanted her to write poetry, Slye's early interest in nature attracted her to biology. After her father's death, she had to earn money for school, and in 1895, she entered the University of Chicago with $40. After recovering from exhaustion, she completed her studies at Brown University and became professor of psychology and pedagogy at Rhode Island State Normal School. Slye returned to Chicago as a graduate assistant and began research on "waltzing mice" to find out about the possibility of inheriting cancer. She used her meager allowance to feed her mice instead of herself, eventually collecting information on over 150,000 mice. In 1911, she joined the staff of the Sprague Memorial Institute, where better facilities and more funds helped her conclude that susceptibility to cancer was inherited but that the disease was not contagious. In 1919, she became the director of the Cancer Laboratory at the University of Chicago, and in 1922, she became assistant professor of pathology, rising to associate in 1922 and remaining there until her retirement in 1944. Evidence in 1936 indicated that cancer involved more than one gene, and she had to modify her own view of a single Mendelian recessive character as the cause, but her insight about heredity and cancer retained respect. Among her awards were gold medals from the American Medical Association and the American Radiological Society and an honorary degree from Brown University. She repeatedly requested that a central record bureau for human cancer statistics be established for future research on heredity and possible external factors affecting cancer, but to no avail. In addition to her medical interests, Slye also published two volumes of poetry.

BIBLIOGRAPHY

McCoy, J. J. *The Cancer Lady: Maud Slye and Her Heredity Studies.* Nashville, TN: T. Nelson, 1977. 0-8407-6552-5, 191p. McCoy closely examines Slye's heredity studies, executed tirelessly and meticulously, in a technical text suitable for young adults.

SMEDLEY, AGNES (1892?-1950)
Journalist   Northwest Missouri

Agnes Smedley was an author and a journalist who sanctioned socialism. She was born in either 1892 or 1894 as the second of five children to an uneducated, alcoholic farmer and his wife. Having few family resources, Smedley did not finish elementary school, but while serving as a teacher in impoverished New Mexico schools, she became interested in education, and after the deaths of her mother and older sister, she left home at 16. She worked as a secretary in Denver, attended the Normal School in Tempe, Arizona, and married. In California with her husband, she attended more classes and learned about socialism. In 1916, after the breakup of her marriage, she went to New York and attended night classes at New York University while working for a magazine. Her interest in socialism increased, and she opposed entry into World War I. In 1918, she was arrested for violating the federal Espionage Act after unwittingly helping an exiled Indian Nationalist. She remained in prison for several weeks before charges were dismissed. The next year, she went to Germany to study and work for Indian independence. On her way to India in 1928, Smedley stopped in China, felt needed, and remained. In Shanghai, she first supported Chiang Kai-shek's Kuomintang government, and when communist authors changed her mind, she lost her job with the *Frankfurter Zeitung* and began writing freelance articles on Chinese life. In 1935, she interviewed participants of the Red Army's "Long March," collected medical supplies, and broadcast English-language programs for communists before going to Yenan to meet Mao Tse-tung. In 1937, she walked hundreds of miles on the Sino-Japanese battlefront, taking notes for her book, *China Fights Back: An American Woman with the Eighth Route Army,* published in 1938. On the journey, she helped establish medical centers and secured Red Cross supplies while simultaneously filing stories with the *Guardian.* Her *Battle Hymn of China,* written and published after her return to America, was her most famous book. Chinese officials granted her request to be buried in China and placed her ashes in Peking's National Memorial Cemetery of Revolutionary Martyrs, the only noncommunist foreigner buried there.

BIBLIOGRAPHY

MacKinnon, Janice R., and Stephen R. MacKinnon. *Agnes Smedley: The Life and Times of an American Radical.* Berkeley: University of California Press, 1988. 0-520-05966-2, 425p. This thorough biography of Smedley reveals her strength.

Smedley, Agnes. *Battle Hymn of China*. 1943. New York: Da Capo Press, 1975. 0–306–70693–8, 528p. Smedley's readable accounting of the years from 1929 to 1941 reveals her support of communism.

SMITH, BESSIE (1894–1937)
Entertainer   Chattanooga, Tennessee

Bessie Smith, "empress of the blues," became a symbol of African American pride and refusal to submit to inferior social status while introducing blues to mainstream America. She was born on April 15, 1894, into a poor family. Her father died before she was two, and her mother and two brothers died within the next 10 years. Smith's sister headed the family while Smith sang on street corners to her brother's guitar accompaniment. At 18, she joined the Moses Stokes traveling troupe as a dancer and met **Ma Rainey**, a member who befriended her but was not responsible for Smith's later success. In 1913, Smith gained fame in Atlanta and the South before moving to Philadelphia and beginning to record with Columbia in New York. Her first record, containing songs of an oral tradition and of a personal strain that appealed to her African American fans, sold 780,000 copies in six months. She became the first African American to broadcast live radio shows in Atlanta and Memphis and to sing for white audiences. During future recordings, she teamed with Louis Armstrong for nine songs as well as with Benny Goodman and others. Although the Great Depression ended her recording contract and left her with few jobs before her death in an automobile accident, her legacy has remained important in the music world. She has also been elected to The National Women's Hall of Fame.

BIBLIOGRAPHY
Albertson, Chris. *Bessie*. New York: Stein and Day, 1972. 0–8128–1406–1, 253p. After interviews with Smith's niece and others who knew her, Albertson examines Smith in a readable, well-documented text.
Feinstein, Elaine. *Bessie Smith*. New York: Viking, 1985. 0–670–80642–0, 104p. This brief overview of Smith's life quotes her friends and acquaintances as it lauds her achievements.

SMITH, EMMA HALE (1804–1879)
Religious Leader   Harmony, Pennsylvania

Emma Hale Smith became a prominent Mormon leader as the wife of the prophet Joseph Smith. She was born on July 10, 1804, the seventh of eleven children of a strict Methodist farmer and his wife. Smith met her husband, a diviner or spryer, while he was trying to help a farmer find a lost silver mine. When her father refused to allow the marriage, she eloped in 1827. Smith's husband supposedly talked with angels, and she wrote on paper his dictation of rules from Egyptian characters on tablets that she was not allowed to see, which resulted in the *Book of Mormon*. Smith evidently believed her husband since she promoted his work and led the church's women's organization, the Female Relief Society, while raising four surviving children of nine. When Smith, her husband, and other Mormons settled in Nauvoo, Illinois, the group attracted thousands of converts. Smith's husband secretly began to practice polygamy, and in 1843, he dictated an official revelation saying that polygamy was God's law. Over Smith's objections, her husband collected nearly 50 wives. When Smith's husband was murdered by anti-Mormons the next year, she remained in Nauvoo while other Mormons migrated further west. In 1847, she married a non-Mormon but remained true to her religion although opposed to polygamy. Her son, Joseph Smith III, started an antipolygamous Mormon group known as the Reorganized Church of Jesus Christ of Latter-Day Saints, and Smith actively supported him.

BIBLIOGRAPHY

Cheville, Roy Arthur. *Joseph and Emma Smith, Companions for Seventeen and a Half Years*. Independence, MO: Herald, 1977. 0-8309-0174-4, 206p. This researched biography of Smith examines her relationship with her husband.

Newell, Linda King, and Valeen Tippetts Avery. *Mormon Enigma: Emma Hale Smith*. Urbana: University of Illinois Press, 1994. 0-252-06291-4, 394p. Newell and Avery show Smith as a loving woman whose Mormon friends betrayed her when they married her husband under his law of polygamy.

SMITH, JESSIE WILLCOX (1863–1935)
Artist   **Philadelphia, Pennsylvania**

Jessie Willcox Smith was a painter whose children's book illustrations brought her fame. She was born on September 8, 1863, as the youngest of four children to an investment broker and his wife. After a private school education, Smith began training to teach kindergarten but discovered a love of drawing. She entered the School of Design for Women in Philadelphia and continued work at the Pennsylvania Academy of the Fine Arts under Thomas Eakin. A few of her illustrations appeared in *St. Nicholas*, but her best work began with Howard Pyle at Drexel Institute. She completed several commissions before winning national acclaim and a bronze medal at the Charleston Exposition in 1902. Her intense work ethic led her friends to call her "the Mint" when her illustrations for magazines and advertisements earned her a large income. Among the publications in which her illustrations appeared were *Ladies' Home Journal*, *Collier's*, *Scribner's*, *Harper's*, the *Century*, and *Good Housekeeping*, with her color covers gracing the latter for 15 consecutive years. She preferred, however, to illustrate children's books including Robert Louis Stevenson's *A Child's Garden of Verses*, **Louisa May Alcott**'s *Little Women*, Charles Kingsley's *Water Babies*, George MacDonald's *At the Back of the North Wind*, and Johanna Spyri's *Heidi*. Throughout her career, she illustrated over 60 books and created over 450 separate drawings for other publications. Although Smith never married, she supported 11 children at various times during her life and contributed to orphanages and other charities. Among her additional awards were the Mary Smith Prize and a silver medal at the Panama Pacific Exposition.

BIBLIOGRAPHY

Nudelman, Edward D. *Jessie Willcox Smith: American Illustrator.* Gretna, LA: Pelican, 1990. 0–88289–786–1, 144p. A brief biography precedes a series of Smith's color illustrations.

Schnessel, S. Michael. *Jessie Willcox Smith.* London: Studio Vista, 1977. 0–289–70805–2, 224p. This biography of Smith examines her life and her career.

SMITH, KATE   (1909–1986)
Singer   Greenville, Virginia

Kate Smith was one of the most popular singers of the twentieth century. She was born Kathryn Elizabeth Smith on May 1, 1909, to a wholesale magazine distributor and his wife. Although Smith failed to talk until she was four, she was singing at church socials one year later and for troops at army camps in the Washington area during World War I. She studied nursing for a few months but chose to become a singer. In 1926, after opening in an Atlantic City review, she became a star on Broadway. At the time she was 17 years old and weighed nearly 200 pounds. A Columbia Records representative heard her sing and suggested that she focus on singing instead of comedy, and her first major booking lasted for a record 11 weeks. In 1931, on May 1, her twenty-second birthday, she began a 15-minute nightly radio show and performed the song that became her trademark, "When the Moon Comes Over the Mountain." Within six months, she had a sponsor, a long-term contract, and a large salary. In 1938, she began a successful daytime radio show during which she commented on current affairs and gave advice. The same year, she first sang Irving Berlin's "God Bless America." After its huge success, Smith and Berlin donated their subsequent royalties from it to the Boy and Girl Scouts of America. In 1950, Smith started the *Kate Smith Variety Hour* on television, and when the network tried to drop the show five years later, it received 400,000 protest letters. During her career, Smith recorded almost 3,000 songs, with at least 600 of those making the hit parade. She made over 15,000 radio broadcasts and received more than 25 million fan letters. During World War II, she was named one of the most popular women in America. She sold over $107 million in war bonds in 18 hours of work on the CBS radio network and over $600 million during World War II. President Roosevelt once introduced her to King George VI of England, saying, "This is Kate Smith. Miss Smith is America."

BIBLIOGRAPHY

Hayes, Richard K. *Kate Smith: A Biography.* Jefferson, NC: McFarland, 1995. 0–7864–0053–6, 306p. Hayes uses interviews with Smith and others in his biography.

Pitts, Michael R. *Kate Smith: A Bio-Bibliography*. Westport, CT: Greenwood Press, 1988. 0-313-25541-5, 261p. Pitts, in his thoroughly researched and documented critical study of Smith, includes a short biography.

SMITH, LILLIAN EUGENIA (1897-1966)
Reformer and Author
Jasper, Florida

Lillian Smith was a reformer and author. She was born on December 12, 1897, as the seventh of ten children to religious parents who subjected her to religious revivals, sexual taboos, and racial prejudices. Smith began studying at Piedmont College but had to leave to help the family when her father lost his business in 1915. As a talented musician, she was able to return to school in 1917 at the Peabody Conservatory. In 1922, she became music director at a Methodist school in Huchow, China, where discrimination based on race and class continued to disturb her. When her parents became ill in 1925, she left China to nurse them and to manage their camp. At the camp, Smith met Paula Snelling, and based on their shared beliefs, they developed a lifelong friendship. Smith began writing, and in 1936, she and Snelling published a little magazine, *Pseudopodia* (renamed the *North Georgia Review* and then *South Today*). As the first white southern journal to publish writing by African American scholars and artists, it grew to a circulation of 10,000 before ceasing in 1945. Smith published her first novel, *Strange Fruit*, in 1944, but the post office deemed its interracial love obscene. Her second book, *Killers of the Dream*, denounced segregation. Hostility toward her work damaged sales of future books, and arsonists destroyed manuscripts, over 13,000 letters, and private papers in three separate fires. Her last book focused on the nonviolent civil rights movement, and African American universities such as Howard, Atlanta, and Fisk honored it. Smith served for many years on the executive board of the Congress of Racial Equality (CORE) until she became too ill with cancer. When she died, she left unfinished work in which she had begun to discuss gender discrimination.

BIBLIOGRAPHY

Blackwell, Louise, and Frances Clay. *Lillian Smith*. New York: Twayne, 1971. No ISBN, 152p. The text examines Smith's writing and life by analyzing her nonfiction and fiction.

Loveland, Anne C. *Lillian Smith, a Southerner Confronting the South: A Biography*. Baton Rouge: Louisiana State University Press, 1986. 0-8071-1343-3, 298p. Loveland posits that Smith deserves accolades as a civil rights pioneer but not as a writer.

Smith, Lillian Eugenia. *How Am I to Be Heard? Letters of Lillian Smith*. Ed. Margaret R. Gladney. Chapel Hill: University of North Carolina Press, 1993. 0-8078-2095-4, 384p. Gladney accompanies this collection of 145 of Smith's letters with biographical essays.

SMITH, MARGARET CHASE (1897–1995)
Congresswoman   Skowhegan, Maine

Margaret Chase Smith was the first woman elected to both branches of Congress and nominated for president by a major political party. She was born on December 14, 1897, as the eldest of six children to the town's barber and his wife. While attending Skowhegan High School, she worked part-time in the local dime store, as a night telephone operator, and as a substutite barber for her father. After she graduated in 1916, she eventually worked for eight years on the *Independent Reporter*, the community's weekly newspaper. After she married at 32, her husband, a wealthy Republican politician of 55, ran for Congress. She worked for him, and after he died suddenly from a heart attack, his constituents elected Smith to succeed him. Smith served Maine for 32 years, from 1941 to 1973, 8 in the House and 24 in the Senate, her first 12 years as the lone female member. She was the Republican Party's first female senator and the second woman in history elected to the Senate. From June 1955 to August 2, 1968, "the Lady from Maine" answered 2,941 votes in succession, saying that she had been doing the job for which she was elected. Her speech against Senator Joseph McCarthy in her famous "Declaration of Conscience" on the Senate floor on June 1, 1950, may have been her most courageous moment. For 15 minutes, she denounced McCarthy and the hate and intolerance of his committee. In 1964, when her name was put into nomination for president at the Republican National Convention, she received 27 votes. In her fifth campaign for the Senate, a younger Democrat upset her, and she began conducting seminars and discussion groups at many colleges and universities throughout the country under the aegis of the Woodrow Wilson National Fellowship Foundation. She was elected to The National Women's Hall of Fame.

BIBLIOGRAPHY

Gould, Alberta. *First Lady of the Senate: A Life of Margaret Chase Smith*. Mt. Desert, ME: Windswept House, 1995. 1-88365-027-5, 150p. This biography for young adults covers Smith's life and career.

Schmidt, Patricia L. *Margaret Chase Smith: Beyond Convention*. Orono: University of Maine Press, 1996. 0-89101-088-2, 392p. Schmidt's carefully and thoroughly researched biography includes interviews with Smith.

Vallin, Marlene Boyd. *Margaret Chase Smith: Model Public Servant*. Westport, CT: Greenwood Press, 1998. 0-313-29163-2, 264p. Vallin examines Smith's political speeches to focus on her beliefs.

Wallace, Patricia Ward. *Politics of Conscience: A Biography of Margaret Chase Smith*. Westport, CT: Praeger, 1995. 0-275-95130-8, 245p. Wallace presents a balanced view of Smith, based on a series of interviews with her and former colleagues and on her personal papers.

SOKOLOW, ANNA (1915?-)
Choreographer   Hartford, Connecticut

Anna Sokolow is a choreographer, dancer, and teacher. She was born either in 1910; on February 20, 1913; or on February 9, 1915 (a date she will not verify). Her father was disabled, and her mother supported her four children with low-paying jobs in the garment industry. Sokolow studied at the School of American Ballet and Metropolitan Opera Ballet School before joining **Martha Graham**'s original dancers in 1930. She began choreographing in 1934, founded her own troupe, and in 1939, started the first modern dance company in Mexico, La Paloma Azul. She was the first to have dancers shivering from head to toe, in groups with tangled limbs, or frozen in fear. She has also conducted pioneering collaborations with experimental jazz composers but has never produced a consistent seasons of performances, never founded a school, and never maintained a studio. The Joffrey Ballet, Alvin Ailey American Dance Theater, the Netherlands Dance Theatre, and London's Ballet Rambert have repeatedly performed *Rooms*, which she choreographed in 1955. She participated in the creation of *Hair* and *Candide* on Broadway and has choreographed works by Samuel Beckett and Tennessee Williams. Because she has never sought grants, she has had few funds with which to build her name. She lives frugally, concerned only with choreographing. She spent time in Israel helping it develop its dance, and Israelis admired her achievements as much as Mexicans did during her earlier career. One of her awards was the Samuel H. Scripps American Dance Festival Award for $25,000, the largest sum given annually to a dance artist, honoring a significant lifetime contribution to American modern dance.

BIBLIOGRAPHY
Warren, Larry. *Anna Sokolow: The Rebellious Spirit.* Princeton, NJ: Princeton University Press, 1991. 0-87127-162-1, 402p. Warren notes that in the hundred interviews conducted for this biography of Sokolow, he heard many different interpretations of similar incidents.

SONTAG, SUSAN (1933-)
Author   New York, New York

Susan Sontag is an author and intellectual. She was born on January 16, 1933, and from an early age was interested in literature and philosophy. She grew up in Tucson, Arizona, and Los Angeles, and after graduation from high school at 15, she enrolled at the University of California, Berkeley. She thought she wanted to study medicine and write, but she realized that she preferred writing. She finished her education in English and philosophy by studying at the University of Chicago, Harvard, and Oxford, England. She began writing essays and book reviews in the early 1960s, and her first novel, *The Benefactor*, was published in 1963. During this time she taught, but by 1966, royalties from her books *Against Interpretation* and *Other Essays* enabled her to write full-time. In her articles for *Partisan Review*,

Harper's, Nation, and the *New York Review of Books,* Sontag lauded European artists and thinkers, and critics noted that her work, as a historian of ideas, has more in common with that of Roland Barthes and Walter Benjamin than with her New York colleagues. In her later career, she has analyzed her battle with cancer and written screenplays. Among her awards are a George Polk Memorial Award, a National Institute and American Academy Award, and the National Book Critics Circle Prize.

BIBLIOGRAPHY

Poague, Leland, ed. *Conversations with Susan Sontag.* Jackson: University Press of Mississippi, 1995. 0–87805–833–8, 287p. In 20 interviews with Sontag that appeared in different publications beginning in 1969, Poague shows the progression of her thought.

Sayres, Sohnya. *Susan Sontag: The Elegaic Modernist.* New York: Routledge, 1990. 0–415–90030–1, 170p. Sayres clearly admires Sontag's work in this critical study of her life and writing.

SPENCER, ANNE (1882–1975)
Poet   Henry County, Virginia

Anne Spencer, a distinguished African American poet during the Harlem Renaissance, was born on February 6, 1882. Her parents separated when she was five, and she and her mother moved to a West Virginia mining town. When her father discovered that she had had no formal education by age 11, he threatened to take her, so her mother enrolled her in a Lynchburg school. She graduated in 1899 as valedictorian, taught for two years, and married. James Weldon Johnson came to Lynchburg in 1917 to organize a chapter of the National Association for the Advancement of Colored People and stayed with her family. When he saw Spencer's poetry, he helped her find a publisher and suggested her pen name. She published her first poem when 38 in *Crisis,* and Johnson published some of her poems in his work, *The Book of American Negro Poetry* (1922). She then appeared in every anthology of African American poetry between 1920 and 1940, although her style and themes reflected the nineteenth century more than the Harlem Renaissance. Her fame made her confident enough to advocate civil rights in Lynchburg, influencing the hiring of African American teachers and the opening of a library for African Americans. At her death, she had completed over 50 poems.

BIBLIOGRAPHY

Greene, J. Lee. *Time's Unfading Garden: Anne Spencer's Life and Poetry.* Baton Rouge: Louisiana State University Press, 1978. 0–8071–0294–6, 204p. Using samples from Spencer's writings as well as her own recollections, Greene's critical biography reveals facets of the times in which Spencer lived.

STANTON, ELIZABETH CADY (1815-1902)
Reformer   Johnstown, New York

Elizabeth Cady Stanton was a women's rights leader. Born on November 12, 1815, she was the fourth of six children of a lawyer and his wife. Her father served in Congress and on the New York Supreme Court. In her father's office, she often heard stories of women who lost their property and their children when their marriages failed. Her father once lamented that she was female, and she decided to make him proud of her by studying languages, riding horseback, and becoming skillful at games. She attended **Emma Willard**'s Troy Female Seminary, graduating in 1832. When in 1840 she married an abolitionist, she removed the term "obey" from their ceremony. In London for the World's Anti-Slavery Convention, Stanton met **Lucretia Mott**, and in Boston, she met other abolitionists including Frederick Douglass, John Greenleaf Whittier, **Lydia Maria Child**, and **Abby Kelley Foster**. In 1847, Stanton asked friends to address her letters to "Elizabeth Cady Stanton," and she and Lucretia Mott began planning the agenda for a woman's rights convention in 1848. In 1851, when Stanton met **Susan B. Anthony**, she impressed Anthony with the importance of woman suffrage, and their partnership began. After the Civil War, Stanton and Anthony created the National Woman Suffrage Association, with Anthony publishing *Revolution*, a women's rights newspaper. Stanton protested sexual abuse and advocated coeducational schools in lectures around the country. In 1881, she and Anthony published the first of three volumes of *History of Woman Suffrage*. In 1890, Stanton became president of the National American Woman Suffrage Association, but her radical stance against religion almost undermined the organization. When she published *The Woman's Bible*, a study of sexism in the Old Testament, in 1895, she lost her leadership. Although she died before woman suffrage became law, her efforts to change attitudes both at home and in England made it possible. She was elected to The National Women's Hall of Fame.

BIBLIOGRAPHY

Banner, Lois W. *Elizabeth Cady Stanton, a Radical for Woman's Rights*. Boston: Little, Brown, 1980. 0-316-08030-6, 189p. This biography, suitable for young adults, is an analysis of Cady Stanton's life.

Griffith, Elisabeth. *In Her Own Right: The Life of Elizabeth Cady Stanton*. New York: Oxford University Press, 1984. 0-19-503440-6, 268p. In her carefully researched and documented critical biography on Cady Stanton, Griffith sees her as a nineteenth-century female revolutionary.

Lutz, Alma. *Created Equal: A Biography of Elizabeth Cady Stanton, 1815-1902*. 1940. New York: Octagon, 1974. 0-374-95167-5, 345p. Lutz used unpublished materials, letters, manuscripts, and interviews to research this biography of Stanton.

Oakley, Mary Ann B. *Elizabeth Cady Stanton*. Old Westbury, NY: Feminist Press, 1972. 0-912670-03-7, 148p. Oakley's documented biography, suitable for young adults, emphasizes Stanton's shocking initiatives.

Stanton, Elizabeth Cady. *Eighty Years and More: Reminiscences, 1815–1897.* 1898. Boston: Northeastern University Press, 1993. 1–55553–136–9, 490p. In this autobiography, Stanton limits her discussion to her private life.

STAUPERS, MABEL KEATON (1890–1989)
Nurse and Activist   Barbados, West Indies

Mabel Keaton Staupers helped African American nurses win recognition for their services during the Great Depression and World War II through desegregating the Army Nurse Corps. She was born on February 27, 1890, and when 13, moved with her family to New York's Harlem community. She then attended the Freedmen's Hospital School (now Howard University) in Washington, DC, graduating with honors. Her marriage to a physician failed, and although relegated at first to private duty nursing like other African American nurses, Staupers helped African American physicians organize the Booker T. Washington Sanitarium, the first in-patient center in Harlem. While on a working fellowship at the Henry Phipps Institute of Tuberculosis in Philadelphia, she observed the lack of respect for and poor treatment of African Americans. In 1922, her survey of Harlem's health needs also indicated poor support. In 1934, as the secretary of the National Association of Colored Graduate Nurses, she worked to integrate nurses into the medical community. She used World War II as a chance to succeed by publicizing the military's refusal to allow more African American nurses to serve their country after the low quota allotted to them was filled. She received accolades for her endeavors, including the Spingarn Medal.

BIBLIOGRAPHY
Staupers, Mabel Keaton. *No Time for Prejudice: A Story of the Integration of Negroes in Nursing in the United States.* New York: Macmillan, 1961. No ISBN, 206p. Although this is not an autobiography, Staupers has written a history of the National Association of Colored Graduate Nurses, in which her participation was central.

STEIN, GERTRUDE (1874–1946)
Author   Allegheny, Pennsylvania

Gertrude Stein was an author and expatriate. She was born on February 3, 1874, the youngest of seven children of a businessman and his wife. Stein lived abroad with her family in Vienna and Paris for a few years before moving to Oakland, California. After her parents' early death, she lived with her mother's sister in Baltimore. She became a student at Harvard Annex (later Radcliffe College), where courses with George Santayana and William James influenced her, and in 1898, she received her degree magna cum laude. She entered Johns Hopkins Medical School but soon left to join her brother Leo in Paris to search art galleries for paintings by Cézanne, Renoir, Daumier, Manet, Gauguin, Matisse, Braque, and Picasso.

Wanting to be known as a writer, however, Stein began translating, and then writing her own work. With no contract for her first book, *Three Lives*, she published it with a vanity press. A California friend, Alice B. Toklas, offered to proofread her work and moved in. Then Stein published *Tender Buttons*, an attempt to write in the Cubist style. During World War I, Stein and Toklas volunteered in the ambulance unit for the American Fund for French Wounded, and afterward, Stein presided over her salon, which many expatriates, including Ernest Hemingway, Sherwood Anderson, and F. Scott Fitzgerald, attended. Stein subsequently lectured in England and garnered the attention that she desired. In 1933, she published *The Autobiography of Alice B. Toklas*, her view of life in Paris supposedly through Toklas's eyes. When World War II started, Stein and Toklas left Paris, but Stein became ill in 1944, and they returned and entertained many American soldiers. Supposedly Stein said on her deathbed, "What is the answer?" and when no one answered, she asked, "In that case, what is the question?" Stein was eccentric but shrewd, knowing what she wanted and striving to obtain it through her hard work.

BIBLIOGRAPHY

Brinnin, John Malcolm. *The Third Rose: Gertrude Stein and Her World*. Reading, MA: Addison-Wesley, 1987. 0-201-05880-4, 428p. Brinnin's well-researched and carefully documented scholarly biography is a recommended, balanced account of Stein's life and writing.

Knapp, Bettina Liebowitz. *Gertrude Stein*. New York: Continuum, 1990. 0-8264-0458-8, 201p. Knapp's biography introduces Stein's life and career to the nonscholar.

Mellow, James R. *Charmed Circle: Gertrude Stein and Company*. 1974. Boston: Houghton Mifflin, 1991. 0-395-47982-7, 528p. Mellow's carefully researched biography of Stein, based on memoirs and letters, examines her friendships and her art collection.

Wagner-Martin, Linda. *Favored Strangers: Gertrude Stein and Her Family*. New Brunswick, NJ: Rutgers University Press, 1995. 0-8135-2169-6, 346p. Wagner-Martin traces Stein's life in her thorough and accessible biography.

Wineapple, Brenda. *Sister Brother: Gertrude and Leo Stein*. New York: Putnam, 1996. 0-399-14103-0, 514p. Wineapple's authoritative, scholarly biography is a detailed examination of Stein's relationship with her brother Leo.

STEINEM, GLORIA (1934-)
Author and Editor   Toledo, Ohio

Gloria Steinem, an author and editor, has been a driving force behind the women's movement for 25 years. She was born on March 25, 1934, to a farmer who divorced his wife when Steinem was 10, leaving her alone to care for her mentally ill mother. Steinem later attended Smith College on scholarship and graduated Phi Beta Kappa. She then broke her engagement to study in India, where the caste system exposed her to the difficulties of an underclass, and in 1973 received her doctorate in human justice from Simmons College. Steinem first worked for the

Independent Research Service before taking a job as a contributing editor for *Glamour*. She helped found *New York* magazine in 1968 and then founded *Ms.* magazine in 1972, with the first issue selling 300,000 copies in eight days. Steinem worked for *Ms.* as editor and columnist until 1986. One of her earliest articles, "I Was a Playboy Bunny," described life as a Playboy bunny during two weeks of employment. In 1988, she shifted to a publishing house. While advocating women's rights, Steinem also supported civil rights, peace movements, and farm workers. Politically, she has been active in the campaigns of Democrats including Robert Kennedy, **Shirley Chisholm**, and George McGovern. She founded the National Women's Political Caucus in 1971, and the *Ms.* Foundation for Women, and helped found both the Coalition of Labor Union Women and Voters for Choice. Among her awards are the Penney-Missouri journalism award, the Woman of the Year for *McCall's* magazine, the Ceres Medal, election to The National Women's Hall of Fame, and nine citations from *World Almanac* as one of the 25 most influential women in America.

BIBLIOGRAPHY

Heilbrun, Carolyn G. *The Education of a Woman: The Life of Gloria Steinem*. New York: Dial, 1995. 0-385-31371-3, 451p. Heilbrun had many interviews with Steinem and people who knew her, visited places she lived, and examined her memorabilia at Smith College for this biography.

Steinem, Gloria. *Moving Beyond Words*. New York: Simon and Schuster, 1994. 0-671-64972-8, 319p. Steinem's collection of six essays reveals the woman's movement from her personal experience.

———. *Outrageous Acts and Everyday Rebellions*. 1983. New York: Henry Holt, 1995. 0-8050-4202-4, 406p. This collection of Steinem's best essays traces her development as a journalist and feminist.

Stern, Sydney Ladensohn. *Gloria Steinem: Her Passions, Politics, and Mystique*. Secaucus, NJ: Carol, 1997. 1-55972-409-9, 501p. Stern examines Steinem's development in a carefully documented and balanced biography, based on interviews with her associates.

STETSON, AUGUSTA E. (1842-1928)
Religious Leader   Waldoboro, Maine

Augusta Emma Simmons Stetson was a religious leader. She was born on October 12, 1842 (and died on the same day in 1928), the daughter of a carpenter and architect and his wife. The family attended the local Methodist church, and when Stetson learned to play piano, she became the church organist at 14. Later, she attended Lincoln Academy in Maine. After her marriage during the Civil War to a veteran, she went with him to England and India for his shipbuilding business, but weak health forced them to return to Boston to live with Stetson's parents. To support her husband, Stetson decided to become an orator, a talent she had developed in school. In 1884, she attended one of **Mary Baker Eddy**'s lectures on Christian Science. Recognizing Stetson's leadership abilities, Eddy appointed her one of five Boston preachers (readers) and then asked her to go to New York to organize the Christian Scientists. In 1888, 17 people formed a church and ordained Stetson as pastor of the First Church of Christ Scientist in New York. Three years later she organized an institute to train members of the congregation. Her church grew larger than the home church in Boston, and Eddy's fear of Stetson's competition led Eddy to limit the tenure of readers to three years. Stetson resigned her post, but in 1909, when Eddy's board of directors revoked Stetson's license to preach, Stetson continued to instruct students. Stetson thought that Eddy would change her mind, but as she waited, she decided that the experience was a test to guide her into deeper spiritual understanding. Since she espoused music and singing, she started the Choral Society of the New York City Christian Science Institute, and Stetson's students continued to follow her, arranging for her to broadcast on the radio five times each week until her death.

BIBLIOGRAPHY

Weatherbe, Gail M. *Augusta E. Stetson: Apostle to the World.* Cuyahoga Falls, OH: Emma, 1990. 1-879135-06-X, 322p. In this biased biography, Weatherbe used Stetson's letters to find out what motivated her to support Mary Baker Eddy.

STETTHEIMER, FLORINE (1871–1944)
Artist   Rochester, New York

Florine Stettheimer was an artist. She was born on August 19, 1871, as the fourth of five children to a banker who left his wife while the children still lived at home. Stettheimer studied with private tutors before working with Robert Henri during the 1890s. When her family went abroad to conserve money, Stettheimer studied with artists in Germany. At the beginning of World War I, she and two sisters opened a New York art salon which attracted such luminaries as **Georgia O'Keeffe** and Marcel Duchamp. In 1916, Stettheimer held a one-woman show with walls draped in white. When no one purchased her paintings, she refused to exhibit more than one or two paintings in museum group shows. As the years passed, she gained a reputation as an artist who would not sell her work, while her style changed from what she had been taught to her own personal expression. She began painting her family and friends in their own environments, and her *Family Portrait No. 2*, owned by the Museum of Modern Art, reveals her eclecticism. In 1934, she designed sets and costumes for the Virgil Thomson–**Gertrude Stein** opera *Four Saints in Three Acts*. Her use of cellophane and feathers won her acclaim, and she began her series of large masterpieces called *Cathedrals* with the subjects of Fifth Avenue, Broadway, Wall Street, and Art. She had wanted to have her paintings buried with her, but she decided to allow her sister to manage them. In 1946, the Museum of Modern Art gave her a memorial show, and 20 years later, Columbia University established a room in its Art Center for her work.

BIBLIOGRAPHY

Bloemink, Barbara J. *The Life and Art of Florine Stettheimer*. New Haven, CT: Yale University Press, 1995. 0-300-06340-7, 303p. In Bloemink's thorough academic biography, she identifies and analyzes Stettheimer's work.

Sussman, Elisabeth. *Florine Stettheimer: Manhattan Fantastica*. New York: Harry N. Abrams, 1995. 0-8109-6815-0, 143p. Sussman includes illustrations as well as photographs of Stettheimer and her work in this biography.

STOKES, ROSE PASTOR (1879–1933)
Activist   Augustów, Poland

Rose Pastor Stokes was an activist. She was born on July 18, 1879, to Jewish parents, but her father died soon after her birth, and Stokes took the name of her mother's second husband. The family immigrated to London, and she attended school. When she was 11, the family moved to Cleveland, Ohio, and Stokes had to contribute support to her six younger siblings. She worked in a cigar factory and may have earned extra money by reading aloud to the workers. In 1900, she published several poems in the Yiddish *Jewish Daily News* of New York City and began receiving two dollars a week for regular contributions. In 1903, the family moved to the Bronx, and she began working as an assistant editor of the *Daily News*, where she wrote an advice column. Stokes also became a lecturer for her wealthy New Yorker husband's organization, the Intercollegiate Socialist Society. As a leader from the working class, Stokes advised women workers about problems she had once faced and participated in the New York restaurant and hotel workers' strike of 1912. Stokes continued publishing articles, but in World War I, she and her husband left the Socialist Party because of its antiwar stance. After the Russian Revolution in 1917, Stokes returned to the party but was indicted and sentenced to 10 years in prison under the wartime Espionage Act for a letter to the *Kansas City Star* condemning the government's profiteering and for supposedly interfering with military recruitment. A higher court overturned her conviction, but she moved philosophically to the extreme and joined the Communist Party in 1919. In 1922, she was an American delegate to the Fourth Congress of the Communist International in Moscow. Afterward, she stood on picket lines in New York, wrote articles for *Pravda* and the *Worker* (later the *Daily Worker*), made speeches, ran for office, was arrested, and exhibited paintings at the Society of Independent Artists in 1925. She and her husband diverged ideologically, and after their divorce, friends collected money for her unsuccessful cancer treatment in Europe.

BIBLIOGRAPHY

Stokes, Rose Pastor. *I Belong to the Working Class: The Unfinished Autobiography of Rose Pastor Stokes*. Athens: University of Georgia Press, 1992. 0-8203-1383-1, 173p. Stokes's ideas of the the early twentieth century revealed in this readable biography remain relevant.

Zipser, Arthur, and Pearl Zipser. *Fire and Grace: The Life of Rose Pastor Stokes*. Athens: University of Georgia Press, 1989. 0-8203-1133-2, 348p. Zipser and Zipser elucidate Stokes's concerns in their biography based on extensive research in primary sources.

STONE, LUCY (1818-1893)
Reformer   West Brookfield, Massachusetts

Lucy Stone was an activist for women's rights. She was born on August 13, 1818, as the eighth of nine children to a farmer and tanner who ruled his children and wife. Stone saw the hard life of her mother, and at age 12, she began rising early to help her. When Stone read in the Bible that men should rule women, she suspected a mistranslation and decided to learn Greek and Hebrew so that she could find the original, a declaration that her father ridiculed. When Stone began teaching at 16, the disparity between salaries for women and for men dismayed her. At 25, she enrolled in Oberlin College, supporting herself with housework and teaching. She then learned Hebrew and Greek, saw that passages had been misinterpreted, and when she later became an orator, used her knowledge to shock her audience into listening. In 1847, she graduated as the first Massachusetts woman to have a college degree. **Abby Kelley Foster** suggested that Stone lecture for the American antislavery movement, but Stone's inclusion of women's rights led to censure. In 1850, at the first national women's rights convention in Worcester, Massachusetts, her speech convinced **Susan B. Anthony** to join the group. Stone then began lecturing widely on woman suffrage. In 1855, before agreeing to marriage, she demanded the right to keep her own name and to continue her work. She relinquished her career to care for her child, although after the Civil War ended, she and her husband helped establish the American Woman Suffrage Association, with **Julia Ward Howe** as president. Stone then founded the weekly newspaper *Woman's Journal*, with Mary A. Livermore as editor. An innovator in life, Stone did the same after death by becoming the first person cremated in New England. She was elected to The National Women's Hall of Fame.

BIBLIOGRAPHY

Blackwell, Alice Stone. *Lucy Stone, Pioneer of Woman's Rights*. 1930. Detroit: Grand River, 1971. No ISBN, 313p. Blackwell's biography of her mother is a balanced examination of Stone's achievements.

Hays, Elinor Rice. *Morning Star: A Biography of Lucy Stone, 1818-1893*. 1961. New York: Octagon Books, 1978. 0-347-93756-7, 339p. This well-researched and documented biography of Stone, based on the Blackwell papers, recounts her contributions.

Kerr, Andrea Moore. *Lucy Stone: Speaking Out for Equality*. New Brunswick, NJ: Rutgers University Press, 1992. 0-8135-1859-8, 301p. Kerr's readable scholarly biography, based on manuscript collections and printed primary sources, analyzes Stone's personal life and marriage.

Lasser, Carol, and Marlene Deahl Merrill, eds. *Friends and Sisters: Letters Between Lucy Stone and Antoinette Brown Blackwell*. Urbana: University of Illinois Press, 1987. 0-252-01396-4, 278p. These letters between Stone and Antoinette Brown Blackwell reveal their close relationship between 1846 and 1893 although none date from the 1860s.

STORER, MARIA LONGWORTH (1849–1932)
Music Patron and Potter   Cincinnati, Ohio

Maria Longworth Nichols Storer was a music patron and ceramist. She was born into a wealthy family as the third child on March 20, 1849. She received a good education, and at 19, she married an older man who shared her interests in music and art. With him, she founded the Cincinnati May Music Festival. When they went to the Philadelphia Centennial Exposition of 1876 and saw Japanese pottery items, Storer became intensely interested. She returned home to open Ohio's first art pottery and worked there daily for the next 10 years. With the help of a chemist, she developed a glaze that gave the pottery a deep tone, and her recognition included a gold medal at the 1889 Paris Exposition. She won a second gold medal at the Paris Exposition of 1900 for her decorative work in bronze. After Storer remarried when her first husband died, she went to Washington, where her husband served in Congress before becoming a diplomat. When they went to Madrid, Storer helped organize an American women's charity drive to help Spanish prisoners in the Philippines. She continued to be involved in charity work at other posts filled by her husband and after they returned to America in 1906.

BIBLIOGRAPHY
Boehle, Rose Angela. *Maria Longworth: A Biography*. Dayton, OH: Landfall Press, 1990. 0-913428-71-X, 168p. This researched and documented biography of Storer is based on diaries, letters, and interviews with her descendants.

STOWE, HARRIET BEECHER (1811–1896)
Author   Litchfield, Connecticut

Harriet Elizabeth Beecher Stowe was an author and a philanthropist. She was born on June 14, 1811, the seventh of eight children of a minister and his wife. Her mother died when Stowe was four, and her father, wishing that Stowe had been male, controlled her life. She began attending school at age eight and was welleducated before beginning to teach at sixteen. The *Western Monthly Magazine* had a contest in 1834 which Stowe won for her short piece, "Uncle Lot," but her life changed two years later when she married a professor of biblical literature. She had five children in seven years, and she had to help support the family financially by writing. After her husband went to Bowdoin to teach, Stowe ran a small school in their home. When she read the works on slavery by **Lydia Maria Child** and Theodore Weld, Stowe became angry and wrote *Uncle Tom's Cabin*. It was first serialized in the *National Era*, an antislavery paper published in Washington, DC, during 1851. People in the South hated her, but others loved the book, and it was translated into more than 23 languages. Her subsequent book, *Key to Uncle Tom's*

Cabin, revealed innumerable sources and their accounts of slavery. Two years later, Stowe visited Europe, where her book and her reputation had preceded her. Other books followed, and she published many articles in the *Atlantic Monthly*, the *Independent*, and the *Christian Union*. She was elected to The National Women's Hall of Fame.

BIBLIOGRAPHY

Gerson, Noel Bertram. *Harriet Beecher Stowe: A Biography*. Westport, CT: Praeger, 1976. 0-275-34070-8, 218p. In this straightforward biography of Stowe, Gerson recounts her life.

Hedrick, Joan D. *Harriet Beecher Stowe: A Life*. New York: Oxford University Press, 1994. 0-19-506639-1, 507p. Hedrick's definitive biography, using previously unavailable materials including Stowe's correspondence, examines Stowe and her writing from a feminist perspective. Pulitzer Prize.

Scott, John Anthony. *Woman Against Slavery: The Story of Harriet Beecher Stowe*. New York: Crowell, 1978. 0-690-00701-9, 169p. This biography, suitable for young adults, examines both the moral and religious background which gave Stowe the basis for her antislavery novel, *Uncle Tom's Cabin*.

Wilson, Robert Forrest. *Crusader in Crinoline: The Life of Harriet Beecher Stowe*. 1941. Westport, CT: Greenwood Press, 1972. 0-8371-6191-6, 706p. Wilson's carefully researched, documented, and readable biography of Stowe covers her life and work in detail. Pulitzer Prize.

STREEP, MERYL (1949-)
Actor   Summit, New Jersey

Meryl Streep is an actor. She was born Mary Louise Streep on June 22, 1949, as one of three children, to a pharmaceutical executive and a commercial artist. She started studying music as a young girl and began preparing to become an opera singer by the time she was 12. In her public school, she was a performer in musicals and the homecoming queen. In 1971, after she received her degree from Vassar, she enrolled first at Dartmouth College and then on a scholarship at Yale University's School of Drama, where she completed her M.F.A. in 1975. The same year, she made her Broadway debut, and for her second play won a Tony nomination. She began acting in films in 1977 with a small role in *Julia*. In 1978, she won an Emmy for the miniseries *Holocaust*, and the same year, she won an Academy Award nomination for *The Deer Hunter*. She won the Academy Award the next year for her work in *Kramer vs. Kramer* and again in 1982 for *Sophie's Choice*, cementing her position as a top box office star. In 1989, she won the Cannes Film Festival Best Actress Award. In 1995, she received her tenth Academy Award nomination, and two years later, she made her debut as an executive producer. Other honorary degrees and awards include New York Film Critics Circle Awards, Golden Globe Awards, and the **Bette Davis** Lifetime Achievement Award.

BIBLIOGRAPHY

Maychick, Diana. *Meryl Streep: The Reluctant Superstar*. New York: St. Martin's, 1984. 0-312-53066-8, 166p. For this popular readable biography of Streep, Maychick interviewed many of her colleagues.

Pfaff, Eugene E., and Mark Emerson. *Meryl Streep: A Critical Biography*. Jefferson, NC: McFarland, 1987. 0-89950-287-3, 148p. This researched, documented, readable, and recommended biography of Streep gives an overview of her life and career.

Smurthwaite, Nick. *The Meryl Streep Story*. New York: Beaufort, 1984. 0-8253-0229-3, 128p. Smurthwaite states that his biography attempts to give a progress report of Streep's first decade as a professional actor.

STREISAND, BARBRA (1942–)
Actor and Entertainer   Brooklyn, New York

Barbra Streisand is an actor, producer, director, and entertainer. She was born Barbara Joan Streisand on April 24, 1942, as one of two children, to an English teacher who died when she was 15 months old and a clerk. Her mother remarried when Streisand was nine, but her stepfather left five years later. Streisand attended Erasmus Hall High School, where she was an honor student, and she studied acting briefly before singing in nightclubs and making her first appearance on the Broadway stage in *I Can Get It for You Wholesale* in 1962. Two years later, her performance in the Broadway musical *Funny Girl* made her a major star. In 1963, she released a series of best-selling record albums that featured original interpretations of popular songs. Her career in motion pictures began with the film version of *Funny Girl* in 1968, and she made seven other movies during the next six years. She made her directorial debut in 1983 in her film *Yentl*, in which she also starred. She has continued to record throughout her career, and has collected 27 gold record albums and 10 platinum ones. She also performs in Las Vegas concerts. Among her awards are Grammy Awards, Emmy Awards, a Tony Award, and a Directors Guild of America Award.

BIBLIOGRAPHY

Bly, Nellie. *Barbra Streisand: The Untold Story*. New York: Windsor, 1994. 0-7860-0051-1, 348p. Bly's recommended and balanced popular biography of Streisand examines her relationships.

Dennen, Barry. *My Life with Barbra: A Love Story*. Amherst, NY: Prometheus, 1997. 1-57392-160-2, 281p. Dennen establishes himself as the person who helped Streisand polish her performances in preparation for fame.

Edwards, Anne. *Streisand: A Biography*. Boston: Little, Brown, 1997. 0-316-21138-9, 600p. In a thorough and balanced biography, based on interviews with a number of sources, Edwards recognizes Streisand's enormous talent.

Riese, Randall. *Her Name Is Barbra: An Intimate Portrait of the Real Barbra Streisand*. New York: St. Martin's, 1994. 0-312-95391-7, 667p. Riese carefully researched Streisand's life to find anecdotes that describe her career and life for a balanced, definitive biography.

Spada, James. *Streisand: Her Life.* New York: Crown, 1995. 0-517-59753-5, 552p.
Spada's presentation of Streisand emphasizes the diversity of her talent.

STRONG, ANNA (1885-1970)
Journalist   Friend, Nebraska

Anna Louise Strong was a radical journalist and writer. Born on November 24,
1885, she was eldest of three children of Oberlin College graduates, a
Congregational minister and his stalwart wife. Strong's mother became a major
influence before her death at sea in 1903 when Strong was 18. After graduation
from Oberlin, Strong acquired her Ph.D. from the University of Chicago in
philosophy. Interested in reform, she began to organize pacifist programs and to
direct child welfare exhibits, eventually working for **Julia Lathrop** at the
Children's Bureau. After the United States entered World War I, Strong began
writing antiwar articles for a socialist newspaper in Seattle. In 1921, she went to
Poland to assist famine victims and continued on to Russia, where she supported
the Bolsheviks and taught English to Leon Trotsky. In 1925, she visited China, and
when she returned in 1927, she recorded the communist retreat to Siberia. She
began to raise money for the John Reed Children's Colony, and after it failed,
spent part of each year in the Soviet Union until 1949, when the Soviets denounced
her for supporting Mao Tse-tung. She died in Beijing and is buried at the National
Memorial Cemetery of Revolutionary Martyrs.

BIBLIOGRAPHY
Strong, Anna Louise. *I Change Worlds: The Remaking of an American.* 1935. Seattle: Seal
     Press, 1979. 0-931188-05-9, 422p.   In a recommended autobiography, Strong
     reveals her shift from capitalist to communist.
Strong, Tracy B., and Helene Keyssar. *Right in Her Soul: The Life of Anna Louise Strong.*
     New York: Random, 1983. 0-394-51649-4, 399p.   In their well-researched
     biography of Strong, the authors present many facts for readers to assess.

SULLIVAN (MACY), ANNE (1866-1936)
Educator   Feeding Hills, Massachusetts

Annie Sullivan Macy was **Helen Keller**'s teacher and lifelong friend. She was born
on April 14, 1866. Her illiterate father deserted his three children when Sullivan
Macy was ten, and her mother died when she was eight. Sullivan Macy, nearly
blind from a childhood fever, and her younger brother, lame from tuberculosis,
went to a state almshouse; a few months later, her brother died. Sullivan Macy had
heard of the Perkins Institute for the Blind in Boston, and when an official from
the State Board of Charities visited the almshouse, she appealed to go there. At 14,
she enrolled, and the next year, a benefactor at the boarding house where she
worked paid for an eye operation which gave her limited sight. She became an avid
reader and graduated from the school in 1886 as the valedictorian in her class. That

same year, the Perkins director sent her to Alabama to become governess for a seven-year-old child who was both blind and deaf. Sullivan Macy realized that the overprotected and pampered child, Helen Keller, was also intelligent, and she patiently worked with her. By spelling out the word "water" in Keller's hand and running water over her hand, she taught Keller that things had names. Sullivan Macy later said that she taught Keller using any method that occurred to her, but realized that she had to constantly communicate with Keller for learning to proceed. Sullivan Macy helped Keller prepare for entrance exams to Radcliffe College, and during Keller's four years at the school, Sullivan Macy attended all her classes, spelled out all of the lectures in Keller's hand, and studied with her for five to six hours each day. After Sullivan Macy and Keller moved to a farm they had purchased in 1904, John Macy, a Harvard instructor who had helped Keller with her autobiography the previous year, proposed. She eventually married him but refused to leave Keller. He left in 1912, although they never divorced. After 1916, Sullivan Macy and Keller recreated the story of her teaching Keller on the vaudeville circuit for two years. Sullivan Macy's health began to fail; by 1935, she became completely blind, and died the next year. She received several honors for her work.

BIBLIOGRAPHY

Keller, Helen. *Teacher: Anne Sullivan Macy*. 1955. Westport, CT: Greenwood Press, 1985. 0-313-24738-2, 247p. Keller's tribute reveals the inventiveness that Sullivan Macy used to teach Keller.

Lash, Joseph P. *Helen and Teacher: The Story of Helen Keller and Anne Sullivan Macy*. New York: Delacorte, 1980. 0-440-03654-2, 811p. In this biography on Keller and Sullivan Macy, Lash examines Keller's productivity during the 32 years after Sullivan Macy's death and decides that Sullivan Macy allowed Keller to be herself.

SWAIN, CLARA A. (1834–1910)
Missionary and Physician   **Elmira, New York**

Clara A. Swain was a physician who served as a missionary in India. She was born on July 18, 1834, as the tenth child in a religious family. She began reading at a young age and started teaching as a teenager. After studying at a seminary, Swain resumed teaching but wanted to become a doctor, and in 1865, she began medical training at the Castile Sanitarium. Then she attended Woman's Medical College of Pennsylvania, and in 1869 received her medical degree. Attracted to evangelism, Swain decided to work in Bareilly, India, under the Woman's Foreign Missionary Society of the Methodist Episcopal Church. She and **Isabella Thoburn** sailed together in 1869, and Swain began to treat patients as soon as she arrived. She also lectured on anatomy, physiology, and other topics to seventeen females, fourteen from the local orphanage and three married women. Her practice grew, and in 1873 she opened a six-room dispensary. In less than eight months, she had treated 1,600 patients, giving each a prescription accompanied by a verse from the Bible in Hindi, Persian, and Urdu. The next year, she opened the first hospital for women in India. By the following year, she had treated 2,000 patients with over 5,000 prescriptions. In 1885, the royal family asked her to become palace physician, and hoping to bring Christian influence into the area, she agreed, remaining with them for the next 10 years. She also continued to lecture, emphasizing the importance of good drainage and the unlawfulness of female infanticide. For her years of service, the area honored her by renaming her building the Clara Swain Hospital.

BIBLIOGRAPHY

Swain, Clara A. *A Glimpse of India*. 1909. New York: Garland, 1987. 0-8240-0677-1, 366p. In these letters to members of her family, Swain recounts her experiences in India.

Wilson, Dorothy Clarke. *Palace of Healing: The Story of Dr. Clara Swain, First Woman Missionary Doctor*. London: Hodder and Stoughton, 1969. 0-340-10779-0, 245p. Wilson read Swain's letters, visited her hospital in India, and conducted interviews to create this fictional biography, suitable for young adults.

SWALLOW, ELLEN HENRIETTA. *See* RICHARDS, ELLEN SWALLOW

SZOLD, HENRIETTA (1860–1945)
Activist and Religious Leader   Baltimore, Maryland

Henrietta Szold was the founder of Hadassah, the Women's Zionist Organization. She was born on December 21, 1860, as the oldest of eight daughters to a rabbi and his wife. Her family spoke German; her father, who had emigrated from Hungary, taught her French and Hebrew; and she learned English after emigrating. She used her languages to help her father translate Hebrew until his death in 1902. She attended the Western Female High School, graduating first in her class, and then becoming principal and teacher. Szold wrote articles for the *Jewish Messenger*, using the pseudonym "Sulamith," and attended lectures at Johns Hopkins. Concerned about Russian Jewish immigrants in Baltimore, she established a night school, one of the first of its kind in the United States, which helped immigrants adapt to their new language and culture. It served over 5,000 students before it closed. Szold also served as editorial secretary of the Jewish Publication Society of America, and then as general editor, writer, and translator of Jewish classics until 1916. After her father's death, she and her mother went to Palestine. When she saw the poor conditions and the need for medical help, she returned and founded Hadassah (Hebrew for Esther, the heroine of Purim), with herself as president. In 1916, she organized a large medical unit for Palestine, and when it arrived in the fall of 1918, it contained 44 doctors, nurses, dentists, nutritionists, sanitary engineers, and administrators. She moved to Palestine and, in 1924, became the first woman elected to the World Zionist executive body. Szold then established Lemaan ha-Yeled (later renamed the Szold Foundation) to improve child welfare and to research juvenile problems. In 1933, she became director of Youth Aliyah, a worldwide movement to rescue young victims of Nazism for rehabilitation in Israel. In the last years of her life, Szold was regarded as the "Mother of the Yishuv," the Jewish settlement in Palestine.

BIBLIOGRAPHY

Dash, Joan. *Summoned to Jerusalem: The Life of Henrietta Szold*. New York: Harper and Row, 1979. 0-06-010963-7, 348p. In her readable and recommended analytical biography, Dash emphasizes Szold's life and work.

Gidal, Nachum. *Henrietta Szold: The Saga of an American Woman*. New York: Gefen, 1997. 965-229-162-5, 150p. Gidal knew Szold, and his biographical overview is basically a series of revealing photographs of her life and work.

Krantz, Hazel. *Daughter of My People: Henrietta Szold and Hadassah*. New York: Dutton, 1987. 0-525-67236-2, 145p. Primary sources, including Szold's own writings after age 49, tell her story in a biography for young adults.

Lowenthal, Marvin. *Henrietta Szold, Life and Letters*. 1942. Westport, CT: Greenwood Press, 1975. 0-8371-5998-9, 350p. Lowenthal used Szold's letters and those of her family in a readable biography.

Shargel, Baila R. *Lost Love: The Untold Story of Henrietta Szold*. Philadelphia: Jewish Publication Society, 1997. 0-8276-0629-X, 382p. Shargel discusses Szold's exchange of letters with Dr. Louis Ginzberg, a man 13 years her junior, thinking that he returned her love.

$\mathcal{T}$

TALLCHIEF, MARIA (1925–)
Ballerina   **Fairfax, Oklahoma**

Maria Tallchief performed as a professional ballerina. She was born on January 24, 1925, to an Osage father and a mother of Irish, Scottish, and Dutch heritage. Her family soon discovered that she had perfect pitch, and her mother arranged for her and her sister to sing at rodeos and benefits scheduled near their home. Tallchief moved to Los Angeles at age eight and studied ballet with Bronislava Nijinska, and at twelve, she gave a recital in which she first played the Chopin *E Minor Concerto* on the piano and then danced. Three years later, Nijinska encouraged her onstage at the Hollywood Bowl. She decided to dance rather than play piano and gained recognition in featured roles with the Ballet Russe de Monte Carlo such as Balanchine's *Danses Concertantes* and *La Somnambula*. She married Balanchine, and even though their marriage ended after five years, their collaboration continued. From 1947 to 1965, Tallchief performed with the New York City Ballet, dancing as its prima ballerina until 1960. She founded the Chicago City Ballet in 1979 and has been artistic director of the Lyric Opera Ballet. She has also performed in films. Among her honorary degrees and awards are the *Dance Magazine* Award, the Capezio Award, a Kennedy Center Honors Award for Lifetime Achievement, and election to The National Women's Hall of Fame.

BIBLIOGRAPHY
Lang, Paul. *Maria Tallchief: Native American Ballerina*. Springfield, NJ: Enslow, 1997. 0–89490–866–9, 128p. This biography for young adults focuses on Tallchief's background and career.

Livingston, Lili Cockerille. *American Indian Ballerinas*. Norman: University of Oklahoma Press, 1997. 0-80612-896-8, 328p.   For a collective biography acknowledging the Native American contributions to ballet, Livingston interviewed Tallchief.

Myers, Elisabeth P. *Maria Tallchief: America's Prima Ballerina*. New York: Grosset and Dunlap, 1967. No ISBN, 175p. This biography for young adults relates Tallchief's story.

Tallchief, Maria. *Maria Tallchief: America's Prima Ballerina*. New York: Henry Holt, 1997. 0-8050-3302-5, 351p. Tallchief remembers the people who taught her to dance and her career as a ballerina.

TAMIRIS, HELEN (1905–1966)
Ballerina   New York, New York

Helen Tamiris was a dancer and choreographer. She was the youngest of five children, born on April 24, 1902, to a tailor and his wife, both Jewish immigrants. As a young child, Tamiris wanted to be a dancer, and she took lessons at **Lillian Wald**'s Henry Street Settlement. Against her father's wishes, she auditioned for the Metropolitan Ballet School. She received a scholarship for study, and after graduating from high school, joined the company. She left the Metropolitan in 1923 and toured South America with the Bracale Opera Company. When she returned, she danced in nightclubs and revues as Senorita Tamiris. In 1924, she danced in the Music Box Revue with **Fanny Brice**, but in 1927, she decided to perform on the concert stage, choreographing her own dances and designing and stitching her costumes. In her second solo concert, she introduced two Negro spirituals, and began her crusade to reform dance, premiering 12 works over the next years. She wanted her dancing to "express the spirit" of her race, and she went to Austria as the first American woman invited to perform. She then returned to New York and opened her School of American Dance. During the 1930s, she was active in the new form of modern dance with **Martha Graham** and **Doris Humphrey** while using jazz along with spirituals to develop social-protest themes in her work. She encouraged **Hallie Flanagan** to include dance in the Federal Theatre Project and served as its principal choreographer from 1937 to 1939. During the same years, she gave benefit performances for the *Daily Worker* and for the Lenin Memorial Meeting in 1936, earning herself the epithet "Red sympathizer." In 1937, concerned about the needs of dancers, she merged her Dance Association with two other groups to form the American Dance Association. Tamiris choreographed a skating ballet in the musical *Up in Central Park* (1944) on Broadway, which ran for 500 performances, and 10 additional shows including *Annie Get Your Gun* and *Fanny*. Among her awards are the first *Dance* Magazine Award and a Tony Award.

BIBLIOGRAPHY
Schlundt, Christena L. *Tamiris: A Chronicle of Her Dance Career, 1927–1955*. New York: New York Public Library, 1972. 0-87104-233-9, 94p.   Schlundt uses

programs and clippings, unpublished materials, and other sources in her documented biography of Tamiris.

TAN, AMY (1952–)
Author   Oakland, California

Amy Tan is an Asian American author. She was born on February 19, 1952, to a minister and electrical engineer and a vocational nurse. She attended San Jose State for her undergraduate and graduate degrees and studied further at the University of California in Berkeley. After her schooling, she worked as a consultant with programs for disabled children and then as a reporter, managing editor, and associate publisher for *Emergency Room Reports* (now *Emergency Medicine Reports*), and as a freelance technical writer until 1987. In 1989, she published *The Joy Luck Club*, a book about women much like her mother and aunt, and critics applauded it. She followed it with *The Kitchen God's Wife* two years later, which also received good reviews. Although she began writing fiction as therapy for her workaholic tendencies, she discovered in it her unique voice. Among her awards are the Commonwealth Club Gold Award and the Bay Area Book Reviewers Award.

BIBLIOGRAPHY
Huntley, E. D. *Amy Tan.* Westport, CT: Greenwood Press, 1998. 0–313–30207–3, 184p. Huntley's critical biography examines Tan's life and work.

Kramer, Barbara. *Amy Tan, Author of "The Joy Luck Club."* Springfield, NJ: Enslow, 1996. 0–89490–699–2, 112p. Kramer used quotes from published interviews and reviews to reveal Tan's initial rebellion toward her heritage.

TANDY, JESSICA (1909–1994)
Actor   London, England

Jessica Tandy was an actor. She was born on June 7, 1909, the third child and only daughter of a rope manufacturer and salesman and his wife. Her father died when she was 12, and her mother had to teach night school and work as a clerk to supplement her income as headmistress at a school for retarded children. Tandy studied at Dame Alice Owen's Girls' School, where she read literary classics, attended the theater, and visited museums. Tandy decided to be an actor in her teen years and took drama lessons on Saturdays and studied Shakespeare in the evening. In 1924, she began dramatic training in London after she had made her professional debut in a small backroom theater in London's Soho district. She then began touring, and in 1932, won acclaim as Manuela in *Children in Uniform*. She appeared in more than two dozen plays during the next decade, preferring classical theater, which she had first performed as Olivia in *Twelfth Night* with the Oxford University Dramatic Society. In 1940, after playing Cordelia in *King Lear*, she immigrated to the United States to earn money to support her daughter. She married Hume Cronyn in 1942 and became a naturalized citizen. Her first important role in New York was Blanche DuBois in the original production of *A Streetcar Named Desire* in 1947. The play ran for more than two years, and Tandy won a Tony Award and a New York Drama Critics Circle Award for her work. During her career, she played over 150 roles on stage, in films, and on television, with some of these performances opposite Cronyn. Among her honors were Tony Awards, the *Sarah Siddons Award, Drama Desk Awards, and an Academy Award for one of her last films, *Driving Miss Daisy*.

BIBLIOGRAPHY

Barranger, Milly S. *Jessica Tandy: A Bio-Bibliography*. Westport, CT: Greenwood Press, 1991. 0-313-27716-8, 150p. Barranger follows a biographical profile of Tandy's life with thorough information about her career.

TARBELL, IDA (1857–1944)
Journalist   Erie, Pennsylvania

Ida Minerva Tarbell was an investigative journalist and lecturer. She was born on November 5, 1857, the eldest of three surviving children of the first manufacturer of wooden tanks for the oil industry and a former schoolteacher. Early interested in science and human rights, Tarbell abandoned religion and thought that education was the way to avoid marriage and housekeeping. She attended Allegheny College as one of five women in her class and received her degree in 1880. After teaching for two years, she joined the staff of the *Chautauquan* for the next eight. Then in 1891, she subsidized a trip to Paris by contributing articles to *Scribner's*. The editor of *McClure's* saw her work, liked the articles she wrote for his magazine, and invited her to join his staff. Her text accompanying Napoleon prints in a series of articles increased the magazine's circulation enormously, and her volume of the pieces *A Short Life of Napoleon Bonaparte*, published in 1895, sold over 100,000 copies. In 1900, she began research on Standard Oil Company. Prejudiced against big business since childhood, she started investigating, and her exposure of misdeeds in *The History of the Standard Oil Company* earned the name "muckraking" from the "Man with the Muckrake" in John Bunyan's *Pilgrim's Progress*. Tarbell left *McClure's* and began co-editing *American Magazine*, a publication she partially owned, until 1915. She then lectured on the Chautauqua circuit and wrote several popular biographies, including eight books on Abraham Lincoln. Later she served as a member of government conferences and committees. In 1926, she went to Italy and interviewed Mussolini. Although a feminist in practice, Tarbell did not support woman suffrage and alienated its advocates whom she met in her later years, including **Anna Howard Shaw** and **Carrie Chapman Catt**.

BIBLIOGRAPHY

Brady, Kathleen. *Ida Tarbell: Portrait of a Muckraker*. 1984. Pittsburgh, PA: University of Pittsburgh Press, 1989. 0-8229-5807-4, 286p. Brady thoroughly researched

Tarbell's life for information about her career and presents it in a recommended, balanced biography.

Camhi, Jane Jerome. *Women Against Women: American Anti-Suffragism, 1880–1920.* Brooklyn, NY: Carlson, 1994. 0-926019-65-1, 328p. Camhi devotes a full chapter to Tarbell in which she discusses her role as an antisuffragist.

Kochersberger, Robert C., ed. *More than a Muckraker: Ida Tarbell's Lifetime in Journalism.* Knoxville: University of Tennessee Press, 1994. 0-87049-829-0, 242p. Kochersberger introduces 26 of Tarbell's journalistic pieces on a wide range of topics with a brief biography and an overview of her career.

Tarbell, Ida M. *All in the Day's Work: An Autobiography.* 1939. Boston: Hall, 1985. 0-8398-2881-0, 412p. Tarbell's autobiography is also a social history of the times in which she lived.

TAUSSIG, HELEN BROOKE (1898–1986)
Physician   **Cambridge, Massachusetts**

Helen Taussig was a physician who founded pediatric cardiology and co-developed the successful "blue baby" operation, first performed in 1944. She was born on May 24, 1898, to a Harvard economist and his wife. Her father helped her overcome reading difficulties resulting from dyslexia using what he had learned from his German immigrant physician father, who had studied problems of visually impaired children. She attended college at Radcliffe and the University of California, where she was a tennis champion and a member of Phi Beta Kappa. She studied medicine, first at Harvard as a special student because women were not admitted, then at Boston University, and finally at Johns Hopkins, graduating in 1927. In 1930, she began teaching at Johns Hopkins University where she remained until 1963, becoming a full professor in 1959. She began her study of birth defects of the heart while head of a heart clinic at Johns Hopkins and became interested in rheumatic fever because she had to learn to use fluoroscopy, then a relatively new X-ray technique, to study congenital malformations of the heart. Her association with Dr. Alfred Blalock led to their developing techniques for uncommon birth defects of the heart and encouraged other doctors to explore diagnostic and therapeutic advances. When the tranquilizer Thalidomide caused serious birth defects among European babies, Taussig investigated the epidemic in West Germany and stopped the drug's use in the United States. During her retirement years, Taussig studied deformed hearts in birds at the University of Delaware. Among her awards and honors were the Chevalier Legion of Honor (France), induction into The National Women's Hall of Fame, the Presidential Medal of Freedom, and election as the first woman president of the American Heart Association. She was also a member of the Academy of Arts and Sciences and of the American Academy of Pediatrics. She donated her body to Johns Hopkins for research.

BIBLIOGRAPHY

Baldwin, Joyce. *To Heal the Heart of a Child: Helen Taussig, M.D.* New York: Walker, 1992. 0–8027–8166–7, 128p. Baldwin focuses on Taussig's career in this young adult biography, enumerating the hurdles she had to overcome.

TAYLOR, ELIZABETH (1932–)
Actor   London, England

Elizabeth Rosemond Taylor is an actor. She was born on February 27, 1932, as one of two children to an art dealer and his American actor wife. The family was evacuated from London in 1939, and Taylor attended high school in Los Angeles. In 1941, Universal Pictures signed her to a contract, and the next year, she made her screen debut in *There's One Born Every Minute.* At 12, she achieved child-star status in Metro-Goldwyn-Mayer's *National Velvet.* Critics first acclaimed her as a serious actor after her role in *Giant* in 1956. In 1963, she appeared on television, and almost 20 years later, she made her Broadway stage debut in *The Little Foxes* for which she won a Tony Award nomination. Two years later, she began producing. She was nominated for an Academy Award three times before winning them for *Butterfield 8* and *Who's Afraid of Virginia Woolf?* In 1985, Rock Hudson's death from AIDS led her to become founding co-chair of the American Foundation for AIDS Research, and in 1993, she founded her own Elizabeth Taylor Foundation for AIDS. In 1993, she was presented the American Film Institute Life Achievement Award and a Jean Hersholt Award from the Academy of Motion Picture Arts and Sciences. Other awards include the Cecil B. De Mille Award for life achievement and the Screen Actors Guild Life Achievement Award.

BIBLIOGRAPHY

Heymann, C. David. *Liz: An Intimate Biography of Elizabeth Taylor.* New York: Carol, 1995. 1–55972–267–3, 526p. For his detailed and balanced biography of Taylor, Heymann interviewed over 1,000 of her friends, lovers, and colleagues.

Latham, Caroline, and Jeannie Sakol. *All About Elizabeth: Elizabeth Taylor, Public and Private.* New York: Onyx, 1991. 0–451–40282–0, 342p. In this unconventional biography of Taylor, the authors wrote short commentaries on events for which they felt an affinity with Taylor.

Robin-Tani, Marianne. *The New Elizabeth.* New York: St. Martin's, 1988. 0–312–90949–7, 177p. This popular biography of Taylor gives an overview of her life.

Spoto, Donald. *A Passion for Life: The Biography of Elizabeth Taylor.* New York: HarperCollins, 1995. 0–06–017657–1, 401p. Spoto's chronological biography of Taylor offers informative analyses of her movies.

Walker, Alexander. *Elizabeth: The Life of Elizabeth Taylor.* New York: Weidenfeld, 1991. 0–8021–1335–4, 423p. In his biography of Taylor, Walker dwells on the best about her life.

TAYLOR, LUCY HOBBS (1833–1910)
Dentist   Franklin County, New York

Lucy Beaman Hobbs Taylor was the first American woman to earn a dental degree. She was born on March 14, 1833, as the seventh of ten children to a farmer and his wife, who died when Taylor was ten. Her father's second wife died two years later, and Taylor went to boarding school at Franklin Academy. She began teaching and studying medicine with a local physician, but when she tried to study medicine in Cincinnati, the school would not accept women. Another physician gave her private instruction and suggested she enter dentistry. In 1861, the Ohio College of Dental Surgery refused her admission based on her sex. Instead, she opened her own office in Iowa. In 1865, she served as a delegate from Iowa to the American Dental Association's convention in Chicago, and when she reapplied to school, she was accepted. After four months, she graduated as a doctor of dental surgery. She went to Chicago, married, and taught dentistry to her husband. They developed an extensive practice, with Taylor focusing on women and children. In 1886, when she retired, she joined several organizations and served as president of the Ladies' Republican Club. She also supported woman suffrage. Taylor led the way for women to gain admission to dental schools by her perseverance and her excellence in her profession.

BIBLIOGRAPHY
Behrman, Carol H. *Miss Dr. Lucy*. Washington, DC: Review and Herald, 1984. 0–8280–0231–2, 96p. This fictional biography for young adults describes Taylor's difficulties while trying to become a dentist.

TAYLOR, SUSIE KING (1848–1912)
Educator and Nurse   Georgia

Susie Baker King Taylor was an African American teacher, laundress, and nurse during the Civil War. She was born in Georgia on a plantation, but after she moved to Savannah with her grandmother, she met two white children who taught her to read and write, illegal skills for African Americans prior to the Civil War. When she went to the Sea Islands after the Civil War erupted, Union soldiers made her teach the freed slave children during the day, and at night she taught adults. After marrying a soldier in the United States Colored Troops, she became both a laundress and a nurse for the Union Army, working with **Clara Barton** in 1863. When the war ended, she opened a school in Savannah for the freed African Americans. She soon went to work for a wealthy white family, traveling to New England with them in the summer. In Boston, she met and married Russell Taylor, remained, and became a founding member of the Corps 67 Women's Relief Corps and then president of the organization in 1893. When she went south for one more visit in 1898 to see her dying son, she saw that segregation continued, even in the post-Reconstruction era. She wrote about her experiences during the Civil War in

My Life in Camp with the 33rd United States Colored Troops but never received a pension for her work.

BIBLIOGRAPHY

Booker, Simeon. *Susie King Taylor, Civil War Nurse.* New York: McGraw-Hill, 1969. No ISBN, 127p. This biography for young adults, based on Taylor's autobiography, details her work.

Taylor, Susie King. *A Black Woman's Civil War Memoirs.* New York: M. Wiener, 1988. 0–910129–85–1, 154p. Taylor's autobiography reveals what life was like during the Civil War for African Americans.

TEASDALE, SARA (1884–1933)
Poet
St. Louis, Missouri

Sara Teasdale was a lyric poet with a unique sense of rhythmic line. She was born on August 8, 1884, as one of four children to a wholesale dealer and his wife. Teasdale, much younger than her siblings, often felt lonely and shy while growing up. She went to a small school near her home and enjoyed reading the poetry of *Christina Rossetti and Heinrich Heine before beginning to write her own poems. After she graduated from Hosmer Hall, she and her mother went to New York City and Europe, a trip that introduced Teasdale to art. The actor *Eleanora Duse fascinated her, and Teasdale wrote a series of sonnets after seeing her photograph in 1907. The same year, her monologue "Guenevere," published in a St. Louis weekly, *Reedy's Mirror*, gained her critical attention. After her marriage in 1915, she moved to New York and published *Love Songs*, for which she received the Poetry Society of America's annual award. She continued working although often in poor health. During the next 10 years, she and her husband developed different interests and divorced. In 1931, the suicide of her close friend and former suitor, Vachel Lindsay, distressed her, and she left for England to escape. She worked on her biography of Christina Rossetti but fell ill and returned to New York before recovering. A deep depression followed, and she committed suicide in early 1933. Her best collection of poetry, *Strange Victory*, appeared after her death.

BIBLIOGRAPHY

Carpenter, Margaret Haley. *Sara Teasdale: A Biography.* Norfolk, VA: Pentelic Press, 1977. 0–913110–03–5, 377p. Based on unpublished materials and letters to Teasdale from correspondents including Vachel Lindsay, Carpenter's carefully researched and well-documented biography also reveals childhood influences on Teasdale.

Drake, William. *Sara Teasdale, Woman and Poet.* 1979. Knoxville: University of Tennessee Press, 1989. 0–87049–606–9, 304p. Drake used letters, unpublished poems, and notebooks to present a balanced, recommended picture of Teasdale.

Schoen, Carol. *Sara Teasdale.* Boston: Twayne, 1986. 0–8057–7473–4, 190p. In a researched and documented critical biography of Teasdale, Schoen emphasizes the importance that she placed on lyrics.

TEKAKWITHA, KATERI (1656–1680)
Religious Leader   Auriesville, New York

Catherine Tekakwitha, known as "The Lily of the Mohawks," was a convert to Catholicism who extended charity toward all. She was born in 1656 as one of two children to a Mohawk warrior and his Christian Algonquin wife whom the Mohawks had captured. Both parents and her brother died in the smallpox epidemic around 1660, but Tekakwitha (also known as Tegakwita, Tegah-Kouita, or Tegakouita) recovered, although pockmarked and with weak eyesight. Her father's brother adopted her, and from his family, she learned the Mohawk traditions. Tekakwitha met French missionaries who visited the Mohawks in 1666, and in 1675, she requested instruction in Catholicism, against her uncle's wishes. In 1676, she was baptized and given the name Catherine. Her tribe condemned her decision by stoning her for refusing to work on Sundays. She then joined a group of Christian Mohawks on the south shore of the St. Lawrence River in Canada, and there she began following an ascetic life although not a member of a religious order. She refused marriage, remained a virgin, fasted, and offered charity wherever needed. Although depriving herself physically, she always participated fully in the work of the tribe. She died at 24, and in 1932, a request went to the Catholic Church that it investigate the "Cause of Catherine Tekakwitha" as a candidate for beatification and canonization. In 1943, the decree of heroicity was issued, and on June 22, 1980, she was named Blessed Kateri Tekakwitha.

BIBLIOGRAPHY

Brown, Evelyn M. *Kateri Tekakwitha: Mohawk Maid.* 1958. San Francisco: Ignatius Press, 1991. 0-89870-380-8, 178p. This fictional biography of Tekakwitha for young adults discusses her life and her conversion to Catholicism.

Bunson, Margaret. *Kateri Tekakwitha.* Huntington, IN: Our Sunday Visitor, 1993. 0-87973-786-7, 56p. Although undocumented, this biography of Tekakwitha for young adults gives a straightforward account of the difficulties in her life and her mysticism.

Daughters of St. Paul. *Blessed Kateri Tekakwitha, Mohawk Maiden.* Boston: Daughters of St. Paul, 1980. 0-8198-1100-9, 92p. This brief hagiography of Tekakwitha, suitable for young adults, recounts her devotion to God and the process of becoming a saint.

McCauley, Marlene. *Adventures with a Saint: Kateri Tekakwitha, Lily of the Mohawks.* Phoenix: Grace House, 1992. 0-9633633-0-1, 209p. This hagiography extols Tekakwitha and includes a variety of supporting documents.

TEMPLE (BLACK), SHIRLEY (1928–)
Actor and Ambassador   Santa Monica, California

Shirley Temple (Black), ambassador for the United States, was an actor. She was born on April 23, 1928, to a father with a seventh grade education who became an astute banker and a mother who had Temple Black on stage at age three. Temple Black learned early that doing what was expected of her saved time, and her first director isolated her from the other children to keep her from becoming unruly. Away from work, she enjoyed playing outside and raising rabbits which she rented to the studio for one dollar each. At age eight, she was the most popular film star in Hollywood, receiving 135,000 presents for her birthday, and by nine, she had the seventh highest income in America, $307,014. The following year, each of her four films earned $300,000. She met many famous people, including **Eleanor Roosevelt**, **Amelia Earhart**, and J. Edgar Hoover. She was the youngest person to appear on *Time* magazine's cover, to be listed in *Who's Who*, and to receive an Academy Award. An instructor educated her at the studio until she was 12, and then she completed her schooling at Westlake School for Girls. She retired from film at 22, to work 19 years as a mother, a wife, and a volunteer. In 1972, she had breast cancer, and her acknowledgment of her mastectomy gained public support and gave comfort to others in her state. She then spent another 19 years in public service as a Republican ambassador to Ghana from 1974 to 1976, a member of the United States delegation to the United Nations, and as Chief of Protocol under President Gerald Ford. She initiated a one-week training program for ambassadors that included instruction on acceptable behavior if taken hostage. She later became the ambassador to the former Czechoslovakia. Among her awards are a Kennedy Center Honors Award for Lifetime Achievement.

BIBLIOGRAPHY

David, Lester, and Irene David. *The Shirley Temple Story*. New York: Putnam, 1983. 0–399–12798–4, 224p. This well-researched and documented biography re-creates the story of Temple Black's childhood career and international fame.

Edwards, Anne. *Shirley Temple, American Princess*. New York: Morrow, 1988. 0–688–06051–X, 444p. Edwards's biography of Temple Black reveals her admiration for her accomplishments.

Hammontree, Patsy Guy. *Shirley Temple Black: A Bio-Bibliography*. Westport, CT: Greenwood Press, 1998. 0–313–25848–1, 304p. Hammontree examines Temple Black's various careers, from child star to diplomat, in this critical biography.

Temple, Shirley. *Child Star: An Autobiography*. New York: McGraw-Hill, 1988. 0–07–005532–7, 546p. Temple covers her childhood, her dominating mother, her first marriage to an abusive husband, and her sliding career, ending her story in 1953.

Windeler, Robert. *The Films of Shirley Temple*. Secaucus, NJ: Citadel, 1978. 0–8065–0615–6, 256p. In addition to an undocumented biographical essay, Windeler includes photographs from and discussions of all of Temple Black's films.

TERRELL, MARY CHURCH (1863–1954)
Educator and Reformer   Memphis, Tennessee

African American Mary Church Terrell was a supporter of civil rights and suffrage throughout her life. She was born on September 23, 1863, into a middle-class Memphis family as its oldest child. Her parents tried to shelter her from racism, but as she became aware of discrimination, she decided to fight it by excelling academically. After her parents divorced, she graduated from Oberlin College, teaching first at Wilberforce University and then at the M Street Colored High School in Washington. Terrell decided to visit Europe, and after returning two years later, refused to accept racial inequality. She believed that African American women had to unite, and she became the co-founder and first president of the National Association of Colored Women. The group begin to establish kindergartens, nurseries, and Mother Clubs which addressed both social and economic conditions. She started fund raising for schools of domestic science and homes for girls, the elderly, and the sick. She saw herself as a "New Woman" who could help outside the confines of women's groups. In 1904, she delivered an address in German (she spoke three languages fluently) at the International Congress of Women in Berlin which described the numerous achievements of the African American race. After her anger at continued ill-treatment of African American servicemen during World War II, she became militant and led a fight to require restaurants in Washington, DC, to seat African Americans by filing a case against an owner who refused to serve her. Before her death, she won the right to eat anywhere in Washington, DC, and the Supreme Court ruled for desegregation of the public schools.

BIBLIOGRAPHY

Jones, Beverly Washington. *Quest for Equality: The Life and Writings of Mary Eliza Church Terrell*. Brooklyn, NY: Carlson, 1990. 0-926019-19-8, 352p. Jones's biography includes selections from Terrell's essays and speeches.

Terrell, Mary Church. *A Colored Woman in a White World*. Ed. Nellie Y. McKay. New York: Macmillan, 1996. 0-7838-1421-6, 436p. A documented introductory overview of Terrell's life precedes her recommended autobiography.

THOBURN, ISABELLA (1840–1901)
Missionary   **St. Clairsville, Ohio**

Isabella Thoburn was a Methodist missionary to India. She was born on March 29, 1840, as the ninth of ten children, to a farmer who died when she was ten and his wife. She attended public schools and then the Wheeling Female Seminary. After teaching and studying art at the Cincinnati Academy of Design, she joined the Methodist Church at 19. Her brother, a Methodist missionary in India, returned home in 1866 and told her that Indian women responded more readily to female missionaries. Three years later, the Woman's Foreign Missionary Society of the Methodist Church formed and approved Thoburn for service to India. She and **Clara A. Swain** went together in 1869, and Thoburn joined her brother in Lucknow. Thoburn started a new school in the middle of a bazaar for six Christian girls, four of whom were Hindustani. In two months, she had 17 students. The next year, the Woman's Foreign Missionary Society established a boarding school, and in 1874, Thoburn expanded her work from Lucknow to a school in Cawnpore, 45 miles away. Thoburn became teacher, mother, and nurse to her students, and the strain of constant contact deteriorated her health. She took a furlough to the United States in 1880 but filled her time with speaking engagements. In 1882, she returned to India, and six years later, started a collegiate department which eventually became Lucknow Woman's College. On her second furlough, Thoburn heard about the new deaconess movement for Methodist women, and she joined **Lucy Rider Meyer** in Chicago for a year before superintending a new Methodist deaconess home and hospital in Cincinnati. She took two more tours to India, and after her death there, Lucknow Woman's College became the Isabella Thoburn College.

BIBLIOGRAPHY

Thoburn, J. M. *Life of Isabella Thoburn.* 1903. New York: Garland, 1987. 0-8240-0678-X, 373p.   This undocumented biography of Thoburn offers background on her work and accomplishments.

THOMPSON, DOROTHY (1894–1961)
Journalist   Lancaster, New York

Dorothy Thompson was a journalist. She was born on July 9, 1894, the oldest of three children of a Methodist minister and his wife. Thompson's mother died when Thompson was eight, and her father remarried. Since Thompson disliked her moralistic stepmother, she went to Chicago to live with relatives. After attending Lewis Institute, she entered Syracuse University on a scholarship and graduated in two years. In Europe in 1920, she interviewed the Irish independence leader Terence MacSwiney and co-authored a report on striking Fiat workers with her companion, Barbara De Porte. The International News Service carried both articles. After she published an article on the attempt of Charles, grandnephew of Emperor Franz Josef, to reestablish the Hapsburg monarchy, the *Philadelphia Public Ledger* and the *New York Evening Post* appointed her chief of their Central European bureaus, headquartered in Berlin. In 1927, she married Sinclair Lewis and returned to the United States, but in the year after the birth of her son, she chose to spend the winter of each year working in Europe. When she decried American nonintervention in Germany and denounced Hitler's policies, Nazi Germany expelled her, confirming her status as an internationally respected political journalist. In 1936, she began her newspaper column, "On the Record," for the *New York Herald Tribune,* which was syndicated to over 170 daily papers from 1941 to 1948. On radio, she expressed concern for refugees and privately helped friends obtain visas to leave Europe. *Time* magazine rated her the second most popular woman, after **Eleanor Roosevelt**. Although not anti-Israel, her open support of Palestinian Arabs, when concerned about problems of displacement resulting from the creation of a Zionist state, caused alarm. In the 1950s, she voiced her anticommunist position and argued for world disarmament in her monthly column for *Ladies' Home Journal.* Her global understanding helped others focus on issues important to the world.

BIBLIOGRAPHY

Kurth, Peter. *American Cassandra: The Life of Dorothy Thompson.* Boston: Little, Brown, 1990. 0-316-50723-7, 587p. After reading Thompson's personal papers and consulting articles by other journalists, Kurth finds her to be an early twentieth-century force.

Sanders, Marion K. *Dorothy Thompson: A Legend in Her Time.* Boston: Houghton Mifflin, 1973. 0-395-15467-7, 428p. Sanders used private papers, correspondence, diaries, and other sources, including interviews, to reveal Thompson's character and to trace her career.

Sheean, Vincent. *Dorothy and Red.* Boston: Houghton Mifflin, 1963. No ISBN, 363p. This carefully documented and researched biography of Thompson begins when she met Sinclair Lewis in Berlin.

THURSBY, EMMA CECILIA (1845-1931)
Concert Vocalist   Williamsburg, New York

Emma Cecilia Thursby was a concert singer and music educator. She was born on February 21, 1845, as the second of five children to a rope manufacturer and his French-Dutch wife. Thursby's parents encouraged her early interest in music, and she first sang publicly in church at the age of five. After her father's death in 1859, she left school and began teaching music to help support the family. Thursby thought opera immoral, and she sang only in churches or concert halls after the Civil War, including Henry Ward Beecher's Plymouth Church in Brooklyn. In 1872, she went to Italy briefly for study, and in New York developed her vocal flexibility and range of middle C to E flat above the staff. By 1874, she had a national reputation, and when she began touring, under a $100,000 contract, she appeared with Mark Twain at the Redpath Lyceum. When the Broadway Tabernacle lured her from another church in 1876, it offered her an annual salary of $3,000, the highest paid to any American church soloist at the time. In 1878 and 1880, she debuted in London, Paris, and Germany. In Paris again in 1881, she was the first American to receive the commemorative medal of the Société des Concerts of the Paris Conservatoire. Her rave reviews in both Europe and America added pressure for her to sing opera, but she resisted. In 1895, after family deaths and exhaustion, she made her last major appearance and then devoted herself to teaching, with one of her most successful students being **Geraldine Farrar**. While most singers trained in Europe, Thursby stayed distinctly American both in both musical execution and lifestyle.

BIBLIOGRAPHY

Gipson, Richard McCandless. *The Life of Emma Thursby.* 1940. New York: Da Capo Press, 1980. 0-306-76016-9, 470p. Gipson based his researched and documented biography on Thursby's sister's collection of diaries, letters, programs, newspaper and periodical notices, medals, certificates of honor, photographs, manuscripts, and music as well as his own interviews with Thursby before she died.

TIBBLES, SUSETTE LA FLESCHE. *See* LA FLESCHE (TIBBLES), SUSETTE

TRUTH, SOJOURNER (c. 1797–1883)
Slave, Reformer, and Activist   Hurley, New York

Sojourner Truth was an abolitionist and women's rights activist. She was born Isabella Van Wagener into slavery as the tenth of 12 children, with Dutch her first language. After she and a fellow slave had five children, and just before New York abolished slavery in 1827, Isaac Van Wagener set her free. A Quaker friend helped her fight a court battle to recover her son who had been sold illegally into slavery in the South, and she became the first African American to win a court case against a white man. Truth had visions and heard voices which led her begin working and preaching with a religious missionary. She left New York City in 1843, changed her name to Sojourner Truth, and traveled throughout the Northeast preaching, singing, and debating. During her trips, she heard about abolitionism and then about the women's rights movement. Her charisma attracted crowds wherever she appeared, and she spoke fervently on the horrors of slavery and the value of women, saying "Ain't I a woman?" In the 1850s, she went to Michigan, and when the Civil War began, she solicited food and clothing for African American volunteer regiments. After the war, she encouraged the government to resettle African Americans in the Midwest and continued to impart her story. She was elected to The National Women's Hall of Fame.

BIBLIOGRAPHY
Fitch, Suzanne Pullon, and Roseann M. Mandziuk. *Sojourner Truth as Orator: Wit, Story, and Song.* Westport, CT: Greenwood Press, 1997. 0–313–30068–2, 238p. Fitch and Mandziuk use primary sources to address biographical discrepancies and to explicate contradictory speech texts.

Gilbert, Olive, ed. *Narrative of Sojourner Truth.* 1850. Mineola, NY: Dover, 1997. 0–486–29899–X, 74p. Truth uses third person narrative to describe her life as a slave and afterwards.

Mabee, Carleton, and Susan Mabee Newhouse. *Sojourner Truth—Slave, Prophet, Legend.* New York: New York University Press, 1993. 0–8147–5484–8, 293p. Mabee and Newhouse carefully researched newspapers and correspondence to write this effective and balanced biography about Truth.

Painter, Nell Irvin. *Sojourner Truth: A Life, a Symbol.* New York: Norton, 1996. 0–393–02739–2, 370p. Painter's accessible scholarly biography reveals Truth as a woman with a superb sense of humor who made her audiences both laugh and cry as she detailed the horrors of slavery.

Stetson, Erlene, and Linda David. *Glorying in Tribulation: The Lifework of Sojourner Truth.* East Lansing: Michigan State University Press, 1994. 0–8701–3337–3, 242p. Stetson and David work to reveal the real Truth in their biography, which examines the perceptions of those who knew Truth and how she influenced them.

TUBMAN, HARRIET ROSS (1820?–1913)
Slave and Reformer   Dorchester County, Maryland

African American Harriet Tubman, a leading abolitionist, earned the name Moses for the risks she took to lead over 200 slaves to freedom in the North along the Underground Railroad. She was born Araminta in 1820, as one of the eleven children of slaves, and chose to be called Harriet after her mother. When she was a child, an overseer accidentally struck her on the head, and throughout her life she suffered from narcoleptic seizures. After her marriage in 1844, she feared being sold into the South, and in 1849, she escaped. When she returned for her free African American husband nine months later, he had remarried. Back in Philadelphia, she saved the money she earned working as a domestic until she could rescue her sister and her children. This liberation was the first of many that she completed during her trips south. She knew that slaves could escape successfully if they did exactly as she said, and she often held a loaded revolver on them to keep them focused on the task. During the Civil War, she became the only woman in military history to plan and execute an armed expedition against military forces when she went into the South for the Union Army as spy, scout, and nurse. After she won a pension from the government, she established a home for aged ex-slaves who could no longer work. She also helped with relief associations and raised funds for others. Her home has been designated a national historic landmark, and the first stamp in the African American Heritage USA series boasted her picture.

BIBLIOGRAPHY
Bentley, Judith. *Harriet Tubman*. New York: Watts, 1990. 0-531-10948-8, 144p. Bentley uses primary sources in this authoritative biography for young adults.

Bradford, Sarah H. *Harriet Tubman, the Moses of Her People*. 1869. Bedford, MA: Applewood, 1993. 1-55709-217-6, 149p. This documented biography is dated stylistically and semantically but reveals Tubman's life from a historical point of view.

Carlson, Judy. *Harriet Tubman: Call to Freedom*. New York: Fawcett Columbine, 1989. 0-449-90376-1, 116p. This fictional biography of Tubman for young adults is undocumented.

McClard, Megan. *Harriet Tubman: Slavery and the Underground Railroad*. Englewood Cliffs, NJ: Silver Burdette, 1991. 0-382-09938-9, 133p. This researched and documented examination of Tubman's life for young adults also addresses her role.

Taylor, M. W. *Harriet Tubman*. New York: Chelsea House, 1990. 1-55546-612-5, 112p. Taylor's biography on Tubman for young adults is based on primary sources.

TUCKER, SOPHIE (1884–1966)
Singer and Entertainer   Russia

Sophie Tucker was a singer and entertainer known as "The Last of the Red Hot Mamas." She was born Sophie Abuza on January 13, 1884, to Russian Jews who had fled their country for America. The family moved to Boston when Tucker was eight, and she met entertainers who were patrons of her father's restaurant. She learned their songs and received extra money singing them for other diners. A failed marriage and a child delayed her ambitions, but she left her son with her family and went to New York, renaming herself Sophie Tucker. In 1906, she sang in an amateur hour, secured an agent, and started working in vaudeville. Because she was overweight and not particularly attractive, her manager made her sing in blackface, but several years later, when her makeup was lost en route, the audience liked her without it. In 1909, she became a "headliner" with top billing for the Ziegfeld Follies. In 1929, she made several films and tried musicals but realized that nightclubs were best to showcase her talent because she could say what she wanted and sing what pleased the audience. She always supported her family, and when her income increased in 1910, she bought her parents a home and provided money for their retirement. When she earned more than her family needed, she gave to many charities. In 1945, she set up the Sophie Tucker Foundation, donating profits from her autobiography and revenues from her *Golden Jubilee* album. In 1955, the foundation endowed a chair in theater arts at Brandeis University. She donated more than $4 million to charity after singing gratis at orphanages and prisons and performing many benefits during her 62-year career. Among her awards were election to the Friars Club and a Citation of Merit from the Mayor of New York City.

BIBLIOGRAPHY

Freedland, Michael. *Sophie: The Sophie Tucker Story.* London: Woburn, 1978. 0-7130-0153-4, 221p. Freedland uses Tucker's correspondence and interviews in his undocumented biography.

Tucker, Sophie. *Some of These Days: The Autobiography of Sophie Tucker.* Garden City, NY: Doubleday, Doran, 1945. No ISBN, 309p. In her autobiography, Tucker sprinkles her memories with anecdotes about her early career.

TYLER, ANNE (1941–)
Author   Minneapolis, Minnesota

Anne Tyler is an author. She was born October 25, 1941, the daughter of a chemist and his wife. Her family lived in Quaker communes before settling in the North Carolina mountains. She attended high school in Raleigh, and at 16, entered Duke University, where Reynolds Price, then a promising young novelist who had attended her high school, encouraged her to write, even though she was majoring in Russian. She graduated Phi Beta Kappa from Duke and entered Columbia University for graduate study. She returned to Duke as a Russian bibliographer, and after a year, became assistant to the librarian at McGill University Law Library. She finally began to pursue her writing after moving to Baltimore, with her Iranian husband, and her first book to receive adequate critical attention was her fifth novel, *Celestial Navigation*, in 1974. Since that time, her literary reputation has grown steadily and solidly, with critics currently considering her one of America's most accomplished writers. Although often set in the South, her novels do not fit the general expectations of "southern" literature because their settings are more often timeless than specific. Her women characters, although fulfilling traditional female roles, are often stronger than the men with whom they associate. Her awards include the Award for Literature from the American Academy and Institute of Arts and Letters and the Pulitzer Prize. She is a member of the American Academy and Institute of Arts and Letters.

BIBLIOGRAPHY

Croft, Robert W. *Anne Tyler: A Bio-Bibliography*. Westport, CT: Greenwood Press, 1995. 0-313-28952-2, 172p. This critical biography details Tyler's life and analyzes her fiction and her reviews.

Evans, Elizabeth. *Anne Tyler*. New York: Twayne, 1993. 0-8057-3985-8, 173p. Evans examines both Tyler's books and book reviews in a critical text.

Petry, Alice Hall. *Understanding Anne Tyler*. Columbia: University of South Carolina Press, 1990. 0-87249-716-X, 267p. Petry tries to dispel the labels of woman's writer and southern writer that have become attached to Tyler to show that many other influences are visible in her life and work.

Salwak, Dale, ed. *Anne Tyler as Novelist*. Iowa City: University of Iowa Press, 1994. 0-87745-479-5, 226p. This collection of 17 essays covers a variety of topics in Tyler's writing.

U

UCHIDA, YOSHIKO (1921–1992)
Author   Alameda, California

Yoshiko Uchida was a Japanese American author. She was born on November 24, 1921, to a manager for a large Japanese corporation and his wife, both Japanese immigrants. She grew up in Berkeley and graduated from the University of California in 1942 before being evacuated to the Tanforan assembly center near San Francisco and then interned at the Topaz relocation center with other Japanese Americans. At Topaz, Uchida served as a volunteer teacher, and the next year, the National Japanese American Student Relocation Council got her released to attend graduate school at Smith College. After receiving her M.Ed. Degree in 1944, she taught at the Frankford Friends School in Philadelphia and served as secretary of the Institute of Pacific Relations in New York. When she returned to California, she published *The Dancing Kettle and Other Japanese Folk Tales*, the first of her 28 books. In 1952, she went to Japan on a Ford Foundation fellowship to collect more tales, and she included these in a later book. She decided during this trip that Sansei (third-generation Japanese Americans) needed to know more about the lives of their parents. Later in her career, she became more political in her work as she began writing for older audiences. Two award-winning books, *Journey to Topaz* (1971) and *Journey Home* (1978), examined the wartime internment of Japanese Americans through the eyes of a young girl interned in Topaz. For adults, she wrote *Picture Bride*, a story about Japanese women coming to the United States at the beginning of the twentieth century for arranged marriages. She won honors from the American Library Association and the Commonwealth Club of California.

BIBLIOGRAPHY

Uchida, Yoshiko. *The Invisible Thread: An Autobiography.* Englewood Cliffs, NJ: Messner, 1991. 0-671-74163-2, 136p. Uchida describes growing up in Berkeley, California, as a *Nisei* (second-generation Japanese American) and her family's internment in a Nevada concentration camp during World War II.

———. *Desert Exile: The Uprooting of a Japanese American Family.* Seattle: University of Washington Press, 1982. 0-295-95898-7, 154p. In this autobiographical memoir, Uchida remembers the internment of her family during World War II.

V

VAN LEW, ELIZABETH L. (1818–1900)
Spy   Richmond, Virginia

Elizabeth L. Van Lew was a Federal agent during the Civil War. She was born on October 17, 1818, as one of three children to a wealthy hardware merchant and his society wife. Before the Civil War, Van Lew had developed her antislavery views, and in the 1850s, the family freed their house servants and reportedly purchased members of their former slaves' families from other masters and freed them. Van Lew supported the Union openly during the Civil War and carried food, books, and clothing to Federal officers in Libby Prison. She may also have helped them escape, but her social standing was high enough in Richmond to keep others from accusing her. In 1864, she supposedly removed the body of Colonel Ulric Dahlgren from the city after he had been disgraced in public for carrying secret papers which Van Lew said were forgeries. Near the end of that year, as the Union Army neared Richmond, she began to dress and act strangely so that people called her "Crazy Bet," but she was using her behavior as a cover for maintaining five relay stations between the city and Federal headquarters down the river, with her servants carrying messages along the route in the soles of their workshoes. After the Confederates left the city on April 2, 1865, Van Lew raised a large American flag over her house. When Grant became president, he appointed her postmistress of Richmond, and after Hayes became president, she went to Washington to work at the Post Office Department. During the last years of her life, she fought for women's rights by protesting her tax assessments, saying that she had no representation in government. After her death, sympathizers from Massachusetts erected a monument at her gravesite.

BIBLIOGRAPHY

Nolan, Jeannette Covert. *Yankee Spy, Elizabeth Van Lew*. New York: Messner, 1970. 0-671-32337-7, 190p.   This researched fictional biography of Van Lew is appropriate for young adults.

Van Lew, Elizabeth L. *A Yankee Spy in Richmond: The Civil War Diary of Crazy Bet Van Lew*. Mechanicsburg, PA: Stackpole, 1996. 0-8117-0554-4, 166p. The text includes letters and the diary Van Lew kept while serving as a Union spy in Richmond, Virginia, during the Civil War.

Zeinert, Karen. *Elizabeth Van Lew: Southern Belle, Union Spy*. Parsippany, NJ: Dillon, 1995. 0-87518-608-4, 160p. In this biography for young adults, Zeinert uses Van Lew's personal writings to recreate her life and the social history of Richmond during the Civil War.

VAUGHAN, SARAH (1924-1990)
Singer   Newark, New Jersey

African American Sarah Vaughan earned the names "Sassy" and "The Divine One" for her jazz vocalizations and piano accompaniment. She was born on March 27, 1924, to musical parents; her father was a carpenter, and her mother a laundress. Vaughan began singing with her mother in the church choir and taking piano lessons from her at age seven. By 12, Vaughan had become a soloist and played with the high school orchestra. She won the amateur night at Harlem's Apollo Theater in 1943 and joined Earl "Fatha" Hines's band, where she met other jazz players, including Dizzy Gillespie and Charles Parker. She made her first record in 1944, and her recording in 1946 of Tadd Dameron's "If You Could See Me Now" is a modern classic. The same year, Vaughan began her solo career and married a man who helped her polish her performance with voice and stagecraft lessons. In 1958, her recording of "Broken-Hearted Melody" was her first million-selling hit. Also in 1958, she divorced her husband but continued to mature as a "musician's musician." She understood the intricacies of music and of jazz, and with her three-octave range, she displayed them throughout her career of extensive touring and recording. Among her awards are an Emmy Award and Grammy Awards.

BIBLIOGRAPHY

Gourse, Leslie. *Sassy: The Life of Sarah Vaughan*. 1993. New York: Da Capo Press, 1994. 0-306-80578-2, 302p. Gourse uses newspaper reviews, album notes, and interviews with those who knew Vaughan to follow her career.

Ruuth, Marianne. *Sarah Vaughan*. Los Angeles: Melrose Square, 1994. 0-87067-786-1, 192p. This undocumented biography of Vaughan for young adults covers her life and her career.

VICTOR, FRANCES FULLER (1826–1902)
Author and Historian   Rome, New York

Frances Fuller Victor was an author and a historian. She was born on May 23, 1826, as the oldest of five daughters in a family that journeyed west when she was four. After settling in Ohio around 1839, she attended a female seminary, and during her teens began to write poetry. She published in the New York *Home Journal*, and her first book, *Anizetta, the Guajira: or the Creole of Cuba*, was published in Boston in 1848. Victor's father died in 1850, and she returned to the family home, where she married and separated before rejoining her sister, who had also married, in New York. In 1851, they published *Poems of Sentiment and Imagination* together. After her divorce in 1862, Victor married her sister's brother-in-law and went with him to the Pacific coast. She began writing under the name Florence Fane as a regular contributor to both *Golden Era* and the *San Francisco Bulletin*. After her husband resigned from the navy, Victor began investigating local history in the places they lived. She interviewed many pioneers, examined family papers and archives, and began to integrate her thorough research into her books. In 1878, a historical promoter hired her to help prepare his proposed *History of the Pacific States*. She agreed and remained with the project through its 28 volumes, finishing in 1890. Although given no credit, Victor wrote at least eight of the volumes and contributed to at least three more. In her later life, she studied the Native Americans in Oregon and wrote *The Early Indian Wars of Oregon*. Her carefully documented histories have served as a basis for later studies of the fields about which she wrote.

BIBLIOGRAPHY
Martin, Jim. *A Bit of a Blue: The Life and Work of Frances Fuller Victor*. Salem, OR: Deep Well, 1992. 0-9632066-0-5, 277p. Using unpublished primary sources as well as secondary sources and Victor's writing, Martin has written a carefully researched and documented examination of her life and career.

VORSE, MARY HEATON (1874–1966)
Activist and Journalist   New York, New York

Mary Heaton Vorse was a journalist and author. She was born on October 9, 1874, to an older man and his second wife, who had five much older children from her first marriage. Vorse's mother tutored her, and Vorse attended school before going to Paris at age 16 to study art. When she was 24, she married an explorer who loved boats, and they lived in both New York and Europe. Based on these early years of marriage, Vorse published her first book, *The Breaking In of a Yachtsman's Wife*, in 1908. When she and her husband moved to an old house in Provincetown, Massachusetts, she became symbolically attached to the house and disliked leaving. Her love for the place attracted other New York writers, and this group became the nucleus of the Provincetown Players, with her wharf serving as the locale for the company's first production. In 1910, both her husband and her mother died within one day, and since her father had lost much income during the San Francisco earthquake of 1906, Vorse had to support herself and her children. In 1912, she went to Lawrence, Massachusetts, during the textile mill strike to help the striking workers' children, and after discovering that all family members needed aid, she began a lifelong commitment to labor reform. She joined **Elizabeth Gurley Flynn** in demanding a political solution to oppressive labor tactics. She covered other strikes and published articles about them in *Harper's Magazine*, the *Nation*, and the *New Republic*. Her work created a history of the labor movement and its evolving militancy, including unemployment in New York in 1914 and the metal miners of Minnesota strike in 1916. Her book *Men and Steel* details the strikes in 1919 and 1920. In 1922, she went to the Soviet Union to report on the Russian famine. In the 1930s, workers wanted better wages, and after World War II, Walter Reuther and the United Auto Workers impressed her. After disagreeing with the illegalities of longshoremen on strike in 1952, Vorse asserted that she could be pro-labor without being pro-union. In 1962, she received the United Workers' Social Justice Award for her long support of laborers.

BIBLIOGRAPHY

Garrison, Dee. *Mary Heaton Vorse: The Life of an American Insurgent.* Philadelphia: Temple University Press, 1989. 0–87722–601–6, 377p.   Garrison's carefully researched, readable, and documented scholarly text reveals Vorse's life and work.
Vorse, Mary Heaton. *A Footnote to Folly: Reminiscences of Mary Heaton Vorse.* 1935. New York: Arno Press, 1980. 0–405–12865–7, 407p. Vorse's autobiography reveals her strong character and writing skills.

$\mathcal{W}$

WALD, LILLIAN D. (1867–1940)
Reformer and Nurse   Cincinnati, Ohio

Lillian D. Wald was a public health nurse and a social reformer. She was born on March 10, 1867, as the third of four children to an optical goods dealer and his wife. During her happy childhood, Wald enjoyed music and books and attended Miss Cruttenden's English-French Boarding and Day School before applying to Vassar at age 16. Refused admission based on her age, she decided instead to attend the New York Hospital training school for nurses. After her graduation, she enrolled in the Woman's Medical College of New York for further training. Concurrently, she began organizing home nursing classes for immigrants on New York's Lower East Side. When she made a house call at a tenement and witnessed the living conditions, she quit medical school and devoted herself to public health nursing. In 1895, banker Jacob H. Schiff financed Wald's establishment of the "Nurses' Settlement" on Henry Street. Eleven residents moved in, nine of them nurses. In 1902, her nurses influenced the New York City Board of Health to start the first public school nursing program in the country. By 1913, 92 nurses from the Henry Street Settlement were making 200,000 annual visits. Wald expanded settlement activities to aid the unemployed and to become a center for civic, social, educational, and philanthropic work. In 1915, she opened a neighborhood playhouse in the facility. Wald led campaigns against tuberculosis, for improved housing, and for more parks and playgrounds. Although she never married, her concern for children kept her at the front of the child welfare movement, and she and **Florence Kelley** founded the National Child Labor Committee to have legislation passed outlawing child labor. Wald suggested the federal Children's

Bureau to Theodore Roosevelt, who created it and chose **Julia Lathrop** to direct it. At the beginning of World War I, Wald helped organize the American Union Against Militarism, and during the influenza epidemic of 1918–1919, she became chairman of the Nurses' Emergency Council. After the war, she helped found the League of Free Nations Association. She has been elected to The National Women's Hall of Fame.

BIBLIOGRAPHY

Block, Irvin. *Neighbor to the World: The Story of Lillian Wald*. New York: Crowell, 1969. No ISBN, 181p. In a biography for young adults, Block tells Wald's story.
Daniels, Doris. *Always a Sister: The Feminism of Lillian D. Wald*. New York: Feminist Press, 1989. 0–935312–90–0, 207p. Daniels tells about Wald's life and achievements from a feminist viewpoint.

WALKER, ALICE (1944–)
Author and Poet   Eatonton, Georgia

Alice Malsenior Walker focuses on African American women to reveal their culture in her novels. She was born on February 9, 1944, to sharecroppers as the youngest of eight children. Five brothers taught her to defend herself not only at home but also in the white world, where she might be cheated or mistreated. After her brother accidently shot her in the eye with a BB gun, she thought that others could see her scar. She retreated inside and read most of the time, and this activity helped her graduate as valedictorian of her class before she entered Spelman College. She transferred to Sarah Lawrence College in 1963, a world outside the confinement of her southern childhood. While there, she debated whether to commit suicide or to terminate an unwanted pregnancy. She chose the latter, but her decision long haunted her. In 1967, after marrying a white civil rights lawyer, she received a grant that allowed her to complete her first novel, *The Third Life of Grange Copeland*. She held teaching jobs at various colleges before her poetry published in 1973 won the **Lillian Smith** Award and was nominated for a National Book Award. A collection of her short stories the same year won an award from the National Institute of Arts and Letters. In 1977, she won a Guggenheim Foundation Fellowship, and in 1982, *The Color Purple* was nominated for the National Book Critics Circle Award and won both the Pulitzer Prize and the American Book Award before it was adapted in film. She has continued to write and receive other awards.

BIBLIOGRAPHY

Gentry, Tony. *Alice Walker*. New York: Chelsea House, 1993. 0–7910–1884–9, 105p. Gentry's researched biography of Walker's life and career for young adults includes accompanying photographs.
Walker, Alice. *Anything We Love Can Be Saved: A Writer's Activism*. New York: Random, 1997. 0–679–45584–1, 225p. In autobiographical essays suitable for young adults, Walker unites a variety of subjects under the rubric of activism.

————. *In Search of Our Mothers' Gardens: Womanist Prose*. San Diego: Harcourt Brace Jovanovich, 1983. 0–15–144525–7, 397p. Included are Walker's essays, speeches, and letters spanning the years 1967 to 1983 that reveal her growing awareness of being a feminist or "womanist."

————. *The Same River Twice: Honoring the Difficult*. New York: Scribner, 1996. 0–684–81419–6, 302p. Walker reflects on the 10 years following the filming of *The Color Purple*.

Winchell, Donna Haisty. *Alice Walker*. New York: Twayne, 1992. 0–8057–7642–7, 152p. Winchell's critical biography, researched and documented, examines Walker's life and her work.

WALKER, MADAM C. J. *See* WALKER, SARAH BREEDLOVE

WALKER, MAGGIE LENA (1867–1934)
Banker   Richmond, Virginia

Maggie Lena Walker wanted to provide employment for African American women through cooperation and support. She was born on July 15, 1867, to an Irish-born newspaper correspondent father and a mother who worked for the spy **Elizabeth Van Lew**. Walker helped her mother support her siblings by picking up and delivering clothes for her mother to launder. After graduation from school, Walker became a teacher, but her marriage ended that career. During her school days, Walker had a close affiliation with her church and had joined the Good Idea Council No. 16 of the Independent Order of St. Luke, a mutual aid society supporting the African American community. Walker held all of the lower offices and became the Right Worthy Grand Chief in 1890. In 1895, at the group's convention, she suggested the creation of a Juvenile Department, and she was elected its Grand Matron, a job she held for the remainder of her life. Her business skills improved, and she made preparations to become a banker by spending several hours a day in the Merchants' National Bank of Richmond, training to manage St. Luke Penny Savings Bank after its opening in 1903. The bank eventually separated from the Independent Order of St. Luke and merged with other banks, and Walker became board chairman of the first African American bank in Richmond, the Consolidated Bank and Trust Company. She served on many committees and councils, earning accolades for her work.

BIBLIOGRAPHY
Branch, Muriel Miller, and Dorothy Marie Rice. *Pennies to Dollars: The Story of Maggie Lena Walker*. North Haven, CT: Linnet, 1997. 0–208–02453–0, 100p. In a biography for young adults based on Walker's speeches and diaries, Branch and Rice tell of Walker's rise from poverty.

WALKER, MARGARET (1915–1998)
Author and Poet   Birmingham, Alabama

African American Margaret Walker was a poet and novelist who gained critical acclaim for her work. Born on July 7, 1915, into a well-educated family, Walker was surrounded with books and music. Her father could speak five languages and read three more, and her mother was a college-educated music teacher. She finished high school at 14 and college at 19. Her poetry career began when she was 11 after her parents moved to New Orleans; when Langston Hughes visited her high school, she asked his advice. He suggested that she keep writing but leave the South. She attended Northwestern University and received more encouragement, joining the Federal Writers Project in Chicago, where she worked with **Gwendolyn Brooks**. At the project's end, she went to the University of Iowa and completed her first book of poetry. Critics have called the publication of *For My People* (1942) one of the most important events in African American literary history because Walker became the first African American poet to be chosen for the Yale University Series of Younger Poets. She had to teach to eat, however, and after a marriage and four children, she did not publish again until 1966, when her novel, *Jubilee*, a fictional treatment of her great-grandmother's life, appeared. In the interim, she received honors and completed her Ph.D. at the University of Iowa. At Jackson State University, where she served as professor, she founded the Institute for the Study of History, Life and Culture of Black People. She also wrote essays, other volumes of poetry, and biography.

BIBLIOGRAPHY

Giovanni, Nikki. *A Poetic Equation: Conversations Between Nikki Giovanni and Margaret Walker*. 1974. Washington, DC: Howard University Press, 1983. 0-88258-003-5, 148p. This conversation between Giovanni and Walker exposes Walker's attitude about her writing and the world.

Walker, Margaret. *How I Wrote "Jubilee" and Other Essays on Life and Literature*. New York: Feminist Press, 1990. 1-55861-004-9, 157p. Walker divulges the process of creating *Jubilee* in a collection including 14 speeches and essays spanning the years 1943 to 1988.

WALKER, MARY EDWARDS (1832–1919)
Physician   Oswego, New York

Mary Edwards Walker was a physician. She was born on November 26, 1832, as one of six children to a farmer who taught himself medicine and his wife. She studied in public schools before attending the Falley Seminary and entering Syracuse Medical College. She graduated in 1855, practiced a short time in Ohio, and returned to Rome, New York, where she married a fellow medical student with whom she practiced for several years. She quickly adopted **Amelia Jenks Bloomer**'s costume, and as Walker became more interested in dress reform, she began contributing to *Sibyl*, a reformist publication. When the Civil War began,

Walker went to Washington, but when she could not obtain a commission as an army surgeon, she worked as an unpaid volunteer in the Patent Office Hospital and helped organize the Women's Relief Association to aid women visiting soldiers billeted in the city. After going to New York City to earn her degree from the Hygeio-Therapeutic College, she returned to work in battle zone tent hospitals. In 1863, she finally won an appointment as an assistant surgeon in Tennessee and donned the same uniform as her male officer colleagues. When she crossed enemy lines to help civilians, Confederates captured and imprisoned her for several months. After her release, she served as a supervisor in a Kentucky hospital for women prisoners and as director of an orphanage in Tennessee, but her dictatorial methods alienated her subordinates. In 1865, at the end of the war, she was the only woman to be awarded the Congressional Medal of Honor. She then became active in woman suffrage but thought the proposed Equal Rights Amendment was "trash." Her conflicts with family and neighbors continued, but she always wore her Medal of Honor, although it was officially withdrawn in 1917.

BIBLIOGRAPHY

Hall, Marjory. *Quite Contrary: Dr. Mary Edwards Walker.* New York: Funk and Wagnalls, 1970. No ISBN, 160p. In a fictional biography for young adults, Hall explores Walker's life as a nonconformist.

Leonard, Elizabeth D. *Yankee Women: Gender Battles in the Civil War.* New York: Norton, 1994. 0–393–03666–9, 308p. Letters and journals form the basis of this collective biography, which explores Walker's determination for equal treatment.

Snyder, Charles McCool. *Dr. Mary Walker: The Little Lady in Pants.* 1962. New York: Arno Press, 1974. 0–405–06122–6, 166p. Snyder used the Walker family records, anecdotes from those who knew them, and Walker's own words to create his researched and documented biography of Walker and her career.

WALKER, SARAH BREEDLOVE (1867–1919)
Businesswoman   **Delta, Louisiana**

Madam C. J. Walker created an industry of hair goods and preparations for African Americans before she became a philanthropist and political activist. On December 23, 1867, she was born Sarah Breedlove to former slaves living on a cotton plantation. They died by the time she was seven, and when she was ten, she became a domestic, following that job with marriage at fourteen. Her husband died in 1887 when her daughter A'Lelia was two. After working for 17 more years, she moved to Denver, married, and began promoting her hair products. She built her business, became wealthy, and began giving money to worthy causes such as establishing the Young Men's Christian Association in African American communities and supporting African American schools. She became outspoken about political issues and served as the keynote speaker at National Association for the Advancement of Colored People (NAACP) fund-raisers while advocating a woman's ability to run a business and become a millionaire as she had. She was elected to The National Women's Hall of Fame.

BIBLIOGRAPHY

Bundles, A'Lelia Perry. *Madam C. J. Walker.* New York: Chelsea House, 1991. 1-55546-615-X, 110p. In this researched biography of Walker for young adults, Bundles presents her life and career with accompanying photographs.

Lommel, Cookie. *Madam C. J. Walker.* Los Angeles: Melrose Square, 1993. 0-8706-7597-4, 192p. Lommel's biography of Walker for young adults explores her determination to build her business.

WALLACE, LILA ACHESON (1889–1984)
Publisher and Philanthropist   **St. Paul, Minnesota**

Lila Acheson Wallace was a publisher, the creator of *Reader's Digest*, and a philanthropist. She was born on December 25, 1889, the daughter of a Presbyterian minister and his wife. She grew up in small Midwestern towns before moving to Tacoma, Washington, and graduating from the University of Oregon. She taught school, and during World War I, she organized centers for women working in war industries in the eastern states. In 1921, she married a man who wanted to create a journal. After borrowing $5,000, the two began to publish *Reader's Digest* in 1922, marketing it by direct mail from their basement underneath a Greenwich Village speakeasy. The magazine's circulation grew rapidly, rising from 1,500 to 200,000 in 1929 and to about 27 million (worldwide) in 48 editions and 19 languages by the mid-1990s. Wallace's husband served as editor from 1921 to 1965 and as chairman from 1921 to 1973. Wallace and her husband wanted the magazine to generate a positive tone, and they included affirmative articles on a wide range of topics. With the enormous wealth earned from the magazine, the two began many philanthropies, including the restoration of Claude Monet's house and grounds at Giverny, France, and preservation of temples at Abu Simbel in Egypt. For their contributions, Wallace and her husband received the United States Presidential Medal of Freedom. The Lila Wallace–*Reader's Digest* Fund has become the largest private funder of culture and the arts in the United States. When she died, Wallace was worth more than $250 million, the wealthiest woman in the country.

BIBLIOGRAPHY

Canning, Peter. *American Dreamers: The Wallaces and Reader's Digest.* New York: Simon and Schuster, 1996. 0-684-80928-1, 379p. Based on memories and interviews, Canning, a former manager for the *Reader's Digest*, relates the history of the publication and those who founded it.

Heidenry, John. *Theirs Was the Kingdom: Lila and Dewitt Wallace and the Story of the Reader's Digest.* New York: Norton, 1993. 0-393-03466-6, 701p. Heidenry interviewed former *Reader's Digest* employees to uncover some of the truths about the magazine and its founders.

WALTERS, BARBARA (1931-)
Broadcast Journalist   Boston, Massachusetts

Barbara Walters is an internationally respected broadcast journalist. She was born on September 25, 1931, to the founder of the "Latin Quarter" nightclubs and his wife. She attended Sarah Lawrence College and graduated with a degree in English in 1953. She began her career as a writer for local East Coast television stations before getting a job in 1961 as a writer and researcher for the *Today* show. Beginning in 1963, she appeared in isolated episodes on the show, and the next year, she was promoted to regular status, where she stayed until becoming an anchor in 1974. In 1972, she was one of three woman reporters accompanying President Nixon on his trip to China, and her experience on this assignment plus other coups raised her salary to $1 million a year for five years, more than her male colleagues received. In 1976, she began co-anchoring the *ABC Evening News*, and during this time arranged the first joint interview between Egypt's President Anwar Sadat and Israel's Prime Minister Menachem Begin. She also had a series of interviews with people sometimes unwilling to talk to others, including Princess Grace of Monaco, *Sophia Loren, **Diana Ross**, **Elizabeth Taylor**, Sean Connery, and Ronald Reagan. After serving as a correspondent for *World News Tonight* in 1979, she appeared intermittently on the ABC news magazine show *20/20* until 1984, when she began co-hosting. In 1997, she began hosting *The View*, a twice-weekly daytime talk and information show. Among her honorary degrees and honors are Emmy Awards, a Silver Satellite Award, the George Foster Peabody Award, induction into the Television Academy Hall of Fame, and being named one of America's 100 Most Important Women of the Century in both *Good Housekeeping* and *Ladies' Home Journal* magazines.

BIBLIOGRAPHY
Malone, Mary. *Barbara Walters: TV Superstar*. Hillside, NJ: Enslow, 1990. 0-89490-287-3, 128p. Malone interviewed Walters and consulted electronic and print media for this balanced biography for young adults.

Oppenheimer, Jerry. *Barbara Walters: An Unauthorized Biography*. New York: St. Martin's, 1990. 0-312-03806-2, 368p. In his biography, Oppenheimer emphasizes that Walters's strong will and hard work helped her to advance in the competitive profession of television broadcasting.

WARD, NANCY (1738?-1822)
Tribal Leader   Chota, Tennessee

Nancy Ward was a Cherokee leader, sometimes known as the "**Pocahontas** of the West." She was born around 1738, most likely to a member of the Delaware tribe who had become a member of the matriarchal Wolf tribe at his marriage to Tame Doe, Ward's mother. Ward was married young to Kingfisher of the Dear clan and bore two children. In 1775, when her husband died in the battle of Taliwa between the Cherokees and the Creeks, she took his place in battle and helped the

Cherokees win decisively. For her courage, she was named Agi-ga-u-e (Beloved Woman). She headed the influential Woman's Council and was a member of the Council of Chiefs. She then married a white trader and had a daughter before leaving the Cherokee Nation. Although her husband returned to his South Carolina home and later married a white woman, he and Ward seemed to have communicated after this time, and she maintained good relations with white settlers in eastern Tennessee. During the American Revolution, she warned Tennessee leader John Sevier about a pro-British Cherokee attack. The same year, while colonial troops were destroying other Cherokee villages, they spared Ward's village. After warning of a second Cherokee attack, her family was again protected. During peace negotiations, Ward urged friendship with the Cherokee because she realized that the white men would remain. Having learned to make butter and cheese from one of the settlers, Ward bought cattle, and after the war, she taught her people how to raise them. As she aged, she begged the Cherokee not to relinquish any more of their land, but she could not save them.

BIBLIOGRAPHY

Adams, Robert G. *Nancy Ward, Beautiful Woman of Two Worlds*. Chattanooga, TN: Hampton House, 1979. No ISBN, 109p. For this fictional biography, suitable for young adults, Adams has gathered available facts and combined them with legends about Ward.

Alderman, Pat. *Nancy Ward, Cherokee Chieftainess*. Johnson City, TN: Overmountain Press, 1978. No ISBN, 86p. Although basically a script for a television program about Ward, the text places her in her time and examines her accomplishments.

Felton, Harold W. *Nancy Ward, Cherokee*. New York: Dodd, Mead, 1975. 0-396-07072-8, 89p. A brief young adult biography of Ward focuses on her aid to her Cherokee people and her assistance to the colonists during the American Revolution.

WARDE, MARY FRANCES XAVIER (1810?–1884)
Religious   Abbeyliex, Ireland

Sister Mary Frances Xavier Warde was the American founder of the Sisters of Mercy. She was born around 1810 as the youngest of six children to a successful merchant and his wife, who died soon after Warde was born. Warde remained on the family lands of Bellbrook and received her education from private tutors and from her older sister. Her thorough understanding of religious matters surprised her examiners, and they allowed her to receive Communion at a younger age than her peers. She and her older brother often secretly read from one of her mother's favorite books on *Teresa of Ávila. When Warde was confirmed, she chose the name "Teresa," without divulging her reason. Warde's father lost his land when she was 17, and she went to Dublin and met *Catherine McAuley. Warde joined McAuley's Convent of the Sisters of Mercy, thinking then and throughout her life that McAuley was the ultimate woman of God. Warde became the first Sister of Mercy to be professed by Mother Catherine in the first Convent of Mercy before

Warde went to Carlow, Naas, and Wexford to establish new convents. At age 33, she received the call to go to the United States to establish a Sisters of Mercy mission in Pittsburgh for the lonely Irish immigrants working there. Her superiors knew that being somewhat assertive and determined, but also gracious and loving, with the ability to "charm the birds from the trees," Warde would be more successful than other sisters. After she and six other sisters, the "First Seven," went to Pittsburgh, people in other areas of the country summoned her to start convents for them. She went to New Hampshire, Maine, and the West, establishing her last Mercy Convent 40 years after her arrival. Warde's convents served the poor, the sick, and the illiterate. She also helped non-Catholic adults through her interpretation of the Scripture, her love of music, and her fondness for beautiful gardens. After her death in one of the dormitories where she had always housed herself, hundreds lined the streets of Manchester, New Hampshire, to honor her, and many churches dedicated windows in memory of her service to them and to God.

BIBLIOGRAPHY

Healy, Kathleen. *Frances Warde: American Founder of the Sisters of Mercy.* New York: Seabury Press, 1973. 0-8164-1139-5, 535p. This carefully researched biography reveals Warde's importance as a pioneer in American life.

WARREN, MERCY (OTIS) (1728–1814)
Author and Historian   **Barnstable, Massachusetts**

Mercy Otis Warren was a poet and historian. The third of 13 children, she was born on September 14, 1728 to a farmer who served as judge of the county court of common pleas and his wife. Warren's parents educated their sons but not their daughters; however, she often listened to her brothers' tutors and their political discussions. At 26, she married a Harvard graduate. As the colonies' conflict with England grew, Warren's home served as a place for men to discuss their options. She began writing political satire in closet dramas, and her first play, *The Adulateur*, appeared in the Boston newspaper *Massachusetts Spy* in 1772. She published several others, disguising Tories with evil names, in the following years. She and her husband were unjustly accused of supporting Shays's Rebellion, probably because she vocally opposed the ratification of the federal Constitution in 1788 in her *Observations on the New Constitution.* She also annoyed citizens by supporting the French Revolution. Throughout, she worked on a three-volume *History of the Rise, Progress and Termination of the American Revolution,* finally published in 1805. In it, she gave her personal opinions about people she had known during the fray, with her attitude about John Adams severing their friendship. Warren was a feminist in her time because she resented the lack of education for women and hated being excluded from activities specifically limited to men. She accepted her subordinate role only because she thought it would be better for the family, although not for her.

BIBLIOGRAPHY

Anthony, Katharine Susan. *First Lady of the Revolution: The Life of Mercy Otis Warren.* 1958. Port Washington, NY: Kennikat Press, 1972. 0–8046–1656–6, 258p. Anthony calls Warren "First Lady of the Revolution," and documents the claim with background on her life.

Fritz, Jean. *Cast for a Revolution: Some American Friends and Enemies, 1728–1814.* Boston: Houghton Mifflin, 1972. 0–395–13945–7, 400p. Fritz's carefully researched view of Warren relies on Warren's point of view and those who knew her.

Zagarri, Rosemarie. *A Woman's Dilemma: Mercy Otis Warren and the American Revolution.* Wheeling, IL: Harlan Davidson, 1995. 0–88295–924–7, 187p. This carefully researched and scholarly examination of Warren reveals that she used her intelligence to accomplish what she wanted to do.

WATERS, ETHEL (1896–1977)
Singer   Chester, Pennsylvania

African American Ethel Waters was a blues and jazz singer as well as an actor. She was born on October 31, 1896, as the result of her 12-year-old mother being raped, and her grandmother raised her in the slums of Philadelphia. She made her professional debut at age five in a church production. At 13, she married a man 10 years her senior, at her mother's encouragement, but they soon separated. In 1917, she began appearing with a vaudeville troupe, becoming the first woman to sing W. C. Handy's "St. Louis Blues." After going to New York's Harlem in 1919, she became one of its best known performers. In 1927, she began acting, first on Broadway and then in films. The first African American to perform in an Irving Berlin all-white Broadway hit, *As Thousands Cheer*, she sang "Heat Wave," and she was the first African American woman to star in a Broadway drama when she took the lead as Hagar in *Mamba's Daughters*. She received an Academy Award nomination for her work in *Pinky*, and she also garnered praise for her work in *A Member of the Wedding*. In the early 1950s, she was one of three major female actors along with **Katharine Cornell** and **Helen Hayes**. Among those with whom she made recordings were Duke Ellington and Benny Goodman. She joined Billy Graham's crusades in the late 1950s, continuing to perform her songs, especially "His Eye Is on the Sparrow," while dealing with a difficult private life.

BIBLIOGRAPHY

DeKorte, Juliann. *Finally Home.* Old Tappan, NJ: Revell, 1978. 0–8007–0934–9, 128p. The nurse who cared for Waters as she prepared to die had known her for many years, and she discloses their friendship and the importance of "Mom" (Waters) in her life and in the lives of others.

Knaack, Twila. *Ethel Waters: I Touched a Sparrow.* Waco, TX: World, 1978. 0–8499–0084–0, 128p. As Waters's companion and helper after 1970, Knaack knew Waters well, and she illuminates Waters's physical and emotional concerns during these years while a member of the Billy Graham organization.

Waters, Ethel. *His Eye Is on the Sparrow: An Autobiography.* New York: Da Capo Press, 1992. 0–306–80477–8, 278p. Waters's autobiography reveals the sordidness of her early life, the prejudices toward her as an African American, and the final successes that she enjoyed in her long career.

————. *To Me It's Wonderful*. New York: Harper and Row, 1972. No ISBN, 162p. In this autobiography, Waters has a conversation with the reader in which she reveals her loving personality and her strong spiritual beliefs.

WEBER, LOIS   (1881–1939)
Film Director   Allegheny, Pennsylvania

Lois Weber was a film director, author, and actor. She was born on June 13, 1881, as the second of two daughters to an upholsterer and decorator and his wife. Weber showed her musical skills at an early age, singing in church and school choirs and skillfully playing the piano. She toured at 16 as a concert pianist but disliked the life, and when she returned home, she sang with the Church Army at rescue missions and on the streets. Wanting to be an opera singer and actor, she played in repertory and stock, but she and her husband decided that they needed to work in films if they were going to avoid further separation. The two worked on experimental "talking films," with Weber writing scenarios and recording the dialogue on phonograph records to play with the action. Weber acted, directed, wrote stories, found locations, cut film, and completed any other necessary jobs for Rex Studios, later Universal Studios. By 1915, Weber had become a director, and in 1916 was Universal's highest paid nonacting staff member, male or female. She and her husband opened Lois Weber Productions, although she continued to release her work through Universal. She had popular successes, including a film with *Anna Pavlova, but she preferred to address controversial issues such as birth control, anti-Semitism, and women in a male-dominated society. Professionals recognized her talent and her knowledge, and she enjoyed long-term success because she tried, through her films, to reach as many people as possible. Weber wrote and directed most of her 40 feature films and her hundreds of short films.

BIBLIOGRAPHY
Slide, Anthony. *Lois Weber: The Director Who Lost Her Way in History*. Westport, CT: Greenwood Press, 1996. 0-313-29945-5, 179p. Slide documents Weber's important contributions in his recommended biography.

WELCH, RAQUEL (1940–)
Actor and Author   Chicago, Illinois

Latina American Rachel Welch is an internationally known actor. Born Rachel Tejada on September 5, 1940, to a Bolivian immigrant mechanical engineer and an American mother, she moved with her family to La Jolla, California, when only two. She took music and dance in high school, determining that she wanted to act, and at 15, won her first beauty contest. She married a high school sweetheart, but after five years and two children, they divorced. She eventually met Pat Curtis, and together they began to market her image. Although her provocative photographs appeared on 90 European and 20 American magazine covers, she continued to perform in undistinguished movies. Finally, in 1975, her performance in *The Four Musketeers* won her a Golden Globe Award for best actress. She replaced **Lauren Bacall** in a Broadway play, *Woman of the Year*, and won critical acclaim. As president of her own production company, Welch develops new projects for herself. In 1990, the Los Angeles Hispanic Women's Council named her Woman of the Year.

BIBLIOGRAPHY

Haining, Peter. *Raquel Welch: Sex Symbol to Super Star*. New York: St. Martin's, 1984. 0–312–66396–X, 224p. Haining's popular biography of Welch, with photographs, examines her response to being a sex symbol along with her life and career.

WELLS-BARNETT, IDA B. (1862–1931)
Journalist   Holly Springs, Mississippi

African American Ida Bell Wells-Barnett advocated women's rights, civil rights, and economic rights throughout her life as a journalist. She was born on July 16, 1862, as the eldest daughter of slaves who had seven more children. All of the children went to school, with Wells-Barnett's mother often going to classes with her children so that she herself could learn to read and write. When a yellow fever epidemic swept through town in 1878, Wells-Barnett's parents and a brother died, and she had to assume leadership of the family at 16. She passed the teacher's exam and got a job. In 1884, she bought a train ticket which the conductor declined to take as long as she sat in the white coach. She refused to move, and conductors physically forced her from the train. She hired an African American lawyer and sued the railroad, and after no action on the case, she hired a white lawyer and won $500. After the editor of her local newspaper left, Wells-Barnett became editor and wrote a column under the pen name "Iola" about her people's concerns. When three of her African American colleagues, upstanding citizens, were lynched in 1892, she realized that white men had lied by crying "rape" in order to lynch men not guilty of the crime. Her subsequent editorial infuriated the white community, and after she left on a trip, someone destroyed her offices. She continued her investigation of the incident from afar before marrying an African American activist who supported her efforts. Throughout her life, she assisted African American initiatives; however, she opposed Booker T. Washington by agreeing with Marcus Garvey that white exploitation evolved from problems within the African American community. She continued to work for and worry about the future of African Americans until her death. Funds from her Negro Fellowship League helped open Chicago's first African American kindergarten. She was later elected to The National Women's Hall of Fame.

BIBLIOGRAPHY

Klots, Steve. *Ida Wells-Barnett*. New York: Chelsea House, 1994. 0-7910-1885-7, 127p. Klots explores Wells-Barnett's contributions in his researched biography for young adults.

Nazel, Joseph. *Ida B. Wells*. Los Angeles: Melrose Square, 1995. 0-87067-785-3, 208p. This biography of Wells-Barnett for young adults covers her life and her career.

Thompson, Mildred I. *Ida B. Wells-Barnett: An Exploratory Study of an American Black Woman*. Brooklyn, NY: Carlson, 1990. 0-926019-21-X, 289p. Thompson used archival records, newspapers, secondary sources, and an interview with one of Wells-Barnett's descendants as sources for his biography.

Townes, Emilie Maureen. *Womanist Justice, Womanist Hope*. Atlanta: Scholars Press, 1993. 1-55540-682-3, 228p. Townes examines Wells-Barnett's moral and social perspectives in this critical biography.

Wells-Barnett, Ida B. *Crusade for Justice: The Autobiography of Ida B. Wells*. Chicago: University of Chicago Press, 1970. 0-226-89342-1, 434p. In the preface to her autobiography, Wells-Barnett compares herself to Joan of Arc, fighting alone for her beliefs.

WELTY, EUDORA (1909-)
Author   Jackson, Mississippi

Eudora Welty is an author. She was born on April 13, 1909, as the oldest of three children to northerners, a teacher-turned-insurance-company president and his wife, a teacher. Since Welty's family read together, she recognized good literature early in her life. After public schools, she attended Mississippi State College for Women and then the University of Wisconsin, where she received her degree in 1929. Her father, believing she would be unable to earn a living by writing, encouraged her to study advertising at the Columbia University Graduate School of Business in New York. Welty's father died suddenly in 1931, and she returned to work with local newspapers and a radio station before becoming a publicity agent for the Works Progress Administration (WPA) in 1933. She reported and interviewed people throughout Mississippi and took hundreds of photographs, documenting the hardship and the dignity of rural lives. She could only arrange a small one-woman show in 1936, but in 1971 some of the pictures appeared in *One Time, One Place: Mississippi in the Depression; A Snapshot Album*. She published her first story, "Death of a Traveling Salesman," in the literary magazine *Manuscript* in 1936. Between 1937 and 1939, *Southern Review* accepted six of her stories, and she became friends with other writers, including **Katherine Anne Porter**. She won the Pulitzer Prize for *The Optimist's Daughter*. Welty served as the Library of Congress consultant in American letters during 1958. Her other awards include the Presidential Medal of Freedom and a National Medal of the Arts. She belongs to the American Academy and Institute of Arts and Letters.

BIBLIOGRAPHY

Evans, Elizabeth. *Eudora Welty*. New York: F. Ungar, 1981. 0-8044-2187-0, 173p. Evans examines Welty's life and work.

Kreyling, Michael. *Author and Agent: Eudora Welty and Diarmuid Russell*. New York: Farrar, Straus and Giroux, 1991. 0-374-10727-0, 215p. Using 23 years of correspondence between Welty and her editor, Diarmuid Russell, Kreyling has created a work that reveals the development of Welty's career.

Waldron, Ann. *Eudora Welty: A Writer's Life*. New York: Doubleday, 1998. 0-385-47647-7, 512p. Waldron's balanced, unauthorized biography of Welty presents the complexities of her life and work.

Welty, Eudora. *One Writer's Beginnings*. 1984. New York: Warner, 1991. 0-446-39328-2, 114p. In these essays constituting a literary autobiography, Welty discusses various influential aspects of her life. American Book Award.

WEST, MAE (1892–1980)

Actor   Brooklyn, New York

Mae West was an actor, comedienne, author, and singer. She was born on August 17, 1892, as one of three children to a heavyweight boxer and his wife, a German immigrant corset designer. As a young girl, her education consisted of dance lessons at an academy. She made her vaudeville debut at age six at the Brooklyn's Royal Theatre's amateur night and followed it by appearing in *Little Nell the Marchioness*. She then joined a stock company for four years before touring the vaudeville circuit, performing in a Coney Island acrobatic act at 15. She made her Broadway debut in 1911 and became a vaudeville headliner, "The Baby Vamp," in 1913. In 1926, she made her Broadway writing, directing, and producing debut in *Sex*. The police closed the play and sentenced her to 10 days in jail plus a $500 fine for obscenity. She was again arrested for performing in *The Drag*, a play dealing with homosexuality in which she played Catherine the Great. In 1928, she wrote and starred in *Diamond Lil*, a hit play, and four years later, made her film debut. In 1933, she made her screenwriting debut with *I'm No Angel*. In 1935, she was the highest paid woman in the United States, making $480,833. But two years later, she was banned from radio for 12 years for her suggestive dialogue. In 1943, she made her penultimate film, and in 1970, she wrote her own scenes for *Myra Breckinridge*, earning $350,000 for 10 days of work. During the interim, she toured in stage revivals and in a nightclub concert act. Her popularity led sailors to name their inflatable life jackets in honor of her overly emphasized "assets," and ensured her a place in *Webster's Dictionary*.

BIBLIOGRAPHY

Bavar, Michael. *Mae West*. New York: Pyramid, 1975. 0-515-03868-7, 159p. This popular biography of West, emphasizing her movies, repeats some of her racy dialogue.

Eells, George, and Stanley Musgrove. *Mae West: A Biography*. Boston: Morrow, 1982. 0-688-00816-X, 351p. Eells and Musgrove interviewed people who knew West and added research to give a realistic picture of West's life and career.

Leider, Emily Wortis. *Becoming Mae West*. New York: Farrar, Straus and Giroux, 1987. 0-374-10959-1, 431p. Leider's carefully researched, thorough, and recommended biography of West focuses on her early life and the establishment of her career.

Leonard, Maurice. *Mae West: Empress of Sex*. Secaucus, NJ: Carol, 1992. 1-55972-151-0,
    422p. This readable, undocumented popular biography of West covers her life and
    career.
Sochen, June. *Mae West: She Who Laughs, Lasts*. Arlington Heights, IL: I. Davidson,
    1992. 0-88295-891-7, 153p. Sochen's well-researched scholarly biography of West
    examines her career.

WHARTON, EDITH (1862–1937)
Author   New York, New York

Edith Newbold Jones Wharton was an author. She was born on January 24, 1862,
the youngest by many years of three children of a real estate owner and his wife.
She spent winters in New York and summers on Long Island or in Newport,
Rhode Island, and observed the world of the wealthy. Economically depressed at
the end of the Civil War, her family went to Europe for six years, living in Italy,
France, and Germany. Wharton read and learned the language of each country.
When she returned to America, a governess taught her, and at 16, she wrote a
volume of poetry which was privately published before she made her debut in
society. In 1885, she married a Boston banker 13 years older than she, but they had
little in common, and to escape the dullness of marriage, she began to write
seriously. Her stories appeared in *Scribner's*, *Harper's*, and the *Century*. After
purchasing a house in Newport, Wharton became interested in interior decoration
and wrote *The Decoration of Houses* to encourage a return to classicism; the book
sold well and influenced the design and furnishing of her contemporaries' homes.
In 1902, when she was 40, she published her first novel, *The Valley of Decision*. *The
House of Mirth*, published in 1905, signaled the beginning of her major productive
period, with early books revealing the high caliber of her work. During World
War I, she organized relief efforts for orphans in both Belgium and France for
which she won the Cross of the Legion of Honor from France and the Chevalier of
the Order of Leopold from Belgium. In 1920, her book *The Age of Innocence*
lamented the destructiveness of the war and won a Pulitzer Prize. She continued to
collect honorary degrees and other awards including election to the National
Institute of Arts and Letters, to the American Academy of Arts and Letters, and to
The National Women's Hall of Fame.

BIBLIOGRAPHY

Benstock, Shari. *No Gifts from Chance: A Biography of Edith Wharton*. New York:
    Scribner, 1994. 0-684-19276-4, 546p. Benstock consulted government records,
    legal and medical documents, and recently available letters to write her thorough,
    recommended biography, suitable for young adults.
Dwight, Eleanor. *Edith Wharton: An Extraordinary Life*. New York: Abrams, 1994.
    0-8109-3971-1, 296p. Dwight examines the variety of subjects about which
    Wharton wrote in her recommended biography.
Goodman, Susan. *Edith Wharton's Inner Circle*. Austin: University of Texas Press, 1994.
    0-292-72771-2, 165p. Goodman examines Wharton's friendships, revealed in

private papers, to uncover their influence on her writing in this recommended, carefully researched biography.

Lewis, R.W.B. *Edith Wharton: A Biography.* 1975. New York: Fromm International, 1985. 0-88064-020-0, 592p. Lewis used previously inaccessible papers for his definitive literary biography of Wharton. Pulitzer Prize.

Price, Alan. *The End of the Age of Innocence: Edith Wharton and the First World War.* New York: St. Martin's, 1996. 0-312-12938-6, 238p. Wharton's unpublished letters and archival records of the relief organizations she supported form the basis of Price's biography.

WHEATLEY, PHILLIS (1753–1784)
Slave and Poet   Gambia, West Africa

Phillis Wheatley was the first African American author to publish her work. She was born around 1753 in Gambia, West Africa, probably as a member of the Fulani tribe. When her master bought her in 1761, off a slave ship, Wheatley was reportedly losing her baby teeth and was probably around seven or eight years old. The family recognized her intelligence and provided her with instruction in reading and writing. She also learned Latin well enough to translate Ovid's *Metamorphoses.* She began writing poetry when 14, and her first published work, *An Elegiac Poem, on the Death of the Celebrated Divine. . . George Whitefield* (1770) received attention from the family's Bostonian friends. After her poetry was published in England, her reputation spread abroad as well. Many of her poems espoused peace and freedom, a topic that may have displeased her masters; however, John Wheatley freed her when she returned from a trip to London in 1773. After his death in 1778, she had no resources, and marriage to a free African American was unsuccessful because he failed in business and could support neither her nor their children. Wheatley worked as a servant because she could not survive on the proceeds from her writing. She died in poverty at a young age.

BIBLIOGRAPHY

Jensen, Marilyn. *Phillis Wheatley: Negro Slave of Mr. John Wheatley of Boston.* Scarsdale, NY: Lion, 1987. 0-87460-326-9, 233p. This accessible biography of Wheatley for young adults serves as a background for treatment of slaves during the Colonial period.

Richmond, M. A. *Phillis Wheatley.* New York: Chelsea House, 1988. 1-55546-683-4, 111p. Using background from the times in which Wheatley lived, Richmond has gathered information about her life and her work in a biography for young adults.

Robinson, William Henry. *Phillis Wheatley and Her Writings.* New York: Garland, 1984. 0-8240-9346-1, 464p. Based on letters and Wheatley's poems, Robinson believes that Wheatley's poetry created the African American literary tradition.

WHITE, ALMA (1862–1946)
Evangelist   Kinniconick, Kentucky

Alma Bridwell White was the founder of the Pillar of Fire Church. She was born on June 16, 1862, as the seventh of 11 children to a tannery and farm owner and his wife. Because she hated the drudgery on the meager farm, she decided to become a teacher. White's parents, although having little education, encouraged her, and she attended Vanceburg Seminary and spent a year at Millersburg Female College before going to Montana to teach. She met and married a Methodist ministry student who allowed her to lead hymns or prayers and sometimes preach. In 1893, she experienced her sanctification and decided that she wanted to conduct her own services. She started revival meetings, but the Methodist hierarchy disapproved of her and of the emotional outbursts she elicited. White then organized an independent sect called the Methodist Pentecostal Union in 1901, which, in 1917 became the Pillar of Fire Church, with White claiming that she was offering the pure "Methodism" of John Wesley, Methodism's founder. White, the senior bishop and the first female bishop of any church, was president of the board of trustees. She conducted all Pillar of Fire activities and preached three or four times a day, crossing the country tirelessly and the Atlantic 58 times. She purchased radio stations in Denver and New Jersey, edited seven magazines, and established seven schools. In 1921, the Alma White College in New Jersey received authorization to grant degrees in arts and sciences. During the church's first 20 years, membership increased from 230 to 4,044 in 46 congregations, and its property increased to a value of $4 million. In addition to her church work, White wrote over 200 hymns and several volumes of poetry. After World War I, she supported the reconstitution of the Ku Klux Klan and its creed of white supremacy, claiming in *The Ku Klux Klan in Prophecy* that heroes in the Old and New Testament were actually Klansmen. When White was 70, she began oil painting and produced over 300 mountain landscapes before her death. Her vital religious organization showed that Americans were willing to experiment with their spiritual growth.

BIBLIOGRAPHY
Stanley, Susie Cunningham. *Feminist Pillar of Fire: The Life of Alma White*. Cleveland, OH: Pilgrim Press, 1993. 0–8298–0950–3, 162p. Stanley used White's unpublished writings to divulge the complexity of her character.
White, Alma. *Looking Back from Beulah*. 1902. New York: Garland, 1987. 0–8240–0681–X, 377p. In this autobiography of her childhood and career, White traces the steps that led to establishing the Pillar of Fire Church.

WHITE, ELLEN GOULD HARMON (1827–1915)
Religious Leader   Gorham, Maine

Ellen Gould Harmon White was co-founder of the Seventh-Day Adventist Church. She was born on November 26, 1827, as one of a set of twins to a hatter and his wife who had six other children. An older girl hit her with a stone when

White was nine, disfiguring her face and leaving her emotionally distraught. She was unable to concentrate on her school work or use a pen, and her formal education ended. Her first religious experience occurred when she was 13. Two years later, she was baptized, and after two more years, she supposedly fell into a trance during an intimate women's prayer group and reported that she had seen a vision of people on a pilgrimage to the City of God. She claimed 2,000 more visions during her lifetime. In 1845, at 18, she began her itinerant ministry, advocating observance of the Sabbath and adherence to the Decalogue, two beliefs of New England pietists. She married an Adventist preacher in 1846, and they began publishing a paper, *Present Truth*, which became *Advent Review and Sabbath Herald*. In 1851, White wrote about her visions and expanded her interests to child-centered education and abolitionism. After she and her husband moved to Battle Creek, Michigan, in 1855, their home quickly became an active stop on the Underground Railroad. In 1860, the groups with which she and her husband had associated met and chose the name "Seventh-Day Adventists," with White's interpretation of the Scriptures forming the basis for the church's beliefs. She opposed tea, coffee, drugs, and meat but approved exercise and water intake. In 1866, she helped Dr. John Harvey Kellogg found the Western Health Reform Institute (later the Battle Creek Sanitarium). After her husband's death, White traveled in Europe and Australia, where she established a school and wrote 15,000 pages of letters and testimonies. Throughout her life, she published over 50 books, many pamphlets, and 4,600 articles, seemingly to make up time lost when she could not hold a pen. When White died from complications of a fractured hip, over 4,000 people attended her funeral.

BIBLIOGRAPHY

Douglass, Herbert E. *Messenger of the Lord: The Prophetic Ministry of Ellen G. White.* Nampa, ID: Pacific Press, 1998. 0-8163-1657-0, 640p. This comprehensive and recommended examination of White's life and work places her within her time.

Knight, George R. *Meeting Ellen White: A Fresh Look at Her Life, Writings, and Major Themes.* Hagerstown, MD: Review and Herald, 1996. 0-8280-1089-7, 127p. Knight's popular, undocumented biography of White discusses her life.

Lantry, Eileen E. *Why Me, Lord? The Story of Ellen White.* Boise, ID: Pacific Press, 1988. 0-8163-0734-2, 80p. Lantry warns readers not to use her fictional biography for young adults as a historical source for what White said and did.

Noorbergen, Rene. *Ellen G. White, Prophet of Destiny.* New Canaan, CT: Keats, 1972. 0-87983-014-X, 241p. This researched and documented biography of White examines her life and work.

Numbers, Ronald L. *Prophetess of Health: Ellen G. White and the Origins of Seventh-Day Adventist Health Reform.* 1976. Knoxville: University of Tennessee Press, 1992. 0-87049-712-X, 335p. Numbers looks at White's relationship to medicine while she formed the tenets of the Seventh-Day Adventists.

WHITE, HELEN MAGILL (1853-1944)
Educator   Providence, Rhode Island

Helen Magill White was an educator and the first American woman to earn a Ph.D. degree. She was born on November 28, 1853, as the oldest of six children to a Quaker educator and his wife. As a child prodigy, she enrolled as the only female in her father's school, the Boston Public Latin High School, before entering Swarthmore College at age 16. She graduated in 1873 as the second of six students in the school's first graduating class after her father became president. She remained at Swarthmore for another two years to read classics before going to Boston University and receiving her Ph.D. in Greek in 1877. She then went to Cambridge University in England for four years, winning a scholarship in her second term. When she returned to the United States, she became principal of a private school before organizing and directing a nonsectarian school for girls in Massachusetts. Although the school was successful, she resigned in 1887 under pressure from irate trustees who did not appreciate her attempts to obtain better facilities, and she began teaching at Evelyn College, a women's annex to Princeton University. The same year she went to a conference of the American Social Science Association to read a paper and met Andrew Dickson White, who had recently resigned as president of Cornell University. He suggested that she apply as "directoress" of Sage College for Women at Cornell, but she decided to teach physical geography in Brooklyn instead. She realized that, at 35, she had jeopardized her career by speaking her mind, but she married White and went with him on diplomatic duties to Russia and Germany. She enjoyed the cultural life, and although a superb conversationalist, she began to lose interest in equal rights, universal suffrage, and militancy. To assuage her disappointment at being denied the career that a brilliant educated woman should have had, White immersed herself in music appreciation.

BIBLIOGRAPHY
Altschuler, Glenn C. *Better than Second Best: Love and Work in the Life of Helen Magill*. Urbana: University of Illinois Press, 1990. 0-252-01669-6, 175p. Using Magill's letters and diary, Altschuler has reconstructed her life and aborted career.

WHITMAN, NARCISSA PRENTISS (1808-1847)
Pioneer and Missionary   Prattsburg, New York

Narcissa Prentiss Whitman, one of the first two American white women to cross the Contential Divide, was a missionary to Native Americans. She was born on March 14, 1808, as the third of nine children to a landowner and mill operator and his wife. Family devotions influenced her decision to join the Presbyterian Church when she was 10, and at 16, she decided to become a missionary. She attended Franklin Academy in Prattsburg, and she may also have entered **Emma Willard**'s Troy Female Seminary. Whitman taught for a few years befor she heard a Congregationlist minister appeal for recruits to become missionaries to the Native

Americans in the West. When the American Board of Commissioners for Foreign Missions refused to accept her because she was unmarried, another recruit, physician Marcus Whitman, proposed to her. She received her appointment, and at 27, she married and began a four-month journey, reaching her destination of Waiilatpu, Oregon, on September 1, 1836, where she and her husband set up a mission. Whitman taught in the school they established and managed the domestic life, raising 11 foster children. In 1839, after her two-year-old daughter accidently drowned, her own eyesight began deteriorating, and, feeling that the Native Americans were not interested in the missionary's message, Whitman became despondent. When the mission board decided to close the mission in 1842, Whitman's husband left for a year to plead for its cause. When he returned, he found that the Native Americans also feared the white infiltration of their lands and connected the Whitmans with the problem because many of the pioneers stopped at the Waiilatpu mission. When pioneers brought an epidemic of measles, many Native American children, who had no immunity, died, and on November 29, 1847, the Native Americans retaliated, killing 11 members of the mission and taking 47 prisoners. Whitman and her husband died in the raid, paying with their lives for their idealism.

BIBLIOGRAPHY

Drury, Clifford Merrill. *Marcus and Narcissa Whitman and the Opening of Old Oregon.* Glendale, CA: A. H. Clark, 1973. 0–870–62104–1, 911p. Drury uses the letters and diaries of both Narcissa Whitman and her husband Marcus as well as other primary sources in a well-researched and carefully documented examination.

Jeffrey, Julie Roy. *Converting the West: A Biography of Narcissa Whitman.* Norman: University of Oklahoma Press, 1991. 0–8061–2359–1, 238p. Jeffrey examines Whitman's life as woman, wife, and religious leader.

Whitman, Narcissa Prentiss. *The Letters of Narcissa Whitman.* Fairfield, WA: Ye Galleon Press, 1986. 0–87770–386–8, 245p. A short biography precedes Whitman's letters.

———. *Where Wagons Could Go.* Lincoln: University of Nebraska Press, 1997. 0–8032–6606–5, 280p. This version of Whitman's letters and diaries contains commentary about the events that may actually have occurred.

WHITNEY, GERTRUDE V. (1875–1942)
Sculptor and Art Patron New York, New York

Gertrude Vanderbilt Whitney was a sculptor and an art patron. She was born on January 9, 1875, as the fourth of seven children to wealthy parents. Private tutors at home and in Europe educated her, and her father's interest in art was a major influence. Shortly after her marriage in 1896, she devoted herself to sculpture. She trained in both New York and Paris, opening a studio in Greenwich Village during 1907, and winning her first prize the next year for a sculpture called *Pan*. The following year, she won an award for the best architectural design from the Architectural League of New York. Among her notable creations were the *Aztec Fountain* for the Pan American Building and the *Titanic Memorial*, both in

Washington, DC; the *Victory Arch*, the *Washington Heights War Memorial*, and the *Peter Stuyvesant Monument*, in New York City; the *Saint-Nazaire Monument* in Saint-Nazaire, France; and the *Columbus Memorial*, in Palos, Spain. Simultaneously, she became a patron of contemporary American art by purchasing the work of younger, unknown American artists. She developed the Whitney Studio, and it became a place for artists to gather and exhibit. In 1929, she donated her large collection of American artists' work to the Metropolitan Museum of Art and offered money to fund a building. Her gift was rejected, and with the help of **Juliana Force**, she established the Whitney Museum of Modern Art the following year. For her philanthropy, she received several honorary degrees. In 1940, she was elected to the National Academy of Design.

BIBLIOGRAPHY

Friedman, B. H. *Gertrude Vanderbilt Whitney: A Biography*. Garden City, NY: Doubleday, 1978. 0–385–12994–7, 684p. Friedman used Whitney's diaries and daybooks to re-create her life.

Stasz, Clarice. *The Vanderbilt Women: Dynasty of Wealth, Glamour, and Tragedy*. New York: St. Martin's, 1991. 0–312–06486–1, 449p. In a well-researched, balanced, and readable collective biography, Stasz evaluates Vanderbilt's unconventional life.

WILDER, LAURA INGALLS (1867–1957)
Author   Lake Pepin, Wisconsin

Laura Ingalls Wilder was an author. She was born on February 7, 1867, as the second of four daughters to a homesteader who moved the family around looking for a better life. As a young girl, her education was sporadic, but Wilder passed a teaching test at 15. In 1885, she married a man 10 years her senior, and they began homesteading, with Wilder also working as a seamstress. Her daughter, Rose, born in 1886, eventually went to California and became a journalist. Rose encouraged her mother to write about her experiences, and Wilder wrote columns about farm households while editing for the *Missouri Ruralist* from 1911 to 1924, and working with the Mansfield Farm Loan Association. She also sold articles to the *St. Louis Star*, *McCall's*, and *Country Gentleman*. In 1931, Wilder wrote *Little House in the Big Woods*, from a child's point of view, about the feelings of male unrest and the patience of women pioneers in establishing homes in the wilderness during the mid-1800s. All except one of the books in the *Little House* series earned a Newbery Honor award. In 1954, the American Library Association established the Laura Ingalls Wilder Award for an author who has made a substantial contribution to children's literature in her honor, and Wilder was the first recipient. Since their publication, Wilder's books have sold nearly 25 million copies, remaining favorites because of their careful construction and their re-creation of a loving family living through difficult times.

BIBLIOGRAPHY

Anderson, William. *Laura Ingalls Wilder: A Biography*. New York: HarperCollins, 1992. 0–06–020113–4, 240p. Anderson's biography of Wilder chronicles her life.

Hines, Stephen W. *I Remember Laura: Laura Ingalls Wilder*. Nashville, TN: Nelson, 1994. 0–7852–8206–8, 274p. Hines has included some of Wilder's writings, recollections of friends and family, newspaper articles, and recipes from people who knew the family in this biography.

Miller, John E. *Becoming Laura Ingalls Wilder: The Woman Behind the Legend*. Columbia: University of Missouri Press, 1998. 0–8262–1167–4, 306p. Miller uses sources including deed claims, local newspapers, census records, and original manuscripts to uncover Wilder's life between the ages of 18 and 50.

Zochert, Donald. *Laura: The Life of Laura Ingalls Wilder*. Chicago: Regnery, 1976. 0–8092–8174–0, 260p. To research Wilder's life, Zochert traveled to the places Wilder mentioned in the "Little House" books, but the undocumented biography includes additional facts to emphasize that her fictional account was adjusted reality.

WILLARD, EMMA (1787–1870)
Educator   Berlin, Connecticut

Emma Hart Willard was an educator. She was born on February 23, 1787, as the sixteenth of seventeen children to a farmer and the ninth of ten children to his second wife. Willard learned about farm life, but her father discussed politics with her and encouraged her to use her intellect. When she turned 13, she taught herself geometry, and at 15, she enrolled in Berlin Academy. Two years later, she began teaching at the academy, and the following year, she taught the older children in her home. In 1806, she took charge of the academy while continuing study in Hartford. She married in 1809, and four years later, when her husband suffered financially, Willard opened a school, the Middlebury Female Seminary, in her home. Not allowed to attend classes at Middlebury College, she taught herself subjects to, in turn, teach her students. When she asked the governor of New York to support state-aided schools for females, the legislators disagreed, but her pamphlet on the subject, *An Address to the Public; Particularly to the Members of the Legislature of New-York, Proposing a Plan for Improving Female Education*, was an important document defining a need in American life. New York's Governor DeWitt Clinton encouraged her to come to his state, and when the Troy, New York, Common Council agreed to raise $4,000 for a female academy, Willard went to that city and opened the Troy Female Academy in 1821. Willard wrote many of her own textbooks, and within 10 years, her model school made money. Her school offered instructions on manners, and students cleaned their rooms, wore uniforms, and sometimes suffered demerits. She graduated 200 teachers before the first normal school opened in the United States. After relinquishing control of the school in 1838 to her daughter, Willard began traveling throughout the country and abroad, advocating educational reform at the World's Educational Convention in London. When she died, her school was renamed the Emma Willard School.

BIBLIOGRAPHY

Lutz, Alma. *Emma Willard: Pioneer Educator of American Women*. 1964. Westport, CT: Greenwood Press, 1983. 0-313-24254-2, 143p. In her biography of Willard, Lutz includes much information about her concerns.

WILLARD, FRANCES (1839-1898)
Reformer and Activist   Churchville, New York

Frances Elizabeth Caroline Willard was an activist. She was born on September 28, 1839, as one of five children to a cabinet-making farmer and his wife. Her family moved twice when she was young because of her father's health, and while growing up on the American frontier, she attended school whenever she could. In 1857, her father allowed her to attend Milwaukee Female College and then North Western Female College. After graduation, she taught briefly before going abroad as a paid companion. In Berlin, Paris, and Rome, she attended lectures and studied languages, and to earn money for extra expenses, wrote articles for newspapers at home. When she returned, she became president of the Evanston College for Ladies, which opened in 1871, but conflicts with the president of nearby Northwestern, a former fiancé, forced her to leave after three years. She started a state temperance organization, helped found the National Woman's Christian Temperance Union (WCTU), and began lecturing to groups around the country. In 1886, she started receiving a salary for her efforts, using the slogan, "For God and Home and Native Land" to encourage women's support of temperance. As a young girl whose brother could vote, Willard had long been resentful that she had no vote, and she supported **Lucy Stone**'s American Woman Suffrage Association while remaining friendly with **Susan B. Anthony** and her National Woman Suffrage Association. In 1891, the WCTU became international, with Willard adding the elimination of drug traffic to its mission. Her work showed many women the importance of politics within their own homes, but as she aged, she began thinking that education, rather than prohibition, might be the way to stop alcoholism. After her death, the state of Illinois commissioned **Helen Farnsworth Mears** to sculpt Willard's statue for Statuary Hall in the United States Capitol Building.

BIBLIOGRAPHY

Bordin, Ruth Birgitta Anderson. *Frances Willard: A Biography*. Chapel Hill: University of North Carolina Press, 1986. 0-8078-1697-3, 294p. In a biography well-documented with diaries and papers, Bordin expresses Willard's causes.

Gifford, Carolyn De Swarte, ed. *Writing Out My Heart: Selections from the Journal of Frances E. Willard*. Urbana: University of Illinois Press, 1995. 0-252-02139-8, 474p. This volume contains selections from journals Willard kept while a young woman.

Leeman, Richard W. *Do Everything Reform: The Oratory of Frances E. Willard*. Westport, CT: Greenwood Press, 1992. 0-313-27487-8, 210p. This critical researched and documented biography of Willard analyzes her life and her speeches.

Willard, Frances Elizabeth. *How I Learned to Ride the Bicycle: Reflections of an Influential Nineteenth Century Woman*. 1895. Sunnyvale, CA: Fair Oaks, 1991. 0–933271–04–2, 104p. Willard describes her life of action from her tomboy days in Wisconsin to her position as head of the women's temperance movement.

WILLEBRANDT, MABEL WALKER (1889–1963)
Attorney   **Woodsdale, Kansas**

Mabel Willebrandt, the "First Lady of the Law," was an assistant attorney general of the United States. She was born in a sod dugout on May 23, 1889, to parents who taught and edited newspapers on the frontier. Willebrandt learned to read at home but was later expelled from Park College for disagreeing with the faculty's religious beliefs. After marriage, she began teaching and became principal of several grammar schools before beginning law classes at the University of Southern California, where she received her LL.B in 1916 and her LL.M. in 1917. Advocating legal assistance for the poor, she then became Los Angeles's unpaid assistant public defender. In 1915, she worked on over 2,000 cases involving women while establishing her private practice. One of her achievements was demonstrating to a judge that both male and female should appear for a charge of prostitution. During World War I, she became head of the Legal Advisory Board for draft cases. Warren G. Harding then appointed her an assistant attorney general of the United States in 1921. As the second woman in the position, after Annette Abbott Adams, she oversaw tax, prison, and prohibition matters. Although not originally a supporter of prohibition, the responsibility of enforcing the law changed her approach. Her success at having several attorneys dismissed after shoddily prosecuting prohibition violations, however, cost her votes for an appointment to the federal bench in California. Earning the name "Prohibition Portia," she solved several important cases and argued before the Supreme Court over 40 times. She also helped establish the first federal prison for women. She left government to specialize in radio, tax, and aeronautical law, and became the first woman to head a committee of the American Bar Association, the Committee on Aeronautical Law, where she met **Amelia Earhart** and **Jacqueline Cochran**. She then established the Federal Radio Commission's authority to allocate radio licenses based on a geographical area's need. She also advocated the end of sex discrimination by supporting the hiring of more qualified women lawyers in the Justice Department. Several colleagues thought that she could have been president had she been male.

BIBLIOGRAPHY
Brown, Dorothy M. *Mabel Walker Willebrandt: A Study of Power, Loyalty, and Law*. Knoxville: University of Tennessee Press, 1984. 0–87049–402–3, 328p. Brown's carefully researched biography of Willebrandt, based on letters and interviews with family and colleagues, reveals her life and career.

WILLS, HELEN (1905–1998)
Athlete   Centerville, California

Helen Wills Moody was an athlete. She was born on October 6, 1905, the daughter
of a doctor and his wife. Her father first taught her tennis, but when she was 14, her
parents gave her a membership to the Berkeley Tennis Club, where a volunteer
coach arranged daily matches for her. Her first attempt to win the national junior
championship in 1921 was successful. The next year, she became the
second-youngest United States national champion. While continuing to compete,
she attended the University of California and graduated Phi Beta Kappa with a
degree in fine arts. In 1924, she went to Europe for the first time, and although she
reached the Wimbledon finals, she lost. She won the next eight finals, and her
record stood until 1990, when **Martina Navratilova** won her ninth singles title.
Wills became the first American-born woman recognized internationally as an
athlete. The press called her "Little Miss Poker Face" because her face lacked
expression during her intense concentration. During a match, she focused on
"every shot, every shot, every shot." She competed for 15 years, winning 31 Grand
Slam titles and changing tennis clothes for women by abandoning long, inhibiting
skirts. She held the world's top ranking for eight years, not losing a set during 180
consecutive matches between 1927 and 1933. She won four French
championships, earned gold medals in singles and doubles at the 1924 Olympics,
and won doubles or mixed doubles at the United States and French Opens and at
Wimbledon 12 times with eight different partners. After playing Suzanne Lenglen,
the European tennis champion, Wills changed her game because she learned that
strength would not regularly defeat finesse. After retiring from competitive tennis,
Wills maintained a studio where she sold her paintings and illustrated articles she
wrote for the *Saturday Evening Post*, remaining interested in the progress and
changes in tennis.

BIBLIOGRAPHY
Engelmann, Larry. *The Goddess and the American Girl: The Story of Suzanne Lenglen and
    Helen Wills.* New York: Oxford University Press, 1988. 0–19–504363–4, 464p.
    Engelmann interviewed Wills for this collective biography.

WILSON, EDITH BOLLING GALT (1872–1961)
First Lady   Wytheville, Virginia

Edith Bolling Galt Wilson was First Lady of the United States. She was born on
October 15, 1872, as one of eleven children to a genteel but poor lawyer and his
wife. She attended colleges in Virginia for two years, but although she accurately
judged character and exhibited common sense, she was not a scholar. She had been
a widow for seven years when she met President Woodrow Wilson in 1915 after
the death of his first wife. He began writing her almost every day, and they married
the same year. Wilson remained at her husband's side throughout his presidency,
showing an interest in all aspects of domestic and foreign policy. Her husband read

diplomatic dispatches and important state papers to her while she decoded messages using his secret code. In 1919, she went with him to the Paris Peace Conference. Although people do not know Wilson's specific role in the White House after her husband's stroke on October 2, 1919, some think that she functioned as the unnamed president of the country. Although she denied making important decisions during the period, there is evidence to both support and refute her claim. Scholars know that she tried to influence her husband to accept limitations on U.S. involvement in the League of Nations in the Treaty of Versailles, but he refused, and the treaty was defeated in the Senate. After her husband died, Wilson managed the publication of his papers and supported organizations bearing his name, including the Woodrow Wilson Foundation, the Woodrow Wilson Birthplace Foundation, and the Woodrow Wilson School of Public and International Affairs at Princeton University.

BIBLIOGRAPHY

Ross, Ishbel. *Power with Grace: The Life Story of Mrs. Woodrow Wilson.* New York: Putnam, 1975. 0–399–11459–9, 374p. Rose shows her high regard for Wilson in this biased biography.

Smith, Gene. *When the Cheering Stopped: The Last Years of Woodrow Wilson.* New York: Morrow, 1964. No ISBN, 307p. This biography examines the last 17 months of the Wilson presidency and Edith Wilson's role as her husband's advisor.

Wilson, Edith Bolling Galt. *My Memoir.* 1939. New York: Arno Press, 1980. 0–405–12868–1, 386p. Wilson's memoir of her life during her husband's last years makes him much more personable than other works.

WINFREY, OPRAH (1954–)
Television Personality, Actor, and Film Producer   **Kosciusko, Mississippi**

African American Oprah Winfrey, a television personality, hosts a respected talk show currently concerned with helping people have better lives. She was born January 29, 1954, to unmarried parents, and she lived with her maternal grandmother on a farm where she learned to read by three and reached the third grade at six. She returned to her welfare mother in Milwaukee, and men in and close to her family subjected her to sexual abuse. She then went to live with her father, a respected citizen of the Nashville community, attended school, and began broadcasting the news on a local radio station. With a scholarship she won in an oratorical contest, she entered Tennessee State University. While still in college, she won several beauty contests and became the first woman co-anchor on Nashville television. After she graduated, she worked in Baltimore before moving to Chicago and a television show that aired opposite *Donahue*. Within one month, she had equaled Donahue's ratings, and within two years, the show became *The Oprah Winfrey Show*, expanded to an hour. In 1985, as an actor, she won an Academy Award nomination for her performance in *The Color Purple*, and in 1998, she starred in *Beloved*. Her television show has garnered Emmy Awards, she received the Spingarn Medal in 1994, and has been elected to The National

Women's Hall of Fame. Winfrey has become one of the world's wealthiest women, a reward for her hard work.

BIBLIOGRAPHY

Bly, Nellie. *Oprah! Up Close and Down Home*. New York: Kensington, 1993. 0-8217-4613-8, 383p. This popular, partially documented biography of Winfrey presents an overview of her life and career.

King, Norman. *Everybody Loves Oprah! Her Remarkable Life Story*. New York: Morrow, 1987. 0-688-07396-4, 222p. This readable and carefully researched but undocumented popular biography describes Winfrey's life and rapid rise to fame.

Mair, George. *Oprah Winfrey: The Real Story*. Secaucus, NJ: Carol, 1994. 1-55972-250-9, 376p. Winfrey's friends and colleagues aided Mair's biography.

Nicholson, Lois. *Oprah Winfrey*. New York: Chelsea House, 1994. 0-7910-1886-5, 111p. In this researched biography for young adults, Nicholson covers Winfrey's life and career.

Patterson, Lillie, and Cornelia H. Wright. *Oprah Winfrey: Talk Show Host and Actress*. Hillside, NJ: Enslow, 1990. 0-89490-289-X, 128p. In a balanced biography for young adults, Patterson and Wright describe Winfrey's life from childhood through her successful television career.

WINNEMUCCA, SARAH (1844?-1891)
Tribal Chief   **Humboldt Sink, Nevada**

Sarah Winnemucca, a leader of the Piute tribe, has often been called "the most famous Indian woman of the Pacific Coast." She was born around 1844 as Toc-me-tony (Shell Flower), the fourth of nine children of the Piute chief Winnemucca II. As a child, Winnemucca used her gift for languages to learn Spanish and English in addition to three Indian dialects. After staying with a stagecoach company agent as his daughter's companion for a year, Winnemucca became a Christian and took the name Sarah. In 1860, she entered St. Mary's Convent in San Jose, California, as her dying grandfather had requested, but she had to leave after three weeks, when parents of white girls complained about their daughters attending school with a Native American. The same year, the Piute war resulted in the establishment of a Piute reservation in northern Nevada, but when corrupt Indian agents did nothing to help the people adjust to the ways of the whites, many Piutes starved. In 1865, after several Piutes stole cattle, soldiers killed Piute women, children, and old men while the tribe's warriors were away hunting. Winnemucca's baby brother was murdered, and within the year her mother and a sister also died. When many Piutes went to military posts for rations, they needed Winnemucca's abilities as a translator, and she served in this capacity many times. In 1878, after hearing that the Bannocks had captured her father, she walked over 100 miles to find and rescue him. After the war, Winnemucca returned to San Francisco to lecture once again about the wrongs against her tribe. This time the press responded to her indictments of Indian agents, and she went to Washington to relay the information to the secretary of the interior and President Rutherford

B. Hayes. The men made promises which they did not fulfill, and Winnemucca again went east to solicit aid. Her book, *Life Among the Piutes*, resulted from these lectures. In Boston, she met **Elizabeth Peabody**, and Peabody began helping Winnemucca in any way she could. Although in poor health, Winnemucca returned to teach Piute children in Nevada. After her death, the whites called her "Princess," and the Piutes called her "Mother." She was later elected to The National Women's Hall of Fame.

BIBLIOGRAPHY

Canfield, Gae Whitney. *Sarah Winnemucca of the Northern Paiutes*. Norman: University of Oklahoma Press, 1983. 0-8061-1814-8, 306p. Canfield used primary and secondary sources to reveals Winnemucca's influence on the Northern Piutes.

Gehm, Katherine. *Sarah Winnemucca: Most Extraordinary Woman of the Paiute*. Phoenix, AZ: O'Sullivan Woodside, 1975. 0-89019-030-5, 196p. In a readable but undocumented biography for young adults, Gehm recounts Winnemucca's life.

Morrison, Dorothy Nafus. *Chief Sarah: Sarah Winnemucca's Fight for Indian Rights*. New York: Atheneum, 1980. 0-689-30752-7, 170p. In a well-researched biography for young adults, Morrison lauds Winnemucca and her achievements.

Scordato, Ellen. *Sarah Winnemucca: Northern Paiute Writer and Diplomat*. New York: Chelsea House, 1992. 0-7910-1710-9, 127p. This well-researched biography for young adults describes Winnemucca's life and her use of her translation skills to help her people.

WOLCOTT, MARION POST (1910-1990)
Photographer   Montclair, New Jersey

Marion Post Wolcott was a photographer who recorded scenes from the Great Depression. She was born on June 7, 1910, to a physician and a registered nurse. Wolcott's mother loved the arts, in contrast to her somewhat staid husband, and when they divorced, her mother went to New York City and began crusading for birth control with **Margaret Sanger**. While Wolcott attended boarding schools in Connecticut, she became interested in art. She then enrolled in the New School for Social Research in New York and later Vassar College. Although she enjoyed teaching, she also liked sculpture and photography. When she began photographing the artists with whom she associated, she recognized photography as her greater talent and began selling pictures to magazines including *Vogue*. In 1936, she went to Philadelphia to work for the *Evening Bulletin*, and in 1938, she shifted to the Farm Security Administration to take photographs of people suffering from the Great Depression to gain support for the government's New Deal program. She drove alone through the South, taking over 15,000 pictures of buildings, people, and unproductive land to capture the essence of the Depression's deprivation for rural families. Wolcott also photographed conditions in the West. After her marriage in 1941, she decided to devote her time to raising her children, but when her husband's employment took the family to Iran, Pakistan, India, and Egypt, Wolcott photographed scenes in those countries. In the late 1970s, a resurgence of interest in the Great Depression led to gallery and museum exhibitions featuring her work, which in Wolcott's words "documented . . . quality of life, the causes of malaise in . . . society—and the world." Honors she received included the **Dorothea Lange** Award, the Distinguished Photographer Award, and a one-woman show at Syracuse University.

BIBLIOGRAPHY

Hendrickson, Paul. *Looking for the Light: The Hidden Life and Art of Marion Post Wolcott.* New York: Knopf, 1992. 0-394-57729-9, 297p. Hendrickson discovered that Wolcott completed most of her photographs in three years, and after interviewing her, created a detailed, intelligent biography.

Hurley, F. Jack. *Marion Post Wolcott: A Photographic Journey.* Albuquerque: University of New Mexico Press, 1989. 0-8263-1114-8, 228p. Hurley's researched and documented biography of Wolcott gives a balanced and thorough look at her life and career.

WOODHULL, VICTORIA (1838–1927)
Reformer   Homer, Ohio

Victoria Claflin Woodhull was a social reformer and candidate for president of the United States. She was born on September 23, 1838, into a family of 10 children, to a drifter and his wife. The family moved when problems occurred, and Claflin's education was intermittent. After performing in her family's traveling medicine show, Woodhull married a physician at age 15. She had two children, but when her sister Tennessee came to live with the family, Woodhull's alcoholic husband disappeared. After Woodhull met a Civil War veteran, Colonel Blood, she divorced her first husband and secured a marriage license, but no records of a second marriage have been discovered. He accompanied Woodhull to New York City, where she and her sister opened a successful brokerage firm, Woodhull, Claflin & Company, probably financed by Tennessee's friend, Cornelius Vanderbilt. Woodhull and Colonel Blood collaborated with a philosopher who endorsed free love in his "Pantarchy" movement, which Woodhull advocated in the first issue of *Woodhull & Claflin's Weekly* along with short skirts, legalized prostitution, world government, and exposure of Wall Street fraud. In 1871, Woodhull became the leader of Marx's International Workingmen's Association and published an English translation of the *Communist Manifesto*. After she pleaded for woman suffrage before the Judiciary Committee of the United States House of Representatives, the suffragists nominated her for president of the United States in 1872. When Woodhull went to England in the late 1870s, she met and married a wealthy English banker, became a philanthropist, and with the help of her daughter, published the *Humanitarian*, a journal emphasizing eugenics. An early patron of aviation, she offered a prize of $5,000 in 1914 for the first transatlantic flight.

BIBLIOGRAPHY

Gabriel, Mary. *Notorious Victoria: The Life of Victoria Woodhull, Uncensored.* Chapel
    Hill, NC: Algonquin, 1998. 1–56512–132–5, 372p.   In her well-researched,
    recommended biography, based on Woodhull's articles, speeches, and letters as well
    as newspapers of the time, Gabriel pursues the thesis that Woodhull refused to
    accept nineteenth-century sexual and social mores.

Goldsmith, Barbara. *Other Powers: The Age of Suffrage, Spiritualism, and the Scandalous
    Victoria Woodhull.* New York: Knopf, 1998. 0–394–55536–8, 531p. Goldsmith used
    letters, diaries, conversations recorded in shorthand, public and private writings,
    trial transcripts, and newspapers of the day to re-create the connection among
    women's rights, spiritualism, and Woodhull's life in her recommended biography.

Meade, Marion. *Free Woman: The Life and Times of Victoria Woodhull.* New York:
    Knopf, 1976. 0–394–83035–0, 174p. Meade's informative biography, appropriate
    for young adults, traces Woodhull's life.

Underhill, Lois Beachy. *The Woman Who Ran for President: The Many Lives of Victoria
    Woodhull.* New York: Penguin, 1996. 0–14–025638–5, 347p. Underhill uses newly
    available material to explore the life of Woodhull in a recommended biography.

WOODWARD, ELLEN S. (1887–1971)
Government Official   Oxford, Mississippi

Ellen Woodward served the federal government in the administrations of Franklin
D. Roosevelt and Harry S. Truman, first in women's work relief programs in the
New Deal and then as a member of the Social Security Board. She was born on July
11, 1887, as one of five children to a lawyer and United States senator and his wife.
Her mother died when Woodward was seven, and Woodward often accompanied
her father to court to hear him argue his cases. She attended local schools and Sans
Souci College before receiving a music certificate. After her marriage and the birth
of her child, she became a leader in community affairs of her home in Louisville,
Mississippi, and helped her husband successfully campaign for the state legislature.
When her husband died suddenly the next year, she was elected as the second
woman to serve in the Mississippi House of Representatives. She refused reelection
to become director of the Mississippi State Board of Development. Roosevelt then
appointed her to the Works Progress Administration (WPA) as an assistant
administrator in charge of emergency relief programs for women. She provided
assistance to nearly 500,000 women with no other means of support and developed
work programs in sewing, management, and public health. In 1936, she added
cultural project duties and support for 250,000 writers, musicians, actors, and
artists. With this expansion, she became the second highest-ranking female official
in the government, behind **Frances Perkins**. She then joined the Social Security
Board, working to expand the program to women and dependent children, trying
to find new employment opportunities for women, and offering unemployment
insurance compensation to women. In 1943, she became a delegate to the United
Nations Relief and Rehabilitation Administration where she observed German
camps for displaced persons after World War II. Under President Truman, she

directed the Office of Inter-Agency and International Relations of the Federal
Security Administration (FSA). After her retirement in 1954, she remained active
in civic organizations.

BIBLIOGRAPHY
Swain, Martha H. *Ellen S. Woodward: New Deal Advocate for Women.* Jackson:
    University Press of Mississippi, 1995. 0-87805-756-0, 275p. Primary sources reveal
    Woodward's life and contributions to government programs, especially during the
    New Deal, to help women.

WOODWORTH-ETTER, MARIA (1844–1924)
Evangelist   Lisbon, Ohio

Maria Beulah Woodworth-Etter was an evangelist. She was born on July 22, 1844,
and at age 13, she converted at a revival meeting of the Disciples of Christ. She
wanted to join the ministry although she knew that the church would not ordain
female ministers. After her marriage and the loss of five of six children, she again
felt a call at a revival meeting in 1879. She began to preach locally, and by 1883,
people attending her services began to reach trancelike states which she described
as the baptism of the Holy Spirit. The next year, she began preaching for the
Church of God, incorporating healing into her rituals, and remained both
successful and controversial for the next 20 years. Large crowds throughout the
United States came to pray for baptism of the Holy Ghost and of fire with her in
ceremonies, much like those of the Pentecostal Church, although excluding the
glossolalia. In 1891, Woodworth-Etter divorced her husband for his adultery, and
in 1902, she remarried, hyphenating her second husband's name and her own. In
1904, the Church of God refused to allow her to preach, claiming that she did not
follow church tenets, but the same year, people began to speak in tongues at her
evangelistic services. For several years, the Pentecostal movement's controversies
kept her from joining, but by 1912, she had become an active Pentecostal healing
evangelist, with thousands attending her Dallas revival during its six months. The
next year, she attracted many people to revivals in Pasadena, California, and
Chicago. Her last two books, *Spirit-Filled Sermons* (1921) and *Marvels and Miracles*
(1922), helped spread the Pentecostal movement after their translation into many
languages.

BIBLIOGRAPHY
Warner, Wayne E. *The Woman Evangelist: The Life and Times of Charismatic Evangelist
    Maria B. Woodworth-Etter.* Metuchen, NJ: Scarecrow Press, 1986. 0-8108-1912-0,
    340p. This well-researched biography, using contemporary newspaper accounts of
    Woodworth-Etter, reveals her status as Aimee McPherson's evangelist precursor.
Woodworth-Etter, Maria Beulah. *Signs and Wonders.* 1916. New Kensington, PA:
    Whitaker House, 1997. 0-8836-8299-0, 569p. In this thorough and recommended
    autobiography, Woodworth-Etter recounts all of the influences in the development
    of her spiritual life.

WRIGHT, ELIZABETH EVELYN (1872–1906)
Educator   Talbotton, Georgia

Elizabeth Evelyn Wright established Voorhees College for African American students. She was born as the seventh of 21 children to a former slave and illiterate carpenter and his Cherokee wife. She had difficulty getting an education because her school opened only periodically, and as a result, Wright wanted to make educational opportunities available for others. She enrolled in Tuskegee Institute in 1888 although she was not sufficiently prepared, and worked to support herself and pay her tuition. Always in poor health, she had to adjust her work and study schedule, but a white woman eventually helped her succeed. She wanted to establish an institution similar to Tuskegee in South Carolina, but problems persisted throughout her four attempts, with local whites burning the building materials at least twice. Finally, in the spring of 1897, she opened the Denmark (South Carolina) Industrial School on the second floor of a local store. With the help of a white attorney and state senator, she obtained the money for 20 acres, and opened this site in the fall of the same year. Wright served as the school's principal and fund-raiser. In 1901, Ralph Voorhees, a New Jersey philanthropist, donated money for 200 acres, and Wright renamed the school in his honor. Wright married in 1906, but died four months later. In 1964, after a series of metamorphoses, Voorhees became a four-year college.

BIBLIOGRAPHY
Morris, J. Kenneth. *Elizabeth Evelyn Wright, 1872–1906: Founder of Voorhees College.* Sewanee, TN: University of the South, 1983. No ISBN, 273p. Morris visited places in South Carolina and Wright's home in Georgia, conducted interviews, examined pictures, and found other primary sources to reconstruct Wright's faith, dedication, and courage in this carefully researched and thorough biography.

WRIGHT, FRANCES (1795–1852)
Activist and Author   Dundee, Scotland

Frances Wright was an author and reformer. She was born on September 6, 1795, as the second of three children to a wealthy, radical linen merchant and his wife, who died when Wright was two. Relatives raised her, and at 21, Wright went to live with a great-uncle who taught moral philosophy. Wright read widely in the college library, especially books about the United States, and she decided to visit. In 1818, she and her sister went to New York to live, and during that time, Wright wrote a play which was actually produced, although it closed after three performances. In 1821, she returned to England and published the correspondence written during her trip in *Views of Society and Manners in America*, an important travel memoir of the early nineteenth century. The same year, she met the Marquis de Lafayette in France, and he asked her to return with him to the United States. Wright did, and she remained. In 1825, after traveling up the Mississippi, she wrote *A Plan for the Gradual Abolition of Slavery in the United States without Danger of*

Loss to the Citizens of the South, in which she suggested that slaves labor on public land with their profits going to their owners as payment for freedom. She tried her own idea, but it failed. She then attacked racially segregated schools, religion, and sexual taboos. Against organized religion, she purchased a small church near New York's Bowery and made it a "Hall of Science" were she lectured, and with her good friend from the New Harmony community in Indiana, published the *Free Enquirer*, in which she condemned capital punishment and promoted a higher status for women in all areas of life. She subsequently focused on education, becoming a central figure in New York's working class movement and founding the Association for the Protection of Industry and for the Promotion of National Education. After several years in Paris during which her sister died and she married, Wright returned to America with her husband and daughter, and in a new series of lectures, began lambasting contemporary society. Although she died without fame or fanfare, later generations realized that she had identified many of the American social issues that needed reform, and she was elected to The National Women's Hall of Fame.

BIBLIOGRAPHY

Bartlett, Elizabeth Ann. *Liberty, Equality, Sorority: The Origins and Interpretation of American Feminist Thought*. Brooklyn, NY: Carlson, 1994. 0–926019–62–7, 184p. Bartlett's study of female intellectuals, including Wright, posits that she pursued feminism.

Morris, Celia. *Fanny Wright: Rebel in America*. 1984. Urbana: University of Illinois Press, 1992. 0–252–06249–3, 337p. Morris examined primary sources in a recommended biography to explore the contradictions in Wright's life.

Perkins, Alice J. G., and Theresa Wolfson. *Frances Wright, Free Enquirer*. 1939. Philadelphia: Porcupine, 1972. 0–87991–008–9, 393p. This scholarly biography examines Wright's life and her contributions to American liberalism.

WRIGHT, PATIENCE (1725–1786)
Sculptor and Spy   Bordentown, New Jersey

Patience Lovell Wright was a sculptor and spy. She was born in 1725 as one of seven children to an affluent Quaker farmer and his wife. The family, at his insistence, was vegetarian, and everyone wore white. When in her early 20s, Wright left for Philadelphia, where she married and raised children. After her husband's death 21 years later, she began to model wax. By 1771, she had created a traveling waxwork exhibit of contemporary famous people which was exhibited in Charleston, Philadelphia, and New York. After a fire destroyed much of her work in New York, she went to England, where Benjamin Franklin introduced her to leading citizens including *Catherine Macaulay and Benjamin West. Wright soon created wax figures of these and other Londoners. Wright's interest in politics never wavered, and while in London, she supposedly passed information to Benjamin Franklin and to members of Congress after listening to women gossip. Supposedly John Hancock cited her efforts in a letter of 1785. One unsubstantiated story is that she hid messages in her wax figures and then sent them to her sister, a Philadelphia wax museum owner, who in turn informed the Patriots. Wright went to Paris in 1780 to show her wax figures, but *Madame Tussaud had already claimed the city with her own wax monuments, and Wright returned to London. Wright had little schooling, but talent made her America's first professional sculptor, and her one known piece of extant work is a wax figure of Lord Chatham now in Westminster Abbey.

BIBLIOGRAPHY

Sellers, Charles Coleman. *Patience Wright, American Artist and Spy in George III's London*. Middletown, CT: Wesleyan University Press, 1976. 0-8195-5001-9, 281p. This readable biography of Wright discusses the technique of her waxworks, her experiences in London, and her possible role as a spy.

𝒴

YALOW, ROSALYN (1921-)
Physicist

New York, New York

Rosalyn Sussman Yalow is a medical physicist who won the Nobel Prize for Physiology. She was born on July 19, 1921, as one of two children to a small business owner, son of Russian immigrants, and his German immigrant wife. Neither of Yalow's parents attended high school, but they encouraged her to succeed. Yalow learned to read before entering kindergarten and, while still in high school, became interested in mathematics and then chemistry. She graduated from Hunter College, where she added physics to her interests, and received her Ph.D. in physics from the University of Illinois in 1945. She returned to Hunter to lecture for four years before she began consulting in nuclear physics at the Bronx Veterans Administration Hospital, where she remained until 1970 as physicist and assistant chief of the radioisotope service. With her colleague, Solomon A. Berson, she began investigating various medical applications of radioactive isotopes. She combined techniques from radioisotope tracing and immunology to develop radioimmunoassay (RIA), a very sensitive and simple method for measuring minute concentrations of biological and pharmacological substances in blood or other fluid samples. They first applied RIA to detecting insulin concentration in the blood of diabetics, but researchers soon adapted the method to hundreds of other applications. In 1973, she became director of the Solomon A. Berson Research Laboratory, and three years later, she was the first woman to be awarded the Albert Lasker Prize for basic medical research. In 1977, she received the Nobel Prize for her work. In 1988, she received the National Medal of Science. She is a member of the American Academy of Arts and Sciences, the National Academy of

Sciences, the American College of Nuclear Physicians, and the National Women's Hall of Fame. She is a fellow of the New York Academy of Sciences and of the American College of Radiology. Of her many awards, she refused the Federal Woman's Award in 1961 because it was restricted to women. The numerous awards she has accepted come from organizations including the American Diabetes Association, the American Association of Clinical Chemists, the American College of Physicians, the Academy of Sciences, the American Medical Association, and election to The National Women's Hall of Fame. She has also received many honorary degrees.

BIBLIOGRAPHY

Dash, Joan. *The Triumph of Discovery: Women Scientists Who Won the Nobel Prize.* Englewood Cliffs, NJ: Messner, 1991. 0–671–69332–8, 148p. In this collective biography for young adults, Dash overviews Yalow's life and achievements.
Straus, Eugene. *Rosalyn Yalow, Nobel Laureate: Her Life and Work in Medicine.* New York: Plenum, 1998. 0–306–45796–2, 292p. This readable, well-researched, and documented biography reveals Yalow's life and career.

YEZIERSKA, ANZIA (c. 1880–1970)
Author   Plotsk, Russia

Anzia Yezierska was an author. She was born around 1880 (or the date she claimed, October 19, 1883), as one of eight or nine children, to a Talmudic scholar and his wife. The family immigrated to America in 1890 or 1895, and Yezierska was renamed Hattie Mayer. In a family that decried education for females, Yezierska attended night classes in East Side settlement houses and told officials of Teachers College at Columbia University, when trying to gain admittance, that she had a high school education. She received a degree in domestic science in 1904, and although she hated the subject, it was the only free education she could find. She reverted to her real name when she started to write, and in 1915 she published her first story, "The Free Vacation House," in which she described how charity can wound the poor. Her 1919 story, "The Fat of the Land" won the O'Brien Prize. In 1920, she published her first book, *Hungry Hearts*, and when Samuel Goldwyn bought it for $20,000, she went to Hollywood to adapt it for the screen. She returned to New York, refusing a screenwriting contract because the movie environment stifled her creativity. After two marriages and a child, she relinquished her child to the father before asking John Dewey to help her secure accreditation to teach. He allowed her to audit his seminar on social and political philosophy, and their romantic involvement began the next year. Dewey encouraged Yezierska's writing, and she again published. During the Great Depression, she joined the Works Progress Administration Writers' Project, working with Richard Wright, but by 1950, she was selling only a few reviews and essays to the *New York Times*, the *Reporter*, *Commentary*, and other journals. In all her writing, she empathized with the poor and the oppressed.

BIBLIOGRAPHY

Dearborn, Mary V. *Love in the Promised Land: The Story of Anzia Yezierska and John Dewey*. New York: Free Press, 1988. 0-02-908090-8, 212p. In an attempt to explain how Yezierska and John Dewey formed a friendship and then had an affair, Dearborn examines their lives.

Henriksen, Louise Levitas. *Anzia Yezierska: A Writer's Life*. New Brunswick, NJ: Rutgers University Press, 1988. 0-8135-1268-9, 327p. Yezierska's daughter, Henriksen used previously unavailable personal documents and letters for her balanced biography.

Schoen, Carol. *Anzia Yezierska*. Boston: Twayne, 1982. 0-8057-7358-4, 142p. Schoen used unpublished papers, letters, and Yezierska's writing to create a documented biography.

$\mathscr{Z}$

ZAHARIAS, BABE DIDRIKSON (1914–1956)
Athlete   Port Arthur, Texas

Mildred Ella Didrikson Zaharias, known as Babe, was one of the great female athletes to have competed in sport. She was born on June 26, 1914, as the sixth of seven children to Norwegian immigrants, a carpenter and his wife who had won skating championships in Norway. Zaharias played sandlot baseball with the males in her neighborhood and became a high school basketball star. After taking a job as a typist at the Employers Casualty Company of Dallas, she led the company basketball team to two finals and a national championship. In 1930 and 1931, she was a member of the women's All-America basketball team. After her introduction to track in 1930, she won eight events and tied for a ninth within two years. In 1932, in the Los Angeles Olympic Games, she won the 80-meter hurdles and the javelin throw. A third gold medal was disallowed because she used a then-unacceptable Western roll to win the high jump. The same year, she began to play golf casually, but from 1934, she played golf exclusively. In 1938, she married a professional wrestler whose support allowed her to refuse prize money in professional tournaments so that she could regain her amateur status. In 1946, as an amateur, she won the United States Women's Amateur golf tournament. In 1947, she won 17 consecutive golf championships, including the British Ladies' Amateur, of which she was the first American winner. As a professional again in 1948, she won the United States Women's Open three times, and through 1951 was the leading money winner among woman golfers. Zaharias made most of the $1 million that she collected in her lifetime playing golf, although she was also a tennis tournament winner, a bowler with a 170 average, and a diving champion.

Six times Woman Athlete of the Year, she was named the Woman Athlete of the Half-Century in 1950. She was later elected to The National Women's Hall of Fame.

BIBLIOGRAPHY

Cayleff, Susan E. *Babe: The Life and Legend of Babe Didrikson Zaharias*. Urbana: University of Illinois Press, 1995. 0-252-01793-5, 327p. Using letters and interviews with people who knew Didrikson Zaharias, Cayleff's carefully documented biography attempts to present her complex life in the male sports world.

Johnson, William O., and Nancy P. Williamson. *Whatta-Gal: The Babe Didrikson Story*. Boston: Little, Brown, 1977. 0-316-46943-2, 224p. This biography, suitable for young adults, is based mainly on accounts of Didrikson's career in *Newsweek* magazine.

Lynn, Elizabeth A. *Babe Didrikson Zaharias*. New York: Chelsea House, 1989. 1-55546-684-2, 111p. This biography for young adults traces Didrikson Zaharias's career as athlete with photographs to accompany the text.

ZAKRZEWSKA, MARIE ELIZABETH   (1829–1902)
Physician   Berlin, Germany

Marie Elizabeth Zakrzewska was a physician. She was born on September 6, 1829, as one of six children to a Prussian army pensioner and his wife of gypsy ancestry. Zakrzewska attended school from the age of eight, but after six years, her father insisted that she stay home and learn housework like other German girls. She spent most of her time at home reading medical works secured from her mother's midwifery courses. At 18, Zakrzewska applied to the Charité Hospital in Berlin, and in 1852, a year after graduating, she became the school's chief midwife and a professor. Although she was successful, male opposition to her position rose, and she left for the United States and the new Female Medical College in Philadelphia. To make money after their arrival, she and her two sisters sold their knitting, but in 1854, Dr. *Elizabeth Blackwell took her as a pupil, insisting that Zakrzewska learn English and study for an M.D. degree. Blackwell arranged for Zakrzewska to attend the Cleveland Medical College of Western Reserve as one of four women in a class of 200, and she survived the ordeal to graduate in 1856. Because of the intense prejudice against women physicians in New York, no one would rent her rooms to work, and she finally opened her practice in Blackwell's back room. In 1857, Zakrzewska became a resident physician and manager of the new New York Infirmary for Women and Children. Two years later, she accepted an offer to be professor of obstetrics and diseases of women and children at the New England Female Medical College of Boston, where she stayed until 1862. The same year, she founded the New England Hospital for Women and Children to provide medical care for women by women, to allow women to study medicine, and to train nurses. She remained until 1887 as attending physician. Concerned about the poor, Zakrzewska took many charity cases at the hospital and also made house calls. In time, she supported other movements such as antislavery and woman suffrage, and as one of the first members of the New England Women's Club, she lectured on women's hygiene.

BIBLIOGRAPHY

Zakrzewska, Marie. *A Woman's Quest: The Life of Marie E. Zakrzewska, M.D.* 1924. Ed. Agnes C. Vietor. New York: Arno Press, 1972. 0-405-04486-0, 514p. Zakrzewska's autobiography gives insight into the influences in her life and what she endured to become a physician.

Appendix A: Notable Women by Year of Birth

d. 1617	Pocahontas
d. 1660	Dyer, Mary
1591	Hutchinson, Anne Marbury
1612?	Bradstreet, Anne
1656	Tekakwitha, Kateri
1700	Musgrove, Mary
1722	Pinckney, Eliza
1725	Wright, Patience
1728	Warren, Mercy (Otis)
1736	Brant, Molly (Mary)
1736	Lee, Mother Ann
1738?	Ward, Nancy
1743	Jemison, Mary
1744	Adams, Abigail Smith
1753	Wheatley, Phillis
1760	Sampson (Gannett), Deborah
1762?	Rowson, Susanna Haswell
1768	Madison, Dolley
1769	Merry, Ann Brunton
1769	Royall, Anne Newport
1774	Seton, Elizabeth Ann
1777?	Kaahumanu
1781	Gratz, Rebecca
1784	Eldridge, Elleanor
1786	Sacajawea
1787	Willard, Emma
1788	Hale, Sarah Josepha
1789	Sedgwick, Catharine Maria
1792	Grimké, Sarah Moore
1793	Mott, Lucretia
1795	Jackson, Rebecca

1795	Wright, Frances
1797	Lyon, Mary
1797?	Truth, Sojourner
1800	Beecher, Catharine Esther
1802	Child, Lydia Maria (Francis)
1802	Dix, Dorothea (Lynde)
1803	Crandall, Prudence
1804	Peabody, Elizabeth Palmer
1804	Smith, Emma Hale
1805	Grimké, Angelina Emily
1807	Palmer, Phoebe
1808	Whitman, Narcissa Prentiss
1810	Foster, Abby Kelley
1810	Fuller (Ossoli), Margaret
1810	Rose, Ernestine L.
1810?	Warde, Mary Frances Xavier
1811	Fern, Fanny
1811	Stowe, Harriet Beecher
1813	Haughery, Margaret
1813	Jacobs, Harriet A.
1815	Carroll, Anna Ella
1815	Miner, Myrtilla
1815	Stanton, Elizabeth Cady
1816	Cushman, Charlotte
1817	Bickerdyke, Mary Ann
1818	Bloomer, Amelia Jenks
1818	Keckley, Elizabeth
1818	Mitchell, Maria
1818	Stone, Lucy
1818	Van Lew, Elizabeth L.
1819	Howe, Julia Ward

1819	Pinkham, Lydia	1842	Richards, Ellen Swallow
1820	Anthony, Susan Brownell	1842	Stetson, Augusta E.
1820	Crosby, Fanny	1843	Lowell, Josephine Shaw
1820	Keene, Laura	1844	Boyd, Belle
1820?	Tubman, Harriet Ross	1844	Cassatt, Mary
1821	Barton, Clara Harlowe	1844	Fay, Amy
1821	Eddy, Mary Baker	1844?	Winnemucca, Sarah
1822	Agassiz, Elizabeth Cabot	1844	Woodworth-Etter, Maria
1823	Cary, Mary Ann Shadd	1845?	Lewis, (Mary) Edmonia
1823	Chesnut, Mary Boykin Miller	1845	Thursby, Emma Cecilia
1824	Frémont, Jessie Benton	1846	Green, Anna Katharine
1824	Larcom, Lucy	1847	Ream, Vinnie
1825	Blackwell, Antoinette Brown	1847	Shaw, Anna
1825	Harper, Frances E. W.	1848	Taylor, Susie King
1825	Robinson, Harriet Hanson	1849	Jewett, Sarah Orne
1826	Craft, Ellen	1849	Lazarus, Emma
1826	Victor, Frances Fuller	1849	Meyer, Lucy Rider
1827	Howland, Emily	1849	Storer, Maria Longworth
1827	White, Ellen Gould Harmon	1850	Lease, Mary
1829	Zakrzewska, Marie Elizabeth	1851	Chopin, Kate
1830	Dickinson, Emily	1851	Lathrop, Rose Hawthorne
1830	Hosmer, Harriet	1852	Calamity Jane
1830	Jackson, Helen Hunt	1852	Freeman, Mary Wilkins
1830?	Jones, Mary (Mother)	1852	Hooks, Julia Britton
1830	Lockwood, Belva	1852	Käsebier, Gertrude
1831	Bradwell, Myra Colby	1853	Belmont, Alva Vanderbilt
1831	Dodge, Mary Mapes	1853	White, Helen Magill
1832	Alcott, Louisa May	1854	La Flesche (Tibbles), Susette
1832	Walker, Mary Edwards	1855	Beaux, Cecilia
1833	Ney, Elisabet	1855	Palmer, Alice Freeman
1833	Taylor, Lucy Hobbs	1856	Blatch, Harriot Stanton
1834	Duniway, Abigail	1856	Mead, Lucia Ames
1834	Fields, Annie	1857	Tarbell, Ida
1834	Furbish, Kate	1858	Cooper, Anna Julia
1834	Swain, Clara A.	1858	Drexel, Katharine Mary
1835	Brown, Olympia	1858	Lathrop, Julia
1836	Holley, Marietta	1858	Nutting, Mary Adelaide
1837	Coppin, Fanny Jackson	1859	Catt, Carrie (Chapman)
1837	Forten (Grimké), Charlotte L.	1859	Kelley, Florence
1838	Fearing, Maria	1859	La Follette, Belle Case
1838	Fletcher, Alice Cunningham	1860	Addams, Jane
1838	Lili'uokalani	1860	Gilman, Charlotte Perkins
1838	Woodhull, Victoria	1860	Low, Juliette Gordon
1839	Schofield, Martha	1860	Monroe, Harriet
1839	Willard, Frances	1860	Moses, Anna (Grandma Moses)
1840	Moon, Lottie	1860	Oakley, Annie
1840	Thoburn, Isabella	1860	Szold, Henrietta
1841	Edmonds, Sarah Emma Evelyn	1861	Russell, Lillian
1841	Richards, Linda	1861	Schumann-Heink, Ernestine
1842	Jacobi, Mary Putnam	1862	Fuller, Loie

1862	Wells-Barnett, Ida B.	1876	Beard, Mary Ritter
1862	Wharton, Edith	1876	Force, Juliana
1862	White, Alma	1876	Lloyd, Alice
1863	Bailey, Florence Merriam	1877	Duncan, Isadora
1863	Smith, Jessie Willcox	1877	Moskowitz, Belle
1863	Terrell, Mary Church	1877	St. Denis, Ruth
1864	Bly, Nellie	1878	Abbott, Grace
1864	Coolidge, Elizabeth Sprague	1878	Gilbreth, Lillian
1865	de Wolfe, Elsie	1878	Mitchell, Lucy Sprague
1865	Fiske, Minnie Maddern	1879	Astor, Nancy Witcher
1865	La Flesche (Picotte), Susan	1879	Barrymore, Ethel
1866	Blaine, Anita McCormick	1879	Burroughs, Nannie Helen
1866	Sullivan (Macy), Anne	1879	Fisher, Dorothy Canfield
1867	Beach, Amy Marcy	1879	Roberts, Lydia Jane
1867	Powell, Maud	1879	Sanger, Margaret
1867	Wald, Lillian D.	1879	Stokes, Rose Pastor
1867	Walker, Maggie Lena	1880	Grimké, Angelina Weld
1867	Walker, Sarah Breedlove	1880	Keller, Helen
1867	Wilder, Laura Ingalls	1880	Rankin, Jeannette
1868	Austin, Mary Hunter	1880?	Yezierska, Anzia
1868	Robins, Margaret Dreier	1881	Antin, Mary
1869	Cameron, Donaldina	1881	Bernstein, Aline
1869	Dressler, Marie	1881	Evans, Alice Catherine
1869	Hamilton, Alice	1881	Phillips, Lena Madesin
1869	Lovejoy, Esther Pohl	1881	Weber, Lois
1869	Slye, Maud	1882	Davis, Frances Elliott
1871	Hawes, Harriet Boyd	1882	Farrar, Geraldine
1871	Homer, Louise	1882	Fauset, Jessie Redmon
1871	Hope, Lugenia Burns	1882	Hunter, Jane Edna
1871	Sabin, Florence	1882	Perkins, Frances
1871	Stettheimer, Florine	1882	Spencer, Anne
1872	Adams, Maude	1883	Ames, Jessie Daniel
1872	Dennett, Mary Ware	1883	Brown, Charlotte Hawkins
1872	Farrand, Beatrix	1883	Cunningham, Imogen
1872	Mears, Helen Farnsworth	1883	Harrison, Hazel
1872	Morgan, Julia	1884	Allen, Florence Ellinwood
1872	Wilson, Edith Bolling Galt	1884	Roosevelt, Eleanor
1872	Wright, Elizabeth Evelyn	1884	Teasdale, Sara
1873	Cather, Willa (Sibert)	1884	Tucker, Sophie
1873	Glasgow, Ellen	1885	Campbell, Lucie E.
1874	O'Neill, Rose Cecil	1885	Paul, Alice
1874	Rockefeller, Abby Aldrich	1885	Strong, Anna
1874	Stein, Gertrude	1886	Doolittle, Hilda (H.D.)
1874	Vorse, Mary Heaton	1886	Hollingworth, Leta Stetter
1875	Adams, Harriett Chalmers	1886	Hunter, Clementine
1875	Bethune, Mary McLeod	1886	Rainey, Ma
1875	Dunbar-Nelson, Alice Moore	1887	Beach, Sylvia
1875	Martin, Anne	1887	Benedict, Ruth
1875	Parsons, Elsie Clews	1887	Ferber, Edna
1875	Whitney, Gertrude V.	1887	Moore, Marianne

1887	O'Keeffe, Georgia	1899	Nevelson, Louise
1887	Post, Marjorie Merriweather	1899	Page, Ruth
1887	Woodward, Ellen S.	1900	Arzner, Dorothy
1888	Loos, Anita	1900	Hayes, Helen
1888	Marion, Frances	1900	Le Sueur, Meridel
1888	McMein, Neysa	1900	Mitchell, Margaret
1889	Wallace, Lila Acheson	1900	Moorehead, Agnes
1889	Willebrandt, Mabel Walker	1901	Mead, Margaret
1890	Flanagan, Hallie	1901	Seeger, Ruth Crawford
1890	Flynn, Elizabeth Gurley	1902	McClintock, Barbara
1890	McPherson, Aimee Semple	1903	Baker, Ella
1890	Porter, Katherine Anne	1903	Bernard, Jessie
1890	Staupers, Mabel Keaton	1903	Hawes, Elizabeth
1891	Brice, Fanny	1903	Hurston, Zora Neale
1891	Gilpin, Laura	1903	Luce, Clare Boothe
1891	Harkness, Georgia Elma	1904	Bourke-White, Margaret
1891	Larsen, Nella	1904	Crawford, Joan
1892	Buck, Pearl Sydenstricker	1905	de Mille, Agnes
1892	Flanner, Janet	1905	Fields, Dorothy
1892	Millay, Edna St. Vincent	1905	Hellman, Lillian
1892?	Smedley, Agnes	1905	Jones, Loïs Mailou
1892	West, Mae	1905	McCardell, Claire
1893	Cornell, Katharine	1905	Tamiris, Helen
1893	Holm, Hanya	1905	Wills, Helen
1893	Pickford, Mary	1906	Baker, Josephine
1894	Graham, Martha	1906	Hopper, Grace
1894	Smith, Bessie	1906	Lindbergh, Anne Morrow
1894	Thompson, Dorothy	1907	Carson, Rachel
1895	Allen, Gracie	1907	Enters, Angna
1895	Humphrey, Doris	1907	Hamilton, Grace Towns
1895	Hunter, Alberta	1907	Kuhlman, Kathryn
1895	King, Carol Weiss	1908	Davis, Bette
1895	Lange, Dorothea	1908	Fisher, Mary Frances Kennedy
1895	McDaniel, Hattie	1908	Krasner, Lee
1896	Coleman, Bessie	1908	Petry, Ann
1896	Pesotta, Rose	1909	Hepburn, Katharine
1896	Sandoz, Mari	1909	Merman, Ethel
1896	Waters, Ethel	1909	Smith, Kate
1897	Anderson, Marian	1909	Tandy, Jessica
1897	Bogan, Louise	1909	Welty, Eudora
1897	Day, Dorothy	1910	Cochran, Jacqueline
1897	Earhart, Amelia	1910	Dunham, Katherine
1897	Ponselle, Rosa	1910	Maynor, Dorothy
1897	Rincon de Gautier, Felisa	1910	Wolcott, Marion Post
1897	Smith, Lillian Eugenia	1911	Ball, Lucille
1897	Smith, Margaret Chase	1911	Bishop, Elizabeth
1898	Abbott, Berenice	1911	Jackson, Mahalia
1898	Guggenheim, Peggy	1911	Rogers, Ginger
1898	Sage, Kay	1912	Child, Julia
1898	Taussig, Helen Brooke	1912	Jones, Margo

1912	McCarthy, Mary	1928	Frankenthaler, Helen
1912	Russell, Rosalind	1928	Ozick, Cynthia
1912	Sarton, May	1928	Sexton, Anne
1913	Olsen, Tillie	1928	Temple (Black), Shirley
1913	Parks, Rosa	1929	Marshall, Paule
1913	Rukeyser, Muriel	1929	Onassis, Jacqueline Kennedy
1914	Ray, Dixy Lee	1929	Rich, Adrienne
1914	Zaharias, Babe Didrikson	1929	Sills, Beverly
1915	Holiday, Billie	1930	Fornés, María Irene
1915?	Sokolow, Anna	1930	Hansberry, Lorraine
1915	Walker, Margaret	1930	Huerta, Dolores Fernandez
1916	Grable, Betty	1930	O'Connor, Sandra Day
1916	Mendoza, Lydia	1931	Moreno, Rita
1917	Brooks, Gwendolyn	1931	Morrison, Toni
1917	Deren, Maya	1931	Schuyler, Philippa
1917	Graham, Katharine	1931	Walters, Barbara
1917	Hamer, Fannie Lou	1932	Cline, Patsy
1917	Horne, Lena	1932	Fossey, Dian
1917	McCullers, Carson	1932	Plath, Sylvia
1918	Bailey, Pearl	1932	Taylor, Elizabeth
1918	Fitzgerald, Ella	1933	Ginsburg, Ruth Bader
1918	Ford, Betty	1933	Richards, Ann
1918	Hayworth, Rita	1933	Sontag, Susan
1919	Catlett, Elizabeth	1934	Lorde, Audre
1919	Comden, Betty	1934	MacLaine, Shirley
1919	Robinson, Julia	1934	Rainer, Yvonne
1920	Abzug, Bella	1934	Steinem, Gloria
1920	Childress, Alice	1935	Ferraro, Geraldine Anne
1920	Higgins, Marguerite	1936	Burnett, Carol
1921	Friedan, Betty	1936	Dole, Elizabeth
1921	Holliday, Judy	1936	Hamilton, Virginia
1921	Uchida, Yoshiko	1936	Hesse, Eva
1921	Yalow, Rosalyn	1936	Jordan, Barbara
1922	Clark, Eugenie	1936	Moore, Mary Tyler
1922	Garland, Judy	1937	Albright, Madeleine
1923	Callas, Maria	1937	Fonda, Jane
1923	Dandridge, Dorothy Jean	1938	Lord, Bette Bao
1924	Bacall, Lauren	1938	Mohr, Nicholasa
1924	Chisholm, Shirley	1938	Oates, Joyce Carol
1924	Vaughan, Sarah	1938	Ponce, Mary Helen
1925	Lansbury, Angela	1938	Reno, Janet
1925	O'Connor, Flannery	1939	Edelman, Marian Wright
1925	Tallchief, Maria	1940	Kingston, Maxine Hong
1926	Monroe, Marilyn	1940	Rudolph, Wilma
1927	Bombeck, Erma	1940	Welch, Raquel
1927	Carter, Rosalynn	1941	Baez, Joan
1927	Gibson, Althea	1941	Tyler, Anne
1927	King, Coretta Scott	1942	Ferré, Rosario
1927	Price, (Mary) Leontyne	1942	Franklin, Aretha
1928	Angelou, Maya	1942	Mora, Pat

1942	Robinson, Rubye Doris Smith	1948	McAuliffe, Christa
1942	Streisand, Barbra	1948	Silko, Leslie
1943	Giovanni, Nikki	1949	Streep, Meryl
1943	Jamison, Judith	1950	Goldberg, Whoopi
1943	Joplin, Janis	1950	Naylor, Gloria
1943	King, Billie Jean	1951	Ride, Sally Kristen
1944	Ross, Diana	1952	Cofer, Judith Ortiz
1944	Walker, Alice	1952	Tan, Amy
1945	Farrell, Suzanne	1954	Cisneros, Sandra
1945	Hawn, Goldie	1954	Evert, Chris
1945	Mankiller, Wilma	1954	Winfrey, Oprah
1945	Midler, Bette	1956	Jemison, Mae
1946	Cher	1956	Navratilova, Martina
1946	Chung, Connie	1957	Lopez, Nancy
1946	Field, Sally	1958	Estefan, Gloria
1946	Minnelli, Liza	1958	Madonna
1946	Parton, Dolly	1959	Lin, Maya Ying
1946	Ronstadt, Linda	1962	Foster, Jodie
1947	Clinton, Hillary Rodham	1962	Joyner-Kersee, Jacqueline

Appendix B: Notable Women by Title, Occupation, or Main Area of Interest

Activist

Abzug, Bella
Anthony, Susan Brownell
Beard, Mary Ritter
Belmont, Alva Vanderbilt
Brant, Molly (Mary)
Carroll, Anna Ella
Carter, Rosalynn
Catt, Carrie (Chapman)
Dennett, Mary Ware
Dunbar-Nelson, Alice Moore
Fonda, Jane
Forten (Grimké), Charlotte L.
Friedan, Betty
Fuller (Ossoli), Margaret
Grimké, Angelina Emily
Grimké, Sarah Moore
Hamer, Fannie Lou
Hamilton, Grace Towns
Jacobs, Harriet A.
King, Coretta Scott
La Flesche (Tibbles), Susette
La Follette, Belle Case
Martin, Anne
Mead, Lucia Ames
Paul, Alice
Robinson, Harriet Hanson
Robinson, Rubye Doris Smith
Rose, Ernestine L.
Rukeyser, Muriel
Shaw, Anna
Staupers, Mabel Keaton
Stokes, Rose Pastor
Szold, Henrietta
Truth, Sojourner
Vorse, Mary Heaton
Willard, Frances
Wright, Frances

Actor

Adams, Maude
Bacall, Lauren
Ball, Lucille
Barrymore, Ethel
Cher
Cornell, Katharine
Crawford, Joan
Cushman, Charlotte
Dandridge, Dorothy Jean
Davis, Bette
Dressler, Marie
Field, Sally
Fiske, Minnie Maddern
Fonda, Jane
Foster, Jodie
Garland, Judy
Goldberg, Whoopi
Grable, Betty
Hawn, Goldie
Hayes, Helen
Hayworth, Rita
Hepburn, Katharine
Holliday, Judy

Keene, Laura
Lansbury, Angela
MacLaine, Shirley
Madonna
McDaniel, Hattie
Merry, Ann Brunton
Minnelli, Liza
Monroe, Marilyn
Moorehead, Agnes
Moreno, Rita
Parton, Dolly
Pickford, Mary
Rogers, Ginger
Rowson, Susanna Haswell
Russell, Rosalind
Streep, Meryl
Streisand, Barbra
Tandy, Jessica
Taylor, Elizabeth
Temple (Black), Shirley
Welch, Raquel
West, Mae
Winfrey, Oprah

Ambassador
Luce, Clare Boothe
Roosevelt, Eleanor
Temple (Black), Shirley

Anthropologist
Benedict, Ruth
Dunham, Katherine
Fletcher, Alice Cunningham
Hurston, Zora Neale
Mead, Margaret
Parsons, Elsie Clews

Archaeologist
Hawes, Harriet Boyd

Architect
Lin, Maya Ying
Morgan, Julia

Art Patron
Force, Juliana
Guggenheim, Peggy
Whitney, Gertrude V.

Artist
Beaux, Cecilia
Cassatt, Mary
Catlett, Elizabeth
Frankenthaler, Helen
Hesse, Eva
Hunter, Clementine

Jones, Loïs Mailou
Krasner, Lee
Lewis, (Mary) Edmonia
McMein, Neysa
Mears, Helen Farnsworth
Mohr, Nicholasa
Moses, Anna (Grandma Moses)
O'Keeffe, Georgia
O'Neill, Rose Cecil
Sage, Kay
Smith, Jessie Willcox
Stettheimer, Florine

Astronaut
Jemison, Mae
Ride, Sally Kristen

Astronomer
Mitchell, Maria

Athlete
Evert, Chris
Gibson, Althea
Joyner-Kersee, Jacqueline
King, Billie Jean
Lopez, Nancy
Navratilova, Martina
Rudolph, Wilma
Wills, Helen
Zaharias, Babe Didrikson

Attorney
Abzug, Bella
Allen, Florence Ellinwood
Bradwell, Myra Colby
Cary, Mary Ann Shadd
Clinton, Hillary Rodham
Dole, Elizabeth
Ferraro, Geraldine Anne
Ginsburg, Ruth Bader
Jordan, Barbara
King, Carol Weiss
Lockwood, Belva
O'Connor, Sandra Day
Phillips, Lena Madesin
Reno, Janet
Willebrandt, Mabel Walker

Author
Adams, Harriett Chalmers
Alcott, Louisa May
Angelou, Maya
Antin, Mary
Austin, Mary Hunter
Beecher, Catharine Esther
Bishop, Elizabeth

Bombeck, Erma
Buck, Pearl Sydenstricker
Carson, Rachel
Cather, Willa (Sibert)
Chesnut, Mary Boykin Miller
Child, Julia
Child, Lydia Maria (Francis)
Childress, Alice
Chopin, Kate
Cisneros, Sandra
Cofer, Judith Ortiz
Dodge, Mary Mapes
Dunbar-Nelson, Alice Moore
Fauset, Jessie Redmon
Ferber, Edna
Ferré, Rosario
Fields, Annie
Fisher, Dorothy Canfield
Fisher, Mary Frances Kennedy
Flanner, Janet
Freeman, Mary Wilkins
Frémont, Jessie Benton
Friedan, Betty
Fuller (Ossoli), Margaret
Gilman, Charlotte Perkins
Gilpin, Laura
Glasgow, Ellen
Green, Anna Katharine
Hamilton, Virginia
Harper, Frances E. W.
Hawes, Elizabeth
Holley, Marietta
Howe, Julia Ward
Hurston, Zora Neale
Jackson, Helen Hunt
Jewett, Sarah Orne
Keller, Helen
Kingston, Maxine Hong
La Flesche (Tibbles), Susette
Larsen, Nella
Le Sueur, Meridel
Lindbergh, Anne Morrow
Loos, Anita
Lord, Bette Bao
Marion, Frances
Marshall, Paule
McCarthy, Mary
McCullers, Carson
Mitchell, Margaret
Mohr, Nicholasa
Morrison, Toni
Naylor, Gloria
Oates, Joyce Carol
O'Connor, Flannery
Olsen, Tillie
Ozick, Cynthia

Petry, Ann
Ponce, Mary Helen
Porter, Katherine Anne
Rowson, Susanna Haswell
Sandoz, Mari
Sarton, May
Sedgwick, Catharine Maria
Silko, Leslie
Smith, Lillian Eugenia
Sontag, Susan
Stein, Gertrude
Steinem, Gloria
Stowe, Harriet Beecher
Tan, Amy
Tyler, Anne
Uchida, Yoshiko
Victor, Frances Fuller
Walker, Alice
Walker, Margaret
Warren, Marcy (Otis)
Welch, Raquel
Welty, Eudora
Wharton, Edith
Wilder, Laura Ingalls
Wright, Frances
Yezierska, Anzia

Aviator
Cochran, Jacqueline
Coleman, Bessie
Earhart, Amelia

Ballerina
Farrell, Suzanne
Tallchief, Maria
Tamiris, Helen

Banker
Walker, Maggie Lena

Biologist
Carson, Rachel

Botanist
Furbish, Kate

Broadcast Journalist
Chung, Connie
Walters, Barbara

Businesswoman
Ball, Lucille
Beach, Sylvia
Duniway, Abigail
Eldridge, Elleanor
Graham, Katharine

Haughery, Margaret
Musgrove, Mary
Pinckney, Eliza
Pinkham, Lydia
Walker, Sarah Breedlove

Cabinet Member
Albright, Madeleine
Dole, Elizabeth
Reno, Janet

Charity Worker
Gratz, Rebecca

Chef
Child, Julia

Chemist
Richards, Ellen Swallow

Choreographer
de Mille, Agnes
Dunham, Katherine
Enters, Angna
Graham, Martha
Holm, Hanya
Page, Ruth
Sokolow, Anna

Clergy
Blackwell, Antoinette Brown
Brown, Olympia
Shaw, Anna

Composer
Beach, Amy Marcy
Campbell, Lucie E.
Hunter, Alberta
Schuyler, Philippa
Seeger, Ruth Crawford

Computer Engineer
Hopper, Grace

Concert Vocalist
Thursby, Emma Cecilia

Congresswoman
Abzug, Bella
Chisholm, Shirley
Ferraro, Geraldine Anne
Jordan, Barbara
Luce, Clare Boothe
Rankin, Jeannette
Smith, Margaret Chase

Dancer
de Mille, Agnes
Duncan, Isadora
Dunham, Katherine
Enters, Angna
Fuller, Loie
Graham, Martha
Holm, Hanya
Humphrey, Doris
Jamison, Judith
Page, Ruth
Rogers, Ginger
St. Denis, Ruth

Dentist
Taylor, Lucy Hobbs

Director
Jones, Margo
Keene, Laura

Dollmaker
O'Neill, Rose Cecil

Dramatist
Flanagan, Hallie
Fornés, María Irene
Grimké, Angelina Weld
Hansberry, Lorraine
Hellman, Lillian
Luce, Clare Boothe

Dressmaker
Keckley, Elizabeth

Editor
Dodge, Mary Mapes
Hale, Sarah Josepha
Monroe, Harriet
Onassis, Jacqueline Kennedy
Steinem, Gloria

Educator
Abbott, Grace
Agassiz, Elizabeth Cabot
Beecher, Catharine Esther
Bethune, Mary McLeod
Brown, Charlotte Hawkins
Burroughs, Nannie Helen
Campbell, Lucie E.
Cary, Mary Ann Shadd
Chisholm, Shirley
Cooper, Anna Julia
Coppin, Fanny Jackson
Crandall, Prudence
Dunbar-Nelson, Alice Moore
Forten (Grimké), Charlotte L.

Hooks, Julia Britton
Howland, Emily
Lloyd, Alice
Lyon, Mary
McAuliffe, Christa
Miner, Myrtilla
Mitchell, Lucy Sprague
Mora, Pat
Nutting, Mary Adelaide
Palmer, Alice Freeman
Peabody, Elizabeth Palmer
Richards, Linda
Roberts, Lydia Jane
Schofield, Martha
Sullivan (Macy), Anne
Taylor, Susie King
Terrell, Mary Church
White, Helen Magill
Willard, Emma
Wright, Elizabeth Evelyn

Entertainer
Allen, Gracie
Baker, Josephine
Brice, Fanny
Burnett, Carol
Cline, Patsy
Estefan, Gloria
Fitzgerald, Ella
Franklin, Aretha
Garland, Judy
Holiday, Billie
Horne, Lena
Joplin, Janis
Madonna
Merman, Ethel
Midler, Bette
Minnelli, Liza
Moore, Mary Tyler
Oakley, Annie
Parton, Dolly
Rainey, Ma
Ross, Diana
Russell, Lillian
Smith, Bessie
Streisand, Barbra
Tucker, Sophie

Environmentalist
Carson, Rachel

Evangelist
Kuhlman, Kathryn
Lee, Mother Ann
McPherson, Aimee Semple
Palmer, Phoebe

White, Alma
Woodworth-Etter, Maria

Fashion Designer
Hawes Elizabeth
McCardell, Claire

Film Director
Arzner, Dorothy
Deren, Maya
Foster, Jodie
Marion, Frances
Weber, Lois

Film Producer
Deren, Maya
Foster, Jodie
Winfrey, Oprah

Filmmaker
Rainer, Yvonne

First Lady
Adams, Abigail Smith
Carter, Rosalynn
Clinton, Hillary Rodham
Ford, Betty
Madison, Dolley
Onassis, Jacqueline Kennedy
Roosevelt, Eleanor
Wilson, Edith Bolling Galt

Geneticist
McClintock, Barbara

Government Official
Astor, Nancy Witcher
Hamilton, Grace Towns
Perkins, Frances
Ray, Dixy Lee
Richards, Ann
Rincon de Gautier, Felisa
Woodward, Ellen S.

Guide
Sacajawea

Healer
Kuhlman, Kathryn

Historian
Beard, Mary Ritter
Victor, Frances Fuller
Warren, Mercy (Otis)

Horticulturist
Pinckney, Eliza

Hostess
Fields, Annie

Humanitarian
Adams, Harriett Chalmers
Buck, Pearl Sydenstricker
Dix, Dorothea (Lynde)

Hymn Writer
Crosby, Fanny

Ichthyologist
Clark, Eugenie

Indian Captive
Jemison, Mary

Industrial Engineer
Gilbreth, Lillian

Interior Decorator
de Wolfe, Elsie

Journalist
Bly, Nellie
Cary, Mary Ann Shadd
Duniway, Abigail
Fern, Fanny
Higgins, Marguerite
La Follette, Belle Case
Royall, Anne Newport
Smedley, Agnes
Strong, Anna
Tarbell, Ida
Thompson, Dorothy
Vorse, Mary Heaton
Wells-Barnett, Ida B.

Judge
Allen, Florence Ellinwood

Labor Leader
Flynn, Elizabeth Gurley
Huerta, Dolores Fernandez
Jones, Mary (Mother)
Pesotta, Rose

Landscape Architect
Farrand, Beatrix

Lecturer
Adams, Harriett Chalmers
Sampson (Gannett), Deborah

Librettist
Comden, Betty
Fields, Dorothy

Literary Critic
Bogan, Louise

Mathematician
Robinson, Julia

Microbiologist
Evans, Alice Catherine

Military Official
Hopper, Grace

Mill Girl
Larcom, Lucy
Robinson, Harriet Hanson

Missionary
Cameron, Donaldina
Coppin, Fanny Jackson
Fearing, Maria
Lyon, Mary
Moon, Lottie
Swain, Clara A.
Thoburn, Isabella
Whitman, Narcissa Prentiss

Music Patron
Coolidge, Elizabeth Sprague
Storer, Maria Longworth

Naturalist
Agassiz, Elizabeth Cabot

Newspaper Publisher
Graham, Katharine

Nurse
Barton, Clara Harlowe
Bickerdyke, Mary Ann
Davis, Frances Elliott
Nutting, Mary Adelaide
Richards, Linda
Staupers, Mabel Keaton
Taylor, Susie King
Wald, Lillian D.

Nutritionist
Roberts, Lydia Jane

Opera Singer
Anderson, Marian
Callas, Maria
Farrar, Geraldine
Homer, Louise
Ponselle, Rosa
Price, (Mary) Leontyne
Schumann-Heink, Ernestine

Sills, Beverly

Ornithologist
Bailey, Florence Merriam

Pantomimist
Enters, Angna

Pathologist
Slye, Maud

Philanthropist
Blaine, Anita McCormick
Haughery, Margaret
Lowell, Josephine Shaw
Post, Marjorie Merriweather
Robins, Margaret Dreier
Rockefeller, Abby Aldrich
Wallace, Lila Acheson

Photographer
Abbott, Berenice
Bourke-White, Margaret
Cunningham, Imogen
Gilpin, Laura
Käsebier, Gertrude
Lange, Dorothea
Wolcott, Marion Post

Physician
Hamilton, Alice
Jacobi, Mary Putnam
La Flesche (Picotte), Susan
Lovejoy, Esther Pohl
Meyer, Lucy Rider
Sabin, Florence
Shaw, Anna
Swain, Clara A.
Taussig, Helen Brooke
Walker, Mary Edwards
Zakrzewska, Marie Elizabeth

Physicist
Yalow, Rosalyn

Pianist
Beach, Amy Marcy
Fay, Amy
Harrison, Hazel
Schuyler, Philippa

Pioneer
Calamity Jane
Duniway, Abigail
Jemison, Mary
Whitman, Narcissa Prentiss

Poet
Angelou, Maya
Bishop, Elizabeth
Bogan, Louise
Bradstreet, Anne
Brooks, Gwendolyn
Cofer, Judith Ortiz
Dickinson, Emily
Doolittle, Hilda (H.D.)
Giovanni, Nikki
Grimké, Angelina Weld
Larcom, Lucy
Lazarus, Emma
Lorde, Audre
Millay, Edna St. Vincent
Monroe, Harriet
Moore, Marianne
Plath, Sylvia
Rich, Adrienne
Rukeyser, Muriel
Sarton, May
Sexton, Anne
Silko, Leslie
Spencer, Anne
Teasdale, Sara
Walker, Alice
Walker, Margaret
Wheatley, Phillis

Political Consultant
Moskowitz, Belle

Politician
Catt, Carrie (Chapman)
Lease, Mary
Martin, Anne

Potter
Storer, Maria Longworth

Primatologist
Fossey, Dian

Princess
Pocahontas

Psychologist
Hollingworth, Leta Stetter

Public Administrator
Abbott, Grace

Publisher
Beach, Sylvia
Wallace, Lila Acheson

Reformer
Addams, Jane
Ames, Jessie Daniel
Baker, Ella
Blaine, Anita McCormick
Blatch, Harriot Stanton
Bloomer, Amelia Jenks
Brown, Olympia
Cameron, Donaldina
Child, Lydia Maria (Francis)
Craft, Ellen
Day, Dorothy
Dennett, Mary Ware
Dix, Dorothea (Lynde)
Dyer, Mary
Edelman, Marian Wright
Foster, Abby Kelley
Hope, Lugenia Burns
Howland, Emily
Hunter, Jane Edna
Jackson, Helen Hunt
Jacobs, Harriet A.
Kelley, Florence
Lathrop, Julia
Low, Juliette Gordon
Lowell, Josephine Shaw
Miner, Myrtilla
Mott, Lucretia
Parks, Rosa
Pesotta, Rose
Robins, Margaret Dreier
Sanger, Margaret
Smith, Lillian Eugenia
Stanton, Elizabeth Cady
Stone, Lucy
Terrell, Mary Church
Truth, Sojourner
Tubman, Harriet Ross
Wald, Lillian D.
Willard, Frances
Woodhull, Victoria

Regent
Kaahumanu

Religious
Drexel, Katharine Mary
Lathrop, Rose Hawthorne
Seton, Elizabeth Ann
Warde, Mary Frances Xavier

Religious Leader
Eddy, Mary Baker
Harkness, Georgia Elma
Hutchinson, Anne Marbury
Jackson, Rebecca

Meyer, Lucy Rider
Smith, Emma Hale
Stetson, Augusta E.
Szold, Henrietta
Tekakwitha, Kateri
White, Ellen Gould Harmon

Ruler
Kaahumanu
Lili'uokalani

Sculptor
Hesse, Eva
Hosmer, Harriet
Mears, Helen Farnsworth
Nevelson, Louise
Ney, Elisabet
Ream, Vinnie
Whitney, Gertrude V.
Wright, Patience

Singer
Baez, Joan
Bailey, Pearl
Dandridge, Dorothy Jean
Hunter, Alberta
Jackson, Mahalia
Maynor, Dorothy
Mendoza, Lydia
Ronstadt, Linda
Smith, Kate
Tucker, Sophie
Vaughan, Sarah
Waters, Ethel

Slave
Craft, Ellen
Fearing, Maria
Jacobs, Harriet A.
Keckley, Elizabeth
Truth, Sojourner
Tubman, Harriet Ross
Wheatley, Phillis

Social Worker
Abbott, Grace
Moskowitz, Belle

Sociologist
Bernard, Jessie

Soldier
Edmonds, Sarah Emma Evelyn
Sampson (Gannett), Deborah

Spy
Boyd, Belle
Van Lew, Elizabeth L.
Wright, Patience

Stage and Costume Designer
Bernstein, Aline

Supreme Court Justice
Ginsburg, Ruth Bader
O'Connor, Sandra Day

Television Personality
Winfrey, Oprah

Theatrical Producer
Flanagan, Hallie
Jones, Margo
Keene, Laura

Theologian
Harkness, Georgia Elma

Translator
Sacajawea

Tribal Leader
Mankiller, Wilma
Musgrove, Mary
Ward, Nancy
Winnemucca, Sarah

Violinist
Powell, Maud

Zoologist
Ray, Dixy Lee

Appendix C: Notable Women by Ethnicity

African Americans

Anderson, Marian
Angelou, Maya
Bailey, Pearl
Baker, Ella
Baker, Josephine
Bethune, Mary McLeod
Brooks, Gwendolyn
Brown, Charlotte Hawkins
Burroughs, Nannie Helen
Campbell, Lucie E.
Cary, Mary Ann Shadd
Catlett, Elizabeth
Childress, Alice
Chisholm, Shirley
Coleman, Bessie
Cooper, Anna Julia
Coppin, Fanny Jackson
Craft, Ellen
Dandridge, Dorothy Jean
Davis, Frances Elliott
Dunbar-Nelson, Alice Moore
Dunham, Katherine
Edelman, Marian Wright
Eldridge, Elleanor
Fauset, Jessie Redmon
Fearing, Maria
Fitzgerald, Ella
Forten (Grimké), Charlotte L.
Franklin, Aretha
Gibson, Althea
Giovanni, Nikki
Goldberg, Whoopi
Grimké, Angelina Weld
Hamer, Fannie Lou

Hamilton, Grace Towns
Hamilton, Virginia
Hansberry, Lorraine
Harper, Frances E. W.
Harrison, Hazel
Holiday, Billie
Hooks, Julia Britton
Hope, Lugenia Burns
Horne, Lena
Hunter, Alberta
Hunter, Clementine
Hunter, Jane Edna
Hurston, Zora Neale
Jackson, Mahalia
Jackson, Rebecca
Jacobs, Harriet A.
Jamison, Judith
Jemison, Mae
Jones, Loïs Mailou
Jordan, Barbara
Joyner-Kersee, Jacqueline
Keckley, Elizabeth
King, Coretta Scott
Larsen, Nella
Lewis, (Mary) Edmonia
Lorde, Audre
Marshall, Paule
Maynor, Dorothy
McDaniel, Hattie
Morrison, Toni
Naylor, Gloria
Parks, Rosa
Petry, Ann
Price, (Mary) Leontyne

Rainey, Ma
Robinson, Rubye Doris Smith
Ross, Diana
Rudolph, Wilma
Schuyler, Philippa
Smith, Bessie
Spencer, Anne
Staupers, Mabel Keaton
Taylor, Susie King
Terrell, Mary Church
Truth, Sojourner
Tubman, Harriet Ross
Vaughan, Sarah
Walker, Alice
Walker, Maggie Lena
Walker, Margaret
Walker, Sarah Breedlove
Waters, Ethel
Wells-Barnett, Ida B.
Wheatley, Phillis
Winfrey, Oprah
Wright, Elizabeth Evelyn

Asian Americans
Chung, Connie
Kingston, Maxine Hong
Lin, Maya Ying
Lord, Bette Bao
Tan, Amy
Uchida, Yoshiko

Latina Americans
Baez, Joan
Cisneros, Sandra
Cofer, Judith Ortiz
Estefan, Gloria
Ferré, Rosario
Fornés, María Irene
Hayworth, Rita
Huerta, Dolores Fernandez
Lopez, Nancy
Mendoza, Lydia
Mohr, Nicholasa
Mora, Pat
Moreno, Rita
Ponce, Mary Helen
Rincon de Gautier, Felisa
Ronstadt, Linda
Welch, Raquel

Native Americans
Kaahumanu
La Flesche (Picotte), Susan
La Flesche (Tibbles), Susette
Lili'uokalani
Mankiller, Wilma
Musgrove, Mary
Pocahontas
Sacajawea
Silko, Leslie
Tallchief, Maria
Tekakwitha, Kateri
Ward, Nancy

Index

Numbers in **bold** indicate main entry.

About the Author

LYNDA G. ADAMSON is Professor of Literature and Chair of the English Department at Prince George's Community College in Maryland. She is also author of *Notable Women in World History* (Greenwood, 1998), *Recreating the Past* (Greenwood, 1994), *A Reference Guide to Historical Fiction for Children and Young Adults* (Greenwood, 1987), *Literature Connections to American History, K–6* (1998), *Literature Connections to American History, 7–12* (1998), *Literature Connections to World History, 7–12* (1998), *Literature Connections to World History, K–6* (1998), *American Historical Fiction: An Annotated Guide to Novels for Adults and Young Adults* (1999), and *World Historical Fiction: An Annotated Guide for Adults and Young Adults* (1999).